Handbook of
Marketing
Second Scales
Edition

I dedicate this book to *Patti, Anna,* and *Wallace*

—Bill Bearden

I dedicate this book to my loving wife, *Susan*

—Rick Netemeyer

William O. Bearden / Richard G. Netemeyer

Handbook *of* Marketing

Second
Edition Scales

Multi-Item Measures for Marketing
and Consumer Behavior Research

Published in Cooperation With the Association for Consumer Research

SAGE Publications
International Educational and Professional Publisher
Thousand Oaks London New Delhi

For information:

 SAGE Publications, Inc.
2455 Teller Road
Thousand Oaks, California 91320
E-mail: order@sagepub.com

SAGE Publications Ltd.
6 Bonhill Street
London EC2A 4PU
United Kingdom

SAGE Publications India Pvt. Ltd.
M-32 Market
Greater Kailash I
New Delhi 110 048 India

Printed in the United States of America

Library of Congress Cataloging-in-Publication Data

Bearden, William O., 1945-
    Handbook of marketing scales: Multi-item measures for
marketing and consumer behavior research / by William O. Bearden
and Richard G. Netemeyer. — 2nd ed.
        p.   cm. — (Association for consumer research series)
    ISBN 0-7619-1000-X (cloth; acid-free paper)
    1. Marketing research.   2. Consumer behavior—Research.
I. Netemeyer, Richard G., 1956-   . II. Title.   III. Series.
    HF5415.3.B323   1998
        658.8′3—ddc21   98-25452

99   00   01   02   03   10   9   8   7   6   5   4   3   2

Acquiring Editor:	Harry Briggs
Editorial Assistant:	Anna Howland
Production Editor:	Diana E. Axelsen
Editorial Assistant:	Nevair Kabakian
Typesetter/Designer:	Janelle LeMaster
Cover Designer:	Candice Harman

CONTENTS

Chapter Three: Values

General Values

Values Related to Environmentalism and Socially Responsible Consumption

Values Related to Materialism and Possessions/Objects

Chapter Four: Involvement, Information Processing, and Price Perceptions

Chapter Five: Reactions to Advertising Stimuli

Measures Related to Ad Emotions and Ad Content

Measures Related to Ad Believability/Credibility

Measures Related to Children's Advertising

Chapter Six: Attitudes About the Performance of Business Firms, Satisfaction and Post-Purchase Behavior, Social Agencies, and the Marketplace

Consumer Attitudes Toward Business Practices and Marketing

Scales Related to Post-Purchase Behavior: Consumer Discontent

Business Ethics

Business Attitudes Toward the Marketplace

Chapter Seven: Sales, Sales Management, Organizational Behavior, and Interfirm-Intrafirm Issues

Sales, Sales Management, and Organizational Behavior Issues

Job Satisfaction Measures

Other Measures Related to Interfirm Issues

PREFACE

Most of the measures summarized in this second edition of the book were originally published in marketing- and consumer-related journals or conference proceedings. In addition, the social psychology and organizational behavior literatures, as well several books, contributed measures to this volume. We would like to thank *all* the publishers that granted us permission to reprint the measures summarized in this volume. In particular, we are grateful to the following publishers and their corresponding publications:

American Marketing Association
Journal of Marketing
Journal of Marketing Research
Journal of Public Policy & Marketing
AMA Proceedings
250 South Wacker Drive, Suite 200
Chicago, IL 60606-5819

Association for Consumer Research
ACR Proceedings
63 TNRB
Brigham Young University
Provo, UT 84602

University of Chicago Press
Journal of Consumer Research
5801 South Ellis
Chicago, IL 60637

American Psychological Association
Journal of Personality and Social Psychology
Journal of Applied Psychology
Personality and Social Psychology Bulletin
2nd Floor
750 1st Street, N.E.
Washington, DC 20002-4242

1

Introduction

BACKGROUND

This volume represents an updated, second edition of a compilation of multi-item, self-report measures developed and/or frequently used in consumer behavior and marketing research. As with the first edition, we hope researchers will find this volume useful in many ways. First, the book should be helpful in reducing the time it takes to locate instruments for survey research in marketing and consumer behavior, and given that a number of constructs have several measures, the book should provide researchers with options to consider. Second, a number of the measures in this volume have been used in several studies. Therefore, the book should serve as a partial guide to the literature for certain topic areas and may spur further refinement of existing measures in terms of item reduction, dimensionality, reliability, and validity. This text may also help identify those areas where measures are needed, thus encouraging further development of valid measures of consumer behavior and marketing constructs. Finally, we hope that the book will serve as an impetus to advance knowledge. By using the same measures across several studies, comparison and integration of results may be enhanced.

CRITERIA FOR MEASURE SELECTION

The primary emphasis of this edition has been to update the first edition and improve it in terms of "usability." For the most part, this second edition includes measures from articles whose major objective (or at least one of the major objectives) was measurement development. As with the first edition, we have not compiled single-item measures or multi-item measures that lacked estimates of construct validity. Also, no claim is made that this volume contains every multi-item measure relevant to marketing and con-

sumer behavior. We undoubtedly have omitted some relevant and psychometrically sound measures published in periodicals that we did not include in our "search" procedures (see below) or just plain "missed" through oversight. Our intent was to include only those published measures subjected to some minimal developmental procedures. Throughout the search process for this second edition, "judgment calls" were made with regard to what measures to include and what measures to exclude. Also, several authors sent us copies of their scales (that we were unaware of). In most cases, we included these scales, given that they met the general criteria for inclusion stated below.

Criteria for inclusion:
   a. The measure had a reasonable theoretical base and/or conceptual definition.

   b. The measure was composed of several (i.e., at least three) items or questions.

   c. The measure was developed within the marketing or consumer behavior literature and was used in, or was relevant to, the marketing or consumer behavior literature.

   d. At least some scaling procedures were employed in scale development.

   e. Estimates of reliability and/or validity existed.

What was excluded:
   a. Single-item measures—though important in many studies, the task of compiling them was not a focus of this text.

   b. Multi-item measures that did not meet the above five criteria. For example:

1

1. Multi-item measures based on "face validity" alone and

2. Multi-item measures included in studies as dependent or independent variables that were not derived through scale development procedures.

SEARCH PROCEDURES

Two procedures were used in the search for scales included in this second edition: (a) an on-line computer search of publications in marketing and consumer behavior and (b) a visual search of the major publications in marketing/consumer behavior. Except where noted, our additional search for this edition was restricted to the period of 1992-1997, as 1992 was the year the first edition was completed. We also added three marketing/consumer behavior periodicals to our search, the *Journal of Consumer Affairs* (1984-1997), the *Journal of Consumer Psychology* (1991-1997), and *Marketing Letters* (1990-1997). As such, we examined all (or most) issues currently in print. The following publications were consulted for additions and revisions to include in this second edition:

American Marketing Association Summer
    Educators' Conference Proceedings
Association for Consumer Research Proceedings
Journal of the Academy of Marketing Science
Journal of Advertising
Journal of Advertising Research
Journal of Business Research
Journal of Consumer Affairs
Journal of Consumer Psychology
Journal of Consumer Research
Journal of Marketing
Journal of Marketing Research
Journal of Public Policy and Marketing
Journal of Retailing
Marketing Letters
Psychology & Marketing

FORMAT OF THE BOOK AND PRESENTATION OF MEASURES

The format of this second version is similar to that of the first version. First, we have divided the scales into six general topical areas (with subtopics) and have devoted a chapter to each topical area. (See Table of Contents.) The six areas are (a) *Traits and Individual Differences Variables*, covered in Chapter 2; (b) *Values*, covered in Chapter 3; (c) *Involvement, Information Processing, and Price Perceptions*, covered in Chapter 4; (d) *Reactions to Advertising Stimuli*, covered in Chapter 5; (e) *Attitudes About the Performance of Business Firms, Satisfaction and Post-Purchase Behavior, Social Agencies, and the Marketplace*, covered in Chapter 6; and (f) *Sales, Sales Management, Organizational Behavior, and Interfirm-Intrafirm Issues*, covered in Chapter 7.

As in the first edition, topic areas were chosen in terms of marketing mix and consumer behavior variables. Still, the placement of certain scales into topic areas involved some subjectivity. For example, many *values* can be considered *traits or individual difference variables* and vice versa, and several *individual difference variables* could be viewed as *variables relating to information processing*. Thus, we made "judgment calls" regarding the topical categorization of several of the measures. For each topic and subtopic area, scales are presented in alphabetical order. This second edition also contains an "Index" of all scales, subscales, factors, and dimensions (also listed in alphabetical order). We hope that the addition of an index will make this volume a little more "user-friendly" than the first edition.

For each scale summarized, we have provided the following information using the outline shown below. *If information from the original source (or other sources) for a particular subheading was not available or applicable*, we noted this by stating "N/A."

a. **Construct:** the definition and/or theoretical base of the construct as provided by the authors of the scale.

b. **Description:** the description of the measure including the number of items, scale points, scoring procedures, and dimensionality.

c. **Development:** how the scale was developed (i.e., the general procedures used to derive the final form of the scale from the original scale development article).

d. **Samples:** the samples used in scale development and validation.

e. **Validity:** estimates of validity (i.e., reliability, convergent, discriminant, and nomological validity) from development of the scale. In many cases, actual estimates are provided. In articles performing numerous tests of validity, however, a summary of the pattern of results, along with some example findings that provided evidence of validity, is offered.

f. **Scores:** mean and/or percentage scores on the scale from the original development article.

g. **Sources:** the source(s) of the scale (the authors who developed the scale and the publication(s) the scale first appeared in).

h. **Other evidence:** other evidence of validity (i.e., reliability, convergent, discriminant, and nomological validity) and scores from applications of the scale other than the original source. In general, we restricted "other evidence" to one to three applications of the scale in the marketing and consumer behavior literature.

i. **Other sources:** Sources from select applications of the scale (e.g., the sources in which "other evidence" was found).

j. **References:** critical references from articles pertaining to the topic area other than those of the source of the scale and other sources. These references typically involve description of the construct domain or definition.

k. **Scale items:** the actual items in the scale, dimensions to which the items belong, items that require reverse scoring, and, where applicable, directions for using the scale.

CAVEATS AND CAUTIONS

A number of caveats and cautions regarding the use of this text are warranted. For each measure, we have tried to provide a reasonably complete description of the scale itself, the procedures used to develop the scale, and some of the available evidence regarding the reliability and validity of each scale. The articles on which the scales are based, however, vary greatly in depth, length, and detail. Consequently, the summaries themselves depend on the characteristics of the original source(s), and within any one write-up or summary, the information included in the outline categories often required some creative assignment. For example, in some articles it was not always clear when scale development procedures ended and subsequent validation began. Hence, the outlines for each scale are best viewed as a means of organizing the presentation, not as a definitive guide.

In addition, this volume is not intended to be a substitute for careful evaluation of available measures or the development of valid measures for use in specific studies. The inclusion of a scale in the volume does not ensure an acceptable level of quality. In fact, the detail and sophistication of the procedures underlying some of the scales vary dramatically. Prospective users of these measures are encouraged to refer to the original source(s) and to make their own detailed evaluation prior to use of any measure in their research. (See "Evaluation of Measures" in the next several pages.) Finally, it is hoped that the enhanced availability of the scales in this volume will not lead to the blind inclusion of "additional variables" on data collection instruments without sufficient theoretical justification.

EVALUATION OF MEASURES

In using, evaluating, or developing multi-item scales, a number of guidelines and procedures are recommended to help ensure that the measure is as psychometrically sound as possible. These procedures are outlined in the psychometric literature, and the discussion that follows borrows heavily from this literature. Also, the discussion that follows should not be interpreted as a definitive guide to scale development. The reader is strongly urged to consult the relevant literature when considering measurement development or evaluation (e.g., American Psychological Association 1985; Bohrnstedt and Borgatta 1981; Carmines and Zeller 1979; Churchill 1979; Clark and Watson 1995; Cortina 1993; DeVillis 1991; Nunnally and Bernstein 1994; Peter 1979, 1981; Robinson, Shaver, and Wrightsman 1991; Spector 1992).

Construct Definition and Domain

First, the scale should be based on a solid theoretical definition, with the construct's domain thoroughly delineated and outlined. This definition, and its attendant description, should entail what is included in the domain of the construct, what is excluded from the construct's domain, and the a priori dimensionality of the construct's domain. The theoretical definition, the domain of the construct, and its dimensionality should be derived from a thorough review of the existing literature and, ideally, expert opinion.

Content Validity

The scale items should exhibit "content" or "face" validity. That is, on the surface, they should appear consistent with the theoretical domain of the construct. In development, it is generally recommended that a number of items be generated that "tap the domain of the construct," that the items be screened by judges with expertise in the literature, and that several pilot tests on samples from relevant populations be conducted to trim and refine the pool of items (Churchill 1979; DeVillis 1991; Robinson et al. 1991). Furthermore, shorter and simpler items (ones that are easier to process and understand) are generally easier to respond to and are more reliable (Carmines and Zeller 1979; Churchill 1979; Churchill and Peter 1984; Converse and Presser 1986; Robinson et al. 1991; Spector 1992; Sudman and Bradburn 1982). Thus, items should be representative of the construct they are proposed to measure, and they should be easy to respond to (i.e., avoid jargon or difficult wording, double-barreled items, and ambiguous wording).

Scale Dimensionality

A construct's domain can be hypothesized as uni- or multidimensional. Thus, the scale (or subscales/factors) used to operationalize the construct should reflect the hypothesized dimensionality. Given that scale (factor) unidimensionality is considered prerequisite to reliability and validity, assessment of unidimensionality should be considered (Gerbing and Anderson 1988; Hattie 1985; McDonald 1981). Thus, a scale's empirical factor structure should reflect the dimensionality theorized.

A number of procedures have been employed to check the dimensionality of a scale (i.e., item analysis as well as exploratory and confirmatory factor analysis). One somewhat agreed upon technique is confirmatory factor analysis, in which several multi-item factors (and relations among the factors) can be specified and evaluated on criteria used to assess dimensionality (e.g., fit indices, presence of within/across factor correlated measurement errors, degree of cross-loading, presence of "methods" factors). The reader is strongly urged to consult the literature when examining dimensionality of measures (e.g., Anderson and Gerbing 1988; Anderson, Gerbing, and Hunter 1987; Clark and Watson 1995; Floyd and Widaman 1995; Gerbing and Anderson 1988; Hattie 1985; Kumar and Dillon 1987a, 1987b; McDonald, 1985; Nunnally and Bernstein 1994).

Reliability

Two broad types of reliability are referred to in the psychometric literature: (a) test-retest—the correlation between the same person's score on the same set of items at two points in time, and (b) internal consistency—the correlation among items or sets of items in the scale for all who answer the items.

Test-Retest. The stability of a respondent's item responses over time has not been assessed in scale use or development as frequently as internal consistency. This has been the case across disciplines (Robinson et al. 1991), and marketing and consumer behavior are no exceptions. Less than half of the scales in this text offer test-retest coefficients, but more than 90% offer some estimate of internal consistency reliability. It is unfortunate that test-retest estimates are available for so few of the scales in the marketing and consumer behavior literature, and those planning scale development work should give a priori consideration to assessing test-retest reliability in addition to other procedures of evaluating reliability and validity.

Internal Consistency. Items composing a scale (or subscale) should show high levels of internal consistency. Some commonly used criteria for assessing internal consistency are individual corrected item-to-total correlations, the inter-item correlation matrix for all scale items or items proposed to measure a given scale dimension, and a number of reliability coefficients (Bohrnstedt, Mohler, and Muller 1987; Churchill 1979; Cortina 1993; DeVillis 1991; Nunnally and Bernstein 1994; Peter 1979; Robinson et al. 1991). A recently used rule of thumb for corrected item-to-total correlations is that they should be .50 or greater to retain an item (e.g., Bearden, Netemeyer, and Teel 1989; Shimp and Sharma 1987). Rules of thumb for individual correlations in the inter-item correlation matrix vary (i.e., Robinson et al. [1991] recommend levels of .30 or better as exemplary).

The most widely used internal consistency reliability coefficient is Cronbach's (1951) coefficient alpha. (Others, such as split-halves and rank order coefficients, are available, but given the widespread use of coefficient alpha, we will limit our discussion to alpha.) A number of rules of thumb for what constitutes an acceptable level of coefficient alpha also exist. Some estimates go as low as .70 or .60 (Robinson et al. 1991). Regardless, scale length must be considered. As the number of items increases, alpha will tend to increase, and, because parsimony is also a concern in measurement (Carmines and Zeller 1979; Clark and Watson 1995; Cortina 1993), an important question is "how many items does it take to measure a construct?" The answer to this question depends partially on the domain and dimensions of the construct. Naturally, a construct with a wide domain and multiple dimensions will require more items to adequately tap the domain/dimensions than will a construct with a narrow domain and few dimensions. Given that most scales are self-administered and respondent fatigue and/or noncooperation need to be considered, it would seem that scale brevity is often a concern (cf. Bohrnstedt et al. 1987; Carmines and Zeller 1979; Churchill and Peter 1984; Cortina 1993; DeVillis 1991; Nunnally and Bernstein 1994).

With the advent of structural equation modeling, other tests of internal consistency are available. Composite reliability (Werts, Linn, and Jöreskog 1974), which is similar to coefficient alpha, can be calculated directly from the LISREL, EQS, or AMOS output (cf. Fornell and Larcker 1981). A more stringent test of internal stability involves assessing the amount of variance captured by a construct's measure in relation to the amount of variance due to measurement error. An advocated rule of thumb is that the variance extracted by the construct's measure is greater than .50 (Fornell and Larcker 1981). By using a combination of the criteria above (i.e., item-to-total correlations, examining the inter-item correlation matrix, coefficient alpha, composite reliability, and variance extracted estimates), researchers can develop scales in an efficient manner without sacrificing internal consistency.

Robinson et al. (1991) recently noted that it is possible to derive a scale with high internal consistency by writing the same items in different ways (i.e., "empirical redundancy"). Though slight wording variations between items will ensure high inter-item correlations and internal consistency estimates, they may detract from adequately tapping content domain. Internal consistency of a scale is highly desirable but must be balanced by sampling of item content, proper item wording, and other validity checks.

Finally, many scale development articles and texts recommend the use of "reverse-worded" items. These items clearly can have face validity and reduce the potential for acquiescence bias in responding. Still, one must consider the potential for a "methods" factor (or other threats to dimensionality) when using reverse-worded items. (For a discussion and application, the reader is urged to see Herche and Engellend [1996]).

Construct Validity

Beyond content validity, dimensionality, and reliability, a number of other validity issues must be considered in scale use and development, including convergent, discriminant, nomological, and known group validity. (These types of validity have been collectively referred to as "construct validity.") Again, a number of procedures and rules of thumb exist and should be considered.

Convergent, Discriminant, and Nomological Validity. Convergent validity refers to the degree to which two measures designed to measure the same construct are related. Convergence is found if the two measures are highly correlated. Discriminant validity assesses the degree to which two measures designed to measure similar, but conceptually different, constructs are related. A low to moderate correlation is often considered evidence of discriminant validity.

Multitrait multimethod matrices (MTMM) have often been used to assess convergent and discriminant validity where maximally different measurement methods (i.e., self-report vs. observational) are required (Campbell and Fiske 1959; Churchill 1979; Peter 1981). An early advocated rule of thumb for convergent validity is that the correlation between two measures designed to assess the same construct should be statistically significant and "sufficiently large to encourage further examination of validity" (Campbell and Fiske 1959, p. 82). Early advocated criteria for discriminant validity were (a) entries in the validity diagonal should be higher than the correlations that occupy the same row and column in the hetero-method block, (b) convergent validity coefficients should be higher than the correlations in the hetero-trait-mono-method triangles, and (c) the pattern of correlations should be the same in all the hetero-trait triangles (Campbell and Fiske 1959). Although these criteria have been criticized as problematic and vague (Peter 1981), they do offer some guidance as to what constitutes convergent and discriminant validity. Our discussion of MTMM here has been extremely brief and oversimplified, and the reader is strongly urged to consult the original source (Campbell and Fiske 1959) and a number of critical evaluations and updates (e.g., Bagozzi 1980; Bagozzi, Yi, and Phillips 1991; Kenny and Kashay 1992; Kumar and Dillon 1992; Peter 1981; Schmitt, Coyle, and Saari 1977; Schmitt and Stults 1986; Widaman 1985).

Nomological validity has been defined as the degree to which predictions from a formal theoretical network containing the concept under scrutiny are confirmed (Campbell 1960). It assesses the degree to which constructs that are theoretically related are actually empirically related (i.e., their measures correlate significantly in the predicted direction). Rules of thumb for nomological validity also exist but have been criticized as well (Peter 1981). As with internal consistency, structural equation packages have been used recently to assess the convergent, discriminant, and nomological validity of scale measures. MTMM procedures via structural equations are tenable where variance in the measures is partitioned as trait, method, and error variance (e.g., Bagozzi 1980, Bollen 1989; Kenny and Kashay 1992; Kumar and Dillon 1992; Schmitt and Stults 1986; Werts and Linn 1970; Widaman 1985). Convergent and discriminant validity is assessed via chi-square maximum likelihood tests and related fit statistics. Similarly, the empirical relationships among theoretically related measures (i.e., nomological validity) can also be assessed with structural equation models. Several books (e.g., Bollen 1989; Hayduk 1987, 1996; Hoyle 1995; James, Mulaik, and Brett 1982; Schumacker and Lomax 1996) and articles (e.g., Anderson and Gerbing 1988; Bagozzi et al. 1991; Bentler and Chou 1987) illustrate modeling techniques, evaluative criteria, and rules of thumb for what constitutes an acceptable level of validity.

Known Group Validity. Known group validity asks the question "Can the measure reliably distinguish between groups of people who should score high on the trait and low on the trait?" As examples, a person who is truly conservative should score significantly higher on a conservatism scale than a person who is liberal, and salespeople in the retail car business and the large computer business should differ in their levels of customer orientation (Saxe and Weitz 1982). Thus, mean score differences between groups for a given scale can be used as evidence of known group validity. An excellent application of known group validity testing can be found in Jarvis and Petty (1996).

Other Issues to Consider

Other issues warrant some discussion regarding the development and evaluation of multi-item scales in marketing and consumer research: (a) representative sampling, (b) the provision of normative information, and (c) response set bias.

First, an often neglected issue in scale development, particularly in the marketing and consumer behavior literature, has been representative sampling. Too many scales have been developed using samples of college students only, and in general, results from student samples are difficult to generalize to other populations. (For an excellent review, see Sears [1986].) We are not advocating the discontinuation of using college student samples; however, we are recom-

mending that scale developers go beyond student samples to samples more representative of the population as a whole, or a given population of interest. In essence, the prime consideration in scale evaluation, use, and development is the applicability of the scale and scale norms to respondents who are likely to use them in the future (Robinson et al. 1991).

Another area often overlooked by those who develop scales is the reporting of mean and/or percentage scores and variances (i.e., normative information). A raw score on a measurement instrument is not particularly informative about the position of a person on the characteristic being measured because the units in which the scale is expressed are often interval and unfamiliar (Churchill 1979, p. 72). Scale means, individual item means, and standard deviations across different sample groups represent useful information because they offer a frame of reference and comparison points for the potential scale user.

Finally, increased testing for response set bias is needed in scale development and use in consumer and marketing research. Response set bias refers to a tendency on the part of individuals to respond to attitude statements for reasons other than the content of the statements (Mick 1996; Paulhus 1991; Robinson et al. 1991). What can result is a scale score not truly reflective of how the respondent actually stands on the construct. Two sources of response set bias are commonly cited: acquiescence bias and social desirability bias. Acquiescence bias can take the form of responses that reflect an attitude change in accordance with a given situation, or "yea-saying and nay-saying"— where respondents are willing to go along with anything that sounds good or are unwilling to look at the negative side of an issue (Robinson et al. 1991). Although there are no easy answers regarding the elimination of acquiescence bias, procedures have been recommended (Paulhus 1991; Robinson et al. 1991).

Trying to make a good impression is the most common form of social desirability bias. That is, respondents may purposefully score low on measures assessing undesirable social characteristics (i.e., selfishness) or purposefully score high on measures assessing desirable social characteristics (i.e., altruism). Although some research has shown that the effects of social desirability bias may be overstated (Moorman and Podsakoff 1992), others suggest that such effects still can bias the relationships among variables, particularly those that have a higher propensity for socially desirable responding (Mick 1996). Although this type of bias is difficult to detect and control, several authors do offer procedures and/or scales for examining social desirability bias (Crowne and Marlowe 1960; Mick 1996; Paulhus 1991, 1992; Robinson et al. 1991; Strahan and Gerbasi 1972). These measures and procedures should be considered in scale development and testing.

Summary

In the preceding few pages, we have tried to delineate those most frequently acknowledged concepts and procedures useful for developing, evaluating, and using self-report scale measures. These procedures include examining the theoretical base of the measure, content validity, dimensionality, reliability, construct validity, and issues relating to sample representativeness, scale norms, and response set bias. We have offered only a brief discussion of each of these procedures, and as we have stated throughout, the reader is strongly urged to consult the more thorough sources that we have cited.

REFERENCES

American Psychological Association. (1985). *Standards for Educational and Psychological Tests*. Washington, DC: Author.

Anderson, James C., and David W. Gerbing. (1988). "Structural Equation Modeling in Practice: A Review and Recommended Two-Step Approach." *Psychological Bulletin, 103*, 411-423.

Anderson, James C., David W. Gerbing, and John E. Hunter. (1987). "On the Assessment of Unidimensional Measurement: Internal and External Consistency, and Overall Consistency Criteria." *Journal of Marketing Research, 24*, 432-437.

Bagozzi, Richard P. (1980). *Causal Models in Marketing*. New York: John Wiley.

Bagozzi, Richard P., Youjai Yi, and Lynn W. Phillips. (1991). "Assessing Construct Validity in Organizational Research." *Administrative Science Quarterly, 36*, 421-458.

Bearden, William O., Richard G. Netemeyer, and Jesse E. Teel. (1989). "Measurement of Consumer Susceptibility to Interpersonal Influence." *Journal of Consumer Research, 15*, 473-481.

Bentler, Peter M., and Chih-Ping Chou. (1987). "Practical Issues in Structural Modeling." *Sociological Methods & Research, 16*, 78-117.

Bohrnstedt, George, and Edgar F. Borgatta. (1981). *Social Measurement: Issues*. Beverly Hills, CA: Sage.

Bohrnstedt, George, Peter P. Mohler, and W. Muller (1987). *Empirical Study of the Reliability and Stability of Survey Research Items*. Newbury Park, CA: Sage.

Bollen, Kenneth A. (1989). *Structural Equations With Latent Variables*. New York: John Wiley.

Campbell, Donald T. (1960). "Recommendations for APA Test Standards Regarding Construct, Trait, or Discriminant Validity." *American Psychologist, 15*, 546-553.

Campbell, Donald T., and Donald W. Fiske. (1959). "Convergent and Discriminant Validity by the Multitrait-Multimethod Matrix." *Psychological Bulletin, 56*, 81-105.

Carmines, Edward G., and Richard G. Zeller. (1979). *Reliability and Validity Assessment*. Beverly Hills, CA: Sage.

Churchill, Gilbert A. (1979). "A Paradigm for Developing Better Measures of Marketing Constructs." *Journal of Marketing Research, 16*, 64-73.

Churchill, Gilbert A., and J. Paul Peter. (1984). "Research Design Effects on the Reliability of Rating Scales: A Meta-Analysis." *Journal of Marketing Research, 21*, 360-375.

Clark, Lee Anna, and David Watson. (1995). "Constructing Validity: Basic Issues in Scale Development." *Psychological Assessment, 7*(3), 309-319.

Converse, Jean M., and Stanley S. Presser. (1986). *Survey Questions: Handcrafting the Standardized Questionnaire*. Newbury Park, CA: Sage.

Cortina, J. M. (1993). "What Is Coefficient Alpha? An Examination of Theory and Application." *Journal of Applied Psychology, 78*, 98-104.

Cronbach, Lee J. (1951). "Coefficient Alpha and the Internal Structure of Tests." *Psychometrika, 31*, 93-96.

Crowne, Douglas P., and David Marlowe. (1960). "A New Scale for Social Desirability Independent of Psychopathology." *Journal of Consulting Psychology, 24*, 349-354.

DeVillis, Robert F. (1991). *Scale Development: Theory and Applications*. Newbury Park, CA: Sage.

Floyd, Frank J., and Keith Widaman. (1995). "Factor Analysis in the Development and Refinement of Clinical Assessment Instruments." *Psychological Assessment, 7*(3), 286-299.

Fornell, Claes, and David F. Larcker. (1981). "Evaluating Structural Equation Models With Unobservable Variables and Measurement Error." *Journal of Marketing Research, 18*, 39-50.

Gerbing, David W., and James C. Anderson. (1988). "An Updated Paradigm for Scale Development Incorporating Unidimensionality and Its Assessment." *Journal of Marketing Research, 25*, 186-192.

Hattie, John. (1985). "Methodology Review: Assessing Unidimensionality of Tests and Items." *Applied Psychological Measurement, 9*, 139-164.

Hayduk, Leslie A. (1987). *Structural Equations Modeling With LISREL: Essentials and Advances*. Baltimore, MA: Johns Hopkins University Press.

Hayduk, Leslie A. (1996). *LISREL: Issues, Debates, and Strategies*. Baltimore, MA: Johns Hopkins University Press.

Herche, Joel, and Brain Engellend. (1996). "Reversed-Polarity Items and Scale Dimensionality." *Journal of the Academy of Marketing Science*, 24(4), 366-374.

Hoyle, Rick. (1995). *Structural Equation Modeling: Issues and Applications*. Newbury Park, CA: Sage.

James, Lawrence R., Stanley A. Mulaik, and Jeanne M. Brett. (1982). *Causal Analysis: Assumptions, Models, and Data*. Beverly Hills, CA: Sage.

Jarvis, W. Blair G., and Richard E. Petty. (1996). "The Need to Evaluate." *Journal of Personality and Social Psychology*, 70(1), 172-194.

Kenny, D. A., and D. A. Kashay. (1992). "Analysis of the Multi-Trait Multi-Method Matrix by Confirmatory Factor Analysis." *Psychological Bulletin*, 122, 165-172.

Kumar, Ajith, and William R. Dillon. (1987a). "The Interaction of Measurement and Structure in Simultaneous Equation Models With Unobservable Variables." *Journal of Marketing Research*, 24, 98-105.

Kumar, Ajith, and William R. Dillon. (1987b). "Some Further Remarks on Measurement-Structure Interaction and the Unidimensionality of Constructs." *Journal of Marketing Research*, 24, 438-444.

Kumar, Ajith, and William R. Dillon. (1992). "An Integrative Look at the Use of Additive and Multiplicative Covariance Structure Models in the Analysis of MTMM Data." *Journal of Marketing Research*, 29, 51-64.

McDonald, Roderick P. (1981). "The Dimensionality of Tests and Items." *British Journal of Mathematical and Statistical Psychology*, 34, 100-117.

McDonald, Roderick P. (1985). *Factor Analysis and Related Methods*. Hillsdale, NJ: Lawrence Erlbaum.

Mick, David Glen. (1996). "Are Studies of Dark Side Variables Confounded by Socially Desirable Responding? The Case of Materialism." *Journal of Consumer Research*, 23, 106-119.

Moorman, Robert H., and Phillip Podsakoff. (1992). "A Meta-Analytic Review and Empirical Test of the Potential Confounding Effect of Social Desirability Response Sets in Organizational Behavior Research." *Journal of Occupational and Organizational Psychology*, 56(2), 131-149.

Nunnally, Jum, and Ira H. Bernstein. (1994). *Psychometric Theory* (3rd ed.). New York: McGraw-Hill.

Paulhus, Delroy L. (1991). "Measurement and Control of Response Bias." In J. P. Robinson, P. R. Shaver, and L. S. Wrightsman (Eds.), *Measures of Personality and Social Psychological Attitudes* (pp. 17-59). San Diego: Academic Press.

Paulhus, Delroy L. (1992). "The Balanced Inventory of Desirable Responding." In *Reference Manual, BIDR Version 6*. Vancouver: University of British Columbia.

Peter, J. Paul. (1979). "Reliability: A Review of Psychometric Basics and Recent Marketing Practices." *Journal of Marketing Research*, 16, 6-17.

Peter, J. Paul. (1981). "Construct Validity: A Review of Basic Issues and Marketing Practices." *Journal of Marketing Research*, 18, 133-145.

Robinson, John P., Phillip R. Shaver, and Lawrence S. Wrightsman. (1991). "Criteria for Scale Selection and Evaluation." In J. P. Robinson, P. R. Shaver, and L. S. Wrightsman (Eds.), *Measures of Personality and Social Psychological Attitudes* (pp. 1-15). San Diego: Academic Press.

Saxe, Robert, and Barton A. Weitz. (1982). "The SOCO Scale: A Measure of the Customer Orientation of Salespeople." *Journal of Marketing Research*, 19, 343-351.

Schmitt, Neal, Brian W. Coyle, and Bryce B. Saari. (1977). "A Review and Critique of Multitrait-Multimethod Matrices." *Multivariate Behavioral Research*, 12, 447-478.

Schmitt, Neal, and Daniel M. Stults. (1986). "Methodology Review: Analysis of Multitrait-Multimethod Matrices." *Applied Psychological Measurement*, 10, 1-22.

Schumacker, Randall E., and Richard G. Lomax. (1996). *A Beginners Guide to Structural Equation Modeling*. Mahwah, NJ: Lawrence Erlbaum.

Sears, David O. (1986). "College Sophomores in the Laboratory: Influences of a Narrow Data Base on Social Psychology's View of Human Nature." *Journal of Personality and Social Psychology*, 51, 515-530.

Shimp, Terence A., and Subhash Sharma. (1987). "Consumer Ethnocentrism: Construction and Validation of the CETSCALE." *Journal of Marketing Research*, 24, 280-289.

Spector, Paul E. (1992). *Summated Rating Scale Construction: An Introduction*. Newbury Park, CA: Sage.

Strahan, Robert, and Kathleen C. Gerbasi. (1972). "Short, Homogeneous Versions of the Marlowe-Crown Social Desirability Scale." *Journal of Clinical Psychology*, 28, 191-193.

Sudman, Seymour, and Norman M. Bradburn. (1982). *Asking Questions*. San Francisco: Jossey-Bass.

Werts, Charles E., and Robert L. Linn. (1970). "Cautions in Applying Various Procedures for Determining the Reliability and Validity of Multiple-Item Scales." *American Sociological Review, 34,* 757-759.

Werts, Charles E., Robert L. Linn, and Karl G. Jöreskog. (1974). "Interclass Reliability Estimates: Testing Structural Assumptions." *Educational and Psychological Measurement, 34,* 25-33.

Widaman, Keith F. (1985). "Hierarchically Nested Covariance Structure Models for Multitrait-Multimethod Data." *Applied Psychological Measurement, 9,* 1-26.

2

Traits and Individual Difference Variables

SCALES RELATED TO INTERPERSONAL ORIENTATION, NEEDS/PREFERENCES, AND SELF-CONCEPT

INNER-OTHER DIRECTEDNESS: SOCIAL PREFERENCE SCALE
(Kassarjian 1962)

Construct: The I-O scale is designed to assess two of the social character types proposed by Riesman (1950) in his book *The Lonely Crowd*. These two types are inner-directed and other-directed people. Inner-directed persons turn to their own inner values and standards for guidance in their behavior, while other-directed persons depend upon the people around them to give direction to their actions (Kassarjian 1962, p. 213). Inner-directed persons are thought to be driven by their need for accomplishment, while other-directed persons are motivated by the need for approval from others. The I-O Preference Scale (i.e., the preference for inner- versus other-directedness) is designed to place people along a continuum from other- to inner-directedness.

Description: The scale consists of 36 forced-choice items. Each item consists of an incomplete statement and two responses, one inner-directed and one other-directed. Respondents select the response that they agree with most and provide their degree of agreement with each item. (See instructions in Kassarjian [1962, p. 226].) The other-directed answer is assigned a value of –2; the inner-directed answer is assigned a value of +2. A constant of 72 is added to the total score to avoid negative values. Consequently, the scale can range from 0 (complete other-direction) to 144 (complete inner-direction).

Development: Little detail was provided by Kassarjian (1962, p. 217) regarding the development of the 36-item scale. In a preliminary study, first-person-worded statements with forced-choice response formats were found superior to other procedures. Only those items that consistently elicited varied responses and that contributed to scale internal consistency were retained for the final scale. Item reliability was verified using test-retest procedures. A number of validation procedures were also performed.

Samples: UCLA undergraduates served as subjects in all preliminary studies. The validation studies were carried out with both graduate and undergraduate students, while the general distribution of scores was examined on a stratified sample of Los Angeles residents. The final test reported by Kassarjian (1962, p. 217) involved 150 undergraduate students.

10

Validity: Item-to-total correlations ranged from .32 to .94. A 4-week test-retest administration on a sample of 52 undergraduates yielded a reliability coefficient of .85. Correlations between the I-O scale and an index of behaviors (e.g., hobbies, sports, social activity) ranged from .55 to .69 across various combinations of the student samples. These behaviors were expected to vary between other- and inner-directed individuals. Evidence of discriminant validity was provided by low correlations with two personality characteristic measures (e.g., the SI-scale of the MMPI) thought similar to but different from social character, and low correlations with an Asch-type measure of social conformity. A significant difference in means ($t = 4.98$, $p < .05$) between two samples of undergraduate students selected from varying majors to represent predictable differences in other-directed individuals (e.g., education, social welfare majors) and inner-directed individuals (e.g., natural sciences, philosophy majors) was also obtained.

While city dwellers were found more other-directed than rural residents, other demographic comparisons were largely nonsignificant. However, additional evidence of validity was provided by lower scores on a 25-item version of the I-O scale for a general population sample (i.e., older and, hence, more inner-directed) as compared to student respondents.

Scores: The average score for the undergraduate sample of 150 was 72.2 ($SD = 16.93$) (with a range of 22 to 109). A sample of 96 graduate students had a significantly higher mean of 86.97 ($SD = 17.85$) (i.e., significantly more inner-directed). The undergraduate mean scores for the varying academic majors were 79.4 and 93.9 for the other- and inner-directed groups, respectively.

Source: Kassarjian, Waltraud M. (1962). "A Study of Riesman's Theory of Social Character." *Sociometry*, *25*, 213-230. Scale items taken from pp. 226-230.

Other evidence: Additional evidence of the validity of the I-O scale as a measure of social character has been provided by its successful application in a number of marketing and consumer contexts by other researchers. (Three of these are cited below; a larger number of successful applications outside of consumer contexts have been reported as well.) This consumer-research-related evidence includes the research by Kassarjian (1965), which found that inner- and other-directed individuals show differential preference for advertisements created to appeal to varying character types. Relationships among social character, innovation proneness, and adoption leadership among farmers were studied by Barban, Sandage, Kassarjian, and Kassarjian (1970). Their results (based on use of a 30-item version of the scale) revealed that social character was normally distributed across the sample of 828 male heads of farm households. In addition, inner-directed subjects were found to be more prone to adopt innovations. Only weak relationships were found between inner-other directedness and adoption leadership and key demographic variables. Support for these findings was provided by Donnelly (1970) in his research involving a survey of 140 housewives. Specifically, it was concluded that the I-O Social Preference Scale was related to the acceptance of five innovative grocery products. The mean score for the 140 housewives in Donnelly's research was 72.2.

Other sources: Barban, Arnold M., C. H. Sandage, Waltraud M. Kassarjian, and Harold H. Kassarjian. (1970). "A Study of Riesman's Inner-Other Directedness Among Farmers." *Rural Sociology*, *35*, 232-243.

Donnelly, James H., Jr. (1970). "Social Character and Acceptance of New Products." *Journal of Marketing Research*, *7*, 111-113.

Kassarjian, Harold H. (1965). "Social Character and Differential Preference for Mass Communication." *Journal of Marketing Research*, *2*, 146-153.

Reference: Riesman, David. (1950). *The Lonely Crowd*. New Haven, CT: Yale University Press.

INNER-OTHER DIRECTEDNESS: SOCIAL PREFERENCE SCALE
(Kassarjian 1962)

1. With regard to partying, I feel
   a. the more the merrier (25 or more people present);
   b. it is nicest to be in a small group of intimate friends (6 or 8 people at most).

2. If I had more time,
   a. I would spend more evenings at home doing the things I'd like to do;
   b. I would more often go out with my friends.

3. If I were trained as an electrical engineer and liked my work very much and would be offered a promotion into an administrative position, I would
   a. accept it because it means an advancement in pay which I need quite badly;
   b. turn it down because it would no longer give me an opportunity to do the work I like and am trained for even though I desperately need more money.

4. I believe that
   a. it is difficult to draw the line between work and play and therefore one should not even try it;
   b. one is better off keeping work and social activities separated.

5. I would rather join
   a. a political or social club or organization;
   b. an organization dedicated to literary, scientific, or other academic subject matter.

6. I would be more eager to accept a person as a group leader who
   a. is outstanding in those activities which are important to the group;
   b. is about average in the performance of the group activities but has an especially pleasing personality.

7. I like to read books about
   a. people like you and me;
   b. great people or adventurers.

8. For physical exercise or as a sport, I would prefer
   a. softball, basketball, volleyball, or similar team sport;
   b. skiing, hiking, horseback riding, bicycling, or similar individual sport.

9. With regard to a job, I would enjoy more
   a. one in which one can show his skill or knowledge;
   b. one in which one gets contact with many different people.

10. I believe
    a. being able to make friends is a great accomplishment in and of itself;
    b. one should be concerned more about one's achievements rather than making friends.

11. It is more desirable
    a. to be popular and well liked by everybody;
    b. to become famous in the field of one's choice or for a particular deed.

12. With regard to clothing,
    a. I would feel conspicuous if I were not dressed the way most of my friends are dressed;
    b. I like to wear clothes which stress my individuality and which not everybody else is wearing.

13. On the subject of social living,
    a. a person should set up his own standards and then live up to them;
    b. one should be careful to live up to the prevailing standards of the culture.

14. I would consider it more embarrassing
    a. to be caught loafing on a job for which I get paid;
    b. losing my temper when a number of people are around of whom I think a lot.

15. I respect the person most who
    a. is considerate of others and concerned that they think well of him;
    b. lives up to his ideals and principles.

16. A child who has intellectual difficulties in some grade in school
    a. should repeat the grade to be able to get more out of the next higher grade;
    b. should be kept with his age group though he has some intellectual difficulties.

17. In my free time
    a. I'd like to read an interesting book at home;
    b. I'd rather be with a group of my friends.

18. I have
    a. a great many friends who are, however, not very intimate friends;
    b. few but rather intimate friends.

19. When doing something, I am most concerned with
    a. "what's in it for me" and how long will it last;
    b. what impression others will get of me for doing it.

20. As leisure-time activity, I would rather choose
    a. woodcarving, painting, stamp collecting, photography, or a similar activity;
    b. bridge or other card game, or discussion groups.

21. I consider a person most successful, when
    a. he can live up to his own standards and ideals;
    b. he can get along with even the most difficult people.

22. One of the main things a child should be taught is
    a. cooperation;
    b. self-discipline.

23. As far as I am concerned,
    a. I am only happy when I have people around me;
    b. I am perfectly happy when I am left alone.

24. On a free evening,
    a. I like to go and see a nice movie;
    b. I would try to have a television party at my (or a friend's) house.

25. The persons whom I admire most are those who
    a. are very outstanding in their achievements;
    b. have a very pleasant personality.

26. I consider myself to be
    a. quite idealistic and to some extent a "dreamer";
    b. quite realistic and living for the present only.

27. In bringing up children, parents should
    a. look more at what is done by other families with children;
    b. stick to their own ideas on how they want their children brought up regardless of what others do.

28. To me, it is very important
    a. what one is and does regardless of what others think;
    b. what my friends think of me.

29. I prefer listening to a person who
    a. knows his subject matter real well but is not skilled in presenting interestingly;
    b. knows his subject matter not as well but has an interesting way of discussing it.

30. As far as I am concerned
    a. I see real advantages to keeping a diary and would like to keep one myself;
    b. I'd rather discuss my experiences with friends than keep a diary.

31. Schools should
    a. teach children to take their place in society;
    b. be concerned more with teaching subject matter.

32. It is desirable
    a. that one shares the opinions others hold on a particular matter;
    b. that one strongly holds onto his opinions even though they may be radically different from those of others.

33. For me it is more important to
    a. keep my dignity (not make a fool of myself) even though I may not always be considered a good sport;
    b. be a good sport even though I would lose my dignity (and make a fool of myself) by doing it.

34. When in a strange city or foreign country, I should have no great difficulty because
    a. I am interested in new things and can live under almost any new conditions;
    b. people are the same everywhere and I can get along with them.

35. I believe in coffee breaks and social activities for employees because
    a. it gives people a chance to get to know each other and enjoy work more;
    b. people work more efficiently when they do not work for too long a stretch at a time and can look forward to a special event.

36. The greatest influence upon children should be
    a. from outside their own age group and from educational sources outside the family since they can be more objective in evaluating the child's needs;
    b. from the immediate family who should know the child best.

NOTES: As stated above in the **Description** section, scoring procedures for the scale are provided in Kassarjian (1962, p. 226). We have not provided these procedures here because of the complexity of them. Though all statements are dichotomous, they are scored on a four-choice basis using columns, where the respondent is asked to choose one column over the others. Thus, the potential user of the scale is referred to Kassarjian (1962) for explicit instructions on scale administration.

INTERPERSONAL ORIENTATION: CAD SCALE
(Cohen 1967)

Construct: The CAD scale is designed to measure a person's interpersonal orientation. The instrument was derived from Horney's (1945) tripartite model. Specifically, the scale is designed to assess compliant, aggressive, and detached interpersonal orientations. Compliant oriented persons are those who desire to be a part of the activities of others (i.e., who move toward others). Aggressive persons are those who want to excel, to achieve success, prestige, and admiration. Detached individuals desire to put emotional distance between themselves and others (i.e., they move away from others) (Cohen 1967, pp. 270-271). The impetus for the scale is based on the expected effects of varying interpersonal orientations on consumer decision making.

Description: The scale consists of 35 items each operationalized using 6-point scales labeled *extremely undesirable* to *extremely desirable*. Ten items each are used to represent the compliant and detached factors. The remaining 15 items reflect the aggressive dimension. Total scores for each subscale are formed by summing item scores within each dimension.

Development: The exact procedures used to develop the initial set of items were not described in Cohen (1967). However, a number of separate analyses were conducted in evaluation of the 35-item, three-factor scale. In support of the measures, seven expert judges agreed that the items demonstrated face validity and reflected their respective dimensions. Several tests for evidence of convergent and predictive validity were performed.

Samples: A series of different undergraduate and graduate student samples was used in the initial development and validation of the CAD scales. For example, the final validation efforts involving the study of a wide range of consumer decisions were based on the responses of 157 undergraduate business students.

Validity: Evidence of convergent validity was provided by correlations of the CAD scale with measures of occupational interpersonal relations. For example, the correlation between the compliant CAD factor and the occupational interpersonal compliant factor was .48 ($p < .01$). As predicted, less aggressive and more compliant subjects exhibited greater "change" in a study of susceptibility to interpersonal influence (Cohen 1967, p. 273).

In addition to the validity evidence cited above, the CAD scale factors were further examined for differences across a number of product and brand purchase decisions. The results indicate that "some products and brands appear to express either compliant, aggressive, or detached responses to life" (Cohen 1967, p. 277). Some of the specific findings include the following. High aggressives exhibited differential brand preferences for deodorant, beer, and dress shirts. Both high and low aggressive and high and low detached students differed in their television viewing preferences.

Scores: Cohen (1967) reports a series of mean scores for each factor. However, in his Appendix, it is noted that "Studies reported in this article have used an earlier 4-point response format" (Cohen 1967, p. 277). Hence, mean scores from the original article are not reproduced here since the final version reported by Cohen (1967) recommends a wider 6-point response format.

Source: Cohen, Joel B. (1967). "An Interpersonal Orientation to the Study of Consumer Behavior." *Journal of Marketing Research*, *4*, 270-278.

© 1967 by the American Marketing Association. Scale items taken from p. 277. Reprinted with permission from the American Marketing Association.

Other evidence: A number of studies have either employed or reevaluated the CAD scale(s). Three of these are cited below.

Ryan and Becherer (1976) reported internal consistency reliability estimates for the three factors as follows: compliant, .72; aggressive, .68; and detached, .51. Though the results of a factor analysis with varimax rotation produced a four-factor solution, most of the items did load on three factors that appeared to represent aggressive, compliant, and detached orientations. In addition, these were the first three factors of the four-factor solution.

Tyagi (1983) reported coefficient alpha estimates of internal consistency of .72, .62, and .63 for the compliant, aggressive, and detached factors, respectively. Intercorrelations among the three factors ranged from −.31 to .25. The results of an MTMM analysis using measures of nurturance, aggression, and autonomy provided mixed but generally positive support for the convergent and discriminant validity of the measures.

Noerager (1979) provided less supportive results. Specifically, the coefficient alpha estimates of internal consistency reliability for the compliant, aggressive, and detached factors were .60, .36, and .43, respectively. The results of a factor analysis of the 35 items did not reveal a pattern of simple structure along the lines predicted by the theoretical justification for the measures (i.e., a three-factor model).

Other sources: Noerager, Jon P. (1979). "An Assessment of CAD: A Personality Instrument Developed Specifically for Marketing Research." *Journal of Marketing Research*, *16*, 53-59.

Ryan, Michael J., and Richard C. Becherer. (1976). "A Multivariate Test of CAD Instrument Construct Validity." In Beverly B. Anderson (Ed.), *Advances in Consumer Research* (Vol. 3, pp. 149-154). Cincinnati, OH: Association for Consumer Research.

Tyagi, Pradeep K. (1983). "Validation of the CAD Instrument: A Replication." In Richard P. Bagozzi and Alice M. Tybout (Eds.), *Advances in Consumer Research* (Vol. 10, pp. 112-114). Ann Arbor, MI: Association for Consumer Research.

Reference: Horney, Karen. (1945). *Our Inner Conflicts*. New York: W. W. Norton.

INTERPERSONAL ORIENTATION: CAD SCALE
(Cohen 1967)

Extremely							*Extremely*
undesirable	*1*	*2*	*3*	*4*	*5*	*6*	*desirable*

1. Being free of emotional ties with others is:

2. Giving comfort to those in need of friends is:

3. The knowledge that most people would be fond of me at all times would be:

4. To refuse to give in to others in an argument seems:

5. Enjoying a good movie by myself is:

6. For me to pay little attention to what others think of me seems:

7. For me to be able to own an item before most of my friends are able to buy it would be:

8. Knowing that others are somewhat envious of me is:

9. To feel that I like everyone I know would be:

10. To be able to work hard while others elsewhere are having fun is:

11. Using pull to get ahead would be:

12. For me to have enough money or power to impress self-styled "big-shots" would be:

13. Basing my life on duty to others is:

14. To be able to work under tension would be:

15. If I could live all alone in a cabin in the woods or mountains it would be:

16. Pushing those who insult my honor is:

17. To give aid to the poor and underprivileged is:

18. Standing in the way of people who are too sure of themselves is:

19. Being free of social obligations is:

20. To have something good to say about everybody seems:

21. Telling a waiter when you have received inferior food is:

22. Planning to get along without others is:

23. To be able to spot and exploit weaknesses in others is:

24. A strong desire to surpass others' achievements seems:

25. Sharing my personal feelings with others would be:

26. To have the ability to blame others for their mistakes is:

27. For me to avoid situations where others can influence me would be:

28. Wanting to repay others' thoughtless actions with friendship is:

29. Having to compete with others for various rewards is:

30. If I knew that others paid very little attention to my affairs it would be:

31. To defend my rights by force would be:

32. Putting myself out to be considerate to others' feelings is:

33. Correcting people who express an ignorant belief is:

34. For me to work alone would be:

35. To be fair to people who do things which I consider wrong seems:

NOTES: The items belonging to the factors are arranged as follows:
Compliant: 2, 3, 9, 13, 17, 20, 25, 28, 32, 35;
Aggressive: 4, 7, 8, 11, 12, 14, 16, 18, 21, 23, 24, 26, 29, 31, 33;
Detached: 1, 5, 6, 10, 15, 19, 22, 27, 30, 34.

NEED FOR COGNITION: NFC
(Cacioppo and Petty 1982)

Construct: Need for cognition (NFC) represents the tendency for individuals to engage in and enjoy thinking (Cacioppo and Petty 1982). Cohen, Stotland, and Wolfe (1955) originally described the need for cognition as a need to structure relevant situations in meaningful, integrated ways and a need to understand and make reasonable the experiential world. The scale has been frequently used in consumer research in examining the effects of persuasive arguments. Among these applications, the concept has been shown to be useful in understanding how argument strength and endorser attractiveness in advertisements may influence consumer attitudes (e.g., individuals high in need for cognition are more influenced by the quality of arguments in an advertisement) (Haugtvedt, Petty, Cacioppo, and Steidley 1988). In addition, it has been shown that individuals low in need for cognition react to the simple presence of a price promotion signal whether or not the price of the promoted brand is reduced (Inman, McAlister, and Hoyer 1990).

Description: The original scale is comprised of 34 items each scored –4 to +4 as follows: +4, *very strong agreement*; +3, *strong agreement*; +2, *moderate agreement*; +1, *slight agreement*; 0, *neither agreement nor disagreement*; –1, *slight disagreement*; –2, *moderate disagreement*; –3, *strong disagreement*; and –4, *very strong disagreement*. An 18-item short form for assessing need for cognition has been proposed by Cacioppo, Petty, and Kao (1984). The items included in both versions are presented here. Some of the items are varied in direction to inhibit response bias. Item scores are summed for an overall index.

Development: An unspecified pool of items was edited (i.e., deleted or revised) for ambiguity. The remaining pool of 45 items was administered to the faculty of a large midwestern university (i.e., a high need for cognition group) and a group of factory line workers from the same community (Cacioppo and Petty 1982, p. 118). The initial sample (combining both groups) included a total of 96 respondents; 84 of the respondents were included in these initial analyses. A series of 2 × 2 (gender by high and low cognition; i.e., gender by faculty/factory line worker) analysis of variance tests were used to delete items that did not discriminate between the high and low groups. Tests for the overall sum for the initial 45 items and the final 34 items revealed a significant main effect for need for cognition but nonsignificant effects for gender and the interaction. Remaining items that failed to correlate significantly with the total score were also eliminated.

Samples: As explained above, 84 university professors and factory workers were used in the Study 1 development of the 34-item NFC measure. The sample was composed of approximately equal numbers of males and females. Participants in Study 2 were 419 introductory psychology students. Study 3 involved 104 (35 males and 69 females) students from the University of Iowa, and 97 student subjects participated in Study 4.

Validity: A single dominant factor from a principal components analysis was interpreted as support for a unidimensional scale composed of 34 items. The correlation between factor loadings in Studies 1 and 2 was .76 ($n = 34$, p .01). Multiple sources of validity evidence are described in Cacioppo and Petty (1982). For example, evidence of discriminant validity was found in Study 2 from low correlations with measures of cognitive style and test anxiety. In Study 3, correlations with intelligence ($r = .39$), social desirability ($r = .08$), and dogmatism ($r = -.27$) were provided as evidence of the scale's validity. In Study 4, a significant hypothesized interaction revealed that high NFC subjects reported enjoying a complex task more than a simple task, while low NFC subjects enjoyed a simple task more than a complex task. Also in Study 4, a modest negative correlation with dogmatism was found ($r = -.23$); however, a significant correlation with a measure of social desirability was revealed ($r = .21$).

Scores: Means and standard deviations were not provided in the cited manuscripts.

Source: Cacioppo, John T., and Richard E. Petty. (1982). "The Need for Cognition." *Journal of Personality and Social Psychology*, *42*(1), 116-131.

© 1982 by the American Psychological Association. Scale items taken from Table 1 (pp. 120-121). Reprinted with permission.

Other evidence: In the development of the short form, Cacioppo et al. (1984) reported coefficient alpha estimates of internal consistency reliability of .90 and .91 for the 18-item and 34-item versions, respectively.

Substantial evidence of the validity of the construct and the measures described here has been provided by a number of studies which have successfully used the Cacioppo and Petty (1982) need for cognition scale. As recent examples, the two studies by Haugtvedt et al. (1988) showed, as predicted from the theory underlying the construct, that individuals high in need for cognition were more influenced by the quality of arguments in advertisements and that individuals low in NFC were influenced more by the peripheral cue endorser attractiveness. Similarly, Inman et al. (1990) used the NFC measure to successfully predict the effects of price signals (i.e., price messages without actual price information).

Epstein, Pacini, Denes-Raj, and Heier (1996) offer a 5-item version of NFC as a factor in their "Rational-Experiential Inventory (REI)." (See the summary of the REI in this chapter.)

Other sources: Cacioppo, John T., Richard E. Petty, and Kao Feng Chuan. (1984). "The Efficient Assessment of Need for Cognition." *Journal of Personality Assessment*, *48*(3), 306-307.

Haugtvedt, Curt, Richard E. Petty, John T. Cacioppo, and Theresa Steidley. (1988). "Personality and Ad Effectiveness: Exploring the Utility of Need for Cognition." In Michael J. Houston (Ed.), *Advances in Consumer Research* (Vol. 15, pp. 209-212). Provo, UT: Association for Consumer Research.

Inman, J. Jeffrey, Leigh McAlister, and Wayne D. Hoyer. (1990). "Promotion Signal: Proxy for a Price Cut." *Journal of Consumer Research*, *17*(June), 74-81.

References: Cohen, A. R., E. Stotland, and D. M. Wolfe. (1955). "An Experimental Investigation of Need for Cognition." *Journal of Abnormal and Social Psychology*, *51*, 291-294.

Epstein, Seymour, Rosemary Pacini, Veronika Denes-Raj, and Harriet Heier. (1996). "Individual Differences in Intuitive-Experiential and Analytical-Rational Thinking Styles." *Journal of Personality and Social Psychology*, *71*(2), 390-505.

NEED FOR COGNITION: NFC
(Cacioppo and Petty 1982)

1. I really enjoy a task that involves coming up with solutions to problems. (b)

2. I would prefer a task that is intellectual, difficult, and important to one that is somewhat important but does not require much thought. (b)

3. I tend to set goals that can be accomplished only by expending considerable mental effort.

4. I am usually tempted to put more thought into a task than the job minimally requires.

5. Learning new ways to think doesn't excite me very much. (a, b)

6. I am hesitant about making important decisions after thinking about them. (a)

7. I usually end up deliberating about issues even when they do affect me personally. (b)

8. I prefer to let things happen rather than try to understand why they turned out that way. (a)

9. I have difficulty in thinking in new and unfamiliar situations. (a)

10. The idea of relying on thought to get my way to the top does not appeal to me. (a, b)

11. The notion of thinking abstractly is not appealing to me. (a, b)

12. I am an intellectual.

13. I only think as hard as I have to. (a, b)

14. I don't reason well under pressure. (a)

15. I like tasks that require little thought once I've learned them. (a, b)

16. I prefer to think about, small daily projects to long-term ones. (a, b)

17. I would rather do something that requires little thought than something that is sure to challenge my thinking abilities. (b)

18. I find little satisfaction in deliberating hard and for long hours. (a, b)

19. I more often talk with other people about the reasons for and possible solutions to international problems than about gossip of tidbits of what famous people are doing.

20. These days, I see little chance for performing well, even in "intellectual" jobs, unless one knows the right people. (a)

21. More often than not, more thinking just leads to more errors. (a)

22. I don't like to have the responsibility of handling a situation that requires a lot of thinking. (a, b)

23. I appreciate opportunities to discover the strengths and weaknesses of my own reasoning.

24. I feel relief rather than satisfaction after completing a task that required a lot of mental effort. (a, b)

25. Thinking is not my idea of fun. (a, b)

26. I try to anticipate and avoid situations where there is a likely chance I'll have to think in depth about something. (a, b)

27. I prefer watching educational to entertainment programs.

28. I think best when those around me are very intelligent.

29. I prefer my life to be filled with puzzles that I must solve. (b)

30. I would prefer complex to simple problems. (b)

31. Simply knowing the answer rather than understanding the reasons or the answer to a problem is fine with me. (a)

32. It's enough for me that something gets the job done, I don't care how or why it works. (a, b)

33. Ignorance is bliss. (a)

34. I enjoy thinking about an issue even when the results of my thoughts will have no outcome on the issue.

NOTES: "a" denotes items requiring reverse scoring; "b" denotes items included in the short form. There were slight wording variations for some items in both versions.

NEED FOR EMOTION: NFE
(Raman, Chattopadhyay, and Hoyer 1995)

Construct: Need for emotion (NFE) is defined as "the tendency or propensity for individuals to seek out emotional situations, enjoy emotional stimuli, and exhibit a preference to use emotion in interacting with the world" (Raman, Chattopadhyay, and Hoyer 1995, p. 537). Though it is suggested that NFE taps mainly into short-term emotions, rather than longer emotional states, NFE should be able to partially explain patterns of individual behavior. Though the constructs of affect intensity, emotional style, and affect orientation are related to NFE, it is felt that NFE is distinct from these constructs. Five aspects of the NFE construct were originally conceptualized: (a) whether a person seeks to be involved in situations where there is a potential for emotion-laden stimuli to be present, (b) whether a person is comfortable with and even enjoys experiencing such situations, (c) whether a person prefers to process emotional information, (d) emotional preferences and general behaviors across situations, and (c) emotion as a single dimension, rather than various emotional subdimensions.

Description: The NFE scale is composed of 12 items scored on 5-point Likert-type scales ranging from *strongly disagree* to *strongly agree*. Item scores are summed to form an overall NFE composite ranging from 12 to 60.

Development: A pool of 48 items was originally generated to reflect five facets of the NFE construct as detailed above; 23 of these items were reverse coded. Via principal components, item, and reliability analyses, the final 12-item form of the scale was derived. Tests of validity were also performed.

Samples: Two undergraduate student samples were used: $n = 203$ for scale development purposes and $n = 212$ for a "hold-out" sample.

Validity: The coefficient alpha estimates of internal consistency were .87 and .84 for the developmental and "hold-out" samples, respectively. For the developmental sample, item-to-total correlations ranged from .46 to .66 across the 12 items. The summed 12-item scale exhibited correlations of .69 with the Affective Orientation Scale (AOS) and .46 with the Need for Cognition scale (NFC) for the developmental sample. For the "hold-out" sample, these correlations were .67 and .31. These correlations were significant ($p < .01$), and were taken as evidence of NFE being distinct from AOS and NFC.

Scores: Means and standard deviations were offered for males and females for the developmental sample. Female subjects ($M = 46.42$, $SD = 8.97$) scored significantly higher on the NFE than did males ($M = 43.83$, $SD = 8.54$; $t = 2.23$, $p < .05$), as hypothesized.

Source: Raman, Nirijan V., Prithviraj Chattopadhyay, and Wayne D. Hoyer. (1995). "Do Consumers Seek Emotional Situations: The Need for Emotions Scale." In Frank Kardes and Mita Sujan (Eds.), *Advances in Consumer Research* (Vol. 22, pp. 537-542). Provo, UT: Association for Consumer Research.
© 1995 by the Association for Consumer Research. Scale items taken from Table 1 (p. 540). Reprinted with permission.

Other evidence: N/A

Other source: N/A

References: N/A

NEED FOR EMOTION: NFE
(Raman, Chattopadhyay, and Hoyer 1995)

1. I try to anticipate and avoid situations where there is a likely chance of my getting emotionally involved.

2. Experiencing strong emotions is not something I enjoy very much.

3. I would rather be in a situation where I experience little emotion than one which is sure to get me emotionally involved.

4. I don't look forward to being in situations that others have found to be emotional.

5. I look forward to situations that I know are less emotionally involving.

6. I like to be unemotional in emotional situations.

7. I find little satisfaction in experiencing strong emotions.

8. I prefer to keep my feelings under check.

9. I feel relief rather than fulfilled after experiencing a situation that was very emotional.

10. I prefer to ignore the emotional aspects of situations rather than getting involved in them.

11. More often than not, making decisions based on emotions just leads to more errors.

12. I don't like to have the responsibility of handling a situation that is emotional in nature.

NOTE: All 12 items require reverse scoring to reflect a higher level of NFE.

NEED TO EVALUATE SCALE: NES
(Jarvis and Petty 1996)

Construct: Evaluation is defined as the assessment of the positive and/or negative qualities of an object. The need to evaluate is assumed to be one of the most pervasive and dominant of human responses. In accordance with this view, Jarvis and Petty (1996, p. 172) view the need to evaluate as the chronic tendency for individuals to engage in evaluative responding. Furthermore, the need to evaluate is believed to be an individual difference variable that affects, and is affected by, numerous socially based attitudes. Thus, the Need to Evaluate Scale (NES) assesses individual differences in the propensity to engage in evaluation.

Description: The NES is composed of 16 items scored on 5-point scales where 1 = *extremely uncharacteristic*, 2 = *somewhat characteristic*, 3 = *uncertain*, 4 = *somewhat characteristic*, and 5 = *extremely characteristic*. Item scores are summed to form an overall NES score that can range from 16 to 80. The NES is considered a single-factor, unidimensional measure.

Development: Numerous recommended scaling procedures were used to derive the final form of the scale and to test for reliability and construct validity. Five studies encompassing numerous samples were used. After generating 46 initial items to reflect the construct, the 16-item NES was derived via inspection of item-to-total correlations, intercorrelations among items, item mean (standard deviation) scores, and face validity from four pilot studies. Study 1 then examined the structure and internal consistency of the NES via principal and confirmatory factor analyses, item analyses, and coefficient alpha. Study 2 examined the validity of the NES by correlating it with related constructs. Study 2 looked at the NES's relation to social and political attitudes, and Study 4 examined the relation to "spontaneous evaluative thoughts." Finally, Study 5 examined the validity of the NES within the context of recalling "autobiographical narratives" from the previous day. All in all, consistent evidence for the dimensionality, internal consistency, and validity of the NES was found.

Samples: The "pilot" studies were composed of $n = 357$ undergraduate psychology students. Three samples of $n = 131$, $n = 160$, and $n = 266$ (all undergraduate psychology students) were used in Study 1. Study 2 used $n = 600$ students, Study 3 used $n = 52$ students; Study 4 used $n = 35$ students (females only), and Study 5 used $n = 93$ students.

Validity: By comparing four different factor structures, including two structures that included the presence of "methods" factors, it was determined that the NES could be reasonably represented by a single, unidimensional 16-item factor (although a two-factor solution offered a better "fit" to the data). (See "Notes" to actual scale items below.) For the three samples of Study 1, coefficient alphas ranged from .82 to 87 for the 16-item NES. Test-retest reliability for a subsample of $n = 70$ over a 10-week period was .84. For Study 2, the coefficient alpha estimate of the NES was .84. As evidence of discriminant validity, the NES was correlated with nine other constructs and a measure of social desirability. The correlations between the NES and affective intensity, desire for control, and need for cognition were .17, .22, and .35 ($p < .05$), respectively. All other correlations were not significant. In support of predictive validity, regression analyses in Study 3 showed significant relations with attitudes toward social and political issues. Finally, Studies 4 and 5 showed that actual evaluative responding behavior could be predicted by NES scores.

Scores: Mean scores were consistently reported by male and female subsamples. For the most part, men scored slightly higher on the NES than did women; however, some of these differences were not significant. Some of the mean scores were 53.21 and 51.05, and 53.20 and 51.05, for males and females, respectively, from Study 1. For Study 2, the mean NES score was 52.80 for males and 50.88 for females ($p < .05$).

Study 3 reported an overall mean score of 53.0, and Study 4 reported an overall mean of 53.6. Individual item means were also reported. Also, the NES was split at the median, or tertiary splits were used, to create high/low or high/medium/low NES groups for purposes of analysis.

Source: Jarvis, W. Blair G., and Richard E. Petty. (1996). "The Need to Evaluate." *Journal of Personality and Social Psychology*, *70*(1), 172-194.

© 1996 by the American Psychological Association. Scale items taken from Table 1 (p. 176). Reprinted with permission.

Other evidence: N/A

Other source: N/A

References: N/A

NEED TO EVALUATE SCALE: NES
(Jarvis and Petty 1996)

1. I form opinions about everything.

2. I prefer to avoid taking extreme opinions.

3. It is very important to me to hold strong opinions.

4. I want to know exactly what is good and bad about everything.

5. I often prefer to remain neutral about complex issues.

6. If something does not affect me, I do not usually determine if it is good or bad.

7. I enjoy strongly liking and disliking new things.

8. There are many things for which I do not have a preference.

9. It bothers me to remain neutral.

10. I like to have strong opinions even when I am not personally involved.

11. I have many more opinions than the average person.

12. I would rather have a strong opinion than no opinion at all.

13. I pay a lot of attention to whether things are good or bad.

14. I only form strong opinions when I have to.

15. I like to decide that new things are really good or really bad.

16. I am pretty much indifferent to many important issues.

NOTES: Items 2, 5, 6, 8, 9, 14, and 16 require reverse scoring and were labeled as a NEVAL(−) or "Preference for Neutrality" factor in a two-factor solution. The remaining items were labeled as a NEVAL(+) or "Need to Evaluate" factor in a two-factor solution.

NEED FOR PRECISION: NFP
(Viswanathan 1997)

Construct: Need for precision (NFP) is defined as "a preference for engaging in a relatively fine-grained mode of processing" (Viswanathan 1997, p. 727). The NFP construct reflects a motivation to engage in relatively fine-grained, precise information processing and engaging in making distinctions that are fine-grained as opposed to course-grained.

Description: The final form of the NFP scale is composed of 13 items scored on 7-point *strongly disagree* to *strongly agree* scales. Item scores are summed, then divided by the number of items in the scale (i.e., 13), to form overall NFP scores that can theoretically range from 1 to 7.

Development: Over nine studies using recommended scaling procedures, the final 13-item form of the scale was derived and extensively tested for dimensionality, internal consistency, and validity. An initial pool of 40 items was generated to reflect the construct. This pool was reduced to 20 items, based on content validity. (Throughout the initial scale development procedures, items were modified, deleted, and replaced.) Twenty items were then empirically tested via exploratory and confirmatory factor analyses, and reliability and item analyses were conducted until the 13-item form of the NFP was obtained.

Samples: Study 1 used 3 samples of $n = 95$, 160, and 90; Study 2 used samples of $n = 177$ and 166; Study 3 used samples of $n = 106$ and 98; Study 4 used a sample of $n = 118$; Study 5 used a sample of $n = 160$; and Studies 6 through 9 used samples of $n = 40$, 30, 50, and 68, respectively. All samples were composed of college students.

Validity: For the two larger samples of Study 2, confirmatory factor analyses showed adequate levels of fit and dimensionality for a single-factor representation of the 13-item NFP. Estimates of internal consistency ranged from .76 to .84 (average of .80) over seven of the samples alluded to above. Test-retest reliability correlations over 1- and 12-week intervals for the samples of Study 3 were .72 and .67. Correlational estimates of validity were numerous. The NFP showed correlations of .27, .36, .28, and .30 ($p < .05$) with measures of need for cognition, preference for numerical information, attitude toward math, and attitude toward statistics, respectively. NFP also showed a correlation of .48 with a "sorting task," and a correlation of $-.25$ with a measure of tolerance for ambiguity. NFP also showed a nonsignificant correlation with a measure of social desirability bias ($r = .13$). (Several other estimates of validity were reported in Table 4, p. 727.)

Scores: Numerous mean scores were reported. For example, the mean (std. dev.) score for the NFP scale at Times 1 and 2 for the samples of Study 3 were 4.54 (.77) and 4.46 (.80) for the 1-week interval sample, and 4.60 (.63) and 4.61 (.66) for the 12-week interval sample. Mean scores were also reported by gender. For example, in Study 4, females ($M = 4.94$) scored higher than did males ($M = 4.52$; $t = 3.61$, $p < .01$) on the NFP.

Source: Viswanathan, Madhubalan. (1997). "Individual Differences in Need for Precision." *Personality and Social Psychology Bulletin, 23*, 717-735.

© 1997 by Sage Publications. Scale items taken from Table 1 (p. 723). Reprinted with permission.

Other evidence: N/A

Other sources: N/A

References: N/A

NEED FOR PRECISION: NFP
(Viswanathan 1997)

1. I enjoy tasks that require me to be exact.

2. Vague descriptions leave me with the need for information.

3. I have a rough rather than exact idea of my opinions on various issues.

4. I do not find it interesting to learn precise information.

5. Thinking is enjoyable when it does not involve exact information.

6. I tend to put things into broad categories as much as possible.

7. I don't see the point in trying to discriminate between slightly different alternatives.

8. I like to express myself precisely even when it is not necessary.

9. I think approximate information is acceptable whereas exact information is not necessary.

10. I am satisfied with information as long as it is more or less close to the facts.

11. I am satisfied with my knowledge about issues as long as I am in the ballpark.

12. I like tasks which require me to look for small differences between things.

13. I like to use precise information that is available to make decisions.

NOTE: Items 3-7 and 9-11 require reverse scoring.

PREFERENCE FOR CONSISTENCY: PFC
(Cialdini, Trost, and Newsom 1995)

Construct: Preference for consistency (PFC) is viewed as "a tendency to base one's responses to incoming stimuli on the implications of existing (prior entry) variables, such as previous expectancies, commitments, and choices" (Cialdini, Trost, and Newsom 1995, p. 318). PFC represents a dispositional preference for or against consistent responding that can be manifested in three domains: (a) the desire to be consistent with one's own responses (internal consistency), (b) the desire to appear consistent to others (public consistency), and (c) the desire that others be consistent (others' consistency).

Description: The PFC has 18 items scored on 9-point Likert-type scales ranging from *strongly disagree* (1) to *strongly agree* (9). A 9-item short form of the scale is also available. Though three domains of the construct were identified, items scores are summed and then divided by the number of items in the scale, to form average PFC scores for both the 18- and 9-item versions. (In scale development, the authors found that the three domains alluded to above were highly correlated, .73 to .87, and thus could be treated as one overall scale.)

Development: An initial pool of 72 items was generated by the authors and other faculty members at Arizona State University. Elimination of redundant items and/or those that lacked face validity trimmed this pool to 60. The 60 items were then further assessed via item-to-total correlations and other distributional properties (sample of $n = 567$) to derive the final forms of the 18- and 9-item versions of the PFC. Numerous estimates of reliability and validity were offered over three more survey-based studies and three experimental studies.

Samples: Four samples of undergraduate psychology students were used to develop and test the reliability and validity of the PFC: $n = 567$ (the initial developmental sample), $n = 230$, $n = 452$, and $n = 224$. The scale was further validated in three experimental studies encompassing samples of $n = 50$, $n = 357$, and $n = 47$ (all college students).

Validity: Estimates of internal consistency were offered in terms of an average over three samples. For the 18-item version, the average coefficient alpha estimate was .89; for the 9-item version, the average coefficient alpha estimate was .84. The average correlation between the 18- and 9-item versions was .95. The PFC showed adequate evidence of discriminant and nomological validity via correlations with related (or hypothesized not to be related) constructs. For example, the correlation of PFC with a measure of "rigidity," personal need for structure, self-consciousness, and the extroversion and openness factors of the Big Five personality dimensions were .48, .47, .25, −.22, and −.38 ($p < .05$), respectively. The PFC was not significantly correlated with measures of social desirability, self-monitoring, locus of control, agreeableness, and neuroticism. Three experiments consistent with balance theory, the foot-in-the-door effect, and cognitive dissonance theory also showed consistent support for the validity of the PFC scale.

Scores: Means scores are reported as averages across the three survey-based studies. For the 18-item version, the mean (std. dev.) was 5.43 (1.19). Median and mode scores of 5.50 and 5.44 were also reported. For the 9-item version, the mean (std. dev.) was 5.36 (1.31). Median and mode scores of 5.39 and 5.17 were also reported. Scores based on median splits in the experimental studies were also reported.

Source: Cialdini, Robert B., Melanie R. Trost, and Jason Newsom. (1995). "Preference for Consistency: The Development of a Valid Measure and the Discovery of Surprising Behavioral Implications." *Journal of Personality and Social Psychology*, 69(2), 318-328.

© 1995 by the American Psychological Association. Scale items taken from Appendix (p. 328). Reprinted with permission.

Other evidence: N/A

Other sources: N/A

References: N/A

PREFERENCE FOR CONSISTENCY: PFC
(Cialdini, Trost, and Newsom 1995)

1. I prefer to be around people whose reactions I can anticipate.

2. It is important to me that my actions are consistent with my beliefs.

3. Even if my attitudes and actions seemed consistent with one another to me, it would bother me if they did not seem consistent in the eyes of others.

4. It is important to me that those who know me can predict what I will do.

5. I want to be described by others as a stable, predictable person.

6. Admirable people are consistent and predictable.

7. The appearance of consistency is an important part of the image I present to the world.

8. It bothers me when someone I depend upon is unpredictable.

9. I don't like to appear as if I am inconsistent.

10. I get uncomfortable when I find my behavior contradicts my beliefs.

11. An important requirement for any friend of mine is personal consistency.

12. I typically prefer to do things the same way.

13. I dislike people who are constantly changing their opinion.

14. I want my close friends to be predictable.

15. It is important to me that others view me as a stable person.

16. I make an effort to appear consistent to others.

17. I'm uncomfortable holding two beliefs that are inconsistent.

18. It doesn't bother me much if my actions are inconsistent.

NOTES: Items 4, 5, 7, 11, 12, 14, 15, 16, and 18 comprise the 9-item short form of the PFC scale. Item 18 requires reverse scoring.

PREFERENCE FOR NUMERICAL INFORMATION: PNI
(Viswanathan 1993)

Construct: Preference for numerical information (PNI) is defined as a "preference or proclivity toward using numerical information and engaging in thinking involving numerical information" (Viswanathan 1993, p. 742). PNI reflects a preference/proclivity, and not necessarily an ability, toward numerical information. The PNI also focuses on numerical information rather than mathematical or statistical domains, and the PNI is considered relevant to a variety of settings rather than a specific context. As such, the PNI encompasses the satisfaction, usefulness, and enjoyment individuals derive from using numerical information.

Description: The PNI scale is composed of 20 items scored on 7-point scales ranging from *strongly disagree* to *strongly agree*. Item scores are summed, and then divided by the number of items in the scale (i.e., 20), to form an overall PNI score that can theoretically range from 1 to 7. It seems that 17- and 8-item versions of the scale are also tenable.

Development: Over eight studies using recommended scaling procedures, the 20-item form of the scale was derived and extensively tested for dimensionality, internal consistency, and validity. An initial pool of 35 items was generated to reflect the construct. This pool was reduced to 20 items, based on content validity. (Throughout the initial scale development procedures, items were modified, deleted, and replaced.) Twenty items were then empirically tested via exploratory (common) factor analyses, and reliability and item analyses, until the 20-item form of the PNI was obtained and tested for internal consistency and validity.

Samples: Studies 1, 2, and 3 used samples of $n = 93$, 160, and 90; Study 4 used a sample of $n = 108$; Study 5 used a sample of $n = 174$; Study 6 used a sample of $n = 106$; Study 7 used a sample of $n = 118$; and Study 8 used a sample of $n = 160$. All samples were composed of college students.

Validity: Given that the final 20-item form of the scale was derived and tested for its psychometrics in Studies 5 through 7, discussion of validity will be restricted to these studies. Although common factor analysis led to the extraction of two factors, the first factor accounted for a large portion of the variance in the data (45.1%), thus offering some evidence for a single-dimension PNI (Study 5). Coefficient alpha estimates for the PNI were .92 to .94 for Studies 5 and 6. (An eight-item short form of the NPI had an alpha of .91.) A test-retest reliability correlation from Study 6 was $r = .91$ ($p < .01$). Studies 7 and 8 examined the scale's validity. In Study 7, PNI was not related to social desirability bias ($r = .03$) and was significantly correlated with need for cognition ($r = .30$) and with grades in statistics/quantitative courses ($r = .43$, $r = .41$, and $r = .47$). Numerous other estimates of validity were reported in Study 8, but these estimates pertain to a 17-item version of the scale. This 17-item version showed correlations of .41 and −.24 ($p < .01$) with measures of need for precision and tolerance of ambiguity, respectively. Numerous correlations between the PNI and attitudes toward math and statistics showed evidence of validity for the scale. Six correlations were reported that ranged from .51 to .74 ($p < .01$).

Scores: Mean scores for the final 20-item version are summarized here. For Study 6, means were 4.64 and 4.62 for the test-retest interval data. In Study 7, the mean for males was 4.51, and the mean for females was 4.76. These two means were not statistically different.

Source: Viswanathan, Madhubalan. (1993). "Measurement of Individual Differences in Preference for Numerical Information." *Journal of Applied Psychology*, *78*(5), 741-752.

   © 1993 by the American Psychological Association. Scale items taken from Table 1 (p. 745). Reprinted with permission.

Other evidence: N/A

Other sources: N/A

References: N/A

PREFERENCE FOR NUMERICAL INFORMATION: PNI
(Viswanathan 1993)

1. I enjoy work that requires the use of numbers.

2. I think quantitative information is difficult to understand.

3. I find it satisfying to solve day-to-day problems involving numbers.

4. Numerical information is very useful in everyday life.

5. I prefer not to pay attention to information involving numbers.

6. I think more information should be available in numerical form.

7. I don't like to think about issues involving numbers.

8. Numbers are not necessary for most situations.

9. Thinking is enjoyable when it does not involve quantitative information.

10. I like to make calculations using numerical information.

11. Quantitative information is vital for accurate decisions.

12. I enjoy thinking about issues that do not involve numerical information.

13. Understanding numbers is as important in daily life as reading or writing.

14. I easily lose interest in graphs, percentages, and other quantitative information.

15. I don't find numerical information to be relevant for most situations.

16. I think it is important to learn and use numerical information to make well-informed decisions.

17. Numbers are redundant for most situations.

18. It is a waste of time to learn information containing a lot of numbers.

19. I like to go over numbers in my mind.

20. It helps me to think if I put down information as numbers.

NOTES: Items 1, 3, 4, 5, 7, 10, 15, and 19 represent an 8-item version of the PNI. The 17-item version has all
items except items 2, 12, and 18. Items 2, 5, 7, 8, 9, 12, 14, 15, 17, and 18 require reverse scoring.

RATIONAL-EXPERIENTIAL INVENTORY: REI
(Epstein, Pacini, Denes-Raj, and Heier 1996)

Construct: Cognitive-Experiential Self Theory (CEST) posits that individuals have two fundamentally different, but parallel, modes of information processing (Epstein 1991): (a) a "rational system" where the individual operates primarily at the conscious level, is intentional, analytical, primarily verbal, and relatively affect free; and (b) an "experiential system" that is more automatic, pre-conscious, holistic, associanistic, primarily nonverbal, and intimately associated with affect (Epstein et al. 1996, p. 391). Based on this conceptualization, Epstein et al. (1996) used 19 items from the Need for Cognition (NFC) scale (Cacioppo and Petty 1982) to reflect the "rational system," and 12 items from the measure presently developed (i.e., the Faith in Intuition (FI) scale) to reflect the "experiential system." These two scales (NFC and FI) constitute the REI.

Description: The REI is composed of two separate scales (factors). The NFC scale is composed of 19 items from Cacioppo and Petty's (1982) scale. The FI scale is composed of 12 items. All items are scored on 5-point scales ranging from *completely false* to *completely true*. Items scores are summed within each scale to form overall scores of need for cognition (NFC) and faith in intuition (FI). Five-item versions of the scales are also available using the same scoring system. However, the 5-item NFC includes some "adapted" wording of items by the authors.

Development: Based on content validity and item-to-total correlations, 19 items were culled from the original NFC to reflect the rational system. The 12 FI items were generated by the authors. With the first sample, principal component analyses indicated that two distinct factors were tenable (i.e., NFC and RI) for the 19-item NFC and 12-item FI. In the second sample, principal components analyses also showed two distinct factors for the 5-item versions of the NFC and FI scales. Both sample offered several estimates of reliability and validity for the two REI scales.

Samples: Two samples were used in scale development and testing: (a) $n = 184$ undergraduate college students and $n = 973$ undergraduate college students.

Validity: Coefficient alpha estimates of internal consistency for the 19-item NFC and 12-item FI scales were .87, and .77, respectively, for the first sample. The correlation between NFC and FI was −.07 (ns). For the second sample, the 5-item versions of NFC and FI showed coefficient alpha estimates of .73 and .72. The correlation between these two 5-item versions was .08 ($p < .01$). Using Sample 1 data, the 5-item versions were found highly correlated to their original, longer versions (i.e., .90 for the 18- and 5-item versions of NFC, and .85 for the 12- and 5-item versions of FI). Numerous correlational estimates of validity were offered for the first sample, as well as differences in correlations between male and female subsamples. For example, for the overall sample, correlations of .26, .34, .41, .25, and −.37 ($p < .05$) were found between NFC and measures of absence of negative overgeneralization, behavioral coping, action-orientation, consciousness, and naive optimism, respectively. Corresponding correlations of these measures with FI were smaller and mostly nonsignificant. FI was found significantly correlated with esoteric thinking (.30), belief in the unusual (.31), and formal superstition (.27). Hypothesized correlational differences between males and females for NFC/FI and many of these measures also were found. In the second sample, both NFC and FI were found significantly correlated with measures of depression (−.24 and −.09, respectively) and self-esteem (−.30 and −.17, respectively). Also, NFC was found to be positively correlated with SAT score and GPA (.28 and .13). Numerous other validity-related tests (i.e., ANOVA and regression) were reported. In sum, strong and consistent evidence for the REI was found.

Scores: For the first sample, the 19-item NFC had a mean (std. dev.) of 64.29 (10.54). Also, males scored significantly higher on NFC ($M = 67.02$) than did females ($M = 63.14$; $t = 2.31$, $p < .05$). The 12-item FI scale had a mean of 41.13 (6.08).

Source: Epstein, Seymour, Rosemary Pacini, Veronika Denes-Raj, and Harriet Heier. (1996). "Individual Differences in Intuitive-Experiential and Analytical-Rational Thinking Styles." *Journal of Personality and Social Psychology*, *71*(2), 390-505.

© 1996 by the American Psychological Association. Scale items taken from Table 2 (p. 394) and Table 5 (p. 399). Reprinted with permission.

Other evidence: N/A

Other sources: N/A

References: Cacioppo, John T., and Richard E. Petty. (1982). "The Need for Cognition." *Journal of Personality and Social Psychology*, *42*, 116-131.

Epstein, Seymour. (1991). "Cognitive-Experiential Self Theory: An Integrative Theory of Personality." In R. Curtis (Ed.), *The Relational Self: Convergence in Psychoanalysis and Social Psychology* (pp. 111-137). New York: Guilford.

RATIONAL-EXPERIENTIAL INVENTORY: REI
(Epstein, Pacini, Denes-Raj, and Heier 1996)

19-Item Need for Cognition (NFC)

1. I would prefer a task that is intellectual, difficult, and important to one that is somewhat important but does not require much thought.

2. I tend to set goals that can be accomplished only by expending considerable mental effort.

3. Learning new ways to think doesn't excite me very much. (a)

4. I have difficulty in thinking in new and unfamiliar situations. (a)

5. The idea of relying on thought to get my way to the top does not appeal to me. (a)

6. The notion of thinking abstractly is not appealing to me. (a)

7. I generally prefer to accept things as they are rather than to question them. (a)

8. I don't reason well under pressure. (a)

9. I would rather do something that requires little thought than something that is sure to challenge my thinking abilities. (a)

10. I find little satisfaction in deliberating hard and for long hours. (a)

11. I prefer to talk about international problems rather than to gossip or talk about celebrities.

12. I don't like to have the responsibility of handling a situation that requires a lot of thinking. (a)

13. I feel relief rather than satisfaction after completing a task that required a lot of mental effort. (a)

14. Thinking is not my idea of fun. (a)

15. I try to anticipate and avoid situations where there is a likely chance I'll have to think in depth about something. (a)

16. I prefer my life to be filled with puzzles that I must solve.

17. I would prefer complex to simple problems.

18. Simply knowing the answer rather than understanding the reasons or the answer to a problem is fine with me. (a)

19. It's enough for me that something gets the job done, I don't care how or why it works. (a)

5-Item Need for Cognition (NFC)

1. I don't like to have to do a lot of thinking. (a)

2. I try to avoid situations that require thinking in depth about something. (a)

3. I prefer to do something that challenges my thinking abilities rather than something that requires little thought.

4. I prefer complex to simple problems.

5. Thinking hard and for a long time about something gives me little satisfaction. (a)

Faith in Intuition (FI)

1. My initial impressions of people are almost always right.

2. I trust my initial feelings about people.

3. When it comes to trusting people, I can usually rely on my "gut feelings."

4. I believe in trusting my hunches.

5. I can usually feel when a person is right or wrong, even if I can't explain how I know.

6. I am a very intuitive person.

7. I can typically sense right away when a person is lying.

8. I am quick to form impressions about people.

9. I believe I can judge character pretty well from a person's appearance.

10. I often have a very clear visual image of things.

11. I have a very good sense of rhythm.

12. I am good at visualizing things.

NOTES: For both versions of the NFC scale, "a" denotes items requiring reverse scoring. Items in the 5-item FI short form are items 1 through 5.

ROMANTICISM-CLASSICISM: RC INDEX
(Holbrook and Olney 1995)

Construct: Drawing on literature based in the history of philosophy, esthetics, art criticism, sociology, and marketing, Holbrook and Olney (1995) form the conceptual base of romanticism-classicism. In essence, the classicist is generally more purposeful, rational, controlled, and risk-averse than the romanticist, and the romanticist is more sensitive, emotional, chaotic, and risk-seeking than the classicist. Romanticism is more closely aligned to aesthetic sensitivity, creativity, and the power of imagination, and classicism is more aligned with economical thinking, rules, and methods. Based on these views, the Romanticism-Classicism Index (RC) was developed.

Description: The RC Index is composed of 55 items measured on 7-point Likert-type scales ranging from *strongly disagree* to *strongly agree*. Twenty-eight of the items reflect romanticism, and 27 reflect classicism. After the classicism items are reverse scored, scores on all 55 items are summed to form one overall RC Index score. A higher score reflects a higher level of "romanticism."

Development: Versions and use of this RC Index were reported upon in Holbrook (1986). The discussion here is limited to what was presented in Holbrook and Olney (1995) in terms of reliability and validity of the instrument. Principal components analysis and coefficient alpha were used to assess scale dimensionality and internal consistency. Using a factorially designed set of travel options/features as dependent variables, the predictive validity of the RC Index was examined, as well as its moderating effect on risk in travel preferences.

Samples: A sample of $n = 117$ MBA students was used.

Validity: A coefficient alpha estimate of internal consistency of .85 was reported for the 55-item RC Index. Principal component analyses extracted 17 eigenvalues greater than 1, but after the first factor, a sharp drop (i.e., elbow) in the scree plot was apparent. Furthermore, the average loading on the first component was .33. Thus, some evidence of a single factor underlying the data was offered. Consistent with Holbrook (1986), females scored significantly higher than did males on the RC Index, $t = 2.63$, $p < .05$. Regression results showed the hypothesized moderating effect of the RC Index on reaction to risk in travel preference, supporting the validity of the RC Index (see Table 1 of Holbrook and Olney 1995, p. 218).

Scores: Mean scores were not reported.

Source: Holbrook, Morris B., and Thomas J. Olney. (1995). "Romanticism and Wanderlust: An Effect of Personality on Consumer Preferences." *Psychology & Marketing*, *12*, 207-222.
    © 1995 by John Wiley & Sons, Inc. Scale items taken from pp. 213-214. Adapted by permission of John Wiley & Sons, Inc.

Other evidence: N/A

Other sources: N/A

Reference: Holbrook, Morris B. (1986). "Aims, Concepts, and Methods for the Representation of Individual Differences in Aesthetic Responses to Design Features." *Journal of Consumer Research*, *13*, 337-347.

ROMANTICISM-CLASSICISM: RC INDEX
(Holbrook and Olney 1995)

1. One should adopt a conservative lifestyle.

2. Truth often involves an element of mysticism.

3. I am a practical person.

4. Sensitivity is a valuable trait.

5. In art, color excites me more than form.

6. A routine way of life is preferable to unpredictability.

7. I think that life is an awesome mystery.

8. Uncertainty is exciting.

9. I am a sensitive person.

10. Progress in science, technology, and education continues to insure a brighter tomorrow.

11. Rigorous training is the true basis of athletic skill.

12. Facts are more important than feelings.

13. I enjoy art that expresses the artist's emotions.

14. A cool head wins every time.

15. Sometimes evil is consistent with greatness.

16. Intuition is a valuable tool.

17. Disorganization is a major flaw.

18. I believe that first impressions are almost always correct.

19. Paintings should attempt to represent their subjects with maximum realism.

20. I am not an emotional person.

21. It is O.K. to be eccentric.

22. I am organized.

23. Every decision deserves to be carefully thought out.

24. I think of myself as eccentric.

25. The heart, not the brain, should be your guide.

26. I like to touch sculpture.

27. People should try to be more tender.

28. Feelings are more important than facts.

29. Idealism is a wonderful quality.

30. Logic can solve any problem.

31. When I am being taken somewhere in an unfamiliar place, I like to know exactly where I am and where I am going.

32. Occasionally it's O.K. to be moody.

33. I am impulsive.

34. In life, unpredictability is preferable to routine.

35. I like to keep my home neat and orderly.

36. One's actions should always be carefully planned.

37. I prefer to live in a certain amount of chaos.

38. One should remain stable at all times.

39. I prefer a routine way of life to an unpredictable one.

40. A nice home is always neat and orderly.

41. I think of myself as a precise person.

42. Absent-mindedness is a lovable characteristic.

43. I think of myself as a natural person.

44. One should always be precise.

45. It is fun to be exposed to people with new ideas.

46. I tend to be a serious person.

47. It's O.K. to daydream a lot.

48. Self-control is all-important.

49. I am precise about where I keep my possessions.

50. I am easily distracted.

51. New ideas are exciting.

52. I am a controlled person.

53. Forgetfulness is forgivable.

54. I have a scientific outlook on most problems.

55. One should always be rational.

NOTES: Items 1, 3, 6, 10, 11, 12, 14, 17, 19, 20, 22, 23, 30, 31, 35, 36, 38, 39, 40, 41, 44, 46, 48, 49, 52, 54, and 55 are items that reflect "classicism" and require reverse scoring. The other items reflect "romanticism."

SELF-ACTUALIZATION–CONSUMER
SELF-ACTUALIZATION TEST: CSAT
(Brooker 1975)

Construct: Based upon Maslow's (1970) description of the self-actualizing person, this measure attempts to assess consumer self-actualization. The self-actualizing person may be described as one who achieves the full use and exploitation of talents, capacities, and potential. Specifically, the following 16 characteristics were assumed to underlie the construct and were used as the basis for developing the consumer-related item pairs: comfortable perceptions with reality; acceptance of self and others; spontaneity, simplicity, and naturalness; problem-centering; detached; autonomy; freshness of appreciation; feeling for mankind; interpersonal relations; democratic; discrimination between means and ends; philosophical sense of humor; creativeness; resistance to enculturation; resolution of dichotomies; and peak experiences.

Description: The test contains 20 items of the A vs. B variety. Each item receiving a self-actualizing response receives a score of 1 and is scored 0 otherwise. Scores are then summed to form an overall index which can range from 0 to 20 (Brooker 1975, p. 567).

Development: An initial set of over 150 pairs of actualizing and nonactualizing items were developed. Items were written for all traits except "peak experience." A panel of four faculty judges evaluated the items for self-actualizing content. Subjects (*n* = 319) responded to the items, varied in order to address respondent fatigue. Items were selected using a combination of corrected item-to-total correlations balanced with the need to have items reflecting the various dimensions. The final scale contains items representing 14 of the 16 traits identified by Maslow (1970). Test-retest reliability was also assessed.

Samples: A convenience sample of 319 subjects (186 females) responded to the initial set. The average of age of respondents was 30.6 years. Thirty-five MBA students participated in the first test-retest administration. Another sample of 24 was also used.

Validity: Item-to-total correlations ranged from .12 to .40. Based on the responses of 35 MBA students, the Spearman test-retest correlation, as an estimate of reliability, was 0.57. A similar test using a more heterogeneous sample of 24 respondents resulted in an estimate of .67. Evidence of content validity was said to be provided by the representation of the various traits (i.e., 14 of the 16 traits) in the final 20-item set. Evidence of concurrent validity was provided by differences in CSAT scores and those using or not using ecologically beneficial products (i.e., certain types of gasoline and detergents). Higher scores for females and older subjects were also cited as evidence of known group validity. Differences between those scoring high and low on the CSAT measure in terms of several personal characteristics were also argued to represent support for the measure. For example, those scoring above the median were found to be "more relaxed, more outdoorsy, more secure, happier, more outgoing, more homebodyish, more natural, and nondrinkers" (Brooker 1975, p. 573).

Scores: For the sample used to develop the test (*n* = 319), test scores ranged from 2 to 19 with a mode of 10 and a median of 10.4.

Source: Brooker, George. (1975). "An Instrument to Measure Consumer Self-Actualization." In Mary Jane Schlinger (Ed.), *Advances in Consumer Research* (Vol. 2, pp. 563-575). Ann Arbor, MI: Association for Consumer Research.
© 1975 by the Association for Consumer Research. Scale items taken from pp. 567-568. Reprinted with permission.

Other evidence: N/A

Other sources: N/A

Reference: Maslow, Abraham H. (1970). *Motivation and Personality* (2nd ed.). New York: Harper & Row.

SELF-ACTUALIZATION–CONSUMER
SELF-ACTUALIZATION TEST: CSAT
(Brooker 1975)

(Detached)
1. *a. Information from publications such as Consumer Reports is quite valuable to me in deciding on costly purchases.
   b. I find publications of little use to me; I prefer personal recommendations for expensive purchases.

(Accepting of Self, Others)
2. *a. Usually, I am not upset when products fail to meet my expectations.
   b. I am often upset when products fail to meet my expectations.

(Feeling for Mankind)
3. *a. When one helps a friend make a purchase, it's enough to know the assistance was needed.
   b. When one helps a friend make a purchase, I think it's only proper that one is thanked for the help.

(Democratic Character Structure)
4. *a. All people are worthy of respect.
   b. Some people are not worthy of respect.

(Resolution of Dichotomies)
5. a. It is more fun to give a gift than to decide what to give.
   *b. Deciding what to give for a gift is as much fun as giving it.

(Spontaneity, Simplicity)
6. a. I usually feel more confident when I know I am dressed in the latest fashion.
   *b. I am at ease regardless of how I am dressed.

(Detached)
7. *a. When I am shopping for myself, I make my decisions without help from others.
   b. I often look to people I know for help when buying something for myself.

(Freshness of Appreciation)
8. a. I like advertisements I see often more than those I have seen only a few times.
   *b. I find myself trying to avoid advertisements I have seen before.

(Means-End Relationships)
9. a. Money may not be everything, but it's got a big lead over whatever is second.
   *b. It's true, money can't buy happiness.

(Autonomy; Independence)
10. *a. The things I desire for the good life are often different from those chosen by others in my economic class.
    b. The things I would choose for the good life are similar to the choices of others in my economic class.

(Freshness of Appreciation)
11. a. I am often bored.
    *b. I am seldom bored.

(Sense of Humor)
12. a. I like jokes that are slightly off-color.
    *b. I like jokes that make me think.

(Problem Centered)
13.   *a. Activities like charity work and community service attract me.
     b. I am so busy doing day-to-day things I can't be bothered thinking about volunteer work.

(Sense of Humor)
14.   a. I prefer comedians who imitate famous people.
     *b. I prefer comedians who comment on the present time.

(Accepting of Self, Others)
15.   a. When I go on a buying spree, I often regret it later.
     *b. I seldom regret a buying spree.

(Resistance to Enculturation)
16.   *a. Being fashionable or chic holds no interest for me.
     b. It is important to me to be fashionable or chic.

(Perceptions of Reality)
17.   *a. When I am nervous or anxious, I usually try to avoid buying things.
     b. When I am nervous or anxious, I often find buying something new helps me feel better.

(Interpersonal Relationships)
18.   a. It is usually wise to present yourself to people in such a way that they will like you.
     *b. It is unwise to present anything but your true self to people.

(Perceptions of Reality)
19.   a. I am reluctant to try new products until I can find out if they are good.
     *b. I often try new things just because they look interesting or good.

(Resistance to Enculturation)
20.   *a. I could probably live under any economic system and be just as happy.
     b. I can imagine myself being happy living only in one kind of economic system.

NOTES: Parentheses represent characteristics or trait; *indicates the self-actualizing response.

SELF-CONCEPT CLARITY: SCC
(Campbell, Trapnell, Heine, Katz, Lavallee, and Lehman 1996)

Construct: Self-concept clarity (SCC) is defined as the "extent to which the contents of an individual's self-concept (e.g., perceived personal attributes) are clearly and confidently defined, internally consistent, and temporally stable" (Campbell, Trapnell, Heine, Katz, Lavallee, and Lehman 1996, p. 141). SCC is considered related to, yet distinct from, aspects of self-identity (i.e., achievement, status, self-esteem). SCC is a perceptual, belief-based variable. As such, these beliefs may not necessarily be accurate relative to one's behavior.

Description: The SCC scale has 12 items scored on 5-point Likert-type scales ranging from *strongly disagree* to *strongly agree*. Item scores are summed to form an SCC scale score that ranges from 12 to 60. The scale represents a single factor and can be considered unidimensional.

Development: Three studies, encompassing four large samples and three international subsamples, were conducted to derive the final form of the SCC scale and examine dimensionality, reliability, and validity. A pool of 40 items was culled from other sources and/or generated by the authors. Twenty of these items were then selected based on initial internal consistency and item redundancy estimates. Then, 12 items that loaded most highly on a single factor were retained (using three samples in Study 1). Both principal components and maximum likelihood factor analyses were used to assess dimensionality. Numerous estimates of reliability and validity followed across two more studies.

Samples: In Study 1, three samples of undergraduate students were used: $n = 471$, $n = 608$, and $n = 465$. A subset of $n = 155$ of the first sample was used in Study 2. In Study 3, samples of $n = 80$, $n = 196$, and $n = 100$ Japanese students from the University of British Columbia or from two Japanese universities were compared to samples of $n = 112$, $n = 90$, and $n = 82$ Canadian students at the University of British Columbia.

Validity: Across the three samples of Study 1, coefficient alpha estimates of internal consistency were .86, .86, and .85 for the final 12-item SCC scale. Inter-item correlations ranged from .10 to .58, and item-to-total correlations ranged from .35 to .66 (on average) across the three samples. Test-retest reliability correlations over 4- and 5-month intervals for subsamples of Sample 1 and Sample 3 (i.e., $n = 155$ and $n = 61$) were .79 and .70, respectively. Factor analyses (both principal components and maximum likelihood) showed evidence of a single dimension underlying the 12 items. Numerous correlations with related variables showed evidence of discriminant and nomological validity for the SCC scale. For example, across the three samples of Study 1, the SCC scale showed correlations of .67, .62, and, .60 with a measure of self-esteem. The SCC showed correlations of –.51, –.50, and –.49 with a measure of negative affectivity. Significant nomological correlations were also found between the SCC scale and measures of self-consciousness, extroversion, and openness. The scale did show modest correlations to social desirability (.32-.33). Study 2 showed a similar pattern of results in terms of the validity of the SCC scale. In Study 3, hypothesized mean-level differences between Canadian (Western Culture) and Japanese (Eastern Culture) students were found. As predicted, the mean SCC scale scores for the Canadian students were higher than the mean SCC scale scores for the Japanese students for all three samples of Study 3 ($p < .01$). In sum, across samples and studies, the SCC scale showed consistent evidence of reliability and validity.

Scores: Several mean scores were reported. For the overall SCC scale, Study 1 means (std. devs.) were 42.12 (8.19), 39.68 (8.16), and 38.86 (8.06). Means were also reported for male and females separately (see Table 2, p. 145 of Campbell et al. [1996]). Means for the Canadian subsamples of Study 3 were 41.72, 39.30, and 38.02. Means for the Japanese subsamples of Study 3 were 34.41, 35.01, and 34.35. Individual item means (std. devs.) are offered in Table 1 of Campbell et al. (1996, p. 145).

Source: Campbell, Jennifer, Paul D. Trapnell, Steven J. Heine, Ilana M. Katz, Loraine F. Lavallee, and Darrin R. Lehman. (1996). "Self-Concept Clarity: Measurement, Personality Correlates, and Cultural Boundaries." *Journal of Personality and Social Psychology*, *70*(1), 141-156.
© 1996 by the American Psychological Association. Scale items taken from Table 1 (p. 145). Reprinted with permission.

Other evidence: N/A

Other sources: N/A

References: N/A

SELF-CONCEPT CLARITY: SCC
(Campbell, Trapnell, Heine, Katz, Lavallee, and Lehman 1996)

1. My beliefs about myself often conflict with one another.

2. On one day I might have one opinion of myself and on another day I might have a different opinion.

3. I spend a lot of time wondering about what kind of person I really am.

4. Sometimes I feel that I am not really the person that I appear to be.

5. When I think about the kind of person I have been in the past, I'm not sure what I was really like.

6. I seldom experience conflict between the different aspects of my personality.

7. Sometimes I think I know other people better than I know myself.

8. My beliefs about myself seem to change very frequently.

9. If I were asked to describe my personality, my description might end up being different from one day to another day.

10. Even if I wanted to, I don't think I could tell someone what I'm really like.

11. In general, I have a clear sense of who I am and what I am.

12. It is often hard for me to make up my mind about things because I don't really know what I want.

NOTE: Items 1 through 5, 7 through 10, and 12 require reverse scoring.

SELF-CONCEPTS, PERSON CONCEPTS, AND PRODUCT CONCEPTS
(Malhotra 1981)

Construct: Measures are derived for evaluating self-concepts, person concepts, and product concepts. The specific concepts chosen for study were automobiles and actors. (The objective of the research on which the measures are based was to describe the construction of the scales rather than the development of a generalized scale for measuring self-concepts, person concepts, and product concepts [Malhotra 1981, p. 456].) The measure is said to be applicable for coordinating the image of a product with the self-concept(s) of a target market and image of a spokesperson that might be used in testimonial for that product.

Description: The final scale includes 15 semantic differential items anchoring seven-place response formats. The scale is multidimensional and, hence, summed scores are not appropriate. Item scores can be summed within dimensions.

Development: A beginning pool of 70 items was developed from pretest data generated from free associations, repertory grid procedures, and the studies of Osgood, Suci, and Tannenbaum (1957). A panel of four judges was used to reduce the item pool to 27. These items included at least two semantic differential scales for eight factors: evaluative, potency, activity, stability, tautness, novelty, receptivity, and aggressiveness. Based on analysis of the two student surveys described below, the 15-item final scale was developed as follows. First, a series of factor analyses (i.e., principal factoring with iterations followed by varimax rotation) was conducted and examined for stability, loading patterns, uniqueness, and explained variance. Second, hierarchical clustering procedures supported the factor analysis results. As summarized by Malhotra (1981, p. 460), the 15 items were selected using the following criteria: high loadings on the factor they represent; high correlations with other items representing the same factor or cluster; low correlations with items representing other factors or clusters; high stability across self-concepts, auto brands, or actors; uniqueness in the cluster solutions; and high coefficients of multiple correlation with multidimensional space coordinates. Six of the factors are represented by two items each. The tautness and aggressiveness factors are not reflected in the final scale.

Samples: Two surveys were used in the development of the measures. The first survey involved 167 student subjects for three self-concepts (i.e., "ideal," "actual," and "social") and nine brands of automobiles. The second survey involved 187 students (of which 135 had participated in the first survey) for the same three self-concepts and nine actors (i.e., "persons").

Validity: Test-retest estimates were obtained from 135 subjects over a 4-week delay for the ideal, actual, and social self ratings. All correlations were significant. Evidence of stability was also provided through individual level correlations. Coefficient alpha estimates for appropriate factor subscales ranged from .50 to .70 (with a single exception). Evidence provided by the expert panel judgments was cited as support for face validity. Evidence of convergent and discriminant validity was provided from a multitrait-multimethod analysis in which the actors and brands served as traits and the semantic differentials and similarity ratings served as methods. For example, validity coefficients for the autos and actors were . 38 and .49, respectively (Malhotra 1981, p. 463).

Scores: Neither overall nor item mean scores were reported.

Source: Malhotra, Naresh K. (1981). "A Scale to Measure Self-Concepts, Person Concepts, and Product Concepts." *Journal of Marketing Research, 16,* 456-464.

 © 1981 by the American Marketing Association. Scale items taken from Table 3 (p. 462). Reprinted with permission.

Other evidence: N/A

Other sources: N/A

Reference: Osgood, C. E., George J. Suci, and Percy M. Tannenbaum. (1957). *Measurement of Meaning.* Urbana: University of Illinois Free Press.

SELF-CONCEPTS, PERSON CONCEPTS, AND PRODUCT CONCEPTS
(Malhotra 1981)

1. Rugged . . . . Delicate

2. Excitable . . . . Calm

3. Uncomfortable . . . . Comfortable

4. Dominating . . . . Submissive

5. Thrifty . . . . Indulgent

6. Pleasant . . . . Unpleasant

7. Contemporary . . . . Noncontemporary

8. Organized . . . . Unorganized

9. Rational . . . . Emotional

10. Youthful . . . . Mature

11. Formal . . . . Informal

12. Orthodox . . . . Liberal

13. Complex . . . . Simple

14. Colorless . . . . Colorful

15. Modest . . . . Vain

NOTES: Though the scale is considered multidimensional, items belonging to specific dimensions were not explicitly given, nor was the directionality of the items (i.e., the specification of reverse coding) stated by Malhotra (1981).

SELF-SCHEMA SEPARATENESS-CONNECTEDNESS: SC
(Wang and Mowen 1997)

Construct: Self-schema separateness-connectedness (SC) reflects an individual's self-perception in relation to others. A "separated" person has a sense of independence and perceives him/herself as an individual who is distinct from others ("I am me"). The separated person also tends to distinguish him/herself by making clear boundaries between him/herself and others as part of his/her self-identity. A "connected" person has a sense of interdependence and sees him/herself as the continuation of others ("I am a part of others"), or sees others as an extension of the self. The connected person has greater empathy toward others and views important others as "part" of the self.

Description: The SC scale has nine items scored on 5-point scales ranging from *does not describe me at all* to *describes me very well*. Although two factors were found for the SC scale, items scores were summed over all nine items and then averaged (i.e., divided by 9) to form an SC score that can range from 1 to 5. A higher score is indicative of a "separated" schema.

Development: A pool of 60 items was generated to reflect the construct. After judging for content validity (by fellow faculty members), 32 items were retained for further evaluation. Two studies were then conducted to derive the final form of the scale and test its psychometric properties. Via item-to-total correlations and principal components analysis, the nine-item SC was derived (Study 1). Confirmatory factor analyses and tests of validity were also performed in Study 1. Study 2 used an experimental approach within the context of reacting to advertisements to further validate the SC scale.

Samples: Study 1 used a sample of $n = 144$ undergraduate students; 97 of these students were American (i.e., "Western Culture"), and 43 were Asian or African (i.e., "Eastern Culture"). Study 2 used $n = 105$ undergraduate students (actually a subsample of Study 1).

Validity: Though both principal components and confirmatory factor analyses showed two factors for the SC scale (i.e., an Independence/Individuality factor and a Self-Other Boundary factor), a coefficient alpha estimate of .73 was reported for the entire nine-item scale. (In confirmatory factor analysis, the correlation between the two factors was .28.) Loadings from the confirmatory factor analysis ranged from .28 to .77 across the two factors. The nine-item SC showed correlations of .33 and −.18 ($p < .05$) with measures of maintenance of emotional separation and attention to social comparison information, respectively. There was no evidence of contamination from social desirability bias, as its correlation with the SC scale was not significant ($r = .06$). Mean-level differences between males and females, and "Western" vs. "Eastern" cultures, also supported the construct validity of the SC scale. (These are all results from Study 1.) In Study 2, SC scale scores were split into three levels, forming groups of high, medium, and low levels of "separateness." Over several ad-based dependent variable measures, the SC scale showed that "separated" schemas responded more favorably to an ad stressing a separate theme, and "connected" schemas responded more favorably to an ad stressing a connected theme.

Scores: Study 1 reported mean scores by gender and culture. Males ($M = 3.46$) scored higher than did females ($M = 3.12$; $t = 3.38$, $p < .01$), and Western Culture students ($M = 3.42$) scored higher than did Eastern Culture students ($M = 3.10$; $t = 2.75$, $p < .01$).

Source: Wang, Chen Lu, and John C. Mowen. (1997). "The Separateness-Connectedness Self-Schema: Scale Development and Application to Message Construction." *Psychology & Marketing*, *14*, 185-207.

© 1997 by John Wiley & Sons, Inc. Scale items are from Table 1 (p. 192). Adapted by permission of John Wiley & Sons, Inc.

Other evidence: N/A

Other sources: N/A

References: N/A

SELF-SCHEMA SEPARATENESS-CONNECTEDNESS: SC
(Wang and Mowen 1997)

Independence/Individuality Factor

1. I often find that I can remain cool in spite of people around me being excited.

2. I enjoy the way I am rather than the way other people would like me to be.

3. To become an adult means to become myself and to be distinct from others.

4. I feel more comfortable having someone to rely on rather than dealing with my problems alone.

5. I will stick to my own opinions if I think I am right, even if I might lose popularity with others.

Self-Other Boundary Factor

6. I have my own privacy, which I would never share even with my closest family members or partner.

7. There should be a clear boundary between me and others, even with my parents, spouse, and closest friends.

8. I would like to solve my personal problems by myself, even if someone else can help me.

9. Most of the time, I do not get involved in other people's personal problems.

NOTE: Item 4 requires reverse scoring to reflect a higher level of "separateness."

THE SEXUAL IDENTITY SCALE: SIS
(Stern, Barak, and Gould 1987)

Construct: The SIS assesses the degree to which one identifies with a given gender. That is, the measure assesses the degree to which individuals view themselves as more masculine or more feminine regardless of their actual gender (Stern, Barak, and Gould 1987).

Description: The SIS is a four-item measure scored on 5-point scales from *very masculine* to *very feminine*. (See Appendix for scoring details.) The scale is unidimensional, and scores range from a low of 100 for very masculine to a high of 500 for very feminine.

Development: Based on a thorough review of the sex role and age research literatures, four items were generated to measure four aspects of sex role identity. A large sample composed of both men and women was used in assessing the reliability and validity of the SIS.

Sample: A sample of 380 adult men and 380 adult women from the New York/New Jersey area was used in scale reliability and validity analyses.

Validity: Reliability via coefficient alpha was .85 for women, .87 for men, and .96 for the total sample combined. SIS correlations with biological sex ranged from $-.70$ to $-.81$, and the correlation was $-.81$ for the total SIS. Correlations of the SIS with a femininity index were .35 for women and $-.05$ for men. Correlations of the SIS with a masculinity index were $-.21$ for men and $-.07$ for women. A confirmatory factor analysis via LISREL also showed evidence of discriminant and convergent validity for the SIS when compared to the femininity and masculinity indices. Finally, a series of mean tests between the male and female samples showed the expected SIS differences between men and women (i.e., men more strongly identified with masculinity than did women and vice versa).

Scores: Mean scores were reported for both men and women for the overall SIS and each SIS item. The mean of the overall SIS for females was 399.54 ($SD = 60.13$), and the mean for males was 188.62 ($SD = 55.08$). These two means were significantly different, $t = 50.42$, $p < .01$.

Source: Stern, Barbara B., Benny Barak, and Stephen J. Gould. (1987). "Sexual Identity Scale: A New Self-Assessment Measure." *Sex Roles*, *17*, 503-519.

   © 1987 by Plenum Press. Scale items taken from Appendix A (p. 517). Reprinted with permission.

Other evidence: In a study of gender schema and fashion, Gould and Stern (1989) reported an alpha of .97 for the SIS. Furthermore, the SIS exhibited correlations of .38 with fashion consciousness, .42 with an index of femininity, and $-.26$ with an index of masculinity, providing evidence for the SIS's validity.

Other source: Gould, Stephen J., and Barbara B. Stern. (1989). "Gender Schema and Fashion Consciousness." *Psychology & Marketing*, *6*(Summer), 129-145.

Reference: Barak, Benny. (1987). "Cognitive Age: A New Multidimensional Approach to Measure Age Identity." *The International Journal of Aging and Human Development*, *252*, 109-128.

THE SEXUAL IDENTITY SCALE: SIS
(Stern, Barak, and Gould 1987)

Please specify—for each of the following—how MASCULINE or FEMININE you consider yourself to be.

1. I FEEL as though I am . . .

2. I LOOK as though I am . . .

3. I DO most things in a manner typical of someone who is . . .

4. My INTERESTS are mostly those of a person who is . . .

APPENDIX

1 = *very masculine*

2 = *masculine*

3 = *neither masculine nor feminine*

4 = *feminine*

5 = *very feminine*

NOTES: Sexual Identity is a composite measure. The scoring system is derived from the summation/division scoring system used by the Cognitive Age Scale. (See Barak [1987] for scoring procedures.) Scores range from a low of 100 for *very masculine* to a high of 500 for *very feminine*. The SIS index is computed by a weighting procedure in which the score for each of the four items is divided by 4. Users are urged to contact the authors for specific instructions in deriving the SIS Index.

VANITY: TRAIT ASPECTS OF VANITY
(Netemeyer, Burton, and Lichtenstein 1995)

Construct: "Vanity," as delineated by Netemeyer, Burton, and Lichtenstein (1995), has four trait aspects: (a) an excessive concern for physical appearance, (b) a positive (and perhaps inflated) view of one's physical appearance, (c) an excessive concern for personal achievements, and (d) a positive (and perhaps inflated) view of one's personal achievements.

Description: The vanity scales are viewed as four distinct dimensions. The excessive concern for physical appearance dimension is composed of five items, the positive (and perhaps inflated) view of one's physical appearance is composed of six items, and the excessive concern for personal achievements and the positive (and perhaps inflated) view of one's personal achievements dimensions are composed of five items each. All items are scored on 7-point Likert-type scales from *strongly disagree* to *strongly agree*. Item scores are summed within dimensions to form composite scores for each dimension.

Development: Via a review of the literature, formal definitions of the four vanity dimensions were formulated. Numerous items were generated by the authors or culled from various sources to represent the dimensions. Items were judged for representativeness by "experts." A total of 100 items were initially retained for numerous data collection and developmental procedures. Four studies were used to develop the scales, and three more studies were used in further validation procedures. Factor-analytic techniques and reliability analyses were used to assess dimensionality and internal consistency. Correlational and mean difference testing procedures were used to check validity.

Samples: As stated above, a total of seven samples was used in the development and validation of the four vanity dimensions. The first four samples were combinations of students and nonstudents ($n = 277$, $n = 145$, $n = 186$, and $n = 264$). Three other samples were taken from a *Who's Who* directory ($n = 267$), an NCAA Division I football team ($n = 27$), and a fashion model agency ($n = 43$ females).

Validity: Confirmatory factor analyses was used to assess the dimensionality and discriminant validity of the four vanity dimensions. Across samples (where the sample size was large enough), evidence of four distinct vanity dimensions was found. Across the first four samples, internal consistency estimates (i.e., coefficient alpha and composite reliability via LISREL) ranged from .80 to .92 across the four vanity dimensions. For the last three samples, estimates of internal consistency ranged from .77 to .92. Numerous estimates of nomological validity were offered, including significant correlations of the vanity dimensions with narcissism, grandiosity, status concern, materialism, the List of Values (i.e., LOV), clothing concern, dieting behavior, use of cosmetics, and others. Mean-level difference tests also showed evidence of known-group validity, as fashion models scored higher on the "physical" aspects of vanity than did other samples, and the *Who's Who* sample scored higher on the "achievement" aspects of vanity than did other samples.

Scores: Means and standard deviations for the summed composites of the vanity dimensions are offered in Netemeyer et al. (1995, p. 624). Across the seven samples, the mean (and standard deviation) for the concern for physical appearance dimension ranged from 21.32 (6.16) to 25.44 (6.08), the mean (and standard deviation) for the view of physical appearance dimension ranged from 20.60 (7.08) to 26.90 (6.49), the mean (and standard deviation) for the concern for personal achievement dimension ranged from 19.26 (6.81) to 23.14 (6.37), and the mean (and standard deviation) for the view of personal achievement dimension ranged from 20.96 (6.20) to 26.25 (4.68).

Source: Netemeyer, Richard G., Scot Burton, and Donald R. Lichtenstein. (1995). "Trait Aspects of Vanity: Measurement and Relevance to Consumer Behavior." *Journal of Consumer Research*, *21*, 612-626.

    © 1995 by University of Chicago Press. Scale items taken from Appendix (p. 624). Reprinted with permission.

Other evidence: N/A

Other sources: N/A

References: N/A

VANITY: TRAIT ASPECTS OF VANITY
(Netemeyer, Burton, and Lichtenstein 1995)

Concern for Physical Appearance Items

1. The way I look is extremely important to me.

2. I am very concerned about my appearance.

3. I would feel embarrassed if I was around people and did not look my best.

4. Looking my best is worth the effort.

5. It is important that I always look good.

View of Physical Appearance Items

1. People notice how attractive I am.

2. My looks are very appealing to others.

3. People are envious of my good looks.

4. I am a very good-looking individual.

5. My body is sexually appealing.

6. I have the type of body that people want to look at.

Concern for Achievement Items

1. Professional achievements are an obsession with me.

2. I want others to look up to me for my accomplishments.

3. I am more concerned with professional success than most people I know.

4. Achieving greater success than my peers is important to me.

5. I want my achievements to be recognized by others.

View of Achievement Items

1. In a professional sense, I am a very successful person.

2. My achievements are highly regarded by others.

3. I am an accomplished person.

4. I am a good example of professional success.

5. Others wish they were as successful as me.

SCALES RELATED TO CONSUMER COMPULSIVENESS AND IMPULSIVENESS

COMPULSIVE BUYING SCALE
(Valence, d'Astous, and Fortier 1988)

Construct: Although no explicitly stated formal definition for compulsive buying is offered by Valence d'Astous, and Fortier (1988), the symptoms of the construct seem consistent with other views of compulsive buying (Faber and O'Guinn 1988). Valence et al. suggest that compulsive buyers show (a) a high propensity to spend, (b) purchases activated by psychological tension (i.e., a reactive aspect), (c) feelings of guilt after purchase (i.e., post-purchase guilt), and (d) a family environment, particularly parental attitude, that may affect their compulsive behavior.

Description: The final scale is composed of 13 items scored on 5-point "agreement" scales. Item scores can be summed over the 13 items to form an overall composite score of compulsive buying.

Development: As originally conceptualized, four aspects or "symptoms" of compulsive buying were specified. A total of 16 items were generated to reflect these four aspects. However, item analyses showed that the three items reflecting the family environment factor did not correlate highly with the total scale. These three items were dropped to derive the final form of the scale. Via maximum likelihood factor analysis, reliability analyses, correlational analyses, and mean-level difference testing, the internal consistency and validity of the scale were assessed.

Samples: A sample of 10 adult consumers was used to pretest the understandability of the original 16 items. Then, a sample of 38 self-identified compulsive buyers and 38 noncompulsive buyers responded to the items, as well as other scales, for validity testing purposes.

Validity: The final form of the scale exhibited a coefficient alpha estimate of internal consistency of .884. Though three factors with eigenvalues greater than 1 were extracted by maximum likelihood factor analysis, 78% of the variance in the data was explained by the first factor, suggesting a unidimensional scale. The sample of self-identified compulsive buyers scored significantly higher on the scale than did the noncompulsive buyer sample. A positive and significant correlation ($r = .40$) was found between anxiety and the compulsive buying scale. Measures of depression, presence of other addictive behaviors, and extreme nervousness also showed significant relations with the compulsive buying scale.

Scores: Mean scores for the self-identified compulsive buying sample and the noncompulsive buying sample were 42.24 and 28.21, respectively. As stated above, the difference between these means was significant.

Source: Valence, Gilles, Alain d'Astous, and Louis Fortier. (1988). "Compulsive Buying: Concept and Measurement." *Journal of Consumer Policy*, *11*, 419-433.
        © 1988 by Kluwer Academic Publishers. Scale items taken from Table 1 (p. 426). Reprinted with kind permission of Kluwer Academic Publishers.

Other evidence: N/A

Other sources: N/A

Reference: Faber, Ronald J., and Thomas C. O'Guinn. (1988). "Compulsive Consumption and Credit Abuse." *Journal of Consumer Policy*, *11*, 97-109.

COMPULSIVE BUYING SCALE
(Valence, d'Astous, and Fortier 1988)

1. When I have money, I cannot help but spend part or the whole of it.

2. I am often impulsive in my behavior.

3. For me, shopping is a way of facing the stress of my daily life and of relaxing.

4. I sometimes feel that something inside pushed me to go shopping.

5. There are times when I have a strong urge to buy (clothing, books, etc.)

6. At times I have felt somewhat guilty after buying a product, because it seemed unreasonable.

7. There are some things I buy that I do not show to anybody for fear of being perceived as irrational in my buying behavior ("a foolish expense").

8. I often have an unexplainable urge, a sudden and spontaneous desire, to go and buy something in a store.

9. As soon as I enter a shopping center, I have an irresistible urge to go into a shop and buy something.

10. I am one of those people who often respond to direct mail offers (e.g., books, records).

11. I have often bought a product that I did not need, while knowing that I have very little money left.

12. I am a spendthrift.

13. I have sometimes thought "If I had to do it all over again, I would . . ." and felt sorry for something I have done or said.

NOTES: Although not explicitly stated, items are likely scored on 5-point scales ranging from *strongly disagree* to *strongly agree*. Items 1, 2, 9, 10, 11, and 12 represent the "tendency to spend" facet; items 3, 4, 5, and 8 reflect the "reactive" aspect; and items 6, 7, and 13 reflect the "post-purchase guilt" aspect.

COMPULSIVE CONSUMPTION: A DIAGNOSTIC TOOL/CLINICAL SCREENER FOR CLASSIFYING COMPULSIVE CONSUMERS
(Faber and O'Guinn 1989, 1992)

Construct: This abnormal form of consumer behavior is typified by chronic buying episodes of a somewhat stereotyped fashion in which the consumer feels unable to stop or significantly moderate the behavior(s). Although compulsive buying may produce some short-term positive feelings for the individual, it ultimately is disruptive to normal life functioning and produces significant negative consequences (Faber and O'Guinn 1989). As such, compulsive buying shares similarities with other types of compulsive and addictive behaviors. O'Guinn and Faber (1989) and Faber and O'Guinn (1992, p. 459) formally define compulsive buying as "a chronic, repetitive purchasing that becomes a primary response to negative events or feelings."

Description: The measure represents a screening instrument designed to identify compulsive consumers. The initial instrument was composed of the unweighted sum of scores of 14 items (Faber and O'Guinn 1989). Each item was operationalized using 5-point Likert-type scales. The range of the measure is 14 to 70. Lower scores reflect greater agreement or compulsivity. The refined instrument is composed of seven items scored on 5-point scales, and a weighted algorithm-based score is derived as a "screener" to classify individuals as potential compulsive buyers (Faber and O'Guinn 1992).

Development: Development of the initial scale began with a set of 32 variables that assessed psychological, motivational, and behavioral aspects of buying. These items were developed from the literature on other compulsive behaviors, the authors' previous experiences, and a pilot test with a small group of compulsive consumers (Faber and O'Guinn 1989). Those 14 items discriminating ($p <$ .10) between two groups (i.e., the two samples described below) were selected for inclusion in the measure. Using a general population sample, factor analysis of these 14 items revealed only one viable factor. The refined scale employed the items from the initial scale as well as other items that reflected the construct definition. A total of 29 items were selected as potential candidates for the screening instrument. These items were carefully generated from both the existing literature and judgments of therapists and trained observers. Using samples of both self-identified compulsive buyers and respondents from the general population, the final form of the screener was derived. Numerous procedures consistent with scale development as a "classification" tool were employed, including logistic regression, test-retest reliability (via a c coefficient), internal consistency, and principal component analyses. Several validity tests were also performed that assessed the degree to which the screener "correctly" classified compulsive buyers, as well as mean-level difference tests on various psychological variables between compulsive buyers and "general consumers."

Samples: The samples for the initial instrument (Faber and O'Guinn 1989) and the refined screener (Faber and O'Guinn 1992) employed many of the same respondents. As such, these samples will be described (briefly) in tandem. A sample of 388 respondents to a mail survey specifically designed to contact potential "compulsive buyers" was obtained. These individuals were in contact (but not in therapy) with a self-help group for problem consumers. A comparison sample of 292 individuals was obtained after three mailings to a sample of 800 drawn from three Illinois cities of varying sizes. From these samples, smaller samples ($n = 22$) based on classification results from the refined screener as well as randomly generated samples from the general population and self-identified compulsive buyers were compared. Samples of 53 and 54 responding either to a "compulsive buyer ad" or "control ad" (both were newspaper ads) were used to assess the classification rate of the refined screener (Faber and O'Guinn 1992).

Validity: The coefficient alpha estimate of internal consistency reliability for the 14-item initial scale (Faber and O'Guinn 1989) was .83. The refined seven-item version showed a coefficient alpha estimate of .95 (Faber and O'Guinn 1992).

In Faber and O'Guinn (1989), the distributions of the screening measure were examined for both groups. The intersections of the distributions were examined to determine a threshold score (i.e., two standard deviations below the mean for the general distribution) of 42, which also was the modal value for the compulsive sample. Approximately 6% of the general sample was identified as compulsives. Tests of mean differences were made between the 16 compulsives in the general sample and 16 individuals drawn from the compulsive group. These comparisons revealed that the screener measure is capable of identifying compulsives in the general population similar to individuals in the compulsive group but quite different from other members of the general population. Differences were examined for measures of self-esteem, payments for past purchases, general compulsivity, envy, and fantasy.

In Faber and O'Guinn (1992), mean-level difference tests showed that compulsive buyers exhibited lower levels of self-esteem, higher levels of obsessive compulsiveness, high levels of fantasy, higher levels of remorse (guilt), and higher levels of materialism than did a "general consumer" sample. In addition, using rigorous criteria, as a clinical screening instrument, the refined scale was able to correctly classify about 88% of respondents as "compulsive buyers" or "noncompulsive buyers" in the samples used.

Scores: Mean scores are reported for both a "comparison strata" and a "compulsive strata" in Faber and O'Guinn (1989). The mean scores (and standard deviations) were 37.44 (10.74) and 57.33 (7.51) for the compulsive and comparison strata, respectively. The corresponding modal values were 42 and 58.

Source: Faber, Ronald J., and Thomas C. O'Guinn. (1989). "Classifying Compulsive Consumers: Advances in the Development of a Diagnostic Tool." In Thomas K. Srull (Ed.), *Advances in Consumer Research* (Vol. 16, pp. 738-744). Provo, UT: Association for Consumer Research.
© 1989 by the Association for Consumer Research. Scale items taken from Table 1 (p. 741). Reprinted with permission.

Faber, Ronald J., and Thomas C. O'Guinn. (1992). "A Clinical Screener for Compulsive Buying." *Journal of Consumer Research, 19,* 459-469. Scale items taken from Appendix (p. 468).

Other evidence: In two studies, Faber, Christenson, De Zwaan, and Mitchell (1995) found evidence for a "comorbid" link between compulsive buying and binge eating as 24 compulsive buyers (as classified Faber and O'Guinn's [1992] clinical screener) showed higher levels of binge eating, substance abuse, and impulse control disorders than did a matched noncompulsive buying sample (*n* = 24). In another study, Rindfleisch, Burroughs, and Denton (1997) report a coefficient alpha estimate for the seven-item compulsive buying clinical screener of .80. They report correlations of .25, −.26, .24, and .36 with family structure, family resources, family stressors, and material values, respectively, with the compulsive buying screener. They also report results from moderation and mediation analyses showing that compulsive buying is affected by family resources, family structure, and family stressors.

Other sources: Faber, Ronald J., Gary Christenson, Martina De Zwaan, and James Mitchell. (1995). "Two Forms of Compulsive Consumption: Comorbidity of Compulsive Buying and Binge Eating." *Journal of Consumer Research, 22,* 296-304.

Rindfleisch, Aric, James E. Burroughs, and Frank Denton. (1997). "Family Structure, Materialism, and Compulsive Buying." *Journal of Consumer Research, 23,* 312-325.

References: O'Guinn, Thomas C., and Ronald R. Faber. (1989). "Compulsive Buying: A Phenomenological Exploration." *Journal of Consumer Research, 16,* 147-157.

COMPULSIVE CONSUMPTION: A DIAGNOSTIC TOOL/CLINICAL SCREENER FOR CLASSIFYING COMPULSIVE CONSUMERS
(Faber and O'Guinn 1989, 1992)

1. Bought things even though I couldn't afford them.

2. Felt others would be horrified if they knew of my spending habits.

3. If I have any money left at the end of the pay period, I just have to spend it.

4. Made only the minimum payments on my credit cards.

5. Bought myself something in order to make myself feel better.

6. Wrote a check when I knew I didn't have enough money in the bank to cover it.

7. Just wanted to buy things and didn't care what I bought.

8. I often buy things simply because they are on sale.

9. Felt anxious or nervous on days I didn't go shopping.

10. Shopping is fun.

11. Felt depressed after shopping.

12. Bought something and when I got home I wasn't sure why I had bought it.

13. Went on a buying binge and wasn't able to stop.

14. I really believe that having more money would solve most of my problems.

NOTES: The items above are as they originally appeared in Faber and O'Guinn (1989). These 14 items composed the initial instrument. Items that compose the 1992 Faber and O'Guinn clinical screener (i.e., the refined instrument) are items 1 through 6, and 9. Items 1, 2, 4, 5, 6, and 9 are scored on *very often* to *never* scales, and item 3 is scored on a *strongly agree* to *strongly disagree* scale. These item scores can be summed to form an overall scale score, or they can be used to construct the Faber and O'Guinn weighted algorithm for classification purposes, which is as follows:

$$-9.69 + (Q3 \times .33) + (Q2 \times .34) + (Q1 \times .50) + (Q6 \times .47) + (Q5 \times .33) + (Q9 \times .38) + (Q4 \times .31)$$

If a score on the above algorithm is ≤ -1.34, a subject is classified as a compulsive buyer.

IMPULSIVENESS: BUYING IMPULSIVENESS SCALE
(Rook and Fisher 1995)

Construct: Rook and Fisher (1995, p. 306) define buying impulsiveness as "a consumer's tendency to buy spontaneously, unreflectively, immediately, and kinetically." High impulse buyers are more likely to have more "open" shopping lists, are more likely to be receptive to sudden and unexpected buying ideas, and are more apt to experience spontaneous buying stimuli. They tend to be motivated by immediate gratification and are more likely to act on a whim in purchase situations. Also, the high impulse buyer is likely to be prompted by the physical proximity of a desired product and dominated by an emotional attraction to it. In extreme cases, the behavior may by totally stimulus driven—translating into and yielding to a physical response or consumer "spasm" (Rook and Fisher 1995, p. 306).

Description: The buying impulsiveness scale is composed of nine items scored on 5-point Likert-type scales from *strongly disagree* to *strongly agree*. Item scores are summed to form an overall index score than can range from 9 to 45.

Development: A total of 35 items were first generated to reflect the construct's definition. These items were pretested with a sample of 281 students and tested again with a sample 212 undergraduate students. Via numerous recommended scaling procedures, including exploratory and confirmatory factor analyses, reliability analyses, and other correlation-based tests, the final nine-item form of the scale was derived. Several validity checks via mean-level difference testing and correlations with the buying impulsiveness scale and other constructs were performed.

Samples: Three samples were reported on in Rook and Fisher (1995). Two samples were composed of 281 and 212 undergraduate students. A third sample was composed of 104 respondents from a field study conducted in a mall record store.

Validity: Confirmatory factor analytic fit indices showed evidence of unidimensionality for the nine-item scale with one of the undergraduate samples ($n = 212$). Factor loadings were significant and ranged from .60 to .81 across items, and the coefficient alpha estimate of internal consistency was reported to be .88. Hypothesized relationships between "normative evaluation" and the buying impulsiveness scale were also supported. The mall record store sample also showed evidence of a unidimensional scale via confirmatory factor analyses, as well as adequate internal consistency (alpha = .82). Correlations of the buying impulsiveness scale with measures of normative evaluation and actual impulse-related buying behavior were .10, .21, .53, and .21. With the exception of the .10 correlation, all correlations were significant. Numerous other mean-level difference tests also support the validity of the scale.

Scores: Throughout the Rook and Fisher (1995) article, various mean scores on splits of their scale or moderating variable measures were reported. In addition, overall mean scores were reported. For the $n = 212$ sample, the mean (std. dev.) was 25.1 (7.4); and for the $n = 104$ sample, the mean (std. dev.) was 21.5 (7.1).

Source: Rook, Dennis, and Robert J. Fisher. (1995). "Normative Influences on Impulsive Buying Behavior." *Journal of Consumer Research*, 22, 305-313.

    © 1995 by the University of Chicago. Scale items taken from Table 1 (p. 308). Reprinted with permission.

Other evidence: N/A

Other soures: N/A

References: N/A

IMPULSIVENESS: BUYING IMPULSIVENESS SCALE
(Rook and Fisher 1995)

1. I often buy things spontaneously.

2. "Just do it" describes the way I buy things.

3. I often buy things without thinking.

4. "I see it, I buy it" describes me.

5. "Buy now, think about it later" describes me.

6. Sometimes I feel like buying things on the spur of the moment.

7. I buy things according to how I feel at the moment.

8. I carefully plan most of my purchases.

9. Sometimes I am a bit reckless about what I buy.

NOTE: Item 8 requires reverse scoring.

IMPULSIVENESS: IMPULSE BUYING TENDENCY
(Weun, Jones, and Beatty 1997)

Construct: Impulse buying tendency is defined as the "degree to which an individual is likely to make unintended, immediate, and unreflective purchases (i.e., impulse purchases)" (Weun, Jones, and Beatty 1997, p. 306).

Description: The impulse buying tendency scale is composed of five items. Item scores are summed to form an overall index. (Given that the Weun et al. paper appeared as a lengthy abstract, information on scale format was sketchy. The items appear to be Likert-type items scored on 5- or 7-point scales.)

Development: Ten items were originally generated based on the construct definition. Then, over three studies, using exploratory and confirmatory factor analyses, item and reliability analyses, and several validity-based tests, the final form of the scale was derived and validated.

Samples: Again, given that the paper was an abstract, information pertaining to the samples was limited. Two student samples and one nonstudent sample were used for the three studies.

Validity: The final five-item scale showed evidence of unidimensionality, internal consistency, and discriminant and convergent validity. The impulse buying tendency scale also performed better than the Rook and Fisher (1995) measure of impulse buying tendency.

Scores: Neither mean nor percentage scores were reported.

Source: Weun, Seungoog, Michael A. Jones, and Sharon E. Beatty. (1997). "A Parsimonious Scale to Measure Impulse Buying Tendency." In W. M. Pride and G. T. Hult (Eds.), *AMA Educators's Proceedings: Enhancing Knowledge Development in Marketing* (pp. 306-307). Chicago: American Marketing Association.

     © 1997 by the American Marketing Association. Scale items taken from p. 306. Reprinted with permission.

Other evidence: N/A

Other sources: N/A

Reference: Rook, Dennis, and Robert J. Fisher. (1995). "Normative Influences on Impulsive Buying Behavior." *Journal of Consumer Research*, 22, 305-313.

IMPULSIVENESS: IMPULSE BUYING TENDENCY
(Weun, Jones, and Beatty 1997)

1. When I go shopping, I buy things that I had not intended to purchase.

2. I am a person who makes unplanned purchases.

3. When I see something that really interests me, I buy it without considering the consequences.

4. It is fun to buy spontaneously.

5. I avoid buying things that are not on my shopping list.

NOTE: Item 5 requires reverse scoring.

IMPULSIVENESS-CONSUMER IMPULSIVENESS SCALE: CIS
(Puri 1996)

Construct: Puri (1996) offers the CIS to "measure people's chronic values toward impulsiveness" (p. 89). Impulsive behavior results in the choice of an option that offers immediate hedonic benefits but serious long-term consequences. Consistent with existing literature (e.g., Rook 1987), impulsive behavior is viewed as "consumer preference for a smaller, immediate reward over a much larger, later reward, even though they would generally prefer the larger reward" (p. 88). Puri proposes a two-factor framework where the accessibility of the costs versus the benefits of impulsiveness—determined by chronic values or situational characteristics—will influence if consumers behave impulsively or in a controlled manner.

Description: The CIS is a two-factor measure composed of a "prudence" subscale and a "hedonic" subscale. The prudence subscale has seven items, and the hedonic subscale has five. All items are represented by a single adjective where respondents indicate the degree to which each adjective describes them on 7-point scales. Item scores are summed within subscales to form two independent, yet related, indices of prudence and hedonism.

Development: Twenty-five adjectives were originally judged by two doctoral students and one faculty member. Via this procedure, 13 ambiguous items were deleted. The remaining 12 items that compose the final versions of the prudence and hedonic subscales were then subjected to exploratory and confirmatory factor analyses, reliability analyses, and numerous validity checks with three samples. Three experiments were then conducted that supported Puri's two-factor framework of consumer impulsiveness, as well as the validity of the CIS subscales.

Samples: The three samples used in initial scale development were composed of $n = 93$ MBA students, $n = 90$ MBA and Ph.D. students, and $n = 127$ respondents from India. The three experimental samples were $n = 60$ undergraduate students, $n = 134$ undergraduate students, and $n = 73$ MBA and Ph.D. students.

Validity: Via exploratory and then confirmatory factor analyses, it was found that a two-factor model, representing the prudence and hedonic subdimensions, fit the data well. Item-to-factor loadings for these two subdimensions ranged from .53 to .82 within the respective subdimensions. Though the prudence and hedonic subdimensions are considered separate, a coefficient alpha estimate for all 12 items combined was reported to be .82 ($n = 93$ sample). Split-halves reliability was reported to be .83 for all 12 items ($n = 90$ sample). Evidence of discriminant validity was provided via correlations of the two subscales with Market Mavenism, a measure of Social Desirability, and a measure of Internal-External Locus of Control. These correlations were .15, .13, and −.04, respectively, for the hedonic subscale; and .02, .11, and −.08, respectively, for the prudence subscale ($p > .25$ for all correlations using the $n = 93$ sample). Convergent validity was assessed via a correlation of .50 between all 12 items of the CIS and a measure of future orientation and willpower. Numerous mean-level difference tests conducted with the three experimental samples also show support for the validity of the CIS.

Scores: Throughout the text and tables of the Puri (1996) article, mean scores are reported, primarily based on experimental results. It seems that these mean scores are the result of summing the item scores within each of the subdimensions of the CIS and then dividing by the number of scale items per dimension.

Source: Puri, Radhika. (1996). "Measuring and Modifying Consumer Impulsiveness: A Cost-Benefit Accessibility Framework." *Journal of Consumer Psychology*, 5(2), 87-113.

© 1996 by Lawrence Erlbaum Associates, Inc. Scale items taken from Appendix A (p. 112). Reprinted with permission.

Other evidence: N/A

Other sources: N/A

Reference: Rook, Dennis W. (1987). "The Buying Impulse." *Journal of Consumer Research*, *14*, 189-198.

IMPULSIVENESS-CONSUMER IMPULSIVENESS SCALE: CIS
(Puri 1996)

Read each of the following adjectives carefully and indicate how well they would describe you. Circle the number on the scale next to the adjective. Numbers near 1 indicate that the adjective would usually describe you, numbers near 4 indicate that it would sometimes describe you, and numbers near 7 indicate that it would seldom describe you.

		usually would describe me			*sometimes would describe me*			*seldom would describe me*
1.	impulsive	1	2	3	4	5	6	7
2.	careless							
3.	self-controlled							
4.	extravagant							
5.	farsighted							
6.	responsible							
7.	restrained							
8.	easily tempered							
9.	rational							
10.	methodical							
11.	enjoy spending							
12.	a planner							

NOTES: Items 3, 5, 6, 7, 9, 10, and 12 compose the "prudence" subscale. These items also require reverse scoring. Items 1, 2, 4, 8, and 11 compose the "hedonic" subscale. According to the author, respondents scoring above (below) the median on the reverse-scored prudence subscale are classified as prudents (hedonics). All others are classified as moderates (p. 112).

SCALES RELATED TO COUNTRY IMAGE AND AFFILIATION

COUNTRY IMAGE SCALE
(Martin and Eroglu 1993)

Construct: Country image is defined as "the total of all descriptive, inferential, and informational beliefs about a particular country" (Martin and Eroglu 1993, p. 193). Country image is conceptualized as different from attitude toward the products from a given country. Country image can be affected by direct experience with a country, outside sources of information such as advertising or word of mouth, or inferences (correct or incorrect) from past experience with products from a given country.

Description: Although four dimensions of country image were originally conceptualized (i.e., political, economic, technological, and social desirability), the final form of the scale has three dimensions, composed of a five-item political factor, a five-item economic factor, and a four-item technological factor. (It was concluded that the social desirability aspect of the construct was adequately reflected in the three dimensions that were retained.) All items are scored on 7-point semantic differential scales. Item scores can be summed within dimension (factor) to form separate indices for the economic, political, and technological factors, or all 14 item scores can be summed to form one overall country image composite.

Development: Via a two-phase procedure, 60 items were originally generated to reflect the four originally conceptualized dimensions of the construct. In the first phase, students and faculty members were used to generate items, and in the second phase eight doctoral students with varying international backgrounds were used. This pool of 60 items was then trimmed to 29 via expert judging of the representativeness of the items to the construct. Then, with six samples, the final form of the scale was derived and validated using principal component analyses, reliability and item analyses, and other correlational techniques. With these samples, the countries of Japan, the United States, India, and West Germany were used as the focal countries of interest in responding to the scales.

Samples: A sample of 200 undergraduate and graduate students was used to derive the final form of the scale. Samples of 230, 80, 80, 79, and 79 (all students) were used for further reliability and validity checks.

Validity: For the sample $n = 200$, coefficient alpha was reported to be .950 for the entire 14-item country image scale. Alpha estimates for the economic, political, and technological dimensions ranged from .56 to .71. For the $n = 230$ sample, coefficient alpha for the entire 14-item scale was .925. A split-halves coefficient of .78 was also reported for the entire 14-item scale. For the first $n = 80$ sample, coefficient alpha for the entire 14-item scale was .895, with alphas ranging from .686 to .887 for the three country image dimensions (factors). For the second $n = 80$ sample, alpha was .928 for the entire 14-item scale, with alphas ranging from .581 to .761 across the three dimensions. As a test of discriminant validity, the three dimensions of country image were correlated with a measure of an image of products with foreign country of origin using the two $n = 79$ samples. Across all three dimensions, these correlations ranged from .18 to .51 ($p > .19$ for all).

Scores: Neither mean nor percentage scores were reported.

Source: Martin, Ingrid, and Sevgin Eroglu. (1993). "Measuring a Multi-Dimensional Construct: Country Image." *Journal of Business Research*, *28*, 191-210.

© 1993 by Elsevier Science. Scale items taken from Appendix C (pp. 206-207). Reprinted with permission from Elsevier Science.

Other evidence: N/A

Other sources: N/A

References: N/A

COUNTRY IMAGE SCALE
(Martin and Eroglu 1993)

This is a survey to find out what a person thinks about a certain country. To measure this, we will ask you to rate the country that appears at the top of the page against a series of descriptors by placing a check (X) on the scale from one to seven that best reflects *your* judgment. There are no right or wrong answers. We are only interested in how YOU perceive the country.

(COUNTRY NAME)

1. Economically developed   ___:___:___:___:___:___:___   Economically underdeveloped
                                     1   2   3   4   5   6   7

2. Democratic system   Dictatorial system

3. Mass-produced products   Handcrafted products

4. Civilian government   Military government

5. Predominantly industrialized   Predominantly non-industrialized

6. High labor costs   Low labor costs

7. High literacy rates   Low literacy rates

8. Free market system   Centrally planned system

9. Existence of welfare system   Lack of a welfare system

10. Stable economic environment   Unstable economic environment

11. Exporter of agricultural products   Importer of agricultural products

12. Production of high-quality products   Production of low-quality products

13. High standard of living   Low standard of living

14. High level of technological research   Low level of technological research

NOTES: From Tables 2 through 4 in the Martin and Eroglu (1993) article, it is a bit unclear as to which items pertain to which dimensions. Specifically, table descriptor items differ slightly from Appendix C (the source of the actual scale items) descriptor items. Also, with the exception of items 6 and 9, it would seem that all items require reverse coding such that higher scores reflect higher levels of the construct.

COUNTRY-OF-ORIGIN SCALE
(Pisharodi and Parameswaran 1992; Parameswaran and Pisharodi 1994)

Construct: According to Pisharodi and Parameswaran (1992), country of origin is an evolving construct which states that people attach stereotypical "made in" perceptions to products from specific countries and this influences purchase and consumption behaviors in multinational markets. Furthermore, the construct encompasses perceptions of a sourcing country's economic, political, and cultural characteristics, as well as specific product image perceptions (i.e., in the 1992 study automobiles were the focal product, and in the 1994 study Korean and German brands of automobiles and blenders were the focal products).

Description: The final version of the 1992 scale is composed of 24 items scored on 10-point scales ranging from *not at all appropriate* (1) to *most appropriate* (10). The scale has six factors; three relate to general product attitudes (GPA), two relate to general country attitudes (GCA), and one relates to specific product attributes (SPA). The first five factors are applicable across product attitudes and country attitudes (i.e., the GPA and GCA factors), and the last factor (SPA) is specific to automobiles. Item scores can be summed within factors to form factor indices. The scale is considered multidimensional, but items within the factors reflect unidimensional measurement.

The final versions of the 1994 scale are composed of 35 items scored on 10-point scales ranging from *not at all appropriate* (1) to *most appropriate* (10). Depending on the product category (autos vs. blenders) and the country of origin (Korea vs. Germany), scale content in terms of items-to-factors differ slightly. The scale has eight factors; three relate to general product attitudes (GPA), two relate to general country attitudes (GCA), and three relate to specific product attributes (SPA). Item scores can be summed within factors to form factor indices, and the scale is considered multidimensional. Items within the factors reflect unidimensional measurement.

Development: In the 1992 chapter, via an extensive review of the literature, 40 items were generated to reflect the GPA, GCA, and SPA factors. Initially, it was felt that the construct would be best represented by just a three-factor solution (i.e., one factor each for GPA, GCA, and SPA). Responses from a large sample were then used to trim the number of items and assess dimensionality and internal consistency. Using confirmatory factor analysis (via LISREL) and the ITAN package (Gerbing and Hunter 1988), an iterative process that examines inter-item correlations, item-factor loadings, and dimensionality derived the final form of the scale. The final form reflected three factors relating to GPA. Two of the GPA factors stress positive attributes (i.e., labeled GPA2 and GPA3), and one reflects negative attributes (i.e., labeled GPA1). The final form of the 1992 scale also contains one factor relating to SPA (positive attributes).

In the 1994 study, similar procedures were followed in deriving the final form of the scale.

Sampless: A total of 678 adults from a large midwestern metropolitan area responded to the numerous items in the original questionnaire for both the 1992 and 1994 studies.

Validity: For the 1992 study, the fit of the six-factor model, representing the final form of the scale, indicated unidimensionality of items in each of the six factors. Coefficient alpha estimates for the factors were .872, .849, .918, .735, .796, and 819 for GCA1, GCA2, GPA1, GPA2, GPA3, and SPA, respectively.

For the 1994 study, the fit of the eight-factor model, representing the final form of the scale, indicated adequate fit to the data in terms of items to the factors. Coefficient alpha estimates of the factors for the German brands ranged from a low .609 for a three-item SPA2 factor (i.e., blender) to a high of .943 for an eight-item SPA1 factor (i.e., blender). Coefficient alpha estimates of the factors for the Korean brands ranged from a low .586 for a three-item SPA2 factor (i.e., blender) to a high of .924 for an eight-item SPA1 factor (i.e., blender).

Scores: Neither mean nor percentage scores were reported in the 1992 or 1994 studies.

Sources: Pisharodi, R. Mohan, and Ravi Parameswaran. (1992). "Confirmatory Factor Analysis of a Country-of-Origin Scale: Initial Results." In John Sherry and Brian Sternthal (Eds.), *Advances in Consumer Research* (Vol. 19, pp. 706-714). Provo, UT: Association for Consumer Research. © 1992 by the Association for Consumer Research. Scale items taken from Table 1 (p. 708). Reprinted with permission.

Parameswaran, Ravi, and Mohan R. Pisharodi. (1994). "Facets of Country-of-Origin Image: An Empirical Assessment." *Journal of Advertising*, *23*, 44-56. © 1994 by Publisher. Scale items taken from Table 1 (pp. 47-48).

Other evidence: N/A

Other sources: N/A

Reference: Gerbing, David W., and John E. Hunter. (1988). *ITAN: A Statistical Package for Item Analysis With Correlational Data Including Multiple Groups Factor Analysis.* Portland State University, Portland, OR.

COUNTRY-OF-ORIGIN SCALE
(Pisharodi and Parameswaran 1992)

General Country Attitudes: GCA1 Items
1. Well educated
2. Hard-working
3. Achieving high standards
4. Raised standards of living
5. Technical skills

General Country Attitudes: GCA2 Items
1. Similar political views
2. Economically similar
3. Culturally similar

General Product Attitudes: GPA1 Items
1. Unreasonably expensive
2. Imitations
3. Not attractive
4. Frequent repairs
5. Cheaply put together

General Product Attitudes: GPA2 Items
1. Sold in many countries
2. Intensely advertised
3. Advertising information
4. Easily available

General Product Attitudes: GPA3 Items
1. Long lasting
2. Good value
3. Prestigious products

Specific Product Attitudes: SPA Items

1. Workmanship good
2. Handles well
3. Little maintenance
4. Made to last

COUNTRY-OF-ORIGIN SCALE
(Parameswaran and Pisharodi 1994)

General Country Attitudes: GCA Items
C1. Friendly & likable
C2. Artistic & creative
C3. Well educated
C4. Hard-working
C5. Technical education
C6. Achieving high standards
C7. Raised standards of living
C8. Technical skills
C9. Similar political views
C10. Economically similar
C11. Culturally similar
C12. Participates in international affairs

General Product Attitudes: GPA Items
P1. Unreasonably expensive
P2. Luxury products
P3. Meticulous workmanship
P4. Imitations
P5. Known mainly for industrial products
P6. Sold in many countries
P7. Not attractive
P8. Intensely advertised
P9. Frequent repairs
P10. Wide range of models
P11. Long lasting
P12. Advertising informative
P13. Difficult to service
P14. Cheaply put together
P15. High technology
P16. Good value
P17. Easily available
P18. Prestigious product

*Specific Product Attitudes: SPA Items (***Cars***)*
- S1. Good fuel economy
- S2. Exterior styling attractive
- S3. Workmanship good
- S4. Handles well
- S5. Little maintenance
- S6. Very comfortable
- S7. Difficult to get parts
- S8. Quality service
- S9. Made to last
- S10. Overall excellent

*Specific Product Attitudes: SPA Items (***Blenders***)*
- S1. High quality
- S2. Very good workmanship
- S3. Exterior design attractive
- S4. Difficult to find spares
- S5. Compact
- S6. Versatile
- S7. Operate very quickly
- S8. Not durable
- S9. Not safe
- S10. Good value for the money
- S11. Overall excellent

NOTES: For this 1994 version, for *German brands* items C3, C4, and C6 through C8 compose the GCA1 factor (i.e., "people facet"); C9 to C11 compose the GCA2 factor (i.e., the "interaction facet"); items P4, P7, P9, P13, and P14 compose the GPA1 factor (i.e., "undesirable product attributes"); items P6, P7, P12, and P17 compose the GPA2 factor (i.e., "distribution-promotion-based desirable attributes"); items P11, P16, and P18 compose the GPA3 factor (i.e., "product-based general desirable attributes"); items S3, S4, S5, and S9 compose the SPA-**Car** factor; items S1 to S3, S5 to S7, S10, and S11 compose the SPA1-**Blender** factor; and items S4, S8, and S9 compose the SPA2-**Blender** factor.

     For *Korean brands* items C1 to C3 and C6 to C8 compose the GCA1 factor (i.e., "people facet"); C9 to C11 compose the GCA2 factor (i.e., the "interaction facet"); items P4, P7, P9, P13, and P14 compose the GPA1 factor (i.e., "undesirable product attributes"); items P6, P7, and P17 compose the GPA2 factor (i.e., "distribution-promotion-based desirable attributes"); items P11, P15, and P18 compose the GPA3 factor (i.e., "product-based general desirable attributes"); items S3, S4, S5, and S9 compose the SPA-**Car** factor; items S1 to S3, S5 to S7, S10, and S11 compose the SPA1-**Blender** factor; and items S4, S8, and S9 compose the SPA2-**Blender** factor.

ETHNOCENTRISM-CONSUMER ETHNOCENTRISM: CETSCALE
(Shimp and Sharma 1987)

Construct: The CETSCALE is designed to measure consumers' ethnocentric tendencies (i.e., disposition to act in a consistent fashion) related to purchasing foreign- versus American-made products. Consumer ethnocentrism represents the beliefs held by consumers about the appropriateness, indeed morality, of purchasing foreign-made products (Shimp and Sharma 1987, p. 280). The purchase of foreign-made products, in the minds of ethnocentric consumers, is wrong because it hurts the domestic economy, causes loss of jobs, and is unpatriotic.

Description: The scale consists of 17 items scored on 7-point Likert-type formats (*strongly agree* = 7, *strongly disagree* = 1). Item scores are summed to form an overall score ranging from 17 to 119. In its original form, the scale was designed for use on American subjects, as most items contain reference to America or the United States. (A shortened 10-item version using a 5-place response format was also tested in the national consumer goods study described below.) Both versions are considered unidimensional.

Development: Recommended scaling procedures were used in scale development. The CETSCALE was developed using an initial pool of 180 nonredundant items based upon the common wording of responses from an open-ended elicitation study of 800 consumers. Following a judgmental screening of items by a panel of six academics, two purification studies were conducted to develop the final form of the scale. Initially, the development phase addressed seven facets of consumers' orientations toward foreign products. Common factor analysis of the data obtained in the first purification study reduced the item pool to 25 items reflecting the ethnocentrism dimension. From the second purification study, 17 items consistently demonstrated satisfactory reliability in a series of confirmatory factor analyses.

Samples: The respondents were 407 households in the first study. The second study included approximately 320 households from each of three metropolitan areas (Detroit, Denver, Los Angeles) and 575 households from the Carolinas. Using some of these same data, four additional studies were conducted to assess reliability and validity of the scale: (a) four area studies, *n* = 1,535; (b) Carolinas study, *n* = 47; (c) national consumer goods study, *n* = 2000+; and (d) crafted-with-pride study, *n* = 145 involved. Only the crafted-with-pride study involved student subjects.

Validity: The assessment of reliability and validity of the CETSCALE in the original article was stringent and extensive. Only a brief summary is provided here. Interested readers are advised to refer to Shimp and Sharma (1987) for details. Internal consistency estimates of reliability ranged from .94 to .96; test-retest was estimated at .77. Evidence of convergent and discriminant validity was provided by significant and positive correlations of the CETSCALE and measures of patriotism and political-economic conservatism. Extensive tests of nomological validity (in one instance over a 2-year delay) were also presented in support of the scale. Briefly, scale scores were found, as predicted, negatively correlated with varying measures of consumers' beliefs, attitudes, and intentions toward foreign-made products. Other data revealed that origin of manufacturer was more important for high scorers and that higher scorers were biased in favor of American products and in opposition to European and Asian products. Finally, tests of mean differences revealed that scores were highest among individuals whose quality of life and economic situation (and hardships) are threatened by foreign competition (i.e., lower social classes, Detroit respondents).

Scores: Mean scores (std. dev.) for the CETSCALE for the four geographic areas followed a predicted pattern: (a) Detroit, 68.58 (25.96); (b) Carolinas, 61.28 (24.41); (c) Denver, 57.84 (26.10); (d) Los Angeles, 56.62 (26.37). The mean scores for the two-phase student sample used in the crafted-with-pride study resulted in mean scores of 51.92 (16.37) and 53.39 (16.52). Scores also were found to decline predictably across three social classes: upper-lower, 73.63; lower-middle, 64.01; and upper-middle, 51.91.

Source: Shimp, Terence A., and Subhash Sharma. (1987). "Consumer Ethnocentrism: Construction and Validation of the CETSCALE." *Journal of Marketing Research*, *24*, 280-289.

© 1987 by the American Marketing Association. Scale items taken from Table 1 (p. 282). Reprinted with permission.

Other evidence: In a validation study, Netemeyer, Durvasula, and Lichtenstein (1991) used student samples of 71, 73, 70, and 76 from colleges in the United States, Germany, France, and Japan, respectively. Netemeyer et al. (1991) reported alpha levels ranging from .91 to .95 across the four countries studied. In addition, the CETSCALE was correlated with a number of behavioral measures reflecting a consumer ethnocentric bias. Across countries, these correlations offered evidence of nomological validity for the scale. In a more recent study by Sharma, Shimp, and Shin (1995), the 17-item CETSCALE showed an internal consistency estimate of .91. The CETSCALE also showed significant correlations with the social-psychological constructs of openness, $r = -.21$; patriotism/conservatism, $r = .53$; and collectivism, $r = .18$ and $r = .23$, and with the demographic characteristics of education, $r = -.25$, and income, $r = -.15$. The CETSCALE was also shown to be a significant predictor of attitude toward importing various products and perceived economic threat (in regression analyses). The Sharma et al. (1995) study used a sample of 667 Korean consumers.

Other sources: Netemeyer, Richard G., Srinivas Durvasula, and Donald R. Lichtenstein. (1991). "A Cross-National Assessment of the Reliability and Validity of the CETSCALE." *Journal of Marketing Research*, *28*, 320-327.

Sharma, Subhash, Terence A. Shimp, and Jeongshin Shin. (1995). "Consumer Ethnocentrism: A Test of Antecedents and Moderators." *Journal of the Academy of Marketing Science*, *23*(1), 26-37.

References: N/A

ETHNOCENTRISM-CONSUMER ETHNOCENTRISM: CETSCALE
(Shimp and Sharma 1987)

1. American people should always buy American-made products instead of imports.

2. Only those products that are unavailable in the U.S. should be imported.

3. Buy American-made products. Keep America working.

4. American products, first, last and foremost.

5. Purchasing foreign-made products is un-American.

6. It is not right to purchase foreign products.

7. A real American should always buy American-made products.

8. We should purchase products manufactured in America instead of letting other countries get rich off us.

9. It is always best to purchase American products.

10. There should be very little trading or purchasing of goods from other countries unless out of necessity.

11. Americans should not buy foreign products, because this hurts American business and causes unemployment.

12. Curbs should be put on all imports.

13. It may cost me in the long run but I prefer to support American products.

14. Foreigners should not be allowed to put their products on our markets.

15. Foreign products should be taxed heavily to reduce their entry into the U.S.

16. We should buy from foreign countries only those products that we cannot obtain within our own country.

17. American consumers who purchase products made in other countries are responsible for putting their fellow Americans out of work.

NOTE: Items composing the 10-item reduced version are items 2, 4 through 8, 11, 13, 16, and 17.

HISPANICNESS: AN INDEX TO MEASURE "HISPANICNESS"
(Valencia 1985)

Construct: The term "Hispanicness" refers to the rate or degree of acculturation of Hispanic consumers living in the United States (Valencia 1985, p. 118). Acculturation is defined as the process of learning a culture other than the one into which one is born. The impetus for the research is based upon the recognition that the degree of identification the individual feels with a given ethnic group may largely determine the level of commitment regarding cultural norms and the degree of influence exerted by a particular culture (Hirschman 1981). Consequently, differences in consumption preferences should be observed.

Description: The index has six indicators that are summed, with a range for the total score of 6 to 23. The English language ability item is reverse scored. Item scoring procedures for the six questions are shown below. The measure is designed to include the following attributes: strength of ethnic identification, understanding of the English language, extent of Spanish language maintenance, length of time lived in the American culture, and marital relationships (i.e., miscegenation).

Development: The items composing the scale were developed to reflect the attributes of Hispanicness reviewed in the manuscript's introduction. More traditional item-generation procedures were not employed in the development of the scale. However, a series of multiple bilingual translations were used to ensure consistent meaning and interpretation of the items and the survey used to test the index.

Sample: The index was tested on a sample of respondents to a mail survey of residents of New York, Los Angeles, Miami, and San Antonio (i.e., cities with high concentrations of Hispanic residents and including 42% of America's Hispanic population). After excluding responses from inappropriate ethnic groups and incomplete responses, data were available from 178 Hispanic and 288 White respondents (Valencia 1985, p. 119).

Validity: An unspecified reliability estimate of .73 was provided. The correlation between the Hispanic Index and a six-item measure of consumer acculturation was .17 ($p < .05$). The Spearman correlation between the scale and place of birth (i.e., outside or within the United States) was .54 ($p < .01$). In addition, mean differences in shopping opinions and behaviors between Whites and low and high Hispanic groups were cited as further evidence of the scale's validity.

Scores: In an earlier study, index scores ranged from 6 to 19. Other data regarding means were not provided in Valencia (1985).

Source: Valencia, Humberto. (1985). "Developing an Index to Measure 'Hispanicness.'" In Elizabeth C. Hirschman and Morris Holbrook (Eds.), *Advances in Consumer Research* (Vol. 12, pp. 118-121). Provo, UT: Association for Consumer Research.
© 1985 by the Association for Consumer Research. Scale items taken from Table 1 (p. 120). Reprinted with permission.

Other evidence: N/A

Other sources: N/A

Reference: Hirschman, Elizabeth C. (1981). "American Jewish Ethnicity: Its Relationship to Some Selected Aspects of Consumer Behavior." *Journal of Marketing, 45,* 102-110.

HISPANICNESS: AN INDEX TO MEASURE "HISPANICNESS"
(Valencia 1985)

1. Strength of ethnic identification
"How strongly do you identify yourself with the ethnic or racial group you mentioned above?"
1) Very strongly, 2) Strongly, 3) More or less, 4) Weak, 5) Very weak.

2. English language ability
"As you may know, some people in the U.S. are bilingual. If you speak Spanish, please answer the next three questions. Would you say you speak English":
1) Very well, 2) Well, 3) Not well, 4) Not at all.

3. Spanish language spoken at home
"Would you say your family speaks Spanish at home?"
1) All of the time, 2) Most of the time, 3) Sometimes, 4) Not at all.

4. Language preference
"If you had the chance to communicate with someone just as well in English or Spanish, which would you prefer to converse with them?"
1) Spanish, 2) Either Spanish or English, 3) English.

5. Ratio of length of residence in the U.S.
"How long have you lived in the U.S.? _____ Years."
Note: Number of years is divided by age and weighted by 4.

6. Miscegenation
"If married, with which ethnic or racial group does your spouse identify with?"
1) Hispanic/Hispanic spouse or Hispanic single, 2) Hispanic/Anglo spouse,
3) Anglo/Hispanic spouse, 4) Anglo/Anglo spouse or Anglo single.

NOTE: For higher scores to reflect higher levels of Hispanicness, items 1 and 3 through 6 require reverse coding.

SCALES RELATED TO CONSUMER OPINION
LEADERSHIP AND OPINION SEEKING

EXPERTISE: CONSUMER EXPERTISE
(Kleiser and Mantel 1994)

Construct: Kleiser and Mantel adopt the Alba and Hutchinson (1987) view of consumer expertise. Specifically, consumer expertise is considered multidimensional and is defined as "the ability to perform product-related tasks successfully" (Alba and Hutchinson 1987, p. 411). The five dimensions of consumer expertise delineated are (a) *cognitive effort and its inherent automaticity*, which refers to decision making that is performed with minimal effort and without conscious control; (b) *cognitive structure*, which reflects factual knowledge and beliefs that consumers have about products and the ways in which the knowledge is organized; (c) *analysis*, which represents the extent to which consumers access all relevant/important information for a particular task; (d) *elaboration*, which represents the number of intervening facts that must be computed in order for an inference to be made; and (e) *memory*, one's ability to remember product-related information.

Description: The consumer expertise scale has four dimensions. Although five dimensions (as delineated above) were originally hypothesized, scale developmental procedures retained only four dimensions; the *cognitive structure* dimension was omitted. A total of 15 items compose the four dimensions retained. All items are scored on a 7-point Likert-type scales from *strongly disagree* to *strongly agree*, and item scores are summed within dimensions to form dimension composite scores.

Development: Thirty-nine items were generated to reflect the five original dimensions. Using a camera as the focal product, these items were subjected to exploratory factor analyses and an "oblique centroid multiple groups analysis" (*n* = 118). Based on these procedures, 15 items were eliminated. The remaining 24 items were subjected to confirmatory factor analyses (LISREL). From this procedure, the cognitive structure items were dropped and the final 15-item, four-factor structure was retained. (Though a three-factor model combining the "analysis" and "elaboration" dimensions fit the data as well as the four-factor model, the four-factor model was retained.) Estimates of reliability and validity were also offered.

Sample: One sample of *n* = 118 undergraduate students was used.

Validity: Coefficient alpha estimates of internal consistency were .90, .72, .89, and .86 for the cognitive effort, analysis, elaboration, and memory dimensions, respectively. Correlations among the four dimensions ranged from .439 to .864. The .864 correlation was between the "elaboration" and "analysis" dimensions. Still, some evidence (albeit weak) of discriminant validity between these two dimensions was offered. The four dimensions were modeled as antecedents of "product familiarity" in a structural equations analysis. The model fit the data well, and the standardized path estimates from the four dimensions of expertise to product familiarity were .681, .832, .912, and .676 for cognitive effort, analysis, elaboration, and memory, respectively ($p < .01$ for all). Thus, support for the nomological validity of the dimensions of expertise was offered.

Scores: Neither mean nor percentage scores were offered.

Source: Kleiser, Susan B., and Susan Powell Mantel. (1994). "The Dimensions of Consumer Expertise: A Scale Development." In Ravi Achrol and Andrew Mitchell (Eds.), *AMA Summer Educators' Proceedings* (Vol. 5, pp. 20-26). Chicago: American Marketing Association.
© 1994 by the American Marketing Association. Scale items taken from Table 1 (p. 22). Reprinted with permission.

Other evidence: N/A

Other sources: N/A

Reference: Alba, Joseph W., and Wesley Hutchinson. (1987). "Dimensions of Consumer Expertise." *Journal of Consumer Research*, *13*, 411-454.

EXPERTISE: CONSUMER EXPERTISE
(Kleiser and Mantel 1994)

Cognitive effort/automaticity items
1. I automatically know which brands of cameras to buy.
2. I am loyal to one brand of cameras.
3. At the place of purchase, I can visually detect my preferred brand without much effort.
4. I can immediately identify my preferred brand even if it is located with other brands of cameras.
5. When I purchase my preferred brand, I do not pay attention to the other brands of cameras.

Analysis items
1. I enjoy learning about cameras.
2. I will search for the latest information on cameras before I purchase a brand.
3. I keep current on the most recent developments in cameras.

Elaboration items
1. I consider myself knowledgeable on cameras.
2. My knowledge of cameras helps me to understand very technical information about this product.
3. I use my knowledge on cameras to verify that adverting claims are in fact true.

Memory items
1. I can recall almost all existing brands of cameras from memory.
2. I can recognize almost all brand names of cameras.
3. I can recall product-specific attributes of cameras.
4. I can recall brand-specific attributes of the various brands of cameras.

FASHION LEADERSHIP
(Goldsmith, Freiden, and Kilsheimer 1993)

Construct: Goldsmith et al. (1993) follow the views of King and Summers (1967) and Guttman and Mills (1982) in formulating fashion leadership. Specifically, fashion leaders learn about new fashions earlier than the average buyer, and they purchase new fashion items soon after they are introduced into the market. Fashion leaders are more open to the excitement of buying new fashions and enjoy the fashion buying process because of the excitement. They also play a key role in the diffusion of fashion and fashion information. From this conceptual base, measures of fashion leadership were developed for the United States and the United Kingdom.

Description: For both the U.S. and U.K. versions, the fashion leadership scale is composed of five Likert-type items scored on 5-point scales ranging from *disagree* to *agree*. Item scores are summed to form an overall score that can range from 5 to 25. Both versions are considered unidimensional.

Development: The scales were derived from a measure originally proposed by Guttman and Mills (1982). For each country separately (United States and United Kingdom), their 17-item scale was factor analyzed. Five items were retained for each sample. Estimates of internal consistency and validity were offered.

Samples: A sample of $n = 136$ women from a medium-size MSA in the United States and a sample of $n = 115$ women from continuing education classes in London participated in the studies.

Validation: For both the U.S. and U.K. samples, principal axis factor analysis was used to derive the final form of the scale. For the U.S. sample, the five items retained (from the original 17) had factor loadings of .50 or greater. Another factor analysis of the retained five items showed that a single factor accounting for 64% in the data was extracted, offering evidence of a unidimensional scale. Alpha for the five-item scale was .85. Similar procedures were followed for the U.K. sample. The five items retained had loadings greater than .40, and a separate factor analysis of the five items showed a single factor accounting for 50% of the variance in the data. Alpha was .74. Numerous tests of validity were performed based on median splits of the fashion leadership scale (i.e., "low" and "high" leadership groups). In both countries, "high" fashion leaders reported higher levels of clothing spending, fashion magazine readership, shopping frequency, and new fashion items purchased than did "low" fashion leaders. Significant differences for the LOV value of "excitement" were also found for both the U.S. and U.K. samples.

Scores: For the U.S. sample, the mean (std. dev.) score for the fashion leadership scale was 14.1 (3.8), with a median of 13. For the U.K. sample, the mean (std. dev.) was 12.4 (3.0), with a median of 12.

Source: Goldsmith, Ronald E., Jon B. Freiden, and Jacqueline C. Kilsheimer. (1993). "Social Values and Female Fashion Leadership: A Cross-Cultural Study." *Psychology & Marketing*, *10*, 399-412.
© 1993 by John Wiley & Sons, Inc. Scale items taken from Table 2 (p. 405). Adapted by permission of John Wiley & Sons, Inc.

Other evidence: N/A

Other sources: N/A

References: Guttman, J., and M. K. Mills. (1982). "Fashion Life Style, Self-Concept, Shopping Orientation, and Store Patronage." *Journal of Retailing*, *58*(2), 64-86.

King, C. W., and J. O. Summers. (1967). "Technology, Innovation and Consumer Decision Making." In R. Moyer (Ed.), *Changing Marketing Systems, AMA Winter Conference Proceedings* (pp. 63-68). Chicago: American Marketing Association.

FASHION LEADERSHIP
(Goldsmith, Freiden, and Kilsheimer 1993)

1. I am aware of fashion trends and want to be one of the first to try them.

2. I am the first to try new fashion; therefore, many people regard me as being a fashion leader.

3. It is important for me to be a fashion leader.

4. I am confident in my ability to recognize fashion trends.

5. Clothes are one of the most important ways I have of expressing my individuality.

6. I don't spend a lot of time on fashion-related activities.

NOTES: Items 1-4 are used in both the U.S. and U.K. versions. Item 5 is for the U.S. version only, and item 6 is for the U.K. version only. Item 6 also requires reverse scoring.

MARKET MAVEN: PROPENSITY TO PROVIDE
MARKETPLACE AND SHOPPING INFORMATION
(Feick and Price 1987)

Construct: The "market maven" refers to individual consumers with a propensity to provide general shopping and marketplace information. Market mavens are defined formally as "individuals who have information about many kinds of products, places to shop, and other facets of markets, and initiate discussions with consumers and respond to requests from consumers for market information" (Feick and Price 1987, p. 85). The definition is comparable with the definition of opinion leaders in that influence derives from knowledge and expertise, but differs in that the expertise is not product specific (i.e., a more general knowledge of markets). Mavens obtain information because they think it will be useful to others or because it will provide a basis for conversations.

Description: The scale consists of six statements, five of which are operationalized as 7-place scales labeled *strongly disagree* to *strongly agree*. The sixth item has a 7-point response format of *the description does not fit me well at all* to *the description fits me very well*. Item scores are summed to form an overall score, and the range of the scale is from 6 to 42. All items are worded such that greater agreement results in a larger total score (i.e., a greater propensity to provide marketplace information).

Development: An initial pool of 40 items was generated based on the concept definition. This set was reduced to 19 by a panel of marketing academics and practitioners. Using the responses of a pilot sample of 265 MBAs, factor analysis, item-to-total correlations, and coefficient alpha were used to reduce the final scale to six items.

Samples: The main study for which the final instrument was administered involved nationwide telephone interviews (selected by random digit dialing) with 1,531 adult household heads. Sixty-four percent of the sample was female. Subjects were randomly assigned to subsamples; 771 were in the food subsample and 760 in the drug subsample (Feick and Price 1987, p. 87). In addition, 265 part-time MBA students participated in an earlier scale development study. A probability sample of 303 heads of households from a large northeastern city also participated in a study of the discriminant validity of the scale in relation to measures of opinion leadership.

Validity: For the pilot study, coefficient alpha was .84; item-to-total correlations ranged from .51 to .67. For the main study, the estimate of internal consistency reliability was .82, and item-to-total correlations ranged from .48 to .65.

   Validity evidence regarding the concept was provided from responses to queries regarding knowledge of individuals fitting the market maven description (46%) and the importance of those persons in making purchase decisions. Discriminant validity was examined (and supported) through factor analysis of the market maven items and a series of opinion leadership items. The correlation between the maven scale and a measure of opinion leadership was .22. Correlations between the market maven measure and a series of innovativeness variables were positive and significant. For example, the correlations for the food sample ranged from .31 to .34. Discriminant validity evidence was also provided from confirmatory factor analysis of the main study sample.

   Substantial correlational evidence of the scale's validity was provided by a series of proposition tests in which the scale was used to form low, medium, and high groups across which a series of difference tests were performed. In addition, the market maven scale was found correlated as predicted with a series of shopping and individual characteristics. These results confirm expectations regarding the construct and, hence, support the validity of the measure. For example, Feick and Price (1987, p. 94) conclude that market mavens exist, and consumers can identify them and use them in making purchase decisions. Furthermore, the concept was found related to early awareness of new products, provision of information, extensive use of information sources, and market activities such as couponing and reading advertising.

Scores: The mean score and standard deviation based on the sample of 1,531 interviews were 25.6 and 8.5, respectively.

Source: Feick, Lawrence F., and Linda L. Price. (1987). "The Market Maven: A Diffuser of Marketplace Information." *Journal of Marketing*, *51*, 83-97.
           © 1987 by the American Marketing Association. Scale items taken from Appendix (p. 95). Reprinted with permission.

Other evidence: Price, Feick, and Guskey-Federouch (1988) report a telephone interview of 213 subjects. Difference tests across groups revealed evidence for the scale's validity, as mavens were more likely to engage in smart shopping behaviors (i.e., use of coupons, designing grocery budgets) than nonmavens.

Other sources: Price, Linda L., Lawrence F. Feick, and Audrey Guskey-Federouch. (1988). "Couponing Behaviors of the Market Maven: Profile of a Super Shopper." In Michael J. Houston (Ed.), *Advances in Consumer Research* (Vol. 15, pp. 354-349). Provo, UT: Association for Consumer Research.

References: N/A

MARKET MAVEN: PROPENSITY TO PROVIDE MARKETPLACE AND SHOPPING INFORMATION
(Feick and Price 1987)

1. I like introducing new brands and products to my friends.

2. I like helping people by providing them with information about many kinds of products.

3. People ask me for information about products, places to shop, or sales.

4. If someone asked where to get the best buy on several types of products, I could tell him or her where to shop.

5. My friends think of me as a good source of information when it comes to new products or sales.

6. Think about a person who has information about a variety of products and likes to share this information with others. This person knows about new products, sales, stores, and so on, but does not necessarily feel he or she is an expert on one particular product. How well would you say this description fits you?

NOTE: Item 6 is scored from *the description does not fit me well at all* to *the description fits me very well*.

OPINION LEADERSHIP
(King and Summers 1970; Childers 1986)

Construct: The King and Summers measure of opinion leadership summarized here is actually an adaptation of an earlier measure presented by Rogers and Cartano (1962). A more recent revision of the scale by Childers (1986) is also summarized. In King and Summers's (1970) original study of opinion leadership generalization across product categories, a product- or issue-specific seven-item opinion leadership scale was offered. As originally conceptualized, opinion leadership reflects the extent to which individuals give information about a topic and the extent to which information is sought by others from those individuals. Opinion leadership is thought to be a critical determinant of word-of-mouth communication and interpersonal influences affecting the diffusion of new products, concepts, and services.

Description: The original King and Summers scale consists of seven items; five are operationalized using a dichotomous response format while the remaining items have three response possibilities. The total range of the scale is from 7 to 16. The items are worded such that alternative product categories can be inserted into each statement. For example, the first item reads as follows: "In general, do you like to talk about _____ with your friends? Yes__ -1 No__ -2."

The revised Opinion Leadership Scale (Childers 1986) also contains seven items adaptable to different product categories. However, the revised measure contains a modified set of items which are each operationalized via 5-place bipolar response formats. Item scores are summed to form a range of 7 to 35. (Both the King and Summers and the Childers versions are included below.) Childers eventually recommends that item 5 be deleted, resulting in a potential range of 6 to 30.

Development: The scale was developed by modifying an already existing self-designating measure of opinion leadership (Rogers 1961; Rogers and Cartano 1962). The modifications to the Rogers measure included (a) omitting the word "new" in each of six questions to remove bias in favor of innovators, (b) adding a question, and (c) changing the order of questions (King and Summers 1970, p. 46).

Childers (1986) reported two studies in his efforts to investigate the King and Summers measure. The first was designed to evaluate the original scale. His second study was designed to evaluate a revised version in which the response format for all items was changed to 1- to 5-place scales anchored by bipolar adjectives or adjective sets.

Samples: The data on which the King and Summers (1970) measure were evaluated reflected the responses of 1,000 housewives interviewed in 1967. Participants were residents of Marion County, Indiana. Responses were obtained for six product categories (i.e., packaged food products, women's clothing, household cleansers and detergents, cosmetics, large appliances, and small appliances). Respondents were categorized as leaders or nonleaders in a proportion designed to achieve comparability with the opinion leader categorizations of Katz and Lazarfield (1965). Childers's (1986) initial analysis of the King and Summers scale was based on the responses of 110 respondents to a mail survey. His second study, conducted to examine the revised scale, involved the responses of 176 households either adopting or refusing subscription to a cable service.

Validity: Little evidence of validity was offered in the original King and Summers (1970) article. Childers (1986), however, offers several estimates of reliability and validity. An internal consistency reliability estimate of .66 was reported by Childers as well as an average item-to-total correlation of .43. (Deletion of item 7 increased the reliability estimate to .68.) The Childers version was found to correlate with measures of product ownership, product-specific risk, multiple use potential, and creativity/curiosity and to differ as expected across known groups (Childers 1986). For example, a correlation of .28 with a product-specific measure of perceived risk was found. Other results revealed an internal consistency estimate of .83 after deletion of item 5. The average item-to-total correlation improved to .62 (after an r to z transformation). Correlations with four of five validity measures were significant as predicted. Mean scores were found to differ across groups as expected (i.e., the means for premium cable subscribers, basic-only subscribers, and refusers were 20.0, 19.5, and 15.2, respectively).

Scores: Means and standard deviations were not reported in King and Summers (1970). The means for premium cable subscribers, basic-only subscribers, and refusers in Childers's second study were 20.0, 19.5, and 15.2, respectively.

Source: King, Charles W., and John O. Summers. (1970). "Overlap of Opinion Leadership Across Product Categories." *Journal of Marketing Research*, 7, 43-50.
© 1970 by the American Marketing Association. Scale items taken from p. 45. Reprinted with permission.

Childers, Terry L. (1986). "Assessment of the Psychometric Properties of an Opinion Leadership Scale." *Journal of Marketing Research*, 23, 184-188.
© 1986 by the American Marketing Association. Scale items taken from Table 1 (p. 186). Reprinted with permission.

Other evidence: A number of studies have used and/or evaluated some form of the opinion leadership scale. Three of these are briefly described here.
Darden and Reynolds's (1972) administration of a modified (five-item) instrument assessed the opinion leadership of suburban males ($n = 104$) in addition to fraternity ($n = 76$) and nonfraternity ($n = 102$) undergraduate students. They report a split-half reliability estimate of .79. Riecken and Yavas (1983) report KR-20 estimates of reliability ranging from .50 to .82 across five samples for the King and Summers version. Their mean scores ranged from 11.59 to 14.99.
Goldsmith and Desborde (1991) provide some recent and extensive tests for the revised scale (cf. Childers 1986) (based on the responses of 187 undergraduate business students). Record albums were the domain of study. Goldsmith and Desborde (1991) found significant correlations between the revised scale and measures of awareness ($r = .46$), purchase ($r = .32$), and innovativeness ($r = .22$). The overall mean reported by Goldsmith and Desborde (1991) was 19.3 ($SD = 5.66$) for Childers's version. The means for males and females were 20.8 and 17.6, respectively.
Flynn, Goldsmith, and Eastman (1994) also examined the psychometric properties of the Childers's (1986) version of the scale over several products (e.g., jeans, professional clothing, and rock music) and four samples (i.e., $n = 172, 128, 247,$ and 185). They concluded that a six-item version of the scale (i.e., deletion of item 5 below) showed adequate levels of unidimensionality (via structural equation modeling) and internal consistency. Coefficient alpha estimates for this six-item version ranged from .78 to .88 across the four samples.

Other sources: Darden, William R., and Fred D. Reynolds. (1972). "Predicting Opinion Leadership for Men's Apparel Fashions." *Journal of Marketing Research*, 9, 324-328.

Flynn, Leisa Reinecke, Ronald E. Goldsmith, and Jacqueline K. Eastman. (1994). "The King and Summers Opinion Leadership Scale: Revision and Refinement." *Journal of Business Research*, 31, 55-64.

Goldsmith, Ronald E., and Rene Desborde. (1991). "A Validity Study of a Measure of Opinion Leadership." *Journal of Business Research*, 22, 11-19.

Riecken, Glen, and Ugur Yavas. (1983). "Internal Consistency of King and Summers' Opinion Leadership Scale: Further Evidence." *Journal of Marketing Research*, 20, 325-326.

References: Katz, Elihu, and Paul Lazarfield. (1965). *Personal Influence*. Glencoe, IL: Free Press.

Rogers, Everett. (1961). *Characteristics of Agricultural Innovators and Other Adopter Categories* (Research Bulletin 882). Wooster: Ohio Experiment Station.

Rogers, Everett, and David G. Cartano. (1962). "Methods of Measuring Opinion Leadership." *Public Opinion Quarterly*, 26, 435-441.

OPINION LEADERSHIP
(King and Summers 1970)

1. In general, do you like to talk about _____ with your friends?

> Yes_____ -1   No_____ -2

2. Would you say you give very little information, an average amount of information, or a great deal of information about _____ to your friends?

> You give very little information   _____ -1
> You give an average amount of information _____ -2
> You give a great deal of information   _____ -3

3. During the past six months, have you told anyone about some _____?

> Yes_____ -1   No_____ -2

4. Compared with your circle of friends, are you less likely to be asked, about as likely to be asked, or more likely to be asked about _____?

> Less likely to be asked   _____ -1
> About as likely to be asked   _____ -2
> More likely to be asked   _____ -3

5. If you and your friends were to discuss _____, what part would you be most likely to play? Would you mainly listen to your friends' ideas or would you try to convince them of your ideas?

> You mainly listen to your friends' ideas   _____ -1
> You try to convince them of your ideas   _____ -2

6. Which of these happens more often? Do you tell your friends about some _____, or do they tell you about some _____?

> You tell them about _____.   _____ -1
> They tell you about some _____.   _____ -2

7. Do you have the feeling that you are generally regarded by your friends and neighbors as a good source of advice about _____?

> Yes_____ -1   No_____ -2

NOTE: Although not explicitly stated in the original article, it appears that items 1, 3, 6, and 7 require recoding.

OPINION LEADERSHIP
(Childers 1986)

1. In general, do you talk to your friends and neighbors about cable television:

very often				*never*
5	4	3	2	1

2. When you talk to your friends and neighbors about cable television do you:

give a great deal of information				*give very little information*
5	4	3	2	1

3. During the past six months, how many people have you told about cable television?

told a number of people				*told no one*
5	4	3	2	1

4. Compared with your circle of friends, how likely are you to be asked about cablevision?

very likely to be asked				*not at all likely to be asked*
5	4	3	2	1

5. In a discussion of cablevision, would you be most likely to:

listen to your friends' ideas				*convince your friends of your ideas*
5	4	3	2	1

6. In discussions of cable television, which of the following happens most often?

you tell your friends about cable				*your friends tell you about cable*
5	4	3	2	1

7. Overall in all of your discussions with friends and neighbors, are you:

often used as a source of advice				*not used as a source of advice*
5	4	3	2	1

NOTE: Childers (1986) and Flynn et al. (1994) recommend deletion of item 5 (which also apparently requires reverse coding).

OPINION LEADERSHIP AND INFORMATION SEEKING
(Reynolds and Darden 1971)

Construct:	Reynolds and Darden's (1971) view of opinion leadership is similar to that of King and Summers's (1970) conceptualization in that opinion leadership is felt to reflect the extent to which individuals give information about a topic and the extent to which information is sought by others from those individuals. In operationalizing opinion leadership, though, Reynolds and Darden measured an information seeking factor as well because it is thought to be a critical determinant of word-of-mouth communication and interpersonal influences affecting the diffusion of new products, concepts, and services. Reynolds and Darden used clothing as the focal product in their study.
Description:	Reynolds and Darden's opinion leadership scale is composed of five 5-point Likert-type items scored from *strongly disagree* to *strongly agree*. Item scores are summed to form an index of opinion leadership. Their information seeking scale is composed of three 5-point Likert-type items, and scores on these items are also summed to form an overall index of information seeking.
Development:	Items for both scales were generated from other published sources. The appropriateness of these items was then examined through factor, reliability, and validity analyses on a large sample.
Samples:	A sample of 300 housewives was used in the study.
Validity:	Split-halves reliabilities were .79 and .73 for the opinion leadership and information seeking scales, respectively. Factor analysis revealed that the hypothesized two-factor structure (opinion leadership and information seeking) was confirmed. A number of chi-square tests showed support for the validity of both scales.
Source:	Reynolds, Fred D., and William R. Darden. (1971). "Mutually Adaptive Effects of Interpersonal Communication." *Journal of Marketing Research*, 8, 449-454. © 1971 by the American Marketing Association. Scale items taken from Appendix (p. 453). Reprinted with permission.
Other evidence:	N/A
Other sources:	N/A
References:	N/A

OPINION LEADERSHIP AND INFORMATION SEEKING
(Reynolds and Darden 1971)

Opinion leadership

1. My friends and neighbors often ask my advice about clothing fashions.

2. I sometimes influence the types of clothes my friends buy.

3. My friends come to me more often than I go to them for information about clothes.

4. I feel that I am generally regarded by my friends and neighbors as a good source of advice about clothing fashions.

5. I can think of at least two people whom I have told about some clothing fashion in the last six months.

Information seeking

1. I often seek out the advice of my friends regarding which clothes I buy.

2. I spend a lot of time talking with my friends about clothing fashions.

3. My friends or neighbors usually give me good advice on what brands of clothes to buy.

OPINION LEADERS AND OPINION SEEKERS: OL AND OS
(Flynn, Goldsmith, and Eastman 1996)

Construct:

The opinion leader and opinion seeker constructs of Flynn, Goldsmith, and Eastman (1996) are considered domain specific, and not global, patterns of behavior. Opinion leadership occurs when individuals try to influence the purchase behavior of other consumers in specific product fields. Opinion seeking happens when individuals search out advice from others when making a purchase decision. As such, opinion leaders give advice and opinion seekers ask for it (Flynn et al. 1996, p. 138).

Description:

The opinion leadership scale is composed of six items, and the opinion seeker scale is composed of six items. All items are scored on 7-point scales ranging from *strongly disagree* to *strongly agree*. Item scores are summed with the each scale to form indices of opinion leadership (OL) and opinion seeking (OS). Thus, total scores on the scales can range from 6 to 42.

Development:

Across five studies, using recommended scaling procedures, the two scales were developed and validated. Twenty-one items were originally generated to tap the definitions of the constructs. Six Ph.D. students judged the items for representativeness, trimming the pool to 19 items. Then, over five studies employing 1,128 respondents, the scales were developed and validated using several product categories (e.g., rock music, fashionable clothing, "green" purchases). Procedures used included exploratory and confirmatory factor analyses, item and reliability analyses, and correlations with various related constructs to establish validity.

Samples:

The first sample was composed of $n = 224$ undergraduate students, the second sample was composed of $n = 263$ students, the third sample was composed of $n = 391$ students, the fourth sample was composed of $n = 99$ women attending a chamber of commerce professional women's luncheon, and the fifth sample was composed of $n = 162$ students.

Validity:

With the first sample, the final forms of the six-item scales were derived via item analyses. Coefficient alpha estimates of internal consistency were reported to be .86 for OL and .87 for OS. With the second sample, scale dimensionality was assessed via confirmatory factor analyses (EQS). Various indices of fit indicted that both OS and OL were unidimensional measures. Alphas for the two scales were .78 and .88 for OL and OS, respectively. The third study also found support for scale unidimensionality (via EQS confirmatory factor analysis), and the internal consistency estimates were .87 for OL and .88 for OS. The fourth and fifth studies used similar procedures and again found evidence for unidimensional and reliable scales (coefficient alphas of .80 and .86 for OL, and .81 and .93 for OS). Test-retest reliability for a large subsample of Study 5 ($n = 127$) showed test-retest correlations of .82 for OL and .75 for OS. Numerous correlational-based validity checks were done (see Tables 4, 5, and 6 of Flynn et al. 1996). For example, significant, or where hypothesized nonsignificant, correlations were found in the predicted direction between OL and OS and perceived knowledge, innovativeness, enduring involvement with the product category of interest, fashion shopping, status consumption, and "green behavior." Correlations between OS and OL ranged from .15 to .35 across the studies. Furthermore, a convergent validity correlation of .72 was reported between OL and King and Summers's modified opinion leadership scale (Flynn et al. 1994).

Scores:

Means (std. dev.) were reported for four of the five studies. These scores were 22.1 (7.1) and 23.8 (8.8) for OL and OS in Study 2, 24.8 (7.2) and 24.0 (8.0) for OL and OS in Study 3, 21.6 (6.6) and 19.9 (7.1) for OL and OS in Study 4, and 20.3 (7.5) and 20.5 (9.6) for OL and OS in Study 5.

Source: Flynn, Leisa Reinecke, Ronald E. Goldsmith, and Jacqueline K. Eastman. (1996). "Opinion Leaders and Opinion Seekers: Two New Measurement Scales." *Journal of the Academy of Marketing Science, 24*(2), 137-147.

© 1996 by Sage Publications. Scale items taken from Appendix (p. 146). Reprinted with permission.

Other evidence: N/A

Other sources: N/A

Reference: Flynn, Leisa Reinecke, Ronald E. Goldsmith, and Jacqueline K. Eastman. (1994). "The King and Summers Opinion Leadership Scale: Revision and Refinement." *Journal of Business Research, 31*, 55-64.

OPINION LEADERS AND OPINION SEEKERS: OL AND OS
(Flynn, Goldsmith, and Eastman 1996)

Opinion Leadership (OL) Items:

1. My opinion on (PRODUCT CATEGORY) seems not to count with other people.

2. When they choose a (PRODUCT CATEGORY), other people do not turn to me for advice.

3. Other people [rarely] come to me for advice about choosing (PRODUCT CATEGORY).

4. People that I know pick (PRODUCT CATEGORY) based on what I have told them.

5. I often persuade others to buy the (PRODUCT CATEGORY) that I like.

6. I often influence people's opinions about (PRODUCT CATEGORY).

Opinion Seeking (OS) Items:

1. When I consider buying a (PRODUCT CATEGORY), I ask other people for advice.

2. I don't like to talk to others before I buy (PRODUCT CATEGORY).

3. I rarely ask other people what (PRODUCT CATEGORY) to buy.

4. I like to get others' opinions before I buy a (PRODUCT CATEGORY).

5. I feel more comfortable buying a (PRODUCT CATEGORY) when I have gotten other people's opinions on it.

6. When choosing (PRODUCT CATEGORY), other people's opinions are not important to me.

NOTES: Items 1 through 3 of OL require reverse scoring, and items 2, 3, and 6 of OS require reverse scoring.

SCALES RELATED TO INNOVATIVENESS

COGNITIVE AND SENSORY INNOVATIVENESS
(Venkatraman and Price 1990)

Construct: Cognitive (sensory) innovativeness is the preference for engaging in new experiences with the objective of stimulating the mind (senses). Venkatraman and Price (1990) assume that consumer innovativeness is not an undifferentiated construct and that cognitive and sensory innovativeness are differentiated by unique demographic and personality profiles and are related differently to adoption behaviors. Cognitive innovators enjoy thinking for its own sake and have a propensity to devote a great deal of mental energy to solving problems they encounter. Sensory innovators enjoy fantasy and daydreaming and adventurous activities such as skydiving.

Description: The final form of the measure(s) includes eight items for both the cognitive and sensory innovativeness scales. Each scale also includes four internal and four external items. The scores are computed by averaging the scores across the internal and external items within each scale.

Development: The scales included here represent refinement of the 80-item Novelty Experiencing Scale (NES) (Pearson 1970). Details regarding the specifics of item deletion and selection were not presented. The developmental procedures included tests of alternative factor structures (for the final sets of two eight-item scales) using confirmatory factor analysis. (In the second validity study involving nonstudent subjects, a higher-order factor model provided the best fit to the data.) Prior to these LISREL analyses, item correlations with measures of sensation seeking and cognition seeking apparently were used to select items for the final scale versions (Venkatraman and Price 1991). Several other estimates of reliability and validity were gathered.

Samples: The NES items were first examined using a sample of 200 undergraduate students. Participating in the first validation study were 326 undergraduate students; 240 respondents to a mail survey (from an initial sample of 450) participated in the product innovation and demographic characteristic validation study. Of this sample, 59% was male; the average age was 37.2 years.

Validity: Coefficient alpha estimates of reliability (based on the initial sample of 200) were .73 and .69 for the cognitive and sensory scales, respectively. Two follow-up studies were conducted to evaluate the validity of the measures. In the first study ($n = 326$), the two scales were correlated with a series of related measures. Evidence for support of the hypothesized relationships was found. For example, a significant positive correlation ($r = .26, p < .01$) was found between the cognitive innovativeness measure and need for cognition (Cacioppo and Petty 1982). Other correlations in support of the measures include $r = .41$ ($p < .01$) between sensory innovativeness and arousal-seeking tendency (Mehrabian and Russell 1974) and $r = .22$ ($p < .01$) between a measure of impulsivity and sensory innovativeness.

A second validity study ($n = 245$) was conducted to demonstrate that cognitive and sensory innovators differ in their responses to innovations and demographically. The alpha coefficients of reliability for this study were .64 and .70 for the cognitive and sensory scales, respectively. Hypothesized differences with product purchase behavior across products selected to vary in hedonic value were not found. However, partial support for the demographic predictions were observed: Men scored higher on sensory innovativeness, younger respondents scored higher on sensory innovativeness, and higher education was associated with higher cognitive scores.

Scores: Some scale mean scores were presented in Table 6 across demographic groups (Venkatraman and Price 1991, p. 309).

Source: Venkatraman, Meera P., and Linda L. Price. (1990). "Differentiating Between Cognitive and Sensory Innovativeness: Concepts, Measurement, and Implications." *Journal of Business Research*, 20, 293-315.

© 1990 by Elsevier Science. Scale items taken from Table 1 (p. 297). Reprinted with permission from Elsevier Science.

Other evidence: N/A

Other sources: N/A

References: Cacioppo, John T., and Richard E. Petty. (1982). "The Need for Cognition." *Journal of Personality and Social Psychology*, *42*, 116-131.

Mehrabian, Albert, and James A. Russell. (1974). *An Approach to Environmental Psychology*. Cambridge, MA: MIT Press.

Pearson, Pamela H. (1970). "Relationships Between Global and Specific Measures of Novelty Seeking." *Journal of Consulting and Clinical Psychology*, *34*, 199-204.

COGNITIVE AND SENSORY INNOVATIVENESS
(Venkatraman and Price 1990)

Cognitive Innovativeness

1. Finding out the meaning of words I don't know.

2. Trying to figure out the meaning of unusual statements.

3. Thinking about different ways to explain the same thing.

4. Figuring out the shortest distance from one city to another.

5. Analyzing my own feelings and reactions.

6. Discussing unusual ideas.

7. Thinking about why the world is in the shape it is in.

8. Figuring out how many bricks it would take to build a fireplace.

Sensory Innovativeness

1. Being on a raft in the middle of the Colorado River.

2. Having a vivid dream with strange colors and sounds.

3. Riding the rapids in a swift moving stream.

4. Having a strange new feeling as I awake in the morning.

5. Steering a sled down a steep hill covered with trees.

6. Dreaming that I was lying on the beach with the waves running all over me.

7. Walking across a swinging bridge over a deep canyon.

8. Having vivid and unusual daydreams as I was riding along.

DOMAIN-SPECIFIC INNOVATIVENESS: DSI
(Goldsmith and Hofacker 1991)

Construct: Domain- or product category–specific innovativeness reflects the tendency to learn about and adopt innovations (new products) within a specific domain of interest (Goldsmith and Hofacker 1991, p. 211). This definition is consistent with the contention that innovativeness must be identified and characterized on a product category or domain basis (Gatignon and Robertson 1985).

Description: The DSI is a six-item scale where the items are scored on 5-point disagree-agree formats. Item scores are summed to form an overall DSI score, and the DSI is considered unidimensional. There are two versions of the DSI. Each version has three positively worded items and three negatively worded items. Therefore, versions can be used interchangeably and are considered applicable to a wide number of product domains.

Development: Six studies were used in the development and validation of the DSI. In Study 1, an initial pool of 11 items was generated based on the construct's definition and a literature review. (Rock music records/tapes was used as the product of interest.) After a pretest of the items on a small sample, a larger sample responded to the items. Via item analysis, coefficient alpha, and preliminary criterion validity checks, the final six items representing the two versions of the DSI were derived. Study 2 further examined the reliability, validity, and factor structure of the two versions of the DSI (again with rock music as the domain). Studies 3 and 4 used fashion and household entertainment equipment as domains and again looked at the psychometric properties of the scales. Study 5 examined the scale's test-retest reliability, predictive validity, and possible confounds (again with rock music). Finally, Study 6 assessed convergent and discriminant validity using rock music recordings, fashions, and cosmetics as the product categories.

Samples: The samples from each of the above six studies were composed of the following. The pretest sample of Study 1 was 27 students, and the large sample of Study 1 was composed of 309 students. Study 2 was composed of 274 students, and Study 3 used 97 female students. Study 4 used 462 nonstudent adults. A sample of 70 students was used in Study 5, and a sample of 306 (students and nonstudents) was used in Study 6.

Validity: In Study 1, the correlations of the six items with four measures of criterion validity ranged from .26 to .40 across items. Coefficient alpha for Study 2 was .86, and confirmatory factor analysis (via EQS) supported the scales' unidimensionality. Correlations of the DSI with seven criterion validity measures ranged from .07 to .78. In Study 3, alpha for the scale was .82, and the positive and negative halves of the scale had a correlation of −.71. Unidimensionality again was confirmed, and the correlations between the DSI and seven criterion measures ranged from .11 to .80. Study 4 reported an alpha of .81, a unidimensional factor structure, and predictive validity correlations of .41 and .46. Test-retest reliability in Study 5 was .86 (over 15 weeks), and the internal consistency, dimensionality, and predictive validity of the scale were supported. The scale also exhibited low correlations with a measure of social desirability bias (i.e., −.13 to .12). Finally, multitrait-multimethod analysis supported the convergent and discriminant validity of the DSI, and alpha was reported to be .85, .83, and .83 across three different product categories.

Scores: Mean scores were reported for several of the studies. In Study 2, the overall mean was 15.8 (*SD* = 5.20). In Study 3, the mean score was 19.4 (*SD* = 4.64). In Study 4, means of 16.5 (*SD* = 4.80) and 17.3 (*SD* = 4.80) were reported for two product categories.

Source: Goldsmith, Ronald E., and Charles Hofacker. (1991). "Measuring Consumer Innovativeness." *Journal of the Academy of Marketing Science*, *19*, 209-221.
    © 1991 by Sage Publications. Scale items taken from Table 1 (p. 212). Reprinted with permission.

Other evidence: Using a sample of $n = 135$ adult women, Goldsmith and Flynn (1992) report a coefficient alpha estimate for the innovativeness scale of .73. Numerous mean-level difference tests and correlations with related constructs show further evidence for the scales's validity. For example, those respondents scoring 21 or greater on the DSI (i.e., the top 14% of the sample) showed higher mean scores on measures of fashion interest, fashion media habits, fashion shopping, and other fashion-related constructs than did those respondents scoring 20 or less on the DSI. ("Fashionable clothing" was the focal product of the study.) The DSI was also significantly correlated, in the predicted direction, with 15 different fashion-related attitudinal and behavioral statements. These correlations ranged from .24 to .59 ($p < .01$). The overall mean score (std. dev.) for the DSI was 16.6 (4.3).

Other source: Goldsmith, Ronald, and Leisa Reinecke Flynn. (1992). "Identifying Innovators in Consumer Product Markets." *European Journal of Marketing*, 26(12), 42-55.

Reference: Gatignon, Hubert, and Thomas R. Robertson. (1985). "A Propositional Inventory for New Diffusion Research." *Journal of Consumer Research*, 11, 849-867.

DOMAIN-SPECIFIC INNOVATIVENESS: DSI
(Goldsmith and Hofacker 1991)

1. In general, I am among the first (last) in my circle of friends to buy a new _____ when it appears.

2. If I heard that a new _____ was available in the store, I would (not) be interested enough to buy it.

3. Compared to my friends I own a few of (a lot of) _____.

4. In general, I am the last (first) in my circle of friends to know the titles/brands of the latest _____.

5. I will not buy a new _____ if I haven't heard/tried it yet. (I will buy a new _____ if I haven't heard/tried it yet.)

6. I (do not) like to buy _____ before other people do.

NOTES: Items 1, 3, and 4 constitute the negative items in Version 1, and items 2, 5, and 6 constitute the positive items in Version 1. Conversely, items 1, 3, and 4 constitute the positive items in Version 2, and items 2, 5, and 6 constitute the negative items in Version 2. Words/sentences in parentheses denote the positive and negative wording for individual items.

INNOVATIVENESS: CONSUMER INNOVATIVENESS
(Manning, Bearden, and Madden 1995)

Construct: Consistent with the work of Midgley and Dowling (1978) and Hirschman (1980), Manning, Bearden, and Madden (1995) define and measure two aspects of consumer innovativeness: (a) *consumer independent judgment-making* (CIJM), which is defined as the degree to which an individual makes innovation decisions independently of the communicated experience of others; and (b) *consumer novelty seeking* (CNS), which is defined as the desire to seek out new product information.

Description: The CIJM scale is composed of six items, and the CNS scale is composed of eight items. All items are 7-point scales ranging from *strongly disagree* to *strongly agree*. Item scores are summed within each scale to form overall index scores that can range from 6 to 42 for CIJM, and from 8 to 56 for CNS.

Development: Numerous recommended scaling procedures were used to develop and validate the CIJM and CNS scales. After construct definition, 74 items and 60 items were generated by the authors or culled from other sources to reflect CIJM and CNS, respectively. Items were further judged (by the authors) for content validity, retaining 31 items for CIJM and 30 for CNS. Five doctoral students then judged these items for representativeness, trimming the pool of items to 16 each for CIJM and CNS. Three studies, using factor analysis, reliability and item analyses, and numerous validity-related tests, were then conducted to refine and validate the scales.

Samples: The first sample was composed of $n = 141$ adults, the second sample was composed of a combination of university staff members and MBA students ($n = 117$), and the third sample was composed of $n = 71$ adult consumers.

Validity: Using the $n = 141$ sample, via exploratory and then confirmatory factor analyses, the final eight- and six-item forms of the scales were derived. Confirmatory factor fit indices offered evidence of unidimensional scales for both the CIJM and the CNS. Coefficient alpha estimates of internal consistency were .86 and .92, construct reliability estimates (via LISREL) were .85 and .88, and variance extracted estimates (also via LISREL) were .52 and .59 for CIJM and CNS, respectively. Factor loadings ranged from .58 to .89 across the two measures. A hypothesized two-factor solution of CIJM and CNS as separate factors was estimated and fit the data well. The correlation between CIJM and CNS was $-.11$ ($p > .10$).

The $n = 117$ sample also showed evidence of unidimensionality and internal consistency for the scales. Coefficient alpha estimates of internal consistency were .87 and .92, construct reliability estimates (via LISREL) were .87 and .91, and variance extracted estimates (also via LISREL) were .53 and .59 for CIJM and CNS, respectively. Factor loading items to constructs ranged from .47 to .88 for the two scales. Numerous alternative models of the CIJM and CNS scales were estimated, but none fit the data as well as the hypothesized two-factor CIJM-CNS solution. (The correlation between CIJM and CNS was $-.07$, $p > .10$).

The $n = 71$ sample also showed unidimensionality and strong evidence of internal consistency for the CIJM and CNS scales (alphas = .84 for both scales, and the correlation between CIJM and CNS was .15, $p < .01$). As evidence of validity, CNS was found to be correlated with age ($r = -.24$, $p < .05$). Also, CNS showed a standardized path estimate of .40 ($p < .01$) to "actualized novelty seeking," and CIJM showed a path estimate of .19 ($p < .05$) to "new product trial."

Scores: Mean scores (std. dev.) are offered for the first two samples. For the $n = 141$ sample, these scores were 22.44 (8.02) and 32.54 (11.22) for CIJM and CNS, respectively. For the $n = 117$ sample, the scores were 16.94 (6.94) and 32.97 (9.68) for CIJM and CNS, respectively.

Source: Manning, Kenneth C., William O. Bearden, and Thomas J. Madden. (1995). "Consumer Innovativeness and the Adoption Process." *Journal of Consumer Psychology*, 4(4), 329-345.

© 1995 by Lawrence Erlbaum Associates, Inc. Scale items taken from Table 1 (p. 334). Reprinted with permission.

Other evidence: N/A

Other sources: N/A

References: Hirschman, Elizabeth C. (1980). "Innovativeness, Novelty Seeking, and Consumer Creativity." *Journal of Consumer Research*, 7, 283-395.

Midgley, D. F., and G. R. Dowling. (1978). "Innovativeness: The Concept and Its Measurement." *Journal of Consumer Research*, 4, 229-242.

INNOVATIVENESS: CONSUMER INNOVATIVENESS
(Manning, Bearden, and Madden 1995)

CIJM Items

1. Prior to purchasing a new brand, I prefer to consult a friend that has experience with the new brand.

2. When it comes to deciding whether to purchase a new service, I do not rely on experienced friends or family members for advice.

3. I seldom ask a friend about his or her experiences with a new product before I buy the new product.

4. I decide to buy new products and services without relying on the opinions of friends who have already tried them.

5. When I am interested in purchasing a new service, I do not rely on my friends or close acquaintances that have already used the new service to give me information as to whether I should try it.

6. I do not rely on experienced friends for information about new products prior to making up my mind about whether or not to purchase.

CNS Items

1. I often seek out information about new products and brands.

2. I like to go to places where I will be exposed to information about new products and brands.

3. I like magazines that introduce new brands.

4. I frequently look for new products and services.

5. I seek out situations in which I will be exposed to new and different sources of product information.

6. I am continually seeking new product experiences.

7. When I go shopping, I find myself spending very little time checking out new products and brands.

8. I take advantage of the first available opportunity to find out about new and different products.

NOTE: Item 1 of CIJM and item 5 of CNS require reverse scoring.

INNOVATIVENESS: OPENNESS OF INFORMATION PROCESSING
(Leavitt and Walton 1975, 1988)

Construct: Innovativeness is assumed to be a personality trait underlying the adoption of innovations. The construct, as involved in the research on which the following measures are based, has lately been redefined to be termed "openness of information processing" (Leavitt and Walton 1975, 1988). Innovators are described as individuals open to new experiences and novel stimuli; as possessing the ability to transform information about new concepts, ideas, products or services for their own use; and as having a low threshold for recognizing the potential application of new ideas. (NOTE: This scale is still under refinement and interested users are encouraged to contact the authors for additional details regarding these measures. Only the information provided in the most recent faculty working paper is summarized here.)

Description: The 1975 version of the measure(s) consisted of two forms each containing 30 items (24 scale items with 6 filler items). Each statement is evaluated in terms of "how well it fits the respondent's own views." The 5-place scales associated with each statement are labeled as follows: 1, *not well at all*; 2, *not very well*; 3, *fairly well*; 4, *very well*; and 5, *extremely well*. In the original form, item scores are summed to form an overall index. Both positively and negatively worded statements along with several social desirability filler items can be included in each form. (The filler items are discarded in computation of overall scores. Only a few of the items refer directly to the purchase of products and services.)

Development: An initial pool of 144 items was developed from the original definition by a group of three "experts" (Leavitt and Walton 1975, p. 549). Twenty-nine positive items were selected from this group based on item-to-total correlations and consideration of social desirability bias. Next, the 29 items were included in a second study with 33 negative items and a series of psychological scales. Again, two parallel forms were developed using both positive and negative statements and a series of item-to-total correlations.

Samples: The initial set of items was administered to a sample of 300 undergraduate women. The exact nature of the sample was not provided. A second sample involved the responses from 299 women.

Validity: Estimates of internal consistency reliability were .74 and .72 for forms A and B, respectively. The correlation between the two forms was .72. Correlations between the two forms and an index of innovation were .35 and .38. Differences in means scores between users and nonusers of a new food service provided some evidence of known group validity. The results of a factor analysis for both males and females provided some evidence for the validity of the expected loadings.

Scores: Based on one of the original samples using intercept interviews, the mean scores for noninnovators and innovators were 76.5 and 84.1, respectively. Mean scores for Form A for 796 users of a new service and 266 nonusers of a service who were aware of the service were 84.3 and 79.1, respectively (Leavitt and Walton 1988).

Source: Leavitt, Clark, and John Walton. (1975). "Development of a Scale for Innovativeness." In Mary Jane Schlinger (Ed.), *Advances in Consumer Research* (Vol. 2, pp. 545-554). Ann Arbor, MI: Association for Consumer Research.
  © 1975 by the Association for Consumer Research. Scale items taken from Table 1 (pp. 547-548). Reprinted with permission.

Leavitt, Clark, and John R. Walton. (1988). *Openness of Information Processing as a Moderator of Message Effects on Behavior* (Faculty Working Paper). College of Business Administration, Ohio State University.
  © 1988 by Clark Leavitt and John R. Walton.

Other evidence: Goldsmith (1984) reported an internal consistency reliability estimate of .78 for Form B of the scale. Evidence of the nomological validity of the scale was provided by significant correlations with dogmatism ($r = -.38$), empathy ($r = .62$), and self-esteem ($r = .69$) (Goldsmith 1984, p. 63). However, nonsignificant results were obtained for social character and cosmopolitanism. Craig and Ginter (1975) factor analyzed Leavitt and Walton's (1975) version and found seven factors: new is wasteful, social desirability, novelty seeking, risk aversion, style consciousness, satisfaction with status quo, and other directedness (see the following pages). Three of these factors were found to discriminate between innovative and non-innovative samples.

Other sources: Craig, C. Samuel, and James L. Ginter. (1975). "An Empirical Test of a Scale for Innovativeness." In Mary Jane Schlinger (Ed.), *Advances in Consumer Research* (Vol. 2, pp. 555-562). Ann Arbor, MI: Association for Consumer Research.
© 1975 by the Association for Consumer Research. Scale items taken from Table 1 (pp. 557-558).

Goldsmith, Ronald E. (1984). "Some Personality Correlates of Open Processing." *Journal of Psychology*, *116*, 59-66.

References: N/A

INNOVATIVENESS: OPENNESS OF INFORMATION PROCESSING
(Leavitt and Walton 1975, 1988)

Form A

1. I like to take a chance.
2. I don't like to talk to strangers.
3. The unusual gift is often a waste of money.
4. I enjoy looking at new styles as soon as they come out.
5. Buying a new product that has not yet been proven is usually a waste of time and money.
6. Often the most interesting and stimulating people are those who don't mind being original and different.
7. I would like a job that requires frequent changes from one kind of task to another.
8. If people would quit wasting their time experimenting, we would get more accomplished.
9. If I got an idea, I would give a lot of weight to what others think of it.
10. I like to try new and different things.
11. In hunting for the best way to do something, it is usually a good idea to try the obvious way first.
12. I like to wait until something has been proven before I try it.
13. When it comes to taking chances, I would rather be safe than sorry.
14. I like people who are a little shocking.

15. When I see a new brand on the shelf, I often buy it just to see what it is like.

16. I feel that too much money is wasted on new styles.

17. I often try new brands before my friends and neighbors do.

18. I enjoy being with people who think like I do.

19. At work, I think everyone should work on only one thing, thereby becoming more of an expert.

20. I like to experiment with new ways of doing things.

21. In the long run, the usual ways of doing things are the best.

22. Some modern art is stimulating.

23. I like to fool around with new ideas even if they turn out later to be a total waste of time.

24. Today is a good day to start a new project.

Form B

1. I like to experiment.

2. I like to try new products to see what they are like.

3. The changing styles especially in clothes are a waste of money.

4. I like a great deal of variety.

5. I don't like to take chances if I don't have to.

6. Sometimes original and different people make me uneasy.

7. Unless there is good reason for changing, I think we should continue doing things the way they are being done now.

8. I start up conversations with strangers.

9. I feel that the tried and true ways of doing things are the best at work and in my life.

10. I like to spend money on unusual gifts and toys.

11. New products are usually gimmicks.

12. I generally like to try new ideas at work and in my life.

13. I like to see what my friends and neighbors think of a product before I try it.

14. I like new styles in clothes, especially those that are really different.

15. I dread having to start another new project.

16. I take chances more than others do.

17. I can enjoy being with people whose values are very different from mine.

18. People who are shocking are usually trying to impress someone.

19. In hunting for the best way of doing something, it is usually a good idea to look at the situation from a completely different angle—one that wouldn't occur to someone.

20. I would like a job that doesn't require me to keep learning new tasks.

21. I like to look at strange pictures.

22. When I see a new brand on the shelf, I usually pass right by.

23. I would not risk my position at work by putting into effect some new idea that might not work.

24. I'm the kind of person who is always looking for an exciting, stimulating, active life.

NOTES: Although not specified by the original authors, items requiring reverse coding apparently are items 2, 3, 5, 8, 9, 11, 12, 13, 16, 18, 19, and 21 of Form A, and items 3, 5, 6, 7, 9, 11, 13, 15, 18, 20, 22, and 23 of Form B. Recoding these items would reflect a higher level of innovativeness. Also, the "filler" items are not included in the above scales.

INNOVATIVENESS FACTORS: FACTOR ANALYSIS
OF LEAVITT AND WALTON'S ITEMS
(Craig and Ginter 1975)

Factor 1 (New Is Wasteful)

1. The unusual gift is often a waste of money.

2. Some modern art is stimulating.

3. I would rather not waste my time with some new idea.

4. Buying a new product that has not yet been proven is usually a waste of time and money.

5. I would like a job that doesn't require me to keep learning new tasks.

6. The changing styles, especially in clothes, are a waste of money.

Factor 2 (Social Desirability)

1. I am always courteous even to people who are disagreeable.

2. I have never been irked when people express ideas very different from my own.

3. No matter who I am talking to, I am always a good listener.

4. I am always willing to admit when I make a mistake.

5. I have never felt that I was punished without cause.

Factor 3 (Novelty Seeking)

1. I like to experiment with new ways of doing things.

2. I like to fool around with new ideas even if they turn out to be a waste of time.

3. I like to try new and different things.

4. When I see a new brand on the shelf, I often buy it just to see what it's like.

Factor 4 (Risk Aversion)

1. I like to take a chance.

2. When it comes to taking chances, I'd rather be safe than sorry.

3. I like people who are a little shocking.

Factor 5 (Style Consciousness)

1. I enjoy looking at new styles as soon as they come out.

2. The changing styles especially in clothes are a waste of money.

Factor 6 (Satisfaction With Status Quo)

1. I believe in leaving well enough alone.

2. If people would quit wasting their time experimenting, we would get more accomplished.

3. When I see a brand on the shelf, I often buy it just to see what it's like.

Factor 7 (Other Directedness)

1. If I got an idea I would give a lot of thought to what others think.

2. I like to see what my friends and neighbors think of a product before I try it.

NOTES: Many of these items are not part of the scale published by Leavitt and Walton. Apparently, several of these items (particularly the social desirability items) come from an earlier version (possibly item-generation stage) of their scale. In the Craig and Ginter article, item 2 of the "new is wasteful" factor loaded negatively, items 1 and 3 of the "risk aversion" factor loaded negatively on that factor, and item 2 of the "style consciousness" loaded negatively on that factor (Craig and Ginter 1975, pp. 557-558).

INNOVATIVENESS: USE INNOVATIVENESS
(Price and Ridgway 1983)

Construct: Use innovativeness (or variety seeking in product use) involves the use of previously adopted products in novel ways (Price and Ridgway 1983, p. 679). The concept was initially introduced by Hirschman (1980). As conceptualized by Price and Ridgway, use innovativeness encompasses five factors: creativity/curiosity, risk preferences, voluntary simplicity, creative reuse, and multiple use potential.

Description: The scale consists of 44 items designed to reflect the five factors. Each item was operationalized using a 7-place, Likert-type format. The factor labels and corresponding number of items are as follows: (a) creativity/curiosity, 13; (b) risk preferences, 9; (c) voluntary simplicity, 5; (d) creative reuse, 10; and (e) multiple use potential, 7. Item scores can be summed within factors for factor indices and can be summed overall for an overall use innovativeness measure.

Development: An initial set of 70 items was generated to reflect the five factors assumed to underlie use innovativeness. This set also included five voluntary simplicity items from Leonard-Barton (1981). The set of 70 items was reduced to 60 "based on the judgment of several experts." These 60 items were administered to 358 student subjects along with six questions about calculator usage. The final 44 items were selected using the following criteria: high loadings on the anticipated factor, high item-to-total correlations for each subscale or factor, and high item-to-total correlations for the combined scale. These analyses resulted in 4 items being reassigned to another factor and 16 items (predominantly risk-taking and multiple use measures) being eliminated.

Samples: The developmental and validation analyses were performed on a sample of 358 undergraduate student subjects.

Validity: Factor analysis was performed to verify the structure of the scale. A four-factor solution was said to be superior; however, five factors are reported. The inclusion of the five items as a voluntary simplicity factor may have accounted for the inconsistency between the reported results and the final scale depicted in Table 1 (Price and Ridgway 1983, pp. 681-682). Estimates of internal consistency for the subscales were .86 for creativity/curiosity, .70 for risk preferences, .64 for voluntary simplicity, .82 for creative reuse, and .56 for multiple use potential. Again, intercorrelations among the factors range from .14 to .65. Using scores for the total scale, the sample was partitioned into upper, middle, and lower thirds. Analysis of variance tests of mean differences across groups revealed that the calculator usage scores behaved in a predictable pattern. That is, subjects scoring higher on the scale exhibited greater variety in their use of calculators.

Scores: The mean use innovativeness score for the entire scale summed as a whole was 199, varying from a low of 112 to a high of 299 (Price and Ridgway 1983, p. 681).

Source: Price, Linda L., and Nancy M. Ridgway. (1983). "Development of a Scale to Measure Use Innovativeness." In Richard P. Bagozzi and Alice M. Tybout (Eds.), *Advances in Consumer Research* (Vol. 10, pp. 679-684). Ann Arbor, MI: Association for Consumer Research.
© 1983 by the Association for Consumer Research. Scale items taken from Table 1 (pp. 681-682). Reprinted with permission.

Other evidence: N/A

Other sources: N/A

References: Hirschman, Elizabeth C. (1980). "Innovativeness, Novelty Seeking, and Consumer Creativity." *Journal of Consumer Research*, 7, 283-295.

Leonard-Barton, Dorothy. (1981). "Voluntary Simplicity Lifestyles and Energy Conservation." *Journal of Consumer Research*, 8, 243-252.

INNOVATIVENESS: USE INNOVATIVENESS
(Price and Ridgway 1983)

Creativity/Curiosity

1. Knowing how a product works offers almost as much pleasure as knowing that the product works well.

2. I am very creative when using products.

3. I am less interested in the appearance of an item than in what makes it tick.

4. As a child, I really enjoyed taking things apart and putting them back together again.

5. As long as a product works well, I don't really care how it works.

6. Curiosity is one of the permanent and certain characteristics of a vigorous intellect.

7. I am very curious about how things work.

8. I like to build things for my home.

9. If I can't figure out how something works, I would rather tinker with it than ask for help.

10. I never take anything apart because I know I'll never be able to put it back together again.

11. I like to fix things around the house.

12. I have gotten instruction in self-reliance skills (e.g.,carpentry, car tune-up, etc.).

13. I would rather fix something myself than take it to someone to fix.

Risk Preferences

1. When I try to do projects on my own, I'm afraid I will make a worse mess of them than if I had just left them alone.

2. I always follow manufacturer's warnings against removing the backplates on products.

3. When I try to do projects on my own, without exact directions, they usually work out really well.

4. I find very little instruction is needed to use a product similar to one I'm already familiar with.

5. I'm afraid to buy a product I don't know how to use.

6. I'm uncomfortable working on projects different from types I'm accustomed to.

7. I always follow manufacturer's warnings regarding how to use a product.

8. If a product comes in an assembled and an unassembled form, I always buy the assembled form, even though it costs a little more.

9. I like to improvise when I cook.

Voluntary Simplicity

1. I like to make clothing or furniture for myself and my family.

2. I often buy clothing at second hand stores.

3. I often make gifts instead of buying them.

4. When building something, it is better to use things already around the house than to buy materials.

5. I often buy items such as furniture at garage sales.

Creative Reuse

1. I save broken appliances because I might fix them someday.

2. I save broken appliances because I might be able to use the parts from them.

3. I enjoy thinking of new ways to use old things around the house.

4. I find myself saving packaging on products to use in other ways (e.g., egg cartons, L'eggs pantyhose eggs, plastic shopping bags, etc.).

5. When I build something, I can often make do with things I've already got around the house.

6. Even if I don't have the right tool for the job, I can usually improvise.

7. I never throw something away that I might use later.

8. I take great pleasure in adapting products to new uses that the manufacturer never intended.

9. In general, I would rather alter an old product to work in a new situation than purchase a new product specifically for that purpose.

10. After the useful life of a product, I can often think of ways to use the parts of it for other purposes.

Multiple Use Potential

1. I do not enjoy a product unless I can use it to its fullest capacity.

2. I use products in more ways than most people.

3. I often buy a food item for a particular recipe but end up using it for something else.

4. A product's value is directly related to the ways that it can be used.

5. It's always impossible to improve upon a project by adding new features.

6. After purchase of a product such as a stereo or camera, I try to keep track of new accessories that come out into the market.

7. I enjoy expanding and adding onto projects that I'm involved in on a continuing basis.

NOTES: Although not explicitly stated by the authors, it would seem that items 5 and 10 of the "creativity/ curiosity" factor would require recoding to reflect a higher level of this factor. It would also seem that items 3, 4, and 9 of the "risk preference" factor require recoding to reflect a risk aversion preference, and item 5 of the "multiple use potential" factor requires recoding to reflect a higher level of multiple use potential.

UNIQUENESS: DESIRE FOR UNIQUE CONSUMER PRODUCTS: DUCP
(Lynn and Harris 1997)

Construct: The Desire for Unique Consumer Products (DUCP) measures the extent to which consumers hold as a personal goal the acquisition and possession of consumer goods, services, and experiences that few others possess (Lynn and Harris 1997). Antecedents of differences in DUCP include individual differences in the need for uniqueness (Snyder and Fromkin 1980) as well as status aspiration and materialism. Specific consequences of a high DUCP include an increased tendency to acquire and use products that are scarce, innovative, customized, and/or outmoded, as well as a desire to shop at small, unique retail outlets.

Description: The scale consists of eight items designed to load on a single factor. Each item was operationalized using a 5-place bipolar scale ranging from *strongly disagree* to *strongly agree*. Item scores are summed to create the DUCP score.

Development: An initial set of 33 nonredundant items that prima facie appeared to tap a broad array of behaviors and dispositions related to DUCP was generated The items were administered to 240 business students. A principal components factor analysis was performed, and the eight items that loaded most highly on the first unrotated factor were retained. These items were selected because they had high factor loadings (above .50) and represented several different manifestations of the desire for unique consumer products. A maximum likelihood confirmatory analysis on these eight items indicated that a single factor model fit the data well. The consistency and generalizability of the scale were assessed by administering it to 106 working adults. A maximum likelihood confirmatory analysis indicated that a single factor model fit the data well.

Samples: The developmental analyses were conducted on convenience samples of (a) 240 business students and (b) 106 working adults. Test-retest reliability was assessed with a sample of 50 business students, correlation with theoretically relevant constructs was assessed using a sample of 337 business and psychology students, and the relationship between DUCP and a behavioral correlate was assessed using a sample of 119 theater patrons.

Validity: Coefficient alpha estimates for both the student and nonstudent samples were .78. The test-retest reliability (assessed by administering the scale to a new sample of 50 business students, 2 weeks apart) was .85. The validity of the measure was first assessed by measuring its relationship with theoretically related personality scales. Based on a sample of 337 students, the scale is significantly correlated with status aspiration, need for uniqueness, acquisitiveness, power-prestige, competitiveness, informational influence, normative influence, and possessiveness. In addition, the validity of the scale was assessed using an actual consumer behavior and a nonstudent sample of consumers. In one study, the scale was administered to 60 patrons of an "artistic" theater showing unusual movies and 59 patrons of a "second-run" theater showing popular movies. DUCP scores of patrons at the artistic theater were significantly higher than scores of patrons at the second-run theater.

Scores: Mean scores of DUCP for the student samples were 24.8 and 26.2. Mean scores for the nonstudent samples were 26.2 and 25.25. The authors found no correlation with DUCP scores and sex but did find a correlation with age in some studies, such that younger subjects tended to have higher scores.

Source: Lynn, Michael, and Judy Harris. (1997). "The Desire for Unique Consumer Products: A New Individual Differences Scale." *Psychology & Marketing*, *14*, 601-616.

          © 1997 by John Wiley & Sons, Inc. Scale items taken from Table 1 (p. 608). Adapted by permission of John Wiley & Sons, Inc.

Other evidence: N/A

Other sources: N/A

Reference: Snyder, C. R., and H. L. Fromkin. (1980). *Uniqueness: The Human Pursuit of Difference.* New York: Plenum.

UNIQUENESS: DESIRE FOR UNIQUE CONSUMER PRODUCTS: DUCP
(Lynn and Harris 1997)

1. I am very attracted to rare objects.

2. I tend to be a fashion leader rather than a fashion follower.

3. I am more likely to buy a product if it is scarce.

4. I would prefer to have things custom-made than to have them ready-made.

5. I enjoy having things that others do not.

6. I rarely pass up the opportunity to order custom features on the products I buy.

7. I like to try new products and services before others do.

8. I enjoy shopping at stores that carry merchandise that is different and unusual.

SCALES RELATED TO CONSUMER SOCIAL INFLUENCE

ATTENTION TO SOCIAL COMPARISON INFORMATION: ATSCI
(Lennox and Wolfe 1984)

Construct: Attention to social comparison assesses the extent to which one is aware of the reactions of others to one's behavior and is concerned about or sensitive to the nature of those reactions. These individuals care what other people think about them and look for clues as to the nature of others' reactions toward them (Lennox and Wolfe 1984).

Description: The ATSCI is a 13-item scale where the items are scored from 0 (*always false*) to 5 (*always true*). Item scores are summed to form an index.

Development: Three studies were performed to arrive at the final 13-item ATSCI. Each study contained Snyder's (1974) self-monitoring scale, from which the ATSCI is derived. (The items were adjusted to 6-point formats, as Snyder's scale was originally scored in a dichotomous format.) Also included in the studies were several other items and measures hypothesized to be related to various aspects of ATSCI and self-monitoring. Via factor analysis, reliability, and validity checks, the final form of the ATSCI was derived.

Samples: Three student samples ($n = 128$, 224, and 201) were used to develop the ATSCI across the three studies.

Validity: For the third study reported by Lennox and Wolfe ($n = 224$), the ATSCI had an alpha of .83 and was correlated with other measures reflecting concern for the opinions of others: ability to modify self-presentation ($r = .40$), fear of negative evaluation ($r = .64$), and cross-situational variability ($r = .42$).

Scores: Mean scores per item are reported by Lennox and Wolfe (1984, p. 1362) for their $n = 224$ sample.

Source: Lennox, Richard D., and Raymond N. Wolfe. (1984). "Revision of the Self Monitoring Scale." *Journal of Personality and Social Psychology*, *46*, 1349-1364.
    © 1984 by the American Psychological Association. Scale items taken from Table 10 (p. 1362). Reprinted with permission.

Other evidence: In a consumer behavior context, the ATSCI was examined using student samples of 62, 99, 63, and 85 (Bearden and Rose 1990). Bearden and Rose (1990) report alpha estimates for the ATSCI of .85, .83, .88, and .89 across their four studies. Furthermore, correlations of the ATSCI with a number of variables reflecting concern for the opinion of others (e.g., public self-consciousness, $r = .60$, .40, and .46; fear of negative evaluation, $r = .50$; and consumer behavior measures) show strong support for the validity of the ATSCI.

Other source: Bearden, William O., and Randall L. Rose. (1990). "Attention to Social Comparison Information: An Individual Difference Factor Affecting Consumer Conformity." *Journal of Consumer Research*, *16*, 461-471.

Reference: Snyder, Mark. (1974). "The Self-Monitoring of Expressive Behavior." *Journal of Personality and Social Psychology*, *30*, 526-537.

ATTENTION TO SOCIAL COMPARISON INFORMATION: ATSCI
(Lennox and Wolfe 1984)

1. It is my feeling that if everyone else in a group is behaving in a certain manner, this must be the proper way to behave.

2. I actively avoid wearing clothes that are not in style.

3. At parties I usually try to behave in a manner that makes me fit in.

4. When I am uncertain how to act in a social situation, I look to the behavior of others for clues.

5. I try to pay attention to the reactions of others to my behavior in order to avoid being out of place.

6. I find that I tend to pick up slang expressions from others and use them as a part of my own vocabulary.

7. I tend to pay attention to what others are wearing.

8. The slightest look of disapproval in the eyes of a person with whom I am interacting is enough to make me change my approach.

9. It's important to me to fit into the group I'm with.

10. My behavior often depends on how I feel others wish me to behave.

11. If I am the least bit uncertain as to how to act in a social situation, I look to the behavior of others for cues.

12. I usually keep up with clothing style changes by watching what others wear.

13. When in a social situation, I tend not to follow the crowd, but instead to behave in a manner that suits my particular mood at the time.*

NOTE: *Denotes item that is reverse scored.

INTERPERSONAL INFLUENCE: CONSUMER SUSCEPTIBILITY TO INTERPERSONAL INFLUENCE
(Bearden, Netemeyer, and Teel 1989)

Construct: Consumer susceptibility to interpersonal influence is assumed to be a general trait that varies across individuals and is related to other individual traits and characteristics. The construct is defined as the need to identify with or enhance one's image in the opinion of significant others through the acquisition and use of products and brands, the willingness to conform to the expectations of others regarding purchase decisions, and/or the tendency to learn about products and services by observing others or seeking information from others (Bearden et al. 1989, p. 474). That is, the construct is multidimensional in that both normative influences (e.g., value expressive and utilitarian) and informational influences are considered (e.g., Burnkrant and Cousineau 1975; Deutsch and Gerard 1955).

Description: The scale consists of 12 items each operationalized as a bipolar, 7-place rating scale ranging from *strongly agree* to *strongly disagree*. All items are positively worded. The 12 items reflect two correlated dimensions of susceptibility to interpersonal influence. Item scores are summed within each dimension to form normative and informational indices, and they can be summed overall for an overall susceptibility to interpersonal influence score ranging from 12 to 84.

Development: An original pool of 166 items was developed from a review of prior research. The number was reduced to 135 after deletion of ambiguous items and items with essentially identical meaning. Five judges were then used to assign items to categories based upon definitions provided for the three factors. Items that did not receive consistent classification by four of the five judges were eliminated. This process reduced the number of items to 86. The pool of items was further reduced to 62 using a second judgmental procedure. That is, those items not classified as clearly representative of each of the three factors by four marketing faculty judges were eliminated.

The remaining 62 items were interspersed across the three factors and then administered to a convenience sample of 220 adults. Corrected item-to-total correlations for each factor and oblique factor analysis (restricting the solution to three factors) were used to reduce the set of items to 18. Those items with item-to-total correlations below .50 were first deleted. Items not exhibiting simple structure were then eliminated.

The remaining 18 items were examined using confirmatory factor analysis which revealed three items with low reliabilities. For the five items remaining as indicators of informational, utilitarian, and value expressiveness influences, the respective construct reliabilities were .86, .87, and .83. Subsequent tests of convergent and discriminant validity revealed, however, that the value expressiveness and utilitarian factors were not discrete. This finding resulted in a 10-item normative factor. Estimates of construct reliability and shared variance for this factor were .91 and .52.

These 15 items were subsequently examined on a student sample of 141 subjects. Confirmatory factor analysis then supported (after the deletion of three additional items) a 12-item scale reflecting informational (four items) and normative influences (eight items).

Samples: The first administration obtained responses from a convenience sample of 220 adult (nonstudent) subjects. The second administration involved a survey of 141 student subjects. The validity of the scale was then evaluated on separate samples of 47 students in a correlational study involving measures of self-esteem and attention to social comparison information, 35 and 43 students in a two-phase behavioral index study, 72 fraternity and sorority subjects in the external judges study, and a group of 143 students in a study of motivations to comply.

Validity: Coefficient alpha estimates for the informational and normative factors were .82 and .88 ($n = 220$). A small sample of 35 subjects resulted in corresponding test-retest estimates of .75 and .79. Confirmatory factor analysis tests of invariant structure across the two samples also supported the stability of the measures.

The validity of the measures was further examined in five separate studies (see Bearden et al. 1989, pp. 477-479 for details). First, correlations between the two factors and measures of self-esteem and attention to social comparison information provided some evidence of construct validity in that the correlations were in the direction and pattern as expected. The evidence here was strongest for the normative factor. Second, the correlations between the informational factor and the normative factor and a series of self-reported behavioral indices were .37 ($p < .05$) and .15, respectively. Third and fourth, two external judgmental rating procedures also supported the ability of the scale to explain susceptibility to interpersonal influences. Lastly, the normative and informational factor measures were correlated with measures of motivations to comply as predicted. These estimates were .39 and .59 for the informational and normative scales, respectively.

Scores: Mean scores were not reported in the studies cited below. The authors did find that students scored significantly higher than nonstudents.

Source: Bearden, William O., Richard G. Netemeyer, and Jesse E. Teel. (1989). "Measurement of Consumer Susceptibility to Interpersonal Influence." *Journal of Consumer Research, 15,* 473-481.
 © 1989 by University of Chicago Press. Scale items taken from Table 2 (p. 477). Reprinted with permission.

Other evidence: The dimensionality and validity of the scales were further examined by the same authors (Bearden, Netemeyer, and Teel 1990) in a series of follow-up tests on new data and reanalyses of the data presented above. The results of correlating the susceptibility to interpersonal influence measures with a number of personality traits were reported. For the normative factor, example measures and significant correlations include the following: consumer confidence, $r = -.53$; interpersonal orientation, $r = .38$; inner-other directedness, $r = .37$; and extroversion, $r = .16$. In addition, the SUSCEP measures were shown to be more highly correlated with ATSCI and self-esteem than comparable measures developed from Park and Lessig (1977). Confirmatory factor analyses revealed that the two-factor solution was superior to both null and single-factor model solutions in terms of model fit and that the construct reliabilities were similar to those reported by Bearden et al. (1989).

Other source: Bearden, William O., Richard G. Netemeyer, and Jesse E. Teel. (1990). "Further Validation of the Consumer Susceptibility to Interpersonal Influence Scale." In Marvin E. Goldberg, Gerald Gorn, and Richard W. Pollay (Eds.), *Advances in Consumer Research* (Vol. 17, pp. 770-776). Provo, UT: Association for Consumer Research.

References: Burnkrant, Robert E., and Alain Cousineau. (1975). "Informational and Normative Influence in Buyer Behavior." *Journal of Consumer Research, 2,* 206-215.

Deutsch, Morton, and Harold B. Gerard. (1955). "A Study of Normative and Informational Influence Upon Individual Judgment." *Journal of Abnormal and Social Psychology, 7*(November), 1-15.

Park, C. Whan, and Parker V. Lessig. (1977). "Students and Housewives: Differences in Susceptibility to Reference Group Influence." *Journal of Consumer Research, 4,* 102-110.

INTERPERSONAL INFLUENCE: CONSUMER
SUSCEPTIBILITY TO INTERPERSONAL INFLUENCE
(Bearden, Netemeyer, and Teel 1989)

1. I often consult other people to help choose the best alternative available from a product class.

2. If I want to be like someone, I often try to buy the same brands that they buy.

3. It is important that others like the products and brands I buy.

4. To make sure I buy the right product or brand, I often observe what others are buying and using.

5. I rarely purchase the latest fashion styles until I am sure my friends approve of them.

6. I often identify with other people by purchasing the same products and brands they purchase.

7. If I have little experience with a product, I often ask my friends about the product.

8. When buying products, I generally purchase those brands that I think others will approve of.

9. I like to know what brands and products make good impressions on others.

10. I frequently gather information from friends or family about a product before I buy.

11. If other people can see me using a product, I often purchase the brand they expect me to buy.

12. I achieve a sense of belonging by purchasing the same products and brands that others purchase.

NOTES: Normative factor items are 2, 3, 5, 6, 8, 9, 11, and 12; informational factor items are 1, 4, 7, and 10.

**REFERENCE GROUP INFLUENCE: CONSUMER
SUSCEPTIBILITY TO REFERENCE GROUP INFLUENCE**
(Park and Lessig 1977)

Construct: Reference group influence is defined as the influence from an actual or imaginary individual or group conceived of having significant relevance upon an individual's evaluations, aspirations, or behavior. Furthermore, reference group influence has three motivational components (Park and Lessig 1977, p. 102): informational, utilitarian, and value expressive.

Informational influence is accepted from others for its informational content because it enhances the individual's knowledge of his/her environment or his/her ability to cope with some aspect of the environment (e.g., a product purchase).

Utilitarian influence is based on compliance with others. An individual complies because he/she perceives that significant others can mediate rewards or punishments, because the individual's behavior is known or visible to others, or because the individual is motivated to realize a reward or avoid punishment.

Value expressive influence relates to the individual's desire to enhance his/her self-concept in the eyes of others (i.e., the individual identifies with positive referents and dissociates him/herself from negative referents).

Description: The reference group scale is composed of 14 statements each measured along 4-point scales in regard to one's consumer behavior (i.e., *highly relevant* = 4, *medium relevance* = 3, *low relevance* = 2, and *not relevant* = 1). There are five items each for the informational and value expressive dimensions, and four items for the utilitarian dimension. Item scores are summed within dimensions and then divided by the number of items within each dimension to form indices for each dimension.

Development: Informal interviews and author judgment were used to generate 18 items that tapped the three dimensions of reference group influence. These items were pretested with a student sample and then trimmed to the final 14-item scale. A number of reliability and validity tests were then performed on new samples over 20 different product categories.

Samples: A sample of 22 students was used to trim the pool of 18 statements down to 14. A sample of 42 consumers was used in a validity check study, and samples of 100 housewives and 51 and 37 students also participated in validation studies.

Validity: Test-retest reliabilities for the three dimensions ranged from .43 to .78 (for a subsample of 20 of the housewife sample of 100) and .56 to .96 (for a subsample of 13 from one of the student samples). Multitrait-multimethod analyses supported the convergent and discriminant validity of the measures, as across products, the correlations among measures of the same trait were high, and correlations with different traits were low. (Beyond this, little detail was provided by Park and Lessig on their MTMM analyses.) Also, a number of mean difference tests between the housewife and student samples supported the scale's validity. That is, students were more susceptible to reference group influence for products like beer and cigarettes, and housewives were more susceptible to influence for products like furniture.

Scores: A number of mean scores are reported by Park and Lessig (1977, Tables 1, 2, 3, and 4, pp. 106-108). Across the 20 products studied, mean scores ranged from 2.46 to 4.00 for informational influence, 2.33 to 3.95 for utilitarian influence, and 1.93 to 3.97 for value expressive influence.

Source: Park, C. Whan, and V. Parker Lessig. (1977). "Students and Housewives: Differences in Susceptibility of Reference Group Influence." *Journal of Consumer Research, 4*, 102-110.

© 1977 by University of Chicago Press. Scale items taken from Exhibit (p. 105). Reprinted with permission.

Other evidence: Bearden and Etzel (1982) used a slightly modified version of the Park and Lessig measures. Thirteen of the items were used with slight wording changes and measures on 6-point disagree-agree statements (i.e., four items for informational, five for value expressive, and four for utilitarian). Across several product decisions, alphas for the dimensions were .63, .88, and .71 for the informational, value expressive, and utilitarian subscales, respectively. Across several brand decisions, alphas were .70, .80, and .77 for the three dimensions. Average test-retest reliabilities over a 3-week period ranged from .53 to .68 for the dimensions. A number of mean difference tests showed hypothesized differences between the three influence types.

Other source: Bearden, William O., and Michael J. Etzel. (1982). "Reference Group Influence on Product and Brand Purchase Decisions." *Journal of Consumer Research*, 9, 183-194.

References: N/A

REFERENCE GROUP INFLUENCE: CONSUMER SUSCEPTIBILITY TO REFERENCE GROUP INFLUENCE
(Park and Lessig 1977)

Informational Influence

1. The individual seeks information about various brands and products from an association of professionals or independent group of experts.

2. The individual seeks information from those who work with the products as a profession.

3. The individual seeks brand-related knowledge and experience (such as how Brand A's performance compares to Brand B's) from those friends, neighbors, relatives, or work associates who have reliable information about the brands.

4. The brand which the individual selects is influenced by observing a seal of approval of an independent testing agency (such as Good Housekeeping).

5. The individual's observation of what experts do influences his choice of a brand (such as observing the type of car which police drive or the brand of TV which repairmen buy).

Utilitarian Influence

6. To satisfy the expectations of fellow work associates, the individual's decision to purchase a particular brand is influenced by their preferences.

7. The individual's decision to purchase a particular brand is influenced by the preferences of people with whom he has social interaction.

8. The individual's decision to purchase a particular brand is influenced by the preferences of family members.

9. The desire to satisfy the expectations that others have of him has an impact on the individual's brand choice.

Value Expressive Influence

10. The individual feels that the purchase or use of a particular brand will enhance the image which others will have of him.

11. The individual feels that those who purchase or use a particular brand possess the characteristics which he would like to have.

12. The individual sometimes feels that it would be nice to be like the type of person which advertisements show using a particular brand.

13. The individual feels that the people who purchase a particular brand are admired or respected by others.

14. The individual feels that the purchase of a particular brand helps him show others what he is, or would like to be (such as an athlete, successful businessman, good mother, etc.).

SELF-MONITORING SCALE
(Snyder 1974)

Construct: Self-monitoring of expressive behavior and self-presentation were defined originally by Snyder (1974) as self-observation and self-control guided by situational cues to social appropriateness. An instrument was designed to discriminate individual differences in concern for social appropriateness, sensitivity to the expression and self-presentation of others in social situations as cues to social appropriateness of self-expression, and use of these cues as guidelines for monitoring and managing self-presentation and expressive behavior (Snyder 1974). The self-monitoring scale has generated a substantial body of research that continues to develop. The research includes a number of evaluations of the scale that include both supportive and critical evaluations. The scale has been used successfully in a number of consumer behavior studies (e.g., Becherer and Richard 1978) and has implications for salesperson behavior as well.

Description: The scale consists of 25 true-false items. Negatively worded items are reverse scored such that higher scores reflect higher self-monitoring. Labels for each item or situation were "True or Mostly True" and "False or Not Usually True." Five factors were assumed to underlie the original development of items: (a) concern with the social appropriateness of one's self-presentation, (b) attention to social comparison information as cues to appropriate self-expression, (c) the ability to control and modify one's self-presentation and expressive behavior, (d) the use of this ability in particular situations, and (e) the extent to which the person's self-presentation is cross-situationally consistent or variable (Snyder 1974, p. 529). Items are scored 0 or 1 and summed such that scores range from 0 to 25.

Development: A beginning set of 41 true-false items was first administered to 192 Stanford undergraduates. This set included items designed to reflect the above five factors. Items in the final scale were selected based upon their contribution to internal consistency and their ability to discriminate between low and high scorers on the original set.

Samples: Student samples of 192 and 146 from Stanford and Minnesota were used in the initial development of the scale. Subsamples of actors ($n = 24$) and psychiatric patients ($n = 31$) also were used in validity testing.

Validity: The KR-20 and test-retest estimates of reliability were .70 and .83, respectively. The KR-20 estimate reliability for a separate sample of 146 undergraduates was .63. Evidence of discriminant validity was provided by a $-.19$ ($p < .05$) correlation with the Marlowe-Crowne Social Desirability Scale. Modest correlations with measures of Machiavellianism ($r = -.09$) and inner-other directedness ($r = -.19$), among others, were also cited as evidence of discriminant validity.

A series of other studies were conducted to validate the measure. First, 16 fraternity members participated in a peer rating study of other fraternity members which found the SM measure to be related to external peer ratings of self-monitoring, $r = .45$, $p < .05$. Second, differences in mean scores were obtained between a sample of actors, the Stanford student sample, and a sample of psychiatric patients. Third, in a study of taped expressions, high self-monitors were better able than low self-monitors to express arbitrary emotional states in facial and vocal behavior. Also, in a study in which subjects were allowed to look or not to look at social comparison information (i.e., normative social comparison information) prior to an anticipated task, high self-monitors were more likely than low self-monitors to seek out social comparison information.

Scores: The mean scores for the actor and psychiatric patient samples were 18.41 and 10.19, respectively. These means were also said to be significantly above and below the Stanford student sample.

Source: Snyder, Mark. (1974). "Self-Monitoring of Expressive Behavior." *Journal of Personality and Social Psychology*, *30*(4), 526-537.

    © 1974 by the American Psychological Association. Scale items taken from Table 1 (p. 531). Reprinted with permission.

Other evidence: Snyder and Gangestad (1986) also offer an 18-item reduced version of Snyder's (1974) original scale. This version exhibited alpha estimates in excess of .70, and the first unrotated factor accounted for 62% of the scale variance.

    As noted above, the research stimulated by Snyder's (1974) self-monitoring concept, measure, and related work has been extensive. For an excellent review of this work see Snyder and Gangestad (1986). For consumer behavior purposes, only the manuscript by Becherer and Richard (1978), which reproduces the original scale in their *Journal of Consumer Research* article, is referenced here. In that research, self-monitoring was shown to moderate the effects on consumer decisions. Specifically, as expected from the theory underlying the self-monitoring construct, situational factors (as opposed to personal dispositions or personality traits) were suggested as being most related to consumption for high self-monitors. In addition, the data indicated that, among the low self-monitoring group, the relationship between a series of personality measures (e.g., tolerance) and private brand proneness was significant for both social and nonsocial products.

Other sources: Becherer, Richard C., and Lawrence M. Richard. (1978). "Self-Monitoring as a Moderating Variable in Consumer Behavior." *Journal of Consumer Research*, *5*, 159-162.

    Snyder, Mark, and Steve Gangestad. (1986). "On the Nature of Self-Monitoring: Matters of Assessment, Matters of Validity." *Journal of Personality and Social Psychology*, *51*, 125-139.

References: N/A

SELF-MONITORING SCALE
(Snyder 1974)

1. I find it hard to imitate the behavior of other people.
2. My behavior is usually an expression of my true inner feelings, attitudes, and beliefs.
3. At parties and social gatherings, I do not attempt to do or say things that others will like.
4. I only argue for ideas which I already believe.
5. I can make impromptu speeches on topics about which I have almost no information.
6. I guess I put on a show to impress or entertain people.
7. When I am uncertain how to act in a social situation, I look to the behavior of others for cues.
8. I would probably make a good actor.
9. I rarely need the advice of my friends to choose books, movies, or music.
10. I sometimes appear to others to be experiencing deeper emotions than I am.
11. I laugh more when I watch a comedy with others than I do when I watch alone.

12. In a group of people, I am rarely the center of attention.

13. In different situations with different people, I often act like very different people.

14. I am not particularly good at making other people like me.

15. Even if I am not enjoying myself, I often pretend to be having a good time.

16. I am not always the person I appear to be.

17. I would not change my opinions (or the way I do things) in order to please someone else or to win their favor.

18. I have considered being an entertainer.

19. In order to get along and be liked, I tend to be what people expect me to be rather than anything else.

20. I have never been good at games like charades or improvisational acting.

21. I have trouble changing my behavior to suit different people and different situations.

22. At a party I let others keep the jokes and stories going.

23. I feel a bit awkward in company and do not show up quite so well as I should.

24. I can look anyone in the eye and tell a lie with straight face (if for a right end).

25. I may deceive people by being friendly when I really dislike them.

NOTES: A "TRUE" response for items 5 through 8, 10, 11, 13, 15, 16, 18, 19, 24, and 25 reflects high self-monitoring. A "FALSE" response for items 1 through 4, 9, 12, 14, 17, and 20 through 23 also reflects high self-monitoring.

   Items 1, 3, 4, 5, 6, 8, 12, 13, 14, 16, 17, 18, and 20 through 25 represent Snyder and Gangestad's 18-item version.

SELF-MONITORING SCALE: REVISED FORM
(Lennox and Wolfe 1984)

Construct:	Lennox and Wolfe (1984) restrict the concept of self-monitoring to the ability to modify self-presentation and sensitivity to the expressive behavior of others. This more narrow definition of the construct is felt to be more reflective of the forte of the high self-monitor (Lennox and Wolfe 1984).
Description:	The Lennox and Wolfe version of the scale is composed of 13 items each scored on 6-point scales. Subjects are asked to indicate the degree to which each item is reflective of their own behavior: 0 = *certainly, always false*; 1 = *generally false*; 2 = *somewhat false, but with exceptions*; 3 = *somewhat true, but with exceptions*; 4 = *generally true*; and 5 = *certainly, always true*. Seven items represent ability to modify self-presentation, and six items represent sensitivity to the expressive behavior of others. Item scores can be summed within these two factors to form factor indices, or overall to form an overall measure of self-monitoring (Lennox and Wolfe 1984).
Development:	Over four studies, Lennox and Wolfe administered and factor-analyzed Snyder's (1974) original scale and items they generated to measure the construct. In Study 1, they factor-analyzed the original scale and found that several items did not load as hypothesized. In Study 2, they retained 19 of Snyder's original items, added 28 of their own, and factor-analyzed them using the previously described 6-point scoring system. From these 28 items, a four-factor structure was retained. Studies 3 and 4 further analyzed the scale and resulted in the final two-factor scale to measure self-monitoring. Coefficient alpha and a number of validity checks were performed on the final scale.
Samples:	The four samples used for the four studies were all composed of student subjects. Samples sizes were 179, 128, 224, and 201 for the four studies, respectively.
Validity:	The final scale had a coefficient alpha of .75 for the total scale (all 13 items), .77 for the seven-item ability to modify self-presentation factor, and .70 for the six-item sensitivity to the expressive behavior of others ($n = 201$). Correlations with related constructs revealed evidence of construct validity. For example, the overall scale had a correlation of .30 with a measure of individuation and of .17 with private self-consciousness.
Scores:	Mean scores for the total scale and subscales were not provided. Table 9 of Lennox and Wolfe (1984, p. 1361) provides item means and standard deviations.
Source:	Lennox, Richard D., and Raymond N. Wolfe. (1984). "Revision of the Self-Monitoring Scale." *Journal of Personality and Social Psychology*, 46, 1349-1364. © 1984 by the American Psychological Association. Scale items taken from Table 9 (p. 1361). Reprinted with permission.
Other evidence:	N/A
Other source:	N/A
Reference:	Snyder, Mark. (1974). "The Self-Monitoring of Expressive Behavior." *Journal of Personality and Social Psychology*, 30(4), 526-537.

SELF-MONITORING SCALE: REVISED FORM
(Lennox and Wolfe 1984)

Ability to Modify Self-Presentation

1. In social situations, I have the ability to alter my behavior if I feel that something else is called for.

2. I have the ability to control the way I come across to people, depending on the impression I wish to give them.

3. When I feel that the image I am portraying isn't working, I can readily change it to something that does.

4. I have trouble changing my behavior to suit different people and different situations.*

5. I have found that I can adjust my behavior to meet the requirements of any situation I find myself in.

6. Even when it might be to my advantage, I have difficulty putting up a good front.*

7. Once I know what the situation calls for, it's easy for me to regulate my actions accordingly.

Sensitivity to the Expressive Behaviors of Others

1. I am often able to read people's true emotions correctly through their eyes.

2. In conversations, I am sensitive to even the slightest change in the facial expression of the person I'm conversing with.

3. My powers of intuition are quite good when it comes to understanding others' emotions and motives.

4. I can usually tell when others consider a joke to be in bad taste, even though they may laugh convincingly.

5. I can usually tell when I've said something inappropriate by reading it in the listener's eyes.

6. If someone is lying to me, I usually know it at once from that person's manner of expression.

NOTE: *Denotes items that require reverse coding.

3
Values

GENERAL VALUES

LIST OF VALUES: LOV
(Kahle 1983)

Construct: The term "value" has been defined as an enduring prescriptive or proscriptive belief that a specific end state of existence or specific mode of conduct is preferred to an opposite end state or mode of conduct for living one's life (cf. Kahle 1983; Rokeach 1968, 1973).

   The LOV typology draws a distinction between external and internal values, and it notes the importance of interpersonal relations in value fulfillment, as well as personal factors (i.e., self-respect, self-fulfillment) and apersonal factors (i.e., fun, security, excitement) in value fulfillment. In essence, the LOV measures those values that are central to people in living their lives, particularly the values of life's major roles (i.e., marriage, parenting, work, leisure, and daily consumptions). The LOV is most closely tied to social adaptation theory (Kahle, Beatty, and Homer 1986), and many studies suggest that the LOV is related to and/or predictive of consumer behavior and related activities (e.g., Homer and Kahle 1988; Kahle 1983).

Description: The LOV is composed of nine values that can be scored in a number of ways. Each value can be evaluated on 9- or 10-point scales (*very unimportant* to *very important*), or the values can be rank ordered from most to least important. Also, some combination of the two methods can be used where each value is rated on 9- or 10-point scales and then subjects are asked to circle the one or two values that are most important to them in living their daily lives (e.g., Kahle 1983; Kahle et al. 1986; Kahle and Kennedy 1988).

Development: The LOV was developed from a theoretical base of values proposed by Feather (1975), Maslow's (1954) hierarchy of values, Rokeach's (1973) 18 terminal values, and various other contemporaries in values research. The LOV items were derived by culling the values from the above sources from a much larger pool of values to the nine LOV items. For a more detailed discussion of the scale development procedures, see Kahle (1983, 1986) and Kahle et al. (1986).

Samples: The major study on the LOV was conducted with a probability sample of $n = 2,264$ Americans. The study was conducted by the Survey Research Center of the Institute for Social Research at the University of Michigan (Kahle 1983, 1986; Kahle and Kennedy 1988).

Validity: The original study found the LOV to be significantly correlated with various measures of mental health, well-being, adaptation to society, and self (Kahle 1983). Thus, evidence for the nomological validity of the LOV exists.

Scores: Mean scores for the nine values were not directly reported by Kahle (1983); however, the percentage of respondents selecting the one value that is most important to them is available in Kahle (1983). (See also Kahle, Liu, and Watkins [1992] below.)

115

Source: Kahle, Lynn R. (1983). *Social Values and Social Change: Adaptation to Life in America.* New York: Praeger.
© 1983 by Praeger. Scale items taken from Table 3.2 (p. 1361). Reprinted with permission.

Other evidence: The LOV was also tested with a student sample of 193 (of which 122 were foreign students) in terms of predictive ability of consumer-related trends (Kahle et al. 1986), a convenience sample of 356 in terms of comparing it to the Rokeach Value survey (Beatty, Kahle, Homer, and Misra 1985), and, a sample of 831 food shoppers for predictive validity purposes (Homer and Kahle 1988).

Beatty et al. (1985) found that 92% and 85% of respondents who picked any given first value ranked it first or second 1 month later, offering support for the LOV's consistency over time. In one study, using 10-point scales to evaluate each of the nine LOV items, a three-factor representation of the values was found with composite reliability estimates (via LISREL) of .69 for a factor representing internal individual values, .68 for an external values factor, and .58 for an internal interpersonal values factor (Homer and Kahle 1988).

Most studies employing the LOV have focused on the distribution of values across the United States (e.g., Kahle 1986), the predictive validity of the LOV toward consumer behaviors, and/or the relationship of the LOV with other psychological constructs (e.g., Homer and Kahle 1988; Kahle 1983; Kahle et al. 1986). These studies indicate that the LOV was found to be significantly correlated with various measures of mental health, well-being, adaptation to society, and self (Kahle 1983), and predictive of a number of consumer behaviors (Homer and Kahle 1988; Kahle et al. 1986). Furthermore, the hypothesized dispersion of values across areas of the United States was supported (Kahle 1986). In sum, evidence for the nomological and predictive validity of the LOV exists.

In the Homer and Kahle (1988) study, means of the LOV items by various discriminant groups are also reported. In yet another study, LOV rankings from 997 respondents in the United States were compared to LOV rankings from Kahle's (1983) original LOV study (Kahle, Poulos, and Sukhdial 1988). A Spearman rank order correlation between the ranks of the values (i.e., in terms of the percentage of people endorsing the value as the primary value) across the two studies revealed stability in importance placed on different values by the American people over a decade. The correlation for males was .91, for females was .79, and for the sample combined was .83. Kahle et al. (1988) offer numerous breakdowns of the LOV values by gender and age groups.

Mean scores for eight LOV values across four U.S. geographic regions are reported in Kahle et al. (1992). These means scores are based on 7-point scales (*not at all important to me* to *extremely important to me*) and are reproduced in Table 3.1.

TABLE 3.1

Value	Region Order	Mean1	Mean2	Mean3	Mean4
Self-respect	w,e,m,s	6.37	6.55	6.55	6.72
Security	e,m,w,s	6.29	6.29	6.31	6.43
Warm relations with others	e,w,m,s	6.03	6.29	6.31	6.39
Self of fulfillment	m,w,e,s	5.82	5.91	6.03	6.16
Sense of accomplishment	m,w,e,s	6.04	6.14	6.17	6.31
Being well respected	w,e,m,s	5.72	5.97	6.01	6.20
Sense of belonging	w,e,m,s	5.52	5.77	5.81	6.02
Fun and enjoyment in life	m,e,w,s	5.53	5.60	5.67	5.81

NOTE: e = East, m = Midwest, s = South, w = West; total *n* = 442.

Other sources: Beatty, Sharon E., Lynn R. Kahle, Pamela Homer, and Shekhar Misra. (1985). "Alternative Measurement Approaches to Consumer Values: The List of Values and the Rokeach Value Survey." *Psychology & Marketing*, 2(Fall), 181-200.

Kahle, Lynn, Basil Poulos, and Ajay Sukhdial. (1988). "Changes in Social Values in the United States During the Past Decade." *Journal of Advertising Research*, 28, 35-41.

References: Feather, Norman T. (1975). *Values in Education and Society.* New York: Free Press.

Homer, Pamela, and Lynn R. Kahle. (1988). "A Structural Equation Analysis of the Value-Attitude-Behavior Hierarchy." *Journal of Personality and Social Psychology, 54,* 638-646.

Kahle, Lynn. (1986). "The Nine Nations of North America and the Values Basis of Geographic Segmentation." *Journal of Marketing, 50,* 37-47.

Kahle, Lynn, Sharon E. Beatty, and Pamela Homer. (1986). "Alternative Measurement Approaches to Consumer Values: The List of Values (LOV) and Life Style (VALS)." *Journal of Consumer Research, 13,* 405-409.

Kahle, Lynn, and Patricia Kennedy. (1988). "Using the List of Values (LOV) to Understand Consumers." *The Journal of Services Marketing, 2*(Fall), 49-56.

Kahle, Lynn, Ruiming Liu, and Harry Watkins. (1992). "Psychographic Variation Across United States Geographic Regions." In John F. Sherry and Brian Sternthal (Eds.), *Advances in Consumer Research* (Vol. 18, pp. 346-352). Provo, UT: Association for Consumer Research.

Maslow, Abraham H. (1954). *Motivation and Personality.* New York: Harper.

Rokeach, Milton J. (1968). "The Role of Values in Public Opinion Research." *Public Opinion Quarterly, 32,* 547-549.

Rokeach, Milton J. (1973). *The Nature of Human Values.* New York: Free Press.

LIST OF VALUES: LOV
(Kahle 1983)

The following is a list of things that some people look for or want out of life. Please study the list carefully and then rate each thing on how important it is in your daily life, where 1 = very unimportant and 9 = very important.

	Very Unimportant								*Very Important*	%	M
1. Sense of belonging	1	2	3	4	5	6	7	8	9	8.8	7.05
2. Excitement	1	2	3	4	5	6	7	8	9	—	7.08
3. Warm relationships with others	1	2	3	4	5	6	7	8	9	16.2	8.76
4. Self-fulfillment	1	2	3	4	5	6	7	8	9	9.6	8.62
5. Being well respected	1	2	3	4	5	6	7	8	9	8.8	7.55
6. Fun and enjoyment of life	1	2	3	4	5	6	7	8	9	4.5	8.08
7. Security	1	2	3	4	5	6	7	8	9	20.6	7.75
8. Self-respect	1	2	3	4	5	6	7	8	9	21.1	8.97
9. A sense of accomplishment	1	2	3	4	5	6	7	8	9	11.4	8.59

Now reread the items and **circle the one thing that is most important to you in your daily life.**

NOTES: The above scoring format is but one possible format. As indicated earlier, the values can be rank ordered, or respondents can be asked to indicate their top two values and/or use 10-point scales and/or a combination of scoring methods.

In the original study ($n = 2,264$), only 2% of the sample endorsed "excitement" as their top value. Subsequently, excitement was collapsed into the "fun and enjoyment in life" category. The percentages presented above reflect the percentage of respondents who ranked the value as the most important in living their daily lives. The percentage reported for "fun and enjoyment in life" reflects the 2% added to it for those respondents endorsing "excitement" as their top value (Kahle 1983).

The mean values (*M*) are based on 10-point items and were calculated by averaging the values reported in Table 7 of Homer and Kahle (1988). Values 2, 4, 8, and 9 represent the internal individual values factor; values 1, 5, and 7 represent the external dimension values factor; and values 3 and 6 represent the internal interpersonal values factor (Homer and Kahle 1988).

MULTI-ITEM MEASURES OF VALUES: MILOV
(Herche 1994)

Construct: Consistent with the conceptual work of Rokeach (1968) and Kahle (1983), "values" are viewed as enduring beliefs that a specific end state of existence or specific mode of conduct is preferred to an opposite or converse end state or mode of conduct of existence (Herche 1994). In this research, social values, or the socially oriented, life-goal view of values, are measured.

Description: In essence, MILOV is a multi-item operationalization of the list of values (LOV) developed and then further refined by Kahle and colleagues. MILOV contains 44 items covering nine social values. All items are scored on 9-point Likert-type scales probably ranging from *strongly disagree* to *strongly agree*. Item scores can be summed within each value to create separate dimension indices for each value.

Development: Recommended scaling procedures were used to derive MILOV. An initial pool of 400 items was generated to reflect the nine values. After editing for redundancy and ambiguity, the pool was trimmed to 128 items. Using a sample of $n = 333$ college students and exploratory factor analyzes, 63 items were retained based on a consistent pattern of response and face validity. These 63 items were further classified into one of nine categories (i.e., the nine social values) by eight judges with Ph.D.s in marketing. Two more large samples of students were used to further clarify item meaning and the reliability of the scales. These procedures resulted in the final 44-item form of MILOV. With a large adult sample, using exploratory and confirmatory factor analyzes, item and reliability analyses, and several correlational-based tests, the dimensionality, internal consistency, and validity of the MILOV scales were established.

Samples: Samples of $n = 333$, $n = 416$, and $n = 291$ (all students) were used to derive the final form of MILOV. A sample of $n = 8$ marketing Ph.D.s was also used to categorize and judge MILOV items. A sample of $n = 683$ adult U.S. consumers was used to test the psychometric properties of MILOV.

Validity: Via exploratory and confirmatory factor analyses, scale dimensionality was examined. The rotated factor pattern (from exploratory analyses) and the fit indices (from confirmatory analyzes) provide evidence that the nine MILOV measures are distinct dimensions. Item-to-total correlations ranged from .554 to .838 within/across dimensions, and coefficient alpha estimates of internal consistency ranged from .57 to .81 across the nine social values dimensions. (See scale items on the following pages for specific estimates.) Correlations among the nine MILOV dimensions ranged from $-.02$ to .54. Only four of nine correlations of the MILOV dimensions with social desirability were significant, suggesting low contamination of social desirability bias. Across numerous activities and media habit constructs, the MILOV dimensions were compared to the LOV items in terms of predictive validity. In 59 regression models, MILOV performed better than LOV in 58 instances. MILOV dimensions proved to be significant predictors in 49 of 59 models with a median R^2 of .057. The LOV was a significant predictor in 27 of 59 cases with a median R^2 of .026.

Scores: Neither mean nor percentage scores were reported.

Source: Herche, Joel. (1994). *Measuring Social Values: A Multi-Item Adaptation to the List of Values (MILOV)* (Working Paper Report Number 94-101). Cambridge, MA: Marketing Science Institute.

© 1994 by the Marketing Science Institute. Scale items taken from Appendix (pp. 23-25). Reprinted with permission.

Other evidence: N/A

Other sources: N/A

References: Kahle, Lynn R. (1983). *Social Values and Social Change: Adaptation to Life in America.* New York: Praeger.

Rokeach, Milton J. (1968). "The Role of Values in Public Opinion Research." *Public Opinion Quarterly, 32,* 547-549.

MULTI-ITEM MEASURES OF VALUES: MILOV
(Herche 1994)

Security Dimension (alpha = .76)

1. I am often concerned about my physical safety.

2. Knowing that I am physically safe is important to me.

3. My security is a high priority to me.

4. Financial security is very important to me.

Self-Respect Dimension (alpha = .81)

1. I try to act in such a way as to be able to face myself in the mirror the next morning.

2. If one loses one's self-respect, nothing can compensate for the loss.

3. My self-respect is worth more than gold.

4. Even though others may disagree, I will not do anything to threaten my self-respect.

5. More than anything else, I must be able to respect who I am.

6. I will do what I know to be right, even when I stand to lose money.

7. Knowing that I am doing the right thing in a given situation is worth any price.

8. I will not compromise on issues that could cause me to lose my self-respect.

Being Well-Respected Dimension (alpha = .71)

1. I strive to retain a high status among my friends.

2. I am easily hurt by what others say about me.

3. The opinions of others are important to me

4. I care what others think of me.

Self-Fulfillment Dimension (alpha = .77)

1. I treat myself well.

2. I deserve the best, and often give myself what I deserve.

3. I like to buy the best of everything when I go shopping.

4. The finer things in life are for me.

5. Meeting my desires is a full-time job for me.

Sense of Belonging Dimension (alpha = .57)

1. I play an important role in my family.

2. I need to feel there is a place that I can call "home."

3. I feel appreciated and needed by my closest relatives and friends.

4. Being a part of the lives of those with whom I am close is a high priority for me.

Excitement Dimension (alpha = .72)

1. I enjoy doing things out of the ordinary.

2. I strive to fill my life with exciting activities.

3. I thrive on parties.

4. I consider myself a thrill-seeker.

Fun and Enjoyment Dimension (alpha = .79)

1. Having fun is important to me.

2. Recreation is an integral part of my life.

3. I work hard at having fun.

4. Recreation is a necessity for me.

Warm Relationships With Others Dimension (alpha = .70)

1. I often commend others on their efforts, even when they fail.

2. I make a point of reassuring others that their presence is welcomed and appreciated.

3. I try to be as open and genuine as possible with others.

4. Without my close friends, my life would be much less meaningful.

5. I value warm relationships with my family and friends highly.

6. When those who are close to me are in pain, I hurt too.

A Sense of Accomplishment Dimension (alpha = .74)

1. I need to feel a sense of accomplishment from my job.

2. I am disappointed when I am unable to see a project through to the end.

3. "Getting things done" is always high on my "to-do" list.

4. Feedback on my job performance is very important.

5. I tend to set and strive to reach my goals.

THE ROKEACH VALUE SURVEY: RVS
(Rokeach 1968, 1973)

Construct: A value is defined as an enduring prescriptive or proscriptive belief that a specific end state of existence or specific mode of conduct is preferred to an opposite end state or mode of conduct (Rokeach 1968, 1973). These values are considered the important principles guiding one's behavior throughout life.

The Rokeach Value Survey (RVS) is designed to measure two sets of values. One set is composed of 18 terminal values or desired end states of existence (e.g., an exciting life, national security), and the other set is composed of 18 instrumental values, or preferable modes of behavior (e.g., being ambitious, independent).

The importance of values, and specifically the Rokeach Value Survey, to marketing/consumer research cannot be overstated. Two reviews of the relevance of values to consumer behavior can be found in Kahle (1985) and Prakash and Munson (1985).

Description: The 18 values within each category (terminal and instrumental) are alphabetically listed on two separate pages (Form D). Then, subjects are asked to rank order each value as to its importance as a guiding principle in living their life. A 1 indicates the most important value and an 18 the least important. Scale responses are considered ordinal.

Development: The original development of the scale is described in Rokeach (1968, 1973). At first, 12 values were selected to represent each set of values, but due to the omission of salient values and low reliability estimates, both sets of values were expanded to 18 in each category. For the terminal values, an extensive literature review, the author's own judgment, and interviews with students ($n = 30$) and nonstudents ($n = 100$) produced an initial pool of values in the hundreds. Then, through further judgment by the author and empirical analysis examining similarity among items, 18 items were retained.

For the instrumental values, Anderson's (1968) checklist of 555 personality-trait words was used as a base. This list was trimmed to about 200, and then the 18 instrumental values were chosen according to the following criteria: (a) by retaining only one word from a group of synonyms, (b) by retaining those judged to be maximally different or minimally intercorrelated with one another, (c) by retaining those judged representative of important American values, (d) by retaining those that would maximally discriminate across demographic variables, (e) by retaining those values judged to be meaningful in all cultures, and (f) by retaining those items that respondents could admit to without appearing to be immodest or vain.

Initial estimates of predictive validity are offered by Rokeach (1968, 1973), and results and comments pertaining to other applications of the scale outside of marketing/consumer behavior can also be found in Rokeach (1973) and Robinson and Shaver (1973). In fact, the scale has undergone numerous reliability and validity checks across various samples.

Samples: Various samples were used by Rokeach throughout the derivation of the value survey instrument. Some of these samples include 50 policemen, 141 unemployed whites and 28 unemployed blacks, 298 students, and 75 Calvinest students. Other applications of the scale outside the marketing/consumer behavior literature are numerous and have employed a wide range of samples encompassing all types of demographic classifications.

Validity: Test-retest reliability (over a 7-week period) has been in the .70 range and above for the RVS. Other estimates of test-retest reliability for applications of the scale outside marketing/consumer behavior have been in the .70 to .79 range for Form D. In most of these applications, the values were ranked as originally prescribed by Rokeach, and thus more traditional estimates of internal consistency (i.e., coefficient alpha) are rarely reported. As mentioned above, estimates of predictive validity can be found in Rokeach (1968, 1973). For example, the value "salvation" was found to be predictive of religious affiliation and church attendance, and the values of "equality" and "freedom" were predictive of participation in civil rights demonstrations.

Scores: Since the Rokeach survey is a rank order scale, mean scores generally have not been reported. However, a comprehensive table of the frequencies for all 36 values across select demographic characteristics is available in Rokeach (1973, pp. 363-419).

Sources: Rokeach, Milton. (1968). *Beliefs, Attitudes and Values.* San Francisco, CA: Jossey-Bass.
© 1968 by Jossey-Bass, Inc. Reprinted with permission.

Rokeach, Milton. (1973). *The Nature of Human Values.* New York: Free Press.
© 1973 by The Free Press. Scale items taken from Appendix A (pp. 355-361). Reprinted with permission.

Other evidence: In the marketing/consumer behavior literature, samples have comprised both student (Munson and McQuarrie 1988; Reynolds and Jolly 1980; Shrum, McCarty, and Loeffler 1990; Vinson, Munson, and Nakanishi 1977) and nonstudent groups (e.g., Beatty, Kahle, Homer, and Misra 1985; McQuarrie and Langmeyer 1985; Munson and McQuarrie 1988). These applications of the scale have used all 18 terminal and all 18 instrumental values, as well as shortened versions of the scale where 12 instrumental and 12 terminal values are evaluated (Rokeach 1968, 1973). In addition, many of these applications have used various scoring formats including Rokeach's original ranking procedure, anchored endpoint scoring, and Likert-type interval scoring. Several of these applications are briefly discussed below.

Based on the difficulty subjects have had in ranking all 18 terminal and 18 instrumental values, many marketing researchers have attempted alternative scaling formats for the Rokeach values. Vinson et al. (1977) had subjects evaluate the 36 values on an interval scaling format ranging from *important* to *not important*. They report that two distinct dimensions were found (i.e., the terminal and instrumental value dimensions as espoused by Rokeach). However, within the two dimensions, several subdimensions were found. Six factors for the terminal values were found: social harmony, personal gratification, self-actualization, security, love and affection, and personal contentedness. Four factors were found for the instrumental dimension: competence, compassion, sociality, and integrity. Estimates of internal consistency were not reported.

Munson and McIntyre (1979) compared three different scaling formats of the Rokeach values. The three formats were the original format proposed by Rokeach, Likert statements for each of the 36 values ranging from *extremely important* to *extremely unimportant*, and an anchored scaling format. Over a 2-week period, test-retest reliability was estimated via Spearman's rho for each format. For Rokeach's rank order format, rho = .82 and .76 for the terminal and instrumental values, respectively. For the Likert format, rho = .76 and .74 for the terminal and instrumental values, and for the anchored scaling, rho = .73 and .68 for the terminal and instrumental values. Munson and McIntyre concluded that the Likert format was an appropriate alternative to Rokeach's rank order format.

Reynolds and Jolly (1980) also compared three scaling formats including Rokeach's rankings, a Likert-type format, and a paired comparison format for the 18 terminal values and a 12-value subset of the terminal values. Over a 2-week period, test-retest reliability was computed across the formats via Spearman's rho and Kendall's tau. They concluded that the Likert format may not be appropriate based on the results in Table 3.2.

TABLE 3.2

	Rokeach		*Likert*		*Paired*	
	18	*12*	*18*	*12*	*18*	*12*
Rho	.78	.76	.66	.75	.67	.77
Tau	.62	.62	.62	.69	.57	.66

Using Rokeach's ranking procedure, Kahle (1985) found the 18 terminal values to have convergent/discriminant validity when compared to corresponding values from the LOV survey (Kahle 1983).

In a special issue of *Psychology & Marketing* (1985, Vol. 2, No. 4), a number of papers examined the Rokeach Value Survey. For example, McQuarrie and Langmeyer used a 15-value subset of the Rokeach values in studying attitudes toward personal computers. The 15 items were evaluated in relation to home computers using 5-point agree-disagree Likert statements (alpha = .90). Evidence of discriminant validity between the 15-item value measure and related constructs was also reported. Prakash and Munson used the Rokeach ranking procedure for the 36 values but found seven factors underlying the values (i.e., fun and enjoyment, workplace ethics, sapience, autonomy, aesthetics, security, and love).

Munson and McQuarrie (1988) attempted to reduce the Rokeach Value Survey to values most relevant to consumer behavior. In one sample, subjects were asked to identify the 12 values most irrelevant to consumer behavior. In a subsequent sample, subjects evaluated the 24 remaining values on the degree to which they were related to consumer behavior on 3-point scales (i.e., *not related*, *weakly related*, *strongly related*). Coefficient alpha was .94. In another sample, these 24 values were again evaluated on the degree to which they were related to consumer behavior on 5-point scales (i.e., *no*, *weak*, *some*, *definite*, or *strong* relation), with a coefficient alpha of .95. Furthermore, three factors were found to underlie the 24 consumer behavior relevant values—a "values to help fulfill adult responsibilities" factor, a "values to help fulfill lifestyle goals" factor, and a "values to help relieve tension" factor.

In one study, though, all 36 values were assessed on 7-point Likert-type scales, and mean scores are reported for various subsamples (Vinson et al. 1977, p. 251). The mean scores ranged from a low of 4.5 for "social recognition" to a high of 6.6 for "honesty" and "self-respect."

Lastly, Crosby, Bitner, and Gill (1990) had a sample of 418 rank, then rate on 7-point scales, the 18 instrumental and 18 terminal values. Confirmatory factor analysis found three dimensions for the instrumental values: self-direction (9 items), conformity (5 items), and virtuousness (4 items) with composite reliability estimates of .81, .57, and .65, respectively. Correlations among these dimensions ranged from .08 to .59. Three dimensions were also found for the terminal values: self-actualization/hedonism (12 items), idealism (3 items), and security (3 items) with composite reliabilities of .62, .58, and .67, respectively. Correlations among these dimensions ranged from −.44 to .77.

Other sources: Beatty, Sharon E., Lynn R. Kahle, Pamela Homer, and Shekhar Misra. (1985). "Alternative Measurement Approaches to Consumer Values: The List of Values and the Rokeach Value Survey." *Psychology & Marketing*, 2, 181-200.

Crosby, Lawrence A., Mary Jo Bitner, and James D. Gill. (1990). "Organizational Structure of Values." *Journal of Business Research*, 20, 123-134.

Kahle, Lynn R. (1983). *Social Values and Social Change: Adaptation to Life in America.* New York: Praeger.

McQuarrie, Edward F., and Daniel Langmeyer. (1985). "Using Values to Measure Attitudes Toward Discontinuous Innovations." *Psychology & Marketing*, 2, 239-252.

Munson, J. Michael, and S. H. McIntyre. (1979). "Developing Practical Procedures for the Measurement of Personal Values in Cross-Cultural Marketing." *Journal of Marketing Research*, *16*(February), 48-52.

Munson, J. Michael, and Edward F. McQuarrie. (1988). "Shortening the Rokeach Value Survey for Use in Consumer Behavior." In Michael J. Houston (Ed.), *Advances in Consumer Research* (Vol. 15, pp. 381-386). Provo, UT: Association for Consumer Research.

Reynolds, Thomas J., and James P. Jolly. (1980). "Measuring Personal Values: An Evaluation of Alternative Methods." *Journal of Marketing Research*, *17*, 531-536.

Shrum, L. J., John A. McCarty, and Tamara L. Loeffler. (1990). "Individual Differences in Value Stability: Are We Really Tapping True Values?" In Marvin E. Goldberg, Gerald Gorn, and Richard W. Pollay (Eds.), *Advances in Consumer Research* (Vol. 17, pp. 609-615). Provo, UT: Association for Consumer Research.

Vinson, Donald E., J. Michael Munson, and Masao Nakanishi. (1977). "An Investigation of the Rokeach Value Survey for Consumer Research Applications." In William E. Perreault (Ed.), *Advances in Consumer Research* (Vol. 4, pp. 247-252). Provo, UT: Association for Consumer Research.

References: Anderson, N. H. (1968). "Likableness Ratings of 555 Personality-Trait Words." *Journal of Personality and Social Psychology*, 9, 272-279.

Kahle, Lynn R. (1985). "Social Values in the Eighties: A Special Issue." *Psychology & Marketing*, 2, 231-237.

Prakash, Ved, and J. Michael Munson. (1985). "Values, Expectations From the Marketing Systems and Product Expectations." *Psychology & Marketing*, 2, 279-298.

Robinson, J. P., and R. P. Shaver. (1973). *Measures of Social Psychological Attitudes*. Ann Arbor, MI: Survey Research Center, Institute for Social Research.

THE ROKEACH VALUE SURVEY: RVS
(Rokeach 1968, 1973)

Listed below are 18 values in alphabetical order. Your task is to arrange them in order of importance to YOU, as guiding principles in YOUR life. Study the list very carefully and then rank all 18 in terms of their importance to you. Place a "1" next to the value that is the most important as a guiding principle in your life, a "2" next to the second most important value as a guiding principle in your life, a "3" next to the third most important value as a guiding principle in your life, and so on. Again, it is important that you rank all values from 1 to 18.

Work slowly and think carefully. If you change your mind, feel free to change your answers. The end result should truly show how you really feel.

Value	Rank
1. A comfortable life (i.e., a prosperous life)	_____
2. An exciting life (i.e., a stimulating, active life)	_____
3. A sense of accomplishment (i.e., a lasting contribution)	_____
4. A world at peace (i.e., free of war and conflict)	_____
5. A world of beauty (i.e, beauty of nature and the arts)	_____
6. Equality (i.e., brotherhood, equal opportunity for all)	_____
7. Family security (i.e., taking care of loved ones)	_____
8. Freedom (i.e., independence, free choice)	_____
9. Happiness (i.e., contentedness)	_____
10. Inner harmony (i.e., freedom from inner conflict)	_____
11. Mature love (i.e., sexual and spiritual intimacy)	_____
12. National security (i.e., protection from attack)	_____
13. Pleasure (i.e., an enjoyable, leisurely life)	_____
14. Salvation (i.e., saved, eternal life)	_____
15. Self-respect (i.e., self-esteem)	_____
16. Social recognition (i.e., respect, admiration)	_____
17. True friendship (i.e., close companionship)	_____
18. Wisdom (i.e., a mature understanding of life)	_____

When you have finished, go to the next page.

Please rank these 18 values in order of importance, the same as before.

Value	Rank
19. Ambitious (i.e., hard working, aspiring)	_____
20. Broad-minded (i.e., open minded)	_____
21. Capable (i.e., competent, effective)	_____
22. Cheerful (i.e., lighthearted, joyful)	_____
23. Clean (i.e., neat, tidy)	_____
24. Courageous (i.e, standing up for your beliefs)	_____
25. Forgiving (i.e., willing to pardon others)	_____
26. Helpful (i.e., working for the welfare of others)	_____
27. Honest (i.e., sincere, truthful)	_____
28. Imaginative (i.e., daring, creative)	_____
29. Independent (i.e., self-reliant, self-sufficient)	_____
30. Intellectual (i.e., intelligent, reflective)	_____
31. Logical (i.e., consistent, rational)	_____
32. Loving (i.e., affectionate, tender)	_____
33. Obedient (i.e., dutiful, respectful)	_____
34. Polite (i.e., courteous, well-mannered)	_____
35. Responsible (i.e., dependable, reliable)	_____
36. Self-controlled (i.e., restrained, self-disciplined)	_____

NOTES: Items 1-18 are terminal and items 19-36 are instrumental values. Values 4, 6, 8, 12, and 14 compose a social harmony factor; values 1, 2, 3, 13, and 16 compose a personal gratification factor; values 3, 5, 10, 15, and 18 compose a self-actualization factor; values 7 and 14 compose a security factor; values 2, 11, and 17 compose a love and affection factor; values 8 and 9 a personal contentedness factor; values 19, 21, 24, 28, 29, 30, and 31 a competence factor; values 22, 25, 26, and 32 a compassion factor; values 23, 33, and 34 a sociality factor; and values 27, 34, 35, and 36 an integrity factor (Vinson et al. 1977).

Values 6, 13, 14, 17, and 33 compose a fun and enjoyment factor; values 1, 3, 21, 19, 27, and 34 a workplace ethics factor; values 1, 2, 10, 15, 17, and 18 a sapience factor; values 25, 26, 29, and 30 an autonomy factor; values 4 and 5 an aesthetics factor; values 4, 9, and 12 a security factor; and values 11 and 32 a mature love factor. Only values with loadings ≥ ±.30 were reported (Prakash and Munson 1985).

Values 3, 6, 7, 8, 10, 13, 15, 16, and 18 represent the reduced set of terminal values, and values 19, 21, 28, 29, 30, and 36 represent a reduced set of instrumental values (McQuarrie and Langmeyer 1985).

Values 1, 2, 3, 5 through 10, 13, 15, 16, and 18 represent the reduced set of terminal values relevant to consumer behavior, and values 19 through 23, 28, 29, 30, 32, 35, and 36 represent the reduced set of instrumental values relevant to consumer behavior. Furthermore, values 6, 7, 18, 19, 21, 30, 31, 35, and 36 compose an adult responsibilities factor; values 1, 2, 3, 8, 9, 13, and 16 compose a lifestyle goals factor; and values 5, 10, 15, 20, 22, 23, and 28 compose a remove tension factor (Munson and McQuarrie 1988).

Values 3, 10, 11, 14, 15, 17, and 18 represent the self-actualization aspect, and values 1, 2, 9, 13, and 16 represent the hedonism aspect of the self-actualization/hedonism dimension of the terminal values. Values 5, 6, and 8 represent the idealism dimension, and values 4, 7, and 12 represent the security dimension of the terminal values (Crosby et al. 1990). Values 1-3, 5, 10-13, and 18 represent the self-direction dimension of the instrumental values. Values 4, 5, and 15-17 represent the conformity dimension, and values 7-9 and 14 represent the virtuousness dimension of the instrumental values identified by Crosby et al. (1990).

APPENDIX TO GENERAL VALUES

Another value assessment technique has been proposed by Hofstede (1980). Through a lengthy survey of work-related values over 53 cultures (similar in form to VALS), Hofstede identified four value dimensions related to basic anthropological/societal issues (Hofstede and Bond 1984, pp. 419-420): power distance, uncertainty avoidance, individualism vs. collectivism, and masculinity vs. femininity.

> *Power distance* is the extent to which less powerful members of institutions and organizations accept that power is distributed unequally. The basic anthropological/societal issue that "power distance" relates to is social inequality and the amount of authority of one person over others.

> *Uncertainty avoidance* is the extent to which people feel threatened by ambiguous situations and have created beliefs and institutions that try to avoid these. This dimension is related to the way a society deals with conflicts and aggression, and, as the last resort, with life and death.

> *Individualism vs. collectivism*: Individualism is viewed as a situation in which people are supposed to look after themselves and their immediate family only, and collectivism is viewed as a situation in which people belong to in-groups and are opposed to look after them in exchange for loyalty. This dimension reflects a bipolar continuum and is related to the individual's dependence on the group, or his or her self-concept as "I" or "we."

> *Masculinity vs. femininity*: Masculinity is defined as a situation in which the dominant values in society are success, money, and things. Its opposite, femininity, is defined as a situation in which the dominant values in society are caring for others and the quality of life. The anthropological-societal issue to which this dimension relates is the choice of social sex roles and its effects on one's self-concept. These value dimensions show correspondence with the Rokeach values. Though not extensively used in the U.S. marketing/consumer behavior literature, the Hofstede values have seen use in the cross-cultural psychology literature. The interested reader is referred to the following sources.

Sources: Hofstede, Geert. (1980). *Culture's Consequences: International Differences in Work-Related Values.* Beverly Hills, CA: Sage.

Hofstede, Geert, and Michael H. Bond. (1984). "Hofstede's Culture Dimensions: An Independent Validation Using Rokeach's Value Survey." *Journal of Cross-Cultural Psychology*, *15*, 417-433.

Though not a specific personality assessment procedure, a "laddering" technique that ranks the values associated with product attributes has also been proposed. Specifically, laddering refers to an in-depth, one-on-one interviewing technique used to develop an understanding of how consumers translate the attributes of products into meaningful associations with respect to self, following Means-End Theory (e.g., Guttman 1982, 1984; Reynolds and Guttman 1988). For example, a typical laddering format employs a series of direct probes such as "Why is that (attribute, product) important to you?," where the goal is to determine linkages between key perceptual elements across the range of product attributes, consequences of purchase, and values. The networks or "ladders" constructed represent combinations of elements that serve as the basis for distinguishing between and among products in a given product class. The above description is an overly simplistic and brief one. The interested reader is referred to the following sources.

Sources: Guttman, Jonathan. (1982). "A Means-End Chain Model Based on Consumer Categorization Processes." *Journal of Marketing*, *46*, 60-72.

Guttman, Jonathan. (1984). "Analyzing Consumer Orientations Toward Beverages Through Means-End Chain Analysis." *Psychology & Marketing*, *3/4*, 23-43.

Reynolds, Thomas J., and Jonathan Guttman. (1988). "Laddering Theory, Method, Analysis, and Interpretation." *Journal of Advertising Research*, *28*, 11-31.

VALUES RELATED TO ENVIRONMENTALISM
AND SOCIALLY RESPONSIBLE CONSUMPTION

DRINKING AND DRIVING: MOTIVATIONAL
TENDENCIES TO DRINK AND DRIVE: MTDD
(Lastovicka, Murray, Joachimsthaler, Bhalla, and Scheurich 1987)

Construct:	Drinking-driving behaviors are posited to be related to several motivational tendencies and AIOs (Lastovicka, Murray, Joachimsthaler, Bhalla, and Scheurich 1987). The MTDD was derived to determine if it can characterize young males most likely to drink and drive.
Description:	The MTDD scales are composed of five measures that tap related dimensions of the propensity to drink and drive. Each measure is composed of three 4-point Likert-type items scored from *strongly disagree* to *strongly agree* (a total of 15 items). Items can be summed within factors to form indices of each factor.
Development:	The procedures used to develop the measures generally followed guidelines found in the psychometric scaling literature. Preliminary data from convenience samples was used to select the 15 items. Then, via a phone survey of 703 18-24-year-old males, the factor structure, reliability, and validity of the measures were assessed.
Samples:	As stated above, convenience samples were used to develop the items. Then, a sample of 703 18-24-year-old males was used to examine the scale's psychometric properties and relationship to the likelihood of drinking and driving.
Validity:	Via factor analysis and a cross-validation procedure, the dimensionality and reliability of the items were examined. A five-factor solution established a "problem behaviors" factor, a "partying" factor, a "sensation-seeking" factor, a "macho" factor, and a "dissatisfaction with life" factor. Each factor was composed of three items. The Kaiser-Caffrey alpha estimates of the representativeness of the sampling domain of items were .78, .70, .74, .55, and .88 for factors 1 through 5, respectively. A cross-validation procedure (i.e., the stability of the factor solution across splits in the sample) showed coefficients ranging from .88 to .97 across the five factors.
	Means on the lifestyle factors and percentages of respondents reporting drinking and driving behaviors indicated relationships between the measures and drinking-driving behaviors (Lastovicka et al. 1987, Table 2, p. 260).
Scores:	Means on the lifestyle factors by various behavioral-based clusters are reported in Table 2. These means are based on a K-means clustering solution (Lastovicka et al. 1987, p. 260).
Source:	Lastovicka, John L., John P. Murray, Jr., Erich A. Joachimsthaler, Gaurav Bhalla, and Jim Scheurich. (1987). "A Lifestyle Typology to Model Young Male Drinking and Driving." *Journal of Consumer Research, 14,* 257-263.
	© 1987 by University of Chicago Press. Scale items taken from Table 1 (p. 259). Reprinted with permission.
Other evidence:	N/A
Other sources:	N/A
References:	N/A

DRINKING AND DRIVING: MOTIVATIONAL
TENDENCIES TO DRINK AND DRIVE: MTDD
(Lastovicka, Murray, Joachimsthaler, Bhalla, and Scheurich 1987)

1. I frequently skipped classes in high school.

2. I have been suspended from school for fighting on more than one occasion.

3. Except for times when I was sick, I hardly ever missed a day of school.*

4. It seems like no matter what my friends do on a weekend, we almost always end up at a bar getting smashed.

5. A party wouldn't be a party without some liquor.

6. I've been drunk at least five times this month.

7. Taking chances can be fun.

8. I would like to drive a race car.

9. I like to speed in my car.

10. If someone gives me a hard enough time, I'll punch him.

11. It's important for me to act and dress like I'm a tough guy.

12. There should be a gun in every home.

13. My life appears to be coming apart at the seams.

14. I feel like I'm getting a raw deal out of life.

15. Overall, I'd say I'm very happy.*

NOTES: *Denotes reverse scoring. Items 1 to 3 compose the "problem behaviors" factor, items 4 to 6 compose the "partying" factor, items 7 to 9 compose the "sensation-seeking" factor, items 10 to 12 compose the "macho" factor, and items 13 to 15 compose the "dissatisfaction with life" factor.

ENVIRONMENTALLY RESPONSIBLE CONSUMERS: ECOSCALE
(Stone, Barnes, and Montgomery 1995)

Construct: Stone, Barnes, and Montgomery (1995) posited five dimensions of consumer environmental responsibility: (a) consumer knowledge and awareness, (b) consumer desire and willingness to act, (c) consumer ability to act, (d) consumer opinions and attitudes concerning the environment, and (e) consumer behavior toward the environment. "Consumer Environmental Responsibility" is formally defined as "a state in which a person expresses an intention to take action directed toward remediation of environmental problems, acting not as an individual consumer with his/her own economic interests, but through a citizen consumer concept of societal-environmental well-being. Further, this action will be characterized by awareness of environmental problems, knowledge of remedial alternatives best suited for alleviation of the problem, skill in pursuing his or her own chosen action, and possession of a genuine desire to act after having weighed his/her own locus of control and determining that these actions can be meaningful in alleviation of the problem" (Stone et al. 1995, p. 601).

Description: Though five dimensions were originally hypothesized (see "Construct" above), the ECOSCALE has seven dimensions comprising 31 items. All items are scored on 5-point scales ranging from *strongly disagree* to *strongly agree*, or ranging from *never* to *always*. Item scores can be summed within each dimension to form dimension indices, or all 31 item scores can be summed to form one overall ECOSCALE composite.

Development: After a literature review and construct definition, 50 items were generated to reflect the domain of the construct. A group of university professors further examined the items for content validity. Exploratory factor analyses and item analyses were used to derive the final form of the scale, and confirmatory factor analyses were used to assess the dimensionality of each of the seven ECOSCALE dimensions. Estimates of reliability and validity were also offered.

Samples: A sample of $n = 238$ undergraduate students was used to develop the ECOSCALE, and a sample of $n = 215$ college students was used to examine dimensionality and validity.

Validity: Exploratory factor analyses extracted the seven factors (dimensions) of the ECOSCALE that accounted for 86.3% of the variance in the data. Factor loadings (within dimension) ranged from .541 to .956 across the seven dimensions. Item-to-total correlations (within dimension) ranged from .313 to .726 across the seven dimensions. One estimate of internal consistency was offered. The coefficient alpha for the entire 31-item ECOSCALE was .929. (All of these estimates pertain to the $n = 238$ sample.)

With the $n = 215$ sample, seven 1-factor confirmatory models corresponding to the seven dimensions of the ECOSCALE were estimated. Each model showed adequate levels of fit, offering evidence for each dimension's unidimensionality (see Stone et al., Table 4, pp. 609-610). Zero-order correlations among the seven dimensions ranged from .01 to .46. (Except for the .01 correlation, all correlations between ECOSCALE dimensions were significant.) As evidence of predictive validity, the seven ECOSCALE dimensions were correlated with measures of recycling, boycotting products unfriendly to the environment, making lifestyle changes, making personal sacrifices, educating others, and changing political strategy. Thus, a total of 42 correlations were computed. These correlations ranged from .05 to .40. All these correlations were reported to be significant.

Scores: Neither mean nor percentage scores were reported.

Source: Stone, George, James H. Barnes, and Cameron Montgomery. (1995). "ECOSCALE: A Scale for the Measurement of Environmentally Responsible Consumers." *Psychology & Marketing*, *12*, 595-612.

© 1995 by John Wiley & Sons, Inc. Scale items taken from Table 2 (pp. 603-604). Adapted by permission of John Wiley & Sons, Inc.

Other evidence: N/A

Other source: N/A

Reference: N/A

ENVIRONMENTALLY RESPONSIBLE CONSUMERS: ECOSCALE
(Stone, Barnes, and Montgomery 1995)

Opinions and Beliefs Dimension Items

1. The burning of the oil fields in Kuwait, the meltdown in Chernobyl, and the oil spill in Alaska are examples of environmental accidents whose impact is only short term.

2. The United States is the biggest producer of fluorocarbons, a major source of air pollution.

3. The earth's population is now approaching 2 billion.

4. Excess packaging is one source of pollution that could be avoided if manufacturers were more environmentally aware.

5. Economic growth should take precedence over environmental considerations.

6. The earth's resources are infinite and should be used to the fullest to increase the human standard of living.

Awareness Dimension Items

7. The amount of energy I use does not affect the environment to any significant degree.

8. This country needs more restrictions on residential development (construction of a new mall on farmland, new subdivisions, etc.)

9. If I were a hunter or fisherman, I would kill or catch more if there were no limits.

10. In order to save energy, this university should not heat the pool during the winter.

Willing to Act Dimension Items

11. I attend environmental/conversation group meetings (Green Peace, Ducks Unlimited, etc.)

12. I have started/joined consumer boycott programs aimed at companies that produce excess pollution.

13. Whenever no one is looking I litter.

14. Wearing exotic furs and leather is not offensive.

Attitude Dimension Items

15. One of the primary reasons for concern in destruction of the ozone layer is its ability to screen ultraviolet radiation.

16. There is nothing the average citizen can do to help stop environmental pollution.

17. My involvement in environmental activities today will help save the environment for future generations.

18. I would not car pool unless I was forced to. It is too inconvenient.

Action Taken Dimension Items

19. I turn in polluters when I see them dumping toxic liquids.

20. I have my engine tuned to help stop unwanted air pollution.

21. I have my oil changed at installations which recycle oil.

22. The earth is so large that people have little effect on the overall environment.

23. People who litter should be fined $500 and be forced to work on road crews and pick up garbage.

Ability to Act Dimension Items

24. The EPA stands for "Environmental Planning Association" and it is responsible for matters dealing with protection of the environment.

25. I do not purchase products that are known to cause pollution.

26. I vote for pro-environmental politicians.

27. I cut up plastic rings around six-packs of soft drinks.

Knowledge Dimension Items

28. Ivory is a hard white stone that when polished can be used in making piano keys.

29. Acid rain affects only Canada.

30. It is no use worrying about environmental issues: I can't do anything about them anyway.

31. I would describe myself as environmentally responsible.

NOTES: According to the authors, items in the "Willingness to Act," "Action Taken," and "Ability to Act" dimensions are scored on 5-point *never* to *always* scales. All other items are scored on 5-point *strongly disagree* to *strongly agree* scales. Though not specified by the authors, it would seem that items 1, 3, 5, 6, 7, 9, 13, 14, 16, 18, 22, 24, 28, 29, and 30 require reverse scoring such that a higher score reflects a greater level of environmental responsibility. Also, item 9 is specified for "males" only, and item 14 is specified for "females" only.

HEALTH CONSCIOUSNESS SCALE: HCS
(Gould 1988)

Construct: As specified by the author, the Health Consciousness Scale (HCS) seems to tap an overall alertness, self-consciousness, involvement, and self-monitoring of one's health.

Description: The HCS is composed of nine items scored on 5-point scales ranging from 0 to 4. Though four factors relating to HCS were empirically identified (i.e., overall alertness [HA], self-consciousness [HCSC], involvement [HI], and self-monitoring [HSM] of one's health), item scores can be summed to form an overall HCS score ranging from 0 to 36.

Development: Using a sample of $n = 343$ adult respondents, the nine-item HCS was administered and checked for internal consistency and validity. Via confirmatory factor analyses, reliability analyses, and several correlational and mean-level difference tests, the psychometric properties of the HCS were examined.

Samples: One sample of $n = 343$ adult consumers from the northeastern United States responded to the HCS and other measures.

Validity: Confirmatory factor analyses revealed that a first-order 4-factor model and a higher-order model fit the data well. A decision was made to treat the nine HCS items as a single scale. A .93 coefficient alpha estimate of internal consistency was reported for the nine-item HCS. The total HCS score was split at the median to form two groups: high health consciousness and low health consciousness. Some evidence of validity for the HCS was found through t tests between these two groups across 40 health attitude statements. These tests revealed 17 significant differences ($p < .10$ or better).

Scores: Means (std. dev.) were reported for the four factors of the HCS. These scores were 6.44 (3.29) for HCSC, 3.78 (2.40) for HI, 5.51 (1.99) for HA, and 4.28 (2.25) for HSM.

Source: Gould, Stephen J. (1988). "Consumer Attitudes Toward Health and Health Care: A Differential Perspective." *Journal of Consumer Affairs*, 22, 96-118.
© 1988 by The University of Wisconsin Press. Scale items taken from Table 3 (p. 103). Used by permission of The University of Wisconsin Press.

Other evidence: N/A

Other sources: N/A

References: N/A

HEALTH CONSCIOUSNESS SCALE: HCS
(Gould 1988)

1. I reflect about my health a lot.

2. I'm very self-conscious about my health.

3. I'm generally attentive to my inner feelings about my health.

4. I'm constantly examining my health.

5. I'm alert to changes in my health.

6. I'm usually aware of my health.

7. I'm aware of the state of my health as I go through the day.

8. I notice how I feel physically as I go through the day.

9. I'm very involved with my health.

NOTES: Items are scored as 0 = *statement does not describe you at all*, 1 = *statement describes you a little*, 2 = *statement describes you about fifty-fifty*, 3 = *statement describes you fairly well*, and 4 = *statement describes you very well*. As noted before, though item scores were summed to form an overall HCS composite, four factors were identified. Items 1, 2, and 3 compose the HCSC factor, items 4 and 9 compose the HI factor, items 5 and 6 compose the HA factor, and items 7 and 8 compose the HSM factor.

LEISURE: SUBJECTIVE LEISURE SCALES: SLS
(Unger and Kernan 1983)

Construct: In their research, Unger and Kernan (1983) measure leisure from a subjective perspective. Most definitional discussions of leisure from this perspective relate leisure to free time, recreation, and play. From this theoretical base, Unger and Kernan (1983) propose six determinants of leisure: intrinsic satisfaction, perceived freedom, involvement, arousal, mastery, and spontaneity.

Intrinsic satisfaction: leisure is seen as an end unto itself rather than a means to an end.

Perceived freedom: leisure is viewed as free, that is, perceived as voluntary, without coercion or obligation.

Involvement: true leisure means total absorption in an activity, such that it is an escape from daily life.

Arousal: arousal (i.e., novelty seeking, exploration, and risk taking) is present in leisure pursuits.

Mastery: one has the opportunity to test oneself or to conquer the environment through leisure pursuits (i.e., mastery of the activity, mental or physical, is present).

Spontaneity: unlike obligatory events, leisure activities are not routine, planned, or anticipated.

Description: The SLS is a six-factor measure designed to assess the six determinants of leisure discussed above. A total of 26 items are used to measure the six determinants, and all items are scored on 6-point formats from *strongly disagree* (1) to *strongly agree* (6). Scores on items within each dimension can be summed to form indices of each dimension.

Development: Forty-two items were generated to reflect the six determinants of leisure. The items were checked for face validity by a panel of 10 marketing professors and Ph.D. students, resulting in 36 items retained. Various tests for reliability, validity, and factor structure were then performed on the remaining items to derive the final scales over two samples and six leisure scenarios.

Samples: Two samples were used in scale development. (Two other samples were also used to generate the leisure scenarios for validity testing but did not respond to the leisure items.) The first sample consisted of 132 students, and the second sample consisted of 160 nonstudent adults. Three other samples (n = 10, 200, and 123) were also used in preliminary stages (i.e., item editing and pretesting).

Validity: Using the student sample, responses to the 36 items were examined for internal consistency. Two items that decreased internal consistency (on the respective factors) were deleted. Principal components analysis was also used to trim the number of items. Items with loadings lower than .40 on any factor in three or more of the scenarios were deleted, resulting in the final 26-item, six-factor SLS. In the nonstudent sample, the SLS was checked for dimensionality and validity. With this sample, factor analysis revealed that the intrinsic satisfaction and perceived freedom dimensions were not distinct, and the arousal and mastery dimensions were not distinct, suggesting that the hypothesized dimensionality of the SLS requires further testing. Though reliability estimates were performed (i.e., coefficient alpha, split-halves), they were not reported in the article (Unger and Kernan 1983). Numerous concurrent, construct, and nomological validity tests, however, did show support for the validity of the SLS. For example, using the SLS factors as predictors across six different leisure scenarios produced multiple Rs ranging from .05 to .56, with most multiple Rs in the range of .30 and above (see Table 1, p. 389).

Scores: Mean or percentage scores were not reported.

Source: Unger, Lynette, and Jerome B. Kernan. (1983). "On the Meaning of Leisure: An Investigation of Some Determinants of the Subjective Experience." *Journal of Consumer Research*, 9, 381-392.

   © 1983 by University of Chicago Press. Scale items taken from Exhibit 3 (p. 387). Reprinted with permission.

Other evidence: N/A

Other sources: N/A

References: N/A

LEISURE: SUBJECTIVE LEISURE SCALES: SLS
(Unger and Kernan 1983)

Following are statements concerning the situation described below. For each statement, indicate whether you strongly agree, agree, somewhat agree, somewhat disagree, disagree, or strongly disagree **as the statement pertains to the way you feel about the situation**.

[SOME LEISURE RELATED SITUATION IS DESCRIBED HERE]

1. It is its own reward.

2. "Not because I have to but because I want to" would characterize it.

3. I feel like I'm exploring new worlds.

4. I feel I have been thoroughly tested.

5. I could get so involved that I would forget everything else.

6. I wouldn't know the day before that it was going to happen.

7. I enjoy it for its own sake, not for what it will get me.

8. I do not feel forced.

9. There is novelty in it.

10. I feel like I'm conquering the world.

11. It helps me forget about the day's problems.

12. It happens without warning or pre-thought.

13. Pure enjoyment is the only thing in it for me.

14. It is completely voluntary.

15. It satisfies my sense of curiosity.

16. I get a sense of adventure or risk.

17. It totally absorbs me.

18. It is a spontaneous occurrence.

19. I do not feel obligated.

20. It offers novel experiences.

21. I feel like a real champion.

22. It is like "getting away from it all."

23. It happens "out of the blue."

24. Others would not have to talk me into it.

25. It makes me feel like I'm in another world.

26. It is a "spur-of-the-moment" thing.

NOTES: Items 1, 7, and 13 are designed to measure intrinsic satisfaction. Items 2, 8, 14, 19, and 24 are designed to measure perceived freedom. Items 3, 9, 15, and 20 are designed to measure arousal. Items 4, 10, 16, and 21 are designed to measure mastery. Items 5, 11, 17, 22, and 25 are designed to measure involvement. Items 6, 12, 18, 23, and 26 are designed to measure spontaneity.

SOCIAL ISSUES: ANXIETY WITH SOCIAL ISSUES
(Sego and Stout 1994)

Construct: Anxiety with social issues is viewed as a chronic emotional state directed at a social issue that can affect how individuals respond to messages about the issue. Though not hypothesized, four dimensions of anxiety with social issues were identified: (a) an "uncomfortable" factor assessing general societal concern, discomfort, and irritation with an issue; (b) a "tense" factor representing symptoms such as loss of appetite associated with an issue; (c) a "rational" factor assessing a cognitive dimension of a lack of an ability to think rationally about an issue; and (d) a "decisive" factor which assesses discouraging individuals from conversing about an issue, attending media reports about an issue, and intending to support an issue.

Description: A total of 15 items compose the four factors of anxiety with social issues scale. All items are scored on 5-point Likert-type scales ranging from *strongly disagree* to *strongly agree*. Item scores are summed within each factor to create indices for the uncomfortable, tense, rational, and decisive factors.

Development: Fifteen items were either orbitally generated by the authors or culled from existing measures. These items were subjected to principal component analyses using one sample. From this procedure, factors were derived and labeled. Estimates of validity were offered.

Sample: Undergraduate students ($n = 103$) responded to a survey containing the anxiety associated with social issues items. The two issues addressed were AIDS and recycling.

Validity: A four-factor principal component solution explained about 63% of the variance in the data. Factor loadings ranged from .480 to .825 (in absolute value) for a given respective factor. No estimates of internal consistency reliability were offered. Various tests of validity were offered. For example, using the factor scores of the uncomfortable, tense, rational, and decisive factors as predictors of "likelihood of conversing about a social issue," "likelihood of attending to media reports about an issue," and "intent to support an issue" in regression equations showed support for the scale's predictive validity. Nine of 12 regression coefficients for these factor scores were significant ($p < .05$). Furthermore, between 13% and 19% of the variance was explained in the dependent variables by the factor scores for the uncomfortable, tense, rational, and decisive factors.

Scores: Only mean-level factor scores were reported by the two different issues (AIDS and recycling) (Table 2, p. 604).

Source: Sego, Trina, and Patricia Stout. (1994). "Anxiety Associated With Social Issues: The Development of a Scale to Measure an Antecedent Construct." In Chris Allen and Deborah Roedder John (Eds.), *Advances in Consumer Research* (Vol. 21, pp. 601-606). Provo, UT: Association for Consumer Research.
© 1994 by the Association for Consumer Research. Scale items taken from Table 1 (p. 603). Reprinted with permission.

Other evidence: N/A

Other sources: N/A

References: N/A

SOCIAL ISSUES: ANXIETY WITH SOCIAL ISSUES
(Sego and Stout 1994)

"Uncomfortable" Items

1. The situation surrounding (ISSUE) makes me uncomfortable.

2. Discussing or thinking about (ISSUE) makes me irritable.

3. Sometimes I feel restless or jittery about problems associated with (ISSUE).

4. When I think about (ISSUE), sometimes I feel tense.

5. I get over-excited or "rattled" when I talk to others about (ISSUE).

"Tense" Items

1. I often feel anxious about (ISSUE).

2. I sometimes feel physical symptoms of nervousness or anxiety, such as "butterflies in my stomach," or rapid heartbeat, when I think about (ISSUE).

3. Sometimes I get so worried about (ISSUE) and I can not get it out of my head.

4. I worry a lot about problems associated with (ISSUE).

"Lack of Ability to Think Rationally" Items

1. I am able to think about problems associated with (ISSUE) in a rational manner.

2. I always have enough energy when faced with problems associated with (ISSUE).

3. I am usually steady and relaxed when I think about or discuss (ISSUE).

"Decisive" Items

1. I have difficulty thinking clearly or deciding what to do about (ISSUE).

2. When I think about (ISSUE) I become excited.

NOTES: Though not specified by the authors, it would seem that the "Rational" items require reverse coding to reflect a higher level of "irrationality."

SOCIALLY RESPONSIBLE CONSUMPTION BEHAVIOR: SRCB
(Antil and Bennett 1979; Antil 1984)

Construct: Socially responsible consumption is defined as those consumer behaviors and purchase decisions which are related to environmental and resource-related problems and are motivated not only by a desire to satisfy personal needs but also by a concern for the welfare of society in general (Antil 1984; Antil and Bennett 1979).

Description: The SRCB is composed of 40 Likert-type items (agree-disagree) scored on a 5-point basis. Scores on the items are summed to form an overall SRCB index. Thus, the scale is considered unidimensional, and the possible range of scores is 40 to 200.

Development: An initial pool of 138 items was developed from a number of relevant sources based on the definition of the construct. Using recommended scaling procedures that included item analysis, coefficient alpha, and factor analysis (across numerous samples described below), the final scale was derived.

Samples: A number of samples were used in the scale development process (Antil and Bennett 1979). An initial student sample (*n* = 444) was used for deleting ambiguous and redundant items. Item analysis based on this sample resulted in trimming the initial pool of 138 to 59 items. A second student sample (*n* = 321) was used to assess initial reliability and item-to-total correlations, resulting in 42 items being retained. A third nonstudent sample (*n* = 98) was used for reliability and item analysis, resulting in the final 40-item scale. Lastly, two nonstudent samples were used to examine the dimensionality, reliability, and validity of the final scale (*n* = 690 and *n* = 98 Sierra Club members) (Antil 1984).

Validity: The reliability, dimensionality, and validity of the final 40-item scale were assessed with the last two nonstudent samples as follows. Two measures of internal consistency were used to assess the scale's reliability. Guttman's Lambda 3 and Cronbach's alpha were .93 and .92, respectively.

Factor analysis indicated that a single factor underlies the dimension of the scale. The first factor accounted for 78.3% of the variance in a three-factor solution using the eigenvalue greater-than-one rule for retaining factors. Thus, evidence for the unidimensionality of the SRCB was found.

In addition, the SRCB demonstrated convergent and discriminant validity (via multitrait-multimethod analysis) when correlated with measures of traditional social responsibility and ecological concern. For example, the correlation between SRCB and social responsibility was .29, and the correlation between SRCB and ecological concern was .73. Mean score differences also offered evidence of known group validity. The mean score for the *n* = 736 sample (Antil and Bennett 1979) was 144.30, and the mean score for the Sierra Club sample (Antil 1984) was 168.50. The difference between these two means was statistically significant.

Scores: Mean scores for the final two validation samples were reported. For combined samples (*n* = 690 and *n* = 98), the overall mean of the scale was 144.50 (*SD* = 24.3). The mean score for the *n* = 736 sample was 144.30, and the mean score for the Sierra Club sample was 168.50. As stated above, the difference between these last two means was statistically significant.

Sources: Antil, John A., and Peter D. Bennett. (1979). "Construction and Validation of a Scale to Measure Socially Responsible Consumption Behavior." In Karl H. Henion II and Thomas C. Kinnear (Eds.), *The Conserver Society* (pp. 51-68). Chicago: American Marketing Association.

© 1979 by the American Marketing Association. Scale items taken from Appendix (pp. 63-66). Reprinted with permission.

Antil, John A. (1984, Fall). "Socially Responsible Consumers: Profile and Implications for Public Policy." *Journal of Macromarketing*, 18-39.

Other evidence: N/A

Other sources: N/A

References: N/A

SOCIALLY RESPONSIBLE CONSUMPTION BEHAVIOR: SRCB
(Antil and Bennett 1979; Antil 1984)

1. People should be more concerned about reducing or limiting the noise in our society.

2. Every person should stop increasing their consumption of products so that our resources will last longer.

3. The benefits of modern consumer products are more important than the pollution which results from their production and use.*

4. Pollution is presently one of the most critical problems facing this nation.

5. I don't think we're doing enough to encourage manufacturers to use recyclable packages.

6. I think we are just not doing enough to save scarce natural resources from being used up.

7. Natural resources must be preserved even if people must do without some products.

8. All consumers should be interested in the environmental consequences of the products they purchase.

9. Pollution is not personally affecting my life.*

10. Consumers should be made to pay higher prices for products which pollute the environment.

11. It genuinely infuriates me to think that the government doesn't do more to help control pollution of the environment.

12. Nonreturnable bottles and cans for soft drinks and beer should be banned by law.

13. I would be willing to sign a petition or demonstrate for an environmental cause.

14. I have often thought that if we could just get by with a little less there would be more left for future generations.

15. The Federal government should subsidize research on technology for recycling waste products.

16. I'd be willing to ride a bicycle or take a bus to work in order to reduce air pollution.

17. I would probably never join a group or club which is concerned solely with ecological issues.*

18. I feel people worry too much about pesticides on food products.*

19. The whole pollution issue has never upset me too much since I feel it's somewhat overrated.*

20. I would donate a day's pay to a foundation to help improve the environment.

21. I would be willing to have my laundry less white or bright in order to be sure that I was using a nonpolluting laundry product.

22. Manufacturers should be forced to used recycled materials in their manufacturing and processing operations.

23. I think that a person should urge his/her friends not to use products that pollute or harm the environment.

24. Commercial advertising should be forced to mention the ecological disadvantages of products.

25. Much more fuss is being made about air and water pollution than is really justified.*

26. The government should provide each citizen with a list of agencies and organizations to which citizens could report grievances concerning pollution.

27. I would be willing to pay a 5% increase in my taxes to support greater governmental control of pollution.

28. Trying to control water pollution is more trouble than it is worth.*

29. I become incensed when I think about the harm being done to plant and animal life by pollution.

30. People should urge their friends to limit their use of products made from scarce resources.

31. I would be willing to pay one dollar more each month for electricity if it meant cleaner air.

32. It would be wise for the government to devote much more money toward supporting a strong conservation program.

33. I would be willing to accept an increase in my family's total expenses of $120 next year to promote the wise use of natural resources.

34. Products which during their manufacturing or use pollute the environment should be heavily taxed by the government.

35. People should be willing to accept smog in exchange for the convenience of automobiles.*

36. When I think of the ways industries are polluting I get frustrated and angry.

37. Our public schools should require all students to take a course dealing with environmental and conservation problems.

38. I would be willing to stop buying products from companies guilty of polluting the environment even though it might be inconvenient.

39. I'd be willing to make personal sacrifices for the sake of slowing down pollution even though the immediate results may not seem significant.

40. I rarely ever worry about the effects of smog on myself and family.*

NOTE: *Denotes items that are reverse coded.

VOLUNTARY SIMPLICITY SCALE: VSS
(Leonard-Barton 1981; Cowles and Crosby 1986)

Construct: Voluntary simplicity is defined as the degree to which an individual selects a lifestyle intended to maximize his/her control over daily activities and to minimize his/her consumption and dependency (Leonard-Barton 1981). Five basic values underlie a voluntary simplicity lifestyle: material simplicity, self-determination, ecological awareness, human scale, and personal growth.

Material simplicity is non–consumption-oriented patterns of use.

Self-determination is a desire to assume greater control over destiny.

Ecological awareness is recognition of the interdependency of people and resources.

Human scale is a desire for smaller-scale institutions and technology.

Personal growth is a desire to explore and develop the inner life.

Description: The VSS is a multidimensional scale comprising 18 statements that assess the degree to which respondents engage in voluntary simplicity behaviors. Fourteen of the items provided by Leonard-Barton are scored on a 5-point basis on the degree to which a behavior is performed. Two of the items offer six response alternatives, and two are dichotomous (yes-no). Though exact scoring procedures are not offered, scores on the VSS can range up to a high of 90 (Leonard-Barton 1981).

Several versions of the scale are tenable, including 6-, 9-, and 14-item scales (Leonard-Barton 1981), and a version proposed by Cowles and Crosby (1986).

Development: Initially, the scale consisted of nine items; it was subsequently expanded to 19 items and then reduced to an 18-item format (Leonard-Barton 1981). Via a number of scaling procedures, including factor analysis and internal consistency reliability across several studies, the 9- and 19-item versions of the scale were derived. The samples and studies used to arrive at these versions are described below.

Samples: A number of samples were used in the scale development and validation process. The original 9-item version was tested on a sample from Palo Alto, California (n not reported). The expanded 19-item version was tested on data collected by Elgin and Mitchell (1977) with a sample of 423. This 19-item version was also tested on another sample ($n = 215$) of homeowners in California. (Half of this sample were users of solar energy in their home.) Lastly, the 18-item version was administered to 812 California homeowners (see Leonard-Barton 1981).

Validity: Reliability estimates of the 9- and 19-item versions of the scale ranged from alpha of .52 to alpha of .70. (These were the only reliability estimates reported by Leonard-Barton [1981]). It should be noted that these alpha estimates should be viewed with caution as the VSS is composed of six factors and the alphas reported above represent reliability estimates for the summed 9- and 19-item versions.

In the original article (Leonard-Barton 1981), factor analysis was used to determine the dimensionality of the scale, and across samples, a six-factor structure was found. The six factors underlying the five simplicity lifestyle values were labeled as (a) conservation through biking, (b) self-sufficiency in services, (c) recycling of resources, (d) self-sufficiency through making goods, (e) recycling of durable goods, and (f) closeness with nature. Leonard-Barton did not report direct estimates of factor internal consistency but provided factor loadings ranging from .31 to .87 across factors (Leonard-Barton 1981, p. 245).

The 18-item VSS was found to be positively related to education ($r = .16$) and negatively related to age ($n = 812$). The VSS was positively correlated with "mechanical ability" to do one's own repairs ($r = .15$ to .22 across the three versions), investment in energy-conserving equipment (beta = .40 in a regression equation), personal conviction to conserve energy ($r = .27$), and other energy-conserving practices like weather stripping and caulking doors and windows ($r = .21$, $n = 812$), thus providing evidence for the validity of the scale (Leonard-Barton 1981).

Scores: Mean scores on the 18-item version were reported by income level only for a sample of $n = 812$. For families with a 1978 reported household income of less then \$15,000, $M = 35.9$; for families with 1978 income between \$16,000 and \$35,000, $M = 38.2$; and for families with income \$46,000 or more, $M = 35.9$. These mean values were not statistically different from each other (Leonard-Barton 1981).

Sources: Leonard-Barton, Dorothy. (1981). "Voluntary Simplicity Lifestyles and Energy Conservation." *Journal of Consumer Research*, 8, 243-252.

© 1981 by University of Chicago Press. Scale items taken from Appendix (pp. 250-251). Reprinted with permission.

Cowles, Deborah, and Lawrence A. Crosby. (1986). "Measure Validation in Consumer Research: A Confirmatory Factor Analysis of the Voluntary Simplicity Lifestyle Scale." In Richard Lutz (Ed.), *Advances in Consumer Research* (Vol. 13, pp. 392-297). Provo, UT: Association for Consumer Research.

© 1986 by the Association for Consumer Research. Reprinted with permission.

Other evidence: Cowles and Crosby (1986) also examined the VSS with a sample of California and Colorado household consumer panel members ($n = 412$).

Cowles and Crosby (1986) reported composite reliability estimates (via LISREL) for the six factors originally found by Leonard-Barton, and for a three-factor model they proposed. These estimates are reported in Table 3.3.

TABLE 3.3

Factor	Leonard-Barton	Crosby and Cowles
Biking	.880	—
Self-sufficiency/services	.898	—
Recycling resources	.775	—
Recycling durable goods	.827	—
Self-sufficiency/goods	.777	—
Closeness to nature	.865	—
Material simplicity	—	.779
Self-determination	—	.938
Ecological awareness	—	.892

The three factors proposed by Cowles and Crosby are also labeled in Table 3.3. Cowles and Crosby found that the two factor structures fit the data equally well and suggested that their proposed three-factor measure of the VSS was an appropriate alternative to the 18-item, six-factor measure of Leonard-Barton.

Other sources: N/A

Reference: Elgin, Duane, and Arnold Mitchell. (1977, Summer). "Voluntary Simplicity." *The Co-Evolution Quarterly*, 2, 5-18.

VOLUNTARY SIMPLICITY SCALE: VSS
(Leonard-Barton 1981; Cowles and Crosby 1986)

Please indicate the degree to which you engage in each of the following behaviors by circling the appropriate response.

1. Make gifts instead of buying
   a. never
   b. occasionally
   c. frequently
   d. usually
   e. always

2. Ride a bicycle for exercise or recreation
   a. never
   b. once or twice a year
   c. once a month
   d. once a week
   e. every day

3. Recycle newspapers used at home
   a. never recycle newspapers
   b. recycle some
   c. recycle many
   d. recycle most
   e. recycle all newspapers

4. Recycle glass jars/bottles used at home
   a. never recycle jars/bottles
   b. recycle some
   c. recycle many
   d. recycle most
   e. recycle all jars/bottles

5. Recycle cans used at home
   a. never recycle cans
   b. recycle some
   c. recycle many
   d. recycle most
   e. recycle all cans

6. Family members or friends change the oil in the family car
   a. never
   b. sometimes
   c. frequently
   d. usually
   e. always

7. Have gotten instructions in skills to increase self-reliance, for example, in carpentry, car tune-up and repair, or plumbing
   a. never
   b. occasionally (informally from friends)
   c. frequently (informally from friends)
   d. have taken a class
   e. have taken more than one class

8. Intentionally eat meatless main meals
   a. never
   b. occasionally
   c. frequently
   d. usually
   c. always

9. Buy clothing at a secondhand store
   a. none of my clothes
   b. a few items
   c. many items
   d. most of my clothes
   e. all of my clothes

10. Buy major items of furniture or clothing at a garage sale (over $15)
    a. never
    b. rarely
    c. sometimes
    d. fairly often
    e. very often

11. Make furniture or clothing for the family
    a. none
    b. a few small items
    c. some items
    d. many items
    e. most of the clothing or most of the furniture

12. Have exchanged goods or services with others in lieu of payment with money, e.g., repairing equipment in exchange for other skilled work
    a. never
    b. have once
    c. have several times
    d. have many times
    e. do so whenever possible

13. Have a compost pile
    a. yes
    b. no

14. Contribute to ecologically oriented organizations
    a. never have
    b. did contribute once; do not now
    c. occasionally contribute now
    d. contribute regularly to one organization
    e. contribute regularly to two or more organizations
    f. do not know

15. Belong to a cooperative
    a. yes
    b. no

16. Grow the vegetables the family consumes during the summer season
    a. none
    b. some
    c. many
    d. most
    e. all

17. Ride a bicycle for transportation to work
    a. never
    b. occasionally
    c. frequently
    d. usually
    e. always
    f. do not know

18. Ride a bicycle on errands within two miles of home
    a. never
    b. occasionally
    c. frequently
    d. usually
    e. always

NOTES: The reduced six-item scale proposed by Leonard-Barton is composed of items 5, 6, 9, 11, 14, and 18. Leonard-Barton's proposed nine-item version is composed of items 3, 4, 5, 8, 9, 10, 12, 15, and 16. Her 14-item version includes all items *except* 8, 9, 17, and 18. The items composing the six factors found by Leonard-Barton are as follows: conservation through biking is composed of items 2, 17, and 18; self-sufficiency in services is composed of items 6, 7, and 12; recycling of resources is composed of items 3, 4, and 5; self-sufficiency through making goods is composed of items 1 and 11; recycling durable goods is composed of items 9 and 10; and closeness to nature is composed of items 4, 8, 13, 14, and 16. Item 15 did not load above .30 on any factor (Leonard-Barton 1981).

The three-factor structure proposed by Cowles and Crosby (1986) is as follows: material simplicity is composed of items 2, 9, 10, 17, and 18; self-determination is composed of items 1, 6, 7, 11, 12, 13, and 16; and ecological awareness is composed of items 3, 4, 5, 13, and 14. (Items 9 and 10 were allowed to load on the self-determination factor, and the composite reliabilities previously reported reflect the cross-loadings.)

VALUES RELATED TO MATERIALISM AND POSSESSIONS/OBJECTS

BELIEF IN MATERIAL GROWTH SCALE: BIMG
(Tashchian, Slama, and Tashchian 1984)

Construct:	Belief in material growth states that certain individuals place a high value on material comforts and conveniences, value economic effort, and may view actions taken for the common good as working against them (Tashchian, Slama, and Tashchian 1984). The BIMG was designed to measure these beliefs in relation to energy consumption.
Description:	The BIMG consists of 12 statements. (Scoring procedures were not mentioned, but it appears that the statements can be scored on a strongly disagree-strongly agree 5- or 7-point basis and then summed to form an overall BIMG index.) The measure is considered unidimensional (Tashchian et al. 1984).
Development:	The BIMG was developed as part of a larger project investigating attitudes toward energy conservation (Tashchian et al. 1984). In this study, three scales were developed, a scale to measure cynicism toward the mid-1970s energy crisis, a scale to measure belief in technology to solve energy problems, and the BIMG. The procedures just for the BIMG are described below.
	The procedures used to develop the BIMG generally adhere to the scale development process outlined in the psychometric literature. A pool of 50 items was generated to reflect the construct. Then, judges were asked to indicate the degree to which they felt each item was relevant to the definition of the construct on a 4-point scale (i.e., *highly relevant*, *moderately relevant*, *somewhat relevant*, and *not relevant at all*). Items which 75% of the judges agreed were either highly or moderately relevant to the construct were retained. Another measure of interjudge reliability indicated a high level of agreement among judges toward what items should be retained. Item-to-total correlations were used to trim the remaining items in such a fashion as to obtain a short 12-item scale. The 12 remaining items were assessed for reliability and validity within a larger study.
Samples:	A focus group of 25 student judges was used to trim the original pool of 50 items to a more manageable number. A sample of 365 adults was used to assess the reliability and validity of the scale using a systematic area sampling method.
Validity:	The overall coefficient alpha for the final 12-item BIMG was .82 (based on the sample of 365).
	The nomological validity of the scale was assessed by correlating it with a measure of environmental concern, and by examining mean differences on BIMG for high- and low-energy conservation groups. Results show that BIMG was negatively correlated with environmental concern ($r = -.509$), and mean differences show that the low conservation group scored higher on BIMG than the high conservation group. These results support the scale's validity (Tashchian et al. 1984).
Scores:	Mean or percentage scores for the scale were not reported. (Only ANOVA F values were reported for the high and low conservation groups.)
Source:	Tashchian, Armen, Mark E. Slama, and Roobian Tashchian. (1984). "Measuring Attitudes Toward Energy Conservation: Cynicism, Belief in Material Growth, and Faith in Technology." *Journal of Public Policy & Marketing*, 3(2), 134-148.
	© 1984 by American Marketing Association. Scale items taken from Table 4 (pp. 135-136). Reprinted with permission.
Other evidence:	N/A
Other sources:	N/A
References:	N/A

BELIEF IN MATERIAL GROWTH SCALE: BIMG
(Tashchian, Slama, and Tashchian 1984)

1. I always buy the best.

2. Material growth has an irresistible attraction for me.

3. Material growth makes for happier living.

4. Growth in material consumption helps raise the level of civilization.

5. Ownership and consumption of material goods has a high value for me.

6. More is better.

7. Increases in the amount of goods and services produced is not essential to my well being.*

8. I am reluctant to conserve material goods and services when it affects my daily life.

9. I would rather be perfectly comfortable in my home (neither warm or cold) than be slightly comfortable to conserve.

10. I have worked hard to get where I am—and am entitled to the "good things in life."

11. People should heat and cool their homes to the most comfortable temperatures regardless of what the government says.

12. The only way to let everyone know about my high status is to show it.

NOTE: *Denotes items that are reverse scored.

MATERIALISM MEASURE
(Richins 1987)

Construct: Richins (1987) describes materialism in terms of its role in consumer culture as "the idea that goods are a means to happiness; that satisfaction in life is not achieved by religious contemplation or social interaction, or a simple life, but by possession and interaction with goods" (p. 352). This view is consistent with extant writings on materialism (e.g., Belk 1984, 1985).

Description: The scale is a six-item, two-factor measure. The items are scored on a 7-point Likert-type format from *strongly disagree* to *strongly agree*. Item scores are summed within factors to form indices for each factor.

Development: Scale development procedures consisted of generating seven items that tapped the content domain of the construct. Then, based on factor analysis and coefficient alpha, the final six items were derived.

Samples: The sample consisted of a quota sample of 252 adults.

Validity: Factor analysis revealed that four items tapped a personal materialism factor (alpha = .73) and two items tapped a general materialism factor (alpha = .61). The two materialism factors were correlated with measures of perceived realism of TV ads, media exposure, and life satisfaction. The resulting correlations show modest support for the validity of the measure.

Scores: Mean and/or percentage scores were not reported.

Source: Richins, Marsha L. (1987). "Media, Materialism, and Human Happiness." In Melanie Wallendorf and Paul Anderson (Eds.), *Advances in Consumer Research* (Vol. 14, pp. 352-356). Provo, UT: Association for Consumer Research.

    © 1987 by the Association for Consumer Research. Scale items taken from Table 2 (p. 354). Reprinted with permission.

Other evidence: N/A

Other sources: N/A

References: Belk, Russell W. (1984). "Three Scales to Measure Constructs Related to Materialism: Reliability, Validity, and Relationships to Measures of Happiness." In Thomas C. Kinnear (Ed.), *Advances in Consumer Research* (Vol. 11, pp. 291-297). Provo, UT: Association for Consumer Research.

Belk, Russell W. (1985). "Materialism: Trait Aspects of Living in the Material World." *Journal of Consumer Research*, *12*, 265-280.

MATERIALISM MEASURE
(Richins 1987)

1. It is important to me to have really nice things.

2. I would like to be rich enough to buy anything I want.

3. I'd be happier if I could afford to buy more things.

4. It sometimes bothers me quite a bit that I can't afford to buy all the things I want.

5. People place too much emphasis on material things.*

6. It's really true that money can buy happiness.

NOTES: *Denotes reverse scoring. Items 1 through 4 compose the personal materialism factor, and items 5 and 6 the general materialism factor.

MATERIALISM–POST MATERIALISM SCALE
(Inglehart 1981)

Construct: Inglehart (1981) delineates materialism from post materialism as follows: Materialism gives top priority to physical sustenance and safety, while post materialism emphasizes belonging, self-expression, and the quality of life. This delineation is based on a value shift from materialism to post materialism from World War II to the early 1980s. This value shift has conceptual roots in two key hypotheses (Inglehart 1981, p. 881):

Scarcity hypothesis: An individual's priorities reflect the socioeconomic environment—one places the greatest subjective value on those things that are in relatively short supply.

Socialization hypothesis: The relationship between socioeconomic environment and value priorities is not one of immediate adjustment—a substantial time lag is involved, for, to a large extent, one's basic values reflect the conditions that prevailed during one's preadult years.

Description: The materialism–post materialism scale is composed of 12 items, 6 designed to tap materialism (as defined above) and 6 designed to tap post materialism. Scoring procedures for the items are sketchy. Respondents are asked what they personally consider the most important goals among the 12 items and then are classified as exclusively materialist, exclusively post materialist, or a "mixed" type (a combination of the two). Scores are then reported as the percentage of respondents falling into each category across a number of cross-classification variables. In one sample, respondents were asked to rank order their priorities as to the 12 items. Thus, it seems that a rank order scoring procedure is also tenable. A reduced, four-item version of the scale also has seen use.

Development: Little information as to scale development was provided. Statements were generated to tap the materialism–post materialism construct and administered to several cross-cultural samples over numerous time periods. Validity for the measure is offered via several cross-classification variables and percentage scores on the scale.

Samples: Samples included representative samples from several Western nations including Britain, France, West Germany, Belgium, Italy, the Netherlands, Luxembourg, Ireland, Denmark, and the United States, as well as Japan. Longitudinal data was collected across several time periods including 1970- 1979, 1974-1976, and 1976-1979. Also, a sample of 742 candidates for seats in the European parliament was included. Other sample sizes are reported in Tables 4, 6, and 8 of Inglehart (1981). For example, pooled data from nine European Community nations classified 18,292 respondents as materialists, 26,694 respondents as "mixed," and 6,098 respondents as post materialists (Inglehart 1981, Table 4, p. 891).

Validity: Though few classic estimates of reliability (i.e., test-retest correlations, coefficient alpha) were offered, the materialism–post materialism scale showed evidence of discriminant validity. First, for the sample of 742 parliament candidates, a principal components analysis revealed two distinct a priori dimensions as the six items to tap materialism loaded on one factor and the six items designed to measure post materialism loaded on another factor. Second, across most of the cross-classification variables, those respondents who gave top priority to one materialist goal also gave top priority to other materialist items, and likewise, those respondents who gave top priority to one post materialist goal also gave top priority to other post materialist items.

Numerous cross-classifications of the scale with a number of demographic and personality variables show evidence for the scale's validity. These cross-classification variables include age, country, support for and resistance to social change, protest potential, occupation, and support for nuclear power.

Scores: Scores are primarily reported as the percentage of respondents categorized as materialists, post materialists, and "mixed" across numerous cross-classification variables and numerous time periods. Table 4 (p. 891) shows pooled data from nine European Community nations that classified 18,292 respondents as materialists, 26,694 respondents as "mixed," and 6,098 respondents as post materialists. Several other tables offer breakdowns across other variables.

Source: Inglehart, Ronald. (1981). "Post-Materialism in an Environment of Insecurity." *American Political Science Review*, 75, 880-900. Scale items taken from p. 884.

Other evidence: N/A

Other sources: N/A

References: N/A

MATERIALISM–POST MATERIALISM SCALE
(Inglehart 1981)

1. Maintain order in the nation.

2. Give people more say in the decisions of the government.

3. Fight rising prices.

4. Protect freedom of speech.

5. Maintain a high rate of economic growth.

6. Make sure the country has strong defense forces.

7. Give people more say in how things are decided at work and in their community.

8. Try to make our cities and countryside more beautiful.

9. Maintain a stable economy.

10. Fight against crime.

11. Move toward a friendlier, less impersonal society.

12. Move toward a society where ideas count more than money.

NOTES: Items 1, 3, 5, 6, 9, and 10 tap materialism, while the remaining items measure post materialism. Items 1 though 4 compose the four-item version of the scale.

MATERIALISM SCALES
(Belk 1984, 1985)

Construct: Materialism is defined as the importance a consumer attaches to worldly possessions. At the highest level of materialism, such possessions assume a central place in a person's life and are believed to provide the greatest sources of satisfaction and dissatisfaction (Belk 1984, 1985). Furthermore, Belk identifies three subtraits of materialism: possessiveness, nongenerosity, and envy.

Possessiveness is defined as the inclination and tendency to retain control or ownership of one's possessions.

Nongenerosity is defined as an unwillingness to give possessions or share possessions with others.

Envy is defined as the displeasure and ill will at the superiority of another person in happiness, success, reputation, or the possession of anything desirable.

Description: The Belk materialism scale is composed of 24 statements designed to measure the three subtraits alluded to above. The items are scored on 5-point Likert-type scales from *agree* to *disagree*. Item scores are summed within each subtrait to form an overall score for each subtrait, and all 24 items can be summed to form an overall index of materialism. The scales consist of nine items for possessiveness, seven items for nongenerosity, and eight items for envy.

Development: Based on the conceptual domains identified for materialism and its subtraits, initial pools of 30 to 35 items were generated for each subtrait. Through factor analysis, item-to-total correlations, and other measures of internal consistency, seven to nine items were selected for each subtrait based on a student sample of 237 (Belk 1984).

Samples: Two samples were used by Belk (1984) to initially examine the reliability and validity of the scales. For developing the scales, a student sample of 237 was used. Through a number of statistical procedures, the final measures were derived. Belk (1984) also used another larger sample composed of both students and nonstudents ($n = 338$) to validate the scale.

In another sample used to assess mean differences in materialism by generation, 99 subjects from 33 different families responded to the scales (Belk 1985).

Validity: A number of reliability and validity estimates are reported for the scales. In the Belk (1984) study, coefficient alpha estimates for the possessiveness, nongenerosity, and envy subscales were .68, .72, and .80, respectively, for the student sample ($n = 237$). The overall summed scale (24 items) had an alpha of .73. For the larger sample ($n = 338$), these estimates were .57 for possessiveness, .58 for nongenerosity, .64 for envy, and .66 for the overall summed 24-item scale. Based on a subsample of 48 students (from the 338 sample), test-retest reliability estimates were .87 for possessiveness, .64 for nongenerosity, .70 for envy, and .68 for the overall scale. By using multitrait-multimethod analysis, behavioral and photo indices of materialism were correlated with the materialism scales. In these analyses, Belk (1984) found the scales to have adequate levels of convergent and discriminant validity. Also, all three materialism measures were found to be negatively correlated with measures of happiness and satisfaction in life (i.e., −.26 and −.24, respectively). In sum, the original Belk study showed support for the validity of the scale.

Scores: Mean scores for the summed 24-item scale and the original three subtraits are reported for the $n = 338$ sample (Belk 1984, 1985). The mean for the overall scale was 73.4. The means for the possessiveness, nongenerosity, and envy subtraits were 32.86, 18.74, and 21.74, respectively. Mean scores are further broken down by occupation in Belk (1984, p. 294). Belk (1985, p. 271) also reports mean scores for the overall scale and the three original subtraits by family generation.

Sources: Belk, Russell W. (1984). "Three Scales to Measure Constructs Related to Materialism: Reliability, Validity, and Relationships to Measures of Happiness." In Thomas C. Kinnear (Ed.), *Advances in Consumer Research* (Vol. 11, pp. 291-297). Provo, UT: Association for Consumer Research.

    © 1984 by the Association for Consumer Research. Scale items taken from Table 1 (p. 292). Reprinted with permission.

Belk, Russell W. (1985). "Materialism: Trait Aspects of Living in the Material World." *Journal of Consumer Research, 12*, 265-280.

    © 1985 by University of Chicago Press. Scale items taken from Exhibit 1 (p. 270).

Other evidence: In a cross-cultural context, Ger and Belk (1990) looked at a sample of 405 students from several different countries (i.e., Germany, England, France, the United States, and Turkey). Ger and Belk (1990) modified and administered the scale cross-culturally and, based on factor analyses, found a fourth dimension, "tangiblization." Coefficient alpha estimates for the four subscales and total scale were reported for the combined sample and by country subsample. For the combined sample ($n = 405$), alpha estimates were .67 for possessiveness, .69 for nongenerosity, .52 for envy, .56 for tangiblization, and .58 for the overall scale. (See Ger and Belk [1990, p. 188] for alpha estimates by country.) Furthermore, the four subscales were correlated with an index assessing the degree to which 20 products/services were viewed as necessities versus luxury items. The pattern of correlations supported the validity of the scales. For example, correlations of the possessiveness, nongenerosity, envy, and tangiblization factors with the number of items viewed as necessities were .18, −.13, .25, and .10, respectively. Ger and Belk (1990, p. 189) also report mean scores by country for the entire scale and all four subtraits.

    In another study, Ellis (1992) examined the dimensionality of Belk's scale by estimating numerous competing factor structures based on a sample of 148 respondents. Ellis concluded that a three-factor structure (i.e., possessiveness, nongenerosity, and envy) appeared to offer the best specification of the materialism items. Although internal consistency estimates were not provided, individual item-to-factor loadings were (see Table 2), and the correlations among the three factors ranged from −.032 to .431.

    More recently, Micken (1995), using a sample of $n = 278$ adults from a Mid-Atlantic Metropolitan Statistical Area (MSA), reported coefficient alpha estimates of .66, .38, .64, .50, and .65 for the overall scale, the possessiveness subscale, the nongenerosity subscale, the envy subscale, and the "preservation" (i.e., "tangibility") subscale, respectively (see "Notes"). Furthermore, a factor structure based on the four subdimensions and their intended items found very limited support with Micken's data. Micken also reports few significant correlations between Belk's measures and measures of education, age, gender, and income. In sum, she questions some of the psychometric properties of the scale.

Other sources: Ellis, Seth R. (1992). "A Factor Analytic Investigation of Belk's Structure of the Materialism Construct." In John F. Sherry and Brian Sternthal (Eds.), *Advances in Consumer Research* (Vol. 19, pp. 688-695). Provo, UT: Association for Consumer Research.

Ger, Guliz, and Russell W. Belk. (1990). "Measuring and Comparing Materialism Across Countries." In Marvin E. Goldberg, Gerald Gorn, and Richard W. Pollay (Eds.), *Advances in Consumer Research* (Vol. 17, pp. 186-192). Provo, UT: Association for Consumer Research.

Micken, Kathleen. (1995). "A New Appraisal of the Belk Materialism Scale." In Frank Kardes and Mita Sujan (Eds.), *Advances in Consumer Research* (Vol. 22, pp. 398-405). Provo, UT: Association for Consumer Research.

References: N/A

MATERIALISM SCALES
(Belk 1984, 1985)

Possessiveness

1. Renting or leasing a car is more appealing to me than owning one.*

2. I tend to hang on to things I should probably throw out.

3. I get very upset if something is stolen from me, even if it has little monetary value.

4. I don't get particularly upset when I lose things.*

5. I am less likely than most people to lock things up.*

6. I would rather buy something I need than borrow it from someone else.*

7. I worry about people taking my possessions.

8. When I travel, I like to take a lot of photographs.

9. I never discard old pictures or snapshots.

Nongenerosity

10. I enjoy having guests stay in my home.*

11. I enjoy sharing what I have.*

12. I don't like to lend things, even to good friends.

13. It makes sense to buy a lawnmower with a neighbor and share it.*

14. I don't mind giving rides to those who don't have a car.*

15. I don't like to have anyone in my home when I'm not there.

16. I enjoy donating things to charity.*

Envy

17. I am bothered when I see people who buy anything they want.

18. I don't know anyone whose spouse or steady date I would like to have as my own.*

19. When friends do better than me in competition, it usually makes me happy for them.*

20. People who are very wealthy often feel they are too good to talk to average people.

21. There are certain people I would like to trade places with.

22. When friends have things I can not afford it bothers me.

23. I don't seem to get what is coming to me.

24. When Hollywood stars or prominent politicians have things stolen, I really feel sorry for them.*

NOTES: *Denotes reverse scoring. Items 1, 3 through 6, 9, and 15 compose the Ger and Belk (1990) scale for possessiveness. In addition, the phrasing for item 1 was changed from "a car" to "a place to live." Items 7, 10, 11, 12, 16, and 19 make up the Ger and Belk nongenerosity scale. In addition, the phrasing for item 10 was changed from "guests" to "people I like." Items 17, 20, 21, and 23 make up the Ger and Belk envy scale, with an additional item that reads as follows: "If I have to choose between buying something for myself versus someone I love, I would prefer buying for myself."

Ger and Belk's "Tangiblization" measure is composed of items 2 and 8, along with the following three statements. (These three items below have recently been referred to as the "Preservation" subscale):

1. I have a lot of souvenirs.
2. I would rather give someone a gift that lasts than take them to dinner.
3. I like to collect things.

MATERIALISTIC ATTITUDES: MMA
(Moschis and Churchill 1978)

Construct: Materialistic attitude is defined as orientations emphasizing possessions and money for personal happiness and social progress (Moschis and Churchill 1978, p. 607).

Description: The MMA is composed of six Likert-type items scored on a 5-point disagree-agree basis. Item scores are summed to form an overall MMA index.

Development: The selection of items for the MMA was done by summing appropriate items, using item-to-total correlations to purify the measure and coefficient alpha to assess the resultant reliability of the measure (Moschis and Churchill 1978). These items were largely adapted from earlier research assessing racial differences in response to advertising to adolescents (Wackman, Reale, and Ward 1972).

Samples: The scale was developed and tested using a sample of 806 adolescents (ages 12 to 18).

Validity: The coefficient alpha reliability of the scale was reported to be .60. In addition, the MMA was significantly related to measures of social utility in regression analysis (beta = .16) as well as peer communication (beta = .12) and gender (–.20) (i.e., males held stronger materialistic attitudes).

Scores: Mean scores or percentages were not reported.

Source: Moschis, George P., and Gilbert A. Churchill, Jr. (1978). "Consumer Socialization: A Theoretical and Empirical Analysis." *Journal of Marketing Research*, *15*, 599-609.
   © 1978 by the American Marketing Association. Scale items taken from Appendix (p. 607). Reprinted with permission.

Other evidence: N/A

Other sources: N/A

Reference: Wackman, Daniel B., Greg Reale, and Scot Ward. (1972). "Racial Differences in Response to Advertising Among Adolescents." In Eli P. Rubenstein, George A. Comstock, and John P. Murray (Eds.), *Television in Day-to-Day Life* (pp. 543-551). Rockville, MD: U.S. Department of Health, Education, and Welfare.

MATERIALISTIC ATTITUDES: MMA
(Moschis and Churchill 1978)

1. It is really true that money can buy happiness.

2. My dream in life is to be able to own expensive things.

3. People judge others by the things they own.

4. I buy some things that I secretly hope will impress other people.

5. Money is the most important thing to consider in choosing a job.

6. I think others judge me as a person by the kinds of products and brands I use.

MATERIAL VALUES
(Richins and Dawson 1992)

Construct: Richins and Dawson (1992) view materialism as a consumer value in that it involves beliefs and attitudes so centrally held that they guide the conduct of one's life. Based on a review of the materialism literature in a variety of disciplines and on popular notions concerning materialism (Fournier and Richins 1991), three important themes concerning materialism were identified. These themes reflect the values consumers place on material goods and the roles these goods play in their lives:

Possessions as defining "success" is the extent to which one uses possessions as indicators of success and achievement in life, both in judging oneself and others.

Acquisition "centrality" is the extent to which one places possession acquisition at the center of one's life (i.e., this lends meaning to life and guides daily endeavors).

Acquisitions as the pursuit of "happiness" is the belief that possessions are essential to satisfaction and well-being in life.

Description: The scale consists of 18 items encompassing the three factors above (six items for "success," seven for "centrality," and five for "happiness"). The items are scored on a 5-point Likert-type format from *strongly agree* to *strongly disagree*. Item scores are summed within dimensions to form indices for each dimension, and they can be summed overall to form an overall materialism score.

Development: The development of the scale closely followed recommended psychometric scaling procedures. First, a convenience sample of 11 consumers was asked to describe the characteristics of materialistic people they knew in an open-ended format. Items were then generated based on these responses. Items were also generated from previously developed materialism scales and the materialism literature (Belk 1984, 1985; Richins 1987). More than 120 items were generated. These items were then screened for ambiguity and redundancy, resulting in further development samples examining either 50 or 66 potential materialism statements (Richins and Dawson 1992). From these, a pool of 48 items was retained for further analysis. This pool was trimmed to 30 items via exploratory factor analysis, reliability analysis, and social desirability testing. Through a number of other scaling procedures (i.e., factor analysis, reliability analysis, and validity checks) across several samples, a final scale consisting of 18 items was developed.

Samples: As stated above, a convenience sample of 11 consumers was used for item generation. Three samples of students ($n = 448$, 191, and 194) were used in preliminary tests of the scale (Richins and Dawson 1990). Four consumer samples were used in scale development, reliability, and validity checks. Sample sizes were 144, 250, 235, 205. A sample of 58 students was also used to assess test-retest reliability.

Validity: Through factor analyses and reliability analysis, three factors emerged. Over the last three samples, coefficient alpha estimates for the factors ranged from .71 to .75 for centrality, from .74 to .78 for the success factor, and from .73 to .83 for the happiness factor (Richins and Dawson 1992). Alpha for the overall 18-item scale ranged between .80 and .88. Test-retest reliability over a 3-week interval ($n = 58$) was .82, .86, .82, and .87 for the centrality, happiness, success, and overall scales, respectively.

  Numerous tests of validity were performed. First, the scales were examined for social desirability bias. The correlations between social desirability and the subscales and overall materialism scale ranged from $-.03$ to $-.13$, indicating virtually no contamination from social desirability bias.

  The materialism factors were also correlated with measures of life satisfaction, values, self-esteem, self-centeredness, and voluntary simplicity in some or all of the samples to examine the validity of the scales. Across samples, the patterns of correlations showed that the materialism factors exhibited construct validity (Richins and Dawson 1992). For example, the correlation between the overall scale and an item assessing voluntary simplicity was –.21, the correlation between the overall scale and Belk's (1985) nongenerosity scale was .25, and the correlation between the scale and a measure of self-esteem was –.12. These correlations support a priori hypotheses about the materialistic individual. A number of other mean difference tests also add support for the scale's validity.

Scores: Mean scores were reported for three samples for each subscale and the overall scale. For the centrality component, mean scores (std. dev.) ranged from 19.3 (4.0) to 19.8 (4.2). For the happiness component, mean scores ranged from 12.8 (4.1) to 13.3 (4.2). For the success component, mean scores ranged from 13.8 (4.1) to 14.7 (3.9), and for the overall combined scale, mean scores ranged from 45.9 (9.8) to 47.9 (10.2).

Source: Richins, Marsha L., and Scott Dawson. (1992). "Materialism as a Consumer Value: Measure Development and Validation." *Journal of Consumer Research, 19,* 303-316.

© 1992 by University of Chicago Press. Scale items taken from Table 3 (p. 310). Reprinted with permission.

Other evidence: Richins (1994) used the material values scale in a study related to the public and private meanings of possessions. Using samples of $n = 144$ and $n = 119$ adults, she reports coefficient alpha estimates for the entire 18-item scale of .86 and .84 for the two samples, respectively. After pooling the two samples and performing quartile splits on the 18-item scale, she found significant hypothesized differences between the top and bottom quartiles across numerous variables. For example, the "high" materialism group (top quartile) had valued possessions that were more socially visible, more expensive, and less likely to involve interpersonal associations than did the "low" materialism group (bottom quartile). Several other tests relating to materialism and private meanings of possessions supported the scales' validity.

Rindfleisch, Burroughs, and Denton (1997) report a coefficient alpha estimate of .87 for the 18-item material values scale. They report correlations of .21, –.17, .15, and .36 with measures of family structure, family resources, family stressors, and compulsive buying, respectively ($p < .05$ or better). They also report that material values were predicted by "family-related" variables in several mediator and moderator regression analyses.

Other sources: Richins, Marsha. (1994). "Special Possessions and the Expression of Material Values." *Journal of Consumer Research, 21,* 522-533.

Rindfleisch, Aric, James A. Burroughs, and Frank Denton. (1997). "Family Structure, Materialism, and Compulsive Buying." *Journal of Consumer Research, 23,* 312-325.

References: Belk, Russell W. (1984). "Three Scales to Measure Constructs Related to Materialism: Reliability, Validity, and Relationships to Measures of Happiness." In Thomas C. Kinnear (Ed.), *Advances in Consumer Research* (Vol. 11, pp. 291-297). Provo, UT: Association for Consumer Research.

Belk, Russell W. (1985). "Materialism: Trait Aspects of Living in the Material World." *Journal of Consumer Research, 12,* 265-280.

Fournier, Susan, and Marsha L. Richins. (1991). "Some Theoretical and Popular Notions Concerning Materialism." *Journal of Social Behavior and Personality, 6,* 403-414.

Richins, Marsha L. (1987). "Media, Materialism, and Human Happiness." In Melanie Wallendorf and Paul Anderson (Eds.), *Advances in Consumer Research* (Vol. 14, pp. 352-356). Provo, UT: Association for Consumer Research.

Richins, Marsha L., and Scott Dawson. (1990). "Measuring Material Values: A Preliminary Report on Scale Development." In Marvin E. Goldberg, Gerald Gorn, and Richard W. Pollay (Eds.), *Advances in Consumer Research* (Vol. 17, pp. 169-175). Provo, UT: Association for Consumer Research.

MATERIAL VALUES
(Richins and Dawson 1992)

Defining Success

1. I admire people who own expensive homes, cars, and clothes.

2. Some of the most important achievements in life include acquiring material possessions.

3. I don't place much emphasis on the amount of material objects people own as a sign of success.*

4. The things I own say a lot about how well I'm doing in life.

5. I like to own things that impress people.

6. I don't pay much attention to the material objects other people own.*

Acquisition Centrality

1. I usually buy only the things I need.*

2. I try to keep my life simple, as far as possessions are concerned.*

3. The things I own aren't all that important to me.*

4. I enjoy spending money on things that aren't practical.

5. Buying things gives me a lot of pleasure.

6. I like a lot of luxury in my life.

7. I put less emphasis on material things than most people I know.*

Pursuit of Happiness

1. I have all the things I really need to enjoy life.*

2. My life would be better if I owned certain things I don't have.

3. I wouldn't be any happier if I owned nicer things.*

4. I'd be happier if I could afford to buy more things.

5. It sometimes bothers me quite a bit that I can't afford to buy all the things I'd like.

NOTE: *Denotes items that are reverse scored.

NOSTALGIA SCALE
(Holbrook 1993)

Construct: Nostalgia refers to a longing for the past, a yearning for yesterday, or a fondness for possessions and activities associated with days of yore. Holbrook and Schindler (1991) define nostalgia as "a preference (general liking, positive attitude, or favorable affect) *toward objects* (people, places, or things) *that were more common* (popular, fashionable, or widely circulated) *when one was younger* (in early adulthood, in adolescence, in childhood, or even before birth)" (p. 330). Based on these views of nostalgia, Holbrook (1993) developed an index to measure nostalgia.

Description: The Nostalgia Scale is composed of eight items scored on 9-point Likert-type scales ranging from *strong disagreement* (1) to *strong agreement* (9). Item scores can be summed to form an overall score of nostalgia.

Development: Twenty statements were originally generated to represent the domain of the construct. Ten of these items were reverse coded. Exploratory and confirmatory factor analyses, using two samples and "preference for movies" as the stimulus object, were performed. These procedures were used to derive the final eight-item Nostalgia Scale. Assessment of internal consistency and numerous tests of validity were offered.

Samples: Two samples were used to develop, refine, and test the psychometric properties of the scale. The first sample ($n = 167$) was composed of graduate business students and was considered "age homogenous" (i.e., ages ranging from 21 to 34 years; 72 females and 95 males). The second sample ($n = 156$) was composed of nonstudent adults who were "age heterogeneous" (i.e., ages ranging from 21 to 85; 94 females and 62 males).

Validity: Initial confirmatory factor analyses showed a "poor fit" to the original 20 items representing nostalgia. A stepwise procedure was used to eliminate items with low loadings and items that threatened a unidimensional factor structure ($n = 167$). The eight items retained from this procedure showed adequate evidence of unidimensionality, as well as adequate coefficient alpha and construct reliability estimates of internal consistency of .78 (for a summated scale). Factor loadings ranged from .49 to .76 ($p < .01$). For the $n = 156$ sample, the eight-item, single-factor structure was replicated with coefficient alpha and construct reliability estimates of .73. Factor loadings ranged from .34 to .60 ($p < .01$). Preference spaces (i.e., "spatial dimension" analyses) for 62 Oscar-winning movies related to nostalgia showed support for the validity of the scale. Furthermore, the two studies demonstrated that the effects of age and nostalgia may operate independently in shaping consumer preference.

Scores: Factor scores of the Nostalgia Scale were used in the "spatial dimension" analyses. Neither mean nor percentage scores were reported.

Source: Holbrook, Morris. (1993). "Nostalgia and Consumption Preferences: Some Emerging Patterns of Consumer Tastes." *Journal of Consumer Research*, 20, 245-256.
    © 1993 by the University of Chicago. Scale items taken from Table 2 (p. 249) and Appendix (p. 255). Reprinted with permission.

Other evidence: Holbrook and Schindler (1994) used the Nostalgia Scale as a moderator of the effect of object-specific age on time-related patterns of preference. They found support for its moderating effect in numerous regression-based analyses. They also found evidence that the eight-item Nostalgia Scale was unidimensional with a construct reliability estimate of .68 (via confirmatory factor analysis).

Other source: Holbrook, Morris B., and Robert M. Schindler. (1994). "Age, Sex, and Attitude Toward the Past as Predictors of Consumer's Aesthetic Tastes for Cultural Products." *Journal of Marketing Research, 31,* 412-422.

Reference: Holbrook, Morris, and Robert M. Schindler. (1991). "Echoes of the Dear Departed Past: Some Work in Progress on Nostalgia." In Rebecca Holman and Michael R. Solomon (Eds.), *Advances in Consumer Research* (Vol. 18, pp. 330-333). Provo, UT: Association for Consumer Research.

NOSTALGIA SCALE
(Holbrook 1993)

1. They don't make 'em like they used to.

2. Things used to be better in the good old days.

3. Products are getting shoddier and shoddier.

4. Technological change will insure a brighter future.

5. History involves a steady improvement in human welfare.

6. We are experiencing a decline in the quality of life.

7. Steady growth of GNP has brought increased human happiness.

8. Modern business constantly builds a better tomorrow.

NOTES: Items 4, 5, 7, and 8 require reverse scoring. The original 20 items generated to reflect the construct can be found in the Appendix to Holbrook (1993, p. 255).

OBJECTS INCORPORATED INTO THE "EXTENDED SELF" SCALE
(Sivadas and Machleit 1994)

Construct: In developing their measure of objects incorporated into the extended self, Sivadas and Machleit (1994) draw primarily from Belk's (1988) view of extended self. The extended self is composed of the self plus possessions, and it contains the contribution of possessions to individual identity. The extended self is part of one's self-identity that is defined by possessions, body parts, gifts, souvenirs, and mementos. Furthermore, individuals consider objects as a part of who they are, and that a loss of self occurs if these objects or stolen or lost. Sivadas and Machleit developed a scale to assess the degree to which possessions have been incorporated into one's extended self.

Description: Their scale is composed of six items scored on 7-point *strongly disagree* to *strongly agree* scales. Item scores can be summed to form an overall scale score ranging from 6 to 42.

Development: Ten items were originally developed to tap the concept of object incorporated into the extended self. Then, using two samples and some recommended scaling procedures, the final six-item form of the scale was derived. Exploratory and confirmatory factor analyses, item analyses, and some correlational-based tests were conducted to derive the final form of the scale, test scale dimensionality and internal consistency, and offer evidence of validity.

Samples: Two undergraduate student samples of $n = 113$ and $n = 137$ were used to develop and validate the scale.

Validity: Across four product/person categories (i.e., car, shirt, gift, gift giver), a one-factor model representing the six items as a single dimension showed adequate levels of fit ($n = 137$), suggesting a unidimensional measure. Coefficient alpha estimates of internal consistency were .90, .90, .90, and .91, respectively, across the product/person categories listed above. Maximum likelihood factor loadings ranged from .536 to .938 across all product/person categories examined. Evidence of discriminant validity from measures of objects of personal relevance and objects of importance were also performed and supported. Evidence of nomological validity was offered by correlating the objects incorporated into the extended self scale with a measure of possession attachment, a measure of "taking good care of" possessions, and a measure pertaining to gift giving. Nine correlations were computed, and all were significant ($p < .01$), ranging from .26 to .68.

Scores: Neither mean nor percentage scores were reported.

Source: Sivadas, Eugene, and Karen Machleit. (1994). "A Scale to Measure the Extent of Object Incorporation in the Extended Self." In C. Whan Park and Daniel C. Smith (Eds.), *Proceedings of the American Marketing Association Winter Conference* (Vol. 5, pp. 143-149). Chicago: American Marketing Association.
© 1994 by the American Marketing Association. Scale items taken from Table 4 (p. 147). Reprinted with permission.

Other evidence: N/A

Other sources: N/A

Reference: Belk, Russell W. (1988). "Possessions and the Extended Self." *Journal of Consumer Research, 15*, 139-168.

OBJECTS INCORPORATED INTO THE "EXTENDED SELF" SCALE
(Sivadas and Machleit 1994)

1. My _____ helps achieve the identity I want to have.

2. My _____ helps me narrow the gap between what I am and what I try to be.

3. My _____ is central to my identity.

4. My _____ is part of who I am.

5. If my _____ is stolen from me I will feel as if my identity has been snatched from me.

6. I derive some of my identity from my _____.

POSSESSIONS: ATTACHMENT TO POSSESSIONS
(Ball and Tasaki 1992)

Construct: Attachment is defined as "the extent to which an object is owned, expected to be owned, or previously owned by an individual, is used by the individual to maintain his of her self-concept" (Ball and Tasaki 1992, p. 158). Attachment suggests that self-schemata is dependent on ownership of an object, and it includes both private and public facets of the self and possessions.

Description: The attachment scale is composed of nine items scored on 6-point Likert-type scales ranging from *disagree* (1) to *agree* (6). It seems that item scores could be summed to form an overall score for the scale ranging from 9 to 54. In the Ball and Tasaki (1992) article, though, a "weighted mean of attachment" was calculated across a number of product categories and stages of acquisition (p. 165).

Development: Originally, 10 items were generated to reflect the domain of the construct. One item was dropped due to low correlations with other items. The remaining nine items tapped the private and public aspects of attachment. One sample of $n = 331$ (188 college students and 143 other adults) was used for all facets of scale development and validation. Factor analyses, reliability analyses, and correlational and mean-level difference tests were used to examine scale dimensionality, reliability, and validity.

Sample: As stated above, a sample of 331 college students and other adults was used.

Validity: Factor analyses of the nine items revealed that a single factor accounted for 87% of the common variance in the data, offering some evidence for a single dimension. Coefficient alpha for the nine items was .93. Using the attachment scale as a dependent variable, several mean-level difference tests via ANOVA showed support for the scale's validity. Correlations of the attachment scale with measures of the emotional significance of possessions, materialism, and social desirability were .503, .159, and −.069, respectively. The first two correlations were significant ($p < .01$), and the last correlation was not, offering some evidence of nomological validity for the scale with no contamination from social desirability bias.

Scores: In Table 4 (p. 166) , 50 "weighted mean attachment" scores are offered across 10 products and 5 acquisition stages, as well as an overall mean score for each product across the stages combined.

Source: Ball, A. Dwayne, and Lori Tasaki. (1992). "The Role and Measurement of Attachment in Consumer Behavior." *Journal of Consumer Psychology*, *1*(2), 155-172.
  © 1992 by Lawrence Erlbaum Associates, Inc. Scale items taken from Table 1 (p. 162). Reprinted with permission.

Other evidence: N/A

Other sources: N/A

References: N/A

POSSESSIONS: ATTACHMENT TO POSSESSIONS
(Ball and Tasaki 1992)

1. Imagine for a moment someone making fun of your car. How much would you agree with the statement, "If someone ridiculed my car, I would feel irritated."

2. How much do you agree with the statement, "My car reminds me of who I am."

3. Picture yourself encountering someone who would like to get to know you. How much do you think you would agree with the statement, "If I were describing myself, my car would likely be something I mentioned."

4. Suppose someone managed to destroy your car. Think about how you would feel. How much do you agree with the statement, "If someone destroyed my car, I would feel a little bit personally attacked."

5. Imagine for a moment that you lost your car. Think of your feelings after such an event. How much do you agree with the statement, "If I lost my car, I would feel like I had lost a little bit of myself."

6. How much do you agree with the statement, "I don't really have too many feelings about my car."

7. Imagine for a moment someone admiring your car. How much would you agree with the statement, "If someone praised my car, I would feel somewhat praised myself."

8. Think for a moment about whether or not people who know you might think of your car when they think of you. How much do you agree with the statement, "Probably people who know me might sometimes think of my car when they think of me."

9. Imagine for a moment that you have lost your car. Think about going through your daily activities knowing that it is gone. How much do you agree with the statement, "If I didn't have my car, I would feel a little bit less like myself."

NOTES: Respondents were instructed to fill in the blanks mentally with the object being rated (e.g., a car above). Item 6 requires reverse scoring.

POSSESSION SATISFACTION INDEX: PSI
(Scott and Lundstrom 1990)

Construct: The idea of possession satisfaction is derived from the constructs of materialism and attitude toward money. It is felt that possession satisfaction is composed of aspects of these two concepts (Scott and Lundstrom 1990). (No formal definition of the construct is offered.)

Description: The PSI is composed of 20 Likert-type statements scored on 5-point *strongly disagree-strongly agree* formats. The scale is further composed of five factors assessing various aspects of possession satisfaction. Scores on the factors are derived by summing individual item scores within factors. An overall PSI score can be obtained by summing across all 20 items.

Development: Based on expert opinion, 9 items relating to money and 11 items relating to material possessions were generated. These items were pretested for discrimination on a student sample, and an adult sample was used to examine the factor structure and reliability of the measure.

Samples: A student sample (*n* not given) was used to pretest the 20 items. The main sample was drawn from a mall intercept approach using a quota sampling technique such that the sample would be representative of the geographic area considered in terms of demographic characteristics (*n* = 150).

Validity: Based on an initial factor analysis and a multitrait matrix analysis, it was found that the 9 items relating to money and the 11 items relating to material possessions were not distinct. Thus, all 20 items were combined to form one overall scale (PSI). A second factor analysis on the 20 items revealed five factors: (a) what possessions can do, (b) what possessions cannot do, (c) public image, (d) success equals possessions, and (e) more is better. Overall coefficient alpha for the scale was .80. (Alphas for the five factors were not reported.) No other estimates of validity were offered.

Scores: No mean or percentage scores were reported.

Source: Scott, Cliff, and William J. Lundstrom. (1990). "Dimensions of Possession Satisfactions: A Preliminary Analysis." *Journal of Satisfaction, Dissatisfaction and Complaining Behavior*, *3*, 100-104. Scale items taken from Table 4 (p. 102).

Other evidence: N/A

Other sources: N/A

References: N/A

POSSESSION SATISFACTION INDEX: PSI
(Scott and Lundstrom 1990)

1. Money makes life a lot easier.

2. I would rather own property than rent.

3. People with a lot of charge cards are important.

4. Wealthy people are respected.

5. Business has commercialized many meaningful holidays, such as Christmas.

6. Happiness is more important than money.*

7. When I shop, I usually make a purchase.

8. Money isn't everything.*

9. The more I have, the better I feel.

10. Given a choice between a well known brand and a store brand, I would take the store brand.*

11. It isn't important to own a nice car.*

12. It is very important to me how people perceive me.

13. I would take a job for less money if it were more self satisfying.*

14. People enjoy showing others their new possessions.

15. People rate other people by the value of their possessions.

16. Being a success means making a lot of money.

17. It is really true that money can buy happiness.

18. Most of the people I look up to are wealthy.

19. The more I have, the more I want.

20. In general, wealthier people are happier than poor people.

NOTES: *Denotes reverse scoring. Items 1 through 4 compose the "what possessions can do" factor, items 5 through 10 compose the "what possessions cannot do" factor, items 11 through 14 compose the "public image" factor, items 15 through 18 compose the "success equals possessions" factor, and items 19 and 20 compose the "more is better" factor.

APPENDIX TO MATERIALISM AND POSSESSIONS/OBJECTS

A scale related to materialism is the Money Attitude Scale: MAS (Yamauchi and Templer 1982). Given its copyrighted and proprietary nature, only a summary of the MAS is offered here.

MONEY ATTITUDE SCALE: MAS
(Yamauchi and Templer 1982)

Construct: The psychological aspects of money are felt to encompass three broad content areas (Yamauchi and Templer 1982): security, retention, and power-prestige.

Security concerns optimism, confidence, and comfort, and the reverse of pessimism, insecurity, and dissatisfaction associated with having or not having money.

Retention includes parsimony, hoarding, and obsessive personality traits.

Power-prestige comprises aspects of status, importance, superiority, and acquisition through money.

The MAS was designed to measure these content areas of attitude toward money.

Description: The MAS comprises 29 Likert-type statements utilizing *always* and *never* as endpoints (7-point items). Though originally designed to assess the three broad content areas described above, the MAS is considered a four-dimensional scale where scores on items within each dimension are summed to form indices of each dimension. An overall MAS score can also be derived by summing responses to all 29 items.

Development: Sixty-two items were originally generated to reflect the three content domains described above. Through factor analyses, this original pool of items was trimmed to 34 items reflecting five substantive factors. Items with loadings of .40 or above on a given factor were retained, and the five factors accounted for 33.6% of the variance. These five factors were (a) a power-prestige factor, (b) a retention-time factor, (c) a distrust factor, (d) a quality factor, and (e) an anxiety factor. Due to theoretical overlap with the power-prestige factor, the quality factor was deleted. Thus, the final scale consists of 29 items reflecting four factors. Coefficient alpha was used to assess the internal consistency of the MAS, and a number of validity estimates were also performed.

Samples   Two samples were used in scale development and validation. The first sample consisted of 300 adults from two California cities. With this sample, the final 29-item scale was derived from the original pool of 62 items. This sample was used to determine the factor structure, internal consistency, and test-retest reliability of the scale. A second sample of 125 students was used to further examine the reliability and test the validity of the scale.

Validity: Internal consistency estimates of the four factors composing the final scale were .80, .78, .73, and .69 for the power-prestige, retention-time, distrust, and anxiety factors, respectively. Corresponding test-retest reliability estimates for a subsample of 31 (from the original 300) were .88, .95, .87, and .88.

To examine the validity of the scale, the MAS, along with a number of other scales, was administered to a student sample of 125. The four factors of the MAS were found to be correlated with measures of Machiavellianism (.13 to .44), status concern (.23 to .48), time competence (−.04 to −.33), obsessional personality (.04 to .40), and anxiety (−.12 to .55), all in the predicted directions. Thus, evidence for the nomological validity of the MAS was found.

Scores: Mean scores (std. dev.) for the total scale and the four factors were reported for the first sample ($n = 300$). For the total 29-item scale, the mean was 97.69 (15.54). For the four factors, the mean scores were 21.35 (7.45) for the power-prestige factor, 28.83 (8.10) for the retention-time factor, 24.71 (6.08) for the distrust factor, and 22.80 (5.51) for the anxiety factor.

Source: Yamauchi, Kent T., and Donald I. Templer. (1982). "The Development of a Money Attitude Scale." *Journal of Personality Assessment*, *46*, 522-528. Scale items taken from Tables 1-5 (pp. 523-525).

Other evidence: N/A

Other sources: N/A

References: N/A

SUBJECTIVE DISCRETIONARY INCOME SCALE: SDI
(O'Guinn and Wells 1989)

Construct: As originally conceptualized and developed by O'Guinn and Wells (1989), subjective discretionary income (SDI) is a measure of perceived spending power. Specifically, it is "an estimate by the consumer of how much money he or she has to spend on nonessentials" (p. 32). As such, the SDI assesses the capacity to spend and is considered an attitudinal rather than an objective behavioral resource.

Description: The SDI is a three-item scale where the items are scored on 6-point scales ranging from *definitely disagree* to *definitely agree*. Item scores are summed to form an overall SDI index that can range from 3 to 18.

Development: The SDI had actually been used in a variety of proprietary studies over a 14-year period. As such, development is based on consistent results of the three items over a long period of time with numerous large samples.

Samples: For the analyses reported below, samples from DDB Needham Lifestyle Survey from 1984, 1985, and 1986 were used. For each of these years, approximately 3,500 consumers were surveyed with response rates of 74% to 85%.

Validity: Using quartile splits of the SDI, O'Guinn and Wells reported that 20.4% of their sample fell into the "low" SDI level (range of 3-6), 35.2% of their sample fell into the "medium" SDI level (range of 7-10), 32.9% of their sample fell into the "medium-high" SDI level (range of 11-14), and 11.5% of their sample fell into the "high" SDI level (range of 15-18).

O'Guinn and Wells (1989) report that the SDI items had high loadings on a single factor (i.e., > .80) with item-to-total correlations ranging from .57 to .69. They report a correlation of $r = .34$ between the SDI and total family income (TFI) as evidence of discriminant validity and, using logistic regression, show that the SDI was a significant predictor of numerous financial-based products and services (e.g., mutual funds, money market funds, and stock ownership).

Scores: Mean scores were not reported.

Source: O'Guinn, Thomas C., and William D. Wells. (1989). "Subjective Discretionary Income." *Marketing Research: A Magazine of Application and Practice, 1*, 32-41.

© 1989 by the American Marketing Association. Scale items taken from p. 34. Reprinted with permission.

Other evidence: Rossiter (1995) conducted a replication study using an effective sample of $n = 1,187$ Australian households. Rossiter trichotomized the total SDI score and found that 28% of the sample was at a "low" SDI level (a score of 3-6), 66% of the sample was at a "medium" SDI level (a score of 7-11), and 6% of the sample was at a "high" SDI level (a score of 12-15). (Rossiter used 5-point scales for the SDI items.) He reported a coefficient alpha estimate of internal consistency of .57 for the SDI, with item-to-total correlations ranging from .66 to .78 for the three SDI items. A correlation of $r = .25$ was reported between SDI and TFI. In chi-square analyses, the SDI also showed evidence of predictive validity for the purchase/use of numerous financial-based products and services (e.g., mutual funds, money market funds, real estate, and credit card ownership/usage).

Other source: Rossiter, John. (1995). *Spending Power and the Subjective Discretionary Income (SDI) Scale*. Working paper, Australian Graduate School of Management.

References: N/A

SUBJECTIVE DISCRETIONARY INCOME SCALE: SDI
(O'Guinn and Wells 1989)

1. No matter how fast our income goes up we never seem to get ahead.

2. We have more to spend on extras than most of our neighbors.

3. Our family income is high enough to satisfy nearly all of our important desires.

NOTE: Item 1 is reverse scored.

4

Involvement, Information Processing, and Price Perceptions

INVOLVEMENT WITH A SPECIFIC CLASS OF PRODUCTS

AUTOMOBILE INVOLVEMENT: IPCA
(Bloch 1981)

Construct: Product involvement has been viewed as a long-term interest in a product which is based on the centrality of the product to important values, needs, or the self-concept, and is primarily a function of individual differences. Consistent with this conceptualization, Bloch (1981) views product involvement as a construct that affects consumer behavior on an ongoing basis and varies across individuals (ranging from minimal to extremely high levels). Based on this view, a scale to measure involvement with automobiles was developed (Bloch 1981).

Description: The IPCA is composed of 17 Likert-type items (*strongly agree* to *strongly disagree*) scored on a 6-point format. These items are self-administered and can be summed to form an overall score. Furthermore, the IPCA has been found to encompass six factors: (a) enjoyment of driving and usage of cars, (b) readiness to talk to others about cars, (c) interest in car racing activities, (d) self-expression through one's car, (e) attachment to one's car, and (f) interest in cars (Bloch 1981).

Development: The development of the IPCA closely adhered to recommended psychometric procedures found in the scaling literature. Based on the specification of the domain of the construct and a comprehensive literature search, 66 items were initially developed. These items were analyzed by a group of six judges to trim redundant and/or irrelevant statements, resulting in 44 retained items. The 44 items were then purified using a student sample ($n = 381$) via coefficient alpha and item-to-total correlations, resulting in the final 17-item measure. Factor analysis further revealed that the scale could be broken down into six factors. Reliability and validity of the scale were assessed with three more samples.

Samples: Four samples were used throughout the scale development process. The first was a student sample ($n = 381$) for initial purification purposes. The second and third samples were also students ($n = 57$ and $n = 90$) and were used to assess reliability and validity. The fourth sample was composed of 52 members of a sports car club. This sample was used to assess the mean level of involvement for a relevant population.

Validity: A number of reliability tests were performed on the 17-item IPCA. Coefficient alpha internal consistency estimates were reported for two of the student samples. For the first student sample ($n = 381$), alpha was .83, and for the second student sample ($n = 57$), alpha was .79. Test-retest reliability was also assessed for the second student sample after a 2-week interval. Test-retest reliability was .78.

Validity of the scale was assessed by correlating the IPCA with a number of behavioral measures assessing interest in automobiles (using the student sample of 90). The IPCA was significantly correlated with all eight measures of car interest, providing support for the validity of the scale (Bloch 1981). For example, the correlations of the IPCA with measures of purchasing name brand auto supplies, visiting car dealers to see new car models, attending auto races and shows, and performing car repairs were .40, .36, .36, and .28, respectively.

Scores: Mean scores were reported for the third student sample ($n = 90$) and the sports car club sample ($n = 52$). The mean for the student sample was 59.01, and the mean for the sports car club sample was 37.39. The difference in these two means was significant ($p < .01$).

Source: Bloch, Peter H. (1981). "An Exploration Into the Scaling of Consumers' Involvement With a Product Class." In Kent B. Monroe (Ed.), *Advances in Consumer Research* (Vol. 8, pp. 61-65). Provo, UT: Association for Consumer Research.

© 1991 by the Association for Consumer Research. Scale items taken from Table 1 (p. 63). Reprinted with permission.

Other evidence: Shimp and Sharma (1983) factor-analyzed the IPCA with a sample of 696 adult nonstudent respondents to test the dimensionality of the scale. They compared the six-factor solution of Bloch with a number of other factor structures. Through an exploratory factor analysis, Shimp and Sharma found that a three-factor solution accounted for 93.5% of the variance, suggesting that Bloch's six-factor structure may be simplified. Then, Shimp and Sharma estimated 12 confirmatory factor models and found that two- and three-factor models also offered a better fit than the six-factor model. Shimp and Sharma also offered reduced versions of the scale. A 13-item, three-factor version had construct reliabilities of .84, .76, and .67 for factors 1, 2, and 3, respectively. An eight-item, two-factor version had construct reliability estimates of .84 and .76 for an emotional/personal factor and a social status factor, respectively. It was concluded that the eight-item, two-factor version was a reasonable alternative to Bloch's 17-item, six-factor scale. These two factors were also correlated with a number of automobile attribute evaluations as a check on validity. For example, the emotional/personal factor had correlations of .12 and .10 with "status" and "looks." Corresponding correlations with the social status factor were .20 and .18.

Other source: Shimp, Terence, and Subhash Sharma. (1983). "The Dimensionality of Involvement: A Test of the Automobile Involvement Scale." In William R. Darden, Kent B. Monroe, and William R. Dillon (Eds.), *American Marketing Association Winter Educator's Conference: Research Methods and Causal Models in Marketing*. Chicago: American Marketing Association.

References: N/A

AUTOMOBILE INVOLVEMENT: IPCA
(Bloch 1981)

1. It is worth the extra cost to drive an attractive and attention-getting car.

2. I prefer to drive a car with a strong personality of its own.

3. I have sometimes imagined being a race driver.

4. Cars offer me relaxation and fun when life's pressures build up.

5. Sometimes I get too wrapped up in my car.

6. Cars are nothing more than appliances.*

7. I generally feel a sentimental attachment to the cars I own.

8. Driving my car is one way I often use to relieve daily pressure.

9. I do not pay much attention to car advertisements in magazines or on TV.*

10. I get bored when other people talk to me about their cars.*

11. I have little or no interest in car races.*

12. Driving along an open stretch of road seems to "recharge" me in body, mind and spirit.

13. It is natural that young people become interested in cars.

14. When I'm with a friend, we often end up talking about cars.

15. I don't like to think of my car as being ordinary.

16. Driving my car is one of the most satisfying and enjoyable things I do.

17. I enjoy discussing cars with my friends.

NOTES: *Denotes items that are reverse scored. Items 4, 8, 12, and 16 loaded highly (.50 and above) on the "enjoyment of driving and usage of cars" factor. Items 10, 14, and 17 loaded highly on the "readiness to talk to others about cars" factor. Items 3 and 11 loaded highly on the "interest in car racing activities" factor. Items 1, 2, and 13 loaded highly on the "self-expression through one's car" factor. Items 5, 7, and 15 loaded highly on the "attachment to one's car" factor, and items 6, 9, and 10 loaded highly on the "interest in cars" factor (Bloch 1981).

Items 4, 5, 8, 12, and 16 compose factor one of Shimp and Sharma's 13-item, three-factor solution. Items 1, 2, and 15 compose factor 2 of Shimp and Sharma's 13-item, three-factor solution, and items 9, 10, 11, 14, and 17 compose factor 3 of Shimp and Sharma's 13-item, three-factor solution.

Items 4, 5, 8, 12, and 16 compose the emotional/personal factor of Shimp and Sharma's eight-item, two-factor structure, and items 1, 2, and 15 compose the social status factor of Shimp and Sharma's eight-item, two-factor structure.

FASHION INVOLVEMENT INDEX: FII; FASHION INVOLVEMENT FACTOR: FIF
(Tigert, Ring, and King 1976)

Constructs: A fashion involvement continuum can be defined based on the aggregate effect of a variety of important fashion behavioral activities. These activities pertain to five dimensions which make up the FII (Tigert, Ring, and King 1976):

Fashion innovativeness and time of purchase is a continuum ranging from the early adopter and experimental consumer to the late-buying conservative consumer.

Fashion interpersonal communication is a continuum that describes the relative communicative and influential power of the consuming population at conveying fashion involvement.

Fashion interest is a continuum ranging from the highly interested to the totally noninterested in fashion.

Fashion knowledgeability is a continuum ranging from very knowledgeable about fashion, styles, and trends to having no insight into the fashion arena.

Fashion awareness and reaction to changing fashion trends is a continuum ranging from the consumer who actively monitors style trends to the totally nonaware individual.

The Fashion Involvement Factor (FIF) also measures aspects of the above five dimensions yet is believed to be distinct from the FII. All items are positively worded.

Description: The FII is composed of one 3-point question to measure each of the first four dimensions described above, along with a 5-point scale to measure the fifth dimension described above. Thus, scores on this overall measure can range from 5 to 17.

    The FIF is composed of five 6-point Likert-type items (*strongly agree* to *strongly disagree*) that are summed to form an overall score for FIF that can range from 6 to 30.

Development: The final FII was derived using tested measurement technology and earlier field tests, (cf. Tigert et al. 1976). The 6 FIF items were derived from an original pool of 24 AIO/lifestyle statements pertaining to various aspects of fashion. Through principal components analysis, the final 6 statements were chosen from the 24 items.

Samples: The primary sample was composed of 1,000 husband and wife pairs that were part of a special panel from the Toronto Retail Fashion Market Segmentation Research Program.

Validity: None of the traditional estimates of internal consistency (i.e., coefficient alpha) were reported. However, factor loadings for the six FIF items ranged from .32 to .60 for females, and from .39 to .66 for males. In addition, the correlations between the FII and the FIF were .63 for males and .57 for females. Several cross-classification analyses revealed that the more highly involved fashion consumers (based on the FII) were heavier buyers of clothes fashions in terms of both volume and price per unit than less fashion-involved individuals. This offers support for the validity of the FII.

Scores: Mean scores on the FII were 9.7 for females and 8.4 for males. The two means were significantly different at the .01 level. Although mean scores were not reported, the mean for females on the FIF was 6.5% higher than the mean for males ($p < .01$). Other scores broken down by cross-classification are also reported (Tigert et al. 1976, pp. 50-51).

Source: Tigert, Douglas J., Lawrence R. Ring, and Charles W. King. (1976). "Fashion Involvement and Buying Behavior: A Methodological Study." In Beverly B. Anderson (Ed.), *Advances in Consumer Research* (Vol. 3, pp. 46-52). Provo, UT: Association for Consumer Research.

    © 1976 by the Association for Consumer Research. Scale items taken from p. 47 and Table 1 (p. 49). Reprinted with permission.

Other evidence: N/A

Other sources: N/A

References: N/A

FASHION INVOLVEMENT INDEX: FII; FASHION INVOLVEMENT FACTOR: FIF
(Tigert, Ring, and King 1976)

The FII

1. In general, would you say you buy men's (women's) clothing fashions *earlier* in the season, *about the same time*, or *later* in the season than most other men (women)?
   a. Earlier in the season than most other men (women)
   b. About the same time as most other men (women)
   c. Later in the season than most other men (women)

2. Would you say you give *very little information*, *an average amount of information*, or a *great deal of information* about new men's (women's) clothing fashions to your friends?
   a. I give very little information to my friends.
   b. I give an average amount of information to my friends.
   c. I give a great deal of information to my friends.

3. In general, would you say you are *less interested*, *about as interested*, or *more interested* in men's (women's) clothing fashions than most other men (women)?
   a. Less interested than most other men (women)
   b. About as interested as most other men (women)
   c. More interested than most other men (women)

4. Compared with most other men (women), are you *less likely*, *about as likely*, or *more likely* to be asked for advice about new men's (women's) clothing fashions?
   a. Less likely to be asked than most other men (women)
   b. About as likely to be asked as most other men (women)
   c. More likely to be asked than most other men (women)

5. Which one of the statements below best describes *your reaction to changing fashions in men's (women's) clothes*? (Even though there may be no statement listed which exactly describes how you feel, make the best choice you can from the answers listed.)
   a. I read the fashion news regularly and try to keep my wardrobe up to date with the fashion trends.
   b. I keep up to date on all the fashion changes although I don't always attempt to dress according to those changes.
   c. I check to see what is currently fashionable only when I need to buy some new clothes.
   d. I don't pay much attention to fashion trends unless a major change takes place.
   e. I am not at all interested in fashion trends.

NOTES: Questions 1 through 5 measure fashion innovativeness and time of purchase, fashion interpersonal communication, fashion interest, fashion knowledgeability, and fashion awareness and reaction to changing fashion trends, respectively. Also, questions 1 and 5 require reverse coding to reflect a higher interest in fashion.

The FIF

   1. I usually have one or more outfits of the very latest style.
   2. An important part of my life and activities is dressing smartly.
   3. I like to shop for clothes.
   4. I like to think I'm a bit of a swinger.
   5. For my fashion needs, I am increasingly shopping at boutiques or fashion specialty stores rather than department stores.
   6. When I must choose between the two, I usually dress for fashion, not comfort.

INVOLVEMENT GENERAL TO SEVERAL PRODUCT CLASSES

COMPONENTS OF INVOLVEMENT: CP
(Lastovicka and Gardner 1979)

Construct: Lastovicka and Gardner (1979) view involvement as having two major components: normative importance and commitment. Normative importance refers to how connected or engaged a product class is to an individual's values. Commitment refers to the pledging or binding of an individual to his/her brand choice.

Description: The CP is composed of 22 Likert-type statements (*strongly disagree* to *strongly agree*), all on 7-point scales. The original CP is composed of three factors that encompass the two major components. These factors have been labeled familiarity, commitment, and normative importance. The items can be summed within each factor to derive an index for each factor.

Development: The items in the CP were chosen such that they reflect the three factors of involvement discussed above. Each item was evaluated across 14 different product categories. Via Tucker's (1963) three-mode factor analysis, the dimensionality of the CP was determined. This procedure uses an eigenvalue plot to derive the number of factors. The three-factor solution accounted for 72% of the variance in the data.

Sample: A sample of 40 graduate and undergraduate students was used in the scale development process. Each subject rated the 22 items across 14 different product categories, resulting in 560 observations.

Validity: Traditional estimates of reliability (i.e., coefficient alpha, test-retest) were not reported by Lastovicka and Gardner (1979). However, the pattern of factor loadings suggest that three distinct orthogonal factors did exist (Lastovicka and Gardner 1979, pp. 62-63). Though no formal statistical tests for validity were performed, it was also concluded that the CP possessed adequate levels of content, convergent, and discriminant validity.

Scores: Mean and/or percentage scores were not reported for the product classes. However, Lastovicka and Gardner (1979, pp. 66-67) do provide "transformed core matrix" scores across the three factors by high, low, and special interest involvement.

Source: Lastovicka, John L., and David M. Gardner. (1979). "Components of Involvement." In J. C. Maloney and B. Silverman (Eds.), *Attitude Research Plays for High Stakes* (pp. 53-73). Chicago: American Marketing Association.
 © 1979 by the American Marketing Association. Scale items taken from Table 1 (pp. 62-63). Reprinted with permission.

Other evidence: In another study using 421 undergraduate students, Jenson, Carlson, and Tripp (1988) used three product categories to further examine the dimensionality of the CP. Jenson et al. (1988) do not provide estimates of reliability and validity; however, they do report that the CP was best represented by a correlated four-factor solution using LISREL. The four factors they found were labeled importance, knowledge, brand preference, and commitment. They also concluded that involvement may be multidimensional both between and across products.

Other source: Jenson, Thomas D., Les Carlson, and Carolyn Tripp. (1988). "The Dimensionality of Involvement: An Empirical Test." In Melanie Wallendorf and Paul Anderson (Eds.), *Advances in Consumer Research* (Vol. 16, pp. 680-689). Provo, UT: Association for Consumer Research.

Reference: Tucker, L. (1963). "Implications of Factor Analysis of Three-Way Matrices for Measurement of Change." In C. Harris (Ed.), *Problems in Measuring Change*. Madison: University of Wisconsin Press.

COMPONENTS OF INVOLVEMENT: CP
(Lastovicka and Gardner 1979)

1. This is a product that I could talk about for a long time.

2. I understand the features well enough to evaluate the brands.

3. This is a product that interests me.

4. I have a preference for one or more brands in this product class.

5. This is a product for which I have no need whatsoever.*

6. I am not at all familiar with this product.*

7. I usually purchase the same brand within this product class.

8. If I had made a brand choice in this product class before actually making the purchase, I might easily change my intended choice upon receiving discrepant information.*

9. If I received information that was contrary to my choice in this product class, I would—at all costs—keep my choice.

10. I can protect myself from acknowledging some basic truths about myself by using this product.*

11. If my preferred brand in this product class is not available at the store, it makes little difference to me if I must choose another brand.*

12. My use of this product allows others to see me as I would ideally like them to see me.

13. This product helps me attain the type of life I strive for.

14. I can make many connections or associations between experiences in my life and this product.

15. I definitely have a "wanting" for this product.

16. If evaluating brands in this class, I would examine a very long list of features.

17. I use this product to define and express the "I" and "me" within myself.

18. I rate this product as being of the highest importance to me personally.

19. Because of my personal values, I feel that this is a product that **ought** to be important to me.

20. Use of this product helps me behave in the manner that I would like to behave.

21. Because of what others think, I feel that this is a product that should be important to me.

22. Most of the brands in this product class are all alike.*

NOTES: *Denotes items that are reverse scored. Items 1 through 7 compose the familiarity factor, items 8 through 11 compose the commitment factor, and items 12 through 22 compose the normative importance factor (Lastovicka and Gardner 1979).

Items 10, 12 through 15, and 17 through 21 compose the importance factor, items 1 through 3, 16, and 22 compose the knowledge factor, items 4 through 6 compose the brand preference factor, and items 7 through 9 and 11 compose the commitment factor (Jenson et al. 1988).

CONSUMER INVOLVEMENT PROFILES: CIP
(Laurent and Kapferer 1985)

Construct: Laurent and Kapferer (1985) view involvement as a multifaceted construct along five dimensions (i.e., antecedents). Depending on these five antecedents, consequences on consumer behavior will differ across individuals. The five dimensions can be combined to form an overall involvement profile applicable to any product class. The five antecedents are briefly described below (see Laurent and Kapferer 1985, pp. 43-44)

The perceived importance and risk of the product class is its personal meaning and relevance, and the perceived importance of the consequences of a mispurchase.

The subjective probability of making a mispurchase is the probability of a poor brand choice.

The symbolic or sign value attributed by the consumer to the product class, its purchase, or its consumption differentiates functional risk from psychosocial risk.

The hedonic value of the product class is its emotional appeal, its ability to provide pleasure and affect.

Interest is an enduring relationship with the product class.

Description: The CIP is a five-facet measure currently composed of 16 Likert-type statements (*totally disagree* to *totally agree*), all scored on a 5-point basis. The items in each facet are summed to form an overall measure of each facet. The CIP was originally drafted in French and then translated into English.

Development: The development of the CIP followed the recommended scaling procedures found in the psychometric literature. Based on the construct's domain and a comprehensive literature review, a pool of items was generated for each facet. Three preliminary samples were used to purify the measure using 14 different product categories. In the first two samples, items were rejected if they had a significant number of nonresponses or "don't know" answers across product categories. Furthermore, to make the CIP amenable to commercial research, each facet was limited to a maximum of five and a minimum of three items. In the third sample, coefficient alpha was used as a criterion in retaining items. From these samples, the final 16 items composing the CIP were obtained. The third sample was also used to assess validity and dimensionality.

Samples: The first two samples were composed of approximately 100 housewives each, where each person was asked about several products. The third and final sample was composed of 207 housewives recruited on the basis of age, socioeconomic quotas, and usage of at least 2 of the 14 products examined. Face-to-face, in-home interviewing was conducted for two product categories per subject with a systematic rotation of product categories by interviewee.

Validity: Internal consistency reliability was assessed via coefficient alpha ($n = 207$). These estimates were .80, .90, .88, .82, and .72 for perceived importance of the product, symbolic or sign value, hedonic value, perceived importance of the negative consequences of a poor choice, and probability of making a poor choice (mispurchase), respectively.
    Laurent and Kapferer (1985) also ran a factor analysis and found that perceived importance of the product and perceived risk of the negative consequences of a poor choice were not distinct facets. Thus, they were combined to form a single facet of product/risk importance with an alpha of .87. Furthermore, the four facets (i.e., product/risk importance, symbolic or sign value, hedonic value, and probability of a mispurchase) accounted for 66% of the total variance in the CIP. (Because the "interest" facet had not been added to the CIP at the time of its appearance in the *Journal of Marketing Research*, a reliability estimate was not reported.)
    Discriminant validity among the facets of the CIP and trait validity for the CIP facets were reported. The correlations among the four facets ranged from .15 to .53, suggesting evidence of discriminant validity. Further correlational analyses of the four facets with various behavioral

consequences associated with product class involvement showed evidence of construct validity for the CIP. For example, the facets of the CIP explained 71% of the variance in "extensive decision process" relating to product purchase and 28% of the variance in "keeping informed" about a given product class.

Scores: Mean scores for the four facets (i.e., product/risk importance, symbolic or sign value, hedonic value, and probability of a mispurchase) across each of the 14 product categories are reported in Table 3 of Laurent and Kapferer (1985, p. 45). These scores were based on an average product scoring system of 100 and were shown to vary widely across product categories, which further supports the validity of the CIP.

Source: Laurent, Gilles, and Jean-Noel Kapferer. (1985). "Measuring Consumer Involvement Profiles." *Journal of Marketing Research*, 22, 41-53.

    © 1985 by the American Marketing Association. Scale items taken from Table 1 (p. 44). Reprinted with permission.

Other evidence: In two more studies, Kapferer and Laurent (1985, 1986) further examined the reliability and validity of the CIP. From a sample of 1,568 observations over 20 products, a five-item "interest" factor, a three-item "pleasure" factor, a three-item "sign" factor, a three-item "risk importance" factor, and a two-item "risk probability" factor had alphas of .76, .83, .81, .72, and .54, respectively. Factor correlations ranged from .10 to .55 (Kapferer and Laurent 1985). Correlations with various consequences of involvement (i.e., extensive decision making, brand commitment, and reading articles) supported the CIP's nomological validity. For example, as predictor variables, the involvement facets explained 54% of the variance in extensiveness of the decision process, 10% of the variance in brand commitment, and 21% of the variance in readership of articles related to the product category. Kapferer and Laurent (1986) also report mean scores (on the same 100-point scale alluded to above) across the 20 products that support the scale's validity. See also "Notes" below for the Jain and Srinivasan (1990) items.

    More recently, Schneider and Rodgers (1996) proposed an "importance" subscale for the CIP. Their seven-item subscale showed coefficient alpha estimates of internal consistency of .846 and .839 for the evaluation of a health care clinic and financial institution, respectively. The subscale also showed some evidence of unidimensionality, and factor loadings ranged from .578 to .817 across the two products (services) examined. Using their importance subscale as a dependent variable in regression, they found that the "interest/pleasure," "sign," "risk importance," and "risk probability" aspects of the CIP were significant predictors of their importance subscale. See also "Notes" below for the Schneider and Rodgers items.

Other sources: Jain, Kapil, and Narasimhan Srinivasan. (1990). "An Empirical Assessment of Multiple Operationalizations of Involvement." In Marvin Goldberg, Gerald Gorn, and Richard Pollay (Eds.), *Advances in Consumer Research* (Vol. 17, pp. 594-602). Provo, UT: Association for Consumer Research.

    Kapferer, Jean-Noel, and Gilles Laurent. (1985). "Consumer's Involvement Profile: New Empirical Results." In Elizabeth Hirschman and Morris Holbrook (Eds.), *Advances in Consumer Research* (Vol. 12, pp. 290-295). Provo, UT: Association for Consumer Research.

    Kapferer, Jean-Noel, and Gilles Laurent. (1986). "Consumer Involvement Profiles: A New Practical Approach to Consumer Involvement." *Journal of Advertising Research*, 25, 49-56.

    Schneider, Kenneth C., and William C. Rodgers. (1996). "An 'Importance' Subscale for the Consumer Involvement Profile." In Kim Corfman and John Lynch (Eds.), *Advances in Consumer Research* (Vol. 23, pp. 249-254). Provo, UT: Association for Consumer Research.

References: N/A

CONSUMER INVOLVEMENT PROFILES: CIP
(Laurent and Kapferer 1985)

1. When you choose _____, it is not a big deal if you make a mistake.*

2. It is really annoying to purchase _____ that are not suitable.

3. If, after I bought _____, my choice(s) prove to be poor, I would be really upset.

4. Whenever one buys _____, one never really knows whether they are the ones that should have been bought.

5. When I face a shelf of _____, I always feel a bit at a loss to make my choice.

6. Choosing _____ is rather complicated.

7. When one purchases _____, one is never certain of one's choice.

8. You can tell a lot about a person by the _____ he or she chooses.

9. The _____ I buy gives a glimpse of the type of man/woman I am.

10. The _____ you buy tells a little bit about you.

11. It gives me pleasure to purchase _____.

12. Buying _____ is like buying a gift for myself.

13. _____ is somewhat of a pleasure to me.

14. I attach great importance to _____.

15. One can say _____ interests me a lot.

16. _____ is a topic which leaves me totally indifferent.*

NOTES: *Denotes items reverse scored.

Items 1 through 3 represent the "perceived product importance/risk" facet. Items 4 through 7 represent the "probability of a mispurchase" facet. Items 8 through 10 represent the "perceived symbolic/sign" facet. Items 11 through 13 represent the "hedonic/pleasure" facet, and items 14 through 16 represent the "interest" facet.

It should be noted that the 16 items above are from an updated version (circa 1989) of the CIP. The reliability and validity estimates reported on the previous pages pertain to an original 19-item CIP reported in Laurent and Kapferer (1985). Furthermore, the "interest" facet of the CIP was not included in the original Laurent and Kapferer article. As stated before, Laurent and Kapferer originally hypothe-sized five facets as follows:

1. The perceived importance of the product—its personal meaning and relevance.
2. The perceived importance of negative consequences in case of a poor choice (i.e., one facet of perceived risk).
3. The perceived probability of making such a mistake (the other facet of perceived risk).
4. The symbolic or sign value attributed by the consumer to the product, its purchase, or its consumption. This differentiates functional risk from psychosocial risk.
5. The hedonic value of the product, its emotional appeal, its ability to provide pleasure and affect.

However, their factor analysis retained four factors (i.e., product/risk importance, symbolic or sign value, hedonic value, and probability of a mispurchase); more recently, a fifth facet (interest) was added. To our knowledge, the scale is currently represented by the 16 items above, encompassing the five facets below.

1. The perceived importance and risk of the product class: its personal meaning and relevance, and the perceived importance of the consequences of a mispurchase.
2. The subjective probability of making a mispurchase.
3. The symbolic or sign value attributed by the consumer to the product class, its purchase, or its consumption. This differentiates functional risk from psychosocial risk.
4. The hedonic value of the product class, its emotional appeal, its ability to provide pleasure and affect.
5. Interest: an enduring relationship with the product class.

In a more recent study, Jain and Srinivasan (1990) reported coefficient alphas of .76, .57, .72, .82, and .78, respectively, for interest, probability of making a mispurchase, hedonic/pleasure, sign/symbol, and perceived importance/risk facets of the CIP. These estimates are based on the current 16-item CIP. It should be noted, though, that Jain and Srinivasan (1990) translated the items using a semantic differential format, rather than the Likert-type format originally used by Laurent and Kapferer. The Jain and Srinivasan items are listed below.

Jain and Srinivasan (1990) CIP Scale

With regard to the following product category . . .

1. It is not a big deal if I make a mistake in choosing it—It is a big deal if I make a mistake in choosing it.

2. It is really annoying to make an unsuitable purchase—It is not annoying to make an unsuitable purchase.*

3. A poor choice wouldn't be upsetting—A poor choice would be upsetting.

4. I never know if I am making the right purchase—I know for sure that I am making the right purchase.*

5. I feel a bit at a loss in choosing it—I don't feel at a loss in choosing it.*

6. Choosing it isn't complicated—Choosing it is complicated.

7. In purchasing it, I am certain of my choice—In purchasing it, I am uncertain of my choice.

8. It tells something about a person—It doesn't tell anything about a person.*

9. What I buy doesn't reflect the kind of person I am—What I buy reflects the kind of person I am.

10. What I buy says something about me—What I buy doesn't say anything about me.*

11. I enjoy buying it for myself—I do not enjoy buying it for myself.*

12. Buying it feels like giving myself a gift—Buying it doesn't feel like giving myself a gift.*

13. I do not find it pleasurable—I find it pleasurable.

14. I attach great importance to it—I attach no importance to it.*

15. I am not at all interested in it—I am very interested in it.

16. I am indifferent to it—I am not indifferent to it.

NOTES: *Denotes items reverse scored.

Items 1 through 3 represent the "perceived product importance/risk" facet. Items 4 through 7 represent the "probability of a mispurchase" facet. Items 8 through 10 represent the "perceived symbolic/sign" facet. Items 11 through 13 represent the "hedonic/pleasure" facet, and items 14 through 16 represent the "interest" facet.

Schneider and Rodgers (1996) "Importance" Subscale

1. Choosing a _____ is a big decision in one's life.
2. I attach great importance to selecting a _____.
3. I don't usually get overly concerned about selecting a _____.
4. Which _____ I choose doesn't really matter to me.
5. Choosing a _____ takes a lot of careful thought.
6. Decisions about selecting a _____ are serious, important decisions.
7. It means a lot to me to have a _____ to use.·

Items can be scored on 5-point Likert-type scales ranging from *totally disagree* to *totally agree*. Items 3 and 4 require reverse scoring.

ENDURING INVOLVEMENT INDEX
(Bloch, Sherrell, and Ridgway 1986)

Construct: In a study investigating the antecedents and consequences of search, Bloch, Sherrell, and Ridgway (1986, p. 120) viewed involvement as enduring in character, representing a continuing interest or enthusiasm rather than a temporary product interest resulting from purchase requirements.

Description: The Bloch et al. Enduring Involvement Index is composed of five items. The first three items assess the importance of the product category to the individual's social life and career. These three items are measured on 7-point scales from *not important at all* to *extremely important*. The fourth item is an interest item scored on a 4-point format from *not at all interested* to *very interested*, and the fifth item is a frequency of thought item scored on a 5-point scale from *never or almost never* to *very frequently*. Scores from the three-item importance facet can be summed to form an importance index, or all five items can be summed to form an overall enduring involvement index.

Development: Little information as to the development of the index was offered. However, reliability and validity estimates were reported.

Samples: A sample of 679 (usable responses) consumers participated in the study. Subsamples based on interest in clothing and computers, the focal products of the study, were also derived.

Validity: Coefficient alpha estimates of internal consistency were reported for the three-item importance facet. These estimates were .83 and .77 for clothing and computers, respectively. Summed over all five items, the enduring involvement index showed correlations of .70 and .67 (for clothing and computers) for a measure of search, offering evidence of nomological validity.

Scores: Neither mean nor percentage scores were reported.

Source: Bloch, Peter H., Daniel L. Sherrell, and Nancy M. Ridgway. (1986). "Consumer Search: An Extended Framework." *Journal of Consumer Research, 13*, 119-126.
                    © 1986 by University of Chicago Press. Reprinted with permission.

Other evidence: N/A

Other sources: N/A

References: N/A

ENDURING INVOLVEMENT INDEX
(Bloch, Sherrell, and Ridgway 1986)

How important is knowledge of _____ to:

1. The quality of your social life?

2. Your present job or career?

3. Your future job or career plans?

4. How interested are you in the subject of _____?

     _____ Not at all interested
     _____ Slightly interested
     _____ Moderately interested
     _____ Very interested

5. How frequently do you find yourself thinking about _____?

    Never or almost never   _____:_____:_____:_____:_____   Very frequently

NOTES: Items 1 through 3 are scored on a 7-point *not at all important* to *extremely important* format. The product category of interest is inserted where the _____ are.

FOOTE, CONE, AND BELDING INVOLVEMENT SUBSCALE: FCBI
(Ratchford 1987; Vaughn 1986)

Construct: The FCBI conceptualization views involvement as implying personal importance (i.e., relevance), and consequent attention to an object or product (cf. Ratchford 1987; Vaughn 1986). This view is similar to the S-O-R paradigm of Houston and Rothschild (1977) and Zaichkowsky's (1985) concept of involvement as well.

Description: The FCBI is a three-item semantic differential measure. Each item is scored on a 7-point scale, and item scores are summed to form an overall score.

Development: Scale development procedures are described in Ratchford (1987) and generally adhere to prescribed psychometric scaling procedures. Fifty items were originally developed. This pool of items was reduced to 30. These 30 items were tested over five studies for internal consistency, ability to discriminate between products, and respondent understanding. These five studies resulted in the three-item FCBI (Ratchford 1987; Vaughn 1986).

Samples: Five samples were used in the derivation of the final FCBI (i.e., adult samples of 30, 50, 30, 249, and 50), and numerous products were examined (e.g., 75 products for the *n* = 249 sample). In addition, the final scale was administered to a sample of 1,792 adults over 254 possible products.

The first sample of 30 was used to trim the 30 items to 11 items. The decision was also made to trim this 11-item measure to 3 items for the remaining studies. The third, fourth, and fifth studies, as well as the major study (*n* = 1,792), assessed the validity of the final three-item FCBI.

Validity: Internal consistency estimates for the FCBI in Studies 3 through 5 and the major study were .81, .74, .75, and .77, respectively. A measure of consistency for the product ratings across studies was also taken and indicated a very high level of consistency (correlations ranged from .84 to .96). Item-to-factor correlations are also reported by Vaughn (1986) and ranged from .90 to .97 for the three FCBI items on the overall FCBI measure.

Several assessments of validity were also taken. Correlations with ratings from Zaichkowsky's (1985) mean scores, and mean scores reported by Laurent and Kapferer (1985), indicated high correlations with the FCBI (.38 to .86), suggesting convergent validity (using the *n* = 1,792 data). Numerous estimates of discriminant and criterion validity also show support for the FCBI (*n* = 1,792 data).

Scores: Mean scores were reported based on a 100-point scoring system and are plotted for 60 products (see Ratchford 1987, p. 31).

Sources: Ratchford, Brian T. (1987). "New Insights About the FCB Grid." *Journal of Advertising Research*, 27, 24-38.

Scale items taken from Table 1 (p. 28). © 1987; reprinted by permission of the Advertising Research Foundation.

Vaughn, Richard. (1986). "How Advertising Works: A Planning Model Revisited." *Journal of Advertising Research*, 27, 57-66.

Other evidence: N/A

Other sources: N/A

References: Houston, Michael J., and Michael Rothschild. (1977). *A Paradigm for Research on Consumer Involvement.* Unpublished working paper, University of Wisconsin, Madison.

Laurent, Gilles, and Jean-Noel Kapferer. (1985). "Measuring Consumer Involvement Profiles." *Journal of Marketing Research, 22,* 41-53.

Zaichkowsky, Judith Lynne. (1985). "Measuring the Involvement Construct." *Journal of Consumer Research, 12,* 341-352.

FOOTE, CONE, AND BELDING INVOLVEMENT SUBSCALE: FCBI
(Ratchford 1987; Vaughn 1986)

1. Very important decision—very unimportant decision*

2. Decision requires a lot of thought—decision requires little thought*

3. A lot to lose if you choose the wrong brand—little to lose if you choose the wrong brand*

NOTE: *Denotes items that are reverse scored.

GENERAL SCALE TO MEASURE INVOLVEMENT WITH PRODUCTS: GSMI
(Traylor and Joseph 1984)

Construct: Traylor and Joseph (1984) conceptualize involvement as a consumer response to a product, message, medium, or situation. Furthermore, involvement is a response that reflects an individual's sense of self or identity and is activated by external stimuli.

Description: The GSMI is a six-item scale composed of Likert-type statements scored on a 7-point basis (*disagree* to *agree*). The scale is considered applicable to a wide range of products and is also considered unidimensional. An overall GSMI score can be derived by summing the scores on the items.

Development: After a review of the involvement literature and previously developed measures of involvement, 48 items were generated to reflect the construct. These items were checked for face validity and subsequently trimmed to 22 items. The 22 items were then administered to a sample of consumers over three product categories per consumer (65 different products in all). Items with factor loadings of .50 or above on the first factor extracted across all products were retained, resulting in 10 items. A second sample was then used to derive the final six-item scale, where items with factor loadings of .50 or above were retained over 12 different products. This second sample was also used to assess the reliability and validity of the scale.

Samples: Two samples were used in actual scale development. (Twenty focus groups were also used to generate the 65 product categories examined with the first sample.) The first sample consisted of 200 consumers randomly selected in a walk-by traffic district of a large midwestern city. The second sample consisted of a combination of 280 graduate and undergraduate students.

Validity: Coefficient alpha for the six-item GSMI was .92 ($n = 280$). In addition, factor loadings across 12 product categories on the first factor are also reported (Table 1, p. 71). Initial estimates of concurrent and predictive validity show modest support for the scale's overall validity, as the GSMI was related to brand selectivity and frequency of purchase over numerous product categories. For example, there was a correlation of $-.24$ between the scale and purchase frequency of the 12 products as a group.

Scores: Neither mean nor percentage scores were reported.

Source: Traylor, Mark B., and W. Benoy Joseph. (1984). "Measuring Consumer Involvement With Products: Developing a General Scale." *Psychology & Marketing*, *1*, 65-77.
 © 1984 by John Wiley & Sons, Inc. Scale items taken from Table 1 (p. 69). Adapted by permission of John Wiley & Sons, Inc.

Other evidence: N/A

Other sources: N/A

References: N/A

GENERAL SCALE TO MEASURE INVOLVEMENT WITH PRODUCTS: GSMI
(Traylor and Joseph 1984)

1. When other people see me using this product, they form an opinion of me.

2. You can tell a lot about a person by seeing what brand of this product he uses.

3. This product helps me express who I am.

4. This product is "me."

5. Seeing somebody else use this product tells me a lot about that person.

6. When I use this product, others see me the way I want them to see me.

NEW INVOLVEMENT PROFILE: NIP
(Jain and Srinivasan 1990)

Construct: In an effort to compare a number of the scales designed to measure involvement and assess whether involvement is a multifaceted or unidimensional construct, Jain and Srinivasan (1990) developed the NIP. The NIP takes a multidimensional approach to measuring involvement that includes five facets: relevance, pleasure, sign, risk importance, and risk probability. These facets are consistent with Laurent and Kapferer's (1985) approach.

Description: The NIP is composed of 15 semantic differential items. The items are scored on a 7-point basis. There are five factors, each composed of three items (i.e., relevance, pleasure, sign, risk importance, and risk probability). Item scores can be summed within each factor to form indices of each factor.

Development: The NIP was developed with an original pool of 49 items from Zaichkowsky's (1985) PII, McQuarrie and Munson's (1986) RPII, Higie and Feick's (1988) EIS, Laurent and Kapferer's (1985) CIP, and the FCBI (Ratchford 1987; Vaughn 1986). All items were adjusted to a semantic differential format. These items were administered to 375 students across 10 products. Through factor structure comparisons, domain overlap testing, and reliability analysis, the 15-item, five-factor scale was derived.

Sample: A sample of 375 of mostly undergraduate students was used to derive the NIP.

Validity: The internal consistency reliability estimates for the relevance, pleasure, sign, risk importance, and risk probability factors of NIP were .80, .84, .84, .80, and .56, respectively. Correlations among the factors ranged from −.02 to .58. It should be noted that the correlations among the first four factors were relatively strong (i.e., .33 to .58), and the correlations of the risk probability factor with the other four factors were low (i.e., −.02 to .23).

These five factors were also correlated with measures of the consequences of involvement (i.e., information search and brand preference). The pattern of correlations suggests that the five NIP factors possess predictive validity. For example, the NIP factors explained 35% of the variance in information search and 13% of the variance in brand preference.

Scores: Mean scores across the 10 products studied are reported in Table 5 of Jain and Srinivasan (1990, p. 601) for the Zaichkowsky PII and for a recent version of Laurent and Kapferer's CIP. These mean scores are standardized on a 100-point basis. Mean scores for the NIP factors were not reported.

Source: Jain, Kapil, and Narasimhan Srinivasan. (1990). "An Empirical Assessment of Multiple Operationalizations of Involvement." In Marvin Goldberg, Gerald Gorn, and Richard Pollay (Eds.), *Advances in Consumer Research* (Vol. 17, pp. 594-602). Provo, UT: Association for Consumer Research.

© 1990 by the Association for Consumer Research. Scale items taken from Table 2 (pp. 597-598). Reprinted with permission.

Other evidence: N/A

Other sources: N/A

References: Higie, Robin A., and Lawrence F. Feick. (1988). "Enduring Involvement: Conceptual and Methodological Issues." In Thomas K. Srull (Ed.), *Advances in Consumer Research* (Vol. 16, pp. 690-696). Provo, UT: Association for Consumer Research.

Laurent, Gilles, and Jean-Noel Kapferer. (1985). "Measuring Consumer Involvement Profiles." *Journal of Marketing Research, 22,* 41-53.

McQuarrie, Edward F., and J. Michael Munson. (1986). "The Zaichkowsky Personal Involvement Inventory: Modification and Extension." In Paul Anderson and Melanie Wallendorf (Eds.), *Advances in Consumer Research* (Vol. 14, pp. 36-40). Provo, UT: Association for Consumer Research.

Ratchford, Brian T. (1987). "New Insights About the FCB Grid." *Journal of Advertising Research, 27,* 24-38.

Vaughn, Richard. (1986). "How Advertising Works: A Planning Model Revisited." *Journal of Advertising Research, 27,* 57-66.

Zaichkowsky, Judith Lynne. (1985). "Measuring the Involvement Construct." *Journal of Consumer Research, 12,* 341-352.

NEW INVOLVEMENT PROFILE: NIP
(Jain and Srinivasan 1990)

1. Essential—non-essential*

2. Beneficial—not beneficial*

3. Not needed—needed

4. I do not find it pleasurable—I find it pleasurable

5. Unexciting—exciting

6. Fun—not fun*

7. Tells others about me—doesn't tell others about me*

8. Others use to judge me—others won't use to judge me*

9. Does not portray an image of me to others—portrays an image of me to others

10. It is really annoying to make an unsuitable purchase—it is not annoying to make an unsuitable purchase*

11. A poor choice wouldn't be upsetting—a poor choice would be upsetting

12. Little to lose by choosing poorly—a lot to lose by choosing poorly

13. In purchasing it, I am certain of my choice—in purchasing it, I am uncertain of my choice

14. I never know if I am making the right purchase—I know for sure that I am making the right purchase*

15. I feel a bit at a loss in choosing it—I don't feel at a loss in choosing it*

NOTES: *Denotes items that are reverse scored.

Items 1 through 3 compose the relevance factor, items 4 through 6 compose the pleasure factor, items 7 through 9 compose the sign factor, items 10 through 13 compose the risk importance factor, and items 14 through 15 compose the risk probability factor.

PERSONAL INVOLVEMENT INVENTORY: PII
(Zaichkowsky 1985)

Construct: Zaichkowsky (1985, p. 342) defines involvement as a person's perceived relevance of the object based on inherent needs, values, and interests. This definition recognizes past definitions of involvement, and the corresponding scale, the PII, is applicable to advertisements, products, or purchase decisions.

Description: The PII is composed of 20 semantic differential items scored on 7-point scales. Scores on the items are summed to form an overall measure of involvement ranging from a low score of 20 to a high score of 140. As originally developed, the scale was felt to be unidimensional.

Development: Development of the PII closely followed recommended scaling procedures found in the psychometric literature. Based on the construct's definition, 168 word pairs were initially generated to tap the domain of involvement. These items were then judged for content validity by two panels of expert judges and the author, resulting in 30 semantic differential pairs retained. The remaining items were checked for reliability and content validity over a number of samples, resulting in 20 items retained for the final scale. The final version of the PII was then examined again for reliability and construct validity over several samples.

Samples: Several samples were used at the various stages of scale development. Along with the author's judgment, two samples of expert judges ($n = 3$ and $n = 5$) rated the content validity of the 168 items, trimming this initial pool to 30 items. A sample of 152 undergraduate students were then used to assess the internal consistency of the 30 items over two products. Adjective pairs with item-to-total correlations of .50 were retained, resulting in 26 items. Based on a factor analysis, two more adjective pairs were dropped, with the resulting 24 items explaining 70% of the variance in the data (Zaichkowsky 1985).

A second sample comprising 68 undergraduate and 45 MBA students was used to assess test-retest reliability and internal consistency over four product categories (two for the undergraduates and two for the MBAs). (Of this total sample of 113, 32 were lost to attrition, resulting in 81 for the estimates of reliability.) After deleting 4 more items with low item-to-total correlations, the final 20-item scale was formed. (The sample of 45 MBAs was also used to further assess content validity.) Two more samples were used to assess the criterion validity of the 20-item PII. One sample ($n = 68$ undergraduates) was used to elicit the product categories used, and the other sample ($n = 47$ undergraduates) responded to the PII across the products elicited. A final sample used to assess construct validity was composed of 57 clerical/administrative staff members at a major university.

In all, four data sets over numerous product categories were used in the development process (not including the expert judges).

Validity: Several estimates of reliability were obtained by Zaichkowsky. For the second sample ($n = 81$), test-retest reliability was .88, .89, .88, and .93 for the four products studied over a 3-week period. Internal consistency for this sample ranged from alpha = .95 to alpha = .97. Internal consistency was also assessed with the clerical/administrative sample ($n = 57$) over three products with alphas of .97, .99, and .97., and with purchase scenarios via a subsample ($n = 41$) of the clerical/administrative sample over two more products with alphas of .97 and .98.

Several criterion and construct validity tests were also offered by Zaichkowsky. The pattern of means for products to be hypothesized as high, medium, and low involvement supported the PII's criterion validity over two samples (i.e., the $n = 47$ undergraduate students and the $n = 57$ clerical/administrative sample). Furthermore, the correlations of the PII with a number of behavioral measures relating to product involvement showed that the PII possessed adequate levels of construct validity ($n = 57$). For example, the correlations of the PII with a measure of reading about how a product is made ranged from .14 to .37 across three product categories. The correlations of the PII with a measure of comparing product characteristics across brands ranged from .23 to .52 across three product categories, and the correlations of the PII with a measure of having a most preferred brand in a product category ranged from .42 to 68.

Scores: Mean scores across samples and the various products examined were reported (cf. Zaichkowsky 1985, pp. 345-351). An overall grand mean score was reported to be 89.55. In addition, those subjects deemed as low involvement across the products studied scored in the 20-69 range, medium involvement in the 70-110 range, and high involvement in the 111-140 range.

Source: Zaichkowsky, Judith Lynne. (1985). "Measuring the Involvement Construct." *Journal of Consumer Research, 12,* 341-352.

© 1985 by University of Chicago Press. Scale items taken from Appendix A (p. 350). Reprinted with permission.

Other evidence: Mean scores across eight different product categories are reported in Zaichkowsky (1986). A sample of 230 students rated each product category. Automobiles had the highest mean rating on the PII of 131, and cigarettes had the lowest mean rating of 49. Mean scores were also broken down by gender, and many of the differences on the PII between males and females were significant in a direction that supports the PII's validity. See also the next several pages (i.e., revised versions of the PII).

Other source: Zaichkowsky, Judith Lynne. (1986). "The Emotional Aspect of Product Involvement." In Melanie Wallendorf and Paul Anderson (Eds.), *Advances in Consumer Research* (Vol. 14, pp. 32-35). Provo, UT: Association for Consumer Research.

References: N/A

PERSONAL INVOLVEMENT INVENTORY: PII
(Zaichkowsky 1985)

PII Instructions

The purpose of this study is to measure a person's involvement or interest in (product category). To take this measure, we need you to judge (product category) against a series of descriptive scales according to how YOU perceive the product you will be shown. Here is how you are to use these scales.

If you feel that the (product) is **very closely related** to one end of the scale, you should place your check mark as follows:

Unimportant   ✓ :___:___:___:___:___:___   Important
or
Unimportant   ___:___:___:___:___:___: ✓   Important

If you feel that the (product) is **quite closely related** to one or the other end of the scale (but not extremely), you should place your check mark as follows:

Appealing   ___:___:___:___:___: ✓ :___   Unappealing
or
Appealing   ___: ✓ :___:___:___:___:___   Unappealing

If you feel that the (product) seems **only slightly related** to one or the other end of the scale (but not really neutral), you should place your check mark as follows:

Uninterested   ___:___: ✓ :___:___:___:___   Interested
or
Uninterested   ___:___:___:___: ✓ :___:___   Interested

IMPORTANT: 1. Be sure that you check every scale for every (product); do not omit any.

2. Never put more than one check mark on a single scale.

Make each item a separate and independent judgment. Work at fairly high speed through this questionnaire. Do not worry or puzzle over individual items. It is your first impressions, the immediate feelings about the items, that we want. On the other hand, please do not be careless, because we want your true impressions.

The PII Items

1. important—unimportant*

2. of no concern—of concern to me

3. irrelevant—relevant

4. means a lot to me—means nothing to me*

5. useless—useful

6. valuable—worthless*

7. trivial—fundamental

8. beneficial—not beneficial*

9. matters to me—doesn't matter*

10. uninterested—interested

11. significant—insignificant*

12. vital—superfluous*

13. boring—interesting

14. unexciting—exciting

15. appealing—unappealing*

16. mundane—fascinating

17. essential—nonessential*

18. undesirable—desirable

19. wanted—unwanted*

20. not needed—needed

NOTE: *Denotes items that are reverse scored.

Revised Versions of Zaichkowsky's PII

ENDURING INVOLVEMENT SCALE: EIS
(Higie and Feick 1988)

Construct: Higie and Feick (1988) view enduring involvement as an individual difference variable representing an arousal potential of a product or activity that causes personal relevance. Enduring involvement is intrinsically motivated by the degree to which the product or activity is related to the individual's self-image or the pleasure received from thoughts about or use of the product or engaging in the activity (see also Richins and Bloch 1986).

Description: The EIS is a 10-item scale composed of semantic differential pairs from Zaichkowsky's (1985) PII and McQuarrie and Munson's (1986) RPII, as well as items developed by the authors (7-point items). The scale has two factors, a hedonic and a self-expression factor, each composed of five items. Scores on items can be summed within dimensions to form hedonic and self-expression indices, or summed overall to form a measure of enduring involvement.

Development: In an initial study, items were chosen from the PII and RPII. Additional items deemed to have face validity were generated by the authors to reflect two hypothesized factors, hedonism and self-expression. Through item analysis and coefficient alpha, five-and four-item subscales for hedonism and self-expression were retained. In a second study, three additional items were generated for the self-expression subscale. Based on reliability and factor analysis results, the final five-item EIS subscales were derived.

Samples: In the first study, a combination of 255 undergraduate and MBA students was used. In the second study, 180 MBA students were used. Personal computers (PCs) and/or lawnmowers were used as the products examined in the two studies.

Validity: In the first study, coefficient alpha for the five-item hedonic subscale was .88 (for PCs with $n =$ 255). In the second study, the corresponding alpha for this measure was .93. Also, the alpha for the final five-item self-expression subscale was .91 for PCs. The combined 10-item hedonic and self-expression measure for PCs had an alpha of. 89. For lawnmowers (second study), the alphas for the hedonic and self-expressive subscales were .92 and .93, respectively, and the combined 10-item scale had an alpha of .92. The five-item subscales of the EIS, as well as the overall EIS, were correlated with a number of measures pertaining to validity (i.e., information search and provision, and opinion leadership). The pattern of correlations ranged from .18 to .46 and suggest that the EIS possessed adequate levels of discriminant and predictive validity.

Scores: Neither mean nor percentage scores were reported.

Source: Higie, Robin A., and Lawrence F. Feick. (1988). "Enduring Involvement: Conceptual and Methodological Issues." In Thomas Srull (Ed.), *Advances in Consumer Research* (Vol. 16, pp. 690-696). Provo, UT: Association for Consumer Research.
                   © 1988 by the Association for Consumer Research. Scale items taken from Table 1 (p. 694). Reprinted with permission.

Other evidence: See the next several pages for additional revisions of the PII.

Other sources: See the next several pages for additional revisions of the PII.

References: McQuarrie, Edward F., and J. Michael Munson. (1986). "The Zaichkowsky Personal Involvement Inventory: Modification and Extension." In Paul Anderson and Melanie Wallendorf (Eds.), *Advances in Consumer Research* (Vol. 14, pp. 36-40). Provo, UT: Association for Consumer Research.

Richins, Marsha, and Peter H. Bloch. (1986). "After the New Wears Off: The Temporal Context of Product Involvement." *Journal of Consumer Research*, *13*, 280-285.

Zaichkowsky, Judith Lynne. (1985). "Measuring the Involvement Construct." *Journal of Consumer Research*, *12*, 341-352.

ENDURING INVOLVEMENT SCALE: EIS
(Higie and Feick 1988)

1. not fun—fun

2. unappealing—appealing

3. boring—interesting

4. unexciting—exciting

5. dull—fascinating

6. shows nothing—tells me about a person

7. others won't use to judge me—others use to judge me

8. not part of my self image—part of my self image

9. doesn't tell others about me—tells others about me

10. does not portray an image of me to others—portrays an image of me to others

NOTE: Items 1 through 5 compose the hedonic factor, and items 6 through 10 compose the self-expression factor.

PII FOR ADVERTISING: PIIA
(Zaichkowsky 1990)

Construct: In measuring involvement toward advertising, a measure must be able to capture personal rational relevance as well as personal emotional relevance of the ad. Furthermore, an involvement measure directed toward advertising should be able to discriminate between high and low involvement with advertising.

Description: The PIIA is a 10-item semantic differential scale. All items are scored on a 7-point basis. The items are summed to form an overall measure of advertising involvement. The scale is considered unidimensional.

Development: The PIIA was developed along recommended scaling procedures. After a review of the advertising involvement literature, 15 bipolar adjective pairs were added to the original 20-item PII (Zaichkowsky 1985). These 35 items were judged for content validity, and then via item analysis and reliability estimates, the final 10-item PIIA was derived. The PIIA was checked again for content validity, as well as construct validity and dimensionality.

Samples: Four samples and a panel of experts were used in developing the PIIA. The first sample of 54 students was used to assess the internal consistency of the 35 items across two products. Items with low reliability were deleted, resulting in 22 items retained. The second sample of 52 students rated the remaining 22 items on a number of ads and products (twice over a 3-week interval). Again, items with low reliability or redundant items were dropped, resulting in the final 10-item PIIA. Content validity and dimensionality were also assessed with the second sample. Two more student samples of 79 and 53 subjects were used to assess the validity of the scale (Zaichkowsky 1990).

Validity: A number of reliability and validity assessments were performed on the PIIA. With the second sample ($n = 52$), coefficient alpha for the final 10-item PIIA ranged from .91 to .96 across products and ads. For the latter two samples, reported alphas ranged from .68 to .95 across ads. Furthermore, factor analysis ($n = 52$) revealed a unidimensional structure for the PIIA.

The 10-item PIIA was correlated with a number of measures reflecting behavioral response of involvement with products ($n = 52$). The pattern of correlations suggest an adequate level of construct validity for the PIIA. For example, the correlations between the PIIA and a measure of interest in reading product information ranged from .15 to .40 across three product categories. The correlations between the PIIA and a measure of comparing product attributes across brands ranged from .21 to .50, and the correlations between the PIIA and a measure of having a most preferred brand ranged from .40 to .66 across the three product categories. Construct validity was also assessed in two studies across a number of ads. The pattern of means and statistical significance tests indicate that the PIIA possessed construct validity and was able to discriminate between groups that showed high and low involvement with ads.

Scores: A number of scores across various ads and treatment levels are reported by Zaichkowsky (1990, Table 3, p. 31). As indicated above, these scores showed that the PIIA was able to discriminate between high- and low-involved groups.

Source: Zaichkowsky, Judith Lynne. (1994). "The Personal Involvement Inventory: Reduction, Revision, and Application to Advertising," *Journal of Advertising, 23*(4), 59-70. Scale items appear on p. 68.

Other evidence: N/A

Other sources: N/A

Reference: Zaichkowsky, Judith Lynne. (1985). "Measuring the Involvement Construct," *Journal of Consumer Research*, 12 (December), 341-352.

PII FOR ADVERTISING: PIIA
(Zaichkowsky 1990)

1. important—unimportant*

2. boring—interesting

3. relevant—irrelevant*

4. exciting—unexciting*

5. means nothing—means a lot to me

6. appealing—unappealing*

7. fascinating—mundane*

8. worthless—valuable

9. involving—uninvolving*

10. not needed—needed

NOTE: *Denotes items that are reverse scored.

RPII AND OPII
(McQuarrie and Munson 1986)

Construct: McQuarrie and Munson (1986) argue that involvement is a multidimensional construct. They also feel that the PII was contaminated with "attitudinal" variables, and thus, some interpretational confounding was evident. Their conceptual view of involvement is somewhat similar to Zaichkowsky's but tries to incorporate risk and sign components into the involvement construct.

Description: The RPII is a multidimensional measure of involvement that includes the dimensions of importance, pleasure, and risk. It is composed of 14 semantic differential items, many of which are derived from Zaichkowsky's original PII. The items are scored on 7-point scales. Items can be summed within dimensions to form indices for each dimension, or all 14 items can be summed to form an overall RPII score.

   The OPII is another involvement measure derived from Zaichkowsky's PII. It is composed of 16 items and may or may not be unidimensional (cf. McQuarrie and Munson 1986, p. 37). The 16 items can be summed to form an overall OPII score.

Development: Four pairs of adjectives from the original PII were deleted because they were considered inappropriate for a non-college-educated population (i.e., superfluous-vital, mundane-fascinating, significant-insignificant, and fundamental-trivial). The remaining 16 items form the OPII. Factor analysis, reliability, and validity estimates were used to examine the OPII.

   The RPII was derived by adding eight new adjective pairs to the OPII. Then, via reliability and factor analysis, the final 14-item RPII was derived. Although four factors were hypothesized (i.e., importance, risk, pleasure, and sign value), three factors were retained (importance, pleasure, and risk).

Sample: Student subjects (80 undergraduates and 56 MBAs) responded to 24 adjective pairs (the OPII items and the 8 new RPII items), over 12 stimulus objects (see McQuarrie and Munson, 1986, p. 37).

Validity: McQuarrie and Munson (1986) report reliability estimates for both the OPII and the RPII. The OPII (16 items) had an alpha of .95. The 14-item RPII (though considered multidimensional) had a coefficient alpha of .93. A factor analysis of the RPII revealed that the scale had three factors, labeled importance (five items), pleasure (six items), and risk (three items), with alphas of .85, .90, and .67, respectively. Correlations among the three factors ranged from .41 to .60.

   Estimates of validity also indicated that both the OPII and the RPII showed evidence of construct validity when correlated with measures reflecting the consequences of involvement (i.e., brand commitment and differentiation, and information search). For example, using the three involvement factors as predictor variables resulted in multiple Rs of .36, .22, and .57 for the prediction of brand commitment, brand differentiation, and information search, respectively.

   Lastly, given its fewer items and multidimensional nature, McQuarrie and Munson (1986) concluded that the RPII is a more parsimonious measure of enduring involvement than the OPII or the PII.

Scores: No mean or percentage scores were reported.

Source: McQuarrie, Edward F., and J. Michael Munson. (1986). "The Zaichkowsky Personal Involvement Inventory: Modification and Extension." In Paul Anderson and Melanie Wallendorf (Eds.), *Advances in Consumer Research* (Vol. 14, pp. 36-40). Provo, UT: Association for Consumer Research.

   © 1986 by the Association for Consumer Research. Scale items taken from Exhibit (p. 38). Reprinted with permission.

Other evidence: See the next several pages (i.e., more revisions of the PII).

Other sources: See the next several pages (i.e., more revisions of the PII).

Reference: Zaichkowsky, Judith Lynne. (1985). "Measuring the Involvement Construct." *Journal of Consumer Research*, *12*, 341-352.

RPII AND OPII
(McQuarrie and Munson 1986)

1. important—unimportant*

2. of no concern—of concern to me

3. irrelevant—relevant

4. means a lot to me—means nothing to me*

5. valuable—worthless*

6. beneficial—not beneficial*

7. matters to me—doesn't matter*

8. uninterested—interested

9. boring—interesting

10. unexciting—exciting

11. appealing—unappealing*

12. useless—useful

13. essential—nonessential*

14. undesirable—desirable

15. wanted—unwanted*

16. not needed—needed

17. fun—not fun*

18. says nothing about me—says something about me

19. tells me about a person—shows nothing*

20. easy to go wrong—hard to go wrong*

21. not risky—risky

22. easy to choose—hard to pick

NOTES: *Denotes items that are reverse scored.

Items 1 through 16 compose the OPII. Items 1 through 4 and 7 compose the RPII importance factor. Items 9 through 11, and 17 through 19 compose the RPII pleasure factor. Items 20 through 22 compose the RPII risk factor.

REVISED RPII: RRPII
(McQuarrie and Munson 1991)

Construct: McQuarrie and Munson (1991) propose a new version of their RPII that captures two facets of involvement: perceived importance and interest. The conceptual base of the RRPII is similar to the conceptual base of the RPII. However, the RRPII captures the two facets of involvement proposed by McQuarrie and Munson (1986) and shows improved criterion validity.

Description: The RRPII is a 10-item semantic differential measure where the items are evaluated on 7-point scales. The scale has two dimensions. Item scores can be summed within each dimension to form indices for each dimension or can be summed over all 10 items for an overall involvement measure.

Development: The original PII (Zaichkowsky 1985) and two new items generated by the authors served as the initial item pool. Over 12 product categories and multiple buying situations, a large sample responded to the 22 items. Eight of the PII items and the two new items were chosen to represent the final scale. The RRPII was then assessed for reliability, factor structure, and various forms of validity.

Samples: A sample of 146 students and 103 nonstudents was used to derive the RRPII and assess its reliability, validity, and dimensionality.

Validity: Internal consistency estimates were reported for the two subscales and the overall RRPII. Across products, the subscales of importance and perceived interest, as well as the overall RRPII, exhibited alphas in the low to mid-.80s range or better. (Three-fourths of the time, alpha was .90 or better.) Test-retest reliability from a subsample of 60 students over three product categories and a 3-week interval ranged from .53 to .78. In 8 of 15 factor analyses, two factors emerged (importance and interest). The correlation between the two factors was reported to be .66 overall.

   Several estimates of validity were also performed. Both the subscales and the RRPII were correlated with measures of attitude, information search, and information processing for three products. Correlations of the importance and interest factors with the attitude measure were .74 and .65. These estimates were lower than the correlation between the PII and the attitude measure (.76) and were taken as evidence of discriminant validity. The RRPII also accounted for more variance in information search and processing (45%) than the PII (40%). The RRPII was also more highly correlated with a number of behavioral outcomes than the PII, and across nine of the products, predictive validity for the RRPII dimensions was found.

Scores: Mean scores for three products over two situations were reported for the 10-item RRPII. For "everyday use," mean scores ranged from 34 to 49, and for "special occasions," mean scores ranged from 51 to 56.

Source: McQuarrie, Edward F., and J. Michael Munson. (1991). "A Revised Product Involvement Inventory: Improved Usability and Validity." In John F. Sherry and Brian Sternthal (Eds.), *Advances in Consumer Research* (Vol. 19, pp. 108-115). Provo, UT: Association for Consumer Research.

   © 1991 by the Association for Consumer Research. Scale items taken from Exhibit (p. 110). Reprinted with permission.

Other evidence: N/A

Other sources: N/A

References: McQuarrie, Edward F., and J. Michael Munson. (1986). "The Zaichkowsky Personal Involvement Inventory: Modification and Extension." In Paul Anderson and Melanie Wallendorf (Eds.), *Advances in Consumer Research* (Vol. 14, pp. 36-40). Provo, UT: Association for Consumer Research.

   Zaichkowsky, Judith Lynne. (1985). "Measuring the Involvement Construct." *Journal of Consumer Research, 12,* 341-352.

REVISED RPII: RRPII
(McQuarrie and Munson 1991)

1. important—unimportant*

2. irrelevant—relevant

3. means a lot to me—means nothing to me*

4. unexciting—exciting

5. dull—neat

6. matters to me—doesn't matter*

7. fun—not fun*

8. appealing—unappealing*

9. boring—interesting

10. of no concern—of concern to me

NOTES: *Denotes items that are reverse scored.

Items 1 through 3, 6, and 10 compose the importance factor. Items 4, 5, and 7 through 9 compose the interest factor.

PURCHASING INVOLVEMENT

PURCHASE DECISION INVOLVEMENT: PDI
(Mittal 1989)

Construct: Purchase decision involvement (PDI) is defined as the extent of interest and concern that a consumer brings to bear upon a purchase-decision task (Mittal 1989). PDI is felt to be analogous to the situational involvement of Houston and Rothschild (1977), has the purchase decision task as its goal object, and is considered a mind-set—not a response behavior (Mittal 1989).

Description: The PDI scale is a four-item measure on 7-point bipolar phrases. The item scores are summed and then divided by four, to form an average score of PDI.

Development: Development of the PDI scale generally followed recommended scaling procedures. An initial pool of nine items was derived via a review of the literature, an open-ended question regarding purchase decision involvement ($n = 20$), and the author's definition of the construct. These items were then administered to 40 consumers over a variety of products. Inter-item correlations, factor analyses, and the author's judgment resulted in the final four items. Then, two more studies assessing the validity of the scale were conducted, as well as a study that assessed the test-retest reliability of the scale.

Samples: Overall, five samples were used in scale development and validation. One sample ($n = 20$) was used for generating items, one sample ($n = 40$) was used to arrive at the final four items, two samples ($n = 256$ nonstudents and $n = 138$ students) were used for validation purposes, and one sample ($n = 85$ students) was used to look at test-retest reliability.

Validity: The first validation study looked at the convergent, discriminant, and criterion validity of the PDI scale ($n = 256$). The factor structure and correlations with product importance/involvement demonstrated convergent and discriminant validity for the PDI scale. Correlations with a measure of consumer information search (.50 for beer and .67 for a camera) indicated criterion validity. The second validation study examined the mean responses to the PDI scale with respect to several product categories ranked with respect to financial and product importance. The pattern of means across the PDI measures suggests that the PDI scale is a valid measure of PDI (Mittal 1989, p. 157, Table 3). For example, the mean scores ranged from a high of 6.27 ($SD = .58$) for eyeglasses (i.e., a high involvement product) to 1.91 ($SD = 1.32$) for pencils (i.e., a low involvement product). Test-retest reliability ($n = 85$) over a 2-week period was .79 for the PDI scale. Although coefficient alpha was not offered, factor loadings for items on the scale ranged from .58 to .88 across three product categories.

Scores: As stated above, mean scores across 15 different products were reported. The mean scores ranged from a high of 6.27 ($SD = .58$) for eyeglasses to 1.91 ($SD = 1.32$) for pencils.

Source: Mittal, Banwari. (1989). "Measuring Purchase-Decision Involvement." *Psychology & Marketing*, *6*, 147-162.
    © 1989 by John Wiley & Sons, Inc. Scale items taken from Figure 1 (p. 152). Adapted by permission of John Wiley & Sons, Inc.

Other evidence: N/A

Other sources: N/A

Reference: Houston, Michael J., and M. L. Rothschild. (1977). *A Paradigm for Research on Consumer Involvement* (Working Paper 11-77-46). Madison: University of Wisconsin Press.

PURCHASE DECISION INVOLVEMENT: PDI
(Mittal 1989)

1. In selecting from many types and brands of this product available in the market, would you say that:

   I would not care at all   I would care a great deal
   as to which one I buy   1 2 3 4 5 6 7   as to which one I buy.

2. Do you think that the various types and brands of this product available in the market are all very alike or are all very different?

   They are alike.   1 2 3 4 5 6 7   They are all different.

3. How important would it be to you to make a right choice of this product?

   Not at all important   1 2 3 4 5 6 7   Extremely important

4. In making your selection of this product, how concerned would you be about the outcome of your choice?

   Not at all concerned   1 2 3 4 5 6 7   Very much concerned.

PURCHASING INVOLVEMENT: PI
(Slama and Tashchian 1985)

Construct: Purchasing involvement is defined as the self-relevance of purchasing activities to the individual (Slama and Tashchian 1985, p. 73). Purchasing involvement is expected to affect consumer decision processes from pre-search to post-search evaluation, as well as attitudes and behaviors toward purchasing.

Description: The PI comprises 33 6-point Likert-type items (*strongly disagree* to *strongly agree*). The items are summed to form an overall purchasing involvement score. Thus, scores on the scale can range from 33 to 198.

Development: Following the literature review and construct definition, 150 items were generated to tap the domain of the construct. This pool of items was trimmed to 75 by a panel familiar with the involvement literature. The remaining pool of items was administered to two samples. Using a number of reliability and validity checks, the final 33-item scale was derived.

Samples: Three samples were used in the scale development process. The first sample consisted of 30 marketing research students familiar with the involvement literature to trim the initial pool of items. Items that at least 75% of these judges agreed on as being reflective of the construct were retained, resulting in 75 items. The second sample consisted of 365 adults from a small southern city. With this sample, the 75 items were trimmed to the final 33-item scale using item-to-total correlations as a guide. Internal consistency and validity of the scale were also assessed with this sample. The third sample, used to assess test-retest reliability, consisted of 76 students.

Validity: Coefficient alpha internal consistency for the PI was .93 ($n = 365$), and test-retest reliability over a 2-week period was .86 ($n = 76$).

    Convergent and discriminant validity of the scale were assessed via a multitrait-multimethod analysis. The correlations between the PI, measures of religious involvement, measures of automobile involvement, and other measures of purchasing involvement indicated that the PI had adequate levels of convergent and discriminant validity. For example, the PI exhibited convergent validity correlations .56 and .48 with other involvement measures. Furthermore, the scale was relatively free of social desirability bias ($r = .06$, ns, $n = 365$).

Scores: Mean scores were reported by various demographic characteristics, including family life cycle, education, income, gender, working status of wife, and race (Slama and Tashchian 1985, p. 78). The mean scores ranged from a low of 136 (for an advanced family life cycle group) to a high of 155.05 (for a married, but wife unemployed, group). The pattern of means and statistical significance tests also show general support for hypothesized predictions pertaining to the validity of the PI (see Table 6, p. 78).

Source: Slama, Mark, E., and Armen Tashchian. (1985). "Selected Socio-economic and Demographic Characteristics Associated With Purchasing Involvement." *Journal of Marketing*, *49*, 72-82.

    © 1985 by the American Marketing Association. Scale items taken from Appendix (pp. 79-80). Reprinted with permission.

Other evidence: N/A

Other sources: N/A

References: N/A

PURCHASING INVOLVEMENT: PI
(Slama and Tashchian 1985)

1. On most purchase decisions the choice I make is of little consequence.*

2. Usually reading about products or asking people about them won't really help you make a decision.*

3. I have little or no interest in shopping.*

4. *Consumer Reports* is not very relevant to me.*

5. I am not interested in bargain seeking.*

6. I am not interested in sales.*

7. You can't save a lot of money by careful shopping.*

8. I often take advantage of coupon offers in the newspapers.

9. Because of my personal values, I feel that "smart purchasing" ought to be important to me.

10. I am usually not annoyed when I find out I could have bought something cheaper than I did.

11. Being a smart shopper is worth the extra time it takes.

12. Even with inexpensive products like shampoo, I will often evaluate a recent purchase and become annoyed because the product doesn't adequately meet my needs.

13. Sales don't excite me.*

14. I am not really committed to getting the most for my money.*

15. For expensive items I spend a lot of time and effort making my purchase decision, since it is important to get the best deal.

16. Consumerism issues are irrelevant to me.*

17. I view the purchasing of goods and services as a rather petty activity, not relevant to my main concerns in life.*

18. It is important to me to be aware of all the alternatives before buying an expensive item.

19. It is important to me to keep up with special deals being offered by the grocery stores in my area.

20. I am too absorbed in more personally relevant matters to worry about making smart purchases.*

21. It is part of my value system to shop around for the best buy.

22. The consumer and business sections of the newspaper are highly relevant to me.

23. If I were buying a major appliance it wouldn't make much difference which brand I chose.*

24. The brands of goods I buy make very little difference to me.*

25. It is not worth it to read *Consumer Reports* since most brands are about the same.*

26. You can save a lot of money by clipping coupons from the newspaper.

27. Thinking about what you are going to buy before going shopping won't make much difference in your long-run expectations.*

28. It doesn't make much sense to get upset over a purchase decision since most brands are about the same.*

29. I am willing to spend extra time shopping in order to get the cheapest possible price on goods of like quality.

30. I pay attention to advertisements for products I am interested in.

31. Shopping wisely is rather a petty issue compared to thinking about how to make more money.*

32. I don't like worrying about getting the best deal when I go shopping; I like to spend money as I please.*

33. I don't like to waste a lot of time trying to get good deals on groceries.*

NOTE: *Denotes items that are reverse scored.

**APPENDIX TO INVOLVEMENT: COMPARING
FOUR MODIFIED INVOLVEMENT SCALES**
(Mittal 1995)

Mittal (1995) compared the psychometric properties of modified versions of four prominent involvement measures. The four were chosen, modified, and compared on the basis that the concept of involvement has the recurrent theme of perceived relevance/importance; namely, it represents "the perceived importance of the stimulus— be that stimulus the product itself or the purchase decision task" (Mittal 1995, p. 664). The four involvement measures examined (and modified) were Zaichkowsky's (1985) Personal Involvement Inventory (PII), Laurent and Kapferer's (1985) Consumer Involvement Profile (CIP), the Foote, Cone, & Belding Involvement (FCB) Grid (Ratchford 1987), and the Mittal (1989) Purchase Decision Involvement (PDI) measure. Using the product/purchase decision categories of beer ($n = 90$), cameras ($n = 80$), jeans ($n = 86$ and $n = 144$), and VCRs ($n = 136$), Mittal (1995) offered the following results from confirmatory factor analyzes (via LISREL) and reliability/item analyses.

A modified five-item PII showed adequate evidence of unidimensionality and internal consistency as a measure of both purchase decision involvement and product involvement. Two modified three-item versions of the CIP product class involvement and purchase decision involvement scales showed adequate evidence of unidimensionality and internal consistency for product class involvement and purchase decision involvement, respectively. A modified three-item PDI showed adequate evidence of unidimensionality and internal consistency as a measure of purchase decision involvement. A modified three-item FCB showed adequate evidence of unidimensionality and internal consistency as a measure of purchase decision involvement. Table 4.1 (Table 2 in Mittal 1995, p. 673) summarizes the results.

TABLE 4.1

	Purchase-Decision Involvement		*Product Involvement*	
	Construct Reliability	*Captured Variance*	*Construct Reliability*	*Captured Variance*
Modified PII	.90	.67	.90	.64
Modified CIP	.80	.59	.75	.51
Modified PDI	.85	.66		
Modified FCB	.84	.64		

Intercorrelations among the scales (for the same product or purchase decision) ranged from .55 to .99. Mittal (1995) offered rank ordered recommendations for the scales in terms of unidimensionality, convergent validity, nomological validity, simplicity, and response set bias (see Table 3, p. 676). However, no one scale was universally endorsed over all these rank ordered criteria. The pages that follow offer the modified versions of the scales.

Source: Mittal, Banwari. (1995). "A Comparative Analysis of Four Scales of Involvement." *Psychology & Marketing, 12,* 663-682.
© 1995 by John Wiley & Sons, Inc. Items taken from Figure 1 (pp. 670-671), and Table 4.1 adapted from Table 2 (p. 673). Adapted by permission of John Wiley & Sons, Inc.

The Modified PII

1. important—unimportant*

2. means a lot to me—means nothing to me*

3. matters to me—does not matter*

4. significant—insignificant*

5. of no concern—of concern to me

NOTES: *Denotes reverse scored items. Items are scored on 7-point scales.

The Modified CIP

Product Class Involvement

1. _____ is very important to me.

2. For me, _____ do (does) not matter.

3. _____ are an important part of my life.

Purchase Decision Involvement

1. I choose _____ very carefully.

2. Which _____ I buy matters to me a lot.

3. Choosing _____ is an important decision for me.

NOTES: Items are scored on 7-point *strongly disagree* to *strongly agree* scales. Item 3 of the product class involvement measure in one of Mittal's (1995) studies was worded "I have a strong interest in _____." Item 2 of Product Class Involvement requires reverse scoring.

The Modified PDI

1. In selecting from many types and brands of _____ available in the market, would you say that:

I would not care at all
as to which one I buy   1 2 3 4 5 6 7   I would care a great deal
                                                       as to which one I buy.

2. How important would it be to you to make a right choice of this product?

Not at all important   1 2 3 4 5 6 7   Extremely important

3. In making your selection of this product, how concerned would you be about the outcome of your choice?

Not at all concerned   1 2 3 4 5 6 7   Very much concerned

22.   A.   I would like to meet some persons who are homosexuals (men or women).
         B.   I stay away from anyone I suspect of being "gay."

23.   A.   I would like to try parachute jumping.
         B.   I would never want to try jumping out of a plane with or without a parachute.

24.   A.   I prefer friends who are excitingly unpredictable.
         B.   I prefer friends who are reliable and predictable.

25.   A.   I am not interested in experience for its own sake.
         B.   I like to have new and exciting experiences and sensations even if they are a little frightening, unconventional or illegal.

26.   A.   The essence of good art is in its clarity, symmetry of form and harmony of colors.
         B.   I often find beauty in the "clashing" colors and irregular forms of modern painting.

27.   A.   I enjoy spending time in the familiar surroundings of home.
         B.   I get very restless if I have to stay around home for any length of time.

28.   A.   I like to dive off the high board.
         B.   I don't like the feeling I get standing on the high board (or I don't go near it at all).

29.   A.   I like to date members of the opposite sex who are physically exciting.
         B.   I like to date members of the opposite sex who share my values.

30.   A.   Heavy drinking usually ruins a party because some people get loud and boisterous.
         B.   Keeping the drinks full is the key to a good party.

31.   A.   The worst social sin is to be rude.
         B.   The worst social sin is to be a bore.

32.   A.   A person should have considerable sexual experience before marriage.
         B.   It's better if two married persons begin their sexual experience with each other.

33.   A.   Even if I had the money I would not care to associate with flighty persons like those in the "jet set."
         B.   I could conceive of myself seeking pleasure around the world with the "jet set."

34.   A.   I like people who are sharp and witty even if they do sometimes insult others.
         B.   I dislike people who have their fun at the expense of hurting the feelings of others.

35.   A.   There is altogether too much portrayal of sex in movies.
         B.   I enjoy watching many of the "sexy" scenes in movies.

36.   A.   I feel best after taking a couple of drinks.
         B.   Something is wrong with people who need liquor to feel good.

37.   A.   People should dress according to some standards of taste, neatness, and style.
         B.   People should dress in individual ways even if the effects are sometimes strange.

38.   A.   Sailing long distances in small sailing crafts is foolhardy.
         B.   I would like to sail a long distance in a small but seaworthy sailing craft.

39.   A.   I have no patience with dull or boring persons.
      B.   I find something interesting in almost every person I talk with.

40.   A.   Skiing fast down a high mountain slope is a good way to end up on crutches.
      B.   I think I would enjoy the sensations of skiing very fast down a high mountain slope.

NOTES: The TAS factor and a high score on the TAS are derived from the following items and their respective answers: 3A, 11B, 16A, 17A, 20B, 21B, 23A, 28A, 38B, and 40B. The ES factor and a high score on the ES are derived from the following items and their respective answers: 4B, 6A, 9A, 10B, 14A, 18A, 19B, 22A, 26B, and 37B. The DIS factor and a high score on the DIS are derived from the following items and their respective answers: 1A, 12A, 13B, 25B, 29A, 30B, 32A, 33B, 35B, and 36A. The BS factor and a high score on the BS are derived from the following items and their respective answers: 2B, 5A, 7B, 8A, 15B, 24A, 27B, 31B, 34A, and 39A.

All versions of the SS are proprietary. The potential user of the SS should write Professor Marvin Zuckerman, Department of Psychology, University of Delaware, Newark, DE 19716 for permission to use the scale. The book from which the SS is drawn is copyrighted under Professor Zuckerman's name.

APPENDIX TO OPTIMUM STIMULATION LEVELS:
REVIEWING/INTEGRATING FOUR OSL MEASURES
(Steenkamp and Baumgartner 1992)

In an excellent review and empirical examination, Steenkamp and Baumgartner (1992) found that four measures of OSL showed adequate levels of convergent validity such that their summed item composite scores could be used as indicators of one overall OSL measure. The four OSL measures examined were (a) the AST-II, a revised version of the Arousal Seeking Tendency Scale (Mehrabian 1978); (b) the SS-V, the Form V Sensation Seeking Scale (Zuckerman 1979); (c) the CSI—Change Seeking Index (Garlington and Shimota 1964); and (d) the NES—Novelty Experiencing Scale (Pearson 1970). Across all measures, item scoring was converted to a +2 to –2 Likert-type format with endpoints of strongly disagree/strongly agree, completely false/completely true, or strongly dislike/strongly like, depending on the measure.

Reliability estimates for the four OSL measures ranged from .806 to .913. (Subscale reliabilities for the SS-V ranged from . 50 to .79, and subscale reliabilities for the NES ranged from .81 to .89.) Correlations among the summed-item composites of the four scales ranged from .411 to .759, and factor loadings (on a one-factor model) for the summed-item composites ranged from .510 to .886, offering evidence for the convergent validity of the four OSL measures.

Over six experiments using behaviors such as gambling and decision making under risk, evidence for the predictive/nomological validity of the four-indicator OSL measure (i.e., the summed-item composites of AST-II, SS-V, CSI, and NES) was found.

Source: Steenkamp, Jan-Benedict E. M., and Hans Baumgartner (1992). "The Role of Optimum Stimulation Level in Exploratory Consumer Behavior." *Journal of Consumer Research*, *19*, 434-448. © 1992 by University of Chicago Press. Reprinted with permission.

References: Garlington, Warren K., and Helen Shimota. (1964). "The Change Seeker Index: A Measure of the Need for Variable Stimulus Input." *Psychological Reports*, *14*, 919-924.

Mehrabian, Albert. (1978). "Characteristic Individual Reactions to Preferred and Unpreferred Environments." *Journal of Personality*, *46*, 717-731.

Pearson, Pamela. (1970). "Relationships Between Global and Specific Measures of Novelty Seeking." *Journal of Consulting and Clinical Psychology*, *43*(2), 199-204.

Zuckerman, Marvin. (1979). *Sensation Seeking: Beyond the Optimal Level of Arousal.* Hillsdale, NJ: Lawrence Erlbaum Associates.

SCALES RELATED TO CONSUMER RESPONSES/STYLES IN THE MARKETPLACE

BRAND PARITY: PERCEIVED BRAND PARITY
(Muncy 1996)

Construct: Brand parity is defined as the "overall perception held by the consumer that the differences between the major brand alternatives in a product category are small" (Muncy 1996, p. 411). As such, when consumers view major brand alternatives as similar, parity is high, and when consumers view brand alternatives as dissimilar, parity is low. In essence, it can be viewed as the opposite of product differentiation.

Description: The brand parity scale is composed of five Likert-type items scored on 5-point scales ranging from *strongly disagree* to *strongly agree*. Item scores can be summed to form an overall brand parity score.

Development: Based on responses from 29 students, eight items were originally generated to reflect the construct. Using several student samples and three iterations, the final five-item scale was derived. Via a confirmatory approach, reliability analyses, and several correlational-based tests over three product categories (i.e., detergent, shampoo, and toothpaste), the structure, internal consistency, and validity of the scale were examined.

Samples: Other than the $n = 29$ student sample and other student samples (n unknown), a sample of $n = 1,200$ "heads of households" was obtained. A response rate of 82% was reported (i.e., $n = 985$). This sample was split evenly over the three product categories ($n = 331$, $n = 327$, and $n = 327$).

Validity: A structural equation model, of which brand parity was a factor, revealed adequate fit over all three product categories, as well as the data combined into one overall sample ($n = 985$). Factor loadings across the three product categories ranged from .619 to .872. Coefficient alpha estimates for the scale ranged from .86 to .91. Path estimates from brand parity to brand loyalty, price sensitivity, and information usefulness were significant and in the predicted direction. Several other correlations also showed evidence of validity for the brand parity scale. For example, for the combined data ($n = 985$), brand parity had correlations of −.704, .734, and −.399 with brand loyalty, price sensitivity, and information usefulness, respectively.

Scores: Neither mean nor percentage scores were reported.

Source: Muncy, James A. (1996). "Measuring Perceived Brand Parity." In Kim Corfman and John Lynch (Eds.), *Advances in Consumer Research* (Vol. 23, pp. 411-417). Provo, UT: Association for Consumer Research.

© 1996 by the Association for Consumer Research. Scale items taken from Appendix 1 (p. 417). Reprinted with permission.

Other evidence: N/A

Other sources: N/A

References N/A

BRAND PARITY: PERCEIVED BRAND PARITY
(Muncy 1996)

1. I can't think of any differences between the major brands of _____.

2. To me, there are big differences between the various brands of _____.

3. The only difference between the major brands of _____ is price.

4. _____ is _____; most brands are basically the same.

5. All major brands of _____ are the same.

NOTES: "_____" is where the product category of interest is inserted for each statement. Item 2 requires reverse scoring.

BRAND PERSONALITY
(Aaker 1997)

Construct: Brand personality is defined as "the set of human characteristics associated with a brand" (Aaker 1997, p. 347). As such, brand personality tends to serve a symbolic or self-expressive function beyond the utilitarian function of product-related attributes. Brand personality is a multidimensional and multifaceted construct (see actual scale items/descriptors) where some dimensions and facets are more relevant and descriptive of certain brands than others.

Description: The brand personality scale has five dimensions and 15 facets that encompass 42 items. Items are scored on 5-point Likert-type scales ranging from *not at all descriptive* (1) to *extremely descriptive* (5) for each brand rated. Item scores are summed within each dimension, and then divided by the number of items within a dimension, to form scores for each dimension that can theoretically range from 1 to 5.

Development: Numerous procedures were used to develop the brand personality dimensions. Initially, a pool of 309 personality trait descriptors was generated and/or drawn from the personality literature and a free-association elicitation procedure involving 16 subjects. Then, using a similar procedure with 25 subjects, this pool was trimmed to 114. Using 37 brands that represented symbolic functions, utilitarian functions, and both symbolic/utilitarian functions, the 114 items were analyzed with a large sample. Via factor, item, and reliability analyses, the final 42-item form for the five dimensions was derived. Using another large sample, the stability of the five dimension structure was further assessed and validated using confirmatory factor and principal components analyzes (using 20 brands as stimuli).

Samples: To help generate the trait descriptors, adult samples of $n = 16$ and $n = 25$ were used. The first large sample consisted of $n = 631$ subjects reflective of the demographic breakdown of the 1992 U.S. Census, and the second large sample was composed of $n = 180$ subjects with a similar demographic breakdown.

Validity: Throughout the development of the scale, several reliability/validity tests were performed. Only a few relevant to the final scale are summarized. Using a subsample of $n = 81$ from the first large sample over a 2-month period, the five brand personality dimensions showed test-retest reliability correlations ranging from .74 to .77. Coefficient alphas estimates of internal consistency ranged from .90 to .95, and item-to-total correlations averaged .85 across the five dimensions. With the second large sample, both confirmatory factor and principal components analyses showed evidence for a stable five-factor model representing the five hypothesized dimensions of brand personality. In sum, high levels of reliability and validity were consistently found over samples and brands.

Scores: Mean scores (with standard deviations) were reported for all 42 items and for the five dimensions in an appendix (Aaker 1997, p. 354). Just the dimension means will be listed here. They are as follow: 2.72 (.99) for Sincerity, 2.79 (1.05) for Excitement, 3.17 (1.02) for Competence, 2.66 (1.02) for Sophistication, and 2.49 (1.08) for Ruggedness.

Source: Aaker, Jennifer. (1997). "Dimensions of Brand Personality." *Journal of Marketing Research*, *34*, 347-356.
   © 1997 by the American Marketing Association. Scale items taken from Appendix A (p. 354). Reprinted with permission.

Other evidence: N/A

Other sources: N/A

References: N/A

BRAND PERSONALITY
(Aaker 1997)

Trait (item)	Facet	Dimension
down-to-earth	down-to-earth	sincerity
family-oriented		
small-town		
honest	honest	
sincere		
real		
wholesome	wholesome	
original		
cheerful	cheerful	
sentimental		
friendly		
daring	daring	excitement
trendy		
exciting		
spirited	spirited	
cool		
young		
imaginative	imaginative	
unique		
up-to-date	up-to-date	
independent		
contemporary		
reliable	reliable	competence
hard-working		
secure		
intelligent	intelligent	
technical		
corporate		
successful	successful	
leader		
confident		
upper-class	upper-class	sophistication
glamorous		
good looking		
charming	charming	
feminine		
smooth		
outdoorsy	outdoorsy	ruggedness
masculine		
Western		
tough	tough	
rugged		

BRAND TRUST: PERCEIVED BRAND TRUST
(Hess 1995)

Construct: The brand trust conceptualization used by Hess (1995) is based on the premise that a brand is trusted by the consumer to the degree that the brand is perceived as being altruistic, reliable, honest, and competent, and that the consumer knows what to expect from a brand. Of these aspects, the brand trust scale assesses brand honesty, altruism, and reliability.

Description: The brand trust scale is composed of 11 items over three dimensions. Items are scored on 5-point scales ranging from *totally disagree* to *totally agree*. Item scores can be summed over all 11 items for a total brand trust score, or item scores can be summed within dimensions to form dimension scores for honesty, altruism, and reliability.

Development: Twenty items were initially generated to tap the conceptualization of the construct (i.e., altruistic, reliable, honest, competent, and knowing what to expect from a brand). Then, with two small pilot studies items were deleted and added such that a total of 38 items were used in a larger study for the purpose of deriving the final form of the scale. In the larger study, factor, item, and reliability analyses were used to derive the scale and examine reliability and validity. (This scale was developed with "cars" as the focal product.)

Samples: The pilot studies were composed of $n = 45$ undergraduate college students and $n = 40$ car owners. The larger sample was composed of $n = 260$ car owners.

Validity: A three-factor model, representing the reliability, honesty, and altruism dimensions, showed an adequate fit via confirmatory factor analyses. Correlations among the factors (dimensions) ranged from .46 to .57. Coefficient alpha estimates of internal consistency were .86, .81, .83, and .78 for the entire 11-item brand trust scale and the honesty, altruism, and reliability dimensions, respectively. The entire scale and each dimension were correlated with measures of satisfaction with brand of car, commitment to a brand of car, and intent to repurchase a brand of car. All correlations (12 in total) were significant and ranged from .41 to .78, supporting the validity of the scale and its dimensions. (All validity estimates are from the $n = 260$ sample.)

Scores: Mean (std. dev.) scores were reported for the $n = 260$ sample and were as follow: 20.57 (7.33) for the entire 11-item brand trust scale, 6.98 (3.01) for honesty, 8.85 (3.58) for altruism, and 4.74 (2.41) for reliability. Individual item mean scores and standard deviations also were reported (p. 22).

Source: Hess, Jeffrey S. (1995). "Construction and Assessment of a Scale to Measure Consumer Trust." In Barbara B. Stern and George M. Zinkhan (Eds.), *1995 AMA Educator's Proceedings* (Vol. 6, pp. 20-26). Chicago: American Marketing Association.
    © 1995 by the American Marketing Association. Scale items taken from Table 1 (p. 22). Reprinted with permission.

Other evidence: N/A

Other sources: N/A

References: N/A

BRAND TRUST: PERCEIVED BRAND TRUST
(Hess 1995)

1. _____ is interested in more than just selling me a car and making a profit.

2. There are no limits to how far _____ will go to solve a problem I might have.

3. _____ is genuinely committed to my satisfaction.

4. _____ will do whatever it takes to make me happy.

5. When I see a _____ advertisement I believe the information in it is accurate.

6. Most of what _____ says about its cars is true.

7. I think some of _____ claims about its cars are puffed up to make them seem better than they really are.

8. If _____ makes a claim or promise about its product, it's probably true.

9. My _____ is very reliable.

10. I feel I know what to expect from my _____.

11. If I bought another car from _____ I feel like I would know what to expect.

NOTES: Items 1-4 represent the altruism dimension, items 5-8 represent the honesty dimension, and items 9-11 represent the reliability dimension. Item 7 requires reverse scoring.

EMOTIONS: CONSUMPTION EMOTIONS SET: CES
(Richins 1997)

Construct: Based on the conceptual work of Clore, Ortony, and Foss (1987), and Ortony, Clore, and Collins (1988), emotion is viewed as a "valenced affective reaction to perceptions of situations" (Richins 1997, p. 127). This view excludes from the domain of emotions descriptors referring to (a) non-valenced cognitions such as interest and surprise, (b) bodily states such as sleepy and droopy, and (c) subjective evaluations of people such as self-confident or feeling abandoned. Based on this view, the Consumption Emotion Set (CES) was developed to assess the range of emotions most frequently experienced in consumption situations.

Description: The author proposed a few versions of the CES. The first version covers 16 identifiable clusters comprising 43 descriptors (i.e., items). Another version includes the 16 identifiable clusters as well as an "other items" category. A third version includes nine more descriptors beyond those in the first two versions. Throughout the developmental process, Richins used 4-point scales as response categories for each descriptor (i.e., *not at all likely* [0] to *very likely* [3], or *never, rarely, sometimes,* and *often,* or *not at all, a little, moderately,* and *strongly*). However, she notes that other scoring formats are tenable (p. 143). It seems that mean scores can be computed for each subscale (cluster) by correcting the means for differences in subscale length (most likely summing descriptor [item] scores within a given cluster and then dividing by the number of descriptor [items] in that cluster).

Development: Over six studies using several scaling procedures, the final versions of the CES were derived. Based on open-ended surveys and prior literature, a pool of 285 descriptors was first generated. Using the Clore et al. (1987) conceptualization as a guide, this pool was trimmed to 175 descriptors. (These procedures constituted Study 1.) Using some well-thought-out decision rules, Studies 2 and 3 reduced the pool of descriptors to 97. Studies 4 through 6 used several quantitative techniques to refine the number of descriptors to "clusters" or emotion subscales and to test their reliability, validity, and superiority over other emotion-based measures of consumption. Multidimensional Scaling (MDS) was used in Study 4 to define the clusters (subscales). Rigorous decision rules based on the MDS solutions were used to retain items. MDS, canonical correlation, and regression were used to compare the CES to existing measures of emotions in consumption in Study 5. Study 6 used discriminant analysis and ANOVA to demonstrate the predictive validity of the CES for three different consumption situations (i.e., automobiles, recreation-based products, and sentimental products).

Samples: Study 1 used samples of $n = 49$ undergraduate college students and $n = 48$ adult consumers. Study 2 used $n = 120$ undergraduate students. Study 3 used $n = 258$ adult consumers and $n = 203$ undergraduate students. Study 4 used a combination of $n = 448$ MBA and undergraduate students. Study 5 used $n = 256$ undergraduate students and $n = 194$ student respondents. Study 6 used four samples ranging in size from $n = 80$ to $n = 139$. Some of the Study 6 respondents were subset samples from Study 5.

Validity: As stated above in "Development," several procedures were used. Those relating to validity are briefly summarized here. Reliability was assessed via coefficient alpha for the three-item subscales. The correlation between items was used as a reliability estimate for two-item subscales (see items on the following pages). The MDS solutions, canonical correlations, and regression models of Study 5 generally showed that the CES captured more variance in the range of emotions than did other measures of consumption-based emotions. Also, for those consumption situations where sentimental value of the product was evident, those CES emotion clusters (i.e., subscales) emphasizing sentiment (i.e., feelings of love) showed greater predictive validity than did those more associated with negative feelings, such as anger or fear. Similar supportive validity results were found for the CES with respect to automobile and recreational products purchase situations.

Scores: Mean scores across purchase situations are graphed in Richin's Figure 6 (p. 143).

Source: Richins, Marsha L. (1997). "Measuring Emotions in the Consumption Experience." *Journal of Consumer Research*, 24, 127-146.

   © 1997 by the University of Chicago. Scale items taken from Appendix (p. 144-145). Reprinted with permission.

Other evidence: N/A

Other sources: N/A

References: Clore, Gerald, Andrew Ortony, and Mark A. Foss. (1987). "The Psychological Foundations of the Affective Lexicon." *Journal of Personality and Social Psychology*, *53*, 751-755.

   Ortony, Andrew, Gerald L. Clore, and Allan Collins. (1988). *The Cognitive Structure of Emotions.* Cambridge, UK: Cambridge University Press.

EMOTIONS: CONSUMPTION EMOTIONS SET: CES
(Richins 1997)

Cluster (subscale)	Descriptor
Anger (alpha = .91, .87)	Frustrated Angry Irritated
Discontent (r = .73, .67)	Unfulfilled Discontented
Worry (alpha = .77, .77)	Nervous Worried Tense
Sadness (alpha = .83, .72)	Depressed Sad Miserable
Fear (alpha = .82, .74)	Scared Afraid Panicky
Shame (alpha = .82, .85)	Embarrassed Ashamed Humiliated
Envy (r = .39, .46)	Envious Jealous
Loneliness (r = .55, .59)	Lonely Homesick
Romantic Love (alpha = .82, .82)	Sexy Romantic Passionate

Cluster (subscale)	Descriptor
Love (alpha = .86, .86)	Loving Sentimental Warm Hearted
Peacefulness (r =. 55, .68)	Calm Peaceful
Contentment (r = .60, .58)	Contented Fulfilled
Optimism (alpha = .82, .86)	Optimistic Encouraged Hopeful
Joy (alpha = .91, .88)	Happy Pleased Joyful
Excitement (alpha = .88, .89)	Excited Thrilled Enthusiastic
Surprise (N/A, alpha = .81)	Surprised Amazed Astonished
Other items	Guilty Proud Eager Relieved

NOTES: The "Other items" correspond to a second version where these items are not specified to an identifiable cluster. An expanded CES (third version) included the following items: awed, carefree, comforted, helpless, impatient, longing, nostalgic, protective, and wishful.

EMOTIONS: DIMENSIONS OF EMOTIONS: PAD
(Mehrabian and Russell 1974)

Construct: Emotional reactions to one's environment can be characterized by the three response dimensions of pleasure, arousal, and dominance. These dimensions are conceptualized to be relatively independent from one another (Mehrabian and Russell 1974, pp. 18-20).

Pleasure refers to a positive affective state that is felt to be distinguishable from preference, liking, positive reinforcement, and approach avoidance.

Arousal is a feeling state that varies along a single dimension from sleep to frantic excitement.

Dominance is based on the extent to which one feels unrestricted or free to act in a variety of ways.

Description: The PAD is composed of 18 semantic differential items scored on a +4 to −4 basis. There are six items representing each dimension described above. Item scores are summed within dimensions to form indices.

Development: Initially, 28 adjective pairs were generated by the authors. Then, based on 40 different hypothetical situations, 134 students responded to the 28 items. The responses were factor analyzed, and the six items in each dimension with the highest factor loadings were retained. In a second study, five additional items for dominance were generated, and the resulting 23 items were presented to another sample, and then factor analyzed. Based on the rule of eigenvalue greater than one, and again choosing the six items in each dimension with the highest loadings on their respective factors, a three-factor, 18-item version was retained (i.e., the final version of the PAD). The scale was then assessed for reliability and validity in another study.

Samples: Three student samples of 134, 163, and 214 were used in the initial scale development and validation.

Validity: From the third study ($n = 214$), estimates of internal consistency and test-retest reliability were performed. Internal consistency reliability was .81 for pleasure, .50 for arousal, and .77 for dominance. Test-retest (over 4 to 7 weeks) was .72, .69, and .77 for pleasure, arousal, and dominance, respectively. As originally conceptualized, the PAD dimensions were considered independent of one another. Factor analysis results across the three studies revealed low and mostly nonsignificant correlations among the three factors, ranging from −.07 to .26, providing evidence that the dimensions are distinct.

The PAD factors were also used as independent variables to predict a number of emotional states and traits (i.e., anxiety, neuroticism, sensitivity to rejection). The results suggest predictive validity for the three PAD dimensions (Mehrabian and Russell 1974, Table 3.4, p. 47). For example, multiple *R*s for the three PAD dimensions as predictor variables ranged from .24 to .73.

Scores: Appendix A (Mehrabian and Russell 1974, pp. 206-215) offers normalized scores for the PAD dimensions across 65 scenarios.

Source: Mehrabian, Albert, and James Russell. (1974). *An Approach to Environmental Psychology.* Cambridge, MA: MIT Press.
© 1974 by the MIT Press. Scale items taken from pp. 206-215. Reprinted with permission.

Other evidence: Although the scale has been used numerous times in social psychology applications, only evidence from consumer behavior studies is reviewed here.

Holbrook, Chestnut, Oliva, and Greenleaf (1984), in a study of how emotions affect enjoyment of games, used a 7-point format for the PAD dimensions and found coefficient alpha estimates of .89, .89, and .88 for pleasure, arousal, and dominance, respectively. Holbrook et al. (1984) also reported that the PAD dimensions were related to complexity and performance.

Havlena and Holbrook (1986) looked at how the PAD dimensions related to various consumption experiences by comparing PAD to another index of emotional response (i.e., Plutchik 1980).

A reduced set of 12 PAD items was used. On a sample of 10 MBAs, coefficient alpha for each PAD dimension exceeded .90. Intrajudge reliability among the 10 respondents ranged from .79 to .95 for the PAD dimensions (7-point scales were used for the PAD items). The correlations between the PAD dimensions and the other emotional index showed evidence of convergent validity. For example, average correlations between the PAD dimensions and the other index were .81 and .71 (based on vector spaces derived through discriminant and canonical analyses). Furthermore, the PAD was judged to be a better method for assessing emotions toward consumption experiences than the other index.

Other sources: Havlena, William J., and Morris Holbrook. (1986). "The Varieties of Consumption Experience: Comparing Two Typologies of Emotions in Consumer Behavior." *Journal of Consumer Research*, *13*, 394-404.

Holbrook, Morris B., Robert W. Chestnut, Terence A. Oliva, and Eric A. Greenleaf. (1984). "Play as Consumption Experience: The Roles of Emotions, Performance, and Personality in the Enjoyment of Games." *Journal of Consumer Research*, *11*, 728-739.

Reference: Plutchik, Robert. (1980). *Emotions: A Psychoevolutionary Synthesis.* New York: Harper & Row.

EMOTIONS: DIMENSIONS OF EMOTIONS: PAD
(Mehrabian and Russell 1974)

Each pair of words below describes a feeling dimension. Some of the pairs might seem unusual, but you may generally feel more one way than the other. So, for each pair, put a check mark (Example: ___ : ✓ : ___) to show how you feel about _____. Please take your time so as to arrive at a real characteristic description of your feelings.

Pleasure

1. happy—unhappy

2. pleased—annoyed

3. satisfied—unsatisfied

4. contented—melancholic

5. hopeful—despairing

6. relaxed—bored

Arousal

7. stimulated—relaxed

8. excited—calm

9. frenzied—sluggish

10. jittery—dull

11. wide awake—sleepy

12. aroused—unaroused

Dominance

13. controlling—controlled

14. influential—influenced

15. in control—cared for

16. important—awed

17. dominant—submissive

18. autonomous—guided

NOTES: All items must be recoded to reflect higher levels of the traits. The reduced set of items used by Havlena and Holbrook (1986) are items 1 through 4 for pleasure, items 7, 8, 9, and 12 for arousal, and items 13, 14, 17, and 18 for dominance.

HEDONIC AND UTILITARIAN CONSUMER ATTITUDES
(Batra and Ahtola 1991)

Construct: The premise that consumer attitudes are inherently bidimensional is the basis for the utilitarian and hedonic conceptualization used by Batra and Ahtola (1991). "Utilitarian" attitudes are more instrumental and concerned with the expectations of consequences of product usage, are based on assessment of functional brand/product attributes, and are more concerned with practical usefulness or benefits derived from a brand/product. "Hedonic" attitudes are based more on affective gratification derived from sensory product/brand attributes. Hedonic attitudes are more experiential and related to how much pleasure a consumer derives from a brand/product. These two dimensions are related, yet distinct, where one dimension might be more relevant to certain products/brands than the other dimension. Still, these two dimensions are not mutually exclusive for many products/brands.

Description: The final scale contains eight semantic differential items that cover the two dimensions (four items for the utilitarian and hedonic dimensions, respectively). Items are scored on 7-point scales, and item scores can be summed within dimensions to form a utilitarian attitude score and a hedonic attitude score.

Development: Scale development used an iterative process over three studies. In the first study, 16 items were generated to reflect the two dimensions; in the second study, 9 items were initially used to reflect the two dimensions; and in the third study, 23 items were used to initially reflect the dimensions. In each study, exploratory and confirmatory factor analyses were used to derive and verify a two-dimensional (i.e., utilitarian and hedonic) attitude structure over numerous products and brands as stimuli. From these studies, four-item scales were derived and further tested for dimensionality, reliability, and validity.

Samples: The three samples used in the three studies were $n = 59$, $n = 180$ (college students), and $n = 93$ (college students).

Validity: In the first two studies, confirmatory factor models using three items each for the utilitarian and hedonic components were estimated that showed adequate fit, discriminant validity, and internal consistency. However, given that the authors recommend four items each, the discussion of validity will be restricted to their four-item scales. In the third study, the two-factor structure showed adequate levels of fit and discriminant validity (via confirmatory factor analysis). For example, over 18 product/brand-related behaviors, discriminant validity was achieved in 13 of 18 comparisons. Coefficient alpha estimates of internal consistently exceeded .75 for the utilitarian dimension for 14 of the 18 behaviors, and they exceeded .80 for the hedonic dimension for 15 of the 18 behaviors. Average variance extracted estimates exceeded .52 for both components over all 18 product/brand-related behaviors. Both dimensions also showed evidence of predictive validity for attitudes hypothesized as primarily utilitarian product/brand-oriented, or primarily hedonic product/brand-oriented in structural equation models.

Scores: Neither mean nor percentage scores were reported.

Source: Batra, Rajeev, and O. Ahtola. (1991). "Measuring the Hedonic and Utilitarian Sources of Consumer Attitudes." *Marketing Letters*, 2(2), 159-170.
    © 1991 by Kluwer Academic Publishers. Scale items taken from Table 1 (p. 163) and Table 2 (p. 167). Reprinted with kind permission from Kluwer Academic Publishers.

Other evidence: Crowley, Spangenberg, and Hughes (1992) found mixed results for the factor structure supported by Batra and Ahtola (1991). Using a sample of $n = 151$ college students across 24 product categories, Crowley et al. found that for some products a two-factor (i.e., utilitarian and hedonic) structure adequately fit the data, but for other products, one- or three-factor models were better representations. They also found that the correlation between the four-item hedonic and utilitarian dimensions averaged .81 over the 24 products. However, they did report high levels of internal consistency for the four-item utilitarian and hedonic dimensions. Pooled across product categories, coefficient alpha estimates of internal consistency were .85 and .89 for the hedonic and utilitarian dimensions, respectively.

Other source: Crowley, Ayn E., Eric R. Spangenberg, and Kevin Hughes. (1992). "Measuring the Hedonic and Utilitarian Dimensions of Attitudes Toward Product Categories." *Marketing Letters*, *3*(3), 239-249.

References: N/A

HEDONIC AND UTILITARIAN CONSUMER ATTITUDES
(Batra and Ahtola 1991)

Utilitarian Items	Hedonic Items
useful—useless	pleasant—unpleasant
valuable—worthless	nice—awful
beneficial—harmful	agreeable—disagreeable
wise—foolish	happy—sad

HEDONIC AND UTILITARIAN CONSUMER ATTITUDES
(Spangenberg, Voss, and Crowley 1997)

Construct: Building on the conceptual work of Holbrook and Hirschman (1992), Batra and Ahtola (1991), and others, Spangenberg, Voss, and Crowley (1997) developed measures of utilitarian and hedonic consumer attitudes. Similar to other authors, Spangenberg et al. (1997) view utilitarian attitudes as more instrumental and concerned with the more functional consequences of product usage. Hedonic attitudes are based more on affective/emotive gratification derived from sensory product/brand attributes, are more experiential, and are related to how much pleasure a consumer derives from a brand/product. However, Spangenberg et al. suggest that hedonic attitudes are experienced at both cognitive and affective levels, but utilitarian attitudes are dominated by cognition. They also posit that the affective/cognitive nature of hedonic attitudes gives rise to emotional desires that compete with utilitarian motives of product purchase.

Description: The utilitarian and hedonic dimensions are composed of 12 items each. All items are 7-point semantic differential scales. Item scores are summed within each dimension to form overall attitude scores for utilitarian and hedonic dimensions.

Development: Via a literature review and pretest, 27 items were generated to reflect the two dimensions. With a large sample, using both exploratory and confirmatory factor analyses, item-to-total correlations, and reliability analyses, the final 12-item forms of the two dimensions were derived. Estimates of dimensionality, internal consistency, and validity were reported.

Sample: The sample for the main study was composed of $n = 608$ undergraduate students.

Validity: Over numerous brands/products, factor analyses showed evidence for a two-dimensional structure (i.e., the hypothesized utilitarian and hedonic dimensions). Construct reliability was .91 or greater for both dimensions, average variance extracted estimates were .47 or above for both dimensions, item-to-total correlations ranged from .57 to .86 over the two dimensions, and factor loading ranged from .58 to .90 over the two dimensions (for analyses involving brand names and product categories). Evidence of validity was offered via ANCOVA and regression-based tests of the hedonic and utilitarian dimensions' relationships with measures of need for cognition, sensation seeking, and involvement (pp. 238-239).

Scores: Neither mean nor percentage scores were reported.

Source: Spangenberg, Eric R., Kevin E. Voss, and Ayn E. Crowley. (1997). "Measuring the Hedonic and Utilitarian Dimensions of Attitude: A Generally Applicable Scale." In Merrie Brucks and Deborah J. MacInnis (Eds.), *Advances in Consumer Research* (Vol. 24, pp. 235-241). Provo, UT: Association for Consumer Research.

   © 1997 by the Association for Consumer Research. Scale items taken from Table 1 (p. 238). Reprinted with permission.

Other evidence: N/A

Other sources: N/A

References: Batra, Rajeev, and O. Ahtola. (1991). "Measuring the Hedonic and Utilitarian Sources of Consumer Attitudes." *Marketing Letters*, 2(2), 159-170.

   Holbrook, Morris, B., and Elizabeth C. Hirschman. (1982). "The Experiential Aspects of Consumption: Consumer Fantasies, Feelings, and Fun." *Journal of Consumer Research, 9*, 132-140.

HEDONIC AND UTILITARIAN CONSUMER ATTITUDES
(Spangenberg, Voss, and Crowley 1997)

Utilitarian Items	*Hedonic Items*
useful/useless	dull/exciting
practical/impractical	not delightful/delightful
necessary/unnecessary	not sensuous/sensuous
functional/not functional	not fun/fun
sensible/not sensible	unpleasant/pleasant
helpful/unhelpful	not funny/funny
efficient/inefficient	not thrilling/thrilling
beneficial/harmful	not happy/happy
handy/not handy	not playful/playful
unproductive/productive	enjoyable/unenjoyable
problem solving/not problem solving	cheerful/not cheerful
effective/ineffective	amusing/not amusing

HEDONIC AND UTILITARIAN SHOPPING VALUES
(Babin, Darden, and Griffin 1994)

Construct: Drawing on previous literature that examined utilitarian and hedonic attitudes/motives for shopping (e.g., Batra and Ahtola 1991; Holbrook and Hirschman 1982), Babin, Darden, and Griffin (1994) describe utilitarian and hedonic shopping value. Utilitarian shopping value is based on the premise that shopping is task-related and rational, reflecting a work mentality. Utilitarian shopping is viewed more as an "errand" or "work" where shopping is functional, and the shopper successfully completes his/her shopping task. Hedonic shopping value is more festive, playful, and fun. It reflects the entertainment value and emotional worth derived from shopping as a pleasurable experience. Hedonic shopping is viewed as enjoyable and as an "escape" or adventure. The scales developed by Babin et al. (1994) reflect the degree to which consumers derived hedonic and/or utilitarian value from a shopping trip.

Description: The utilitarian shopping value scale is composed of 4 items, and the hedonic shopping value scale is composed of 11 items. All items are scored on 5-point Likert-type scales. Item scores can be summed within each scale to create composite scores for the two scales.

Development: Several recommended procedures were used to derive the final 4- and 11-item forms of the scales. Based on focus group interviews and a literature review, 71 items were initially generated to reflect utilitarian and hedonic shopping value. After item judging, 53 items were retained for the first study. Via principal components, confirmatory factor, and item and reliability analysis, a 20-item, two-factor structure corresponding to the utilitarian/hedonic scale dimensions was derived. A second study reduced these 20 items to the final 4- and 11-item scales using confirmatory factor analysis and reliability analysis. Estimates of dimensionality, internal consistency, and validity were offered. A third study examined the psychometric properties of the scales.

Samples: The sample for the first study was composed on $n = 125$ college students. The sample for the second study was composed of $n = 404$ adult consumers. The sample for the third study was composed of $n = 485$ mall shoppers.

Validity: A two-factor structure representing the hypothesized dimensionality of the 4-item utilitarian and 11-item hedonic shopping value scales fit the data well in the second study. The correlation between the two scales was .16; coefficient alpha estimates of internal consistency were .80 and .93 for the utilitarian and hedonic scales, respectively. Factor loadings ranged from .56 to .83 (in absolute value), and item-to-total correlations ranged from .54 to .80 (in absolute value). Hypothesized correlations with related constructs provided evidence of scale validity. For example, the hedonic shopping value scale had correlations of .56, .34, .47, and .61 ($p < .01$) with measures of experiential shopping motives, compulsive buying, pleasure, and arousal, respectively. Corresponding correlations of these measures with the utilitarian scale were −.02 (ns), −.08 (ns), .31, and .26. (Other correlational estimates are also reported in Table 3, p. 651.) The third study also showed support for the hypothesized two-factor utilitarian/hedonic shopping value structure via confirmatory analysis with a correlation of .25 between the scales.

Scores: Neither mean nor percentage scores were reported.

Source: Babin, Barry J., William R. Darden, and Mitch Griffin. (1994). "Work and/or Fun: Measuring Hedonic and Utilitarian Shopping Value." *Journal of Consumer Research, 20,* 644-656.
  © 1994 by University of Chicago Press. Scale items taken from Table 1 (p. 649) and Table 2 (p. 651). Reprinted with permission.

Other evidence: N/A

Other sources: N/A

References: Batra, Rajeev, and O. Ahtola. (1991). "Measuring the Hedonic and Utilitarian Sources of Consumer Attitudes." *Marketing Letters*, 2(2), 159-170.

Holbrook, Morris, B., and Elizabeth C. Hirschman. (1982). "The Experiential Aspects of Consumption: Consumer Fantasies, Feelings, and Fun." *Journal of Consumer Research*, 9, 132-140.

HEDONIC AND UTILITARIAN SHOPPING VALUES
(Babin, Darden, and Griffin 1994)

Hedonic Items

1. This shopping trip was truly a joy.

2. I continued to shop, not because I had to, but because I wanted to.

3. This shopping trip truly felt like an escape.

4. Compared to other things I could have done, the time spent shopping was truly enjoyable.

5. I enjoyed being emerged in exciting new products.

6. I enjoyed this shopping trip for its own sake, not just for the items I may have purchased.

7. I had a good time because I was able to act on "the spur-of-the-moment."

8. During the trip, I felt the excitement of the hunt.

9. While shopping, I was able to forget my problems.

10. While shopping, I felt a sense of adventure.

11. This shopping trip was not a very nice time out.

Utilitarian Items

1. I accomplished just what I wanted to on this shopping trip.

2. I couldn't buy what I really needed.

3. While shopping, I found just the items(s) I was looking for.

4. I was disappointed because I had to go to another store(s) to complete my shopping trip.

NOTE: Item 11 of the hedonic scale and items 2 and 4 of the utilitarian scale require reverse scoring.

LOCAL RETAILER SHOPPING LOYALTY
(Hozier and Stem 1985)

Construct: The local retailer shopping loyalty scale is designed to measure the degree to which consumers desire to shop in their local community rather than "outshopping." The scale assesses aspects of consumer beliefs that they owe it to the community to shop locally and are loyal to community stores.

Description: The scale is composed of 10 items scored on 4-point scales with descriptors of *never* (1), *occasionally* (2), *frequently* (3), and *always* (4). Item scores are summed to form an overall score that can theoretically range from 10 to 40.

Development: Little information as to scale development was offered. The 10 items were chosen from a "previous" principal axis factor analysis.

Sample: One sample of $n = 705$ adult consumers was used.

Validity: A test-retest reliability correlation of .87 was reported. The local retailer shopping loyalty scale showed correlations of .51, .37, and −.20 with a single-item "loyalty" question, a percentage measure of in/local shopping, and a measure of leakage (amount of shopping outside the local area), respectively.

Scores: Neither mean nor percentage scores were reported.

Source: Hozier, George C., and Donald E. Stem, Jr. (1985). "General Retail Patronage Loyalty as a Determinant of Consumer Outshopping Behavior." *Journal of the Academy of Marketing Science*, *13*(1), 32-46.

   © 1985 by Sage Publications. Scale items taken from Table 1 (p. 36). Reprinted with permission.

Other evidence: N/A

Other sources: N/A

References: N/A

LOCAL RETAILER SHOPPING LOYALTY
(Hozier and Stem 1985)

1. I will pay slightly more for products if I can buy them locally.

2. I shop outside my local retail area before looking to see what is offered locally.

3. I shop at local stores because it is important to help my community.

4. I shop locally because the convenience outweighs the other advantages of shopping outside the community.

5. I shop locally to support the local merchants and business district.

6. Shopping at local stores is an enjoyable experience.

7. I will increase my interest in local stores when more goods/services are available through them.

8. Because I am more familiar with local stores, I prefer shopping locally than out of town.

9. I shop locally even when the selection/variety of goods is poor.

10. I am loyal to my local shopping area.

NOTES: Item 2 requires reverse scoring, and, though not specified by the authors, item 7 seems to require reverse scoring to reflect a greater level of local retailer loyalty.

MOOD SHORT FORM: MSF
(Peterson and Sauber 1983)

Construct: The term "mood" or "mood state" has a wide range of usage and definitions (cf. Peterson and Sauber 1983 and Gardner 1985 for critical reviews). However, most definitions of mood agree that "mood" has a state of emotional or affective arousal that is varying and transient. The transient and varying nature of mood is emphasized in MSF (Peterson and Sauber 1983).

Description: The MSF is a four-item scale composed of Likert-type statements scored on 5-point formats (*strongly disagree* to *strongly agree*). Item scores are summed to form a unidimensional MSF index.

Development: A large pool of items was generated to reflect the content domain of mood. Some items were drawn from Mehrabian's (1972) nonverbal communication scale and the Mood Adjective Check List (Nowlis 1965), as well as other items generated by the authors. This pool of items was then administered to a sample and factor analyzed, resulting in six items retained. After further item analysis and reliability checks, the four-item MSF was derived.

Samples: A sample of 323 undergraduate business students was used for scale development purposes. A subset of this sample ($n = 177$) was also used for test-retest reliability purposes. Four more samples were used to investigate other psychometric properties of the MSF: $n = 1,434$, $n = 713$, $n = 248$, and $n = 114$ (all nonstudents).

Validity: Coefficient alpha for the scale was reported to be .78, .74, and .77 for the samples of 1,434, 713, and 248, respectively. Test-retest reliability over a 30-day period ($n = 177$) was .18, indicating that mood does vary over time. Validity checks revealed that the MSF was marginally correlated with measures of satisfaction with the future (a beta weight of .22) and confidence in the American economic system (a beta weight of .24).

Scores: Mean scores were reported for the samples of 1,434, 713, and 248 and were 8.2, 7.8, and 8.1, respectively. (Scores could range from a low of 4 to a high of 20.)

Source: Peterson, Robert A., and Matthew Sauber. (1983). "A Mood Scale for Survey Research." In Patrick Murphy et al. (Eds.), *American Marketing Association Educator's Proceedings* (pp. 409-414). Chicago: American Marketing Association.
© 1983 by the American Marketing Association. Scale items taken from Table 1 (p. 411). Reprinted with permission.

Other evidence: N/A

Other sources: N/A

References: Gardner, Meryl P. (1985). "Mood States and Consumer Behavior: A Critical Review." *Journal of Consumer Research*, *12*, 281-300.

Mehrabian, Albert. (1972). *Nonverbal Communications*. Chicago: Aldine-Atherton.

Nowlis, V. (1965). "Research With the Mood Adjective Check List." In S. S. Tomkins and C. E. Izard (Eds.), *Affect, Cognition, and Personality*. New York: Springer.

MOOD SHORT FORM: MSF
(Peterson and Sauber 1983)

1. Currently, I am in a good mood.

2. As I answer these questions I feel cheerful.

3. For some reason I am not very comfortable right now.*

4. At this moment I feel edgy or irritable.*

NOTE:　*Denotes items that are reverse scored.

RETAIL CROWDING: PERCEPTION OF RETAIL CROWDING
(Machleit, Kellaris, and Eroglu 1994)

Construct: Perceived retail crowding is experienced when the "density" (i.e., the number of people and objects in a limited space) restricts or interferes with shopping activities or when the amount of environmental stimuli exceeds coping capacity. As such, perceived retail crowding is posited as two-dimensional: (a) a human crowding dimension and (b) a spatial crowding dimension. These dimensions encompass the restrictive movement and closed feeling aspects of perceived retail crowding.

Description: The perceived retail crowding scale recommended by the authors is composed of seven items covering two dimensions. Four items tap the "human" dimension, and three items tap the "spatial" dimension. All items are scored on 7-point Likert-type scales, and item scores can be summed to form overall dimension scores for the human and spatial aspects of retail crowding.

Development: Nine items were initially generated by the authors to tap the two dimensions of the construct. Over three studies using exploratory and confirmatory factor analyses, along with item and reliability analyses, the final four- and three-item dimensions were derived. Estimates of validity were also offered.

Samples: In the first study, $n = 76$ undergraduate college students were used. In the second study, a sample of $n = 140$ shoppers at a campus bookstore was used (86% were college students). The third study used samples of $n = 117$ and $n = 114$ of shoppers at Kroger and K-mart stores in the Midwest.

Validity: Although three studies were conducted, the final form of the scale was reported in the third study only. As such, the discussion here will be restricted to the third study (albeit the first two studies showed strong evidence for the dimensionality and internal consistency of four-item versions of both dimensions). In the third study, a two-factor confirmatory model representing the four-item human and three-item spatial dimensions fit the data well for both samples. The correlation between the two dimensions were .66 and .40 for the Kroger and K-mart samples, respectively. Tests of discriminant validity between the two dimensions were supported. Coefficient alpha estimates of internal consistency were .93 and .89 for the human dimension, and .86 and .69 for the spatial dimension. Average variance extracted estimates were .50 or greater for both dimensions over both samples, and factor loadings ranged from .59 to .99 across dimensions and samples. Correlations with "satisfaction with shopping experience" were mostly negative and significant as hypothesized, offering some evidence of nomological validity.

Scores: Scale/dimension scores were not reported.

Source: Machleit, Karen, M., James J. Kellaris, and Sevgin A. Eroglu. (1994). "Human Versus Spatial Dimensions of Crowding Perceptions in Retail Environments: A Note on Their Measurement and Effect on Shopper Satisfaction." *Marketing Letters*, *5*(2), 183-194.
        © 1994 by Kluwer Academic Publishers. Scale items taken from Table 2 (p. 189). Reprinted with kind permission of Kluwer Academic Publishers.

Other evidence: N/A

Other sources: N/A

References: N/A

RETAIL CROWDING: PERCEPTION OF RETAIL CROWDING
(Machleit, Kellaris, and Eroglu 1994)

Human Dimension

1. The store seemed very crowded to me.

2. The store was a little too busy.

3. There wasn't much traffic in this store during my shopping trip.

4. There were a lot of shoppers in the store.

Spatial Dimension

1. The store seemed very spacious.

2. I felt cramped shopping in this store.

3. The store felt confining to shoppers.

NOTES: Item 3 of the human dimension and item 1 of the spatial dimension require reverse scoring to reflect higher levels of retail crowding.

RETAIL STORE IMAGE—CONSUMER RETAIL STORE IMAGE: CIRS
(Dickson and Albaum 1977)

Construct: Though no formal definition was offered, consumer image of retail store was felt to encompass attitudes toward retail prices, products, store layout and facilities, service and personnel, promotion, and "others" (Dickson and Albaum 1977).

Description: The CIRS is composed of 29 7-point semantic differential items designed to measure the aforementioned attitudes. The item scores are summed to form an overall CIRS index.

Development: Adjective pairs were generated via depth interviews with 27 consumers. A total of 31 pairs was generated. Another sample of students was then used to trim this pool of items to the final 29-item form. Another study was then performed to assess scale reliability and factor structure.

Samples: Three samples were used throughout scale development: a sample of 27 consumers for item generation, a sample of 59 students to trim the item pool, and a sample of 82 (composed of students and their spouses) to check reliability and the factor structure.

Validity: Test-retest reliability (based on a subsample of 30 from the sample of 82) over a 2-week period was .91. The Spearman rank order reliability coefficient (split-halves) was .88. Factor analysis of the 29 items extracted five factors accounting for more than 50% of the variance in examining supermarket/discount stores, and six factors accounting for more than 50% of the variance in examining department/shoe stores.

Scores: Neither mean nor percentage scores were offered.

Source: Dickson, John, and Gerald Albaum. (1977). "A Method for Developing Tailor-made Semantic Differentials for Specific Marketing Content Areas." *Journal of Marketing Research*, *14*, 87-91.
© 1977 by the American Marketing Association. Scale items taken from Table 2 (p. 89). Reprinted with permission.

Other evidence: N/A

Other sources N/A

References: N/A

RETAIL STORE IMAGE—CONSUMER RETAIL STORE IMAGE: CIRS
(Dickson and Albaum 1977)

1. crammed merchandise—well spaced merchandise
2. bright store—dull store*
3. ads frequently seen by you—ads infrequently seen by you*
4. low quality products—high quality products
5. well organized layout—unorganized layout*
6. low prices—high prices*
7. bad sales on products—good sales on products
8. unpleasant store to shop in—pleasant store to shop in
9. good store—bad store*
10. inconvenient location—convenient location
11. low pressure salesman—high pressure salesman*
12. big store—small store*
13. bad buys on products—good buys on products
14. unattractive store—attractive store
15. unhelpful salesman—helpful salesman
16. good service—bad service*
17. too few clerks—too many clerks
18. friendly personnel—unfriendly personnel*
19. easy to return purchases—hard to return purchases*
20. unlimited selection of products—limited selection of products*
21. unreasonable prices for value—reasonable prices for the value
22. messy—neat
23. spacious shopping—crowded shopping*
24. attracts upper class customers—attracts lower class customers*
25. dirty—clean
26. fast checkout—slow checkout*
27. good displays—bad displays*
28. hard to find items you want—easy to find items you want
29. bad specials—good specials

NOTES: *Denotes items that are reverse scores. Dickson and Albaum note that items 1, 2, 5, 8, 14, 22, 23, 25, 27, and 28 could be used as a "shopping environment" factor, and that items 6, 7, 13, 21, and 29 could be used as a "product promotion-price" factor.

RETAIL STORE IMAGE: SIS
(Manolis, Keep, Joyce, and Lambert 1994)

Construct: Based on the work of Zimmer and Golden (1988), Manolis, Keep, Joyce, and Lambert (1994) posit a three-dimensional model of retail store image: (a) a general store attributes dimension, (b) an appearance-related dimension, and (c) a salesperson/service dimension.

Description: The SIS is composed of 10 items covering the three hypothesized dimensions. The items use 7-point semantic differential pairs as descriptor endpoints. Item scores can be summed within dimensions to form overall scores for each of the three dimensions.

Development: Forty-five items were originally generated to reflect the construct. Using a small convenience sample (i.e., focus groups were formed from $n = 37$), with store pictures as stimuli, this initial pool of items was trimmed to 23. Ten items were retained from scale purification processes. These 10 items were subjected to confirmatory factor analyses to test the dimensionality, discriminant validity, and internal consistency of the dimensions.

Samples: A small convenience sample of $n = 37$ was used to trim items from the initial pool. A sample of $n = 720$ shoppers from the San Francisco Bay area was used in the main study.

Validity: The data for the main study were analyzed in aggregate and by three store types (i.e., subsamples of approximately $n = 240$ each). For the subsample data, a three-factor model corresponding to the hypothesized store image dimensions was supported. Although some of correlations between dimensions were relatively high, tests of discriminant validity also supported the three-dimensional structure. These correlations ranged from .39 to .88 across the three subsamples. Average variance extracted estimates per dimension ranged from .40 to .60 over the three subsamples. Standardized factor loadings were .46 across dimensions and subsamples. Measurement invariance tests across the three subsamples (i.e., aggregating the data for multigroup analysis) were also supported.

Scores: Only individual item scores were offered (Table 2, p. 637).

Source: Manolis, Chris, William W. Keep, Mary L. Joyce, and David R. Lambert. (1994). "Testing the Underlying Structure of a Store Image Scale." *Educational and Psychological Measurement*, *54*, 628-645. © 1994 by Sage Publications. Scale items taken from Table 1 (p. 631).

Other evidence: N/A

Other sources: N/A

Reference: Zimmer, Mary R., and Linda L Golden. (1988). "Impressions of Retail Stores." *Journal of Retailing*, *64*, 265-293.

RETAIL STORE IMAGE: SIS
(Manolis, Keep, Joyce, and Lambert 1994)

General Store Attributes Dimension

1. The store has a: good selection of merchandise—bad selection of merchandise.

2. The store has a: good reputation—bad reputation.

3. Overall, I have a: good impression —bad impression.

4. The store is: high class—low class.

5. The store is: doing well—in trouble.

6. The store's layout is: good —bad.

Appearance-Related Dimension

1. The store has a: good appearance—bad appearance.

2. The store is in: good physical condition—bad physical condition.

Salesperson-Service Dimension

1. The store offers: good service—bad service.

2. The store's salesperson made a: good impression—bad impression.

NOTE: The semantic differential descriptor endpoints follow each statement.

SHOPPING STYLES: CONSUMER STYLES INVENTORY: CSI
(Sproles and Kendall 1986; Sproles and Sproles 1990)

Construct: The authors identify eight consumer shopping/decision making styles with the following characteristics (Sproles and Sproles 1990, p. 137):

Perfectionist/High Quality Conscious: the degree to which a consumer searches carefully and systematically for the best quality in products.

Brand Consciousness/Price Equals Quality: a consumer's orientation toward buying the more expensive, well-known national brands.

Novelty and Fashion Conscious: consumers who appear to like new and innovative products and gain excitement from seeking out new things.

Recreational and Shopping Conscious: the extent to which a consumer finds shopping a pleasant activity and shops just for the fun of it.

Price Conscious/Value for the Money: a consumer with a particularly high consciousness of sale prices and lower prices in general.

Impulsiveness/Careless: one who tends to buy on the spur of the moment and to appear unconcerned about how much he or she spends (or getting "best buys").

Confused by Overchoice: a person perceiving too many brands and stores from which to choose and who likely experiences information overload in the market.

Habitual/Brand Loyal: a characteristic indicating a consumer who repetitively chooses the same favorite brands and stores.

Description: The CSI is composed of 39 items that cover the eight styles described above. Also, for each style, a three-item short form of the scale is available (i.e., 24 items in total). All items are scored on 5-point Likert-type scales ranging from *strongly disagree* to *strongly agree*. Item scores are summed within each style separately to create composite scores for each style.

Development: Originally, 48 items seemed to have been generated to reflect the eight styles (i.e., six items per each style). Via principal components analysis with a large sample, the final-item form of the eight styles was derived. Estimates of reliability and validity (relationships with other constructs) were offered.

Sample: One sample of $n = 482$ usable responses was obtained. The subjects were all high school students in home economics classes.

Validity: Coefficient alpha estimates for the longer and three-item versions of the style scales ranged from .41 to .76 (see actual scale items). Factor loadings across the eight styles ranged from .41 to .75 (in absolute magnitude). Correlations among the eight styles (from an oblique factor rotation) ranged from .14 to .29. The eight styles were correlated with measures of "learning style" and were used as dependent variables with different learning styles as predictors. Multiple Rs for five of the eight styles as dependent variables ranged from .25 to .36. Canonical correlations also provided estimates of validity for the eight styles.

Scores: Mean scores for the three-item versions of the scales are reported in Table 3 (Sproles and Kendall 1986, p. 275). These mean scores ranged from 8.7 for "brand consciousness" to 11.8 for "recreational shopping conscious."

Sources: Sproles, George B., and Elizabeth Kendall. (1986). "A Methodology for Profiling Consumers' Decision-Making Styles." *Journal of Consumer Affairs*, 20, 267-279.

© 1986 by The University of Wisconsin Press. Scale items taken from Table 1 (pp. 272-273). Reprinted by permission of The University of Wisconsin Press.

Sproles, Elizabeth Kendall, and George B. Sproles. (1990). "Consumer Decision-Making Styles as a Function of Individual Learning Styles." *Journal of Consumer Affairs*, 24 134-147.

© 1990 by The University of Wisconsin Press.

Other evidence: N/A

Other sources: N/A

References: N/A

SHOPPING STYLES: CONSUMER STYLES INVENTORY: CSI
(Sproles and Kendall 1986; Sproles and Sproles 1990)

Perfectionist/High Quality Conscious (seven-item alpha = .74, three-item alpha = .69)

1. Getting very good quality is very important to me.

2. When it comes to purchasing products, I try to get the very best or perfect choice.

3. In general, I usually try to buy the best overall quality.

4. I make a special effort to choose the very best quality products.

5. I really don't give my purchases much thought or care.*

6. My standards and expectations for products I buy are very high.

7. I shop quickly, buying the first product or brand I find that seems good enough.*

Brand Consciousness/Price Equals Quality (six-item alpha = .75, three-item alpha = .63)

1. The well-known national brands are for me.

2. The more expensive brands are usually my choices.

3. The higher the price of the product, the better the quality.

4. Nice department and specialty stores offer me the best products.

5. I prefer buying the best selling brands.

6. The most advertised brands are usually very good choices.

Novelty and Fashion Conscious (five-item alpha = .74, three-item alpha = .76)

1. I usually have one or more outfits of the very newest style.

2. I keep my wardrobe up-to-date with the changing fashions.

3. Fashionable, attractive styling is very important to me.

4. To get variety, I shop different stores and choose different brands.

5. It's fun to buy something new and exciting.

Recreational and Shopping Conscious (five-item alpha = .76, three-item alpha = .71)

1. Shopping is not a pleasant activity to me.*

2. Going shopping is one of the enjoyable activities of my life.

3. Shopping the stores wastes my time.*

4. I enjoy shopping just for the fun of it.

5. I make shopping trips fast.*

Price Conscious/Value for the Money (alpha = .48)

1. I buy as much as possible at sale prices.

2. The lowest price products are usually my choice.

3. I look carefully to find the best value for the money.

Impulsiveness/Careless (five-item alpha = .48, three-item alpha = .41)

1. I should plan my shopping more carefully than I do.

2. I am impulsive when purchasing.

3. Often I make careless purchases I later wish I had not.

4. I take the time to shop carefully for best buys.*

5. I carefully watch how much I spend.*

Confused by Overchoice (four-item alpha = .55, three-item alpha = .51)

1. There are so many brands to choose from that I often feel confused.

2. Sometimes it's hard to choose which stores to shop.

3. The more I learn about products, the harder it seems to choose the best.

4. All the information I get on different products confuses me.

Habitual/Brand Loyal (four-item alpha = .53, three-item alpha = .54)

1. I have favorite brands I buy over and over.

2. Once I find a product or brand I like, I stick with it.

3. I go to the same stores each time I shop.

4. I change brands I buy regularly.*

NOTES: *Denotes items that require reverse scoring. The first three items (i.e., 1, 2, and 3) of every style represent the three-item versions.

STYLE OF PROCESSING SCALE: SOP
(Childers, Houston, and Heckler 1985)

Construct: Childers, Houston, and Heckler (1985) conceptualize processing style as a preference and propensity to engage in a verbal and/or visual modality of processing information about one's environment.

Description: The SOP is a 22-item scale, where the items are scored from 1 (*always true*) to 4 (*always false*). Eleven items reflect a visual processing style, and 11 items reflect a verbal processing style. The scale can be broken down into two components by summing item scores within components, or used to compute a summed overall score of SOP representing a point on a continuum reflecting a preference for one of the two processing styles (Childers et al. 1985).

Development: After defining the construct and reviewing the literature, items from existing measures of processing style and newly generated items were used as an initial pool. Six items from Richardson's (1977) VVQ and 36 new items were generated. These 42 items were then administered to a sample and trimmed to 22 items based on item-to-total correlations. The reliability, validity, and structure of the 22-item SOP were examined in later samples.

Samples: A sample of 35 undergraduate students was used to trim the initial pool of items from 42 to 22. A sample of 106 undergraduate students was used to examine the reliability, validity, and structure of the SOP (Childers et al. 1985).

Validity: The 11-item verbal component and the 11-item visual component of the SOP had alphas of .81 and .86, respectively. The alpha of the overall 22-item SOP was .88. Furthermore, factor analysis revealed that the SOP was best represented by a two-factor structure (i.e., 11 items for the verbal and 11 items for the visual components).

Correlations of the SOP with other measures of processing style demonstrated discriminant validity for the SOP, and correlations of the SOP with measures of ad recall ($r = -.34$) and recognition ($r = -.31$) showed evidence of criterion validity for the SOP.

Scores: No mean and/or percentage scores were reported.

Source: Childers, Terry L., Michael J. Houston, and Susan Heckler. (1985). "Measurement of Individual Differences in Visual Versus Verbal Information Processing." *Journal of Consumer Research*, *12*, 125-134.

© 1985 by University of Chicago Press. Scale items taken from Exhibit (p. 129). Reprinted with permission.

Other evidence: N/A

Other sources: N/A

Reference: Richardson, Alan. (1977). "Verbalizer-Visualizer: A Cognitive Style Dimension." *Journal of Mental Imagery*, *1*, 109-126.

STYLE OF PROCESSING SCALE: SOP
(Childers, Houston, and Heckler 1985)

The aim of this exercise is to determine the style or manner you use when carrying out different mental tasks. Your answers to the questions should reflect the manner in which you typically engage in each of the tasks mentioned. There are no right or wrong answers, we only ask that you provide honest and accurate answers. Please answer each question by circling one of the four possible responses. For example, if I provided the statement "I seldom read books," and this was your **typical** behavior, even though you might read one book a year, you would circle the ALWAYS TRUE response. Responses can range from 1 = *always true* to 4 = *always false.*

1. I enjoy doing work that requires the use of words.

2. There are some special times in my life that I like to relive by mentally "picturing" just how everything looked.*

3. I can never seem to find the right word when I need it.*

4. I do a lot of reading.

5. When I'm trying to learn something new, I'd rather watch a demonstration than read how to do it.*

6. I think I often use words in the wrong way.*

7. I enjoy learning new words.

8. I like to picture how I could fix up my apartment or a room if I could buy anything I wanted.*

9. I often make written notes to myself.

10. I like to daydream.*

11. I generally prefer to use a diagram rather than a written set of instructions.*

12. I like to "doodle."*

13. I find it helps to think in terms of mental pictures when doing many things.*

14. After I meet someone for the first time, I can usually remember what they look like, but not much about them.*

15. I like to think of synonyms for words.

16. When I have forgotten something I frequently try to form a mental "picture" to remember it.*

17. I like learning new words.

18. I prefer to read instructions about how to do something rather than have someone show me.

19. I prefer activities that don't require a lot of reading.*

20. I seldom daydream.

21. I spend very little time trying to increase my vocabulary.*

22. My thinking often consists of mental "pictures" or images.*

NOTES: *Denotes items that are reverse scored. Items 1, 3, 4, 6, 7, 9, 15, 17, 18, 19, and 21 compose the verbal component. Items 2, 5, 8, 10 through 14, 16, 20, and 22 compose the visual component.

SCALES RELATED TO TIME USAGE AND HOUSEHOLD ROLES

POLYCHRONIC ATTITUDE INDEX: PAI
(Kaufman, Lane, and Lindquist 1991)

Construct: Polychronic time use is defined in terms of combining activities such that several goals can be attained at the same time. Thus, two or more activities are performed in the same time block at the same time. Conceptually, it is proposed that polychronic time use is a strategic process whereby individuals enrich their time budgets producing the output of more than 24 hours of single, monochronic time use (Kaufman, Lane, and Lindquist 1991, p. 394). The PAI was designed to measure attitudes toward polychronic time use.

Description: The PAI is composed of four items measured on 5-point *strongly agree* to *strongly disagree* Likert-type scales. The item scores are summed to form an overall PAI, and the PAI is considered unidimensional.

Development: Based on the conceptual description and a literature review, 15 statements were initially generated to tap the domain of the construct. With two student sample pretests, item-to-total correlations were used to delete 11 items, resulting in the final four-item version of the PAI. Dimensionality, reliability, and validity checks were also performed on a later sample.

Samples: As stated above, the PAI items were initially pretested on two student samples (*n* not specified). The final version of the scale was administered to a sample of 310 (42% male and 58% female) in the Philadelphia metropolitan area.

Validity: Factor analysis revealed that the PAI was unidimensional and had a coefficient alpha of .68. The PAI was negatively correlated with a measure of role overload (–.15), and the pattern of correlations of the PAI with activity statements reflecting polychronic time use showed modest evidence of validity (range of .02 to .13 in absolute value). The PAI was also found to be positively correlated with education, employment, and club membership.

Scores: Neither mean nor percentage scores were reported.

Source: Kaufman, Carol Felker, Paul M. Lane, and Jay D. Lindquist. (1991). "Exploring More Than 24 Hours a Day: A Preliminary Investigation of Polychronic Time Use." *Journal of Consumer Research*, *18*, 392-401.

    © 1991 by University of Chicago Press. Scale items taken from Appendix A (p. 400). Reprinted with permission.

Other evidence: N/A

Other sources: N/A

References: N/A

POLYCHRONIC ATTITUDE INDEX: PAI
(Kaufman, Lane, and Lindquist 1991)

1. I do not like to juggle several activities at the same time.

2. People should try not to do too many things at once.

3. When I sit down at my desk, I work on one project at a time.

4. I am comfortable doing several things at the same time.

NOTE: Items 1, 2, and 3 require reverse scoring.

ROLE OVERLOAD OF THE WIFE
(Reilly 1982)

Construct: Role overload for a housewife is defined as the conflict that occurs when the sheer volume of behavior demanded of the wife exceeds her available time and energy (Reilly 1982). This definition is consistent with the organizational behavior literature view of role overload (House and Rizzo 1972; Rizzo, House, and Lirtzman 1970).

Description: The role overload scale is composed of 13 Likert-type items scored on a 5-point basis from *strongly disagree* to *strongly agree*. Item scores are summed to form an overall index of role overload.

Development: The author and several doctoral students wrote a number of items to reflect the construct. These items were administered to a sample of housewives, and items with low item-to-total correlations were eliminated, resulting in the final 13-item scale. Reliability and validity estimates were also obtained.

Samples: A sample of 106 married women responded to the scale.

Validity: Coefficient alpha for the scale was .88, and item-to-total correlations ranged from .50 to .80. Correlations with other constructs showed some evidence of validity. For example, correlations of the scale with women's work attitude and work status were .15 and .17, respectively.

Scores: Neither mean nor percentage scores were provided.

Source: Reilly, Michael D. (1982). "Working Wives and Convenience Consumption." *Journal of Consumer Research*, 8, 407-417.
        © 1982 by University of Chicago Press. Scale items taken from Appendix A (p. 417). Reprinted with permission.

Other evidence: In a study of time use (Kaufman, Lane, and Lindquist 1991), the role overload scale had a coefficient alpha of .86 and was negatively correlated with a measure of time use (−.146), offering further evidence of the scale's reliability and validity.

Other source: Kaufman, Carol Felker, Paul M. Lane, and Jay D. Lindquist. (1991). "Exploring More Than 24 Hours a Day: A Preliminary Investigation of Polychronic Time Use." *Journal of Consumer Research*, 18, 392-401.

References: House, Robert L., and John R. Rizzo. (1972). "Role Conflict and Ambiguity as Critical Variables in a Model of Organizational Behavior." *Organizational Behavior and Human Performance*, 7, 467-505.

Rizzo, John R., Robert J. House, and Sidney Lirtzman. (1970). "Role Conflict and Ambiguity in Complex Organizations." *Administrative Science Quarterly*, 15, 150-163.

ROLE OVERLOAD OF THE WIFE
(Reilly 1982)

1. I have to do things which I don't really have the time and energy for.

2. There are too many demands on my time.

3. I need more hours in the day to do all the things which are expected of me.

4. I can't ever seem to get caught up.

5. I don't ever seem to have any time for myself.

6. There are times when I cannot meet everyone's expectations.

7. Sometimes I feel as if there are not enough hours in the day.

8. Many times I have to cancel my commitments.

9. I seem to have to overextend myself in order to be able to finish everything I have to do.

10. I seem to have more commitments to overcome than some of the other wives I know.

11. I find myself having to prepare priority lists (lists which tell me which things I should do first) to get done all the things I have to do. Otherwise, I forget because I have so much to do.

12. I feel I have to do things hastily and maybe less carefully in order to get everything done.

13. I just can't find the energy in me to do all the things expected of me.

SPOUSAL CONFLICT AROUSAL SCALE: SCAS
(Seymour and Lessne 1984)

Construct: Conflict arousal in a spousal decision-making setting can be defined as the level of dyadic discordance resulting from the initiation of a joint purchase decision between husband and wife (Seymour and Lessne 1984). Four components underlie conflict arousal in consumer decision making.

Interpersonal need is the level of strength of bonds in establishing and maintaining the desire to interact with another individual (i.e., the dyad members of husband and wife).

Power is the ability to influence others and resist being subject to their wills (i.e., the dyad members of husband and wife).

Involvement is the degree to which an individual is willing to engage in complex combinations of decision alternatives.

Utility is the level of motivation to acquire a product derived from the product's ability to satisfy individual wants.

Description: The SCAS is a 20-item scale where all the items are scored on 7-point Likert-type formats (*strongly disagree* to *strongly agree*). The scale is further broken down into the four components above, with each component being represented by five items. Item scores can be summed within components to form component scores. However, a recommended overall scoring procedure is offered by Seymour and Lessne (1984) (see Appendix).

Development: A pool of 44 items was generated to tap the four components. (The items were generated for a car purchase scenario.) A sample of 132 married subjects then responded to the 44 items, and items with less than a .50 item-to-total correlation on the respective components were eliminated, resulting in 33 items. Factor analysis was then used to assess dimensionality and further reduce the number of items, resulting in the final 20-item SCAS. Two other samples of married subjects were also used to further assess reliability and validity (Seymour and Lessne 1984).

Samples: Three samples of married subjects were used by Seymour and Lessne (1984). A sample of 132 was used for initial scale reduction, dimensionality, and reliability. A subsample from this group ($n = 121$) was also used to assess various forms of reliability. A sample of 90 married people was used to assess discriminant and convergent validity as well as reliability. Finally, a sample of 46 husbands and wives was used to assess predictive validity.

Validity: A number of reliability estimates were reported. Coefficient alpha for the four SCAS components ranged from .79 to .89, and item-to-total correlations (within each component) ranged from .64 to .86 ($n = 121$). Test-rest reliability was .81 over a 3-week period for the 20 items. In addition, the hypothesized factor structure was shown to be stable over time. Concurrent validity estimates were also high, ranging from .40 to .81 across the four components ($n = 121$).

In the $n = 90$ sample, a multitrait-multimethod matrix involving the SCAS component measures and other measures assessing aspects of spousal conflict indicated strong convergent validity for the utility, involvement, and power components and marginal support for the interpersonal need component. In addition, discriminant validity was not found between the utility and involvement components.

The sample of 46 husbands and wives was used to assess predictive validity by correlating the SCAS with a behavioral measure of conflict arousal. A correlation of .40 was found between the two measures, supporting the predictive validity of SCAS.

Scores:	Direct mean scores were not reported. The SCAS uses a linear transformation procedure to derive an overall score of conflict arousal that ranges from 0 to 1 (see Appendix).
Source:	Seymour, Daniel, and Greg Lessne. (1984). "Spousal Conflict Arousal: Scale Development." *Journal of Consumer Research*, *11*, 810-821. © 1984 by University of Chicago Press. Scale items taken from Exhibit 1 (pp. 815-816). Reprinted with permission.

Other evidence: N/A

Other sources: N/A

References: N/A

SPOUSAL CONFLICT AROUSAL SCALE: SCAS
(Seymour and Lessne 1984)

The following survey is an attempt to understand your opinions in your roles as a consumer and family member. Each spouse should fill out a **separate survey**. Please **do not** discuss your responses before or during the time you are responding to the survey. All information contained herein is for research purposes only and will be treated anonymously.

1. An automobile, like many other products, is an expression of social image.

2. In making a decision as to which automobile to buy, it is important to get as much information as possible regardless of the time or cost involved.

3. A great deal of personal satisfaction can be gotten from buying an automobile.

4. The type of automobile one buys often represents their level of personal achievement.

5. Because buying an automobile can be a fairly complex decision, a "satisfactory" solution is better than taking a great deal of energy to try and find the "best" solution.*

6. The greater the number of automobiles considered when buying an automobile, the better the results.

7. If information could be seen in terms of dollars, it is reasonable to spend a great deal of money for information before making an automobile purchase.

8. The function that an automobile performs is **not** very important to me.*

9. With the exception of price, there is not much difference between one automobile and another.

10. I get a great deal of enjoyment out of using an automobile.

11. In general, I do **not** have a large amount of experience in the "ways of the world."*

12. I think my (husband/wife) trusts my ability to make a choice which affects our family.

13. I believe that criticism of my (husband/wife's) actions is a natural part of any close relationship.

14. If I were lonely, my first thought would be to seek my (husband/wife's) companionship.*

15. When I know something is important to my (husband/wife), I always try to satisfy (his/her) wishes.*

16. In general, I derive a great deal of satisfaction out of researching a difficult problem and making a decision.

17. I consider myself to be a fairly attractive individual.

18. I would forgive my (husband/wife) for practically anything.*

19. I do need a partner who will listen to my problems.*

20. It would be hard for me to get along without my (husband/wife).*

NOTES: * Denotes items that are reverse scored. Items 13, 15, 16, 19, and 20 compose the interpersonal need component. Items 1, 3, 4, 8, and 10 compose the utility component. Items 2, 5, 6, 7, and 9 compose the involvement component, and items 11, 12, 14, 17, and 18 compose the power component. Although "automobile" is used as the focal product in several of the above items, it is felt that other "high ticket" purchases can be used interchangeably in the statements (Seymour and Lessne 1984, p. 812).

APPENDIX

Derivation of Conflict Arousal Score

Conflict arousal score = TCI − 1.33(DCI)/280

A linear transformation is needed to derive the above equation where:

TCI = total conditional influence which is equal to the sum of the husband's and wife's score on the 20-item SCAS.

DCI = the difference in conditional influence which is equal to the husband's score minus the wife's score on the 20-item SCAS.

The values 1.33 and 280 are constants such that the conflict arousal score ranges from 0 to 1, higher scores reflecting a higher level of conflict.

Thus, the following should hold true:

1. As DCI increases, conflict arousal decreases.

2. As TCI increases, conflict arousal increases.

3. When TCI is at a maximum of 280 (i.e., 20 items × 7 point scales across both husband and wife), and DCI is at a minimum (i.e., husband's SCAS score minus wife's SCAS score equals 0), the conflict arousal score should be 1.

4. When DCI is at a minimum of 120 (i.e., the maximum of any spouse's SCAS is 140 minus the minimum of any spouse's SCAS is 20), and TCI equals 160, the conflict arousal score is 0.

5. The maximum conflict arousal score is 1, and the minimum is 0.

TIME ORIENTATION
(Amyx and Mowen 1995)

Construct: Time orientation refers to a customer's willingness to delay or expedite gains (i.e., obtaining a reward or something of value) and losses (i.e., giving up something of value) (Amyx and Mowen 1995). As such, this construct encompasses a "future" time aspect which stresses a willingness to delay gains for long-term expectations, and a "present" time aspect stressing immediate gratification over long-term interests.

Description: The time orientation scale is composed of seven items scored on 5-point Likert-type scales ranging from *strongly disagree* to *strongly agree*. Item scores are summed to form an overall time orientation scale that can theoretically range from 7 to 49.

Development: A number of items, some generated by the authors and some culled from existing measures relating to time orientation, were generated to reflect the construct. Via an iterative process using principal components and common factor analyses, the final 7-item form of the scale was derived. Estimates of reliability and an experiment showing evidence of validity were offered.

Samples: Samples of $n = 261$ and $n = 246$ college students were used to develop the scale and tests its validity.

Validity: Coefficient alpha for the final seven-item scale was .66, and factor loadings ranged from .35 to .65 ($n = 261$). With the experimental sample ($n = 246$), scale scores were split at the median to form "future" and "present" time orientation groups. These groups were used as independent variables predicting scores on the dependent variables of "likelihood of buying" and "paying" now or in the future (with a car as the focal product). Mean level differences showed a modest but consistent level of support for the validity of the time orientation scale.

Scores: Mean, median, and mode scores for the scale were 28.59, 28, and 25, respectively ($n = 246$).

Source: Amyx, Douglas, and John C. Mowen. (1995). "Advancing Versus Delaying Payments and Consumer Time Orientation: A Personal Selling Experiment." *Psychology & Marketing*, *12*, 243-264.

                    © 1995 by John Wiley & Sons, Inc. Scale items taken from Table 1 (p. 250). Adapted by permission of John Wiley & Sons, Inc.

Other evidence: N/A

Other sources: N/A

References: N/A

TIME ORIENTATION
(Amyx and Mowen 1995)

1. If I really want to buy something, I frequently make the purchase quickly and think about the consequences later.

2. I tend to spend money as soon as I earn it.

3. I am the type of person who likes to slowly save up money in order to make large purchases.

4. I enjoy going shopping and buying on impulse.

5. I tend to think about alternatives a great deal before I buy things.

6. I always pay off my credit card bill each month.

7. If I have purchased something through mail order, I like to have the company express mail it, so I will get it more quickly.

NOTE: To reflect a higher level of "present time" orientation, items 3, 5, and 6 require reverse scoring.

SCALES RELATED TO PRICING PERCEPTIONS

PRICE PERCEPTION SCALES
(Lichtenstein, Ridgway, and Netemeyer 1993)

Construct: Lichtenstein, Ridgway, and Netemeyer (1993) offer a conceptual view of perception of price in a "negative role" and a "positive role." In a negative role, price represents the amount of money that must be given up to engage in a given purchase transaction. In a positive role, the price cue has been used as a signal to indicate quality, thus positively affecting purchase. Consistent with this view, the authors offer five constructs representing the negative role of price and two representing the positive role of price.

In the negative role,

Value consciousness is defined as a concern for price paid relative to quality received,

Price consciousness is the degree to which the consumer focuses exclusively on paying low prices,

Coupon proneness is defined as an increased propensity to respond to a purchase offer because the coupon form of the purchase offer positively affects purchase evaluations (Lichtenstein, Netemeyer, & Burton, 1990),

Sale proneness is defined as an increased propensity to respond to a purchase offer because the sale form in which the price is presented positively affects purchase evaluations (Lichtenstein et al. 1990), and

Price mavenism is defined as the degree to which an individual is a source for price information for many kinds of products and places to shop for the lowest prices, initiates discussions with consumers, and responds to requests from consumers for marketplace price information (see Feick and Price 1987).

In the positive role,

Price-quality schema is defined as the generalized belief across product categories that the level of the price cue is related positively to the quality level of the product, and

Prestige sensitivity is defined as favorable perceptions of the price cue based on feelings of prominence and status that higher prices signal to other people about the purchaser.

Description: Multi-item scales were developed to measure each of the seven constructs listed above. All items are scored on 7-point Likert-type scales ranging from *strongly disagree* to *strongly agree*. Item scores are summed within each scale to form overall indices for each of the seven constructs.

Development: Recommended scaling procedures were used to develop the measures. A large pool of items was initially generated to reflect the constructs. These items were culled from existing measures, generated by the authors, or generated by other marketing faculty/Ph.D. students. Given that measures of value consciousness, coupon proneness, and price-quality schema existed (e.g., Lichtenstein et al. 1990), the 69 items in this pool were restricted to items for the other four constructs. These 69 items were administered to a large sample of nonstudent adult consumers. Via factor and item analyses, the pool was further trimmed to 50 items. These 50, along with 21 items reflecting the value consciousness, coupon proneness, and price-quality schema measures, were evaluated by a field study-based sample. Via confirmatory factor analyses, reliability and item analyses, and numerous correlational based tests, the final forms of the scales were derived and tested for dimensionality, reliability, and predictive validity.

Samples: Two large samples of adult consumers ($n = 341$ and $n = 582$) were used to develop, refine, and check the reliability and validity of the measures.

Validity: With the second large sample, single-factor confirmatory models were estimated for each of the seven scales. Items were eliminated that exhibited low loadings and/or threatened scale dimensionality. This procedure resulted in the final forms of the scales. A series of two-factor models showed evidence for discriminant validity among the seven scales. A higher-order factor model representing value consciousness, price mavenism, price consciousness, sale proneness, and coupon proneness as first-order dimensions of the "negative role" of price, and price-quality schema and prestige sensitivity as first-order dimensions of the "positive role" of price, also found support. The standardized path estimates (lambdas) from the first- to the higher-order factors ranged from .549 to .833. The correlation between the higher-order "negative role" and "positive role" factors was $-.234$. The correlations among the seven scales ranged from $-.03$ to .58. Across all scales, coefficient alpha and composite reliability estimates ranged from .78 to .90. The seven price perception scales were used to predict, across several regression equations, numerous marketplace behaviors including readership of *Consumer Reports*, price recall accuracy and ability, sales responsiveness, and coupon redemption. Significant explained variance estimates in these dependent variables ranged from .04 to .50.

Scores: Means (std. dev.) were reported for each of the seven scales. These scores were 39.00 (7.34) for value consciousness, 18.12 (8.29) for price mavenism, 21.96 (7.64) for price consciousness, 23.55 (8.26) for sale proneness, 19.18 (7.78) for coupon proneness, 14.97 (5.21) for price-quality schema, and 19.11 (8.73) for prestige sensitivity.

Source: Lichtenstein, Donald R., Nancy M. Ridgway, and Richard G. Netemeyer. (1993). "Price Perceptions and Consumer Shopping Behavior: A Field Study." *Journal of Marketing Research*, *30*, 234-245.

   © 1993 by the American Marketing Association. Scale items taken from Appendix (pp. 243-244). Reprinted with permission.

Other evidence: N/A

Other sources: N/A

References: Feick, Lawrence, F. and Linda L. Price. (1987). "The Market Maven: A Diffuser of Marketplace Information." *Journal of Marketing*, *51*, 83-97.

Lichtenstein, Donald R., Richard G. Netemeyer, and Scot Burton. (1990). "Distinguishing Coupon Proneness From Value Consciousness: An Acquisition-Transaction Utility Theory Perspective." *Journal of Marketing*, *54*, 54-67.

PRICE PERCEPTION SCALES
(Lichtenstein, Ridgway, and Netemeyer 1993)

Negative Role of Price Scales

Value Consciousness

1. I am very concerned about low prices, but I am equally concerned about product quality.

2. When grocery shopping, I compare the prices of different brands to be sure I get the best value for the money.

3. When purchasing a product, I always try to maximize the quality I get for the money I spend.

4. When I buy products, I like to be sure that I am getting my money's worth.

5. I generally shop around for lower prices on products, but they still must meet certain quality requirements before I will buy them.

6. When I shop, I usually compare the "price per ounce" information for brands I normally buy.

7. I always check prices at the grocery store to be sure I get the best value for the money I spend.

Price Consciousness

1. I am not willing to go to extra effort to find lower prices.

2. I will grocery shop at more than one store to take advantage of low prices.

3. The money saved by finding lower prices is usually not worth the time and effort.

4. I would never shop at more than one store to find low prices.

5. The time it takes to find low prices is usually not worth the effort.

Coupon Proneness

1. Redeeming coupons makes me feel good.

2. I enjoy clipping coupons out of the newspaper.

3. When I use coupons, I feel that I am getting a good deal.

4. I enjoy using coupons regardless of the amount I save by doing so.

5. Beyond the money I save, redeeming coupons gives me a sense of joy.

Sale Proneness

1. If a product is on sale, that can be a reason for me to buy it.

2. When I buy a brand that's on sale, I feel that I am getting a good deal.

3. I have favorite brands, but most of the time I buy the brand that's on sale.

4. I am more likely to buy brands that are on sale.

5. Compared to most people, I am more likely to buy brands that are on special.

Price Mavenism

1. People ask me for information about prices for different types of product.

2. I'm considered somewhat of an expert when it comes to knowing the prices of products.

3. For many kinds of products, I would be better able than most people to tell someone where to shop to get the best buy.

4. I like helping people by providing them with price information about many types of products.

5. My friends think of me as a good source of price information.

6. I enjoy telling people how much they might expect to pay for different kinds of products.

Positive Role of Price Scales

Price-Quality Schema

1. Generally speaking, the higher the price of the product, the higher the quality.

2. The old saying "you get what you pay for" is generally true.

3. The price of a product is a good indicator of its quality.

4. You always have to pay a bit more for the best.

Prestige Sensitivity

1. People notice when you buy the most expensive brand of a product.

2. Buying a high price brand makes me feel good about myself.

3. Buying the most expensive brand of a product makes me feel classy.

4. I enjoy the prestige of buying a high priced product.

5. It says something to people when you buy the high priced version of a product.

6. Your friends will think you are cheap if you consistently buy the lowest priced version of a product.

7. I think others make judgments about me by the kinds of products and brands I buy.

8. Even for a relatively inexpensive product, I think that buying a costly brand is impressive.

NOTES: Items 1, 3, 4, and 5 of the price consciousness scale require reverse scoring. The price mavenism scale was adapted from the "market maven" scale of Feick and Price (1987).

VALUE CONSCIOUSNESS AND COUPON PRONENESS: VC AND CP
(Lichtenstein, Netemeyer, and Burton 1990)

Constructs: Value consciousness is defined as a concern for paying lower prices, subject to some quality constraint, and coupon proneness is defined as an increased propensity to respond to a purchase offer because the coupon form of the purchase offer positively affects purchase evaluations (Lichtenstein, Netemeyer, and Burton 1990). Based on these two conceptual definitions and a distinction between the two constructs grounded in transaction utility theory, the VC and CP scales were developed.

Description: The VC and CP scales are composed of seven and eight Likert-type items, respectively (*strongly agree* to *strongly disagree*). All the items are scored on a 7-point basis. Scores on the items are summed within each scale to form overall VC and CP scores.

Development: Consistent with the psychometric scaling literature, a pool of 66 items (33 for each construct) was generated based on the definitions of VC and CP and existing literature. Two expert judge panels were used to screen ambiguous and redundant items and to check for content validity. This trimmed the initial pool of items to 15 for VC and 25 for CP. Factor analysis and various estimates of reliability were then used to further purify the scales and assess the dimensionality and internal consistency of the scales. This resulted in the final seven-item VC and eight-item CP scales.

Samples: Two samples were used in the scale development process. The first consisted of 263 students. The second sample consisted of 350 nonstudent adults from a southeastern SMSA.

Validity: Based on the student sample, the composite reliability estimates for the VC and CP scales were .80 and .88, respectively. Via confirmatory factor analysis, tests of discriminant validity revealed that VC and CP measures were related yet distinct measures. The correlation between VC and CP was .36 for the student sample.

With the nonstudent sample, composite reliability estimates again were .80 and .88 for the VC and CP scales, and tests of discriminant validity revealed that the two measures were distinct, supporting the scale's discriminant validity. The VC-CP correlation was .24 for the nonstudent sample. In addition, the VC and CP measures were correlated with a number of cognitive and behavioral measures theoretically related to VC and CP. The pattern of correlations suggest that the VC and CP measures exhibited nomological validity (Lichtenstein et al. 1990). For example, CP explained between 15.5% and 24.4% of the variance in measures of coupon redemption. VC was significantly correlated with measures of enduring product involvement (.26), product knowledge (.43), price knowledge (.41), and information from *Consumer Reports* (.20).

Scores: No mean or percentage scores were reported.

Source: Lichtenstein, Donald R., Richard G. Netemeyer, and Scot Burton. (1990). "Distinguishing Coupon Proneness From Value Consciousness: An Acquisition-Transaction Utility Theory Perspective." *Journal of Marketing, 54,* 54-67.
© 1990 by the American Marketing Association. Scale items taken from Appendix A (pp. 64-65). Reprinted with permission.

Other evidence: Lichtenstein, Ridgway, and Netemeyer (1993) used a five-item version of CP and the seven-item version of VC. One-factor confirmatory models offered support for the unidimensionality of the two scales, and coefficient alpha estimates of internal consistency were .78 or above for the two scales. These two scales were further correlated (in the predicted direction) with measures of price mavenism, price consciousness, sale proneness, price-quality schema, and prestige sensitivity. These correlations ranged from −.03 to .58. Furthermore, both CP and VC were significant predictors of several marketplace behavior variables including readership of *Consumer Reports*, price recall accuracy and ability, sales responsiveness, and coupon redemption, across several regression equations.

Other source: Lichtenstein, Donald, R., Nancy M. Ridgway, and Richard G. Netemeyer. (1993). "Price Perceptions and Consumer Shopping Behavior: A Field Study." *Journal of Marketing Research*, *30*, 234-245.

References: N/A

VALUE CONSCIOUSNESS AND COUPON PRONENESS: VC AND CP
(Lichtenstein, Netemeyer, and Burton 1990)

Value Consciousness (VC)

1. I am very concerned about low prices, but I am equally concerned about product quality.

2. When grocery shopping, I compare the prices of different brands to be sure I get the best value for the money.

3. When purchasing a product, I always try to maximize the quality I get for the money I spend.

4. When I buy products, I like to be sure that I am getting my money's worth.

5. I generally shop around for lower prices on products, but they still must meet certain quality requirements before I will buy them.

6. When I shop, I usually compare the "price per ounce" information for brands I normally buy.

7. I always check prices at the grocery store to be sure I get the best value for the money I spend.

Coupon Proneness (CP)

1. Redeeming coupons makes me feel good.

2. I enjoy clipping coupons out of the newspaper.

3. When I use coupons, I feel that I am getting a good deal.

4. I enjoy using coupons regardless of the amount I save by doing so.

5. I have favorite brands, but most of the time I buy the brand I have a coupon for.

6. I am more likely to buy brands for which I have a coupon.

7. Coupons have caused me to buy products I normally would not buy.

8. Beyond the money I save, redeeming coupons gives me a sense of joy.

NOTE: Items 1-4 and 8 constitute the reduced version form of coupon proneness (Lichtenstein et al., 1993).

5

Reactions to Advertising Stimuli

MEASURES RELATED TO AD EMOTIONS AND AD CONTENT

EMOTIONAL PROFILE—STANDARDIZED EMOTIONAL PROFILE: SEP
(Holbrook and Batra 1987b)

Construct: The purpose of designing the Standardized Emotional Profile (SEP) was to create a parsimonious scale of multi-item indices that can be used to assess emotional responses to print ads or television ads. This set of scales is especially useful in exploring the effects attributable to the nonverbal components of advertising (cf. Holbrook and Batra 1987b). The dimensions of the SEP, as well as subdimensions, were defined as follows:

Pleasure refers intuitively to such feelings as joy, affection, gratitude, and pride. Subdimensions were labeled as faith, affection, and gratitude.

Arousal reflects interest, activation, surprise, and involvement. Subdimensions were labeled as interest, activation, and surgency.

Domination involves a sense of helplessness, sadness, fear, and distrust. Subdimensions were labeled as sadness, fear, and skepticism.

Description: The final SEP consists of 27 items. An example of the 7-point format for responding to each item is as follows:

	Very						Not at all
I felt . . . BORED	___	: ___	: ___	: ___	: ___	: ___	: ___

Subdimension scores are based on the sum of the items in each subdimension, and though not specified, dimension scores can be derived by summing the subdimension scores within dimensions.

Development: Holbrook and Batra (1987b) derived a large set of items based on a review and synthesis of literature (Mehrabian and Russell 1974; Schlinger 1979; Wells 1964; Wells, Leavitt, and McConville 1971). Through author judgment, 109 items reflecting 29 emotions were used as the initial item pool. In a purification study, they reduced the items to a more compact battery of scales accounting for the most variance in emotional responses to advertising content.

Specifically, the authors used the 109 items in response to 72 TV commercials to (a) assess the reliability of emotions toward advertising, (b) isolate the key underlying dimensions of emotional response to TV commercials, and (c) select a more parsimonious battery of scales for the purpose of constructing the SEP (cf. Holbrook and Batra 1987b, pp. 101-102). Twelve judges rated the 72 commercials on the 109 items using the 7-point format described above. Across items, Holbrook and Batra (1987b, p. 103) viewed judges as items in constructing a 12-item multijudge index for assessing reliability across the 72 commercials. The overall mean of this interjudge reliability was .52. Next, each of the 29 emotions was formed by combining three or four items (based on the scores of the 12 judges). The multi-item reliabilities for these emotions range from .47 to .96, with a mean of .81. Then, in a principal components analysis, a three-dimensional solution (pleasure, arousal, and domination) with eigenvalues of 13.6, 4.9, and 2.8 that accounted for 73.3% of the variance in the data was retained. Although this effort did not result in the final form of the SEP, estimates of concurrent validity were then assessed. The three dimensions were further reduced to form the final 27-item SEP via the following four procedures: (a) elimination of items whose multijudge reliability was less than .50, (b) elimination of a subdimension whose multi-item reliability fell below .80, (c) retention of the three subdimensions that loaded most strongly on each dimension, and (d) for those subdimensions with four rather than three items, elimination of the item with the lowest multijudge reliability.

Sample(s):   The SEP ratings were provided by 12 adult females recruited from the community (but not associated with the business school). As stated above, 72 commercials were chosen to provide a judgmental representation of a range of emotions likely to be found in television advertisements.

Validity: Specific estimates of reliability and validity were offered only for preliminary versions of the SEP. However, the four procedures used to derive the final form of the SEP suggest internal consistency estimates of .80 or above. Furthermore, concurrent validity for a preliminary version of the SEP showed that the three dimensions had significant beta weights for predicting the five ad criteria of ad approval, agreement, disagreement, favorable predisposition, and unfavorable predisposition. Multiple Rs for these dependent variables were .92, .83, .84, .90, and .85, respectively.

Scores: Mean scores for the scales were not reported by Holbrook and Batra (1987b).

Source: Holbrook, Morris B., and Rajeev Batra. (1987b). "Toward a Standardized Emotional Profile (SEP) Useful in Measuring Responses to the Nonverbal Components of Advertising." In S. Hecker and David W. Stewart (Eds.), *Nonverbal Communications in Advertising* (pp. 95-109). Lexington, MA: D. C. Heath.

    © 1987 by D. C. Heath. Scale items taken from Table 7-6 (p. 108). Reprinted with permission.

Other evidence: Portions of the above analyses are also reported in Holbrook and Batra (1987a). Further evidence of the nomological validity of the SEP is also offered by Holbrook and Batra (1987a). Their Table 6 (p. 417) reveals that the ad content factors of emotional, threatening, mundane, sexy, cerebral, and personal explained 72% of the variance in pleasure, 69% of the variance in arousal, and 16% of the variance in dominance. Furthermore, when the SEP was used as a predictor of Aad and Abrand, significant beta weights for the three SEP dimensions were found (i.e., .29, .63, and −.23 in predicting Aad for pleasure, arousal, and dominance, respectively).

Other source: Holbrook, Morris B., and Rajeev Batra. (1987a). "Assessing the Role of Consumer Responses to Advertising." *Journal of Consumer Research*, *14*, 404-419.

References: Mehrabian, Albert, and James A. Russell. (1974). *An Approach to Environmental Psychology.* Cambridge, MA: MIT Press.

    Schlinger, Mary. (1979). "A Profile of Responses to Commercials." *Journal of Advertising Research*, *19*, 37-46.

    Wells, William D. (1964). "EQ, Son of EQ, and the Reaction Profile." *Journal of Marketing*, *28*, 45-52.

    Wells, William D., Clark Leavitt, and Maureen McConville. (1971). "A Reaction Profile for TV Commercials." *Journal of Advertising Research*, *22*, 11-17.

EMOTIONAL PROFILE—STANDARDIZED EMOTIONAL PROFILE: SEP
(Holbrook and Batra 1987b)

Dimension	Subdimension	Items
Pleasure	Faith	Reverent
		Worshipful
		Spiritual
	Affection	Loving
		Affectionate
		Friendly
	Gratitude	Grateful
		Thankful
		Appreciative
Arousal	Interest	Attentive
		Curious
		Interested[a]
	Activation	Aroused
		Active
		Excited
	Surgency	Playful
		Entertained
		Lighthearted
Domination	Sadness	Sad
		Distressed
		Sorrowful
	Fear	Fearful
		Afraid
		Anxious
	Skepticism	Skeptical
		Suspicious
		Distrustful

a. This item was added to complete the Interest subdimension.

EMOTIONAL QUOTIENT SCALE (EQ) AND REACTION PROFILE
(Wells 1964a)

Construct: An important dimension of ad recall is emotional appeal. Wells (1964a) developed two scales that assess emotional reaction to ads. The first is the Emotional Quotient Scale (EQ), which measures a "global" emotional reaction toward ads, and the second is the Reaction Profile, which assesses three specific emotional reactions toward ads:

Attractiveness: the physical appeal of the ad.

Meaningfulness: the degree to which the ad delivers a message the respondent understands, will accept, and will find personally significant.

Vitality: the vividness of the ad.

Both scales were originally designed to test emotional reactions to print advertisements.

Description: The EQ is composed of 12 Likert-type statements (6 favorably worded and 6 unfavorably worded). A scale score is derived by summing the number of agreements with the favorable items and the number of disagreements with the unfavorable items, then dividing by 12 and multiplying by 100. Thus, an individual's score can range from 0 to 100.

The Reaction Profile is a 25-item scale operationalized as a series of semantic differential scales, 12 for attractiveness, 9 for meaningfulness, and 5 for vitality (one item overlapped on the attractiveness and vitality dimensions). All items are scored on 8-point scales, and item scores can be summed within dimensions, then averaged by the number of items in each dimension, to form scores for each dimension.

Development: For the EQ, items were generated such that they would discriminate between high and low appeal ads. Then, 100 consumers rated the items with respect to 18 to 24 print ads designed to differ in emotional appeal over three progressive refinement procedures. Item analysis was performed over the three procedures, and the 12-item EQ was derived.

The Reaction Profile was created from a pool of 26 semantic differential scales. Twenty of these scales were originally titled "Son of EQ" and were designed to measure emotional dimensions not tapped by EQ. The remaining six items were generated to reflect other words and phrases respondents might think of when reacting to ads. A large sample of housewives responded to the 26 items after viewing 48 full-page print advertisements (i.e., 50 respondents rated each ad). Through a series of tests (via ANOVA and factor analysis), items were eliminated that failed to distinguish between persons who differ in the quality being measured and that failed to measure the same quality as other items within the same dimensions. This resulted in the final 25-item Reaction Profile. Then, using two large samples, the predictive validity of the Reaction Profile was examined.

Samples: For the EQ, a sample of 100 consumers was used to develop the scale. For the Reaction Profile, a sample of 100 housewives responded to the "Son of EQ" items, and a sample of 600 housewives responded to the total Reaction Profile for scale development and refinement. Two more samples of 190 housewives and 950 consumers responded to the Reaction Profile for assessing predictive validity (Wells 1964a).

Validity: Little evidence of validity was offered for the EQ, and the validity evidence for the Reaction Profile was restricted to factor analysis and predictive validity. Factor analysis of the Reaction Profile supported the three-factor structure of attractiveness, meaningfulness, and vitality. With ad recall as the dependent variable, the predictive validity of the Reaction Profile dimensions was examined. The multiple correlation between the three dimensions of the Reaction Profile and ad recall was .94 (using cluster scores as predictors). For the $n = 950$ sample, the multiple correlations between the Reaction Profile dimensions and recall were .94 across 10 black and white ads and .75 across 19 color ads (Wells 1964a).

Scores: Neither mean nor percentage scores were offered by Wells (1964a).

Source: Wells, William D. (1964a). "EQ, Son of EQ, and the Reaction Profile." *Journal of Marketing*, *28*, 45-52.

        © 1964 by American Marketing Association. Scale items taken from Table 1 (p. 46), Table 3 (p. 48), Table 5 (p. 49), and Table 6 (p. 50). Reprinted with permission.

Other evidence: An abbreviated version of the Reaction Profile was employed to predict recall and recognition scores (Wells 1964b). These versions were three-item subscales from the "attractiveness" and "meaningfulness" factors. (The items were scored on 7-point scales.) The correlations between the attractiveness subscale and recognition and recall measures across 20 ads were .55 and .31, respectively. The correlations between the meaningfulness subscale and recognition and recall measures were .40 and .52, offering evidence of nomological validity.

        Zinkhan and Fornell (1985) compared the Wells Profile to a version of Leavitt's (1970) profile. For the Wells profile, 20 different print ads were used. Four hundred subjects were recruited by an advertising agency and prescreened to confirm they were members of the target audience of the particular ad. For each individual ad, 20 subjects were exposed to a print ad along with other material that might appear in a national magazine. Each subject was exposed to only one ad. After exposure, the subjects completed a version of the reaction profile in which scale items were randomly rotated. In general, the dimensional structure was confirmed for Wells's profile, as the coefficient of congruence (which measures the fit between the hypothesized structure and the rotated solutions) was very high (CC = .94). Furthermore, the attractiveness and meaningfulness factors had significant beta weights for the prediction of attitude toward the brand (i.e., .55 and .14), and attractiveness had a significant beta weight for the prediction of purchase intention (.29), offering evidence of predictive validity.

Other sources: Wells, William D. (1964b). "Recognition, Recall, and Rating Scales." *Journal of Advertising Research*, *4*, 2-8.

        Zinkhan, George M., and Claes Fornell. (1985). "A Test of Two Consumer Response Scales in Advertising." *Journal of Marketing Research*, *22*, 447-452.

Reference: Leavitt, Clark. (1970). "A Multidimensional Set of Rating Scales for Television Commercials." *Journal of Applied Psychology*, *54*, 427-429.

EMOTIONAL QUOTIENT SCALE (EQ) AND REACTION PROFILE
(Wells 1964a)

Emotional Quotient Scale (EQ)

1. This ad is very appealing to me.
2. I would probably skip this ad if I saw it in a magazine.
3. This is a heart-warming ad.
4. This ad makes me want to buy the brand it features.
5. This ad has little interest for me.
6. I dislike this ad.
7. This ad makes me feel good.
8. This is a wonderful ad.
9. This is the kind of ad you forget easily.
10. This is a fascinating ad.
11. I'm tired of this kind of advertising.
12. This ad leaves me cold.

Reaction Profile

1. Beautiful/ugly
2. Pleasant/unpleasant
3. Gentle/harsh
4. Appealing/unappealing
5. Attractive/unattractive
6. In good taste/in poor taste
7. Exciting/unexciting
8. Interesting/uninteresting
9. Worth looking at/not worth looking at
10. Comforting/frightening
11. Colorful/colorless
12. Fascinating/boring
13. Meaningful/meaningless
14. Convincing/unconvincing
15. Important to me/unimportant to me
16. Strong/weak
17. Honest/dishonest
18. Easy to remember/hard to remember
19. Easy to understand/hard to understand
20. Worth remembering/not worth remembering
21. Simple/complicated
22. New/ordinary
23. Fresh/stale
24. Lively/lifeless
25. Sharp/washed out

NOTES: For the Emotional Quotient Scale, items 1, 3, 4, 7, 8, and 10 represent the favorably worded items, and the remaining items represent the unfavorably worded items.

For the Reaction Profile, items 1 through 12 represent the "attractiveness" factor, items 13 through 21 represent the "meaningfulness" factor, and items 22 through 25 and item 11 represent the "vitality" factor (Wells 1964a). All items require reverse coding to reflect higher scores. Items 1, 2, and 5 were the items used by Wells (1964b) to represent "attractiveness," whereas items 13, 15, and 20 were used to operationalize "meaningfulness."

FEELINGS TOWARD ADS
(Edell and Burke 1987)

Construct: Feelings toward the ad are felt to be composed of both positive affective feelings toward a given ad and negative affective feelings toward a given ad. Furthermore, positive affective feelings are composed of "warm" and "upbeat" feelings toward the ad. These feelings affect both attitude toward the ad and attitude toward the brand (Edell and Burke 1987).

Description: The feelings toward the ad scales were originally composed of 65 items comprising three subdimensions: upbeat feelings (32 items), warm feelings (13 items), and negative feelings (20 items). A 52-item version of the scale was also used in Edell and Burke's Study 2, where 26, 14, and 12 items were used to measure upbeat, warm, and negative feelings, respectively. All items are measured on 5-point scales, and scores on items within each subdimension are summed to form indices of each subdimension.

Development: A pool of 169 feelings (items) gleaned from previous research served as the initial pool of items (Wells 1964; Wells, Leavitt, and McConville 1971). Sixty subjects viewed 16 TV ads in a theater setting. The 16 ads were selected to represent a variety of products and executional styles. After viewing the ads, the subjects were given the list of feelings and asked to indicate which feelings they experienced while viewing the ads. Sixty items checked by at least 50% of the sample were retained. Also, nine more items that were mentioned via an open-ended task (but not on the checklist) were added, resulting in 69 items. Two studies then examined the dimensionality and reliability of the items. From the first study, 65 items were retained for the original scale. Four items were dropped that did not load highly on any factor (i.e., less than .50). In the second study, the shorter 52-item version was derived by eliminating items with item-to-total correlations greater than .90 (i.e., redundant items).

Samples: In the first study, a sample of 29 people was used, and in the second study, a sample of 32 people was used. Both samples were obtained via announcements on a university campus.

Validity: In the first study, factor analysis retained 65 of the 69 items. Three factors were retained from the factor analysis. Coefficient alpha estimates for the three factors were .98, .96, and .93 for the upbeat, negative, and warm feelings factors, respectively. For the reduced versions of the scales (i.e., Study 2), corresponding alpha estimates were .95, .89, and .90. In both studies, the three dimensions of feelings toward the ad were related to measures of Aad and Abrand, providing evidence of predictive validity. For example, in Study 1, standardized regression coefficients for the prediction of Aad and Abrand ranged from $-.02$ to .32 for upbeat feelings, $-.09$ to $-.55$ for negative feelings, and $-.02$ to .18 for warm feelings. Also, R^2 estimates for the prediction of transformational and informational ads for the three subscales as predictors ranged from .63 to .78 across high/low conditions of transformational/informational ad content.

Scores: Mean or percentage scores were not reported.

Source: Edell, Julie A., and Marian Chapman Burke. (1987). "The Power of Feelings in Understanding Advertising Effects." *Journal of Consumer Research, 14*, 421-433.
   © 1987 by University of Chicago Press. Scale items taken from Table 1 (p. 424). Reprinted with permission.

Other evidence: Burke and Edell (1989) looked at the predictive power of the feelings scales (slightly modified versions) with a sample of 191 people recruited via announcements and newspaper ads on a university campus. Coefficient alpha estimates were .95, .89, and .88 for the upbeat, warm, and negative scale dimensions, respectively. All three dimensions were found to be related to several affective-based measures of Aad and Abrand. For example, across six Aad/Abrand type dependent variables, standardized predictive coefficients ranged from $-.02$ to .80 for upbeat feelings, $-.19$ to .72 for warm feelings, and $-.02$ to .48 for negative feelings.

Other source: Burke, Marian Chapman, and Julie Edell. (1989). "The Impact of Feelings on Ad-Based Affect and Cognition." *Journal of Marketing Research*, 26, 69-83.

References: Wells, William D. (1964). "EQ, Son of EQ, and the Reaction Profile." *Journal of Marketing*, 28, 45-52.

Wells, William D., Clark Leavitt, and Maureen McConville. (1971). "A Reaction Profile for TV Commercials." *Journal of Advertising Research*, 22, 11-17.

FEELINGS TOWARD ADS
(Edell and Burke 1987)

Instructions: We would like you to tell us how the ad you just saw made you **feel**. We are interested in **your reactions** to the ad, **not** how you would describe it. Please tell us how much you felt each of these feelings while you were watching this commercial. If you felt the feeling very strongly . . . put a "5"; strongly . . . put a "4"; somewhat strongly . . . put a "3"; not very strongly . . . put a "2"; not at all . . . put a "1."

Column 1	Column 2	Column 3
1. active	angry	affectionate
2. adventurous	annoyed	calm
3. alive	bad	concerned
4. amused	bored	contemplative
5. attentive	critical	emotional
6. attractive	defiant	hopeful
7. carefree	depressed	kind
8. cheerful	disgusted	moved
9. confident	disinterested	peaceful
10. creative	dubious	pensive
11. delighted	dull	sentimental
12. elated	fed-up	touched
13. energetic	insulted	warm-hearted
14. enthusiastic	irritated	
15. excited	lonely	
16. exhilarated	offended	
17. good	regretful	
18. happy	sad	
19. humorous	skeptical	
20. independent	suspicious	
21. industrious		
22. inspired		
23. interested		
24. joyous		
25. lighthearted		
26. lively		
27. playful		
28. pleased		
29. proud		
30. satisfied		
31. stimulated		
32. strong		

NOTES: Column 1 represents the "upbeat" factor, column 2 represents the "negative" factor, and column 3 represents the "warm" factor. Item numbers 1, 3 through 13, 18 through 25, and 27 through 32 of the first column compose the reduced version of the upbeat factor used in Study 2 of Edell and Burke (1987). Items 4 through 11 and 15 through 20 of the second column compose the reduced version of the negative factor in Study 2 of Edell and Burke (1987). Items 1 through 11 and 13 of column 3 compose the reduced version of the warm factor in Study 2 of Edell and Burke (1987).

In the Burke and Edell (1989) study, items 1, 3 through 13, 18 through 25, and 27 through 32 of column 1 compose the warm factor. An additional item, "silly," was also used as an item for this factor. Items 4 through 11 and 15 through 20 of column 2 compose the negative factor items used in the Burke and Edell (1989) study. Items 1 through 11 and 13 of column 3 compose the warm factor in the Burke and Edell (1989) study.

INFORMATIONAL AND TRANSFORMATIONAL AD CONTENT
(Puto and Wells 1984)

Construct: An informational advertisement was defined as an ad that provides consumers with factual, relevant brand data in a clear and logical manner such that they have greater confidence in their ability to assess the merits of buying the brand after having seen the advertisement. An important aspect of the definition is that the ad becomes informational if consumers perceive it as such. For an ad to be judged informational, it must reflect the following characteristics: (a) present factual, relevant information about the brand; (b) present information which is immediately and obviously important to the potential consumer; and (c) present data which the consumer accepts as being verifiable. A transformational advertisement is one that associates the experience of using (consuming) the advertised brand with a unique set of psychological characteristics which typically would not be associated with the brand experience to the same degree without exposure to the advertisement. Specifically, the advertisement itself links the brand with the capacity to provide the consumer with an experience that is different from the consumption experience which would normally be expected to occur without ad exposure. For an ad to be judged transformational, it must reflect the following characteristics: (a) the experience of using the product must be made richer, warmer, more exciting, and/or more enjoyable than that obtained solely from an objective ad description; and (b) the experience of the advertisement and the experience of using the brand must be so tightly connected that the consumers cannot remember the brand without recalling the experience generated by the advertisement. The transformation occurs when the descriptors are explicitly related by consumers to the experience of owning or consuming the advertised brand. Advertisements can be classified as belonging to one of four basic categories: (a) high transformational/low information, (b) low transformational/high information, (c) high transformational/high information, and (d) low transformational/low information (Puto and Wells 1984, p. 638).

Description: Puto and Wells's measures include 23 items scored on 6-point *strongly agree* to *strongly disagree* scales. Fifteen of the items tap the transformation construct, while the eight remaining relate to the information construct. The responses are averaged across the items within each subscale to form indices of each subscale.

Development: Scale items which were considered candidates for inclusion on the informational scales were derived from items used in prior research on the informational content of advertisements (e.g., Aaker and Norris 1982). Additionally, a set of items was generated from the definition of informational advertisements. Although research with respect to the emotional and experiential aspects of transformation was also examined, the majority of this research was concerned with measuring empathetic tendencies of individuals. Because the research objectives of this study were concerned with products, it was necessary to develop original items for this aspect of the transformational scale. Personal relevance aspects of the transformation scale were derived from the viewer response profile measures (Schlinger 1979). In sum, a total of 23 items were retained to represent the transformational and informational measures.

To test these items, approximately 400 television commercials were reviewed, and 20 were selected for the initial study. The two basic criteria for commercial selection were that they (a) were mainly informational or mainly transformational, and (b) promoted products of interest to the test audience. From these 20 commercials, 5 were kept as informational ads and 8 as transformational ads (i.e., 13 in all).

Subjects were then exposed to the 13 commercials, and immediately after seeing each commercial, they reported their prior exposure to the commercial and their overall opinion of each ad. Lastly, subjects responded to the 23 transformational and informational items with respect to the commercials. Reliability and validity checks were then assessed.

Samples: Two judges, knowledgeable of the definitions of informational and transformational ads but blind to prior classifications of the ads, independently judged the commercials with respect to the information and transformation constructs. The subjects were 130 undergraduate psychology students.

Validity: Reliability coefficients were computed separately for each commercial and then averaged across the 13 test commercials. The average internal consistency reliability estimates across advertisements were .73 and .88 for the information and transformation scales, respectively. The mean scale values for the information and transformation scales for each commercial differed at the $p < .01$ level (one-tailed t test). These differences reflect the authors' a priori assessment of an ad either being primarily informational or primarily transformational, and offer evidence for the validity of the scales. (Those commercials below the 3.5 midpoint were classified as being "low" on the specific dimension, whereas those above it were classified as being "high.")

Scores: Means and standard deviations for each commercial were presented in Table 4 (p. 642) of the Puto and Wells (1984) study. As an example, the mean information and transformation scores for the first advertisement (i.e., an informational toothbrush advertisement) were 4.00 ($SD = .69$) and 3.08 ($SD = .70$), respectively.

Source: Puto, Christopher P., and William D. Wells. (1984). "Informational and Transformational Advertising: The Differential Effects of Time." In Thomas C. Kinnear (Ed.), *Advances in Consumer Research* (Vol. 11, pp. 638-643). Provo, UT: Association for Consumer Research.

    © 1984 by the Association for Consumer Research. Scale items taken from Table 1 (p. 641). Reprinted with permission.

Other evidence: N/A

Other sources: N/A

References: Aaker, David, A., and Donald Norris. (1982). "Characteristics of TV Commercials Perceived as Informative." *Journal of Advertising Research*, 22, 61-70.

    Schlinger, Mary. (1979). "A Profile of Responses to Commercials." *Journal of Advertising Research*, 19, 37-46.

INFORMATIONAL AND TRANSFORMATIONAL AD CONTENT
(Puto and Wells 1984)

1. I learned something from this commercial that I didn't know before about (this brand).

2. I would like to have an expertise like the one shown in the commercial.

3. The commercial did not seem to be speaking directly to me.

4. There is nothing special about (this brand) that makes it different from the others.

5. While I watched this commercial, I thought how this brand might be useful to me.

6. The commercial did not teach me what to look for when buying (this product).

7. This commercial was meaningful to me.

8. This commercial was very uninformative.

9. (This brand) fits my lifestyle very well.

10. I could really relate to this commercial.

11. Using (this brand) makes me feel good about myself.

12. If they had to, the company could provide evidence to support the claims made in this commercial.

13. It's hard to give a specific reason, but somehow (this brand) is not really for me.

14. This commercial did not really hold my attention.

15. This commercial reminded me of some important facts about (this brand) which I already knew.

16. If I could change my lifestyle, I would make it less like the people who use (this brand).

17. When I think of (this brand), I think of this commercial.

18. I felt as though I were right there in the commercial, experiencing the same thing.

19. I can now accurately compare (this brand) with other competing brands on matters that are important to me.

20. This commercial did not remind me of any experiences or feelings I've had in my own life.

21. I would have less confidence in using (this brand) now than before I saw this commercial.

22. It is the kind of commercial that keeps running through your head after you've seen it.

23. It's hard to put into words, but this commercial leaves me with a good feeling about using (this brand).

NOTES: ( ) denotes brand name of the advertised product. Items 1, 4, 6, 8, 12, 15, 19, and 21 compose the informational content measure. The remaining items compose the transformational content scale.

Although reverse coding is not specified by the authors, it seems that items 3, 6, 8, 12, 14, and 20 need such coding to reflect higher transformational and informational scores.

**JUDGMENT OF ADS-VIEWER JUDGMENT OF ADS:
THE PERSUASIVE DISCLOSURE INVENTORY (PDI)**
(Feltham 1994)

Construct: The persuasive discourse perspective is based upon the Aristotelian theory of rhetoric. As applied to marketing stimuli, the theoretical components of the PDI measure are ethos, pathos, and logos (cf. McGuire 1969). Ethos refers to persuasive appeals that concentrate on the source rather than the message. Studies of advertising effects that have examined emotional or affective appeals fall within the definition of pathos. A logos appeal provides evidence or information about a concept from which a consumer can form beliefs (Feltham 1994, pp. 531-532). Pathos and logos have been viewed by some as different ends of a continuum that considers the message. Feltham suggests that the subscales be used as individual message facets.

Description: Seventeen bipolar adjective sets, operationalized using a 7-place response format, constitute the PDI scale. The three factors are scored as the sum across the five, five, and seven items designed to reflect Ethos, Logos, and Pathos, respectively.

Development: Items were generated from a lexicon of philosophical terms, an encyclopedia of philosophy, speech communication literature, and consultation with colleagues. Subjects from the first sample responded to the scale for 16 stimuli (5 movie clips and 11 advertisements). The items were examined for within-factor item-to-total correlations. These correlation coefficients ranged from .63 to .91. Mean scores were said to vary as predicted across the 16 stimuli. The average coefficient alpha estimates for Ethos, Logos, and Pathos were .89, .86, and .82, respectively. These analyses led to the deletion and addition of several items. Results from the second administration also suggested several additional adjustments to improve within-factor intercorrelations and to reduce cross-correlations among the Ethos, Pathos, and Logos subscales.

Samples: The initial sample was a convenience sample of 19 adult volunteers (average age 42.3). The second sample was composed of students enrolled in four introductory marketing classes ($n =$ 25, 19, 15, and 20). Additional replications that provided additional unreported supportive results were obtained from convenience samples of 15 MBA students and seven choir members.

Validity: A second study involved the reactions of the student subjects to nine new stimuli. The average item-to-total correlations for the second study were .79, .78, and .74 for the Pathos, Ethos, and Logos subscales. The average reliability estimates were .83, .79, and .89 for Ethos, Logos, and Pathos, respectively.

Scores: Mean scores for the first sample varied across the program and ad stimuli used to develop the scale. The Ethos scores ranged from 14.7 to 29.5 (possible range 5 to 35). Similar scores for the Logos and Pathos subscales ranged from 16.7 to 33.2 (possible 5 to 35) and 13.2 to 33.4 (possible range 7 to 49), respectively.

Source: Feltham, Tammi S. (1994). "Assessing Viewer Judgement of Advertisements and Vehicles: Scale Development and Validation." In Chris T. Allen and Deborah Roedder-John (Eds.), *Advances in Consumer Research* (Vol. 21, pp. 531-535). Provo, UT: Association for Consumer Research.
© 1994 by the Association for Consumer Research. Scale items taken from Exhibit 2 (p. 534). Reprinted with permission.

Other evidence: N/A

Other sources: N/A

Reference: McGuire, William J. (1969). "The Nature of Attitude and Attitude Change." In Gardner Lindzey and Elliot Aronson (Eds.), *The Handbook of Psychology: Vol. 3. The Individual in a Social Context* (pp. 136-314). Reading, MA: Addison-Wesley.

JUDGMENT OF ADS-VIEWER JUDGMENT OF ADS:
THE PERSUASIVE DISCLOSURE INVENTORY (PDI)
(Feltham 1994)

Please check the box which you feel best describes the commercial you just saw.

Ethos Scale Items

   E1. unbelievable/believable

   E2. not credible/credible

   E3. not trustworthy/trustworthy

   E4. unreliable/reliable

   E5. undependable/dependable

Logos Scale Items

   L1. not rational/rational

   L2. not informative/formative

   L3. does not deal with facts/deals with facts

   L4. not knowledgeable/knowledgeable

   L5. not logical/logical

Pathos Scale Items

   P1. does not affect my feelings/affects my feelings

   P2. does not touch me emotionally/touches me emotionally

   P3. is not stimulating/is stimulating

   P4. does not reach out to me/reaches out to me

   P5. is not stirring/is stirring

   P6. is not moving/is moving

   P7. is not exciting/is exciting

NOTE: Exhibit 1 of Feltham (1994, p. 533) provides the original order of items.

REACTION PROFILE: LEAVITT'S REACTION PROFILE
(Leavitt 1970)

Construct: The likability or emotional reaction to ads is what Leavitt (1970) attempts to measure. Specifically, Leavitt set out to assess the dimensions on which viewers affectively rate TV commercials.

Description: The original Leavitt profile consisted of 45 single-word or phrase descriptors designed to capture reactions to television commercials. These 45 descriptors formed eight factors reflecting different dimensions of emotional reactions to ads. All items were scored on a 5-point basis from *does not fit* to *fits extremely well*. Though not specified, it seems that item scores can be summed within dimensions to form indices of each dimension.

Development: An original pool of 525 words or phrases was generated to reflect possible affective reactions toward TV ads. Four filtering procedures were then employed to trim the items to the final 45 descriptors. First, over 11 commercials, 30 respondents evaluated one third of the original pool. Words checked by 20% or more of the sample were retained. Then, on a 5-point scale, 110 respondents rated the remaining items over 11 commercials. Via ANOVA, those items that significantly discriminated among commercials were retained, resulting in 206 items. These 206 were then factor analyzed. Redundant words and descriptors with loadings of less than .50 were eliminated, resulting in 73 items. The 73 items were refactored, and 45 items with loadings of .50 or greater were retained. Although another sample was used to rate 250 more items (over 11 new commercials), the 45-item scale was retained.

Sample: Samples of 30, 110, and 110 persons were used to develop and factor-analyze Leavitt's profile.

Validity: Little evidence of reliability or validity was offered. Of the eight factors extracted, the energetic factor accounted for 55% of the total variance, personal relevance accounted for 22%, sensuality accounted for 9%, familiarity 5%, and novelty, authoritative, and disliked accounted for 3%, 2%, and 2%, respectively.

Scores: Neither mean nor percentage scores were reported by Leavitt (1970).

Source: Leavitt, Clark. (1970). "A Multidimensional Set of Rating Scales for Television Commercials." *Journal of Applied Psychology*, 54, 427-429.

 © 1970 by the American Psychological Association. Scale items taken from Table 1 (p. 428). Reprinted with permission.

Other evidence: Wells, Leavitt, and McConville (1971) derived a modified 30-item version of the Leavitt profile encompassing six factors: humor, vigor, sensuousness, uniqueness, personal relevance, and irritation (five items per factor). Over 10 antismoking commercials, the personal relevance factor had a correlation of .80 with a measure of "personal product response," and an overall measure of recall had a correlation of −.64 with the sensuousness factor. Furthermore, rating scores across factors for three different commercials supported the validity of the reduced profile.

 With a sample of 155, Sullivan and O'Connor (1983) examined an abridged version of Leavitt's profile over four public service announcements (PSAs). Five factors were extracted: stimulating, monotonous, relevant, irritating, and likable, accounting for 27.3%, 16.75%, 26.1%, 17.5%, and 12.4% of the variance, respectively. However, none of the factors exhibited significant beta weights for the prediction of behavioral intentions toward the messages from the PSAs.

 Zinkhan and Fornell (1985) looked at a 27-item reduced version of Leavitt's profile using 400 subjects and 20 different ads. The coefficient of congruence (which measures the fit between the hypothesized structure and the rotated solution) was moderate (CC = .58) for four factors examined (i.e., energetic/amusing, personal relevance, familiarity, and sensuousness). The validity of the four factors for predicting attitude toward the brand and purchase intention was also examined. The beta coefficients for all four factors were significant for predicting A-brand (i.e., .37, .13, −.23, and .31 for energetic/amusing, relevance, familiarity, and sensuous, respectively). The beta coefficients for predicting purchase intention were significant for energetic/amusing (.11) and personal relevance (.11).

Other sources: Sullivan, Gary L., and P. J. O'Connor. (1983). "Search for a Relationship Between Viewer Responses to the Creative Aspects of Televised Messages and Behavioral Intention." In R. P. Bagozzi and A. M. Tybout (Eds.), *Advances in Consumer Research* (Vol. 10, pp. 32-35). Ann Arbor, MI: Association for Consumer Research.

Wells, William D., Clark Leavitt, and Maureen McConville. (1971). "A Reaction Profile for TV Commercials." *Journal of Advertising Research*, *11*, 11-17.

Zinkhan, George M., and Claes Fornell. (1985). "A Test of Two Consumer Response Scales in Advertising." *Journal of Marketing Research*, 22, 447-452.

References: N/A

REACTION PROFILE: LEAVITT'S REACTION PROFILE
(Leavitt 1970)

Energetic Factor
1. Lively
2. Exhilarated
3. Vigorous
4. Enthusiastic
5. Energetic
6. Excited

Amusing Factor
7. Merry
8. Jolly
9. Playful
10. Joyful
11. Amusing
12. Humorous

Personal Relevance Factor
13. Important to me
14. Helpful
15. Valuable
16. Meaningful for me
17. Worth remembering
18. Convincing

Authoritative Factor
19. Confident
20. Business-like
21. Consistent-in-style
22. Responsible
23. Frank
24. Dependable

Sensual Factor

25. Lovely
26. Beautiful
27. Gentle
28. Serene
29. Tender
30. Sensitive

Familiarity Factor

31. Familiar
32. Well-known
33. Saw before

Novel Factor

34. Original
35. Unique
36. Imaginative
37. Novel
38. Ingenious
39. Creative

Disliked Factor

40. Phony
41. Terrible
42. Stupid
43. Irritating
44. Unimportant to me
45. Ridiculous

NOTES: Items 2 through 6 compose the "vigor" factor of Wells et al. (1971). Items 7 through 9, 11, and 12 compose their "humor" factor. Items 12, 15, 16, 17, and an added item (i.e., "for me") compose their "personal relevance" factor. Items 25, 27, 28, 29, and an added item (i.e., "soothing") compose their "sensuousness" factor. Items 34 through 38 compose their "uniqueness" factor, and items 40 through 43 and 45 compose their "irritation" factor. Wells et al. (1971) suggest a scoring procedure of fits *extremely well* (5) to fits *not well at all* (1).

Items 1, 6, 11, 35, 36, and 39 and two other items ("clever" and "new") represent Sullivan and O'Connor's (1983) "stimulating" factor. All new items for their "monotonous" factor were generated; they were "dull," "sluggish," "old," and "repetitious." Items 14, 16, 17, 18, 23, and four new items (i.e., "believable," "natural," "realistic," and "informative") represent their "relevant" factor. Their "irritating" factor is composed of item 42 and four new items (i.e., "in poor taste," "silly," "confusing," and "unclear"). Lastly, item 31 and three new items (i.e., "attractive," "agreeable," and "soothing") compose their "likable" factor (Sullivan and O'Connor 1983).

Items 1 through 12 reflect the "energetic/amusing" factor of Zinkhan and Fornell (1985). Their "personal relevance," "sensuousness," and "familiarity" items were identical to those of the original Leavitt profile reported above.

RELEVANCE, CONFUSION, AND ENTERTAINMENT
(Lastovicka 1983)

Construct: Three copy-testing concepts were examined by Lastovicka (1983) with respect to convergent and discriminant validity. These concepts were (Lastovicka 1983, p. 16)

Relevance: questioning the meaningfulness of the ad and its product with respect to the viewer's need

Confusion: the degree to which the commercial is perceived as being misunderstood

Entertainment: an overall positive evaluation or feeling, as opposed to irritation with respect to a commercial's execution.

Description: Sixteen structured questions were administered using a Likert-type format with a scale range from 1 (*strongly disagree*) to 6 (*strongly agree*). Item scores are summed within each factor to form indices of relevance, confusion, and entertainment. Thus, the scale is multidimensional.

Development: With respect to the three concepts of relevance, confusion, and entertainment, two measurement methods were applied: (a) structured questioning using Likert-type "disagree-agree" multiple scales, many of which were culled from Schlinger's (1979) VRP; and (b) open questioning in which viewers were asked to retrospectively list their thoughts while viewing the commercials. Each student answered the open-ended question and then answered a battery of 16 structured questions. Checks on product relevance (i.e., beer, blue jeans, soft drinks, and automobiles) showed that 83% of the respondents had used or purchased some brand from each of the four different product classes represented in the six test ads during the month preceding the study. The open-ended question read as follows: "What were your thoughts while you viewed the television commercial?" The 16 structured items were selected from Leo Burnett Storyboard Test research. These selected items loaded highly on empirically derived factors measuring the dimension of interest. Again, each item was used with a 1-6 (*strongly disagree* to *strongly agree*) scale. Confirmatory factor analysis (via LISREL) of the 16 items empirically supported the battery of items into the three subscales of relevance, confusion, and entertainment. Scale reliability was also assessed, as well as validity.

Sample: The sample consisted of 634 undergraduates from a university business school. Each subject was exposed to one of six different 60-second television commercials in a classroom setting. Each student answered the open-ended question and the 16 structured questions.

Validity: Some of the major results of the Lastovicka (1983) study are summarized as follows. Modest support for the convergent and discriminant validity of the standardized versions of the relevance, confusion, and entertainment dimensions was found as a three-factor model of relevance, confusion, and entertainment provided a strong fit to the data (chi-square = 11.91, $df = 7$, $p = .11$). Scale reliabilities were reported for each dimension: relevance (.85), confusion (.73), and entertainment (.87). The intercorrelations among the three subscales were .68 for relevance-entertainment, −.68 for relevance-confusion, and −.59 for confusion-entertainment.

Scores: Mean scores were not offered by Lastovicka (1983).

Source: Lastovicka, John L. (1983). "Convergent and Discriminant Validity of Television Commercial Rating Scales." *Journal of Advertising*, *12*(2), 14-23.
    Scale items taken from Table 2 (p. 17). © 1993; reprinted by permission of the *Journal of Advertising..*

Other evidence: N/A

Other sources: N/A

Reference: Schlinger, Mary. (1979). "A Profile of Responses to Commercials." *Journal of Advertising Research, 19,* 37-46.

RELEVANCE, CONFUSION, AND ENTERTAINMENT
(Lastovicka 1983)

Relevance

1. During the commercial I thought how the product might be useful for me.

2. I felt as though I was right there in the commercial experiencing the same thing.

3. The commercial was meaningful to me.

4. The ad did not have anything to do with me or my needs.*

5. The commercial gave me a good idea.

6. As I watched I thought of reasons why I would buy or not buy the product.

Confusion

7. I clearly understood the commercial.*

8. The commercial was too complex. I was not sure what was going on.

9. I was not sure what was going on in the commercial.

10. I was so busy watching the screen, I did not listen to the talk.

11. The commercial went by so quickly that it just did not make an impression on me.

Entertainment

12. The commercial was lots of fun to watch and listen to.

13. I have seen this commercial before.*

14. I have seen this commercial so many times that I am tired of it.*

15. I thought the commercial was clever and quite entertaining.

16. The ad was not just selling—it was entertaining me. I appreciated that.

NOTE: *Denotes items that are reverse scored.

RESPONSE PROFILE-VIEWER RESPONSE PROFILE: VRP
(Schlinger 1979)

Construct: The Viewer Response Profile gauges affective reactions to advertisements. It focuses on the emotional component of communication effects and indicates how people feel after seeing a commercial rather than what they know (Schlinger 1979, p. 37). The VRP assesses seven facets relating to how people feel about an advertisement, as follows:

Entertainment is the degree to which a commercial is pleasurable, enjoyable, and fun to watch.

Confusion is the degree to which the viewer feels that the commercial is difficult to follow.

Relevant news is the degree to which viewers feel that the commercial has told them something important and interesting about a brand, or some useful information.

Brand reinforcement is the degree to which the ad reinforces existing positive attitudes toward the brand.

Empathy is the degree to which viewers participate vicariously in events, feelings, and behaviors that are shown in the ad. This empathy can be positive or negative.

Familiarity is the degree to which viewers see commercials as unusual and different either from advertising in general or from current campaigns for the product category or brand.

Alienation is the degree to which the ad is felt to be irrelevant or irritating (i.e., negative judgments about the message or the execution of the message).

Description: The VRP is composed of 32 Likert-type items on 7-point scales from *strongly disagree* to *strongly agree*. There are seven items for entertainment, four for confusion, five for relevant news, two for brand reinforcement, five for empathy, three for familiarity, and six for alienation. Item scores are summed within the facets and then divided by the number of items in each facet to form indices for each facet.

Development: A number of procedures, samples, and analyses were used in scale development. Six hundred statements were initially generated based on the open-ended responses of 400 viewers to 14 commercials and storyboards. This pool of items was trimmed to 139 items (both positively and negatively worded) via subjective judgment. Then, two samples, one of 500 women for 25 different commercials (20 women per commercial) and one of 500 for 10 commercials (50 per commercial) responded to the items. Via factor analyses, these two studies retained 70 items that had loadings of .50 or greater on a given factor and discriminated among commercials. Two more large samples were used to further trim the pool of items over a total of 82 commercials and 377 storyboards. Across several factor analyses, the final 32-item, seven-factor scale was derived. A number of reliability and validity checks using new samples were also performed.

Samples: As stated above, several samples were used in scale development and validation: samples of $n = 400$ in item generation, two samples of $n = 500$ women each in item purification, and two more samples of $n = 1,504$ and $n = 1,871$ men and women in item purification. Also, at least five more samples ranging in size from 12 to 50 were used to assess the reliability and validity of the VRP. (As stated by Schlinger [1979, p. 46], more than 5,000 individual interviews were conducted in development and validation of the VRP over a 5-year period.)

Validity: Test-retest reliability ranged from .62 for familiarity to .96 for brand reinforcement. Though coefficient alpha was not reported, item-factor loadings ranged from .33 to .88 over the first four samples (i.e., 500, 500, 1,504, and 1,871) discussed above.

A number of mean differences provided support for the validity of the scale. In addition, the VRP factors were used as independent variables to predict ad awareness. The VRP facets explained 52% of the variance in ad awareness, offering evidence of predictive validity.

Furthermore, the VRP was strongly correlated with the Wells, Leavitt, and McConville (1971) reaction measure, offering evidence of convergent validity (i.e., together, the VRP and Wells et al.'s measure accounted for 78% of the variance when jointly factor analyzed).

Scores: A number of mean scores are presented in Tables 3, 4, and 5 of Schlinger (1979, pp. 43-44). These scores range from 3.8 to 5.3 for entertainment, 2.1 to 2.6 for confusion, 2.8 to 4.9 for relevant news, 3.8 to 5.6 for brand reinforcement, 2.5 to 3.9 for empathy, 2.1 to 3.5 for familiarity, and 2.6 to 3.6 for alienation.

Source: Schlinger, Mary. (1979). "A Profile of Responses to Commercials." *Journal of Advertising Research, 19*, 37-46.
Scale items taken from Table 1 (p. 40). © 1979; reprinted by permission of the Advertising Research Foundation.

Other evidence: Stout and Rust (1993) used 44 items from a longer list of 52 items employed by Schlinger. The coefficient alpha estimates were .90, .74, .90, .82, .72, and .65 for the factors Relevant News, Brand Reinforcement, Stimulation, Empathy, Familiarity, and Confusion, respectively. These variables were then used in a series of television commercial analyses. The results reported suggest that emotional response measures may complement the VRP, rather than being redundant with the VRP (Stout and Rust 1993, p. 61).

Other source: Stout, Patricia A., and Roland Rust. (1993). "Emotional Feelings and Evaluative Dimensions of Advertising: Are They Related?" *Journal of Advertising, 22*, 61-70.

Reference: Wells, William, Clark Leavitt, and Maureen McConville. (1971). "A Reaction Profile for TV Commercials." *Journal of Advertising Research, 11*, 11-17.

RESPONSE PROFILE-VIEWER RESPONSE PROFILE: VRP
(Schlinger 1979)

Entertainment

1. The commercial was lots of fun to watch and listen to.

2. I thought it was clever and entertaining.

3. The enthusiasm of the commercial is catching—it picks you up.

4. The ad wasn't just selling the product—it was entertaining me and I appreciate that.

5. The characters (or persons) in the commercial capture your attention.

6. It's the kind of commercial that keeps running through your mind after you've seen it.

7. I just laughed at it—I thought it was very funny and good.

Confusion

8. It was distracting—trying to watch the screen and listen to the words at the same time.

9. It required a lot of effort to follow the commercial.

10. It was too complex. I wasn't sure of what was going on.

11. I was so busy watching the screen, I didn't listen to the talk.

Relevant News

12. The commercial gave me a new idea.

13. The commercial reminded me that I'm dissatisfied with what I'm using now and I'm looking for something better.

14. I learned something from the commercial that I didn't know before.

15. The commercial told about a new product I think I'd like to try.

16. During the commercial I thought how that product might be useful to me.

Brand Reinforcement

17. That's a good brand and I wouldn't hesitate recommending it to others.

18. I know that the advertised brand is a dependable, reliable one.

Empathy

19. The commercial was very realistic—that is, true to life.

20. I felt that the commercial was acting out what I feel at times.

21. I felt as though I was right there in the commercial experiencing the same thing.

22. That's my idea—the kind of life that commercial showed.

23. I liked the commercial because it was personal and intimate.

Familiarity

24. This kind of commercial has been done many times . . . it's the same old thing.

25. I've seen this commercial so many times—I'm tired of it.

26. I think this is an unusual commercial. I'm not sure I've seen another like it.*

Alienation

27. What they showed didn't demonstrate the claims they were making about the product.

28. The ad didn't have anything to do with me or my needs.

29. The commercial did not show me anything that would make me want to use their products.

30. The commercial made exaggerated claims. The product would not live up to what they said or implied.

31. It was an unrealistic ad—very far fetched.

32. The commercial irritated me—it was annoying.

NOTE: *Denotes items that are reverse scored.

SEXUAL EMBEDS IN ADVERTISING: VASE SCALES
(Widing, Hoverstad, Coulter, and Brown 1991)

Construct: These measures are designed to assess several attitudinal aspects or viewpoints regarding the use of sexual embeds in print advertisements. Six dimensions with the following definitions were derived (Widing, Hoverstad, Coulter, and Brown 1991, p. 4).

Moral refers to whether the subjects feel that the use of sexual embeds in ads is morally harmful to the viewer.

Objectionable is a measure of general reaction and refers to whether subjects personally object to the use of sexual embeds in advertising.

Manipulative refers to whether subjects find the use of sexual embeds to be manipulative of viewers' attitudes.

Controlled refers to whether subjects find that the use of sexual embeds requires tighter control.

Widespread refers to the subject's perception of how frequently sexual embeds are used in advertising.

Useful as a Tool is the subject's perception of the economic benefits of using sexual embeds in ads.

Description: The six dimensions are each operationalized using 9-point bipolar semantic differential formats. Three separate phrases are used to reflect each of the six factors. Subjects are requested to respond to each of the randomly dispersed 18 items following the introductory statement: "I feel the use of sex in advertising that the viewer is not intended to be consciously aware of is. . . ." Item scores are summed within each dimension to form indices for each dimension. Thus, VASE is considered multidimensional.

Development: The specific procedures for developing the initial item pool or overall scale were not described. However, a number of reliability and validity tests were performed.

Sample: Undergraduate student subjects ($n = 107$) were used in the evaluation of the measures; 51 were female.

Validity: The reliability of the six three-item dimensions was reported. Following exposure and discussion regarding several ads including sexual embeds, coefficient alpha estimates of internal consistency reliability were as follows: .87 (Moral), .84 (Objectionable), .79 (Manipulative), .89 (Controlled), .90 (Widespread), and 82 (Tool).

Some modest evidence of validity was provided by a series of correlations with measures of attitudes toward three advertisements varying in their inclusion of overt sex or sexual embeds. For example, the Objectionable scale was positively correlated with attitudes toward an "Edge" ad ($r = .29$, $p < .05$) and a "Calvin" ad ($r = .05$, $p < .05$) as expected. (See Table 11 in Widing et al. 1991, p. 7.) In addition, the correlations were generally significantly different from correlations obtained between the four scales and attitudes toward an ad not containing overt sex or sexual embeds. Evidence of validity for the fifth and sixth scales (i.e., Widespread and Tool) was not provided.

Scores: Mean scores for the measures were not presented.

Source: Widing, Robert E., II, Ronald Hoverstad, Ronald Coulter, and Gene Brown. (1991). "The VASE Scales: Measures of Viewpoints About Sexual Embeds in Advertising." *Journal of Business Research*, 22, 3-10.

© 1991 by Elsevier Science. Scale items taken from p. 4. Reprinted with permission from Elsevier Science.

SEXUAL EMBEDS IN ADVERTISING: VASE SCALES
(Widing, Hoverstad, Coulter, and Brown 1991)

I feel the use of sex in advertising that the viewer is not intended to be consciously aware of is . . .

Moral

1. Morally harmful—not at all morally harmful.

2. A cause of lower moral values—not at all a cause of lower moral values.

3. A contributor to lower sexual standards—not at all a contributor to lower sexual standards.

Objectionable

4. Very objectionable—not at all objectionable.

5. Not at all offensive—very offensive.

6. Very unethical—not at all unethical.

Manipulative

7. Very manipulative of viewers—not at all manipulative of viewers.

8. A very unfair method of persuasion—not at all an unfair method of persuasion.

9. Not at all exploitative of viewers—very exploitative of viewers.

Controlled

10. Controlled well enough—not at all controlled well enough.

11. Too loosely regulated—not at all too loosely regulated.

12. Restricted well enough—not restricted well enough.

Widespread

13. Very widespread—not at all widespread.

14. Used very frequently—used very infrequently.

15. Very common in advertising—not at all common in advertising.

Useful as a Tool

16. A very effective selling tool—a very ineffective selling tool.

17. Not at all profitable—very profitable.

18. A method to increase sales—a method to decrease sales.

NOTE: Items 5, 9, 11, and 17 require reverse coding.

MEASURES RELATED TO AD BELIEVABILITY/CREDIBILITY

EXPERTISE, TRUSTWORTHINESS, AND
ATTRACTIVENESS OF CELEBRITY ENDORSERS
(Ohanian 1990)

Construct: The celebrity endorser's source credibility is posited to be characterized by three dimensions: the source's expertise, trustworthiness, and attractiveness (Ohanian 1990). In the persuasive communications literature, these three dimensions have been shown to be effective in attitude change studies. Each of the dimensions is briefly defined below.

Expertise: Consistent with the work of Hovland, Janis, and Kelley (1963), Ohanian views expertise as the extent to which the communicator is perceived to be a source of valid assertions about the object/message. This includes the source's competence, expertise, and qualifications with regard to the object/message.

Trustworthiness: Also consistent with Hovland et al. (1963), trustworthiness is viewed as the degree of confidence in the communicator's intent to communicate the assertions he or she considers most valid. This includes both trust and acceptance of speaker and message.

Attractiveness: In this context, attractiveness is referred to as physical attractiveness of the source to the listener, and to a lesser extent, the emotional attractiveness of the source. This includes elements of physical beauty, sexiness, chicness, and elegance.

Description: Each dimension of source credibility is composed of five semantic differential items scored on 7-point scales. Thus, the measure is multidimensional, and scores on each dimension are derived by summing the responses per items within each dimension.

Development: Development of the scale closely adhered to recommended scaling procedures. Based on definitions of the construct dimensions, 182 adjective pairs were initially generated. Based on author judgment and a sample of 38 student judges, this initial pool was trimmed to 104 items. Then, 52 students were supplied with the definitions of the source components and eliminated those items they felt did not represent the definitions, resulting in 72 adjective pairs. Using three celebrity spokespeople and several product categories (derived from a pretest of $n = 40$), two samples responded to the 72 items. Via exploratory factor analysis using stringent a priori decision rules and coefficient alpha statistics, five items within each dimension with the highest item-to-total correlations were retained. The final five-item scales were then subjected to confirmatory factor analysis and multitrait-multimethod (MTMM) analysis using another sample. Reliability and validity checks were also gathered.

Samples: Several samples were used throughout the scale development process. Three samples of 38, 52, and 40 students were used to judge the initial pool of items or generate celebrity names and products required for scale development. Two more samples of 250 and 240 students were used in the exploratory factor analyses to derive the final five-item scales. For the confirmatory factor analyses, two more samples of 138 and 127 nonstudents were used to examine the factor structure and further validate the scales.

Validity: Construct reliability from confirmatory factor analysis (via LISREL) showed strong internal consistency for the three subscales. These estimates were .904 and .893 for attractiveness, .895 and .896 for trustworthiness, and .885 and .892 for expertise across the samples of 138 and 127, respectively. The correlations among the factors across these two samples ranged from .319 to .621, and the hypothesized three-factor model offered the best fit to the data. In sum, the reliability and dimensionality of the scales were supported.

Numerous assessments of convergent, discriminant, and nomological validity are offered by Ohanian (1990, Table 5, p. 48). The correlations across measures used in these analyses range from .145 to .661, and they offer support for the scale's validity. Also, MTMM analysis also supports the discriminant and convergent validity for the measures.

Scores: Mean or percentage scores were not reported.

Source: Ohanian, Roobina. (1990). "Construction and Validation of a Scale to Measure Celebrity Endorsers' Perceived Expertise, Trustworthiness, and Attractiveness." *Journal of Advertising*, *19*, 39-52.

Scale items taken from Appendix (p. 50). © 1990; reprinted with permission of the *Journal of Advertising*.

Other evidence: N/A

Other sources: N/A

Reference: Hovland, Carl I., Irving K. Janis, and Harold H. Kelley. (1963). *Communication and Persuasion.* New Haven, CT: Yale University Press.

EXPERTISE, TRUSTWORTHINESS, AND ATTRACTIVENESS OF CELEBRITY ENDORSERS
(Ohanian 1990)

Attractiveness

1. unattractive—attractive

2. not classy—classy

3. ugly—beautiful

4. plain—elegant

5. not sexy—sexy

Trustworthiness

6. undependable—dependable

7. dishonest—honest

8. unreliable—reliable

9. insincere—sincere

10. untrustworthy—trustworthy

Expertise

11. not an expert—expert

12. inexperienced—experienced

13. unknowledgeable—knowledgeable

14. unqualified—qualified

15. unskilled—skilled

PUBLIC OPINION TOWARD ADVERTISING
(Pollay and Mittal 1993)

Construct: Overall global attitudes toward advertising are depicted as a function of a series of beliefs reflecting three personal use and four societal effects. Personal use factors include product information, social role and image, and hedonic/pleasure. Societal effects include the following four factors: good for the economy, materialism, value corruption, and falsity/no sense. Four distal antecedents were also included in Pollay and Mittal's model of beliefs and attitudes about advertising. "Better living" and "lowers cost of goods" were depicted as antecedents of good for the economy; "sex in ads" and "promotes undesirables" were depicted as distal antecedents of corrupt values.

Description: The seven factors are measured using a total of 27 items distributed in part as follows: product information (3), social image information (3), hedonic amusement (3), good for economy (3), fostering materialism (4), corrupting values (2), and falsity/no sense (3). Other items measure distal constructs. Each item was operationalized via 5-place agree-disagree scales. Further description of the authors' instructions and item allocation is provided in their appendix (Pollay and Mittal 1993, pp. 112-113).

Development: Two convenience samples ($n = 18$ and $n = 30$) responded to a series of open-ended questions. These responses were used to draft the measurement items administered to two larger samples. The initial set of items was administered with a series of similar items from Bauer and Greyser (1968). Principal components factor analysis on both sets of data was used to establish the seven-factor belief structure.

Samples(s): A series of convenience samples was used in item generation. Subsequently, in Sample 1, 188 student subjects with varied background (e.g., ages ranged from 17 to 50) were surveyed during class. Sample 2 consisted of 195 respondents from a southern state consumer panel.

Validity: Evidence of validity was provided from LISREL tests of predictive validity of overall attitudes. Coefficient alpha estimates for those factors with three or more items ranged across the two larger samples from .47 to .78 (see Pollay and Mittal 1993, Table 3, p. 108).

Scores: Factor mean scores in total and across segments of both samples comprising clusters of individuals differing in attitudes toward advertising are provided within the tables reported by Pollay and Mittal (1993, p. 110). As examples, the factor average item scores across the seven factors for the second household sample were as follows: information (3.06), social role (2.35), hedonic (2.71), economic (2.99), materialism (3.59), corrupts values (3.62), and falsity/no sense (3.00).

Source: Pollay, Richard W., and Banwari Mittal. (1993). "Here's the Beef: Factors, Determinants, and Segments in Consumer Criticism of Advertising." *Journal of Marketing*, 57, 99-114.

© 1993 by the American Marketing Association. Scale items taken from Appendix (pp. 112-113). Reprinted with permission.

Other evidence: N/A

Other sources: N/A

Reference: Bauer, R. A., and S. A. Greyser. (1968). *Advertising in America: The Consumer View.* Boston: Harvard University, Graduate School of Business Administration, Division of Research.

PUBLIC OPINION TOWARD ADVERTISING
(Pollay and Mittal 1993)

1. Advertising is essential.

2. Advertising is a valuable source of information about local sales.

3. In general, advertising is misleading.

4. Quite often advertising is amusing and entertaining.

5. Advertising persuades people to buy things they should not buy.

6. Most advertising insults the intelligence of the average consumer.

7. From advertising I learn about fashions and about what to buy to impress others.

8. Advertising helps raise our standard of living.

9. Advertising results in better products for the public.

10. Advertising tells me what people with lifestyles similar to mine are buying and using.

11. Advertising is making us a materialistic society, overly interested in buying and owning things.

12. Advertising tells me which brands have the features I am looking for.

13. Advertising promotes undesirable values in our society.

14. Sometimes I take pleasure in thinking about what I saw or heard or read in advertisements.

15. Advertising makes people buy unaffordable products just to show off.

16. In general, advertising results in lower prices.

17. Advertising helps me know which products will or will not reflect the sort of person I am.

18. In general, advertisements present a true picture of the product advertised.

19. Sometimes advertisements are even more enjoyable than other media contents.

20. In general, advertising helps our nation's economy.

21. Most advertising distorts the values of our youth.

22. Advertising helps me keep up to date about products/services available in the marketplace.

23. Mostly, advertising is wasteful of economic resources.

24. Overall, I consider advertising a good thing.

25. Advertising makes people live in a world of fantasy.

26. There is too much sex in advertising today.

27. Because of advertising, people buy a lot of things they do not really need.

28. My general opinion of advertising is unfavorable.

29. In general, advertising promotes competition, which benefits the consumer.

30. Some products/services promoted in advertising are bad for our society.

NOTES: The instrument measures these constructs with items in parentheses: global attitudes (24, 28, 33), information (2, 12, 22), social role and image (7, 10, 17), hedonic/pleasure (4, 14, 19), good for the economy (20, 23, 29), materialism (11, 15, 25, 27), falsity/no sense (3, 6, 18), and value corruption (13, 21). Bauer-Greyser (1968) items are 1, 5, 6, 8, 9, 16, and 18, of which 6 and 8 are absorbed in the authors' principal constructs, whereas 1 and 5 are supplanted; 8, 9, and 16 measure distal antecedents, as do additional items 26 and 30.

SKEPTICISM TOWARD ADVERTISING
(Obermiller and Spangenberg 1998)

Construct: Skepticism toward advertising is defined as the general tendency toward disbelief of advertising claims. Skepticism is hypothesized as a general trait that varies across individuals and is related to general persuadability. The measure assesses a generalizable characteristic rather than responses to specific ads or ad claims. Moreover, the construct is more limited than concepts such as attitudes toward advertising in general and attitudes toward marketing.

Description: The unidimensional scale consists of nine items operationalized using a 5-place response format ranging from *strongly agree* to *strongly disagree*. The summed scores can range from 9 to 45, with higher scores representing higher skepticism.

Development: A search of relevant literature, brainstorming, and consulting with marketing academics produced 124 statements. Two marketing professors and two advertising executives served as expert judges of the appropriateness of the items following exposure to the construct definition. The judging stage reduced the number to 31 (16 skeptical) items. Twelve items were deleted based upon low item-to-total correlations. Subsequent factor analyses over the first ($n = 304$) and second administrations ($n = 772$) revealed a stable single factor comprising nine items. Confirmatory factor analysis on the second administration data, as well as the first sample, verified the superior fit of a single-factor model relative to competing models.

Samples: The scale was developed and validated using eight different, independent samples ranging in size from 32 to 365 participants. The first and second administrations used in estimation of the final confirmatory factor analyses were 304 undergraduates and 772 nonstudents and secondary students. Five of the subsamples had 174 or more subjects. The mix of samples included a variety of groups including heterogeneous, nonstudent adults; university undergraduate students; MBAs; university faculty; and secondary students.

Validity: A large number of samples and studies are reported by Obermiller and Spangenberg (1998). These tests include substantial evidence of discriminant and predictive validity. Only some of these results are summarized here. Coefficient alpha estimates of internal reliability consistency for the first and second administrations were .85 and .86, respectively. (See Obermiller and Spangenberg [1998], Table 1, p. 171 for a more complete description of fit statistics across the first and second administrations.) Average variance extracted statistics were .33 and .35. Again, a large number of criterion and nomological validity tests, as well as other evidence of reliability, were reported. Some specifics from these analyses include the following results. Evidence of criterion validity was provided by differences in mean scores across student age groups, across industry occupations, and across faculty disciplines as predicted. In addition, the scale was negatively correlated with responses (i.e., likability, believability, and likely influence) to a sample of 13 ads as hypothesized. Correlations with attitude toward marketing, attitude toward advertising, self-esteem, and need for cognition were .49, .48, .25, and .13, respectively. Other evidence was provided regarding a series of behaviors consequent to advertising exposures. In addition, test-retest correlation across a 6-week delay was .66.

Scores: A number of mean scores are reported. For example, mean scores are reported for students and faculty. Overall, students average 28.0, with a breakdown of 27.7 for secondary students, 27.9 for undergraduates, and 29.4 for MBAs. Faculty averaged 33.8, with a breakdown of 36.1 for liberal arts, 33.5 for sciences, and 31.6 for business. Means for adaptations of the measure's target are reported as well.

Source: Obermiller, Carl, and Eric Spangenberg. (1998). "Development of a Scale to Measure Skepticism Toward Advertising." *Journal of Consumer Psychology*, 7(2), 159-186.
© 1998 by Lawrence Erlbaum Associates, Inc. Scale items taken from Table 1 (p. 171). Reprinted with permission.

Other evidence: N/A

Other sources: N/A

References: N/A

SKEPTICISM TOWARD ADVERTISING
(Obermiller and Spangenberg 1998)

1. We can depend on getting the truth in most advertising.

2. Advertising's aim is to inform the consumer.

3. I believe advertising is informative.

4. Advertising is generally truthful.

5. Advertising is a reliable source of information about the quality and performance of products.

6. Advertising is truth well told.

7. In general, advertising presents a true picture of the product being advertised.

8. I feel I've been accurately informed after viewing most advertisements.

9. Most advertising provides consumers with essential information.

TV ADVERTISING BELIEVABILITY SCALE
(Beltramini 1982)

Construct: Ad believability is viewed as the extent to which an ad is capable of evoking sufficient confidence in its truthfulness to render it acceptable to consumers (Beltramini 1982).

Description: The believability scale consists of 10 semantic differentials each operationalized using a 5-place scale response format. The scale is considered applicable to ad claims across various types of products. Scores are derived by averaging over the 10 items, such that higher scores reflect greater believability.

Development: A large pool of items was originally generated and then reduced to the final 10-item scale through a pretest. A large group of students ($n = 584$) then responded to the items for three print ads (i.e., one for tires, one for cars, and one for cigarettes). The scale was then tested for reliability and convergent validity (Beltramini 1982). (Beltramini and Evans [1985] also describe this process.)

Sample: A sample of 584 students was used in the development of the scale.

Validity: Coefficient alpha estimates across the three products were .94, .95, and .95 for tires, cars, and cigarettes, respectively. The high average inter-item correlations across the three products (.61, .69, and .69) offer evidence of convergent validity. Some evidence of discriminant validity was also offered by correlating the scale with a five-item distractor measure. These correlations were .43, .42, and .47 across the three products.

Scores: Mean scores (std. dev.) for the scale across the three ads were 4.55 (1.78), 5.61 (2.08), and 6.28 (1.93) for the tires, cars, and cigarette ads, respectively.

Source: Beltramini, Richard. (1982). "Advertising Perceived Believability Scale." In D. R. Corrigan, F. B. Kraft, and R. H. Ross (Eds.), *Proceedings of the Southwestern Marketing Association* (pp. 1-3). Wichita, KS: Southwestern Marketing Association, Wichita State University.
   © 1982 by the Southwest Marketing Association. Scale items taken from Table 1 (p. 2). Reprinted with permission.

Other evidence: Beltramini (1988) also used the scale to measure the variability and intensity of attitudes toward cigarette warning labels. Questionnaire booklets were administered to business students at a major American university. A total of 727 usable surveys were returned. Cronbach's alpha across four measurements (ads) ranged from .78 to .94, with an average of .90. Furthermore, those who held more firmly that smoking is harmful were found to perceive the ad claim information as significantly more believable than those who held less firmly that smoking is harmful, offering evidence of predictive validity. Mean scores and standard deviations were calculated for the four ads. These means (std. dev.) ranged from 3.54 (1.01) to 4.30 (0.60).

Other source: Beltramini, Richard F. (1988). "Perceived Believability of Warning Label Information Presented in Cigarette Advertising." *Journal of Advertising, 17*(1), 26-32.

Reference: Beltramini, Richard F., and Kenneth R. Evans. (1985). "Perceived Believability of Research Results Information in Advertising." *Journal of Advertising, 14*, 18-24, 31.

TV ADVERTISING BELIEVABILITY SCALE
(Beltramini 1982)

1. Unbelievable / Believable

2. Untrustworthy / Trustworthy

3. Not convincing / Convincing

4. Not credible / Credible

5. Unreasonable / Reasonable

6. Dishonest / Honest

7. Questionable / Unquestionable

8. Inconclusive / Conclusive

9. Not authentic / Authentic

10. Unlikely / Likely

MEASURES RELATED TO CHILDREN'S ADVERTISING

PRESCHOOL NONVERBAL (BRAND) ATTITUDE SCALE: PAS
(Macklin and Machleit 1990)

Construct: Based on the need for a multi-item scale for preschool children, a five-item standardized attitude scale was developed. This "Preschool Attitude Scale" (PAS) was specifically designed for measuring 3- to 5-year-old children's affective attitudes toward products with careful efforts to ensure the scale's age appropriateness. The PAS appears to achieve age-appropriateness and indicates that young people can respond to it in a reliable and valid manner (Macklin and Machleit 1990).

Description: The final version of the scale contains five items (two of which have male and female versions) operationalized by placing five visual scale points per item on 14″ × 5.5″ poster boards. In addition, descriptors were used with each pictorial scale item. Item scores can be summed to form an overall index, and the scale is considered unidimensional. Overall, the PAS presents visual items, requires nonverbal (pointing) responses, and is child-friendly due to its gamelike procedure.

Development: This investigation was divided into four phases. Phase 1 ($n = 91$) was a feasibility study. Phase 2 ($n = 38$) and Phase 3 ($n = 61$) were directed at refinements of the measure and of the procedures for administration, and Phase 4 ($n = 61$) confirmed the results with respect to scale usefulness. In the scale development process, the authors incorporated items similar to the ones that are commonly used in industry (Harrigan and Benzinger 1988) and created several of their own. Originally, seven scale items were developed by placing five visual scale points per item on 14″ × 5.5″ poster boards. Additionally, oral descriptors which were within a child's vocabulary were used with each pictorial scale item. In the first phase of the study, the feasibility of using the measures was assessed. Specifically, the reliability and factor structure of the scale were evaluated. Furthermore, the physical appearance of the scale (horizontal versus vertical scale presentation) was considered (Macklin and Machleit 1990, p. 254). Phase 2 was designed to repeat the Phase 1 study. In addition, the scale's ability to stand up to more difficult tasks was assessed. Two of the original seven items (i.e., the reverse-scored items) were eliminated in this phase. The purpose of Phase 3 was threefold. First, the dimensionality of the scale without using reverse-coded items was assessed. Second, a training session was included in the administration procedure in an effort to help children understand the more subtle distinctions among the points on the scale. Third, three brands within a different product category were evaluated. The purpose of Phase 4 was to address the question, "Does the scale-item basis versus 'product basis' administration procedure make a difference in reliability and predictive validity?" Five scale items were retained in the final version of the PAS. As stated above, numerous reliability, dimensionality, and validity checks were performed across the phases.

Samples: A total of 251 children (ages 3 to 5 years with a relatively equal breakdown across gender) were individually interviewed during the multiphase project ($n = 91, 61, 61$, and 38 for Phases 1 though 4, respectively).

Validity: Although reliability and validity estimates were reported throughout all four phases, we will concentrate on the final two phases (i.e., the final form of the scale). In Phases 3 and 4, the scale consistently exhibited a unidimensional factor structure. In Phase 3, coefficient alpha values were high for each of the three brands of candy rated by the children (.94, .91, and .92). In Phase 4, coefficient alphas ranged from .96 to .97 across the three candy bars rated. Also in Phases 3 and 4, mean differences via MANOVA showed evidence of predictive validity for the scale. Specifically, mean scores were significantly different among candy bars rated as the children's first, second, and third choices.

Scores: Mean attitude scores are reported in Table 2 of the Macklin and Machleit (1990, p. 263) article for both the multi-item PAS and the univariate scale items to facilitate comparison. The overall mean scores for the first, second, and third choice of candies in Phase 3 were 23.60, 20.77, and 16.73, respectively. Mean scores for the first, second, and third choice of candies in Phase 4 were 24.48, 21.88, and 20.10, respectively.

Source: Macklin, M. Carole, and Karen A. Machleit. (1990). "Measuring Preschool Children's Attitude." *Marketing Letters*, *1*(3), 253-265.
    © 1990 by Kluwer Academic Publishers. Scale items taken from Appendix (p. 264). Reprinted with kind permission from Kluwer Academic Publishers.

Other evidence: N/A

Other sources: N/A

References: Harrigan, Judy, and Peter Benzinger. (1988). "Children's Research: Where It's Been, Where It Is Going." *Transcript Proceedings: Second Bi-Annual ARF Workshop on Children's Research* (pp. 5-21). New York: Advertising Research Foundation.

PRESCHOOL NONVERBAL (BRAND) ATTITUDE SCALE: PAS
(Macklin and Machleit 1990)

Happy Faces

  5 = real happy

  4 = somewhat happy

  3 = not happy nor sad

  2 = a little bit sad

  1 = real sad

Big Star

  5 = like a whole lot

  4 = like somewhat

  3 = like a little bit

  2 = don't like a little

  1 = don't like at all

Multiple Stars

  5 = great

  4 = a little bit great

  3 = so-so

  2 = don't like much

  1 = terrible

Smiley

   5 = like a lot

   4 = like some

   3 = like a little

   2 = don't like much

   1 = don't like at all

Jump

   5 = very exciting

   4 = somewhat exciting

   3 = a little exciting

   2 = not very exciting

   1 = not at all exciting

NOTES: Pictorial scale items were mounted on 14″ × 5.5″ poster boards. Scale points are articulated orally by the scale's administrator. Training instructions are available in the Macklin and Machleit (1990, p. 264) article. For "smiley faces" and "jump," both male and female pictorial versions are required.

   The pictorial scales are not reproduced here. The prospective user should consult the source for these scales (cf. Macklin and Machleit 1990, p. 264).

TV ADS: CHILDREN'S ATTITUDES TOWARD TV COMMERCIALS
(Rossiter 1977)

Construct: The scale developed by Rossiter (1977) was designed for the purpose of providing a short, standardized test of children's attitudes toward television commercials. A range of cognitions and affective reactions toward television commercials is reflected in the scale, including the following (Rossiter 1977, p. 180): (a) perceived truthfulness, (b) potential annoying qualities, (c) objectivity in describing advertised products, (d) overall likability, (e) perceived persuasive power, (f) believability of characters, and (g) trustworthiness as guides to product purchase.

Description: After an initial explanation of the rating system by the tester, the finalized version of the instrument is designed for self-administration. The survey consists of seven items which represented the seven components listed above. A 4-point agreement scale is used for each item because the pretest revealed this to be the maximal level of discrimination for most third graders. Because each item is scored 1 to 4, the range of the total scale is 7 to 28. Three of the items are negatively worded. The brevity of the test is commendable given that its intended audience is children (i.e., it can administered in about 5 to 10 minutes, depending on the ages of the children involved).

Development: The test of children's attitudes toward television commercials began with the generation of an initial pool of 12 attitude items that were pretested with a group of 20 third-grade children. Seven items were retained for the final instrument. The items reflected the range of cognitive and affective reactions toward television commercials described above. The retained items were administered in a class setting to 208 children comprising groups of 25 to 30 children at a time. Several reliability tests were performed.

Samples: Following a pretest with a group of 20 third-grade children, the revised attitude test was administered to a sample of 208 children, covering grades 4, 5, and 6 (ages 9 through 12) of a predominately middle-class, suburban Philadelphia primary school. Approximately equal numbers of boys and girls were tested (Rossiter 1977, pp. 180-181).

Validity: Pearson's r was used to assess item intercorrelations. All but two were in the range between .10 and .60, and all were positive. The item-to-total correlations ranged from .49 to .67, indicating an even set of item-test contributions. The coefficient alpha estimate of internal consistency reliability was .69. Two correlational results for the 1-month retest of the instrument were reported, using both Pearson's r and Kendall's tau. These estimates for the scale as a whole were tau = .66 and r = .67.

Scores: Mean scores were not reported in the Rossiter (1977) article.

Source: Rossiter, John R. (1977). "Reliability of a Short Test Measuring Children's Attitudes Toward TV Commercials." *Journal of Consumer Research*, 3, 179-184.

    © 1977 by University of Chicago Press. Scale items taken from Appendix (p. 183). Reprinted with permission.

Other evidence: In a validation study, Bearden, Teel, and Wright (1979) used two samples drawn from separate elementary schools (grades 4 through 6). One sample was of medium- to high-income children (n = 76), and the other was of low-income children (n = 62). Based on the replication sample (i.e., the medium- to high-income group), an alpha of .75 supported the internal consistency of the scale. The corrected item-test correlations ranged from .53 to .70 for the replication study, which was comparable to Rossiter's (1977) study. However, the alpha coefficient for the low-income group was .57, which suggested that the test may have greater internal consistency for middle-income children than for lower-income children. Although the item-test correlations based on the children from the low-income school were within the range of .30 to .80, they were generally lower and more dispersed than those for the moderate- to high-income students. The test-retest Pearson correlation coefficient of .80 for the replication supports the test's overall reliability for medium- to high-income children.

In another study, Lindquist and Belonax (1979) used a sample of approximately 500 children selected from grades 3 through 6 to evaluate the internal consistency and test-retest reliability of the seven-item scale. Four different media were used, including television, children's magazines, radio, and comic books. Minor modifications were made to the scale when gathering data on magazines, radio, and comic books. The alpha (.53) for the television instrument was a bit low for a standard measuring device. The alphas for the magazine and radio commercials were .64 and .66, respectively, while the comic book-based alpha was .70. Test-retest reliability ranged from .44 to .63 across the four media.

Riecken and Samli (1981) also examined the reliability of the scale. A sample of 152 children, ages ranging from 8 to 12 and from a variety of socioeconomic backgrounds, served as subjects. The scale was extended to three specific product categories. In all cases, satisfactory internal consistency and moderate test-retest estimates were found. For example, Cronbach's alpha ranged from .69 to .76, and test-retest ranged from .59 to .63 across three product categories.

Other sources: Bearden, William O., Jesse E. Teel, and Robert R. Wright. (1979). "Family Income Effects on Measurement of Children's Attitudes Toward Television Commercials." *Journal of Consumer Research*, 6, 308-311.

Lindquist, Jay D., and Joseph J. Belonax, Jr. (1979). "A Reliability Evaluation of a Short Test Designed to Measure Children's Attitudes Toward Advertising in Audio-Visual and Print Media." In Jerry C. Olson (Ed.), *Advances in Consumer Research* (Vol. 7, pp. 676-679). Provo, UT: Association for Consumer Research.

Riecken, Glen, and A. Coskun Samli. (1981). "Measuring Children's Attitudes Toward Television Commercials: Extension and Replication." *Journal of Consumer Research*, 8, 57-61.

References: N/A

TV ADS: CHILDREN'S ATTITUDES TOWARD TV COMMERCIALS
(Rossiter 1977)

INSTRUCTIONS:

PRINT YOUR NAME, SCHOOL AND GRADE HERE BEFORE YOU BEGIN.

NAME (First name) _____   (Last Name) _____

SCHOOL _____   GRADE _____

WHAT DO YOU THINK OF THE COMMERCIALS ON TV?
READ EACH QUESTION CAREFULLY, THEN PUT AN X ON THE LINE FOR YOUR ANSWER.

THE BOXES MEAN: YES - I agree very much
yes - I agree
no - I disagree
NO - I disagree very much

1. Television commercials tell the truth. (Truth)

___YES   ___yes   ___no   ___NO

2. Most TV commercials are in poor taste and very annoying. (Annoy)*

___YES   ___yes   ___no   ___NO

3. Television commercials tell only the good things about a product—they don't tell you the bad things. (Good Only)*

___YES   ___yes   ___no   ___NO

4. I like most television commercials. (Like)

___YES   ___yes   ___no   ___NO

5. Television commercials try to make people buy things they don't really need. (Persuade)*

___YES   ___yes   ___no   ___NO

6. You can always believe what the people in commercials say or do. (Believe)

___YES   ___yes   ___no   ___NO

7. The products advertised the most on TV are always the best products to buy. (Best Buy)

___YES   ___yes   ___no   ___NO

MAKE SURE YOU HAVE ANSWERED EVERY QUESTION AND THAT YOUR NAME, SCHOOL
AND GRADE ARE PRINTED AT THE TOP OF THE PAGE.

NOTES: *Denotes that items 2, 3, and 5 are reverse scored. The cognition measured is in parentheses.

6

Attitudes About the Performance of Business Firms, Satisfaction and Post-Purchase Behavior, Social Agencies, and the Marketplace

CONSUMER ATTITUDES TOWARD BUSINESS PRACTICES AND MARKETING

CONSUMER ATTITUDES TOWARD MARKETING AND CONSUMERISM
(Barksdale and Darden 1972)

Construct: Barksdale and Darden (1972) present a battery of items that assess consumer reactions to business policies and practices. As evidenced by the citations listed below, various forms of the items have been adapted and used by a number of other consumer and marketing researchers. The topics addressed include philosophy of business, product quality, advertising, other marketing activities, consumer responsibilities, consumerism, and government regulation.

Description: Forty items grouped into seven categories (i.e., philosophy of business, product quality, advertising, other marketing activities, consumer responsibilities, consumerism, and government regulation) were used to assess consumer attitudes toward marketing and business. Each item was operationalized using a Likert-type 5-place response format (i.e., *strongly agree*, *agree*, *uncertain*, *disagree*, and *strongly disagree*).

Development: The 40 items were chosen after a pretest of 67 items using a sample of 160 adults in three cities (Barksdale and Darden 1972, p. 29). Barksdale and Darden (1972) summarize responses from a nationwide sample of 354 adult consumers for each of the 40 items. Tests of relationships with most individual characteristics revealed that attitudes were generally consistent across most consumer groups (e.g., gender, occupation). However, a number of differences in opinions were noted for younger consumers. Moreover, and as expected, more liberal respondents were generally more critical of marketing and business practices.

Sample: The data were collected by mail survey from an original national sample of 785 consumers randomly selected from telephone directories in each state. Of the 354 complete responses obtained, 61% of the sample was male, 67% described themselves as conservative, 35% were over the age of 55, and 83% were married. A more complete description is offered by Barksdale, Darden, and Perreault (1976, p. 119).

Validity: Direct evidence of validity for the items was not reported for this exploratory study. However, the extensions of this research described below do offer some additional supportive evidence of validity.

Scores: Percentage responses for each of the five agreement categories for all 40 items are reported in Tables 1 through 7. Means and standard deviations can be computed from these frequency distributions.

Source: Barksdale, Hiram C., and William R. Darden. (1972). "Consumer Attitudes Toward Marketing and Consumerism." *Journal of Marketing*, *36*, 28-35.

© 1972 by the American Marketing Association. Scale items and responses taken from Tables 1-7 (pp. 29-33). Reprinted with permission.

Other evidence: A number of authors have used all or parts of the items included in the Barksdale and Darden (1972) battery. A number of these follow-up applications are cited below. In some instances, the results of these studies offer additional support for the usefulness of the Barksdale and Darden (1972) inventory of consumer attitude items.

Barksdale et al. (1976) assessed trends in consumer attitudes by examining changes in item scores across samples taken in 1971, 1973, and 1975. Some of the items were used by LaBarbera and Lazer (1980) in their study of differences between consumers in general and participants in FTC rule making. Darley and Johnson (1993) used adapted versions of some of the items in their study of attitudes toward consumerism in four developing countries.

Varadarajan, Bharadwaj, and Thirunarayana (1994) provide evidence of factor reliabilities and corrected item-to-total correlations within factors. The survey used in their research is an adaptation of the questionnaire originally used by Barksdale and Darden (1972) and those used in follow-ups to the Barksdale and Darden research. For example, coefficient alpha estimates of internal consistency reliability for factors employing the original seven labels range from .53 to .72. Moreover, average factor scores are reported for clusters of Indian marketing and nonmarketing executives. Support for several hypotheses regarding differences in opinions between marketing and nonmarketing executives provides additional support for the items as well.

Other sources: Darley, William K., and Denise M. Johnson. (1993). "Cross-National Comparison of Consumer Attitudes Toward Consumerism in Four Developing Countries." *Journal of Consumer Affairs*, *27*, 37-65.

Dickinson, Virginia H., and James P. Shaver. (1982). "A Test of Consumer Awareness for Adults." *Journal of Consumer Affairs*, *16*, 241-259.

LaBarbera, Priscilla, and William Lazer. (1980). "Characteristics of Consumer Participants in Federal Trade Commission Rule Making." *Journal of Consumer Affairs*, *14*, 405-417.

Varadarajan, P. Rajan, Sundar G. Bharadwaj, and P. N. Thirunarayana. (1994). "Executive Attitudes Toward Consumerism and Marketing: An Exploration of Theoretical and Empirical Linkages in an Industrializing Country." *Journal of Business Research*, *29*, 83-100.

Reference: Barksdale, Hiram C., William R. Darden, and William D. Perreault, Jr. (1976). "Changes in Consumer Attitudes Toward Marketing, Consumerism, and Government Regulation: 1971-75." *Journal of Consumer Affairs*, *10*, 117-135.

CONSUMER ATTITUDES TOWARD MARKETING AND CONSUMERISM
(Barksdale and Darden 1972)

Philosophy of Business

1. Most manufacturers operate on the philosophy that the "consumer" is always right.

2. Despite what is frequently said, "let the buyer beware" is the guiding philosophy of most manufacturers.

3. Competition ensures that consumers pay fair prices.

4. Manufacturers seldom shirk their responsibility to the consumer.

5. Most manufacturers are more interested in making profits than in serving consumers.

Product Quality

6. In general, manufacturers make an effort to design products to fit the needs of consumers.

7. Over the past several years, the quality of most products has not improved.

8. From the consumer's point of view, style changes are not as important as improvements in product quality.

9. Manufacturers do not deliberately design products which will wear out as quickly as possible.

10. Manufacturers often withhold important product improvements from the market in order to protect their own interests.

11. The wide variety of competing products makes intelligent buying decisions more difficult.

12. For most types of products, the differences among competing brands are insignificant and unimportant to consumers.

Advertising

13. Most product advertising is believable.

14. Manufacturers' advertisements are reliable sources of information about the quality and performance of products.

15. Generally, advertised products are more dependable than unadvertised ones.

16. Manufacturers' advertisements usually present a true picture of the products advertised.

Other Marketing Activities

17. Generally speaking, the products required by the average family are easily available at convenient places.

18. In general, the quality of repair and maintenance service provided by manufacturers and dealers is getting better.

19. Generally, product guarantees are backed by the manufacturers who make them.

20. The games and contests that manufacturers sponsor to encourage people to buy their products are usually dishonest.

21. The American marketing system operates more efficiently than those of other countries.

Consumer Responsibilities

22. The problems of consumers are less serious now than in the past.

23. The information needed to become a well-informed consumer is readily available to most people.

24. The average consumer is willing to pay higher prices for products that will cause less environmental pollution.

25. The problems of the consumer are relatively unimportant when compared with the other questions and issues faced by the average family.

26. Many of the mistakes that consumers make in buying products are the result of their own carelessness or ignorance.

27. Consumers often try to take advantage of manufacturers and dealers by making claims that are not justified.

28. For most types of products, consumers do not find it worthwhile to shop around to find the best buy.

29. Concern for the environment does not influence the product choices made by most consumers.

Consumerism

30. Manufacturers seem to be more sensitive to consumer complaints now than they were in the past.

31. When consumers have problems with products they have purchased, it is usually easy to get them corrected.

32. Most business firms make a sincere effort to adjust complaints fairly.

33. From the consumer's viewpoint, the procedures followed by most manufacturers in handling complaints and settling grievances of consumers are not satisfactory.

34. Consumerism or the consumer crusade has not been an important factor in changing business practices and procedures.

35. Ralph Nader and the work he has done on behalf of consumers has been an important force in changing the practices of business.

36. The exploitation of consumers by business firms deserves more attention than it receives.

Government Regulation

37. The government should test competing brands of products and make the results of these tests available to consumers.

38. The government should set minimum standards of quality for all products sold to consumers.

39. The government should exercise more responsibility for regulating the advertising, sales and marketing activities of manufacturers.

40. A Federal Department of Consumer Protection is not needed to protect and promote the interests of consumers.

NOTE: Though not specified by the authors, it would seem that items 2, 5, 7, 10, 11, 12, 20, 26, 27, 29, 33, 34, and 40 require reverse scoring to reflect a more positive attitude toward marketing and consumerism.

CONSUMERISM: ATTITUDES OF CONSUMERS/
BUSINESS PEOPLE TOWARD CONSUMERISM
(Klein 1982)

Construct: The following measures are designed to assess general attitudes of both business people and consumers toward consumerism issues. The scales were designed to be applicable for research on both U.S. and Swedish subjects, including both business executives and consumers. The initial consumerism issues around which items were first constructed included the following: environmental issues, advertising and promotion, product testing consumer education, control and regulation, warranty and service, and public responsibility (Klein 1982, p. 124). Some caution is urged prior to the unquestioned use of the measures described here: Little evidence of reliability and external validation was provided.

Description: The final instrument consists of 20 items reflecting six factors. The factor labels along with the number of statements composing each factor are as follow: (a) most businesses are concerned about and responsive to consumers—5, (b) consumers need protection and education to compete effectively with business—4, (c) generally the quality of products has been decreasing—3, (d) our business system is more efficient than that of most other countries—3, (e) packaging today is essentially honest—2, and (f) business is primarily self-serving in nature—3. Six-point Likert-type rating scales (without a neutral position) were used to operationalize each statement. Respondents are required to indicate their degree of agreement or disagreement with each statement using *strongly disagree* to *strongly agree* bipolar adjective sets. Though not specified, it seems that summing overall items to obtain an overall score and summing items within factors are appropriate.

Development: The initial pool of items was developed from a review of related measures and a brainstorming session. The questionnaire used in the preliminary stages of development included 113 items. Student interviewers from California State University, Long Beach, were used to collect pretest data from samples of 213 and 50 consumers and business persons, respectively. The items were factor analyzed using orthogonal, varimax rotation. Items were retained based upon common meaning (within each factor) and loadings above .50 (Klein 1982). A final version to be used in eventual scale development consisted of 42 items (see the Appendix in Klein [1982]). These 42 items were selected from the pretest results, item-to-total correlations, and consultation with Swedish researchers involved in the project. Data were collected for the 42-item version from 204 Swedish residents and 243 Long Beach residents in 1979. In addition, data were obtained from business samples of 55 and 75 Swedish and American firms, respectively. Uppsala, Sweden, was selected based on its demographic and geographic similarity to Long Beach, California. Factor analysis of these data was used as the primary means of constructing the final 20-item instrument. Only those items loading similarly in both cultures were included in the final scale(s) (Klein 1982, p. 130).

Samples: The first administration (i.e., the pretest of the 113 items) obtained responses from 213 consumers across varying social classes (i.e., upper, middle, and working classes) and census tract divisions in both the U.S and Swedish data collections. In all cases, an attempt was made to collect data from an equal number of male and female consumers. An additional 50 responses were obtained from local business executives. Data also were obtained from 204 Uppsala residents and 243 Long Beach residents in 1979. For the Swedish sample, 57% were female, 40% had no college education, and 58% were below 35 years of age. For the American respondents, 50% were female, 48% had no college work, and 33% were under 35 years of age. Comparable data from 55 Swedish and 75 U.S. business persons were obtained as well.

Validity: No evidence beyond the face validity of the items and the stated consistency of factor analysis results between cultures was provided for the scale.

Scores: Neither total scale, factor, nor item mean scores were provided.

Source: Klein, Gary D. (1982). "Development of a Cross-Cultural Instrument to Measure the Attitudes of Consumers and Business People Toward Consumerism." *Journal of Marketing and Public Policy*, *1*, 123-137.
                     © 1982 by the American Marketing Association. Scale items taken from Table 4 (p. 132). Reprinted with permission.

Other evidence: N/A

Other sources: N/A

References: N/A

CONSUMERISM: ATTITUDES OF CONSUMERS/ BUSINESS PEOPLE TOWARD CONSUMERISM
(Klein 1982)

Business Is Concerned About and Responsive to Consumers

3. Most business firms make a sincere effort to help displeased customers.

12. Most manufacturers really want to fulfill warranty obligations.

22. In general, business firms usually accept responsibility for their products and guarantees.

35. When consumers have problems with products they have purchased, it is usually easy to get them corrected.

38. Most companies' complaint departments back up their products and effectively handle consumer problems.

Consumers Need Protection and Education to Compete Effectively With Business

2. The government should set minimum standards of quality for all products sold to the consumer.

6. More frequent health and safety warnings on packages are necessary to adequately inform the consumer of possible dangers.

7. Business should be legally liable for the pollution it or its products cause.

8. Consumer education should be a required portion of a manufacturer's advertising budget.

The Quality of Products Has Been Decreasing

21. Products that last a long time are a thing of the past.

29. In general, the quality of repairs and maintenance service provided by manufacturers is getting worse.

40. In general, I am dissatisfied with the quality of most products today.

The (U.S./Swedish) Business System Is More Efficient Than That of Most Other Countries

4. Consumers in (the U.S./Sweden) are much more protected by government regulation than in most other countries.

13. (American/Swedish)-made products are less dangerous than those of most other countries.

33. The (American/Swedish) business system operates more efficiently than that of most other countries.

Packaging Today Is Essentially Honest

16. What is seen on the outside of a package is often not what you get on the inside.

26. Package sizes show in a correct way the amount of product contained inside.

Business Is Primarily Self-Serving in Nature

5. All business really wants to do is make the most money it can.

25. The main reason a company is socially responsible is to make more sales.

34. Companies try to influence the government to better their own standing.

NOTES: Item numbers are as they appeared in the original article. To reflect a more positive view toward consumerism, items 21, 29, 40, and 16 require reverse coding.

SATISFACTION WITH SOCIAL SERVICES
(Reid and Gundlach 1984)

Construct: This research attempts to develop a scale for the measurement of consumer satisfaction with social services; that is, it attempts to develop a consumer satisfaction scale of general utility. The measure purports to reflect the elements of social service provision that influence consumer satisfaction. Overall, the items reflect provisions related to satisfaction judgments derived from three attributes:

Relevance: the extent to which a service corresponds to the individual's perception of his or her problem needs,

Impact: the extent to which the service reduces the problem experienced by the client, and

Gratification: the extent to which the service enhances the individual's self-esteem and sense of integrity.

Description: The final scale comprises 34 items reflecting three related subfactors. The dimensions and the corresponding number of items are as follows: (a) relevance, 11 items; (b) impact, 10 items (an eleventh item, shown as item 19 in the scale, was dropped); and (c) gratitude, 13 items. Item wording is varied to inhibit acquiescence bias. Each item is scored from 1 to 5. Total and individual factor scores reflect averages across the number of items involved in each subscale or the total scale. Consequently, the total scale and each subscale range from 1 to 5. A disagree-agree response format was used to operationalize the individual items.

Development: Based on the experience of the authors and questions suggested in related research, a pool of 35 items (see Reid and Gundlach 1984, Table 1, pp. 44-46) was developed. Again, these items were designed to reflect the three attributes of service provision described above. Coefficient alpha estimates of reliability were used to examine the total scale and each of the three subscales. One item (item 19) was dropped based upon the reliability analyses.

Sample: The initial study involved the responses of 166 heads of households of families involved with a Head Start program in Jackson, Michigan. The respondents were predominantly female (81.3%). In addition, most of the respondents reported little education and low family incomes. Utilization data revealed that the subjects were heavy users of various social services.

Validity: The pairwise correlations among the three subscales ranged from .75 to .84. Guttman lambda estimates of reliability for the total scale and the three subscales of relevance, impact, and gratification were .96, .88, .82, and .86, respectively. Some evidence of validity (other than the content of the items themselves) was provided by differences in scores across sample subgroups and analysis of relationships with certain program-related variables. These results are summarized in Tables 3 and 4 of Reid and Gundlach (1984). For example, higher satisfaction scores were obtained for white respondents, while lower scores were found for single and/or divorced respondents. Lower scores were generally observed for the unemployed. Interestingly, satisfaction seemed to have an inverse relationship to program importance, with lower than mean scores being associated with the Department of Social Services and Medicaid, the two services ranked most highly in terms of importance.

Scores: The total scale had a mean and standard deviation of 3.22 and .54, respectively. The relevance and impact factors had means of 3.35 and 3.20, respectively. The mean for the gratitude factor was 3.14.

Source: Reid, P. Nelson, and James H. Gundlach. (1984). "A Scale for the Measurement of Consumer Satisfaction With Social Services." *Journal of Social Service Research*, 7(1), 37-54.
© 1984 by Haworth Press. Scale items taken from Table 1 (pp. 44-46). Reprinted with permission.

Other evidence: N/A

Other sources: N/A

References: N/A

SATISFACTION WITH SOCIAL SERVICES
(Reid and Gundlach 1984)

Relevance Items

1. The social worker took my problems very seriously. (+)

2. If I had been the social worker, I would have dealt with my problems in just the same way. (+)

3. The worker I had could never understand anyone like me. (–)

4. Overall, the agency has been very helpful to me. (+)

5. If a friend of mine had similar problems, I would tell them to go to the agency. (+)

6. The social worker asks a lot of embarrassing questions. (–)

7. I can always count on the worker to help if I'm in trouble. (+)

8. The social agency will help me as much as they can. (+)

9. I don't think the agency has the power to really help me. (–)

10. The social worker tries hard but usually isn't too helpful. (–)

11. The problem the agency tried to help me with is one of the most important in my life. (+)

Impact Items

12. Things have gotten better since I have been going to the agency. (+)

13. Since I've been using the agency my life is more messed up than ever. (–)

14. The agency is always available when I need it. (+)

15. I got from the agency exactly what I wanted. (+)

16. The social worker loves to talk but won't really do anything for me. (–)

17. Sometimes I just tell the social worker what I think she wants to hear. (–)

18. The social worker is usually in a hurry when I see her. (–)

19. I went to the agency with one problem but they ended up helping me on another. (–)

20. No one should have any trouble getting some help from this agency. (+)

21. The worker sometimes says things I don't understand. (–)

22. The social workers are always explaining things carefully. (+)

Gratitude Items

23. I never looked forward to my visits to the social agency. (−)

24. I hope I'll never have to go back to the agency for help. (−)

25. Every time I talk to my worker I feel relieved. (+)

26. I can tell the social worker the truth without worrying. (+)

27. I usually feel nervous when I talk to my worker. (−)

28. The social worker is always looking for lies in what I tell her. (−)

29. It takes a lot of courage to go to the agency. (−)

30. When I enter the agency, I feel very small and insignificant. (−)

31. The agency is very demanding. (−)

32. The social worker will sometimes lie to me. (−)

33. Generally, the social worker is an honest person. (+)

34. I have the feeling that the worker talks to other people about me. (−)

35. I always feel well treated when I leave the social agency. (+)

NOTES: (−) denotes items that are negatively coded; (+) denotes items that are positively coded. Item 19 was deleted from the scale.

SENTIMENT: THE INDEX OF CONSUMER SENTIMENT TOWARD MARKETING
(Gaski and Etzel 1986)

Construct: This measure represents an index of consumer sentiment toward marketing practices. The measure is designed to provide a continuing "barometer of how marketing is doing in the eyes of the consumer public" (Gaski and Etzel 1986, p. 72). The index is offered for several reasons: (a) It may sensitize marketers to consumers' perceptions, (b) it would serve to identify the nature of public relations tasks facing marketing, (c) it should assist in gauging whatever progress is or is not being made, and (d) it may demonstrate marketer concern for public opinion. The measure is designed to reflect composite opinion about four aspects of marketing corresponding roughly to the four elements of the marketing mix: (a) product quality, (b) the prices of products, (c) advertising, and (d) retailing or selling.

Description: Each of the four factors is represented by five Likert-type agree-disagree items which range from –2 to +2. The scale positions are labeled as follows: (1) *agree strongly*, (2) *agree somewhat*, (3) *neither agree nor disagree*, (4) *disagree somewhat*, and (5) *disagree strongly*. After recoding the items such that higher scores reflect more positive opinions, items from each factor are summed and then weighted from 1 (*not at all important*) to 5 (*extremely important*). The range of the index is –200 to +200. The index is computed as the sum[w(j) × sumx(ij)] where j represents one of the four categories and w(j) represents the weight for that category. Thus, though multidimensional, an overall index is derived.

Development: An initial pool of items was developed by the authors in consultation with Market Facts, Inc. personnel. Two items from each factor with low item-to-total correlations were deleted. Data from 50 pretest subjects were used in these purification efforts. The scale was further tested via factor analysis, coefficient alpha, and validity. (Pretest versions of the scale are reported in Gaski and Etzel 1985.)

Samples: The original pool of items (see Gaski and Etzel [1986]) was purified using a pretest sample of 50 subjects from the Consumer Mail Panel of Market Facts, Inc. Data are now being collected annually from a sample of 2,000 members of the Market Facts Panel (*n* = 200,000). The first survey reported in Gaski and Etzel (1986) involved responses from 1,428 individuals to the initial mailing. The panel is designed to reflect U.S. Census data in terms of geographic region, annual income, population density, age, sex, and family size.

Validity: A series of tests was performed in efforts to examine the validity of the index using the responses to the first panel mailing (*n* = 1,428). Estimates of internal consistency reliability ranged from .76 to .82. All within-factor item-to-total correlations exceeded .48. Evidence of discriminant validity was provided by comparisons of the reliability estimates with the factor correlations. The results from principal axis factor analysis with oblique rotation revealed a factor structure consistent with the item content for each of the four factors. Significant evidence of convergent validation was provided by a series of correlations of the Consumer Sentiment Index with overall global impressions (*r* = .63), satisfaction (*r* = .73), and problems (*r* = .63). (These items are also shown in the Appendix in Gaski and Etzel [1986].)

Scores: The mean consumer sentiment score for the first national sample was –14.85 (i.e., slightly in the unfavorable range). The mean attitude score was –12.36 for women and –17.71 for men, *t* = 2.08, *p* < .05.

Source: Gaski, John F., and Michael J. Etzel. (1986). "The Index of Consumer Sentiment Toward Marketing." *Journal of Marketing, 50*, 71-81.

Other evidence: N/A

Other sources: N/A

Reference: Gaski, John F., and Michael J. Etzel. (1985). "A Proposal for a Global, Longitudinal Measure of National Consumer Sentiment Toward Marketing Practice." In Elizabeth C. Hirschman and Morris B. Holbrook (Eds.), *Advances in Consumer Research* (Vol. 12, pp. 65-70). Provo, UT: Association for Consumer Research.

SENTIMENT: THE INDEX OF CONSUMER SENTIMENT TOWARD MARKETING
(Gaski and Etzel 1986)

Product Scale

1. I am satisfied with most of the products I buy.

2. Most products I buy wear out too quickly.*

3. Too many of the products I buy are defective in some way.*

4. The companies that make products I buy don't care enough about how well they perform.*

5. The quality of products I buy has consistently improved over the years.

Advertising Scale

1. Most advertising is very annoying.*

2. Most advertising makes false claims.*

3. If most advertising were eliminated, consumers would be better off.*

4. I enjoy most ads.

5. Most advertising is intended to deceive rather than inform.*

Price Scale

1. Most products I buy are overpriced.*

2. Businesses could charge lower prices and still be profitable.*

3. Most prices are reasonable given the high cost of doing business.

4. Most prices are fair.

5. In general, I am satisfied with the prices I pay.

Retailing/Selling Scale

1. Most retail stores serve their customers well.

2. Because of the way retailers treat me, most of my shopping is unpleasant.*

3. I find most retail salespeople to be very helpful.

4. When I need assistance in a store, I am usually *not* able to get it.*

5. Most retailers provide adequate service.

NOTE: *Denotes items that require reverse coding to reflect a more favorable sentiment toward marketing practices.

SERVICE QUALITY: SERVQUAL
(Parasuraman, Zeithaml, and Berry 1986, 1988)

Construct: The construct of quality as measured by this scale involves perceived quality (as opposed to objective quality). Perceived quality is the consumer's judgment of an entity's overall excellence or superiority, similar to an overall attitude. Perceived service quality is defined as the degree and direction of discrepancy between a consumer's perceptions and expectations (Parasuraman, Zeithaml, and Berry 1986, 1988). Quality is distinguished from satisfaction in that the latter is assumed to involve specific transactions. As part of the conceptualization, expectations are viewed as desires or wants of consumers (not predictions of what will be provided).

Description: The scale is composed of two matched sets of 22 items, each describing expectations for a particular service category and then perceptions of a particular service provider. Both sets of items are operationalized using 7-place bipolar scales labeled *Strongly Agree* (7) to *Strongly Disagree* (1). Approximately half the items are worded negatively, with negative wording indicated by (–) below. Scores for the total scale and each factor range from –6 to +6, with positive scores reflecting perceptions exceeding expectations. Difference scores for the 1-to-7 scales are computed and then averaged over the number of items either in the total scale or for each subscale. Furthermore, five factors constitute the two subscales: tangibility, reliability, responsiveness, assurance, and empathy.

The ensuing scale was developed to contain items appropriate for the multiple service categories used in the construction of the present scale. "Therefore, while SERVQUAL can be used in its present form to assess and compare quality across a wide variety of firms, appropriate adaptation of the instrument may be desirable when only a single service is investigated" (Parasuraman et al. 1988, pp. 27-28).

Development: Ninety-seven items were originally developed to represent 10 dimensions of service quality. Each was cast as an expectation and a perception statement. Responses ($n = 200$) were pooled across five service categories; difference scores were then used as input into "within-dimension" coefficient alpha analyses. These tests resulted in a reduced set of 54 items after deleting those statements with low corrected item-to-total correlations. Oblique factor analysis resulted in further reductions in the number of items and a revision in the dimensionality of the anticipated scale (i.e., 34 items reflecting seven dimensions). Analysis of this initial data then revealed a seven-factor measure comprising 34 items.

Data from the second developmental sample were used to reevaluate the dimensionality and reliability of the 34-item measure. Analysis of the factor loadings (both the pattern and the loading values) in addition to examination of corrected item-to-total correlations resulted in further revisions to the scale. Specifically, two pairs of factors were combined, and several additional items were deleted. These analyses resulted in the final 22-item (actually pairs of items), five-factor scale as described above. Estimates of internal consistency and validity were gathered.

Samples: Initial purification was based upon the responses of a quota sample of 200 adults surveyed by a market research firm in a large southwestern metropolitan mall. Respondents were all above 25 years of age and were equally divided among males and females. Forty recent users (i.e., within 3 months) of five service categories were surveyed. The reduced set of 34 items was reexamined using the responses of 200 recent users of four service providers ($n = 800$).

Validity: The estimates of internal consistency reliability for both the factors and the total scale for the four service companies in the second study were consistently high. The total scale estimates of internal consistency reliability for a linear combination ranged from .87 to .90. Factor analysis of the second phase data and reanalysis of the first wave data supported the dimensionality and expected item loadings for both data sets. Additional evidence of the validity of the scale was provided by mean difference tests across subject groups formed by overall quality ratings (collected in phase 2) for the individual firms. As expected, higher average SERVQUAL scores were obtained for subjects providing more positive responses to the overall rating. Relationships with questions about "recommendations to friends" and "reports of problems" also provided some evidence of the scale's validity. Further supportive evidence was provided by the ability of the subscales to predict overall quality judgments (i.e., R^2 estimates ranged from .27 to .52).

Scores: A series of mean scores is provided in Table 5 of Parasuraman et al. (1988) for the second sample. Across the four categories of services considered, the means are generally slightly negative, suggesting that service expectations generally exceed consumer perceptions. As an example, for the combined scale and across three categories of banking firms (i.e., excellent, good, and fair/poor), the corresponding mean scores were –0.22, –0.92, and –1.61, respectively.

Source: Parasuraman, A., Valerie Zeithaml, and Leonard L. Berry. (1986). *SERVQUAL: A Multiple-Item Scale for Measuring Customer Perceptions of Service Quality* (Report No. 86-108). Cambridge, MA: Marketing Science Institute.

© 1986 by the Marketing Science Institute. Scale items taken from Appendix (pp. 31-34). Reprinted with permission.

Parasuraman, A., Valerie A. Zeithaml, and Leonard L. Berry. (1988). "SERVQUAL: A Multiple-Item Scale for Measuring Consumer Perceptions of Service Quality." *Journal of Retailing, 64,* 12-40. © 1988 by Publisher. Reprinted with permission.

Other evidence: Carmen (1990) tested SERVQUAL in four different service settings, including a business school placement center, a tire store, a dental school patient clinic, and an acute care hospital. The results provide corroborating evidence for the reliability of the scale. Some evidence regarding the need to vary item wording across settings and several questions regarding the uniqueness or structure of the original 10 dimensions were raised.

The overall fit statistics from a confirmatory factor analysis study by Finn and Lamb (1991) using the responses from a telephone survey involving retail shopping experiences did not provide support for the multidimensional (i.e., five correlated factors) measurement model implied by the SERVQUAL scale. However, individual factor reliabilities ranged from .59 to .83.

Cronin and Taylor (1992) found support for a unidimensional measure of a subscale of the SERVQUAL scale they called "SERVPERF." Essentially, SERVPERF represents the 22 items of the PERCEPTIONS aspect of SERVQUAL and can be used as a measure of service quality. (See items listed on the following pages and the Appendix to SERVQUAL.)

Other sources: Carmen, James M. (1990). "Consumer Perceptions of Service Quality: An Assessment of the SERVQUAL Dimensions." *Journal of Retailing, 66,* 33-55.

Cronin, J. Joseph, Jr., and Steven A. Taylor. (1992). "Measuring Service Quality: A Reexamination and Extension." *Journal of Marketing, 56,* 55-68.

Finn, David W., and Charles W. Lamb. (1991). "An Evaluation of the SERVQUAL Scales in a Retail Setting." In Rebecca H. Holman and Michael R. Solomon (Eds.), *Advances in Consumer Research* (Vol. 18, pp. 483-490). Provo, UT: Association for Consumer Research.

References: N/A

SERVICE QUALITY: SERVQUAL
(Parasuraman, Zeithaml, and Berry 1986, 1988)

Expectations

Directions: This survey deals with your opinions of _____ services. Please show the extent to which you think firms offering _____ services should possess the features described by each statement. Do this by picking one of the seven numbers next to each statement. If you strongly agree that these firms should possess a feature, circle the number 7. If you strongly disagree that these firms should possess a feature, circle 1. If your feelings are not strong, circle one of the numbers in the middle. There are no right or wrong answers. All we are interested in is a number that best shows your expectations about firms offering _____ services.

E1. They should have up-to-date equipment.

E2. Their physical facilities should be visually appealing.

E3. Their employees should be well dressed and appear neat.

E4. The appearance of the physical facilities of these firms should be in keeping with the type of services provided.

E5. When these firms promise to do something by a certain time, they should do so.

E6. When customers have problems, these firms should be sympathetic and reassuring.

E7. These firms should be dependable.

E8. They should provide their services at the time they promise to do so.

E9. They should keep their records accurately.

E10. They shouldn't be expected to tell customers exactly when services will be performed. (–)

E11. It is not realistic for customers to expect prompt service from employees of these firms. (–)

E12. Their employees don't always have to be willing to help customers. (–)

E13. It is okay if they are too busy to respond to customer requests promptly. (–)

E14. Customers should be able to trust employees of these firms.

E15. Customers should be able to feel safe in their transactions with these firm's employees.

E16. Their employees should be polite.

E17. Their employees should get adequate support from these firms to do their jobs well.

E18. These firms should not be expected to give customers individual attention. (–)

E19. Employees of these firms cannot be expected to give customers personal attention. (–)

E20. It is unrealistic to expect employees to know what the needs of their customers are. (–)

E21. It is unrealistic to expect these firms to have their customers' best interests at heart. (–)

E22. They shouldn't be expected to have operating hours convenient to all their customers. (–)

NOTES: The items are distributed among the five dimensions of Tangibility (items E1 to E4), Reliability (E5 to E9), Responsiveness (items E10 to E13), Assurance (E14 to E17), and Empathy (items E18 to E22). (–) denotes reverse-coded items.

Perceptions

Directions: The following set of statements relate to your feelings about XYZ. For each statement, please show the extent to which you believe XYZ has the feature described by the statement. Once again, circling a 7 means that you strongly agree that XYZ has that feature, and circling a 1 means that you strongly disagree. You may circle any of the numbers in the middle that show how strong your feelings are. There are no right or wrong answers. All we are interested in is a number that best shows your perceptions about XYZ.

P1. XYZ has up-to-date equipment.

P2. XYZ's physical facilities are visually appealing.

P3. XYZ's employees are well dressed and appear neat.

P4. The appearance of the physical facilities of XYZ is in keeping with the type of services provided.

P5. When XYZ promises to do something by a certain time, it does so.

P6. When you have problems, XYZ is sympathetic and reassuring.

P7. XYZ is dependable.

P8. XYZ provides its services at the time it promises to do so.

P9. XYZ keeps its records accurately.

P10. XYZ does not tell customers exactly when services will be performed. (–)

P11. You do not receive prompt service from XYZ's employees. (–)

P12. Employees of XYZ are not always willing to help customers. (–)

P13. Employees of XYZ are too busy to respond to customer requests promptly. (–)

P14. You can trust the employees of XYZ.

P15. You feel safe in your transactions with XYZ's employees.

P16. Employees of XYZ are polite.

P17. Employees get adequate support from XYZ to do their jobs well.

P18. XYZ does not give you individual attention. (–)

P19. Employees of XYZ do not give you personal attention. (–)

P20. Employees of XYZ do not know what your needs are. (–)

P21. XYZ does not have your best interests at heart. (–)

P22. XYZ does not have operating hours convenient to all their customers. (–)

NOTES: The items are distributed among the five dimensions of Tangibility (items P1 to P4), Reliability (P5 to P9), Responsiveness (items P10 to P13), Assurance (P14 to P17), and Empathy (items P18 to P22). The 22 PERCEPTION items constitute SERVPERF (Cronin and Taylor 1992). (–) denotes reverse-coded items.

SERVICE QUALITY OF RETAIL STORES
(Dabholkar, Thorpe, and Rentz 1996)

Construct: This retail service quality scale development effort represents another extension of the original SERVQUAL measure (Parasuraman, Zeithaml, and Berry 1988). Initially, retail service quality is proposed as a hierarchical factor structure comprising five dimensions (physical aspects, reliability, personal interaction, problem solving, and policy), with three of the five dimensions having two subdimensions (Dabholkar, Thorpe, and Rentz 1996, p. 8). The scale is designed for use in studying retail businesses that offer a mix of goods and services, for assessing levels of service quality, and for detecting needed changes in services provided.

Description: The scale consists of 28 items and five dimensions: physical aspects (6 items), reliability (5), personal interaction (9), problem solving (3), and policy (5). The first three dimensions have subdimensions: physical aspects (i.e., appearance and convenience), reliability (i.e., promises and doing it right), and personal interactions (i.e., inspiring confidence and courteousness/help-fulness). The items corresponding to each subdimension are shown below. Both expectations and perceptions are assessed using 5-place *strongly disagree* (1) to *strongly agree* (5) response formats. To create expectation items, the statements substitute "excellent retail stores" for "this store."

Development: Seventeen of the original 22 SERVQUAL items were selected. Based upon a review of the extant literature and the authors' own qualitative research, an additional 11 items were developed. Justification for the assignment of items to dimensions and subdimensions is described by Dabholkar et al. (1996, p. 8). The subsequent analyses used to validate the scale's structure are based on the perceptions measures only.

Confirmatory factor analysis with partial aggregation (i.e., individual indicators are randomly combined into composite indicators) was used to test the proposed scale structure. Adequate fit was obtained using both samples for the subdimension models, as well as the basic five-dimension models. Details of these analyses are presented by Dabholkar et al. (1996). Support was provided for both the basic dimension model and a second-order model. Construct reliability for the total scale was .74. Reliability estimates for the dimensions and subdimensions ranged from .81 to .92. Some evidence of discriminant validity was offered based on tests of the covariation between the generally highly correlated dimensions.

Samples: An initial sample of 227 retail department store patrons was obtained using university student interviewers. Questionnaires were self-administered and reflected opinions about the store being patronized. Opinions were obtained for seven stores from two department store chains. Of the respondents, 197 were female. A cross-validation sample of 149 patrons from two stores of one of the chains was also surveyed in-store.

Validity: Evidence of predictive validity was offered by correlations ranging from .51 to .70 between the overall scale and its components and measures of intentions to shop and intentions to recommend.

Scores: Item means and standard deviations are depicted in the Appendix (Dabholkar et al. 1996, pp. 14-15). All means were above 4.12 on the 5-place scales.

Source: Dabholkar, Pratibha A., Dayle I. Thorpe, and Joseph O. Rentz. (1996). "A Measure of Service Quality for Retail Stores: Scale Development and Validation. *Journal of the Academy of Marketing Science*, 24(1), 3-16.
© 1996 by Sage Publications. Scale items taken from Appendix (p. 36). Reprinted with permission.

Other evidence: N/A

Reference: Parasuraman, A., Valerie A. Zeithaml, and Leonard L. Berry. (1988). "SERVQUAL: A Multiple-Item Scale for Measuring Consumer Perceptions of Service Quality." *Journal of Retailing*, 64, 12-40.

SERVICE QUALITY OF RETAIL STORES
(Dabholkar, Thorpe, and Rentz 1996)

Physical Aspects

P1. This store has modern-looking equipment and fixtures.

P2. The physical facilities at this store are visually appealing.

P3. Materials associated with this store's service (such as shopping bags, catalogs, or statements) are visually appealing.

P4. This store has clean, attractive, and convenient public areas (restrooms, fitting rooms).

P5. The store layout at this store makes it easy for customers to find what they need.

P6. The store layout at this store makes it easy for customers to move around in the store.

Reliability

P7. When this store promises to do something by a certain time, it will do so.

P8. This store provides its services at the time it promises to do so.

P9. This store performs the service right the first time.

P10. This store has merchandise available when the customers want it.

P11. This store insists on error-free sales transactions and records.

Personal Interaction

P12. Employees in this store have the knowledge to answer customers' questions.

P13. The behavior of employees in this store instill [*sic*] confidence in customers.

P14. Customers feel safe in their transactions with this store.

P15. Employees in this store give prompt service to customers.

P16. Employees in this store tell customers exactly when services will be performed.

P17. Employees in this store are never too busy to respond to customers' requests.

P18. This store gives customers individual attention.

P19. Employees in this store are consistently courteous with customers.

P20. Employees in this store treat customers courteously on the telephone.

Problem Solving

P21. This store willingly handles returns and exchanges.

P22. When a customer has a problem, this store shows a sincere interest in solving it.

P23. Employees in this store are able to handle customer complaints directly and immediately.

Policy

P24. This store offers high quality merchandise.

P25. This store provides plenty of convenient parking for customers.

P26. This store has operating hours convenient to all their customers.

P27. This store accepts most major credit cards.

P28. This store offers its own credit card.

NOTES: Items are distributed across subdimensions as follows: P1-P4, Appearance; P5-P6, Convenience; P7-P8, Promises; P9-P11, Doing It Right; P12-P14, Inspiring Confidence; and P15-P20, Courteousness/Helpfulness.

SERVICE QUALITY: PHYSICAL DISTRIBUTION SERVICE QUALITY
(Bienstock, Mentzer, and Bird 1997)

Construct: The research by Bienstock, Mentzer, and Bird (1997) is another extension of the SERVQUAL measurement approach (Parasuraman, Zeithaml, and Berry 1988). In the present effort, expectations and performance measures are offered as a reliable scale for measuring industrial customer (e.g., manufacturers, wholesalers, retailers, government organizations) perceptions of the physical distribution service quality (PDSQ) received from suppliers. Physical distribution is described as the outbound side of the logistics process. The initial dimensions proposed to underlie PDSQ were timeliness, availability, and conditions (Bienstock et al. 1997, p. 32).

Description: The final scale consists of 15 expectations and performance items. Each statement is operationalized using 7-place scales ranging from *strongly disagree* (1) to *neutral* (4) to *strongly agree* (7). There are six, five, and four items for the timeliness, availability, and conditions dimensions, respectively. Gap scores are formed by subtracting the expectations from the performance scores.

Development: An initial set of 45 items was developed from a review of prior research related to the physical distribution literature and from the results of eight experience interviews. These items were edited and judged by academic colleagues and members of the experience survey pretest (*n* = 8). A second pretest survey of 33 purchasing managers was used to reduce the number of items to 36. Item-to-total correlations, face validity, and frequency of mention in the experience surveys were the criteria used to delete or retain items. Following a random split of the larger follow-up survey, the first portion of the data was used to develop the final 15-item scale. These analyses included an examination of corrected item-to-total correlations, exploratory factor analyses, and confirmatory factory analysis. Items with low reliability were deleted. The structure of the scale was replicated using the second portion of the sample. These efforts resulted in PDSQ being conceptualized as a second-order construct with three dimensions (Bienstock et al. 1997).

Samples: Pretest interviews were first conducted with eight purchasing managers. A second pretest survey of 33 purchasing managers was used to delete items. Subsequent analyses were conducted on the responses of 446 purchasing managers. All participants in the research were members of the National Association of Purchasing Managers.

Validity: A substantial amount of evidence is provided in support of the PDSQ scale and the final set of measures proposed to compose the scale. This evidence is summarized for both halves of the larger survey. These data include reliability estimates for the three dimensions and the overall scale, tests of discriminant and convergent validity, and correlations with measures of global quality and purchase intent. Moreover, supportive results are suggested for both the performance items and the gap difference scores.

Briefly, the estimates of internal consistency reliability ranged from .83 to .97 across dimensions and the total scale for both samples. All indicators had significant *t* values in the confirmatory factor analyses. The overall model fit statistics for the second half of the data included the following statistics: GFI, .90; CFI, .97; and RMSR, .10. Analysis of the squared multiple correlations from structural equation tests indicated that 27% (gap) and 34% (performance) of the variance in global quality was accounted for by the dimensions of PDSQ.

Scores: Dimension mean scores, standard deviations, and intercorrelations are shown in Table 4 (Bienstock et al. 1997, p. 37) for both performance measures and gap difference scores. The same estimates are provided for overall PDSQ scores.

Source: Bienstock, Carol C., John T. Mentzer, and Monroe Murphy Bird. (1997). "Measuring Physical Distribution Service Quality." *Journal of the Academy of Marketing Science*, 25(1), 31-44.

© 1997 by Sage Publications. Scale items taken from Appendix (pp. 41-43). Reprinted with permission.

Other evidence: N/A

Other sources: N/A

Reference: Parasuraman, A., Valerie A. Zeithaml, and Leonard L. Berry. (1988). "SERVQUAL: A Multiple-Item Scale for Measuring Consumer Perceptions of Service Quality." *Journal of Retailing, 64,* 12-40.

SERVICE QUALITY: PHYSICAL DISTRIBUTION SERVICE QUALITY
(Bienstock, Mentzer, and Bird 1997)

Expectations Items

Timeliness

T1. The time between placing and receiving an order should be short.

T2. Delivery should be rapid.

T3. The time between placing and receiving an order should be consistent.

T4. The time it takes my supplier to put my order together should be consistent.

T5. The time between my supplier receiving and shipping my order should be short.

T6. The time it takes my supplier to put my order together should be short.

Availability

A1. Orders should be available in inventory when ordered.

A2. Suppliers should have inventory available near my facility.

A3. If suppliers are notified of possible increases in upcoming orders, they should maintain extra inventory.

A4. Products ordered should be available in inventory.

A5. Products should consistently be available in inventory.

Condition

C1. All orders should be delivered undamaged.

C2. All orders should be accurate (i.e., items should arrive, not unordered items).

C3. All products should be delivered undamaged.

C4. Orders should be packaged conveniently.

Performance Items

Timeliness Items

   T1. The time between placing and receiving an order should be short.

   T2. Delivery should be rapid.

   T3. The time between placing and receiving an order should be consistent.

   T4. The time it takes my supplier to put my order together should be consistent.

   T5. The time between my supplier receiving and shipping my order should be short.

   T6. The time it takes my supplier to put my order together should be short.

Availability Items

   A1. Orders should be available in inventory when ordered.

   A2. Suppliers should have inventory available near my facility.

   A3. If suppliers are notified of possible increases in upcoming orders, they should maintain extra inventory.

   A4. Products ordered should be available in inventory.

   A5. Products should consistently be available in inventory.

Condition Items

   C1. All orders should be delivered undamaged.

   C2. All orders should be accurate (i.e., items should arrive, not unordered items).

   C3. All products should be delivered undamaged.

   C4. Orders should be packaged conveniently.

APPENDIX TO SERVQUAL:
REVIEW AND SOURCES OF SERVQUAL USE

The contribution of Parasuraman, Zeithaml, and Berry (1986, 1988) and the many extensions of the SERVQUAL measurement approach to the study and understanding of service quality are noteworthy. One outcome from their research has been the number of articles that have reevaluated the SERVQUAL conceptualization of service quality. Interested authors are encouraged to read the additional sources cited below and, if needed, to conduct their own literature review. We summarize only some of the published critiques here. Users of SERVQUAL or one of its variations should consider carefully all the possible different models and operationalizations, as well as the assumptions that underlie the SERVQUAL framework. Criticisms regarding the use of difference scores should be considered as well (cf. Brown, Churchill, and Peter 1993).

Cronin and Taylor (1992) test several service quality models, as well as the relationships among service quality, satisfaction, attitude, and purchase intentions. Their research supports measuring service quality as a unidimensional, performance-based construct called SERVPERF, which is equivalent to the 22 PERCEPTION items of the original SERVQUAL measure. Teas (1993) also raises issues related to the use of difference scores (i.e., perceptions-expectations), alternative model configurations, and varying definitions of expectations. Evidence of problems with the P-E service quality framework was found, and the need for additional research is recommended (Teas 1993, p. 28).

Parasuraman, Zeithaml, and Berry (1994) propose three alternative questionnaire formats. Their research suggests that there are psychometric and practical trade-offs in choosing the most appropriate scaling approach. Briefly, the three methods are (a) three-column format in which desired, adequate, and perceived service are assessed with three identical, side-by-side scales; (b) two-column format that generates direct ratings of service-superiority and service-adequacy gaps with identical side-by-side scales; and (c) one-column format in which the previous two gap measures are split into two parts (Parasuraman et al., 1994, pp. 204-205).

Zeithaml, Berry, and Parasuraman (1996) used weighted average performance scores for their five dimensions to operationalize service quality. The scores were then compared to weighted adequate and desired average scores in tests of the effects of performance being above and below the consumer's zone of tolerance. The results of these analyses supported predictions regarding whether customers may remain or defect. Other investigations of service quality that rely on the SERVQUAL framework to some degree include the following: Boulding, Kalra, Staelin, and Zeithaml (1993), Parasuraman, Zeithaml, and Berry (1991), Spreng, MacKenzie, and Olshavsky (1996), and Zeithaml, Berry, and Parasuraman (1993). As such, in measuring service quality, the reader is strongly urged to consult the sources listed below.

Sources: Boulding, William, Ajay Kalra, Richard Staelin, and Valerie A. Zeithaml. (1993). "A Dynamic Process Model of Service Quality: From Expectations to Behavioral Intentions." *Journal of Marketing Research, 30,* 7-27.

Brown, Tom J., Gilbert A. Churchill, Jr., and J. Paul Peter. (1993). "Improving the Measurement of Service Quality." *Journal of Retailing, 69,* 127-139.

Cronin, J. Joseph, Jr., and Steven A. Taylor. (1992). "Measuring Service Quality: A Reexamination and Extension." *Journal of Marketing, 56,* 55-68.

Parasuraman, A., Valerie Zeithaml, and Leonard L. Berry. (1986). *SERVQUAL: A Multiple-Item Scale for Measuring Customer Perceptions of Service Quality* (Report No. 86-108). Cambridge, MA: Marketing Science Institute.

Parasuraman, A., Valerie A. Zeithaml, and Leonard L. Berry. (1988). "SERVQUAL: A Multiple-Item Scale for Measuring Consumer Perceptions of Service Quality." *Journal of Retailing, 64,* 12-40.

Parasuraman, A., Valerie A. Zeithaml, and Leonard L. Berry. (1991). "Refinement and Reassessment of the SERVQUAL Scale." *Journal of Retailing, 67*(4), 420-450.

Parasuraman, A., Valerie A. Zeithaml, and Leonard L. Berry. (1994). "Alternative Scales for Measuring Service Quality: A Comparative Assessment Based on Psychometric and Diagnostic Criteria." *Journal of Retailing*, *70*(3), 201-230.

Spreng, Richard A., Scott B. MacKenzie, and Richard W. Olshavsky. (1996). "A Reexamination of the Determinants of Consumer Satisfaction." *Journal of Marketing*, *60*, 15-32.

Teas, R. Kenneth. (1993). "Expectations, Performance, and Consumers' Perceptions of Quality." *Journal of Marketing*, *57*, 18-34.

Zeithaml, Valerie A., Leonard L. Berry, and A. Parasuraman. (1993). "The Nature and Determinants of Customer Expectations of Service." *Journal of the Academy of Marketing Science*, *21*(1), 1-12.

Zeithaml, Valerie A., Leonard L. Berry, and A. Parasuraman. (1996). "The Behavioral Consequences of Service Quality." *Journal of Marketing*, *60*(2), 31-46.

SOCIAL RESPONSIBILITY SCALE FOR MARKETING PERSONNEL
(Peters 1972)

Construct: A marketing decision maker scoring high in social responsibility is hypothesized to possess four characteristics: (a) concern for his or her firm's practice on the end user, (b) honesty, (c) consistency in social responsibility in all areas of life, and (d) concern for social responsibility beyond the need for immediate return to his or her company. This conceptual definition centers upon the inner orientation of the individual in terms of business ethics and altruism (i.e., concern for the protection and welfare of the customer) (Peters 1972, p. 225).

Description: The scale consists of 26 statements, each operationalized using 5-place bipolar scales labeled *strongly disagree* to *strongly agree*. (There is some indication that the items might have been 7-place scales.) Approximately half the statements require reverse coding. The dimensions were described as related, and thus item scores are summed to represent a total score.

Development: An initial pool of 100 items was reduced to a set of 38 items based on an analysis of the content validity of the items by two expert judges. The 38 items were reduced to the final scale of 26 items "based upon Beta values for high intensity" (Peters 1972, p. 226).

Samples: The results from two samples were described by Peters (1972). These samples included 77 business administration graduate students from the University of Wisconsin and 21 staff members of a corporate marketing department.

Validity: The author described this research as a pilot test; hence, extensive evidence of validity was not provided. The scale did discriminate, however, between individuals scoring high and low in social responsibility as judged by their peers (i.e., other student team members and/or other executives). An initial reliability estimate of .73 was reported for the 38 items.

Scores: The mean score for the 77 students was 104.6 (range 80-128, standard deviation = 11.0) compared to a mean of 104.5 (range 79-121, standard deviation = 10.3) for the 21 marketing executives.

Source: Peters, William H. (1972). "Social Responsibility in Marketing Personnel: Meaning and Measurement." In Helmut Becker (Ed.), *Proceedings of American Marketing Association Educators' Conference* (pp. 224-229). Chicago: American Marketing Association.

© 1972 by the American Marketing Association. Scale items taken from Table 1 (pp. 226-227). Reprinted with permission.

Other evidence: N/A

Other sources: N/A

References: N/A

SOCIAL RESPONSIBILITY SCALE FOR MARKETING PERSONNEL
(Peters 1972)

1. To maximize profits should be the single most important goal of business. (Disagree)

2. The federal regulations concerning packaging of consumer products are anti-business and nothing like them should have been passed by Congress. (Disagree)

3. I would probably quit a company that I felt was unethical in the way they promoted their product. (Agree)

4. We have a long way to go before most companies routinely take the consumer's welfare into consideration when making marketing decisions. (Agree)

5. I am not concerned about the decisions my company makes when I know that I can do nothing to change them.* (Disagree)

6. Business is an institution of society and therefore the problems of society should also be important problems for business to help solve even if there is no immediate monetary reward for the efforts. (Agree)

7. Program content of TV should be mostly under the control of the advertiser. (Disagree)

8. One should not be unduly critical of one's company. After all, everybody tries his best in his own way. (Disagree)

9. There is no real reason to worry about the effects on the public of what is known as "legitimate puffery" in advertising and sales promotion materials. (Disagree)

10. It is the proper role of government to make regulations involving the quality and the promotion of products developed and sold by private industry. (Agree)

11. I often wonder if we are giving the consumer the kind of product they should have.* (Agree)

12. I do not understand people like Ralph Nader, who are always out to make trouble for us. They should leave us alone. After all, business usually does the right thing by the consumer. (Disagree)

13. It is probably best for our society in the long run, if consumer organizations are established and do represent the interests of the consumer before the government and the courts. (Agree)

14. There is basically nothing wrong with using the "buyer beware" concept as a guiding philosophy in one's product development program in industry. (Disagree)

15. I do not think it is basically wrong for a bank to advertise, without qualification, that it is in the best interests of the people to put their money in one of the bank's savings accounts that pays 4½ percent annual interest rate when the rate of inflation in the country is 6 percent. (Disagree)

16. I think it is wrong for a company to encourage the consumer to use more of its product than is needed. (Disagree)

17. There is nothing wrong in a student occasionally cheating on an examination. (Disagree)

18. It is all right if an advertisement implies that your company's product is better than it actually is as long as the ad's copy does not lie outright or break the law. (Disagree)

19. It is not proper to distort evidence about a product's usefulness by quoting the information out of context. (Agree)

20. Generally speaking, I think that students who protest and demonstrate on campus should be expelled from school. (Disagree)

21. I feel that a man's only major responsibility to his family is to provide well for them. (Disagree)

22. I do not feel that a married woman's place has to be in the home. (Agree)

23. Generally speaking, I do not favor the type of fellow who compromises easily so that things will go smoothly. (Agree)

24. The only reason I care what the consumer thinks and wants is because that it is the way to please him and get a bigger share of the market. (Disagree)

25. A good dictator is one who is on our side. (Disagree)

26. The main reason a company should actively take care about the effects of its marketing strategy decisions upon the public's welfare is because this makes for good public relations which in turn makes for more sales. (Disagree)

NOTES: The items are related to the four dimensions as follows: concern for the firm's practices, 1-13; honesty, 14-19; consistency in social responsibility, 20-21; and concern for social responsibility beyond need, 23-26. * Denotes items that were modified for a student sample.

SOCIAL ROLE OF CORPORATIONS: ATTITUDES
TOWARD THE SOCIAL ROLE OF CORPORATIONS
(Williams 1982)

Construct: An individual's attitude toward the social role of corporations was defined as a three-dimensional construct involving opinions (a) about the corporation as a public institution versus beliefs that corporations have predominantly individual rights, (b) regarding whether or not the actions of the corporation should be guided by personal conscience (intuition) or social responsibility (rationality), and (c) about the legitimacy of outside policymakers to influence the policies and goals of corporations.

Description: The scale consists of 23 items, each operationalized using 5-place scales ranging from *strongly disagree* to *strongly agree*. Item scores can be summed for an overall index or summed within factors for factor indices.

Development: A total of 45 statements was included in the original battery of items. A random ordering of the statements was administered to a sample of 145 business students. Within-dimension item-to-total correlations employing a .40 cutoff were used to delete items. In addition, several items with low factor loadings following the item-to-total tests were also deleted. However, the resulting subscales did not correspond to the conceptual dimensionality of three factors; in fact, seven factors were retained. Estimates of test-retest reliability and predictive validity were also obtained.

Samples: The initial development of the scale was conducted using 145 business students. Sixty-one students participated in a subsequent study involving the evaluation of social data. Forty-seven students were involved in a test-retest administration.

Validity: Test-retest estimates for the original set of 45 items ranged from .06 to .75 (most items were from .3 to .7). Similar estimates for the subscales ranged from .40 to .79. Little additional information was provided. A regression equation using the seven subscales as independent predictors explained 28% of the variation in perceptions of the relevance of social data, offering evidence for the scale's predictive validity.

Scores: Mean scores were not provided for either individual factors or the total scale.

Source: Williams, Paul F. (1982). "Attitudes Toward the Corporation and the Evaluation of Social Data." *Journal of Business Research*, *10*, 119-131.

© 1982 by Elsevier Science. Scale items taken from Appendix (pp. 128-130). Reprinted with permission from Elsevier Science.

Other evidence: N/A

Other sources: N/A

References: N/A

SOCIAL ROLE OF CORPORATIONS: ATTITUDES
TOWARD THE SOCIAL ROLE OF CORPORATIONS
(Williams 1982)

1. A large corporation is like a university because both have as their central purpose serving the public interest.

2. The role of the president of a firm like Eastman-Kodak is that of a public servant.

3. The management of a corporation is responsible to many definable interests in society.

4. There exist higher laws, not related to human legislation, which may be discovered by intuition.

5. The internal conduct of business affairs is not a matter for public involvement.

6. Corporations should have as much right to engage in political activity as any other private citizen.

7. The purpose of the corporation can be quite simply summarized as service to society.

8. Representatives of the public, as well as management, should have significant roles in determining the conduct of business affairs.

9. The management of a corporation should do more than the law requires in its concerns with the social impacts of its actions.

10. Right and wrong conduct for business corporations can be meaningfully defined only by the law.

11. A law should be disobeyed when it conflicts with the dictates of one's conscience.

12. Standards for corporate performance must be left to the determination of management.

13. Concern for the welfare of others should be the principle that guides an individual's conduct.

14. Standards for corporate performance come legitimately from the public.

15. The large business corporation should be considered to have the same freedom as do individuals.

16. In doing business, the management of a corporation should do no more than is required by law.

17. Management should be the sole determinant of a corporation's objectives.

18. In all situations, one must accept the authority of the law.

19. It is not appropriate that representatives for the public interest be included on the boards of directors of large corporations.

20. Conscience is a better guide to a manager's actions than whatever the law might say.

21. Since most people are dependent on private industry for employment, corporations should be willing to sacrifice some efficiency in order to provide jobs.

22. Empathy, the ability to walk a mile in the other guy's shoes, is what assures a just society.

23. A business corporation is just like any other corporation.

NOTES: The items are distributed across the dimensions as follows: public—1, 2, 3, 7; private—6, 15, 23; intuitive—4, 9, 11, 20; rational—10, 16, 18; management—5, 12, 17, 19; outsiders—8, 14; and compassion—13, 21, 22.
    Information about statements requiring recoding was not provided. However, Williams (1982, p. 122) states that only items with positive loadings were included.

WELFARE: PUBLIC ATTITUDES REGARDING WELFARE
PROGRAMS: THE ACCEPTANCE OF WELFARE SCALE
(Ahmed and Jackson 1979)

Construct: Acceptance of welfare is defined as a higher-order construct consisting of five facets (Ahmed and Jackson 1979, p. 232), as follow.

Independence from government: a desire to be free from government interference in personal, social, and economic activity versus a belief in the value and importance of government responsibilities for health, welfare, and economic well-being.

Morality of welfare: a general sentiment that government participation in welfare is morally justified and beneficial versus the sentiment that welfare is ethically wrong for both the recipient and government.

Nurturance: a personality trait and value relating to the importance of helping the needy, deprived, and unfortunate.

Work ethic: a belief in the morality of work as an end in itself.

Altruism: the acceptance of generalized responsibility to help, to share, and to be generous toward one's fellow human beings.

Description: The total scale consists of 40 items, each operationalized using 5-place agree-disagree response formats. Eight items (each reflecting four positive and four negatively worded statements) are representative of each of the five factors. The analyses suggest that both the total acceptance of welfare scale and the individual factors (e.g., independence from government) are appropriate for use. Item scores can be summed overall or within factors.

Development: An initial pool of approximately 400 items was developed (i.e., taken and adapted if necessary) to reflect the various issues involved. Items were taken from previous surveys, attitude scales, and personality measures. Item selection for inclusion in the final scale included relevance to scale definition, judged ability to elicit both "anti-" and "pro-" responses, judged freedom from acquiescence bias, and perceived applicability to all age, cultural, and socioeconomic groups (Ahmed and Jackson 1979, p. 233). The final scale was double translated from French to English and vice versa.

Sample: The scale presentation and subsequent tests were based upon the responses of a national sample of 931 Canadian residents surveyed in 1975. Of the participants, 424 were male, and 194 were interviewed in French. The average family income was $11,600.

Validity: The estimate of internal consistency reliability for the total scale was .85. Similar reliability estimates for the individual factor scales were as follows: independence from government, .72; morality of welfare, .62; nurturance, .66; work ethic, .51; and altruism, .68. Correlations among the factors revealed considerable common variance among the factors. Low correlations with a measure of response bias revealed that "response bias was not a problem with these measures" (Ahmed and Jackson 1979, p. 235). Correlations among the five factors and a measure of acceptance of welfare ranged from .48 (work ethic) to .83 (independence from government), offering evidence of convergent validity. Some group differences were also observed. For example, individuals residing in the western provinces were less favorable toward programs than their eastern resident counterparts. Attitudes toward welfare were found independent of marital status, gender, age, education, and income. The five factor subscales were also correlated with opinions regarding a series of welfare issues obtained earlier through another survey of the same respondents. These results (while not described in detail) were said to be supportive of the validity of the measures. For example, the altruism scale was most strongly correlated with willingness to accept a tax increase, whereas nurturance was most strongly correlated with willingness to provide welfare assistance. In general, the strongest relationships were said to be associated with the government scale.

Scores: Only individual item mean scores were reported by Ahmed and Jackson (1979). See Table 2 (pp. 234-235).

Source: Ahmed, Sadrudin A., and Douglas N. Jackson. (1979). "Psychographics for Social Policy Decisions: Welfare Assistance." *Journal of Consumer Research*, 5, 229-239.

Other evidence: N/A

Other sources: N/A

References: N/A

WELFARE: PUBLIC ATTITUDES REGARDING WELFARE PROGRAMS: THE ACCEPTANCE OF WELFARE SCALE
(Ahmed and Jackson 1979)

Independence From Government

1. People should solve their own problems and not have to depend on government help.

2. People should not need the government to help them.

3. The government should not spend money on medical and dental care for low-income groups.

4. Government welfare programs should be cut back because they restrict people's freedom.

5. Retraining unemployed people is an important responsibility of the government.

6. People like deserted wives and children deserve increased support from government.

7. The government should see that every Canadian enjoys the basic necessities of life.

8. The government should speed up its plan to take care for the needy.

Morality of Welfare

1. People who accept welfare for a long time become unable to hold a job.

2. Receiving welfare makes people feel worthless.

3. It is wrong to give people payments when they haven't worked for them.

4. Only a person with no self-respect would accept public assistance.

5. One of the most important government services is to provide public assistance.

6. Welfare is necessary for those who cannot work, like the handicapped.

7. Government spending on welfare is money well spent.

8. Public assistance helps make the poor more productive members of our society.

Nurturance

1. Helping troubled people cope with their problems is very important to me.

2. People in need deserve our sympathy and support.

3. Someone who is disabled will get my attention and aid.

4. People can always count on me for help.

5. If someone is in trouble, it is best not to get involved.

6. It is a waste of time feeling sorry for the poor.

7. Giving sympathy and comfort to people serves no useful purpose.

8. Trying to help the needy often does more harm than good.

Work Ethic

1. If a person is willing to work hard, there is no reason why he should not succeed.

2. I have no sympathy for people who are able to work but choose not to work.

3. A job of any kind, even if the pay is poor, is better than having to be supported.

4. A person deserves to get only things he has worked for.

5. I can understand why a person would choose to live on welfare rather than work.

6. I think that people put too much emphasis on the value of work.

7. I often think that a job keeps a person from getting the most out of life.

8. Hard work is no longer essential for the well-being of society.

Altruism

1. People should pay taxes gladly, because the money goes for good causes.

2. People who have enough for themselves have a responsibility to provide for the needy.

3. Everyone should contribute generously to help those less fortunate.

4. I believe in giving generously to needy organizations.

5. Most charitable organizations are dishonest.

6. Money spent on welfare would be better used to lower taxes.

7. Most of the money given to the poor is wasted.

8. I don't believe in giving anything away for nothing.

NOTES: To reflect a greater acceptance of welfare, items 1-4 of the "independence from government" factor, items 1-4 of the morality of welfare" factor, and items 1-4 of the "work ethic" factor require reverse coding. Items 5-8 of the "nurturance" and "altruism" factors also require reverse coding to reflect a greater acceptance of welfare.

SCALES RELATED TO POST-PURCHASE BEHAVIOR: CONSUMER DISCONTENT

ALIENATION: CONSUMER ALIENATION FROM THE MARKETPLACE
(Pruden, Shuptrine, and Longman 1974)

Construct: Pruden, Shuptrine, and Longman (1974) use Seeman's (1959) theoretical base to define their construct of consumer alienation from the marketplace. The concept encompasses the following five facets.

Powerlessness is the expectancy held by the individual that his own behavior cannot determine the occurrence of the outcomes of reinforcements that he seeks.

Meaninglessness means the individual is unclear as to what he ought to believe—when his minimal standards for clarity in decision making have not been met.

Normlessness is a situation in which social norms regulating behavior are no longer effective rules for individual behavior.

Social isolation refers to isolation or estrangement from society and its culture.

Self-estrangement refers to a person who experiences himself as an alien and can relate more easily to others than he can to himself.

Description: Pruden et al.'s (1974) alienation index is composed of ten 6-point Likert-type items (*strongly agree* to *strongly disagree*). Although the scale was designed to tap the five facets above, item scores are summed to form an overall index.

Development: Four items for each facet were initially generated based on facet definitions and existing literature. A pretest was then used to reduce this pool of 20 items to the final 10-item scale.

Reliability and validity checks were then performed over two samples.

Samples: A sample of 140 (mostly housewives) and a sample of 35 students were used to examine reliability and validity.

Validity: For the sample of 35, the Spearman rank order correlation reliability coefficient was .79. For the sample of 140, the five facets of alienation showed levels of intercorrelations ranging from .14 to .45, and correlations of each facet to the total scale ranged from .16 to .55. No other evidence of validity was offered.

Scores: Neither mean nor percentage scores were reported.

Source: Pruden, Henry, O., F. Kelly Shuptrine, and Douglas S. Longman. (1974). "A Measure of Alienation From the Marketplace." *Journal of the Academy of Marketing Science*, 2, 610-619. © 1974 by Sage Publications. Scale items taken from Table 2 (p. 612).

Other evidence: Shuptrine, Pruden, and Longman (1977) found that business executives were less alienated than consumers. (No other estimates of reliability and validity were provided.)

Other source: Shuptrine, F. Kelly, Henry O. Pruden, and Douglas S. Longman. (1977). "Alienation From the Marketplace." *Journal of the Academy of Marketing Science*, 5, 133-148.

Reference: Seeman, Melvin. (1959). "On the Meaning of Alienation." *American Sociological Review*, 24, 783-791.

ALIENATION: CONSUMER ALIENATION FROM THE MARKETPLACE
(Pruden, Shuptrine, and Longman 1974)

1. There is little use in writing complaint letters to company officials because usually they won't do anything to satisfy an individual consumer.

2. There is little that people like myself can do to improve the quality of the products they sell.

3. Any satisfaction I get from trying new products vanishes a short time after they are purchased.

4. Sometimes, when I look at new products, I wonder if any of them are worthwhile.

5. Many people with fine homes, new cars and other nice things get them only by going over their heads in debt.

6. I sometimes buy products that I really shouldn't buy.

7. The whole idea of fashion and the creation of new styles is not for me.

8. I really like to own things that have well-known brand names.

9. The products and services I buy and use (for example eating, dressing, entertaining, furnishing my house and so on) allow me to really be myself.

10. The way the world is, I have to buy things that other people expect me to rather than to satisfy myself.

NOTES: Items 1 and 2 represent the powerlessness facet, items 3 and 4 represent the meaninglessness facet, items 5 and 6 represent the normlessness facet, items 7 and 8 represent the social isolation facet, and items 9 and 10 represent the self-estrangement facet.

ALIENATION: CONSUMER ALIENATION FROM THE MARKETPLACE
(Allison 1978)

Construct: Consumer alienation from the marketplace was defined as feelings of separation from the norms and values of the marketplace. Such a state was said to include a lack of acceptance of or identification with market institutions, practices, and outputs as well as feelings of separation from the self when one is involved in the consumption role. The marketplace was defined to include the entire spectrum of channels of distribution from the producer to the seller, as well as any support services such as advertising or credit (Allison 1978, p. 570). Alienation from the marketplace was also conceptualized using consumer-adapted definitions for the four sociological constructs of powerlessness, normlessness, social isolation, and self-estrangement. Powerlessness was defined as feelings held by consumers that they are unable to help determine market practices and had an inability to control the market environment or events within the marketplace. Normlessness within the market system is represented by a distrust of business and market practices, often manifested in unclear standards for buyer behavior. Social isolation is characterized by feelings of estrangement from the practices and outputs of market systems, and feelings of self-estrangement arise from an inability to identify with behavior traditionally associated with the consumption role (Allison 1978).

Description: The scale consists of 35 statements, each operationalized using 5-place Likert-type scale response formats ranging from *strongly agree* to *strongly disagree*. Four of the items are positively worded and require reverse scoring. The range of the summed scores is from 35 to 175.

Development: The four sociological constructs of alienation were used to develop a set of 115 attitudinal statements. Approximately half the items were worded positively. This pool of items was reduced to 50 by a panel of 35 undergraduate student judges. These remaining items satisfied two criteria: (a) 75% or more of the judges agreed that the item would differentiate between alienated and nonalienated consumers, and (b) 60% attributed the item to the same alienation dimension. Several pretest interviews in neighborhoods varying in socioeconomic class were used to revise and clarify the wording of the remaining 50 items.

Factor analysis of the data ($n = 368$) revealed that a four-factor solution was most meaningful; however, the factor loadings did not support the validity of the theoretical structure as anticipated (Allison 1978, p. 568). Subsequent coefficient alpha estimates were interpreted as support for a unidimensional scale. Consequently, the original theoretical definition was revised to the definition provided above (i.e., at the beginning of this summary). Additional item-to-total correlation and internal consistency estimates were used to reduce the number of items to the final set composing the 35-item scale.

Samples: Personal interviews were conducted with 400 respondents selected as part of a stratified-by-area sampling procedure. Of these, 386 were usable (Allison 1978). These procedures provided a random sample that was representative of the local population (i.e., Austin, Texas) in terms of gender, age, income, and ethnic origin. The 50 items were, however, self-administered. A convenience sample of 123 graduate business students participated in the test-retest study.

Validity: The 3-week test-retest reliability correlation was .75 ($p < .05$). A series of correlation and mean difference tests was used to examine the validity of the scale. The correlation between the 35-item consumer alienation scale and a general measure of social alienation was .61 ($p < .01$). The correlation between the consumer alienation scale and a measure of belief in government intervention was .45 ($p < .01$). A series of mean difference tests across ethnic and income groups also supported the validity of the scale. Responses of the 386 survey respondents showed that lower-income groups and minority segments were associated with higher average alienation scores, as predicted.

Scores: An analysis of covariance test for the effects of ethnic origin on alienation scores controlling for income resulted in the following adjusted mean scores across groups: white, 108.67; Black, 112.20; and Mexican American, 116.84. Similar analyses across income groups controlling for ethnic origin resulted in adjusted mean scores ranging from 115.45 for individuals with incomes below $4,000 to 104.51 for individuals with incomes over $16,000.

Source: Allison, Neil K. (1978). "A Psychometric Development of a Test for Consumer Alienation From the Marketplace." *Journal of Marketing Research, 15,* 565-575.

© 1978 by the American Marketing Association. Scale items taken from Appendix (pp. 573-574). Reprinted with permission.

Other evidence: The dimensionality, internal consistency, and nomological validity of the scale were evaluated in a follow-up study by Bearden, Lichtenstein, and Teel (1983). Factor analysis of mail survey responses to 748 members of a two-state university consumer panel revealed a three-factor solution for 22 of the 35 items. These factors were subsequently labeled as business ethics, informed choice, and personal norm. Construct reliability estimates for these factors were .83, .67, and .61, respectively. The estimate of internal consistency for the total scale (i.e., for the reduced set of 22 items), allowing for multiple dimensions, was .84. A series of correlations between each of the three factors and measures of life satisfaction, general consumer satisfaction, powerlessness, and satisfaction with four services (e.g., electric and gas) provided modest support for the validity of the three revised consumer alienation factors (Bearden et al. 1983, p. 38).

Other source: Bearden, William O., Donald R. Lichtenstein, and Jesse E. Teel. (1983). "Reassessment of the Dimensionality, Internal Consistency, and Validity of the Consumer Alienation Scale." In Patrick E. Murphy et al. (Eds.), *1985 American Marketing Association Summer Educators' Conference Proceedings* (pp. 35-40). Chicago: American Marketing Association.

References: N/A

ALIENATION: CONSUMER ALIENATION FROM THE MARKETPLACE
(Allison 1978)

1. Most companies are responsive to the demands of the consumer.*

2. It seems wasteful for so many companies to produce the same basic products.

3. Unethical practices are widespread throughout business.*

4. Stores do not care why people buy their products just as long as they make a profit.

5. Shopping is usually a pleasant experience.

6. People are unable to help determine what products will be sold in the stores.

7. Advertising and promotional costs unnecessarily raise the price the consumer has to pay for a product.

8. What a product claims to do and what it actually does are two different things.

9. Mass production has done away with unique products.

10. Misrepresentation of product features is just something we have to deal with.

11. Harmful characteristics of a product are often kept from the consumer.*

12. It is embarrassing to bring a purchase back to the store.

13. I tend to spend more than I should just to impress my friends with how much I have.*

14. Even with so much advertising, it is difficult to know what brand is best.*

15. A sale is not really a bargain but a way to draw people into the store.

16. It is difficult to identify with current trends and fads in fashion.*

17. I often feel sad for buying so many unnecessary products.*

18. Most brands are the same with just different names and labels.

19. A product will usually break down as soon as the warranty is up.*

20. Business is responsible for unnecessarily depleting our natural resources.*

21. It is difficult to identify with business practices today.*

22. One must be willing to tolerate poor service from most stores.*

23. It is difficult to know what store has the best buy.*

24. Business's prime objective is to make money rather than satisfy the consumer.*

25. I often feel frustrated when I fail to find what I want in the store.

26. After making a purchase, I often find myself wondering "why."*

27. It is hard to understand why some brands are twice as expensive as others.*

28. It is not unusual to find out that business has lied to the public.*

29. Buying beyond one's means is justifiable through the use of credit.*

30. It is often difficult to understand the real meaning of most advertisements.

31. Products are designed to wear out long before they are sold.*

32. Most claims of product quality are true.*

33. I am often dissatisfied with a recent purchase.

34. The wide variety of competing products makes intelligent buying decisions more difficult.

35. Advertisements usually present a true picture of the product.*

NOTES: * Denotes the 22 items identified by Bearden et al. (1983) as possessing stability and simple structure. Items 1, 5, 32, and 35 require reverse coding. In addition, items 1, 3, 4, 11, 19, 20, 21, 24, 28, 31, 32, and 35 compose the "business ethics" factor. Items 14, 16, 23, 27, and 34 compose the "informed choice" factor, and items 13, 17, 22, 26, and 29 compose the "personal norm" factor of the Bearden et al. (1983) three-factor structure.

ASSERTIVENESS, AGGRESSIVENESS, AND COMPLAINING BEHAVIOR
(Fornell and Westbrook 1979)

Construct: Assertive behavior was defined by Galassi and Galassi (1977) as a complex set of behaviors emitted by a person in an interpersonal context which expresses that person's feelings, attitudes, wishes, opinions, or rights directly, firmly, and honestly while respecting the feelings, attitudes, wishes, opinions, and rights of other persons. Using this model, Fornell and Westbrook (1979) developed measures of both assertiveness and aggressiveness. The aggressive person does not recognize the potential consequences of his or her actions and does not assume responsibility for them. The person who impels his or her desire for self-assertion to excessive proportions by expressing opinions in a hostile, threatening, or assaultive manner is aggressive (Fornell and Westbrook 1979). The assertive individual stands up for his or her rights without violating the rights of others.

Description: The measures include 19 items, each operationalized using a 6-point agree-disagree response format. Eighteen of the items loaded on seven factors. The last item (see Fornell and Westbrook 1979, p. 108) did not load highly on any factor.

   The seven factors were labeled by Fornell and Westbrook (1979) as follows: F1, submissiveness; F2, vociferousness; F3, congeniality; F4, aggression with undertones of violence; F5, one item favoring enforcement of all laws; F6, tolerance versus intolerance; and F7, shyness. The scores of the items within each factor are summed to form factor indices.

Development: The items were taken from Alberti and Emmons (1974) and Evans (1977). A minimum eigenvalue criterion of one led to a seven-factor solution that explained 61.9% of the variance. Intercorrelations among the factors ranged from under .10 to .20. As shown above, some of the factors include high or low levels of both traits: The two behaviors, then, do not represent manifestations of completely different personality traits. (Note: This research was clearly described by the authors as exploratory, and the measures provided were said to be in need of further validation.)

Samples: Undergraduate students ($n = 119$) responded to a self-administered questionnaire.

Validity: Using the factor scores as independent variables, a series of regression analyses was conducted in which the assertiveness and aggressiveness variables were used to predict a series of grocery shopping self-reports of complaining behavior. The explained variance estimates ranged from .08 to .16. Evidence of predictive validity was provided for the factors F1, submissiveness; F4, aggressive self-assertion; and F6, tolerance. In general, the hypothesis that nonassertive consumers are less likely to resort to complaint actions as a means of reducing frustration is supported by the data.

Scores: Mean scores and standard deviations were not provided.

Source: Fornell, Claes, and Robert A. Westbrook. (1979). "An Exploratory Study of Assertiveness, Aggressiveness, and Complaining Behavior." In William L. Wilkie (Ed.), *Advances in Consumer Research* (Vol. 6, pp. 105-110). Ann Arbor, MI: Association for Consumer Research.

   © 1979 by the Association for Consumer Research. Scale items taken from Table 1 (p. 108). Reprinted with permission.

Other evidence: N/A

Other sources: N/A

References: Alberti, R. E., and M. L. Emmons. (1974). *Your Perfect Right: A Guide to Assertive Behavior* (2nd ed.). San Luis Obispo, CA: Impact.

Evans, C. (1977). *Understanding Yourself.* New York: A&W Visual Library.

Galassi, M. D., and J. P. Galassi. (1977). *Assert Yourself—How To Be Your Own Person.* New York: Human Sciences Press.

ASSERTIVENESS, AGGRESSIVENESS, AND COMPLAINING BEHAVIOR
(Fornell and Westbrook 1979)

1. I often avoid people or situations for fear of embarrassment.

2. When a salesman makes an effort, I find it hard to say no.

3. I find no difficulty in maintaining eye contact, keeping my head upright in a personal conversation.

4. I am openly critical of others' ideas, opinions, and behavior.

5. When a person is highly unfair, I call it to his/her attention.

6. I sometimes show my anger by name-calling or obscenities.

7. I speak out in protest when someone takes my place in line.

8. I find it difficult to compliment or praise others.

9. People who watch bullfights ought to be given a taste of the suffering the bull has to experience.

10. There should be a gun in every home.

11. Man is a dangerous and aggressive animal who is slowly becoming civilized.

12. Sometimes I can feel so angry or annoyed at a person that I feel I could hit him/her.

13. I am in favor of very strict enforcement of all laws.

14. Slow drivers are more of a menace on the roads than fast drivers.

15. The U.S. would be better off if there were no freaks.

16. I am reluctant to speak up in a discussion or a debate.

17. When I meet a stranger, I am usually the first to begin a conversation.

18. I feel uncomfortable stating my views to an authority figure.

19. I dislike arguing with people.

NOTES: The seven factors as labeled by Fornell and Westbrook (1979) are as follow: F1, submissiveness; F2, vociferousness; F3, congeniality; F4, aggression with undertones of violence; F5, one item favoring enforcement of all laws; F6, tolerance versus intolerance; and F7, shyness. Factors to which items belong and scoring procedures were presented by Fornell and Westbrook as follows (no other detail as to scoring was provided): Items 1, 2, and 3 loaded highly on F1. Items 4 through 7 loaded highly on F2. Items 3, 8, and 9 loaded highly on F3. Items 10 through 12 loaded highly on F4. Item 13 loaded highly on F5. Items 14 and 15 loaded highly on F6. Items 16 through 18 loaded highly on F7. (Item 19 did not load highly on any factor.)

TABLE 6.1

Factor	Items	Aggressiveness	Assertiveness
F1	1, 2, 3	—	Low
F2	4, 5, 6, 7	High	High
F3	3, 8, 9	Low	Medium
F4	10, 11, 12	High	—
F5	13	—	—
F6	14, 15	Low	Fairly high
F7	16, 17, 18	Low	Low

ASSERTIVENESS AND AGGRESSIVENESS
(Richins 1983)

Construct: Assertiveness and aggressiveness represent two consumer interaction styles in the market-place—behaviors to maintain one's rights in the marketplace. Interaction style refers to relatively consistent behavior patterns that individuals employ in interpersonal interactions with retail employees (Richins 1983, p. 73). Assertiveness involves standing up for one's rights without infringing upon those of others, whereas aggression involves the use of verbal and nonverbal noxious stimuli to maintain rights (Richins 1983). The research by Richins develops two validated measures, one for each construct. In her research, three interaction situations (i.e., requesting information or assistance, resisting requests for compliance, and seeking remedy for dissatisfaction) and four interaction styles were identified: assertive, nonassertive, aggressive, and resort-to-aggressive. These interaction styles or strategies were based on both a review of existing measures and a series of in-depth personal interviews.

Description: The assertiveness scale consists of three subscales, each containing five items. These subscales are labeled as follows: resisting requests for compliance, requesting information or assistance, and seeking redress. The aggressiveness scale consists of six items. The response format for each item was a 5-point Likert-type scale, where *strongly agree* was scored 5 and *strongly disagree* was scored 1 (Richins 1983, p. 81). Nine of the assertiveness items require reverse coding. Hence, higher scores represent greater assertiveness or aggressiveness. Item scores are summed within subscales (15 items for assertiveness and 6 items for aggressiveness) to form subscale indices.

Development: Seventy-nine items reflecting aggressive and assertive behaviors across the three situations were developed. Initial editing of redundant and ambiguous items in addition to those with strong potential for social desirability bias were deleted. Analysis for each factor separately using item-to-total correlations and principal components resulted in the final 15-item assertiveness scale and the 6-item aggressiveness measure.

Samples: An initial administration for the edited pool of 59 items was given to 118 undergraduate and graduate students. Validation data were collected from a general population mailing and two consumer active groups (i.e., members of a consumer protection group and complainers to a government agency). These efforts resulted in a usable set of 356 respondents.

Validity: Estimates of coefficient alpha (adjusted for dimensionality) for the two measures were .73 for the aggression scale and .87 for the assertiveness measure. Corresponding test-retest estimates were .82 and .83 for the student sample of $n = 112$. Using the responses of 83 college students to the present scales and a series of general assertion and aggression measures, evidence of convergent and discriminant validity were provided from a multitrait-multimethod matrix analysis. For example, correlations of .68 and .42 were provided as evidence of convergent validity for the assertiveness and aggressiveness measures, respectively. Based on the responses of 93 college students to the present measures and a shortened form of the Crowne-Marlowe Social Desirability Scale (1964), corresponding correlations of .13 and −.28 were cited as evidence of limited social desirability bias. Estimates of internal consistency reliability based on the adult validation sample were .80 and .89 for the assertiveness and aggressiveness items, respectively.

Extensive additional evidence was provided by Richins (1983, pp. 77-80). Only some of those results are cited here. More aggressive individuals had more negative attitudes toward business and were more likely to report enjoying making a complaint than nonaggressive individuals, as predicted; the resort-to-aggression group reported the greatest number of complaints; and individuals lowest in both variables took the longest to get off the phone in a follow-up solicitation involving the telephone purchase of craft kits. The assertiveness scale was correlated (modestly) with education and income. Aggressive individuals tended to be younger and male.

Scores: Mean scores were provided for both scales as part of a known group validation. For the mail survey sample, the general population sample was significantly different in terms of assertiveness from the rest of the sample. Mean scores for the general population, consumer protection, and third-party complainer subsamples were 56.5, 58.9, and 58.1, respectively. The means also differed for the aggressiveness factor: third-party complainers, 16.5; general population, 14.5; and consumer protection group, 14.7.

Source: Richins, Marsha L. (1983). "An Analysis of Consumer Interaction Styles in the Marketplace." *Journal of Consumer Research*, *10*, 73-82.

© 1983 by University of Chicago Press. Scale items taken from Appendix (p. 81). Reprinted with permission.

Other evidence: Data were collected in a follow-up validation research effort from two American samples (i.e., 122 general respondents and 234 consumer active respondents) and 304 residents of the Netherlands. (See Richins and Verhage [1987] for details.) Briefly, for the Dutch sample, the estimates of internal consistency reliability were .72 and .77 for the aggressiveness and assertiveness scales, respectively. Corresponding estimates for the American sample were .76 and .80. Confirmatory factor analysis generally supported the factor structure, using the data for both countries. However, the factor analysis results were somewhat stronger in support of the measures for the American data. Scalar equivalence was examined using a series of regression equations in which the scales were used to predict a series of dependent variables and/or behaviors (i.e., seeking redress) for each country. An acceptable level of equivalence was obtained for the aggressiveness measure.

Other source: Richins, Marsha L., and Bronislaw J. Verhage. (1987). "Assertiveness and Aggression in Marketplace Exchanges." *Journal of Cross-Cultural Psychology*, *18*(1), 93-105.

References: N/A

ASSERTIVENESS AND AGGRESSIVENESS
(Richins 1983)

ASSERTIVENESS ITEMS

Resisting Requests for Compliance

1. I have no trouble getting off the phone when called by a person selling something I don't want.

2. I really don't know how to deal with aggressive salespeople.(*)

3. More often than I would like, I end up buying something I don't want because I have a hard time saying no to the salesperson.(*)

4. If a salesperson comes to my door selling something I don't want, I have no trouble ending the conversation.

5. If a salesperson has gone to a lot of trouble to find an item for me, I would be embarrassed not to buy it even if it isn't exactly right.(*)

Requesting Information or Assistance

6. I sometimes don't get all the information I need about a product because I am uncomfortable bothering salespeople with questions.(*)

7. I am uncomfortable asking store employees where products are located in the store.(*)

8. In signing a sales contract or credit agreement, I am reluctant to ask for an explanation of everything I don't understand.(*)

9. If a store doesn't have the size or color of an item I need, I don't mind asking the salesperson to check for the item at other store locations.

10. If a cashier is talking with friends while I am waiting to be waited on, it would not bother me to interrupt the conversation and ask for assistance.

Seeking Redress

11. If a defective product is inexpensive, I usually keep it rather than put up a fuss or complain.(*)

12. I'd rather do almost anything than return a product to the store.(*)

13. I am probably more likely to return an unsatisfactory product than most people I know.

14. I often procrastinate when I know I should return a defective product to the store.(*)

15. I would attempt to notify store management if I thought service in a store was particularly bad.

AGGRESSIVENESS ITEMS

16. I have on occasion told salespeople I thought they were too rude.

17. On occasion, I have tried to get a complaint taken care of by causing a stir which attracts the attention of customers.

18. I get a certain amount of satisfaction from putting a discourteous salesperson in his/her place.

19. Sometimes being nasty is the best way to get a complaint taken care of.

20. I'll make a scene at the store if necessary to get a complaint handled to my satisfaction.

21. Salespeople need to be told off when they are rude.

NOTE   *Denotes items requiring reverse coding.

DISCONTENT: CONSUMER DISCONTENT SCALE
(Lundstrom and Lamont 1976)

Construct: The scale is designed to measure consumers' attitudes toward marketing and marketing-related practices of the business system. Consumer discontent is defined to include the collection of attitudes held by consumers toward (a) the product strategies of business, (b) business communications and information, (c) the impersonal nature of business and retail institutions, and (d) the broader socioeconomic forces that are linked with the business system (Lundstrom and Lamont 1976, p. 374).

Description: The final scale consists of 82 statements operationalized using 6-point scales of *strongly agree*, *agree*, *agree a little*, *disagree a little*, *disagree*, and *strongly disagree*. Individual scores for each statement are summed to form an aggregate measure. Twenty-five of the items are worded as "pro-business." The range of the scale is from 82 to 492.

Development: A beginning pool of 173 items was generated from the literature underlying the four aspects of the construct definition (i.e., product strategies of business, business communications and information, the impersonal nature of business and retail institutions, and socioeconomic and political forces). This initial pool was edited to eliminate ambiguous and redundant items. Ten judges then evaluated the remaining 118 items in an effort to classify the items as either pro- or anti-business. This process eliminated an additional 19 items.

The remaining 99 items were administered to a sample of 309 Denver, Colorado, residents. The set of 99 items was reduced to 84 by deleting those items that did differ significantly ($p < .10$) between the high and low quartiles determined by the total scores on the preliminary set of 99 items. A student sample of 226 students was used to evaluate the reliability of the remaining 84 items and test-retest reliability.

Two additional items were deleted from the scale based on item-to-total correlations using the responses to 280 subjects constituting a third sample. In addition, this sample was split into two groups hypothesized to differ in discontent (i.e., a discontented group and a contented group).

Samples: Four samples were used in various stages of the development. Initial item analysis was conducted on a sample of 309 Denver residents (from an initial sample of 600). A convenience sample of 226 university students was used in a series of reliability tests. From this group, 154 participated in a test-retest administration. A contented group of 100 business members of Rotary and Kiwanis clubs and a discontented group of 180 consumers were involved in the known group test validation. The latter group was selected from members of the Arizona Consumers Council and complainers to the Denver Better Business Bureau.

Validity: The split-half reliability coefficient for the 84-item version was .94 (corrected for scale length). The results of a 6-week test-retest ($n = 154$) revealed a coefficient of reliability of .79. In addition, correlations with measures of agreement response tendency and social desirability bias were not significant. For example, the Spearman rank order correlation between a measure of social desirability bias and the combined scale was –.03. As described above, cited evidence of validity was provided by the face validity of the items, the multiple estimates of reliability, and the known group analyses (cf. Lundstrom and Lamont 1976).

Scores: The mean for a contented group ($n = 100$) was 247, and the mean for a discontented group ($n = 180$) was 354 ($z = 28.2$, $p < .01$).

Source: Lundstrom, William J., and Lawrence M. Lamont. (1976). "The Development of a Scale to Measure Consumer Discontent." *Journal of Marketing Research, 13*, 373-381.

© 1976 by the American Marketing Association. Scale items taken from Appendix A (pp. 379-381). Reprinted with permission.

Other evidence: N/A

Other sources: N/A

References: N/A

DISCONTENT: CONSUMER DISCONTENT SCALE
(Lundstrom and Lamont 1976)

This is a survey to find out what the consumer thinks about business. Below are some statements regarding consumer issues. Please give your own opinion about these statements, i.e., whether you agree or disagree. A simple checkmark in the space provided, is all that is necessary.

1. The business community has been a large influence in raising a country's standard of living. (P)

2. Business profits are too high. (A)

3. Styles change so rapidly a person can't afford to keep up. (A)

4. People who sell things over the telephone are always trying to gyp you. (A)

5. Advertising is a good source of information. (P)

6. Credit makes things too easy to buy. (A)

7. Many times I need assistance in a store and I'm just not able to get it. (A)

8. Warranties would not be necessary if the manufacturer made the product right in thfirst place. (A)

9. Salesmen really take an interest in the consumer and make sure he finds what he wants. (P)

10. Products that last a long time are a thing of the past. (A)

11. Business takes a real interest in the environment and is trying to improve it. (P)

12. Food which is not nutritious is another example of business trying to make a buck and not caring about the consumer. (A)

13. People rate other people by the value of their possessions. (A)

14. Business firms usually stand behind their products and guarantees. (P)

15. When a product is advertised as "new" or "improved" it is the same old thing only in a different package. (A)

16. Industry has an obligation to clean up the waste they have been dumping but they aren't doing it. (A)

17. Chain stores are getting so big that they really don't treat the customer personally. (A)

18. Permanent price controls are the only way to end inflation. (A)

19. The quality of goods has consistently improved over the years. (P)

20. Many times the salesman says one thing to the shopper but he knows it's just the opposite. (A)

21. Many times it's easier to buy a new product rather than trying to fix the old one. (A)

22. The only person who cares about the consumer is the consumer himself. (A)

23. The actual product I buy is usually the same as advertised. (P)

24. It is hard to make a buying decision because of all the products to choose from. (A)

25. The small business has to do what big business says, or else!(A)

26. Most companies have a complaint department which backs up their products and handles consumer problems. (P)

27. Business is the one using up our natural resources (oil, gas, trees, etc.) but it does nothing to replace what has been taken. (A)

28. Many companies listen to consumer complaints but they don't do anything about them. (A)

29. Generally speaking, products work as good as they look. (P)

30. Products fall apart before they have had much use. (A)

31. Products are only as safe as required by government standards, but no more. (A)

32. Stores advertise "special deals" just to get the shopper into the store to buy something else. (A)

33. Companies are helping minorities and the underprivileged by providing them with jobs. (P)

34. The information on most packages is enough to make a good decision. (P)

35. Most salesman who call at home try to force the consumer into buying something. (A)

36. All business really wants to do is to make the most money it can. (A)

37. The business community is actively involved in solving social problems. (P)

38. Most people know that advertising lies a "little." (A)

39. Companies encourage the consumer to buy more than he really needs. (A)

40. The government should enforce ethical business practices. (A)

41. The consumer knows exactly what he is buying with food products because the ingredients are on the package. (P)

42. Companies aren't willing to listen or do anything about consumer gripes. (A)

43. Recycling of products is one way business is cleaning up the environment. (P)

44. Business does not help local residents because it's not profitable. (A)

45. When the consumer is unsure of how good a product is, he can get the correct information from the salesman. (P)

46. The consumer is usually the least important consideration to most companies. (A)

47. Salesman are "pushy" just so they can make a sale. (A)

48. If all advertising were stopped, the consumer would be better off. (A)

49. Sales clerks in stores just don't care about the consumer anymore. (A)

50. Most products are safe when they are used right. (P)

51. Advertised "specials" aren't usually in the store when the shopper goes there. (A)

52. Service departments "pad" the bill by charging for unneeded work. (A)

53. The price I pay is about the same as the quality I receive. (P)

54. Companies try to take a personal interest in each consumer rather than treating him as a number. (P).

55. As soon as they make the sale, most businesses forget about the buyer. (A)

56. Commercials make a person unhappy with himself because he can't have everything he sees. (A)

57. Health and safety warnings on packages are not adequate enough to inform the consumer of possible danger. (P)

58. Service manuals aren't provided for products because the company wants to make money servicing products as well as selling them. (A)

59. What is seen on the outside of a package is many times not what you get on the inside. (A)

60. There are too many of the same types of products which is a waste of money. (A)

61. In general, companies are honest in their dealings with the consumer. (P)

62. Prices of products are going up faster than the incomes of the ordinary consumer. (A)

63. Advertising tempts people to spend their money foolishly. (A)

64. Business profits are high yet they keep on raising their prices. (A)

65. Companies generally offer what the consumer wants. (P)

66. Business has commercialized many meaningful holidays, such as Christmas. (A)

67. The main reason a company does things for society is to make more sales. (A)

68. An attractive package many times influences a purchase that isn't necessary. (A)

69. A large variety of products allow the consumer to choose the one that he really wants. (P)

70. Self-service stores leave the consumer at the mercy of how the product looks. (A)

71. Companies "jazz up" a product with no real improvement, just to get a higher price or sell more. (A)

72. Most of the things I buy are overpriced. (A)

73. Prices are reasonable given the high cost of business. (P)

74. Promotional or "junk" mail is just a waste. (A)

75. Repairs take too long because the right part is not in stock. (A)

76. Advertising tells the shopper about things he would not ordinarily hear about. (P)

77. A warranty or guarantee may be a good one but the service department is often unable to do the work correctly. (A)

78. Repair work is usually done right the first time. (P)

79. Business takes advantage of poor people or minorities by charging higher than normal prices. (A)

80. The stock market is controlled by big financial institutions. (A)

81. Consumer activists, like Ralph Nader, do more harm than good to business. (P)

82. Companies try to influence the government just to better themselves. (A)

NOTES: Items are scored on a 6-point Likert-type scale from *strongly disagree* to *strongly agree*. (P) indicates a pro-business statement, (A) an anti-business statement.

BUSINESS ETHICS

ETHICAL BEHAVIOR IN RESEARCH ORGANIZATIONS
(Ferrell and Skinner 1988)

Construct: Although ethics has been defined as "inquiry into the nature and grounds of morality" (Taylor 1975), Ferrell and Skinner (1988) argue that ethics warrants a special analysis in marketing research organizations. In the case of research organizations, this focus is on honesty in reporting results to clients, including all aspects of a research project.

Description: The ethics scale is composed of six Likert-type statements scored on 6-point scales (*definitely disagree* = 6 to *definitely agree* = 1). Item scores are summed, and the scale is unidimensional.

Development: A pool of 70 items was generated via prestudy interviews with marketing researchers from three organizations. These items were then judged by 11 more researchers, and items were eliminated that lacked face validity. The remaining items were factor analyzed, and items with loadings less than .30 were eliminated. This resulted in the final six-item scale. Reliability and validity estimates were also gathered.

Samples: A sample of 550 marketing researchers from an AMA mailing list was used in the study to develop and validate the scale.

This sample was broken down into subsamples of subcontractors (30%), research firms (45%), and corporate research departments (25%).

Validity: Construct reliability for the six-item scale was .71. Standardized loadings across the items ranged from .43 to .66. In terms of predictive validity, the scale was used as the dependent variable with predictor variables of formalization, centralization, and controls. Across the three subsamples, the ethics scale was positively related to formalization (betas ranged from .18 to .27). Mixed results were found for the other two independent variables.

Scores: No mean or percentage scores were reported.

Source: Ferrell, O. C., and Steven J. Skinner. (1988). "Ethical Behavior and Bureaucratic Structure in Marketing Research Organizations." *Journal of Marketing Research*, 25, 103-109.
   © 1988 by the American Marketing Association. Scale items taken from Appendix (pp. 107-108). Reprinted with permission.

Other evidence: N/A

Other sources: N/A

Reference: Taylor, Paul W. (1975). *Principles of Ethics: An Introduction.* Encino, CA: Dickensen.

ETHICAL BEHAVIOR IN RESEARCH ORGANIZATIONS
(Ferrell and Skinner 1988)

1. Sometimes I compromise the reliability of a study to complete the project.

2. Sometimes I only report part of the data because I know my client may not like the results.

3. I sometimes have to cover up nonresponse and sampling error to please my clients.

4. I have continued a research project after knowing I made errors early.

5. Sometimes I have to alter the sampling design in order to obtain enough respondents.

6. Sometimes I claim to use the latest research techniques as a selling tool, even though I don't use the techniques.

ETHICS: IMPROVING EVALUATIONS OF BUSINESS ETHICS
(Reidenbach and Robin 1990)

Construct: Business ethics is defined as individual ethical judgment in business decision contexts (Reidenbach and Robin 1990). The five major moral philosophies said to underlie the generation of items are justice, relativism, utilitarianism, egoism, and deontology.

Description: The scale comprises eight semantic differential items distributed across three factors as follows: (a) Moral Equity, four items; (b) Relativistic, two items; and (c) Contractualism, two items. Each item is operationalized using 7-place bipolar scales. Item scores can be summed within factors to form factor indices or overall for an overall measure of ethics.

Development: An initial set of 33 items was developed to reflect the five normative philosophies. The categorization was verified using a panel of three expert "ethics literature" judges. Three scenarios (with varying behaviors of questionable ethics) along with the 33 items were administered to a sample of 218 business students (i.e., the item responses reflected opinions about the behaviors in the scenarios). Four scale items were deleted at this stage (with the deletion procedures not specified). Stage 2 involved tests of the factor structure employing both Likert-type and bipolar formats. (No differences across formats were observed.) Examination of the pattern of factor loadings, the size of the loadings, and item-to-total correlations were used to reduce the number of items to 14. From this stage, three factors emerged. In the last phase, 105 small business operators evaluated the three scenarios. Using the same factor analysis and item reduction criteria, the number of items was reduced to eight. Reliability and validity estimates were also obtained.

Samples: A sample of 218 business students was surveyed in the first stage. A sample of 108 retail managers and owners participated in the second phase, and 105 small business operators were the participants in the last phase, in which the number of items was reduced to eight (i.e., the number included in the final scale). A final study involving mail survey responses from 152 business managers was used to evaluate the validity of the scale.

Validity: Factor analysis of the final survey of business managers replicated the anticipated factor structure. In addition, the three-factor solution explained an average of 79% of the variance across the three scenarios. Based on the responses from reaction to three scenarios, a multitrait-multicontext analysis provided some correlational evidence of convergent and discriminant validity. These analyses revealed that the intercorrelations among factors were generally within the .20 to .40 range. The subscale reliabilities ranged from .71 to .92.

The subscales were also correlated with single-item measures of overall perceptions of the ethical nature of the behavior and a measure of behavioral intentions. For the former, the subscales explained an average of 72% of the variance, and for the latter, the subscales explained an average of 34% of the variance. The multiple-item scales were also found to be better predictors of intentions than the single-item, overall measure. Thus, evidence of predictive validity was found.

Scores: Mean scores for the total scale, the subscales, or the individual items were not presented.

Source: Reidenbach, R. Eric, and Donald P. Robin. (1990). "Toward the Development of a Multidimensional Scale for Improving Evaluations of Business Ethics." *Journal of Business Ethics*, 9, 639-653.

© 1990 by Kluwer Academic Publishers. Scale items taken from Table VI (p. 649). Reprinted with permission.

Other evidence: A series of follow-up studies was conducted in an effort to further evaluate the scale (Reidenbach, Robin, and Dawson 1991). Across four studies and 15 trials employing different contexts (i.e., eight scenarios), the factor structure and reliability of the scale were replicated. For example, across the 15 trials, the three-factor solution explained between 57.5% and 82.8% of the variance in the data, with an average of 75%. As predictors of a univariate ethics measure and a measure of ethics intention, the three factors explained between 25% and 83% of the variance in these criterion variables.

Other source: Reidenbach, R. Eric, Donald P. Robin, and Lyndon Dawson. (1991). "An Application and Extension of a Multidimensional Ethics Scale to Selected Marketing Practices and Marketing Groups." *Journal of the Academy of Marketing Science, 19*, 115-122.

References: N/A

ETHICS: IMPROVING EVALUATIONS OF BUSINESS ETHICS
(Reidenbach and Robin 1990)

Moral Equity Dimension

1. Fair/unfair

2. Just/unjust

3. Acceptable to my family/unacceptable to my family

4. Morally right/not morally right

Relativistic Dimension

5. Traditionally acceptable/traditionally unacceptable

6. Culturally acceptable/culturally unacceptable

Contractualism Dimension

7. Violates/does not violate an unspoken promise

8. Violates/does not violate an unwritten contract

NOTE: Items 1 through 6 require recoding to reflect a higher level of morality.

ETHICS: CORPORATE ETHICS SCALE: CEP
(Hunt, Wood, and Chonko 1989)

Construct: As conceptualized by Hunt, Wood, and Chonko (1989), corporate ethics reflects three broad based perceptions: (a) the extent to which employees perceive that managers are acting ethically in their organizations, (b) the extent to which employees perceive that managers are concerned about the issues of ethics in their organization, and (c) the extent to which employees perceive that ethical (unethical) behavior is rewarded (punished) in their organization.

Description: The CEP is a five-item scale that is summed and then divided by five to form an overall index of corporate ethics. All items are scored on 7-point strongly disagree-strongly agree scales. Thus, scores on the scale can range from 1 to 7. The scale is considered unidimensional.

Development: From two studies (Hunt, Chonko, and Wilcox 1984; Hunt et al. 1989), five items from a larger pool of items were chosen for the CEP. Factor analysis and coefficient alpha were used to assess the dimensionality and reliability of the scale.

Sample: A total of 1,246 respondents (499 marketing managers, 417 marketing researchers, and 330 advertising agency managers) were used as the sample in deriving the scale.

Validity: Coefficient alpha for the scale was .78, and factor analysis revealed a unidimensional structure. Furthermore, the CEP was found to be a significant predictor of organizational commitment (i.e., numerous regression coefficients are offered on p. 86), providing evidence of criterion validity for the scale. For example, beta coefficients for the scale ranged from .17 to .58 across four subsamples of the data.

Scores: Mean scores (std. dev.) for the three subsample groups were 5.3 (1.12), 5.08 (1.17), and 5.88 (1.22) for the marketing managers, marketing researchers, and ad agency managers, respectively.

Source: Hunt, Shelby D., Van R. Wood, and Lawrence B. Chonko. (1989). "Corporate Ethical Values and Organizational Commitment in Marketing." *Journal of Marketing*, *53*, 79-90.

© 1989 by the American Marketing Association. Scale items taken from Tables 6 and 7 (p. 317). Reprinted with permission.

Other evidence: N/A

Other sources: N/A

Reference: Hunt, Shelby D., Lawrence B. Chonko, and James B. Wilcox. (1984). "Ethical Problems of Marketing Researchers." *Journal of Marketing Research*, *21*, 309-324.

ETHICS: CORPORATE ETHICS SCALE: CEP
(Hunt, Wood, and Chonko 1989)

1. Managers in my company often engage in behaviors that I consider to be unethical.*

2. In order to succeed in my company, it is often necessary to compromise one's ethics.*

3. Top management in my company has let it be known in no uncertain terms that unethical behaviors will not be tolerated.

4. If a manager in my company is discovered to have engaged in unethical behavior that results primarily in **personal gain** (rather than corporate gain), he or she will be promptly reprimanded.

5. If a manager in my company is discovered to have engaged in unethical behavior that results primarily in **corporate gain** (rather than personal gain), he or she will be promptly reprimanded.

NOTE: *Denotes items that are reverse scored.

ETHICS: MARKETING NORMS ETHICS SCALE
(Vitell, Rallapalli, and Singhapakdi 1993)

Construct: The overall construct assessed by this multidimensional scale is described as the marketing-related norms of marketing practitioners. Norms are defined generally as predetermined guidelines that represent personal values or rules of behavior. Items are said to be reflective of ethical situations faced by marketers in their decision making. The American Marketing Association (AMA) code of ethics was used to drive conceptualization and item generation. Factor analysis was used to derive the factor structure (Vitell, Rallapalli, and Singhapakdi 1993, pp. 331-332).

Description: The scale consists of 25 items, each operationalized using 5-place response formats (1 = *strongly disagree* to 5 = *strongly agree*). The five dimension labels (and numbers of items per dimension) are as follows: price and distribution norms (6), information and contract norms (6), product and promotion norms (5), obligation and disclosure norms (4), and general honesty and integrity (4).

Development: Thirty items were developed reflecting specific ethical situations that marketers face in decision making. Each item was derived from specific elements in the AMA Code of Ethics. Principal components factor analysis with varimax rotation was used to condense the items to five factors and apparently as a means of deleting items.

Samples: A mail survey of a random sample of 2,000 AMA members resulted in a usable sample of 508 practicing marketers, of whom 61% worked in service industries, 52.2% were male, 64% had incomes above $40,000, and 46.3% occupied lower level management positions.

Validity: Coefficient alpha estimates of internal consistency reliability ranged across the five factors from .67 to .87. Evidence of validity was provided by correlations with idealism and relativism and with two dimensions of the Ethics Dimension Questionnaire. A series of regression analyses, in which the norm factors served as dependent variables, was argued as providing evidence of nomological validity.

Scores: Item mean scores are shown in Table 1. All mean scores were above 4.1 on the 5-place response format.

Source: Vitell, Scott J., Kumar C. Rallapalli, and Anusorn Singhapakdi. (1993). "Marketing Norms: The Influence of Personal Moral Philosophies and Organizational Ethical Culture." *Journal of the Academy of Marketing Science, 21*(4), 331-337.

© 1993 by Sage Publications. Scale items taken from Table 1 (p. 333).

Other evidence: N/A

Other sources: N/A

References: N/A

ETHICS: MARKETING NORMS ETHICS SCALE
(Vitell, Rallapalli, and Singhapakdi 1993)

Factor 1: Price and Distribution Norms

All extra-cost added features should be identified.

One should not manipulate the availability of a product for the purpose of exploitation.

Coercion should not be used within the marketing channel.

Undue influence should not be exerted over the resellers' choice to handle a product.

One should not engage in price fixing.

Predatory pricing should not be practiced.

Factor 2: Information and Contract Norms

Information regarding all substantial risks associated with product or service usage should be disclosed.

Any product component substitution that might materially change the product or impact on the buyer's purchase decision should be disclosed.

Outside clients and suppliers should be treated fairly.

Confidentiality and anonymity in professional relationships should be maintained with regard to privileged information.

Obligations and responsibilities in contracts and mutual agreements should be met in a timely manner.

The practice and promotion of a professional code of ethics must be actively supported.

Factor 3: Product and Promotion Norms

Products and services offered should be safe and fit for their intended uses.

Communications about products and services offered should not be deceptive.

False and misleading advertising should be avoided.

High pressure manipulations or misleading sales tactics should be avoided.

Sales promotions that use deception or manipulation should be avoided.

Factor 4: Obligation and Disclosure Norms

One should discharge one's obligations, financial and otherwise, in good faith.

The full price associated with any purchase should be disclosed.

Selling or fund raising under the guise of conducting research should be avoided.

Research integrity should be maintained by avoiding the misrepresentation and omission of pertinent research data.

Factor 5: General Honesty and Integrity

One should always adhere to all applicable laws and regulations.

One should always accurately represent one's education, training and experience.

One must always be honest in serving consumers, clients, employees, suppliers, distributors, and the public.

One should not knowingly participate in a conflict of interest without prior notice to all parties involved.

UNETHICAL BEHAVIOR:
BUYERS' PERCEPTIONS OF UNETHICAL SALES BEHAVIOR
(Lagace, Ingram, and Boorom 1994)

Construct: The focal construct is buyers' perceptions of salespersons' unethical behavior. Ethical salesperson behavior is that set of actions on the part of the salesperson which may be perceived by the consumer as right, just, or morally correct (Lagace, Ingram, and Boorom 1994, p. 119). Examples of unethical behaviors included in the final measure are lying, withholding information, overlooking customer interests, and selling hazardous products.

Description: The scale reflects a single dimension operationalized as the sum or average of 15 items. A 7-place strongly disagree-strongly agree response format was used following each item.

Development: An initial set of 34 items was developed from a literature review of the business ethics literature and two focus groups of buyers. The number and nature of the focus groups was not specified. The physician sample ($n = 90$) was used to purify the measure. Responses reflected opinions about their last salesperson interaction. One item was deleted based on item-to-total correlations. Factor analysis was used to reduce the remaining items to 24, representing a two-factor solution, with coefficient alpha estimates of .94 and .92 for Factors 1 and 2, respectively.

The second sample ($n = 237$) was used to estimate a series of confirmatory factor analysis models. Based on high factor correlations, items with high standardized residuals, and an examination of item content for duplicative items, the scale was further reduced to a single factor comprising 15 items. The remaining one factor scale had a coefficient alpha estimate of .91. The overall fit statistics were said to be satisfactory (GFI = .92, AGFI = .89, and RMSR = .04) (Lagace et al. 1994, p. 121).

Samples: Two samples were used in scale development: 90 physicians and 237 MBA students and their families (also called the general consumer sample).

Validity: Significant negative correlations between the scale and single items assessing perceptions of salespersons' ethics and general trust in salespersons were offered as evidence of validity. These correlations averaged .42 and .20 for the physician and general consumer samples, respectively.

Scores: Mean scores were not reported (i.e., cited Table 3 not presented in paper). While physicians were said to perceive less unethical behavior, neither sample perceived salespersons to be extensively involved in ethical behavior.

Source: Lagace, Rosemary R., Thomas N. Ingram, and Michael L. Boorom. (1994). "An Exploratory Study of Buyers' Perceptions of Salesperson Unethical Behavior: Scale Development and Validation." In Ravi Achrol and Andrew Mitchell (Eds.), *Enhancing Knowledge Development in Marketing* (Vol. 5, pp. 118-123). Chicago: American Marketing Association.

© 1994 by the American Marketing Association. Scale items taken from Table 1 (p. 120). Reprinted with permission.

Other evidence: N/A

Other sources: N/A

References: N/A

UNETHICAL BEHAVIOR:
BUYERS' PERCEPTIONS OF UNETHICAL SALES BEHAVIOR
(Lagace, Ingram, and Boorom 1994)

E16. Falsifies product testimonials

E17. Passes the blame for something s/he did wrong onto someone else

E18. Poses as a market researcher when doing phone calls

E21. Misrepresents guarantees/warranties

E25. Takes advantage of the poor or uneducated

E33. Accepts favors from customers so the seller feels obliged to bend policies

E34. Sells dangerous or hazardous products

E3. Exaggerates benefits of product

E5. Lies about availability in order to make sale

E7. Lies about the competition to make sale

E9. Sells products/services people don't need

E11. Is only interested in own interests, not the clients

E12. Gives answers when s/he doesn't really know answers

E14. Lies to competitors

E28. Approaches "hard sell" tactics

BUSINESS ATTITUDES TOWARD THE MARKETPLACE

CONSERVATISM: MANAGEMENT CONSERVATISM
(Sturdivant, Ginter, and Sawyer 1985)

Construct: This measure is designed to assess "the conservatism of managers' *personal* values" (Sturdivant, Ginter, and Sawyer 1985, p. 17). The assumption underlying the research is that the collective personal values of senior management in a firm will have a substantial impact on corporate goals. The scale is designed to focus on the social and political issues that are of special concern to executives.

Description: The scale consists of 30 items designed to reflect two factors: (a) government/business and the general welfare (16 items) and (b) human rights and responsibilities (14 items). Each statement is operationalized using a 6-place response format: 1 = *agree very much*, 2 = *agree on the whole*, 3 = *agree a little*, 4 = *disagree a little*, 5 = *disagree on the whole*, and 6 = *disagree very much*. The wording of the items (i.e., positive vs. negative) is varied to inhibit response bias. Summed across the two factors (which were reportedly uncorrelated), the scores for the scale could range from 30 to 180, with higher scores reflecting greater conservatism. Summing item scores within factors is also possible to derive factor indices.

Development: The scale was developed from an initial pool of 65 items. The two factors were developed from a series of factor analysis procedures including both oblique and orthogonal rotations and split sample replications ($n = 580$). The two factors were selected based upon explained variance considerations and were named *after* examination of the item content loading on each factor. The factor analyses were also replicated on a subsequent sample of executives ($n = 377$). Several estimates of reliability and validity were obtained.

Samples: Seven different samples (labeled A through G) were used in the development and evaluation of the scale. Most subjects were executives participating in executive development seminars. Two of the samples included MBA student groups ($n = 38$ and $n = 24$). The executive sample sizes were 580, 377, 173, 69, 235, and 28.

Validity: Considerable evidence of reliability and validity is provided in the text of the article and in the appendix to the article. Only some of those results are summarized here. (In addition, the analysis of a series of relationships between conservatism and firm financial performance provided additional evidence regarding the usefulness of the scale.) Estimates of internal consistency reliability for the 16-item factor and the 14-item factor (for Sample A) were .84 and .78, respectively. The linear composite estimate of reliability for the entire scale was .85. For Sample B, the corresponding estimates of reliability were .85, .81, and .86. Based on a 2-week test-retest administration to 24 executive MBA students, the test-retest correlations for Factors 1 and 2 and the total scale were .87, .87, and .92, respectively. Some evidence of discriminant validity was provided from a series of low correlations with measures of a variety of constructs including social desirability, dogmatism, Machiavellianism, and internal-external locus of control. Neither the total scale nor either factor was correlated with social desirability. One measure of authoritarianism was correlated with the total scale ($r = .58$), and dogmatism was correlated with Factor 1 ($r = .30$). Evidence of convergent validity was also provided by correlations with two general conservatism scales.

Scores: Mean scores for 48 companies that were said to vary in terms of social performance were provided. See Figure 1 (Sturdivant et al. 1986, p. 27). The grand mean for the overall scale across groups was 96.3. The subgroup means based on social performance were social activists, 66.4; best, 103.6; honorable mention, 103.9; and worst, 113.8.

Source: Sturdivant, Frederick D., James L. Ginter, and Alan G. Sawyer. (1985). "Managers' Conservatism and Corporate Performance." *Strategic Management Journal*, 6, 17-38.

Other evidence: N/A

Other sources: N/A

References: N/A

CONSERVATISM: MANAGEMENT CONSERVATISM
(Sturdivant, Ginter, and Sawyer 1985)

Government/Business and the General Welfare

1. Corporations have too much influence on the outcome of the presidential elections.

2. Current tax laws allow wealthy individuals to pay less than their fair share.

3. The disadvantaged in our society suffer because of the economic power exerted by large corporations.

4. Tax laws should be changed to close loopholes that allow wealthy individuals to pay proportionately less taxes than low-income individuals.

5. Product quality standards should be set by regulatory agencies to protect consumers.

6. One of the principal purposes of government should be to protect the citizen from the economic power generated by large corporations.

7. Advertising is often a devious method used by companies to lure customers into purchasing their products.

8. To ensure adequate care of the sick, we need to change the present system of privately owned and controlled medical care.

9. Executives of toy producing companies should be subject to jail sentences for failure to inform parents that their products may be hazardous.

10. All individuals, regardless of ability to pay, should be given the same medical care.

11. Business should be required to fund schools that will be used to train and educate handicapped children.

12. Funds for school construction should come from state and federal government loans at no interest or very low interest.

13. Companies should not have business dealings with other companies which ignore their responsibility to protect the environment.

14. The quickened pace of business and competition has taken a heavy toll on the quality of life.

15. Regulatory agencies must be given the power to set and enforce standards for the purpose of guarding against environmental deterioration.

16. Business should give environmental protection groups access to the information they need to properly inform the public.

Human Rights and Responsibilities

1. Government programs to aid the poor usually support those people too lazy to work.

2. The children that are born as a result of racially mixed marriages are detriments to society.

3. Protesters and radicals are good for society even though they may cause a change in normally accepted standards.

4. We would not have so many juvenile delinquents if parents were stricter with their children.

5. There are too many professors in our colleges and universities who are radical in their social and political beliefs.

6. A business should not hire a person if they suspect him of being homosexual.

7. Labor unions should not have the right to strike when the survival of the business is threatened.

8. Inherited racial characteristics play more of a part in the achievement of individuals and groups than is generally known.

9. Police should be able to forcefully enter a person's home if they suspect him of unlawful activity.

10. Many blacks would be executives of major corporations today if they had not been discriminated against in the past.

11. Employers should be able to require their employees to have their hair cut to a specified length.

12. Parents deserve more respect from their children than they receive.

13. Even though the resulting cost may mean a reduction in profits, businesses should set and attempt to meet minority hiring quotas.

14. If experts determine that marijuana has no harmful effects, it should be legalized.

NOTE: Items 1, 2, 4-9, 11, and 12 of the "human rights and responsibilities" factor require recoding to reflect a higher level of management conservatism.

CULTURE: MARKETING CULTURE
(Webster 1993)

Construct: This scale development effort represents an extension of Webster's (1990) earlier research regarding the measurement of the marketing culture of service firms. The marketing culture of a service firm refers to the way marketing "things" are done in the firm (Webster 1993, p. 113). Marketing culture includes the unwritten, the formally decreed, and what actually takes place. It is the pattern of shared values and beliefs that helps individuals understand the marketing function and provides them with norms of behavior. Six dimensions of marketing culture are hypothesized: service quality, interpersonal relationships, selling task, organization, internal communications, and innovativeness.

Description: The revised measure contains 34 items across the six factors: service quality (8), interpersonal relationships (5), selling task (7), organization (5), internal communications (6), and innovativeness (3). Each item is operationalized using a 6-point response format ranging from *no importance* (1) to *necessary* (6). Other response formats were also employed during various stages of the research.

Development: A summary of the steps employed in development of the 34-item scale is presented in Appendix A (Webster 1993, p. 121). Interested users of this measure are encouraged to refer to the original sources. It is unclear in some instances exactly what procedures and samples were employed in the development of the measures proposed by Webster (1993). Briefly, the steps reported by Webster (1993) are as follow. An initial sample of 30 service employees resulted in the identification of 11 additional items. The resulting 49 items (i.e., the additional 11 plus the 38 described by Webster [1990]) were analyzed using data pooled across four industries. Corrected item-to-total and coefficient alpha analyses were used to reduce the number of items to 41. Problems with cross loadings in subsequent exploratory factor analyses reduced the item set further to 34. From Appendix B, overall scale reliability adjusted for linear combination of subdimensions was .94. Factor reliabilities ranged from .75 to .86. Within-factor corrected item-to-total correlations were uniform and high.

Samples: Several additional samples are reported by Webster (1993). (Prior research [Webster 1990] describes other samples used in preliminary scale construction.) First, 30 service employees, selected from companies known for their marketing expertise, were used to evaluate the 38 items described by Webster (1990). Subsequently, the responses of 182 service employees, selected from firms in retail banking, health care, airlines, and repair/maintenance industries, were used to purify the items and develop the eventual 34-item scale. As part of the validation, two additional samples were obtained. These included 400 consumers of four nationally known firms and 192 service firm employees.

Validity: Supportive evidence for the scale was provided by mean differences (i.e., perceptions minus expectations) across groups formed by an overall evaluation single-item measure. Similar mean comparisons across groups differing in their inclination to recommend and complain were also offered as support for the scale. The last employee survey ($n = 192$) provided evidence of the relationship between marketing culture and firm profitability.

Scores: Only factor mean difference scores are reported (Appendix C) (Webster 1993, p. 123).

Source: Webster, Cynthia. (1993). "Refinement of the Marketing Culture Scale and the Relationship Between Marketing Culture and Profitability of a Service Firm." *Journal of Business Research*, *26*, 111-131.

      © 1993 by Elsevier Science. Scale items taken from Appendix D (pp. 124-128). Reprinted with permission from Elsevier Science.

Other evidence: N/A

Other sources: N/A

Reference: Webster, Cynthia. (1990). "Towards the Measurement of Marketing Culture of a Service Firm." *Journal of Business Research*, *21*, 345-362.

CULTURE: MARKETING CULTURE
(Webster 1993)

Service Quality

The firm specifically defining what exceptional service is

The commitment of top management to providing quality service

Systematic, regular measurement and monitoring of employees' performance

Employees' focus on customer needs, desires, and attitudes

The belief of employees that their behavior reflects the firm's image

For employees to meet the firm's expectations

For the firm to place emphasis on employees' communication skills

Employees' attention to detail in their work

Interpersonal Relationships

For the company to be considerate of employees' feelings

For the firm to treat each employee as an important part of the organization

For employees to feel comfortable in giving opinions to higher management

That managers/supervisors have an "open-door" policy

Management's interaction with front-line employees

Selling Task

The firm's emphasis on hiring the right people

The firm providing skill-based training and product knowledge to front-line service providers

The encouragement of creative approaches to selling

The firm's recognition of high achievers in selling

For employees to enjoy pursuing new accounts

For the firm to reward employees, better than competing firms, with incentives to sell

For employees to aggressively pursue new business

Organization

Each employee to be well organized

For careful planning to be characteristic of each employee's daily routine

For employees to prioritize work

Each employee's work area to be well organized

Each employee to manage time well

Internal Communications

The firm having an approved set of policies and procedures which is made available to every employee

That supervisors clearly state what their expectations are of others

That each employee understands the mission and general objectives of the firm

Management's sharing of financial information with all employees

The encouragement of front-line service personnel to become involved in standard-setting

The firm to focus efforts on training and motivating employees

Innovativeness

For all employees to be receptive to ideas for change

The firm keeping up with technological advances

The receptiveness of the company to change

CULTURE: ORGANIZATIONAL CULTURE
(Deshpande, Farley, and Webster 1993)

Construct: Deshpande and Webster (1989, p. 4) defined organizational culture as the pattern of shared values and beliefs that help individuals understand organizational functioning and thus provide them with the norms for behavior in the organization. Subsequently, Deshpande, Farley, and Webster (1993, pp. 25-26) used two dimensions to identify four culture types. The two dimensions describe the continua that range from organic to mechanistic processes and from internal maintenance to external positioning. The four culture types are (a) market culture that emphasizes competitiveness and goal achievement, (b) adhocracy culture that emphasizes entrepreneurship and creativity, (c) clan culture that emphasizes teamwork and cooperation, and (d) hierarchy culture that emphasizes order and regulations.

Description: Complete instructions are provided by Deshpande et al. (1993, p. 34). Briefly, respondents are asked to distribute 100 points across four descriptions (i.e., A, B, C, D) regarding four different issues: (a) kind of organization, (b) leadership, (c) what holds the organization together, and (d) what is important. The four culture scores are computed by adding the four A items for clan, the four B items for adhocracy, the four C items for hierarchy, and the four D items for market. As such, the culture measures represent four different four-item scales that could range from 0 to more than 100.

Development: The culture scale was adapted from Campbell and Freeman (1991) and Quinn (1988). Coefficient alpha estimates of internal consistency reliability were as follow: market, .82; adhocracy, .66; clan, .42; and hierarchy, .71.

Samples: The research is based on 50 sets of four interviews (i.e., 50 quadrads), each representing two interviews from a supplier and two from a customer firm of that supplier (Deshpande et al. 1993, p. 28). These quadrads represent 50 Japanese firms randomly selected from those firms traded on the Nikkei stock exchange in Tokyo.

Validity: Like the evidence cited earlier for the authors' customer orientation measure, evidence in support of validity is provided by the empirical support for the theoretical propositions. For example, market cultures were associated with the best performance, whereas hierarchical cultures were associated with the poorest performance, as predicted.

Scores: Means (std. dev.) pooled across low and high performers were reported as follow: market 106.1 (37.4); adhocracy, 78.9 (26.4); clan, 117.0 (28.8); and hierarchy, 100.9 (31.4).

Source: Deshpande, Rohit, John U. Farley, and Frederick E. Webster, Jr. (1993). "Corporate Culture, Customer Orientation, and Innovativeness in Japanese Firms: A Quadrad Analysis." *Journal of Marketing*, *57*, 23-37.
    © 1993 by the American Marketing Association. Scale items taken from Appendix (p. 34). Reprinted with permission.

Other evidence: N/A

Other sources: N/A

References: Campbell, J. P., and Sarah J. Freeman. (1991). "Cultural Congruence, Strength, and Type: Relationships to Effectiveness." In R. W. Woodman and W. A. Passmore (Eds.), *Research in Organizational Change and Development* (Vol. 5). Greenwich, CT: JAI.

Deshpande, Rohit, and Frederick E. Webster, Jr. (1989). "Organizational Culture and Marketing: Defining the Research Agenda." *Journal of Marketing*, *53*, 3-15.

Quinn, Robert E. (1988). *Beyond Rational Management.* San Francisco: Jossey-Bass.

CULTURE: ORGANIZATIONAL CULTURE
(Deshpande, Farley, and Webster 1993)

Kind of Organization (Please distribute 100 points)

_____Points for A

My organization is a very **personal** place. It is like extended family. People seem to share a lot of themselves.

_____Points for B

My organization is a very **dynamic** and entrepreneurial place. People are willing to stick their necks out and take risks.

_____Points for C

My organization is a very **formalized and structural** place. Established procedures generally govern what people do.

_____Points for D

My organization is very **production oriented**. A major concern is with getting the job done without much personal involvement.

Leadership (Please distribute 100 points)

_____Points for A

The head of my organization is generally considered to be a **mentor, sage,** or a **father or mother figure**.

_____Points for B

The head of my organization is generally considered to be an **entrepreneur**, an **innovator**, or a **risk taker**.

_____Points for C

The head of my organization is generally considered to be a **coordinator**, an **organizer**, or an **administrator**.

_____Points for D

The head of my organization is generally considered to be a **producer**, a **technician**, or a **hard-driver.**

What Holds the Organization Together (Please distribute 100 points)

_____Points for A

The glue that holds my organization together is **loyalty and tradition**. Commitment to this firm runs high.

_____Points for B

The glue that holds my organization together is **commitment to innovation and development**. There is an emphasis on being first.

_____Points for C

The glue that holds my organization together is **formal rules and policies**. Maintaining a smooth-running institution is important here.

_____Points for D

The glue that holds my organization together is the emphasis on **tasks and goal accomplishment**. A production orientation is commonly shared.

What Is Important (Please distribute 100 points)

_____Points for A

My organization emphasizes **human resources**. High cohesion and morale in the firm are important.

_____Points for B

My organization emphasizes **growth and acquiring new resources**. Readiness to meet new challenges is important.

_____Points for C

My organization emphasizes **permanence and stability**. Efficient, smooth operations are important.

_____Points for D

My organization emphasizes **competitive actions and achievement**. Measurable goals are important.

NOTE: The four culture scores are computed by adding the four A items for clan, the four B items for adhocracy, the four C items for hierarchy, and the four D items for market.

CUSTOMER ORIENTATION
(Deshpande, Farley, and Webster 1993)

Construct: Customer orientation is defined as the set of beliefs that puts the customer's interests first, while not excluding those of all other stakeholders such as owners, managers, and employees, in order to develop a long-term profitable enterprise (Deshpande, Farley, and Webster 1993, p. 27). This perspective includes the more deeply rooted values and beliefs that the organization consistently reinforce a customer focus.

Description: Customer orientation is assessed as the sum of nine positively worded items operationalized using a 5-place Likert-type agreement response format. Respondents are requested to answer within the context of a particular market business. Items are constructed such that they can be used for both customers and suppliers.

Development: The customer orientation scale was developed on the basis of extensive qualitative interviewing, a detailed survey of available literature, and pretesting in a small sample of firms (Deshpande et al. 1993, p. 29). Corrected item-to-total correlations and coefficient alpha were used to delete items. Internal consistency estimates of reliability, as evaluated by the suppliers and customers, were .69 and .83, respectively.

Samples: The research is based on 50 sets of four interviews (i.e., 50 quadrads), each representing two interviews from a supplier and two from a customer firm of that supplier (Deshpande et al. 1993, p. 28). These quadrads represent 50 Japanese firms randomly selected from those firms traded on the Nikkei stock exchange in Tokyo.

Validity: Some evidence of validity is provided by the mixed results from the authors' tests of hypotheses. For example, marketers' customer orientation is related positively to business performance, and these effects remained after controlling for organizational culture. However, Japanese managers' reports of their company's customer orientation were not related to performance.

Scores: Overall means (std. dev.) were 32.5 (3.3) and 32.1 (3.2) as evaluated by the supplier and the customer, respectively. Similar estimates were found for both suppliers and customers for low and high performers.

Source: Deshpande, Rohit, John U. Farley, and Frederick E. Webster, Jr. (1993). "Corporate Culture, Customer Orientation, and Innovativeness in Japanese Firms: A Quadrad Analysis." *Journal of Marketing, 57,* 23-37.

 © 1993 by the American Marketing Association. Scale items taken from Appendix (p. 34). Reprinted with permission.

Other evidence: Other evidence of reliability and validity is summarized in the meta-analysis market orientation scale development effort reported by Deshpande and Farley (1996) based on their survey of 82 marketing executives. For example, the estimate of reliability was reported to be .72. The correlation with a validity check measure of market orientation was .66. Evidence of predictive validity was provided by correlations of .28 and .66 with two measures of firm performance. Evidence of discriminant validity was provided by low correlations with measures of organizational climate.

Other source: Deshpande, Rohit, and John U. Farley. (1996, December). *Understanding Market Orientation: A Prospectively Designed Meta-Analysis of Three Market Orientation Scales* (Working Paper Report No. 96-125). Cambridge, MA: Marketing Science Institute.

References: N/A

CUSTOMER ORIENTATION
(Deshpande, Farley, and Webster 1993)

We have routine or regular measures of customer service.

Our product and service development is based on good market and customer information.

We know our competitors well.

We have a good sense of how our customers value our products and services.

We are more customer focused than our competitors.

We compete primarily based on product or service differentiation.

The customer's interest should always come first, ahead of the owners.

Our products/services are the best in the business.

I believe this business exists primarily to serve customers.

EXCELLENCE IN BUSINESS: EXCEL
(Sharma, Netemeyer, and Mahajan 1990)

Construct: Corporate excellence is viewed as those managerial practices and principles that lead to sustained performance (Sharma, Netemeyer, and Mahajan 1990). These principles are posited to be a necessary but not sufficient condition for superior corporate performance. Furthermore, these principles are based on the eight attributes of excellence espoused by Peters and Waterman (1982). These attributes are (a) a bias for action, (b) being close to customers, (c) autonomy and entrepreneurship, (d) being productive through people, (e) an active shared value system among all levels, (f) a simple and lean staff, (g) simultaneous loose-tight properties (i.e., certain core values are centralized while others are decentralized), and (h) "sticking to the knitting" (i.e., a resistance to conglomeracy and a focus on what is known or done best).

Description: The EXCEL scale is a 16-item scale designed to measure the eight attributes of excellence espoused by Peters and Waterman. All items are scored on Likert-type scales from *strongly disagree* to *strongly agree*. Though originally hypothesized to be an eight-factor measure based on the eight attributes, factor analysis revealed a single higher-order factor structure composed of eight secondary factors that reflect the eight attributes of excellence. Thus, the items are summed to form an overall score of excellence, where scores can range from 16 to 112 (Sharma et al. 1990).

Development: The EXCEL scale was developed using recommended scaling procedures. Using the conceptual base of Peters and Waterman (1982), the book was content analyzed by three independent researchers to generate an initial pool of items. Twenty-five items were generated for each attribute (i.e., 200 items). Two expert panels were then used to delete redundant and ambiguous items, trimming the initial pool to 32 items. Both panels were asked to indicate the attribute that each statement reflected. Items were retained that met a stringent a priori decision rule (i.e., for the first panel, seven of eight judges had to agree that the item reflected a given attribute, and for the second panel, 70% agreement was the decision rule for item retention). Two samples were gathered to purify and finalize the scale via a variety of item analyses and reliability and validity tests (Sharma et al. 1990).

Samples: The first expert panel consisted of six business strategy professors and two Ph.D. students in public policy. The second expert panel consisted of 10 additional business strategy professors from four different universities. The first purification sample consisted of 678 business policy/strategy professors drawn from the Academy of Management membership listing. This sample indicated their level of agreement that the statement measured the respective attribute. In addition, 12 firms were rated by seven industry analysts.

Validity: The purification samples produced the final 16-item EXCEL scale. Though eight factors were hypothesized, factor analysis on Sample 1 data ($n = 678$) revealed that a single higher-order factor structure composed of eight secondary factors best fit the data. Coefficient alpha for this version of the scale was .89. Alpha for the industry analyst sample was .90.

The validity of the scale was examined by correlating scores on the scale with financial ratios, measures of stock market performance, and rankings from *Fortune* magazine. These correlations showed strong support for the nomological validity of the EXCEL scale across both samples. For example, the correlation between the Treynor financial index and the EXCEL score was .62 ($p = .05$). The coefficient of concordance between the EXCEL rankings and a set of *Fortune* rankings was .92 ($p = .08$). A coefficient of concordance also indicated a high degree of agreement among the industry analysts (W = .77).

Scores: Mean scores for a computer industry sample are provided in Table 2 of Sharma et al. (1990, p. 326). These scores ranged from a low of 46.80 (for the least excellent firm in the sample) to 95.00 (for the highest evaluated firm).

Source: Sharma, Subhash, Richard G. Netemeyer, and Vijay Mahajan. (1990). "In Search of Excellence Revisited: An Empirical Evaluation of Peters and Waterman's Attributes of Excellence." In William O. Bearden and A. Parasuraman (Eds.), *Enhancing Knowledge Development in Marketing* (Vol. 1, pp. 322-328). Chicago: American Marketing Association.

© 1990 by the American Marketing Association. Scale items taken from Figure 1 (p. 326). Reprinted with permission.

Other evidence: N/A

Other sources: N/A

Reference: Peters, Thomas J., and Robert H. Waterman. (1982). *In Search of Excellence: Lessons From America's Best Run Companies*. New York: Harper and Row.

EXCELLENCE IN BUSINESS: EXCEL
(Sharma, Netemeyer, and Mahajan 1990)

1. The firm encourages employees to develop new ideas.

2. The firm has a small staff that delegates authority efficiently.

3. The firm's top level management believes that its people are of the utmost importance to the company.

4. The firm instills a value system in all its employees.

5. The firm provides personalized attention to all its customers.

6. The firm's top management creates an atmosphere that encourages creativity and innovativeness.

7. The company's values are the driving force behind its operation.

8. The firm is flexible and quick to respond to problems.

9. The company concentrates in product areas where it has a high level of skill and expertise.

10. The firm has a small, but efficient management team.

11. The company develops products that are natural extensions of its product line.

12. The firm truly believes in its people.

13. The firm considers after-the-sale service just as important as making the sale itself.

14. The firm believes in experimenting with new products and ideas.

15. The company believes that listening to what consumers have to say is a good skill to have.

16. The firm is flexible with employees but administers discipline when necessary.

NOTE: The eight attributes and the corresponding items designed to reflect each are as follow: a bias for action, 8; close to the customer, 5, 13, and 15; autonomy and entrepreneurship, 1, 6, and 14; productivity through people, 3 and 12; hands-on value driven, 4 and 7; stick to the knitting, 9 and 11; simple form and lean staff, 2 and 10; and loose-tight properties, 16.

MARKET ORIENTATION
(Narver and Slater 1990)

Construct: Market orientation is the organizational culture that most effectively and efficiently creates the necessary behaviors for the creation of superior value for buyers and thus continuous superior performance for the business (Narver and Slater 1990, p. 21). Furthermore, market orientation consists of three behavioral components (i.e., customer orientation, competitor orientation, and interfunctional coordination) and two decision criteria (i.e., long-term focus and profitability). Each of these is described below.

Customer orientation is the sufficient understanding of one's target buyers to be able to create superior value for them continuously. It requires that the seller know the buyer's entire value chain.

Competitor orientation means that a seller understands the short-term strengths and weaknesses and long-term capabilities and strategies of both the key current and the key potential competitors.

Interfunctional coordination is the coordinated utilization of company resources in creating superior value for target customers at any and all points in the buyer's value chain.

Long-term focus in relation to profits and in implementing each of the three behavioral components is required to be market oriented.

Profitability means that the creation of economic wealth is an overriding objective in market orientation.

Description: The authors describe their scale as a one-dimensional construct but develop multiple-item measures for each of the above facets. The final scale is composed of 15 Likert-type items scored on 7-point scales ranging from *the business unit does not engage in the practice at all* (1) to *the business unit engages in the practice to a very great extent* (7). Indices for the first three components are derived by summing the item scores within components and dividing by the number of items in the component. An overall market orientation index is derived by averaging the item scores across all the items of the three behavioral components. The other two components (i.e., long-term focus and profitability) were not included in calculating the market orientation index because of their low levels of reliability.

Development: Based on a literature review, several items were generated by the authors to tap the domain of the construct. Two expert panels reviewed and judged the items for face validity, and several items were deleted. The remaining items were further examined by six SBU (strategic business unit) managers, and based on their evaluation, items were refined that reflect the final instrument. In a separate study, a number of reliability and validity checks were performed.

Samples: As stated above, two panels of academicians (three in each group) and six SBU managers were used in item generation and face validity analysis. A sample of 371 managers from various SBUs responded to the final form of the scale.

Validity: Coefficient alpha estimates for the six-item customer orientation facet were .85 and .87 (the sample of 371 was split into two groups of 190 and 175). Corresponding estimates for the four-item competitor orientation and five-item interfunctional coordination facets were .72 and .73, and .71 and .73, respectively. For the overall sample, the correlations among these three components ranged from .66 to .73, and alpha for the 15-item scale (i.e., items from the three components as one overall scale) was .88. Thus, these three components exhibited satisfactory levels of reliability.

The three-item long-term focus and three-item profit emphasis components exhibited low levels of internal consistency (i.e., .47 and .48 for the former and .14 and .00 for the latter). Subsequently, they were excluded from further analyses.

Discriminant and concurrent validity of the scale were also assessed. Discriminant validity was examined by correlating the 15-item market orientation measure with a measure of human resource management policy. The correlations between the three components of market orientation and the human resource measure ranged from .45 to .53 and were significantly less than the correlations among the three components of market orientation. This was taken as evidence of discriminant validity. The correlations of the overall scale and the three components with measures for return on assets (ROA), low cost advantage, and the use of a differentiation strategy were used to assess concurrent validity. For ROA, correlations with the overall scale and its three components ranged from .23 to .39. For low cost advantage, corresponding correlations ranged from .18 to .23, and for differentiation strategy, the correlations ranged from .33 to .45. This supports the marketing orientation scale's concurrent validity.

Scores: Mean scores were reported for the overall scale and its components across four different business typologies. For the overall scale, grand mean scores (Narver and Slater 1990, Table 5, p. 28) ranged from 4.28 to 4.77. The grand mean ranges for the customer orientation, competitor orientation, and interfunctional coordination components ranged from 4.53 to 5.05, 4.06 to 5.71, and 4.25 to 4.53, respectively.

Source: Narver, John C., and Stanley F. Slater. (1990). "The Effect of Market Orientation on Business Profitability." *Journal of Marketing*, *54*, 20-35.

© 1990 by the American Marketing Association. Scale items taken from Table 1 (p. 24). Reprinted with permission.

Other evidence: Other evidence of reliability and validity is summarized in the meta-analysis market orientation scale development effort reported by Deshpande and Farley (1996) based on their survey of 82 marketing executives. For example, the estimate of reliability was reported to be .90. The correlation with a validity check measure of market orientation was .46. Evidence of predictive validity was provided by correlations of .40 and .51 with two measures of firm performance. Evidence of discriminant validity was provided by low correlations with measures of organizational climate.

Other source: Deshpande, Rohit, and John U. Farley. (1996, December). *Understanding Market Orientation: A Prospectively Designed Meta-Analysis of Three Market Orientation Scales* (Working Paper Report No. 96-125). Cambridge, MA: Marketing Science Institute.

References: N/A

MARKET ORIENTATION
(Narver and Slater 1990)

In our business unit—

1. Our salespeople regularly share information within our business concerning competitors' strategies.

2. Our business objectives are driven primarily by customer satisfaction.

3. We rapidly respond to competitive actions that threaten us.

4. We constantly monitor our level of commitment and orientation to serving customer's needs.

5. Our top managers from every function regularly visit our current and prospective customers.

6. We freely communicate information about our successful and unsuccessful customer experiences across all business functions.

7. Our strategy for competitive advantage is based on our understanding of customers' needs.

8. All of our business functions (e.g. marketing/sales, manufacturing, R & D, finance/accounting, etc.) are integrated in serving the needs of our target markets.

9. Our business strategies are driven by our beliefs about how we can create greater value for customers.

10. We measure customer satisfaction systematically and frequently.

11. We give close attention to after-sales service.

12. Top management regularly discusses competitors' strengths and strategies.

13. All of our managers understand how everyone in our business can contribute to creating customer value.

14. We target customers where we have an opportunity for competitive advantage.

15. We share resources with other business units.

NOTES: Seven-place response format labeled as follows: 1 = *not at all*, 2 = *to a very slight extent*, 3 = *to a small extent*, 4 = *to a moderate extent*, 5 = *to a considerable extent*, 6 = *to a great extent*, and 7 = *to an extreme extent*. Items 2, 4, 7, 9, 10, and 11 reflect "customer orientation." Items 1, 3, 12, and 14 reflect "competitor orientation." Items 5, 6, 8, 13, and 15 reflect "interfunctional coordination."

MARKET ORIENTATION: MARKOR
(Kohli, Jaworski, and Kumar 1993)

Construct: Market orientation is defined as the organization-wide generation of market intelligence pertaining to current and future needs of customers, dissemination of intelligence within the organization, and responsiveness to it (Jaworski and Kohli 1993, p. 54; Kohli and Jaworski 1990; Kohli, Jaworski, and Kumar 1993, p. 468). This view emphasizes an expanded focus that emphasizes the market, interfunctional coordination with respect to market intelligence, and intelligence processing.

Description: The MARKOR scale consists of 20 items distributed across three factors as follows: intelligence generation, six items; intelligence dissemination, five items; and responsiveness, nine items. Seven of the items require reverse scoring. Items are operationalized using a 5-place response format bounded by *strongly disagree* (1) and *strongly agree* (5) (cf. Deshpande and Farley 1996, p. 16). The authors suggest that, based on their multi-informant data, the 20-item MARKOR scale might best be represented by a factor structure that consists of one general market orientation factor, one factor for intelligence generation, one factor for dissemination and responsiveness, one marketing informant factor, and one nonmarketing informant factor.

Development: An initial set of 25 items was developed by the authors from a series of personal interviews. These field interviews were instrumental in the identification of the three basic components of market orientation. The first pretest reduced the number of items to 21. The second pretest expanded the set of items to 32 (see Appendix A, p. 476). The third pretest resulted in several minor modifications to item wording. The single informant sample reduced the items to the 20 statements composing the final scale. Decisions to delete 12 items were based on low reliability, cross loadings, and high residual covariation. The final model consisted of one general factor and three correlated factors.

Substantial evidence from the extensive confirmatory factor analyses for both the single- and multi-informant analyses are reported by Kohli et al. (1993). These results are too voluminous to be reviewed here. However, for competing models, the following fit statistics are typically reported: chi-square, GFI, NCP, RNI, TLI, and NSNR.

Again, the authors suggest that, based upon their multi-informant data, the 20-item MARKOR scale might best be represented by a factor structure that consists of one general market orientation factor, one factor for intelligence generation, one factor for dissemination and responsiveness, one marketing informant factor, and one nonmarketing informant factor. This conclusion is based on the finding that the dissemination and responsiveness factors lacked discriminant validity. Overall, the model fit statistics were modest, yet the complexity of the model is considerable and run across two separate disparate samples. For example, the GFI and RNI statistics for MOD25 (i.e., the recommended configuration) (Kohli et al. 1993, p. 472) were .68 and .74, respectively.

Samples: Three pretest samples comprised 27 marketing and nonmarketing executives, 7 academic experts, and 7 managers, respectively. The single informant sample comprised 230 members of the American Marketing Association. The multi-informant sample consisted of matched samples of senior marketing and nonmarketing executives from 229 strategic business units from 102 firms (Kohli et al. 1993, p. 469).

Validity: The market orientation factors for the multi-informant data were all correlated with six additional constructs: a global measure of market orientation, top management emphasis on market orientation, interfunctional conflict, market-based rewards, employees' commitment, and subjective performance (see Table 4, p. 475). Overall, these findings were concluded to be moderately supportive of the validity of the market orientation construct (Kohli et al. 1993, p. 473).

Scores: Item means and standard deviations for marketing and nonmarketing executives are shown in Appendix A (Kohli et al. 1993, p. 476).

Source: Kohli, Ajay K., Bernard J. Jaworski, and Ajith Kumar. (1993). "MARKOR: A Measure of Market Orientation." *Journal of Marketing Research, 30,* 467-477.
                         © 1993 by the American Marketing Association. Scale items taken from Appendix A (p. 476). Reprinted with permission.

Other evidence: Other evidence of reliability and validity is summarized in the meta-analysis market orientation scale development effort reported by Deshpande and Farley (1996) based on their survey of 82 marketing executives. For example, the estimate of reliability was reported to be .51. The correlation with a validity check measure of market orientation was .45. Evidence of predictive validity was provided by correlations of .42 and .33 with two measures of firm performance. Evidence of discriminant validity was provided by low correlations with measures of organizational climate.

Other sources: N/A

References: Deshpande, Rohit, and John U. Farley. (1996, December). *Understanding Market Orientation: A Prospectively Designed Meta-Analysis of Three Market Orientation Scales* (Working Paper Report No. 96-125). Cambridge, MA: Marketing Science Institute.

                         Jaworski, Bernard J., and Ajay K. Kohli. (1993). "Market Orientation: Antecedents and Consequences." *Journal of Marketing, 57,* 53-70.

                         Kohli, Ajay K., and Bernard J. Jaworski. (1990). "Market Orientation: The Construct, Research Propositions, and Managerial Implications." *Journal of Marketing, 54,* 1-18.

MARKET ORIENTATION: MARKOR
(Kohli, Jaworski, and Kumar 1993)

Intelligence Generation

In this business unit, we meet with customers at least once a year to find out what products or services they will need in the future.

In this business unit, we do a lot of in-house market research.

We are slow to detect changes in our customers' product preferences. (R)

We poll end-users at least once a year to assess the quality of our products and services.

We are slow to detect fundamental shifts in our industry (e.g., competition, technology, regulation). (R)

We periodically review the likely effect of changes in our business environment (e.g., regulation) on customers.

Intelligence Dissemination

We have interdepartmental meetings at least once a quarter to discuss market trends and developments.

Marketing personnel in our business unit spend time discussing customers' future needs with other functional departments.

When something important happens to a major customer or market, the whole business unit knows about it in a short period.

Data on customer satisfaction are disseminated at all levels in this business unit on a regular basis.

When one department finds out something important about our competitors, it is slow to alert other departments. (R)

Responsiveness

It takes us forever to decide how to respond to our competitors' price changes. (R)

For one reason or another, we tend to ignore changes in our customers' product or service needs. (R)

We periodically review our product development efforts to ensure that they are in line with what customers want.

Several departments get together periodically to plan a response to changes taking place in our business environment.

If a major competitor were to launch an intensive campaign targeted at our customers, we would implement a response immediately.

The activities of the different departments in this business unit are well coordinated.

Customer complaints fall on deaf ears in this business unit. (R)

Even if we came up with a great marketing plan, we probably would not be able to implement it in a timely fashion. (R)

When we find that customers would like us to modify a product or service, the departments involved make concerted efforts to do so.

NOTE: (R) Denotes items that are reverse scored.

MARKET ORIENTATION: SUMMARY SCALE
(Deshpande and Farley 1996)

Construct: Based on a review and analysis of three existing market orientation scales (i.e., Deshpande, Farley, and Webster 1993; Kohli, Jaworski, and Kumar 1993; Narver and Slater 1990), Deshpande and Farley (1996) define market orientation as "the set of cross-functional processes and activities directed at creating and satisfying customers through continuous needs assessment" (p. 14). This inductively derived definition reflects the remaining 10 items composing their "Summary Scale for Market Orientation" developed by a prospectively designed meta-analysis. The emphasis is on needs assessment for customers and not on noncustomer-related activities, such as intelligence on competitors.

Description: The scale comprises 10 positively worded statements, each operationalized using a 5-place Likert-type item response format ranging from 1 = *strongly disagree* to 5 = *strongly agree*.

Development: The scale was developed from the pool of 44 items composing the three scales proposed by Narver and Slater (N-S) (1990), Kohli, Jaworski, and Kumar (K-J-K) (1993), and Deshpande, Farley, and Webster (D-F-W) (1993). The 10 items with the highest loadings on the first factor from factor analysis and low item nonresponse were selected to compose the summary scale. The coefficient alpha estimate of internal consistency reliability was .89. (Prior to these analyses, a number of comparisons across the three separate scales were reported. These analyses included tests of scale reliability, discriminant validity, interrater reliability, and predictive validity.)

Sample: A single sample composed of 82 marketing executives from 27 MSI member companies was used in scale development. The sample represented a variety of American and European firms in a number of different industries.

Validity: Little additional evidence was offered regarding the 10-item summary market orientation scale. However, confidence in the generalizability of the scale was enhanced by findings of no mean differences between American and European countries and across industries. Moreover, no differences across geographic areas and industries were found in correlations of the scale with firm performance measures.

Scores: Mean scores were not reported.

Source: Deshpande, Rohit, and John U. Farley. (1996, December). *Understanding Market Orientation: A Prospectively Designed Meta-Analysis of Three Market Orientation Scales* (Working Paper Report No. 96-125). Cambridge, MA: Marketing Science Institute.

   © 1996 by the Marketing Science Institute. Scale items taken from Appendix 3 (p. 19). Reprinted with permission.

Other evidence: N/A

Other sources: N/A

References: Deshpande, Rohit, John U. Farley, and Frederick E. Webster, Jr. (1993). "Corporate Culture, Customer Orientation, and Innovativeness in Japanese Firms: A Quadrad Analysis." *Journal of Marketing*, 57, 23-37.

   Kohli, Ajay K., Bernard J. Jaworski, and Ajith Kumar. (1993). "MARKOR: A Measure of Market Orientation." *Journal of Marketing Research*, 30, 467-477.

   Narver, John, and Stanley Slater. (1990). "The Effect of Market Orientation on Business Profitability." *Journal of Marketing*, 54, 20-35.

MARKET ORIENTATION: SUMMARY SCALE
(Deshpande and Farley 1996)

Our business objectives are driven primarily by customer satisfaction.

We constantly monitor our level of commitment and orientation to serving customer needs.

We freely communicate information about our successful and unsuccessful competitor experiences across all business functions.

Our strategy for competitive advantage is based on our understanding of customers' needs.

We measure customer satisfaction systematically and frequently.

We have routine or regular measures of customer service.

We are more customer focused than our competitors.

I believe this business exists primarily to serve customers.

We poll end-users at least once a year to assess the quality of our products and services.

Data on customer satisfaction are disseminated at all levels in this business unit on a regular basis.

MARKETING RESEARCH: USE OF MARKET RESEARCH: USER
(Menon and Wilcox 1994)

Construct: Research use is conceptualized initially as action-oriented use, knowledge-enhancing use, and affective use (Menon and Wilcox 1994, p. 3). The scale is designed to assess firms' use of market research studies in making policy and strategy decisions, developing knowledge, promoting organizational learning, and improving organizational confidence. The scale also measures the impact of research study findings on firms, as well as the impact of the research process itself (Menon and Wilcox 1994, p. 2). The final model of research use employed to guide scale development contained six second-order factors: (a) congruous use, (b) incongruous use, (c) cynical use, (d) positive use, (e) process use, and (f) product use. Three pairs of the factors were depicted as being correlated (e.g., process use and product use).

Description: The final scale consists of 18 items, with three items representing indicators for each of the six factors. The items are operationalized using a response format ranging from 0 = *not at all* to 5 = *to a great extent*. The items refer to usefulness of individual research projects.

Development: Following tests for the appropriateness of analyzing responses at the study level, exploratory factor analysis revealed six factors corresponding to the hypothesized conceptual model. (The number of initial items was not provided.) Subsequent factor analyses and item correlations with other constructs were used to revise and delete some of the items. Moreover, correlations among some of the second-order factors were noted. These analyses resulted in a 30-item scale with 5 items remaining for each of the six factors.

Exploratory factor analyses on the second data set ($n = 203$) replicated the item loadings and factor structure. As in the first study results, the distinction between appropriate (i.e., product, congruous, process, positive) and inappropriate (i.e., incongruous, cynical) uses of research was identified. A series of confirmatory factor analyses also supported the model. However, several correlated error terms within facets were required to obtain adequate fit (Menon and Wilcox 1994, p. 14). The final 18-item scale was obtained after deleting two items per factor. A final LISREL model estimated for six factors and 18 items revealed the following statistics: GFI = .93, CFI = .98, centrality index = .94, and RMSR = .07. All construct reliabilities were above .74, and variance extracted estimates ranged from .49 to .62.

Samples: Pretest evaluations and help in item generation were provided by 60 marketing managers from four firms. The first of two subsequent survey data collection efforts reflected responses from managers related to 200 individual research projects. These responses represented input from 105 different managers (95 of the 105 managers reacted to two projects each). The second data collection effort reflected responses to 203 research projects obtained from managers listed in one of two professional directories.

Validity: The second study ($n = 203$) was also intended to provide other evidence of validity. Correlations between the six factors based on the 30-item scale and a series of related constructs were offered as evidence of convergent, discriminant, and nomological validity. For example, greater appropriate use of research is associated with greater quality of the project, and the product facet relates most strongly to a measure of global knowledge enhancement. These results and others are summarized by Menon and Wilcox (1994, pp. 17-18).

Scores: Menon and Wilcox (1994, p. 21) report average factor item scores reflecting usage for the 203 projects in the second study as follows: congruous, 3.8; incongruous, 1.3; positive, 3.4; cynical, 1.5; product, 3.5; and process, 2.8.

Source: Menon, Anil, and James B. Wilcox. (1994, December). *USER: A Scale to Measure Use of Market Research* (Working Paper Report No. 94-108). Cambridge, MA: Marketing Science Institute.
© 1994 by the Marketing Science Institute. Scale items taken from Table 2 (p. 12). Reprinted with permission.

Other evidence: N/A

Other sources: N/A

References: N/A

MARKETING RESEARCH: USE OF MARKET RESEARCH: USER
(Menon and Wilcox 1994)

Congruous

One or more findings of the study had a significant direct impact on a decision.

It is possible that without the research results a different decision would have been made.

It was worth waiting for the research results because some of them materially influenced a decision.

Incongruous

The study was used to make a decision which was inconsistent with at least some of the findings and conclusions.

The results of the study were taken out of context to make a decision.

A decision based on the research project was hard to reconcile with the results of the project.

Cynical

The research was used for appearance's sake.

The study was used for political purposes.

At least in part, the study was used as a scapegoat.

Positive

The study was to validate or confirm our understanding of something.

The research study was used to build awareness and commitment.

The research study was used to promote awareness and appreciation for an issue of importance.

Process

We learned from having to clarify the problem to be addressed by the research.

Apart from what we learned from the results, doing the study was educational.

We gained new insights while providing the researchers with background information on the company, business, and/or competitive situation.

Product

The study results were used to provide new insights.

The study results provided new knowledge about something.

The study results were used to learn something new about our business.

MARKETING RESEARCH: TRUST AND USE OF MARKET RESEARCH
(Moorman, Zaltman, and Deshpande 1992)

Construct: Moorman, Zaltman, and Deshpande (1992) describe the results of their research regarding the relationships between providers and users of marketing research across four different types of user-provider dyads. As part of their study, hypotheses are offered that describe the role of trust as a determinant of the use of marketing research. Measures are described for five key concepts: (a) user trust in researcher, (b) perceived quality of interaction, (c) researcher involvement, (d) commitment to relationship, and (e) research utilization. The first four measures were developed specifically for the study described by Moorman et al. (1992) and are described here. Research utilization was adapted from Deshpande and Zaltman (1982).

Briefly, the following definitions were used to guide measurement development. Trust is defined as a willingness to rely on an exchange partner in whom one has confidence. This definition was adapted to apply to user trust in a researcher. Researcher involvement refers to the extent to which users feel it is important to involve researchers in the design, production, and use of market information. Perceived quality of interactions is the degree to which users view user-researcher interactions as productive. Commitment to the relationship is defined as an enduring desire to maintain a valued relationship (cf. Moorman et al. 1992, p. 316).

Description: User trust in researcher, perceived quality of interaction, and commitment to relationship were operationalized as the average of five, five, and three 7-place, *strongly disagree* to *strongly agree* items, respectively. Researcher involvement assessed the respondent's perceived importance of the researcher's involvement in each of five project activities using 7-place scales bounded by *very unimportant* and *very important*. Instructions asked respondents to reply regarding their most recently completed research project.

Development: A first pretest involving 10 academic colleagues and 10 practitioners was used to judge the appropriateness of items as construct indicators. A second pretest using the responses from 27 researcher users was employed to verify that trust could be differentiated from related concepts such as quality of interaction and commitment. After data collection, the measures were improved by deleting items with low corrected item-to-total correlations. Subsequent factor analyses revealed that items for each variable loaded on a single factor. Coefficient alpha estimates for the four new variables were as follow: TRUST, .84; INTERACT, .86; INVOLVE, .79; and COMMIT, .78 (Moorman et al. 1992, p. 320).

Sample: A total of 779 research users responded to mail surveys from an original eligible sample of 1,719. The sample was generated by calls to 200 top advertising firms. The sample comprised individuals responding to one of four dyads: internal marketing manager-internal marketing researcher (n = 192), internal marketing manager-external marketing researcher (n = 172), internal marketing researcher-external marketing researcher (n = 331), and internal nonmarketing manager-internal marketing researcher (n = 84).

Validity: Evidence of validity is offered from use of the measures in subsequent model and hypothesis tests. The ability of the variables to operate generally as expected within their theoretical framework offers support for measurement validity. Moreover, this conclusion is supported by a number of predicted main and interaction effects. Modest intercorrelations among the five construct measures provide some additional evidence of discriminant validity.

Scores: Means, standard deviations, and variable intercorrelations are presented in Table 2 (Moorman et al. 1992, p. 320).

Source: Moorman, Christine, Gerald Zaltman, and Rohit Deshpande. (1992). "Relationships Between Providers and Users of Market Research: The Dynamics of Trust Within and Between Organizations." *Journal of Marketing Research*, 29, 314-328.
       © 1992 by the American Marketing Association. Scale items taken from Appendix (pp. 325-326). Reprinted with permission.

Other evidence: N/A

Other sources: N/A

Reference: Deshpande, Rohit, and Gerald Zaltman. (1982). "Factors Affecting the Use of Market Research Information: A Path Analysis." *Journal of Marketing Research, 19*, 14-31.

MARKETING RESEARCH: TRUST AND USE OF MARKET RESEARCH
(Moorman, Zaltman, and Deshpande 1992)

User Trust in Researcher

If I or someone from my department could not be reached by our researcher, I would be willing to let my researcher make important research decisions without my involvement.

If I or someone from my department were unable to monitor my researcher's activities, I would be willing to trust my researcher to get the job done right.

I trust my researcher to do things I can't do myself.

I trust my researcher to do things my department can't do itself.

I generally do not trust my researcher. (R)

Perceived Quality of Interaction

Disagreements between my researcher and me tend to be handled productively.

My meetings with my researcher produce novel insights.

My researcher displays a sound strategic understanding of my business in his/her interactions with me.

My researcher is very customer-oriented in his/her interactions with us.

My interactions with my researcher are productive.

Researcher Involvement

For this project, how important was the involvement of your internal researcher in each of the following five activities?
   –Problem definition
   –Research design
   –Data analysis
   –Development of recommendations
   –Implementation of recommendations

Commitment to Relationship

I am committed to my relationship with my researcher.

I consider my researcher to be a part of my department.

I really care about the fate of my working relationship with my researcher.

Research Utilization (adapted from Deshpande and Zaltman 1982)

Without this research information, the decisions would have been very different.

No decision would have been made without this research information.

The majority of the research information from this project was not used.

In your opinion, what proportion of this particular study need not have been done (for whatever reason): _____%

NOTE: (R) denotes reverse-scored item.

7

Sales, Sales Management, Organizational Behavior, and Interfirm-Intrafirm Issues

SALES, SALES MANAGEMENT, AND ORGANIZATIONAL BEHAVIOR ISSUES

Job Satisfaction Measures

JOB CHARACTERISTIC INVENTORY: JCI
(Sims, Szilagyi, and Keller 1979)

Construct: The Job Characteristic Inventory (JCI) measures characteristics of job satisfaction and performance for six areas of the job. These areas, originally described by Turner and Lawrence (1965), are as follow (Sims, Szilagyi, and Keller 1979):

Variety is the degree to which a job requires employees to perform a wide range of operations in their work and/or the degree to which employees must use a variety of equipment and procedures in their work.

Autonomy is the extent to which employees have a major say in scheduling their work, selecting the equipment they will use, and deciding on procedures to be followed.

Task identity is the extent to which employees do an entire or whole piece of work and can clearly identify the results of their efforts.

Feedback is the degree to which employees receive information as they are working which reveals how well they are performing on the job.

Dealing with others is the degree to which a job requires employees to deal with other people to complete the work.

Friendship opportunities is the degree to which a job allows employees to talk with one another on the job and to establish informal relationships with other employees at work.

Description: Thirty items compose the final JCI (Sims et al. 1979, p. 200). Responses for each question were made on 5-point Likert-type scales, some with scale points from *very little* = 1, to *a moderate amount* = 3, to *very much* = 5, and others with scale points from *minimum amount* = 1, to *a moderate amount* = 3, to *a maximum amount* = 5. Scores are averaged across items within each subscale to form subscale indices.

397

Development: After a review of the literature, a questionnaire was administered to a medical center sample that contained 23 items. Many of the items were taken from the Hackman-Lawler (1971) research which investigated employee reactions to job characteristics. In order to improve reliability, other questions which appeared to have face validity were added to the item pool. Based on the results of the validity and reliability analysis of this sample, certain items were deleted from the scale and 14 new items were developed and administered to the manufacturing firm. This resulted in 37 items retained. These 37 items were administered to subjects in a manufacturing firm sample, and based on factor and reliability analyses, the final 30-item JCI was derived. Several estimates of validity were reported.

Samples: The JCI was administered to two highly dissimilar samples. The first sample consisted of 1,161 medical center personnel (containing several subsamples), and the second sample was 192 managers and supervisors employed by a manufacturing organization.

Validity: The range of reliabilities coefficients for the final scale (after a subsequent item analysis) was .72 to .86 across subscales. Factor analysis results confirmed the a priori dimensionality of the JCI across samples, and the scale's validity was also assessed. Multiple discriminant analysis showed that the JCI successfully discriminated among satisfied and dissatisfied employees, offering evidence of predictive validity. Furthermore, correlations of the JCI subscales with measures of task complexity, role ambiguity, adequacy of authority, and warmth showed evidence of discriminant validity in a multitrait-multimethod format. For example, correlations between the JCI subscales and task complexity ranged from .11 to .53, and correlations between the JCI subscales and role ambiguity ranged from −.10 to −.41.

Scores: Mean scores and standard deviations for each subdimension are reported for the two sample groups in Tables 2 and 7 (Sims et al. 1979, pp. 203, 207). For example, the mean scores for the manufacturing sample with respect to the six factors were as follow: variety, 3.46; autonomy, 3.76; feedback, 3.33; task identity, 3.66; dealing with others, 3.68; and friendship, 3.77.

Source: Sims, Henry P., Jr., Andrew D. Szilagyi, and Robert T. Keller. (1979). "The Measurement of Job Characteristics." *Academy of Management Journal, 19,* 195-212.
    © 1979 by *Academy of Management Journal.* Scale items taken from Figure 1 (p. 200). Reprinted with permission.

Other evidence: In a marketing application, Hunt, Chonko, and Wood (1985) used a version of the JCI for four a priori job dimensions of variety, autonomy, identity, and feedback. The sample used was 916 marketing management personnel and marketing researchers. A confirmatory factor analysis was performed. The results indicated a high degree of reliability for all four job dimensions, with reliabilities ranging from .79 to .89, and average variance explained ranging from .48 to .69.

Other source: Hunt, Shelby D., Lawrence B. Chonko, and Van R. Wood. (1985). "Organizational Commitment and Marketing." *Journal of Marketing, 49,* 112-126.

References: Hackman, J. R., and E. E. Lawler. (1971). "Employee Reactions to Job Characteristics." *Journal of Applied Psychology, 55,* 259-286.

    Turner, A. N., and P. R. Lawrence. (1965). *Industrial Jobs and the Worker.* Boston: Harvard University Graduate School of Business Administration.

JOB CHARACTERISTIC INVENTORY: JCI
(Sims, Szilagyi, and Keller 1979)

1. To what extent do you start work that is finished by another employee?

2. How much variety is there in your job?

3. How much are you left on your own to do your own work?

4. How often do you see projects or jobs through to completion?

5. To what extent do you find out how well you are doing on the job as you are working?

6. How much opportunity is there to meet individuals whom you would like to develop friendships with?

7. How much of your job depends upon your ability to work with others?

8. How repetitious are your duties?

9. To what extent are you able to act independently of your supervisor in performing your job function?

10. To what extent do you complete work that has been started by another employee?

11. To what extent do you receive information from your superior on your job performance?

12. To what extent do you have the opportunity to talk informally with other employees while at work?

13. To what extent is dealing with other people a part of your job?

14. How similar are the tasks you perform in a typical work day?

15. To what extent are you able to do your job independently of others?

16. To what extent is your job equivalent to being one small cog in a big machine?

17. To what extent are the results of your work clearly evident?

18. The feedback from my supervisor on how well I'm doing.

19. Friendship from my co-workers.

20. The opportunity to talk to others on my job.

21. The opportunity to do a number of different things.

22. The freedom to do pretty much what I want on my job.

23. The degree to which the work I'm involved with is handled from beginning to end by myself.

24. The opportunity to find out how well I am doing on my job.

25. The opportunity in my job to get to know other people.

26. Working pretty much by myself.

27. The amount of variety in my job.

28. The opportunity for independent thought and action.

29. The opportunity to complete work I start.

30. The feeling that I know whether I am performing my job well or poorly.

31. The opportunity to develop close friendships in my job.

32. Meeting with others in my work.

33. The control I have over the pace of my work.

34. The opportunity to do a job from the beginning to end (i.e., the chance to do a whole job).

35. The extent of feedback you receive from individuals other than your supervisor.

36. To what extent do you do a "whole" piece of work (as opposed to doing part of a job which is finished by some other employee?)

37. The opportunity, in my job, to give help to other people.

NOTES: All 37 items examined are listed above. The final version of the scale is composed of items 2 through 9, 11 through 15, and 18 through 35. The item numbers composing each factor are as follow: variety—2, 8, 14, 21, and 27; autonomy—3, 9, 15, 22, 28, and 33; feedback—5, 11, 18, 24, and 30; dealing with others—7, 13, and 35; task identity—4, 23, 29, and 34; and friendship—6, 12, 19, 20, 25, 31, and 32.

Items 1 through 17 and 36 are scored on the *very little* to *very much* format, and the remaining items are scored on the *minimum amount* to *maximum amount* format.

JOB IN GENERAL: JIG
(Ironson, Smith, Brannick, Gibson, and Paul 1989)

Construct: The JIG was designed to assess overall feelings about one's job. As such, it is considered a global measure of job satisfaction (Ironson, Smith, Brannick, Gibson, and Paul 1989).

Description: The JIG is composed of 18 adjective or short phrase evaluative items concerning feelings about one's job. The format and scoring of the items are the same as those for the JDI (Smith, Kendall, and Hulin 1969). That is, a respondent is asked to write "Y" (for Yes) if an item applies to his work, "N" (for No) if an item does not apply, and "?" if the respondent is undecided. A score of 3 is given to a "Y" answer for a positive item and "N" for a negative item. A score of 2 is given for a "?," and a score of 1 is given to a "Y" for a negative item and "N" for a positive item. The JIG is considered a unidimensional measure of global job satisfaction. Thus, it appears that item scores can be summed to form an overall score.

Development: A pool of 42 adjectives and short phrases from an extensive literature review served as the initial pool of items. Twenty-two of these items were negatively worded. These items were administered to a combined sample (*n* = 1,149). Via item-to-total correlations, principal components analysis, and an index of favorableness, the pool of items was trimmed to a smaller number. Then, with another large sample (*n* = 4,490) from archival data, the index of favorableness was used to reduce the JIG to its final 18-item form. Numerous estimates of reliability and validity were assessed.

Samples: The combined sample of 1,149 was composed of employees from an urban county in Florida. The archival sample of 4,490 was from the Bowling Green Data Archives and was composed of employees of a wide range of job descriptions (i.e., blue-collar, white-collar, professional, etc.). Another large sample of 648 nuclear power plant workers was also collected (see Ironson et al. [1989, pp. 194-195] for a description of the samples and subsamples).

Validity: Principal components analysis of the 18-item JIG showed that the first general factor accounted for 87% of the variance in the data, supporting the scale's unidimensionality. Coefficient alpha for the scale ranged from .91 to .95 across the samples and subsets of the samples. Correlations of the JIG with other measures of job satisfaction ranged from .67 to .80, providing evidence of convergent validity for the scale. Discriminant validity was also demonstrated, as the JIG showed significantly greater validity than the JDI scales in predicting work-related variables. Also, with the nuclear power plant sample, the JIG showed strong evidence of nomological validity. For example, correlations of the JIG with intention to leave, trust in management, and job definition were −.54, .51, and .50, respectively.

Scores: Percentages of those respondents responding favorably to each item are offered in Table 1 of Ironson et al. (1989). These scores range from .23 to .88.

Source: Ironson, G. H., P. C. Smith, M. T. Brannick, W. M. Gibson, and K. B. Paul. (1989). "Construction of a Job in General Scale: A Comparison of Global, Composite, and Specific Measures." *Journal of Applied Psychology*, 74(2), 193-200.
      © 1989 by the American Psychological Association. Scale items taken from Table 1 (p. 195). Reprinted with permission.

References: Smith, Patricia C., Loring M. Kendall, and Charles L. Hulin. (1969). *The Measurement of Satisfaction in Work and Retirement: A Strategy for the Study of Attitudes.* Chicago: Rand McNally.

JOB IN GENERAL: JIG
(Ironson, Smith, Brannick, Gibson, and Paul 1989)

1. pleasant

2. bad*

3. ideal

4. waste of time*

5. good

6. undesirable*

7. worthwhile

8. worst than most*

9. acceptable

10. superior

11. better than most

12. disagreeable*

13. makes me content

14. inadequate*

15. excellent

16. rotten*

17. enjoyable

18. poor*

NOTES: *Denotes items that are reverse coded. See the JDI (Smith et al. 1969) for instructions.

JOB SATISFACTION
(Wood, Chonko, and Hunt 1986)

Construct: Wood, Chonko, and Hunt (1986) characterize job satisfaction as multidimensional. The dimensions of satisfaction were as follows: (a) satisfaction with information, (b) satisfaction with variety and freedom, (c) satisfaction with the ability to complete tasks (i.e., closure), and (d) satisfaction with pay and security.

Description: The job satisfaction measure consists of 14 items scored on a Likert-type format (with 1 = *Strongly Disagree* and 7 = *Strongly Agree*). Item scores are summed within dimensions to form dimension scores, or scores on the 14 items can be summed to form an overall index of satisfaction.

Development: Seven of the job satisfaction items were developed by Wood et al. (1986) from pretested responses, and they focused on various elements of the respondents' jobs. Additionally, seven items were selected from the Job Characteristic Inventory (Sims, Szilagyi, and Keller 1976). These 14 items served both as the initial pool and the final version of the scale. Factor analysis and coefficient alpha was used to judge the scale's dimensionality and reliability.

Sample: A self-administered questionnaire was sent to 4,282 marketing practitioners. The subjects were chosen based on a systematic sample of one out of every four marketing practitioners in the American Marketing Association directory. Educators and students were excluded from the sample. A total of 1,076 usable questionnaires were returned.

Validity: An alpha coefficient of .89 was obtained for the total 14-item satisfaction scale. Alpha coefficients for each of the factors were .93 for information, .88 for variety and freedom, .80 for completion of tasks, and .56 for pay and security. The 14 satisfaction items were factor analyzed, and the four-factor solution of (a) satisfaction with information, (b) satisfaction with variety and freedom, (c) satisfaction with ability to complete tasks, and (d) satisfaction with pay and security was retained. Factor loadings ranged from .51 to .91 on the respective factors, and the four-factor solution accounted for 81% of the variance in the data. Furthermore, correlations of the satisfaction dimensions with income ranged from .08 to .23, providing some evidence of nomological validity.

Scores: Mean scores indicated that the average respondent had a high perceived satisfaction score with respect to job variety, job closure, the job in general, and a marketing career. The overall mean for the 14-item job satisfaction scale was 40.95, with a standard deviation of 2.47. The means and standard deviations for each factor are as follows: satisfaction with information, 13.69 (6.40); satisfaction with variety, 12.91 (6.23); satisfaction with closure, 4.65 (2.37); and satisfaction with pay, 6.78 (3.06).

Source: Wood, Van R., Lawrence B. Chonko, and Shelby Hunt. (1986). "Social Responsibility and Personal Success: Are They Incompatible?" *Journal of Business Research*, *14*, 193-212.

     © 1986 by Elsevier Science. Scale items taken from Appendixes A and B (pp. 207-208). Reprinted with permission from Elsevier Science.

Other sources: N/A

Reference: Sims, Henry P., Jr., Andrew D. Szilagyi, and Robert T. Keller. (1976). "The Measurement of Job Characteristics." *Academy of Management Journal*, *19*, 195-212.

JOB SATISFACTION
(Wood, Chonko, and Hunt 1986)

Satisfaction With Information

1. I am satisfied with the information I receive from my superior about my job performance.

2. I receive enough information from my supervisor about my job performance.

3. I receive enough feedback from my supervisor on how well I'm doing.

4. There is enough opportunity in my job to find out how I am doing.

Satisfaction With Variety

5. I am satisfied with the variety of activities my job offers.

6. I am satisfied with the freedom I have to do what I want on my job.

7. I am satisfied with the opportunities my job provides me to interact with others.

8. There is enough variety in my job.

9. I have enough freedom to do what I want in my job.

10. My job has enough opportunity for independent thought and action.

Satisfaction With Closure

11. I am satisfied with the opportunities my job gives me to complete tasks from beginning to end.

12. My job has enough opportunity to complete the work I start.

Satisfaction With Pay

13. I am satisfied with the pay I receive for my job.

14. I am satisfied with the security my job provides me.

JOB SATISFACTION OF INDUSTRIAL SALESPERSON: INDSALES
(Churchill, Ford, and Walker 1974)

Construct: This scale was designed to measure the job satisfaction construct as it applies to the industrial salesperson. Differences in occupational requirements and work settings make generalizations about satisfaction quite tenuous, and the unique character of the industrial salesperson's role provided the rationale for the development of this scale. Although the construct's domain was originally defined on eight dimensions, seven determinants of job satisfaction were retained: (a) the job itself, (b) fellow workers, (c) supervisors, (d) company policy and support, (e) pay, (f) promotion and advancement, and (g) customers.

Description: The final version of the instrument consisted of 95 items which represent the seven components listed above. A 5-point Likert-type scale format ranging from *strongly disagree* to *strongly agree* was used for each item. Numerical scores for negatively stated items were reversed so that a higher numerical value on any item always indicated more satisfaction. Item scores can be summed within each dimension to form indices for each dimension, or overall to form an overall INDSALES score.

Development: Initially, the construct's domain was defined as consisting of eight determinants of job satisfaction. Through an extensive literature review and open-ended questions with salespeople and a work psychologist, items were generated for each determinant. The initial pool consisted of 185 items. The first purification study reduced the pool to 117 items through several item analytic procedures ($n = 183$). Via factor and reliability analysis of the data from the second purification study ($n = 265$), 95 items that consistently demonstrated satisfactory reliability were retained for the final scale. Furthermore, though the a priori specification of the component structure posited eight dimensions, seven dimensions for the 95 items were retained in the final version. Several other reliability and validity checks were also reported.

Samples: Following open-ended interviews with salespersons in a variety of industries and an experienced psychologist who had worked with industrial salespersons, two purification studies were conducted to develop the final form of the scale. In the first study, the respondents consisted of 183 salespersons randomly selected from the commercial division of a large manufacturer of heating and cooling equipment. In the second study, a more heterogeneous sample consisting of 265 salespersons was drawn from 10 firms in seven different industries ranging from machine tools and computers to cleaning supplies.

Validity: Alpha estimates of internal consistency reliability for the overall scale and each of its components ranged from .82 to .96.

Also, split-half correlations for the total scale were above the .80 level for five of the seven components. Only the fellow worker and the customer component had split-half correlations below .80. An assessment of construct validity was made by examining whether the measure behaves as expected with respect to other related constructs. Specifically, there is a substantial amount of empirical support to suggest that dissatisfied employees tend to quit their jobs more frequently than satisfied employees. The measures obtained were related to turnover in the sample of respondents. Approximately 5 months after the instrument was administered, all the salespersons of the participating firms who had subsequently quit their jobs were contacted. Twelve salespersons had completed both forms of the instrument. The total mean INDSALES score for these salespersons was 47.35, as compared with an average of 50.13 for all other respondents from the same firms. While the difference in test scores was not statistically significant, it was in the predicted direction, $z = 1.10$, $p < .28$.

Scores: The distribution of raw scores obtained in the final administration of the job satisfaction scale was normalized employing the method of "base-line units of unequal size." The normalized scores were then standardized so as to have a mean of 50 and a standard deviation of 10. Table 4 on page 260 presents a sample of the normalized scores for each component as well as the total scale.

Source: Churchill, Gilbert, Neil M. Ford, and Orville C. Walker, Jr. (1974). "Measuring the Job Satisfaction of Industrial Salesmen." *Journal of Marketing Research, 11*, 254-260.

© 1974 by the American Marketing Association. Scale items taken from Table 2 (p. 258). Reprinted with permission.

Other evidence: The satisfaction scales for work, coworkers, supervision, pay, and promotion of the INDSALES and the JDI (Smith, Kendall, and Hulin 1969) were compared from a national sample of 209 salesmen in the health care industry (Futrell 1979). The seven satisfaction scales in INDSALES showed high internal reliability, ranging from .85 to .96. The five satisfaction scales common to INDSALES and the JDI showed evidence of convergent and discriminant validity for IND-SALES, as correlations ranged from .36 to .75 across the corresponding INDSALES and JDI facets.

Childers, Churchill, Ford, and Walker (1980) designed a study to replicate and refine the INDSALES instrument. A mail survey of 113 industrial salespeople was used in the study. A systematic purification process was used to reduce the length of the scale to 61 items with respect to the seven components of job satisfaction. Results showed that the scale reduction was accomplished without compromising its desirable reliability and validity properties. The reliability of the overall scale was .97. The coefficient alphas for the seven facets ranged from .80 to .94. This revised INDSALES measure was also correlated with measures of role conflict and ambiguity. These correlations were –.25 and –.32 for the overall INDSALES score and role ambiguity and conflict, respectively. These correlations offer evidence of nomological validity.

Comer, Machleit, and Lagace (1989) conducted a psychometric assessment of the reduced version of INDSALES (Childers et al. 1980). With the use of a split sample of 295 sales representatives, qualitative techniques were coupled with factor, item, and reliability analyses (via LISREL) to further reduce INDSALES to a balanced 28-item scale with respect to the seven determinants of job satisfaction. The reliabilities of the reduced scale dimensions ranged from .77 to .87, and correlations among the seven facets ranged from .07 to .68, offering evidence of discriminant validity among the facets. Nomological validity was also confirmed. For example, the total score on the 28-item scale was correlated with role ambiguity (–.38), with reward power (.59), with closeness of supervision (.37), and with propensity to leave (–.38). These correlations offer evidence of nomological validity.

A 28-item shortened version of INDSALES was examined by Lagace, Goolsby, and Gassenheimer (1993) on a sample of 311 insurance salespersons. The results of this replication were compared to earlier results reported by Comer et al. (1989), who analyzed the responses of an industrial sample. Overall, the findings support the seven-factor revised scale in which four indicators per factor are employed. For the Lagace et al. (1993) total sample, GFI and AGFI estimates for a seven-factor correlated model were .85 and .82, respectively. Factor reliabilities ranged from .76 to .92, and RMSR was .07. Item indicators and factor intercorrelations are summarized as well. Similar support for the revised scale was provided by the analysis of psychometric properties described earlier by Comer et al. (1989).

Other sources: Childers, Terry L., Gilbert A. Churchill, Neil M. Ford, and Orville C. Walker, Jr. (1980). "Towards a More Parsimonious Measurement of Job Satisfaction for the Industrial Salesforce." In Richard P. Bagozzi et al. (Eds.), *AMA Educator's Conference Proceedings* (pp. 344-349). Chicago: American Marketing Association.

Comer, James M., Karen A. Machleit, and Rosemary R. Lagace. (1989). "Psychometric Assessment of a Reduced Version of INDSALES." *Journal of Business Research, 18*, 291-302.

Futrell, Charles M. (1979). "Measurement of Salespeople's Job Satisfaction: Convergent and Discriminant Validity of Corresponding INDSALES and Job Description Index Scales." *Journal of Marketing Research, 16*, 594-597.

Lagace, Rosemary R., Jerry R. Goolsby, and Jule B. Gassenheimer. (1993). "Scaling and Measurement: A Quasi-Replicative Assessment of a Revised Version of INDSALES." *Journal of Personal Selling and Sales Management, 13*, 65-72.

Reference: Smith, Patricia C., Loring M. Kendall, and Charles L. Hulin. (1969). *The Measurement of Satisfaction in Work and Retirement: A Strategy for the Study of Attitudes.* Chicago: Rand McNally.

JOB SATISFACTION OF INDUSTRIAL SALESPERSON: INDSALES
(Churchill, Ford, and Walker 1974)

The "Overall" Job

1. My work is creative.

2. My work is valuable.

3. I have plenty of freedom on my job to use my own judgment.

4. My job is exciting.

5. My work is satisfying.

6. I'm really doing something worthwhile in my job.

7. I am unproductive in my work.*

8. My work is useless.*

9. My job is interesting.

10. My work is challenging.

11. My job is often dull and monotonous.*

12. My work gives me a sense of accomplishment.

Co-workers

1. My fellow workers are stimulating.

2. The people I work with help each other out when someone falls behind or gets in a tight spot.

3. My fellow workers are boring.*

4. My fellow workers are sociable.

5. My fellow workers are pleasant.

6. My fellow workers are obstructive.*

7. The people I work with are very friendly.

8. My fellow workers are loyal.

9. The people I work with get along well together.

10. My fellow workers are selfish.*

11. My fellow workers are intelligent.

12. My fellow workers are responsible.

Supervision

1. My supervisor is up-to-date.

2. My boss has taught me a lot about sales.

3. My sales manager has the work well organized.

4. My boss does a good job of helping sales representatives develop their own potential.

5. My sales manager has always been fair in his dealings with me.

6. My boss really takes the lead in stimulating sales efforts.

7. My supervisor is intelligent.

8. My sales manager is too interested in his own success to care about the needs of employees.*

9. My sales manager gives credit and praise for work well done.

10. My sales manager lives up to his promises.

11. My sales manager knows very little about his job.*

12. My sales manager is tactful.

13. My sales manager really tries to get our ideas about things.

14. My sales manager doesn't seem to try too hard to get our problems across to management.*

15. My sales manager sees that we have the things we need to do our jobs.

16. My sales manager gets the sales personnel to work together as a team.

Company Policy and Support

1. Compared with other companies, employee benefits here are good.

2. Sometimes when I learn of management's plans I wonder if they know the territory situation at all.*

3. The company's sales training is not carried out in a well-planned program.*

4. I feel that the company is highly aggressive in its sales promotion efforts.

5. Management is progressive.

6. Management keeps us in the dark about things we ought to know.*

7. Management ignores our suggestions and complaints.*

8. Our sales goals are set by the higher-ups without considering market conditions.*

9. Management really know its job.

10. This company operates efficiently and smoothly.

11. Our home office isn't always cooperative in servicing our customers.*

12. I'm satisfied with the way employee benefits are handled around here.

13. We have a real competitive advantage in selling because of the quality of our products.

14. Management is weak.*

15. I have confidence in the fairness and honesty of management.

16. Management here is really interested in the welfare of employees.

17. The company has satisfactory profit sharing.

18. Sales representatives in this company receive good support from the home office.

19. Management here sees to it that there is cooperation between departments.

20. There isn't enough training for sales representatives who have been on the job for a while.*

21. Management fails to give clear-cut orders and instructions.*

Pay

1. My pay is high in comparison with what others get for similar work in other companies.

2. My pay doesn't give me much incentive to increase my sales.*

3. My selling ability largely determines my earnings in this company.

4. My income provides for luxuries.

5. My pay is low in comparison with what others get for similar work in other companies.*

6. In my opinion the pay here is lower than in other companies.*

7. I'm paid fairly compared with other employees in this company.

8. I am very much underpaid for the work that I do.*

9. My income is adequate for normal expenses.

10. I can barely live on my income.*

11. I am highly paid.

Promotion and Advancement

1. My opportunities for advancement are limited.*

2. Promotion here is based on ability.

3. I have a good chance for promotion.

4. Regular promotions are the rule in this company.

5. The company has an unfair promotion policy.*

6. There are plenty of good jobs here for those who want to get ahead.

7. This is a dead-end job.*

8. My opportunities for advancement are reasonable.

Customers

1. My customers are fair.

2. My customers blame me for problems that I have no control over.*

3. My customers respect my judgment.

4. I seldom know who really makes the purchase decisions in the companies I call upon.*

5. My customers are unreasonable.*

6. My customers are friendly.

7. My customers are loyal.

8. My customers are understanding.

9. My customers are inaccessible.*

10. My customers are well organized.

11. My customers expect too much from me.*

12. My customers are trustworthy.

13. My customers are intelligent.

14. My customers are interested in what I have to say.

15. My customers live up to their promises.

NOTES: In their original paper, Churchill et al. (1974) offered a sample of items. A complete enumeration of items for each INDSALES facet is offered above. * Denotes items that require reverse scoring.

The Childers et al. (1980) 61-item version as well as the Comer et al. (1989) 28-item version of INDSALES are offered below.

The "Overall" Job

1. My work is challenging.

2. My job is often dull and monotonous.*

3. My work gives me a sense of accomplishment.

4. My job is exciting.

5. My job does not provide me with a sense of worthwhile accomplishment.*

6. My work is satisfying.

7. I'm really doing something worthwhile in my job.

8. My job is routine.*

9. My job is interesting.

Fellow Workers

10. My fellow workers are selfish.*

11. My fellow workers are intelligent.

12. My fellow workers are responsible.

13. The people I work with are very friendly.

14. My fellow workers are loyal.

15. My fellow workers are stimulating.

16. The people I work with help each other out when someone falls behind or gets in a tight spot.

17. My fellow workers are obstructive.*

18. My fellow workers are pleasant.

Supervision

19. My regional sales manager is tactful.

20. My regional sales manager really tries to get our ideas about things.

21. My regional sales manager is up-to-date.

22. My regional sales manager does a good job of helping salespersons develop their own potential.

23. My regional sales manager has always been fair in dealings with me.

24. My regional sales manager is intelligent.

25. My regional sales manager gets the salesforce to work together as a team.

26. My regional sales manager gives us credit and praise for work well done.

27. My regional sales manager lives up to his/her promises.

28. My regional sales manager knows very little about his/her job.*

Company Policy and Support

29. Management is progressive.

30. Top management really knows its job.

31. This company operates efficiently and smoothly.

32. The formal recognition programs in this company don't give me much incentive to work harder.*

33. I am satisfied with the way our formal recognition programs are administered.

34. Salespersons in my company receive good support form the home office.

35. Management ignores our suggestions and complaints.*

36. Formal recognition programs in our company compare favorably with those of other companies.

37. I do not get enough formal recognition for the work I do.*

38. Recognition awards are based on ability.

39. I have confidence in the fairness and honesty of management.

Pay

40. My pay is high in comparison with what others get for similar work in other companies.

41. My income provides for luxuries.

42. My pay is low in comparison with what others get for similar work in other companies.*

43. In my opinion, the pay here is lower than in other companies.*

44. I am highly paid.

45. I'm paid fairly compared with other employees in this company.

46. My income is adequate for normal expenses.

47. I'm very much underpaid for the work I do.*

Promotion

48. My opportunities for advancement are limited.*

49. Promotion here is based on ability.

50. I have a good chance for promotion.

51. The company has an unfair promotion policy.*

52. There are plenty of good jobs here for those who want to get ahead.

53. This is a dead-end job.*

54. My opportunities for advancement are reasonable.

Customers

55. My customers are fair.

56. My customers are intelligent.

57. My customers are interested in what I have to say.

58. My customers live up to their promises.

59. My customers are trustworthy.

60. My customers are loyal.

61. My customers are understanding.

NOTES: Items 3, 4, 6, and 7 compose Comer et al.'s (1989) job factor; items 10, 13, 16, and 18 compose their fellow workers factor; items 20, 23, 26, and 27 compose their supervision factor; items 29, 30, 31, and 34 compose their policy factor; items 42, 43, 45, and 46 compose their pay factor; items 48, 50, 51, and 52 compose their promotion factor; and items 58 through 61 compose their customer factor. * Denotes items requiring reverse scoring.

APPENDIX TO JOB SATISFACTION

Probably the most commonly used measure of job satisfaction in both the organizational behavior and sales management literature is the JDI: the Job Descriptive Index (Smith, Kendall, and Hulin 1969). The JDI is a copyrighted proprietary measure, and therefore the JDI items are not reproduced here. The potential user of the JDI should contact Professor Patricia Smith, Department of Psychology, Bowling Green State University, Bowling Green, OH 43403. Below, we offer a summary of the JDI.

JOB DESCRIPTION INDEX: JDI
(Smith, Kendall, and Hulin 1969)

Construct: The Job Description Index (JDI) measures employee satisfaction with five dimensions of a job: the type of work, the pay, the opportunities for promotion, the supervision, and the coworkers on the job (Smith, Kendall, and Hulin 1969, p. 69).

Description: For each of the five job-related categories stated above, there is a corresponding list of adjectives or short phrases. The respondent is instructed to indicate whether each word or phrase is descriptive with respect to the particular facet of his/her job. The respondent is asked to write "Y" (for Yes) if the word applies to a facet of his or her work, "N" (for No) if the word does not apply, and "?" if the respondent is undecided. A score of 3 is given to a "Y" answer for a positive item and "N" for a negative item. A score of 2 is given for a "?," and a score of 1 is given to a "Y" for a negative item and "N" for a positive item. An alternative scoring system is also tenable where a score of 0 is given for a "Y" to a negative item and "N" for a positive item. (It is this alternative scoring system that is more widely used.) Thirty-seven of the items were positively worded, and 35 were negatively worded. Thus, the final version of the JDI included a total of 72 scale items. Eighteen items were written for each of the following three job-related areas: work, supervision, and coworkers. Nine scale items were associated with both the pay and promotion categories. Item scores are summed within categories to form indices for each facet, and can be summed overall to derive an overall satisfaction score. Recently, a revised version of the JDI has been proposed (cf. Smith, Kendall, and Hulin 1985, 1987).

Development: The original item pool was developed by selecting items from other job-satisfaction indices and from available lists of adjectives and short phrases which the authors felt tapped various aspects of job satisfaction. This original search generated from 30 to 40 items per category. Initial item analysis discarded items that failed to show significant differences in response frequency between best and worst jobs. After further item analysis and several purification studies, the final 72-item JDI was derived. A number of reliability and validity checks were performed over several samples.

Samples: Using subjects from a wide range of occupational and educational groups, preliminary JDI scales were administered to 17 janitors, 25 secretaries, and 16 cafeteria workers at Cornell University. The first large-scale study used a convenience sample of 317 Cornell University students and Ithaca residents. Based on the results from the group, the scale was revised and administered to 81 randomly selected employees of a New York Farmers' Cooperative. The next sample of subjects included 163 men and 73 women randomly chosen from three companies. In the final item-development study, the JDI was administered to 192 male employees randomly selected from two plants of an electronics firm. Various tests were performed on the scale after the final item-development study. These studies tested a large sample of approximately 2,600 subjects with varying backgrounds.

Validity: Numerous studies were conducted to assess the discriminant and convergent validity of several aspects of job satisfaction.

Specifically, preliminary studies with small groups of janitors, secretaries, and cafeteria workers showed that the JDI score correlated significantly with supervisory ratings and rankings of job satisfaction. The second study was a more extensive attempt to compare two JDI scoring methods and more direct measures of satisfaction involving global ratings and ratings focused on critical incidents. The study also evaluated effects of item selection on validity. A third study was developed to evaluate the validity and soundness of these final JDI scales and the "Faces" rating scale. This study served as the crucial field test of the measures finally selected. A fourth study was performed that showed not only that the discriminability obtained for the several areas applies to total scores cumulated for each area, but also that adequate discriminability exists at the level of specific items which make up the content of total scales. In sum, the original scale development procedures showed evidence of validity for the JDI. For a more extensive review of validation procedures, the interested reader is referred to the original Smith et al. (1969) book.

A variety of data was provided by Smith et al. (1969) on scale reliability. For example, they report random split-half estimates of reliability ranging from .67 to .78 across subscales, and Spearman-Brown reliabilities between .80 and .88 for the $n = 80$ sample. In addition, factor intercorrelations ranged from .28 to .42 for the sample of 980 males, and .16 to .52 for 627 females.

Scores: Mean scores for the five JDI scales are based on a sample of nearly 2,000 male and more than 600 female workers. The samples were obtained by pooling employees across a total of 21 plants, which represented 19 different companies and 16 different Standard Metropolitan Statistical Areas. For the male sample, means (std. dev.) were 36.57 (10.54), 29.90 (14.53), 22.06 (15.77), 41.10 (10.58), and 43.49 (10.02) for work, pay, promotion, supervisor, and coworkers, respectively. Corresponding means for the female sample were 35.74 (9.88), 27.90 (13.65), 17.77 (13.28), 41.13 (10.05), and 42.09 (10.51). A more comprehensive presentation of means and standard deviations can be found in Smith et al. (1969, p. 80).

Sources: Smith, Patricia C., Loring M. Kendall, and Charles L. Hulin. (1969). *The Measurement of Satisfaction in Work and Retirement: A Strategy for the Study of Attitudes.* Chicago: Rand McNally.

Smith, Patricia C., Loring M. Kendall, and Charles L. Hulin. (1985). *The Job Descriptive Index* (Rev. ed.). Bowling Green, OH: Department of Psychology, Bowling Green State University.

Smith, Patricia C., Loring M. Kendall, and Charles L. Hulin. (1987). "The Revised JDI: A Facelift for an Old Friend." *Industrial Organizational Psychologist*, 24(4), 31-33.

Other evidence: The JDI has been extensively used in the work and organizational behavior literature. For an excellent critical review of the JDI, see Kinicki, Carson, and Schriesheim (1990). There have been several applications of the JDI in the marketing literature as well. Two of these are briefly discussed here.

The satisfaction scales for work, coworkers, supervision, pay, and promotion of the INDSALES (Churchill, Ford, and Walker 1974) and the JDI were compared on a national sample of 209 salesmen in the health care industry (Futrell 1979). Alpha estimates for the JDI facets of work, coworkers, supervisor, pay, and promotion were .85, .93, .91, .67, and .88, respectively. Correlations among facets ranged from .19 to .62. Furthermore, the five satisfaction scales common to INDSALES and the JDI show both convergent and discriminant validity, as correlations for the corresponding JDI and INDSALES dimensions ranged from .36 to .75. Mean scores (std. dev.) for the JDI facets of work, coworkers, supervisor, pay, and promotion were 38.80 (10.54), 45.27 (11.68), 40.72 (13.54), 16.99 (5.70), and 12.86 (8.61), respectively.

Over two time periods, Johnston, Parasuraman, Futrell, and Black (1990) reported construct reliabilities for the overall JDI of .85 and .92. In addition, correlations of the JDI with measures of role conflict, role ambiguity, organizational commitment, propensity to leave an organization, and turnover were –.55, –.36, .58, –.59, and –.33, respectively, offering evidence of nomological validity.

Other sources: Futrell, Charles M. (1979). "Measurement of Salespeople's Job Satisfaction: Convergent and Discriminant Validity of Corresponding INDSALES and Job Description Index Scales." *Journal of Marketing Research, 16,* 594-597.

Johnston, Mark W., A. Parasuraman, Charles M. Futrell, and William C. Black. (1990). "A Longitudinal Assessment of the Impact of Selected Organizational Influences on Salespeople's Organizational Commitment During Early Employment." *Journal of Marketing Research, 27,* 333-344.

References: Churchill, Gilbert, Neil M. Ford, and Orville C. Walker, Jr. (1974). "Measuring the Job Satisfaction of Industrial Salesmen." *Journal of Marketing Research, 11,* 254-260.

Kinicki, Angelo, Kenneth A. Carson, and Chester Schriesheim. (1990). *The Construct Validity of the Job Descriptive Index (JDI): Review, Critique, and Analysis.* Working Paper, Arizona State University.

Another job related measure is the Job Diagnostic Survey: the JDS (Hackman and Oldham 1975). Given its length (more than 10 pages) and that it has seen only limited application in the marketing literature, the JDS items and measures were not included in this volume. However, we do offer a summary of the JDS below. The entire JDS and scoring procedures can be found in Hackman and Oldham (1980, Appendix A, pp. 275-294).

JOB DIAGNOSTIC SURVEY: JDS
(Hackman and Oldham 1975, 1980)

Construct: The JDS is intended to (a) diagnose existing jobs to determine if (and how) they might be redesigned to improve employee motivation and productivity, and (b) evaluate the effects of job changes on employees. The JDS is based on a theory of how job design affects work motivation, and it provides measures of (a) objective job dimensions, (b) individual psychological states resulting from these dimensions, (c) affective reactions of employees to the job and work setting, and (d) individual growth need strength (i.e., the readiness of individuals to respond to "enriched" jobs; Hackman and Oldham 1975, p. 159).

Description: The JDS is a multifaceted, multidimensional measure. Within the four facets alluded to above, there are numerous subdimensions. The "objective job dimensions" facet is composed of seven subscales: skill variety, task identity, task significance, autonomy, feedback from the job, feedback from agents, and dealing with others. All these subscales are composed of three items each. The "psychological states" facet is composed of three subdimensions: experienced meaningfulness of the work (4 items), experienced responsibility for the work (6 items), and knowledge of results (4 items). The "affective reactions" facet is composed of seven subdimensions: general satisfaction (5 items), internal work motivation (6 items), satisfaction with job security (2 items), satisfaction with pay (2 items), social satisfaction (3 items), satisfaction with supervision (3 items), and satisfaction with growth (4 items). The "growth need strength" facet is composed of two subdimensions: "would like" format (6 items) and job choice format (12 items). Across facets and dimensions, item scoring varies from 5- to 7- to 10-point scales. Item scores can be summed and then divided by the number of items within a subdimension to form subdimension scores. Also, a motivating potential score (MPS) can be calculated by combining, in a multiplicative fashion, subdimensions of the job dimensions facet. The JDS also contains questions pertaining to biographical characteristics.

Development: The JDS has its developmental origins in previous methodologies (e.g., Hackman and Lawler 1971). In fact, the JDS reported in Hackman and Oldham (1980) represents a revision of the JDS over an extensive period of time. In essence, the JDS has been revised to maximize the substantive richness of the measures while maintaining high levels of reliability and validity. The JDS measures have undergone extensive structure, reliability, and validity analyses over numerous samples.

Sample: The sample on which the "validity" results presented below were based included 658 employees representing 62 different jobs in seven organizations. These jobs included blue-collar, white-collar, and professional workers from various parts of the country in both industrial and service organizations.

Validity: Spearman-Brown internal consistency estimates ranged from .59 to .78 for the subscales of the "job dimensions" facet. Correlations among the subscales ranged from .02 to .51. Spearman-Brown internal consistency estimates ranged from .72 to .76 for the subscales of the "psychological states" facet. Correlations among the subscales ranged from .32 to .64. Spearman-Brown internal consistency estimates ranged from .56 to .84 for the subscales of the "affective responses" facet. Correlations among the subscales ranged from .31 to .67, and Spearman-Brown internal consistency estimates were .88 and .71 for the "would like" and job choice format of the "growth need" facet. The correlation between these two subscales was .50.

    Various estimates of validity were also offered, including correlations among facet scores and mean differences via ANOVA. For example, the MPS showed a median correlation of $-.25$ with absenteeism and .24 with performance effectiveness. Correlations among all subdimensions of the JDS ranged from $-.01$ to .67. Mean differences (Table 3, p. 163) are also reported that support the validity of the JDS (see also Hackman and Oldham [1980]).

Scores: Mean scores for each subdimension are reported in Table 3, p. 165 of Hackman and Oldham (1975).

Sources: Hackman, J. Richard, and Greg Oldham. (1975). "Development of the Job Diagnostic Survey." *Journal of Applied Psychology*, *60*, 159-170.

    Hackman, J. Richard, and Greg Oldham. (1980). *Work Redesign*. Reading, MA: Addison-Wesley.

Other evidence: The JDS has seen extensive use in the organizational behavior literature (cf. Hackman and Oldham 1980). Our discussion of other evidence will be limited to one marketing application of the JDS. Using a sample of 211 industrial salespeople, Becherer, Morgan, and Richard (1982) reported numerous correlations and regression coefficients pertaining to the subdimensions of the JDS. For example, five of the subdimensions of the objective job dimensions facet (i.e., skill variety, task identity, task significance, autonomy, and feedback) showed correlations ranging from .23 to .36 with internal motivation, .14 to .33 with general satisfaction, and .28 to .48 with growth satisfaction. Similar results were reported for the subdimensions of the psychological states facet. For example, meaningfulness of work showed correlations of .52, .69, and .69 with internal motivation, general satisfaction, and growth satisfaction, respectively.

Other source: Becherer, Richard C., Fred W. Morgan, and Lawrence M. Richard. (1982). "The Job Characteristics of Industrial Salespeople: Relationships to Motivation and Satisfaction." *Journal of Marketing*, *46*, 125-135.

Reference: Hackman, J. Richard, and E. E. Lawler III. (1971). "Employee Reactions to Job Characteristics." *Journal of Applied Psychology Monograph*, *55*, 259-286.

Role Perceptions/Conflict

ROLE AMBIGUITY: MULTI-FACETED,
MULTI-DIMENSIONAL ROLE AMBIGUITY: MULTIRAM
(Singh and Rhoads 1991a, 1991b)

Construct: Singh and Rhoads (1991a, pp. 330-331) define role ambiguity as the following: "Perceived role ambiguity is a multidimensional, multifaceted evaluation about the lack of salient information needed to perform a role effectively. Specifically, this evaluation may include ambiguity about role definition, expectations, responsibilities, tasks, and behaviors in one or more facets of the task environment. These facets, in turn, reflect one or more members of the boundary spanner's role set (e.g., customer, boss) and/or activities required to perform a role (e.g, ethical conduct). Finally, each facet may be viewed as a multidimensional evaluation of the ambiguity about that facet." Thus, role ambiguity reflects the salient uncertainties faced by boundary spanners in performing their roles and embraces the entire domain of ambiguity as defined in the literature (e.g., Kahn, Wolfe, Quinn, and Snoek 1964; King and King 1990).

Description: MULTIRAM contains 45 items, scored on 5-point scales from *very certain* to *very uncertain*, reflecting seven facets of role ambiguity. The seven facets are company, boss, customer, ethical conduct, other managers, coworkers, and family. Furthermore, the first four facets listed are considered multidimensional, and thus, MULTIRAM can be estimated as a second-order factor model. Item scores can be summed within facets and within facet dimensions to form indices of each facet or indices of each dimension within the facets.

Development: A number of procedures were used in scale development and validation. From an extensive literature review and six focus groups from an office equipment supplies firm, the definition and domain of the construct were established. From this, 55 items were developed to reflect the construct's domain. Fifty of these items were retained based on responses from a two-group sample of salespeople and service representatives. These 50 items were administered to a large sample, and both first- and second-order factor analysis (using stringent retainment rules) produced the final form of the seven-facet, 13-dimension MULTIRAM. (Estimates of reliability and factor structure were also performed.) The final version of the scale was then administered to another large sample, and the MULTIRAM's factor structure, reliability, and validity were further assessed.

Samples: Several samples were used in scale construction and validation. First, six focus groups consisting of six to eight people (i.e., salespeople and customer representatives) were used to refine the construct and help generate items. Two more samples (*n* unspecified) were used in item trimming. A sample of 472 from the Association of Sales and Marketing Executives was used in the derivation of the final scale, and a sample of 216 of U.S.-based *Fortune* 500 industrial manufacturer personnel was used in the validation study.

Validity: With the two large samples (*n* = 472 and 216), a number of reliability estimates were gathered. The discussion here though will focus on the second large sample. First, the results of the factor analyses with the first sample were largely replicated by the second sample in that the seven-facet, 13-dimension second-order factor structure was validated, offering support for MULTI-RAM's dimensionality and structure. Second, internal consistency and variance extracted estimates were high across dimensions and facets. Composite reliability for the "company" facet was .77 with a variance extracted estimate of .53. The "flexibility," "work," and "promotion" dimensions of the company facet had coefficient alphas of .70, .84, and .75, respectively. The "boss" facet had a composite reliability of .87 and a variance extracted estimate of .77. Its dimensions of "support" and "demands" both had alphas of .86. The "customer" facet had a composite reliability estimate of .81 and a variance extracted estimate of .59. The dimensions of "interaction," "objection," and "presentation" had alphas of .78, .81, and .81, respectively. The "ethical conduct" facet had a composite reliability estimate of .86 with a variance extracted estimate of .55. The "external" and "internal" dimensions of this facet had alphas of .90 and .83, respectively. The "other managers," "coworkers," and "family" facets had composite reliability estimates of .83, .85, and .86, and variance extracted estimates of .71, .74, and .75, respectively. Corresponding coefficient alphas estimates for these facets were .88, .87, and .88.

Convergent and discriminant validity checks were also obtained by correlating the MULTIRAM's facets with the Rizzo, House, and Lirtzman (1970) measure of role conflict and ambiguity ($n = 472$). The correlations of the MULTIRAM facets were consistently higher with role ambiguity (ranging from .18 to .69) than role conflict (ranging from .10 to .50), offering evidence of convergent and discriminant validity. (These results were also replicated with the sample of 216.) Finally, the MULTIRAM facets were also correlated with a number of job-related variables. The pattern of these correlations strongly suggests nomological validity. For example, the MULTIRAM facets' range of correlations with "job satisfaction" was −.23 to −.64, with "job performance" −.21 to −.43, with "job tension" .19 to .51, and with "turnover intentions" .10 to .52. Other correlational estimates also supported MULTIRAM's validity.

Scores: For the two large samples, means were reported for each facet. These mean values were computed by obtaining an equally weighted composite of the dimensions corresponding to the individual facets. For the first large sample, the means (std. dev.) were 2.28 (.72) for company, 2.42 (.85) for boss, 1.71 (.54) for customers, 1.98 (.78) for ethical conduct, 2.32 (.79) for other managers, 2.96 (.68) for coworkers, and 1.98 (.73) for family. For the second large sample, the means (std. dev.) were 2.55 (.66) for company, 2.46 (.86) for boss, 1.92 (.60) for customers, 2.17 (.76) for ethical conduct, 2.93 (.87) for other managers, 2.22 (.638) for coworkers, and 1.97 (.68) for family (Singh and Rhoads 1991b).

Sources: Singh, Jagdip, and Gary K. Rhoads. (1991a). "Boundary Role Ambiguity in Marketing-Oriented Positions: A Multidimensional, Multifaceted Operationalization." *Journal of Marketing Research, 28,* 328-338.

© 1991 by American Marketing Association Scale items taken from Appendix (pp. 337-338). Reprinted with permission.

Singh, Jagdip, and Gary K. Rhoads. (1991b, June). *Boundary Role Ambiguity in Marketing Positions: Scale Development and Validation* (Marketing Science Institute Technical Working Paper, Report #91-115). Cambridge, MA: Marketing Science Institute.

© 1991 by the Marketing Science Institute.

Other evidence: The 45-item MULTIRAM scale was used by Singh (1993) in his study of the organizational determinants of role ambiguity. Estimates of factor reliability are provided for the Sales and Marketing Executive (SME) sample ($n = 472$). Across the seven multi-item factors, reliabilities ranged from .68 to .87. Estimated parameter estimates for the measurement model are provided in Table 3 for the SME sample and an industrial sample ($n = 216$) (Singh 1993, p. 22). Additional evidence regarding the validity of MULTIRAM was provided from tests of structural equation models in which the boundary role facets were correlated as predicted with antecedents (e.g., autonomy, feedback) and outcomes (e.g., performance, job satisfaction) of role ambiguity.

Challagalla and Shervani (1996) also used MULTIRAM in their research on supervisory control. Reliability estimates for supervisor role ambiguity and customer role ambiguity were .91 and .89, respectively. In addition, these measures predicted performance and satisfaction with supervisor as hypothesized.

Other sources: Challagalla, Goutam N., and Tasadduq A. Shervani. (1996). "Dimensions and Types of Supervisory Control: Effects on Salesperson Performance and Satisfaction." *Journal of Marketing, 60,* 89-105.

Singh, Jagdip. (1993). "Boundary Role Ambiguity: Facets, Determinants, and Impacts." *Journal of Marketing, 57,* 11-31.

References: Kahn, R. L., D. M. Wolfe, R. P. Quinn, and J. D. Snoek. (1964). *Organizational Stress: Studies in Role Conflict and Ambiguity.* New York: John Wiley & Sons.

King, L. A., and D. W. King. (1990). "Role Conflict and Role Ambiguity: A Critical Assessment of Construct Validity." *Psychological Bulletin, 107,* 48-64.

Rizzo, J. R., R. J. House, and S. I. Lirtzman. (1970). "Role Conflict and Ambiguity in Complex Organizations." *Administrative Science Quarterly, 15,* 150-163.

ROLE AMBIGUITY: MULTI-FACETED, MULTI-DIMENSIONAL ROLE AMBIGUITY: MULTIRAM
(Singh and Rhoads 1991)

Company

1. How much freedom of action I am expected to have.

2. How I am expected to handle nonroutine activities on the job.

3. The sheer amount of work I am expected to do.

4. Which tasks I should give priority.

5. How much work I am expected to do.

6. How should I handle my free time on the job.

7. What I can do to get promoted.

8. How vulnerable to job termination I am.

9. What is the critical factor in getting promoted.

Boss

10. To what extent my boss is open to hearing my point of view.

11. How satisfied my boss is with me.

12. How far my boss will go to back me up.

13. The method my boss will use to evaluate my performance.

14. How my boss expects me to allocate my time among different aspects of my job.

15. How to meet the demands of my boss.

16. How should I respond to my boss's criticism.

17. What aspects of my job are most important to my boss.

18. The level of professionalism my boss expects of me.

Customer

19. How I am expected to interact with my customers.

20. How much service I should provide my customers.

21. How I should behave (with customers) while on the job.

22. How I am expected to handle my customers' objections.

23. How I am expected to handle unusual problems and situations.

24. How I am expected to deal with customers' criticism.

25. Which specific company strengths I should present to customers.

26. Which specific product benefits I am expected to highlight for customers.

Ethical Conduct

27. If I am expected to lie a little to win customer confidence.

28. If I am expected to hide my company's foul-ups from my customers.

29. How I should handle ethical issues in my job.

30. How top management expects to handle ethical situations in my job.

31. What I am expected to do if I find others are behaving unethically.

32. The ethical conduct my boss expects of me.

Other Managers

33. How managers in other departments expect me to interact with them.

34. What managers in other departments think about the job I perform.

35. How I should respond to questions/criticisms of managers from other departments.

36. How much information I should provide managers from other departments.

Coworkers

37. How my coworkers expect me to behave on the job.

38. How much information my coworkers expect me to convey to my boss.

39. What my coworkers expect me to do for them.

40. The extent to which my coworkers expect me to share my job-related information with them.

41. The kind of attitude my coworkers expect me to have toward the company.

Family

42. About how much time my family feels I should spend on the job.

43. To what extent my family expects me to share my job-related problems.

44. How my family feels about my job.

45. What my family thinks about the ambiguity (e.g., nonroutine job, no fixed hours of work) in my job.

NOTES: Items are scored 1 = *very certain*, 2 = *certain*, 3 = *neutral*, 4 = *uncertain*, and 5 = *very uncertain*. Items 1 and 2 reflect the "flexibility" dimension of the company facet; items 3, 4, 5, and 6 reflect the "work" dimension of the company facet; and items 7, 8, and 9 reflect the "promotion" dimension of the company facet. Items 10 through 13 reflect the "support" dimension of the boss facet; and items 14 through 18 reflect the "demands" dimension of the boss facet. Items 19 through 21 reflect the "interaction" dimension of the customer facet; items 22 through 24 reflect the "objection" dimension of the customer facet; and items 25 and 26 reflect the "presentation" dimension of the customer facet. Items 27 and 28 reflect the "external" dimension of the ethical conduct facet, and items 29 through 32 reflect the "internal" dimension of the ethical conduct facet. The other three facets (i.e., other managers, coworkers, and family) are single dimensions.

ROLE CONFLICT AND ROLE AMBIGUITY
(Rizzo, House, and Lirtzman 1970)

Construct: Both role conflict (RC) and role ambiguity (RA) are important intervening variables that mediate the effects of various organizational practices on individual and organizational outcomes. Role conflict was defined in terms of dimensions of congruency-incongruency or compatibility-incompatibility in the requirements of the role, where congruency or compatibility is judged relative to a set of standards or conditions that impinge upon role performance. RC components were stated as follows:

1. Conflict between the focal person's internal standards or values and the defined role behavior
2. Conflict between the time, resources, or capabilities of the focal person and defined role behavior
3. Conflict between several roles for the same person that require different or incompatible behaviors, or changes in behavior as a function of the situation (i.e., role overload)
4. Conflicting expectations and organizational demands in the form of incompatible policies, conflicting requests from others, and incompatible standards of evaluation.

Role ambiguity is defined in terms of (a) the predictability of the outcome or responses to one's behavior, and (b) the existence or clarity of behavioral requirements, often in terms of input from the environment, which would serve to guide behavior and provide knowledge that the behavior is appropriate (Rizzo, House, and Lirtzman 1970).

Description: The original RC/RA questionnaire consisted of 30 items, 15 for RA (even numbers) and 15 for RC (odd numbers). It is the reduced 6-item RA and 8-item RC measures, however, that are commonly employed for research purposes. Subjects are requested to respond to the items by indicating the degree to which the condition the item describes existed for him/her on a 7-point scale ranging from *very false* to *very true*. Item scores are summed within the RC and RA scales and then divided by the number of items in each scale to form RC and RA scores.

Development: Approximately 350 items were contained in the original pool of items. Based on the results of factor and item analysis, 30 items reflecting role conflict and role ambiguity emerged as separate dimensions, accounting for 56% of the variance in the data. Factor 1 was named role conflict. Of the 15 role conflict items, 9 with loadings greater than or equal to .30 were retained. Factor 2, role ambiguity, also retained 9 items with loadings greater than or equal to .30. Examination of the items revealed that the two factors strongly parallel the theoretical concepts of role conflict and role ambiguity. Reliability analysis was then used to derive the final 6- and 8-item RA and RC scales. A number of validity checks followed.

Samples: The questionnaire was administered to a 35% random sample of the employees in central offices and main plant of a firm and to a 100% sample of the research and engineering division. The total pool of respondents was treated as two separate samples. There were 199 respondents in the first sample and 91 respondents in the second sample. The instrument was administered to groups ranging in size from 10 to 50. Anonymity was assured, and participation was voluntary.

Validity: Coefficient alpha estimates of internal consistency for the 8-item RC scale were .82 and .82 for Samples 1 and 2. Corresponding estimates for the 6-item RA scale were .78 and .81. The correlations between the two scales were .25 and .01 for the two samples, offering evidence of discriminant validity between RC and RA. Nomological validity was assessed by correlating RC and RA with 41 different work-related attitudes and outcomes. The overall pattern of these correlations showed evidence of nomological validity for RC and RA. For example, the correlations between RA and personal recognition were −.43 and −.56 for the two studies. For

RC, corresponding correlations were −.22 and −.11. Correlations between RA and job-induced tension were .12 and .22, and the correlations between RC and tension were .20 and .12. RC and RA were also positively correlated with a measure of propensity to leave the organization.

Scores: The composite means (std. dev.) for role conflict were 4.19 (1.21) and 3.86 (1.21) for the two samples. With respect to role ambiguity, the means were 3.79 (1.08) and 4.03 (1.15) for the two samples.

Source: Rizzo, John R., Robert J. House, and Sidney I. Lirtzman. (1970). "Role Conflict and Ambiguity in Complex Organizations." *Administrative Science Quarterly*, *15*, 150-164.

© 1970 by *Administrative Science Quarterly*. Scale items taken from Table 1 (p. 156). Reprinted with permission.

Other evidence: The RC and RA scales have been extensively used and examined in the organizational behavior literature. For two meta-analytic reviews of role conflict and role ambiguity, see Fisher and Gitelson (1983) and Jackson and Schuler (1985). The scales have also seen wide application in the sales literature. Two of these applications are briefly reviewed here.

In a study of industrial salespeople's job satisfaction, Teas (1983) reported alpha estimates of .88 and .82 for RC and RA. Correlations of RC with job satisfaction, employee feedback, and leadership consideration were −.51, −.31, and −.44, respectively. Corresponding correlations of these variables with RA were −.42, −.40, and −.48.

In another study, Johnston, Parasuraman, Futrell, and Black (1990) reported internal consistency estimates via LISREL of .807 and .846 for the eight-item role conflict measure, and .807 and .815 for the six-item role ambiguity measure. Furthermore, these scales were found related to a number of organizational variables including satisfactory commitment and leadership, offering support for the scales' nomological validity. For example, the correlation of RC with job satisfaction, commitment, and propensity to leave were −.53, −.49, and .45, respectively. Corresponding correlations of these variables with RA were −.36, −.45, and .47.

Other sources: Johnston, Mark, A. Parasuraman, Charles M. Futrell, and William C. Black. (1990). "A Longitudinal Assessment of the Impact of Selected Organizational Influences on Salespeople's Organizational Commitment During Early Employment." *Journal of Marketing Research*, *27*, 333-344.

Teas, R. Kenneth. (1983). "Supervisory Behavior, Role Stress, and the Job Satisfaction of Industrial Salespeople." *Journal of Marketing Research*, *20*, 84-93.

References: Fisher, C. D., and R. Gitelson. (1983). "A Meta-Analysis and Conceptual Critique of Role Conflict and Ambiguity." *Journal of Applied Psychology*, *68*, 320-333.

Jackson, S. E., and R. S. Schuler. (1985). "A Meta-Analysis and Conceptual Critique of Role Ambiguity and Role Conflict in Work Settings." *Organizational Behavior and Human Decision Processes*, *36*, 16-78.

ROLE CONFLICT AND ROLE AMBIGUITY
(Rizzo, House, and Lirtzman 1970)

1. I have enough time to complete my work.

2. I feel certain about how much authority I have.

3. I perform tasks that are too easy or boring.

4. Clear, planned goals and objectives for my job.

5. I have to do things that should be done differently.

6. Lack of policies and guidelines to help me.

7. I am able to act the same regardless of the group I am with.

8. I am corrected or rewarded when I really don't expect it.

9. I work under incompatible policies and guidelines.

10. I know that I have divided my time properly.

11. I receive an assignment without the manpower to complete it.

12. I know what my responsibilities are.

13. I have to buck a rule or policy in order to carry out an assignment.

14. I have to "feel my way" in performing my duties.

15. I receive assignments that are within my training and capability.

16. I feel certain how I will be evaluated for a raise or promotion.

17. I have just the right amount of work to do.

18. I know that I have divided my time properly.

19. I work with two or more groups who operate quite differently.

20. I know exactly what is expected of me.

21. I receive incompatible requests from two or more people.

22. I am uncertain as to how my job is linked.

23. I do things that are apt to be accepted by one person and not accepted by another.

24. I am told how well I am doing my job.

25. I receive an assignment without adequate resources and materials to execute it.

26. Explanation is clear of what has to be done.

27. I work on unnecessary things.

28. I have to work under vague directives or orders.

29. I perform work that suits my values.

30. I do not know if my work will be acceptable to my boss.

NOTES: All the original 30 items are listed above. Items 2, 4, 10, 12, 20, and 26 compose the six-item RA scale, and items 5, 11, 13, 19, 21, 23, 25, and 27 compose the eight-item RC scale. Items 2, 4, 10, 12, 20, and 26 require reverse coding to reflect higher levels of RC and RA.

**ROLE CONFLICT AND ROLE AMBIGUITY SCALES
FOR INDUSTRIAL SALESPEOPLE**
(Ford, Walker, and Churchill 1975)

Construct: Ford, Walker, and Churchill (1975) define role conflict (RC) and ambiguity (RA) as follows. RC is the belief that two or more individuals or groups are making incompatible demands about how a job should be performed. Examples of these individuals or groups include sales manager and customer, sales manager and family, and sales manager and members of other departments. RA is defined as feelings of uncertainty about the kinds of behaviors expected in relation to various role partners. These partners include top management (company policy), sales manager, customer, and family.

Description: The final version of the RC scale consists of 30 possible activity/expectation items across four role-partner groups: company, sales manager, customers, and family. Because all the items were not relevant to all four role-partner groups, the numbers of expectation differences that are possible to calculate for each dyad of role partners are as follows: company-sales manager = 14, company-customers = 14, customer-family = 17, sales manager-customers = 22, and sales manager-family = 11. The total number of expectation differences used to calculate a total perceived conflict score was 68. A 5-point Likert-type scale was used for each RC item, with 1 = *strongly disagree* and 5 = *strongly agree*. The amount of RC was measured by calculating the absolute differences in the respondent's scale scores for the two role partners on each item. A perceived conflict score for each dyad of role partners was calculated across all common items. A total perceived conflict score for the respondent was then calculated by summing the conflict scores for all possible role-partner dyads. With respect to RA, the instrument was constructed to measure the respondent's perceived ambiguity with respect to (a) the company's policies and procedures concerning how job activities should be performed, evaluation criteria concerning job performance, and ways performance is rewarded; (b) the sales manager's expectations concerning performance of job activities and the evaluation criteria used; (c) customers' expectations concerning job performance and their evaluation criteria; and (d) expectations of the family concerning job performance. The final version of the RA scale consisted of 41 items: 21 related to company policies and evaluation criteria, 7 related to the sales manager's expectations, 7 dealing with customer expectations, and 6 were relevant to expectations of family members. Six-point Likert-type scales ranging from *absolutely certain* to *absolutely uncertain* were used for the items. Ambiguity scores for each of the four dimensions were calculated by summing the scores on all items within each component. A total ambiguity score can be calculated by summing the four component scores.

Development: The procedures for scale development included item purification, estimation of reliability and validity, and derivation of scores on the scales. An extensive review of the literature, open-ended interviews with salespersons, and a psychologist who had a number of salespersons as patients were used to define the constructs' domain and generate the initial item pool. The initial RC instrument consisted of 34 items across 84 dyadic expectation comparisons. Forty-six items were selected for the initial RA pool. A purification study, based on responses from 249 salespersons, was performed for each construct. Based on inter-item correlations of the RC items, the total number of dyadic expectation comparisons was reduced from 84 to 68. The final number of RC items was then reduced to a possible of 30 for each group (i.e., company, sales manager, customers, and family). A similar procedure was used to reduce the number of items on the RA instrument from 46 to 41. Estimates of reliability and validity followed.

Samples: To test and refine the initial instrument, a sample of 249 salespeople was randomly drawn from the commercial division of a large heating and cooling equipment manufacturer. Completed questionnaires were received from 74% (183). The revised instrument was tested on a sample of 479 industrial salesmen drawn from 10 firms in seven different industries. A total of 265 salespeople completed the instrument.

Validity: The final 30- and 41-item versions of the role conflict and role ambiguity scales yielded alpha estimates of .85 and .91, respectively. The conflict and ambiguity scales were further evaluated by using a split-half procedure. The resulting corrected correlation coefficient for the split halves of the conflict scale was .67, while the coefficient for the ambiguity scale was .82. The construct validity of each scale was examined by the construction of a multitrait-multimethod matrix. Convergent validity correlations ranged from .40 to .46. Correlations of RC and RA with a measure of job satisfaction were −.24 and −.36, respectively, offering evidence of validity.

Scores: The scores obtained in the final test of the conflict and ambiguity scales were both normalized and standardized. The distributions of raw scores were normalized employing the method of "base-line units of unequal size." The normalized scores were standardized with a mean of 50 and a standard deviation of 10. For RC, the normalized mean score was 35, and for RA it was 101.

Source: Ford, Neil M., Orville C. Walker, Jr., and Gilbert A. Churchill, Jr. (1975). "Expectation-Specific Measures of the Intersender Conflict and Role Ambiguity Experienced by Industrial Salesmen." *Journal of Business Research*, 3, 95-112.

   © 1975 by Elsevier Science. Scale items taken from Appendix (p. 112). Reprinted with permission from Elsevier Science.

Other evidence: N/A

Other sources: N/A

References: N/A

ROLE CONFLICT AND ROLE AMBIGUITY SCALES
FOR INDUSTRIAL SALESPEOPLE
(Ford, Walker, and Churchill 1975)

Role-Conflict Scale

My company expects me:

   1. to expedite orders for my customers.
   2. to follow the "hard sell" approach.
   3. to do systems-design work for my customers.
   4. to show customers how our products can be coordinated with those of our competitors.
   5. to supervise the installation of equipment for my customers.
   6. to "stretch the truth" to make a sale.
   7. to "hold firm" on our normal delivery dates.
   8. to be a technical "trouble-shooter."
   9. to train customers in the use of our equipment.
   10. to be completely honest with my customers.
   11. to handle back charges and adjustments for my customers.
   12. to tailor delivery schedules to my customer's needs.
   13. to negotiate on price.
   14. to do product design work for my customers.
   15. to tailor credit terms to fit the needs of customers.
   16. to perform field tests on newly installed equipment.

My sales manager expects me:

1. to expedite orders for my customers.
2. to perform engineering services for my customers.
3. to do systems-design work for my customers.
4. to show customers how our products can be coordinated with those of our competitors.
5. to supervise the installation of equipment for my customers.
6. to "stretch the truth" to make a sale.
7. to "hold firm" on our normal delivery dates.
8. to be a technical "trouble-shooter."
9. to train customers in the use of our equipment.
10. to be completely honest with my customers.
11. to call on customers even if they are unlikely to place an order.
12. to tailor delivery schedules to my customer's needs.
13. to negotiate on price.
14. to do product design work for my customers.
15. to tailor credit terms to fit the needs of customers.
16. to perform field tests on newly installed equipment.
17. to be available to my customers at all times.
18. to be gone overnight much of the time.
19. to spend little or no time socializing with my customers.
20. to work on weekends.
21. to be a company salesman 24 hours a day.
22. to work in the evenings.
23. to leave my job behind when I go home from work.
24. to include my wife when entertaining my customers.
25. to be available for customer telephone calls at any hour of the night or day.
26. to drink with my customers.
27. to be liberal with my expense account in entertaining customers.
28. to develop close personal relationships with my customers.

My "average" customer expects me:

1. to expedite orders for him.
2. to perform engineering services for him.
3. to do systems-design work for him.
4. to show him how our products can be coordinated with those of our competitors.
5. to supervise the installation of equipment for him.
6. to "stretch the truth" to make a sale.
7. to "hold firm" on our normal delivery dates.
8. to follow the "hard sell" approach.
9. to train him in the use of our equipment.
10. to be completely honest with him.
11. to call upon him even if he is unlikely to place an order.
12. to tailor delivery schedules to him.
13. to negotiate on price.

14. to handle back charges and adjustments for him.
15. to tailor credit terms to fit his needs.
16. to perform field tests on newly installed equipment.
17. to be available to him at all times.
18. to spend little or no time socializing with him.
19. to work on weekends.
20. to work in the evenings.
21. to be available for customer telephone calls at any hour of the night or day.
22. to drink with him.
23. to be liberal with my expense account in entertaining him.
24. to develop close personal relationships with him.

My family expects me:

1. to be available to my customers at all times.
2. to be gone overnight much of the time.
3. to spend little or no time socializing with my customers.
4. to work on weekends.
5. to be a company salesman 24 hours a day.
6. to work in the evenings.
7. to leave my job behind when I go home from work.
8. to include them when entertaining my customers.
9. to be available for customer telephone calls at any hour of the night or day.
10. to drink with my customers.
11. to be liberal with my expense account in entertaining customers.
12. to develop close personal relationships with my customers.

Role-Ambiguity Scale

I AM

1 = completely certain   2 = very certain   3 = moderately certain   4 = somewhat certain   5 = not at all certain

Company policies and evaluations:

1. about the limits of my authority.
2. to what extent I can negotiate on price.
3. about the frequency with which I should call upon my customers.
4. to what extent I can modify normal delivery schedules.
5. to what extent I can extend more liberal credit than normal.
6. to what extent I should be a technical trouble-shooter.
7. what is the best way to close a sale.
8. about how much time I should spend socializing with my customers.
9. about our company rules and regulations.
10. about how to handle back charges and adjustments for my customers.
11. to what extent I should do product design work for my customers.

12. about what is the best way to sell.
13. about how to develop close personal relationships with my customers.
14. about how I should perform my job in order to satisfy my customers.
15. about where to go to get assistance to do my job.
16. about what activities in my job are least important to my sales manager.
17. about how I can best use my expense account in entertaining customers.
18. about how to handle unusual problems or situations.
19. to what extent I should supervise the installation of equipment for my customers.
20. to what extent I should do systems work for my customers.
21. about what kind of engineering services I can offer my customers.

Sales manager's expectations and evaluations:

1. how my sales manager expects me to allocate my time among accounts.
2. how satisfied my sales manager is with my performance on the job.
3. about what activities in my job are most important to my sales manager.
4. about how much time my sales manager feels I should spend on the job.
5. about what my sales manager expects of me in performing my job.
6. about how I should perform my job in order to satisfy my sales manager.
7. about how my sales manager feels I should allocate my time on the job.

Customers' expectations and evaluations:

1. about what my customers expect of me in performing my job.
2. about how frequently my customers expect me to call on them.
3. about how satisfied my customers are with my performance on the job.
4. about what activities in my job are least important to my customers.
5. to what extent I should train customers in the use of our equipment.
6. about what activities in my job are most important to my customers.
7. about the rules and procedures my customers expect me to follow in dealing with them.

Family's expectations and evaluations:

1. about how much time my family feels I should spend on the job.
2. about what my family expects of me in performing my job.
3. about what activities in my job are most important to my family.
4. about what activities in my job are least important to my family.
5. about how satisfied my family is with my job performance.
6. about how I should perform my job in order to satisfy my family.

NOTES: Ford et al. (1975) offered a sample of items. Above is a complete enumeration of their RC and RA items. Note that there are 30 possible RC items. Some were applicable to certain groups, and others were not. Also, the authors did not completely specify which RA items belong to which RA facet. The above assignment reflects our best estimate of items to facets.

ROLE CONFLICT AND ROLE AMBIGUITY SCALES FOR SALESPEOPLE
(Chonko, Howell, and Bellenger 1986)

Construct: Chonko, Howell, and Bellenger (1986) view role conflict (RC) as conflict generated by a combination of sent role expectations and the role expectations of the salespeople. In this sense, their view of RC is analogous to the view of Kahn, Wolfe, Quinn, Snoek, and Rosenthal (1964), who define RC as incompatibility between the expectations of the salesperson and the expectations otherwise associated with the salesperson's position. Sources of RC include one's family, supervisors, customers, personal principles, and the job itself. Role ambiguity (RA) is viewed as the degree to which a sales rep is uncertain about others' expectations with respect to the job, the best way to fulfill known expectations, and the consequences of role performance. Sources of RA include the job, family, supervisors, customers, and the sales organization.

Description: The RC and RA scales are multi-item, multidimensional measures. The RC items are all scored on a 5-point basis ranging from *complete agreement* to *no agreement*. Each source of conflict can be considered a separate dimension of RC. Scores on items are summed within each dimension, and then divided by the number of items in each dimension to form dimension scores. The RA items are scored on a 5-point basis ranging from *completely certain* to *not certain at all*. Each source of ambiguity can be considered a separate dimension of RA, and scores on items are summed within each dimension and then divided by the number of items in each dimension to form dimension scores.

Development: Construction of the RC and RA measures started with personal interviews of salespeople to obtain a more clear understanding of their responsibilities. Open-ended questioning of more salespeople was then performed to elicit possible sources of RC and RA. From these two procedures, a large pool of items was generated. Using a sample of 121 salespeople, the RC and RA measures were refined via item-to-total correlations and factor analysis. Estimates of validity were also made.

Sample: A sample of 121 salespeople from an industrial products firm responded to the RC and RA measures.

Validity: Coefficient alpha estimates for the five sources of ambiguity ranged from .63 to .88. Corresponding estimates for the five sources of conflict ranged from .85 to .92. Correlations between the RC and RA and congruence of performance evaluation indicated some evidence of nomological validity. For RA, family, job, company, supervisors, and customer showed correlations of .16, −.15, .18, .10, and −.12, respectively, with congruence of performance evaluation. For RC, family, job, supervisor, customer, and self principles showed correlations of −.21, −.14, −.17, −.20, and −.02, respectively, with congruence of performance evaluation.

Scores: Mean scores for each dimension (i.e., source) of RC and RA are reported in Table 2, p. 41 of Chonko et al. (1986). Mean scores (std. dev.) for the RA sources ranged from 2.26 (.60) to 2.60 (.77). Corresponding estimates for the RC sources ranged from 2.27 (.76) to 3.29 (1.39).

Source: Chonko, Lawrence B., Roy D. Howell, and Danny Bellenger. (1986). "Congruence in Sales Force Evaluations: Relation to Sales Force Perceptions of Conflict and Ambiguity." *Journal of Personal Selling and Sales Management*, 6, 35-48.

© 1986 by *Journal of Personal Selling and Sales Management*. Scale items taken from Appendices A and B (pp. 44-47). Reprinted with permission.

Other evidence: N/A

Other sources: N/A

Reference: Kahn, R. L., D. M. Wolfe, R. P. Quinn, J. D. Snoek, and R. A. Rosenthal. (1964). *Organizational Stress Studies in Role Conflict and Ambiguity.* New York: John Wiley & Sons.

ROLE CONFLICT AND ROLE AMBIGUITY SCALES FOR SALESPEOPLE
(Chonko, Howell, and Bellenger 1986)

Role-Conflict Measures

Instructions: As an industrial sales representative, you often must satisfy a number of people in the performance of your job. Your sales supervisor, your family, your customers, and you, yourself, have expectations about the activities you should perform in your job and how you should perform these activities. Please circle the number code that best expresses your feeling about the degree of agreement between you and various people with whom you must work. Please use the following scale.

1 = complete agreement   2 = much agreement   3 = moderate agreement   4 = some agreement   5 = no agreement

Family

How much agreement would you say there is between you and your family on . . .

1. the time you spend working.

2. the time you spend socializing with other salespeople.

3. the time you spend socializing with customers.

4. how much you travel on your job.

Job

How much agreement would you say there is between . . .

1. the amount of sales territory I expected to cover and the territory I actually cover.

2. the number of customers I expected to have and the number of customers I actually have.

3. the nonselling tasks I expected to perform and the nonselling tasks I actually perform.

4. the amount of leisure time I expected to have and leisure time I actually have.

Supervisor

How much agreement would you say there is between you and your supervisor on . . .

1. your role in setting sales goals.

2. how often you should report to your supervisor.

3. how much customer research I should provide.

4. how much troubleshooting I should do for my customers.

5. how far I should stretch the truth to make a sale.

6. how much maintenance service you should provide for your customers.

7. how much authority you should have regarding delivery adjustments for your customers.

8. what "acceptable" performance is to you.

9. how you can best help to achieve the organization's objectives.

10. how much authority you should have regarding price negotiations with customers.

11. how much training you should provide your customers.

Customers

How much agreement would you say there is between you and your customers on . . .

1. your performance of field tests for customers.

2. how much training you should provide customers.

3. the extent to which you should develop personal relations with your customers.

4. how you should handle competition in your sales presentation.

5. how you should present the benefits of your firm's product to your customers.

6. how much maintenance service you should provide for your customers.

Self

How much agreement would you say there is between your personal principles and

1. how often your customers offer you favors to bend the rules of your company.

2. how often your customers offer you favors to bend government laws or regulations.

3. how often you try to sell a product to a customer even if you feel that the product has little or no value to the customer.

4. how often you feel pressure to stretch the truth in order to make a sale.

5. how often you feel pressure to apply the "hard sell" in order to make a sale.

Role-Ambiguity Measures

Instructions: In your role as an industrial sales representative, you may not always be clear as to what your supervisor, your customers, and your family expect of you. In general, sales reps tend to be more clear on some things than others. Very few representatives are equally certain about all aspects of their job. Please indicate your degree of certainty regarding the following statements by placing a circle around the appropriate number code.

I AM

1 = completely certain   2 = very certain   3 = moderately certain   4 = somewhat certain   5 = not at all certain

Family

1. about how much time my family feels I should spend on my job.

2. about how much nonwork time I should spend with my customers.

3. how my family feels about my job.

Job

1. how to best close a sale.

2. about how much time I should spend on various aspects of my job.

3. how to handle customer objections.

4. how to file my sales report.

5. how to plan and organize my sales presentations.

6. how to handle unusual problems or situations.

7. when to call on my customers.

8. which of my mannerisms my customers do not like.

9. how I should speak to my customers.

10. of the type of sales personality I should have.

11. where to get assistance in doing my job.

12. how often to call on my customers.

Company

1. about the extent to which I can extend more liberal credit to my customers.

2. how to handle my expense account.

3. to what extent I should be a troubleshooter.

4. to what extent I should provide maintenance service for my customers.

5. about the limits of my authority.

6. to what extent I should train my customers to use our equipment.

7. of my company's rules and regulations.

Manager

1. of the method my supervisor will use to evaluate my performance.

2. how satisfied my supervisor is with my performance.

3. how my sale goals are set.

4. of those aspects of my job that are most important to my supervisor.

5. how my sales commission rates are set.

6. that my performance is a critical factor in the determination of my promotion and advancement.

7. how my supervisor expects me to allocate my time among my accounts.

Customers

1. of the role played by each person I must see in order to make a sale to a customer.

2. who I must see in my customer's organizations in order to make a sale.

3. how satisfied my customers are with my performance.

4. when to call on my customers.

5. what my customers expect of me in performing my job.

6. what aspects of my job are most important to my customers.

7. how much time my customers expect me to socialize with them.

WORK-FAMILY CONFLICT AND FAMILY-WORK CONFLICT SCALES
(Netemeyer, Boles, and McMurrian 1996)

Construct: The following definitions were used to guide the scale development efforts of Netemeyer, Boles, and McMurrian (1996). Work-family conflict (WFC) is a form of interrole conflict in which the general demands of, time devoted to, and strain created by the job interfere with performing family-related responsibilities. Conversely, family-work conflict (FWC) is a form of interrole conflict in which the general demands of, time devoted to, and strain created by the family interfere with performing work-related responsibilities (Netemeyer et al. 1996, p. 401). The assumption is made that WFC and FWC are distinct but interrelated forms of interrole conflict. This conflict is associated with the pressures stemming from membership in multiple groups.

Description: Both the work-family conflict scale and family-work conflict scale are composed of five items each. Item responses are operationalized using a 7-place strongly disagree-strongly agree response format. Items are summed to reflect individual scores for the WFC and FWC measures.

Development: An initial pool of 110 items was generated from a review of related measures used in previously published literature. Faculty judges and further exploratory analyses were used to reduce the pool to 43 items (22 for WFC and 21 for FWC). An exhaustive iterative confirmatory procedure was used to derive the final five-item scales. Items were deleted across the three samples from 43 to 24 to 13 to 10 (i.e., the final 5 WFC and 5 FWC item scales). The heuristics used in item deletion included deleting items with high redundancy, items contributing to within- and across-factor measurement error, and items with extremely high or low factor loadings. Tests of one-factor and two-factor correlated models were used to provide evidence of dimensionality, discriminant validity, and internal consistency. These results are summarized in Table 1 (Netemeyer et al. 1996, p. 404). Briefly, the following average fit statistics (i.e., across the three samples) from the two-factor correlated model estimations were offered: GFI = .91, AGFI = .86, CFI = .95, and TLI = .93. The average construct reliability estimates for WFC and FWC were .88 and .86, respectively. The corresponding averages for average variance extracted were .60 and .57. Subsequent tests of discriminant validity and measurement invariance also supported the validity of the two five-item scales.

Samples: Three samples were used in scale validation. In each case, mail surveys were used to collect the WFC and FWC measures as well as a large number of on- and off-job measures subsequently used in scale validation. Sample 1 comprised 182 elementary and high school teachers and administrators. The median age was 43, and 128 were women. The second sample comprised 162 small business owners. The median age was 45, and 96 were men. The third sample consisted of 186 real estate salespeople. The median age was 48, and 142 were women (Netemeyer et al. 1996, pp. 402-403).

Validity: Correlations with 17 other variables were used to provide further evidence of validity. These correlations are described in Table 3 (Netemeyer et al. 1996, p. 406). Across the samples, 44 of the correlations were significant as predicted. For example, 15 of the 16 correlations related to life satisfaction, relationship satisfaction, and relationship agreement were negative and significant as predicted. Tests of correlation differences between WFC and FWC and related constructs supported expectations as well. For example, WFC was more strongly correlated with the number of hours worked than FWC in all three samples. Lastly, and as predicted, WFC had a higher mean score than the FWC scale across all three samples.

Scores: Mean level difference tests between the two scales were used in scale validation. The means for the WFC scale across the three samples were 15.42, 17.16, and 17.49. The corresponding means for FWC were 9.99, 10.30, and 11.75.

Source: Netemeyer, Richard G., James S. Boles, and Robert McMurrian. (1996). "Development and Validation of Work-Family and Family-Work Conflict Scales." *Journal of Applied Psychology*, *81*(4), 400-410.

                       © 1996 by the American Psychological Association. Scale items taken from Appendix (p. 410). Reprinted with permission.

Other evidence: N/A

Other sources: N/A

References: N/A

WORK-FAMILY CONFLICT AND FAMILY-WORK CONFLICT SCALES
(Netemeyer, Boles, and McMurrian 1996)

Work-Family Conflict Scale

1. The demands of my work interfere with my home and family life.

2. The amount of time my job takes up makes it difficult to fulfill family responsibilities.

3. Things I want to do at home do not get done because of the demands my job puts on me.

4. My job produces strain that makes it difficult to fulfill family duties.

5. Due to work-related duties, I have to make changes to my plans for family activities.

Family-Work Conflict Scale

1. The demands of my family or spouse/partner interfere with work-related activities.

2. I have to put off doing things at work because of demands on my time at home.

3. Things I want to do at work don't get done because of the demands of my family or spouse/partner.

4. My home life interferes with my responsibilities at work such as getting to work on time, accomplishing daily tasks, and working overtime.

5. Family-related strain interferes with my ability to perform job-related duties.

Job Burnout/Tension

BURNOUT IN CUSTOMER SERVICE REPRESENTATIVES
(Singh, Goolsby, and Rhoads 1994)

Construct: Burnout is defined by Maslach and Jackson (1981) as a psychological syndrome or condition that is characterized by three distinct but related dimensions: emotional exhaustion (EE), reduced personal accomplishment (RPA), and depersonalization (DP). EE reflects feelings of being depleted of energy and drained due to excessive psychological demands. RPA is characterized by attributions of inefficacy, reduced motivation, and low self-esteem. DP manifests itself as an uncaring and negative attitude toward others. It is these definitions that guided the scale modifications of Singh, Goolsby, and Rhoads (1994, p. 559). Burnout is depicted as a result of role "stressors" and an antecedent of psychological and behavioral job outcomes.

Description: Boundary spanning burnout is assessed by 24 items (i.e., 8 per dimension). These items reflect adaptations of the original measures of Maslach and Jackson (1981). Items for each dimension are summed and averaged to generate three burnout dimension measures. Items are operationalized using a 6-point scale response format anchored by 1 = *is very much UNLIKE me* to 7 = *is very much LIKE me*. The remaining positions are labeled as well (Singh et al. 1994, p. 568). Within each dimension, there are two items for each of four roles: customers, boss, coworkers, and top management. The three dimension average scores summed across the four roles were used as three indicators of overall burnout in subsequent tests of mediation.

Development: The 24 items were drawn from the scale developed by Maslach and Jackson (1981). The items were modified to include statements about boss, top management, customers, and coworkers. These four role members were identified as being relevant boundary role personnel in preliminary focus group discussions (Singh et al. 1994, p. 562).

Sample: Customer representatives in telemarketing positions for a large multinational firm were surveyed. Of the 351 usable responses, almost 70% were from females. The median age was 31-35 years, and 47% of the sample had been with the company less than 2 years.

Validity: Confirmatory factor analyses revealed that a three-dimensional model provided an acceptable fit to the data. The correlations among the three factors ranged from .30 to .52. The composite reliabilities for the three factors were .80, .81, and .82 for EE, RPA, and DP, respectively (Singh et al. 1994, p. 563). The composite reliability for the second-order burnout construct was .66. Additional supportive evidence for the burnout measures' validity was provided by subsequent structural equation model tests of hypotheses. Specifically, role stressors had a significant positive effect on burnout (0.64), while burnout was inversely related as predicted with psychological (–0.77) and behavioral outcomes (–0.46). Moreover, burnout also partially mediated the direct effects of role stress on important job outcomes.

Scores: The means (std. dev.) for the three factors were as follows: EE, 2.71 (0.87); RPA, 2.34 (0.82); and DP, 2.64 (0.92). These means are compared to other professions in Figure 2 (Singh et al. 1994, p. 564).

Source: Singh, Jagdip, Jerry R. Goolsby, and Gary K. Rhoads. (1994). Behavioral and Psychological Consequences of Boundary Spanning Burnout for Customer Service Representatives." *Journal of Marketing Research, 31*, 558-569.
© 1994 by the American Marketing Association. Scale items taken from Appendix A (p. 568). Reprinted with permission.

Other evidence: N/A

Other sources: N/A

Reference: Maslach, Christina, and Susan E. Jackson. (1981). "The Measurement of Experienced Burnout." *Journal of Occupational Behavior, 2*, 99-113.

BURNOUT IN CUSTOMER SERVICE REPRESENTATIVES
(Singh, Goolsby, and Rhoads 1994)

Depersonalization

1. I feel I treat some customers as if they were impersonal "objects."

2. I feel indifferent toward some of my customers.

3. I feel a lack of personal concern for my boss.

4. I feel I'm becoming more hardened toward my supervisor.

5. I feel I have become callous toward my coworkers.

6. I feel insensitive toward my coworkers.

7. I feel I am becoming less sympathetic toward top management.

8. I feel alienated from top management.

Reduced Personal Accomplishment

1. I feel I perform effectively to meet the needs of my customers.

2. I feel effective in solving the problems of my customers.

3. I feel I am an important asset to my supervisor.

4. I feel my supervisor values my contribution to the firm.

5. I feel my coworkers truly value my assistance.

6. I feel I am a positive influence on my coworkers.

7. I feel I satisfy many of the demands set by top management.

8. I feel I make a positive contribution toward top management goals.

Emotional Exhaustion

1. Working with customers is really a strain for me.

2. I feel I am working too hard for my customers.

3. Working with my boss directly puts too much stress on me.

4. I feel emotionally drained by the pressure my boss puts on me.

5. I feel frustrated because of working directly with coworkers.

6. I feel I work too hard trying to satisfy coworkers.

7. I feel dismayed by the actions of top management.

8. I feel burned out from trying to meet top management's expectations.

NOTE: All items in the Reduced Personal Accomplishment scale are reverse coded.

TENSION: JOB-INDUCED TENSION
(House and Rizzo 1972)

Construct: Job-induced tension is viewed as "the existence of tension and pressures growing out of job requirements, including possible outcomes in terms of feelings or physical symptoms (e.g., tiredness, stiffness, weakness, irritation, digestive problems)" (House and Rizzo 1972, pp. 481-482). The corresponding job-induced tension measure has been used extensively in organizational behavior and sales research.

Description: The job-induced tension scale is composed of seven items originally scored on a *true* = 2, *false* = 1 format. Scores on items are summed and then divided by 7 to form an overall index. The scale is considered unidimensional.

Development: From the description provided by House and Rizzo (1972), 26 items were generated to tap the domain of the construct. Through image covariance factor analysis, item analysis, and Kuder-Richardson reliability analysis, the final seven-item job induced tension scale was derived with a sample of 200 respondents. Numerous estimates of nomological validity were also reported.

Sample: The questionnaire that contained the scale was administered to a sample of the staff, research, development, and engineering personnel at an undisclosed firm. The sample size was $n = 200$.

Validity: The scale had a KR-20 estimate of internal consistency of .825. The scale also showed evidence of nomological validity. For example, the correlations between the job induced tension scale and measures of role conflict and role ambiguity were .20 and .12.

Scores: A mean score of 1.24 ($SD = .28$) was reported for the scale (House and Rizzo 1972, p. 484).

Source: House, Robert, J., and John R. Rizzo. (1972). "Role Conflict and Ambiguity as Critical Variables in a Model of Organizational Behavior." *Organizational Behavior and Human Performance*, 7, 467-505. Scale items taken from Figure 3 (pp. 480-481).

Other evidence: Although the scale has been used on numerous occasions in the organizational behavior literature with evidence of reliability and validity, our discussion of other evidence will be limited to a few marketing applications. Using a sample of 216 pharmaceutical salespeople, Fry, Futrell, Parasuraman, and Chmielewski (1986) reported an internal consistency estimate of .88 for the job-induced tension scale. Evidence of nomological validity was also offered. For example, as an independent variable for the prediction of satisfaction with company support and satisfaction with customers, the job-induced tension scale showed path coefficients of $-.14$ and $-.18$ ($p < .05$), respectively. As a dependent variable, role conflict showed a path coefficient of .39 ($p < .01$) for predicting job-induced tension.

   In another application using a sample of 183 salespeople, Netemeyer, Johnston, and Burton (1990) reported a composite reliability estimate of .82 for the job-induced tension scale (using 5-point items). Furthermore, the scale was significantly correlated with role conflict (.43), role ambiguity (.28), job satisfaction ($-.42$),·and propensity to leave an organization (.30).

Other sources: Fry, Louis W., Charles M. Futrell, A. Parasuraman, and Margaret A. Chmielewski. (1986). "An Analysis of Alternative Causal Models of Salesperson Role Perceptions and Work-Related Attitudes." *Journal of Marketing Research*, 23, 153-163.

   Netemeyer, Richard G., Mark W. Johnston, and Scot Burton. (1990). "Analysis of Role Conflict and Role Ambiguity in a Structural Equations Framework." *Journal of Applied Psychology*, 75, 148-157.

References: N/A

TENSION: JOB-INDUCED TENSION
(House and Rizzo 1972)

1. I feel fidgety or nervous because of my job.

2. Problems associated with work have kept me awake at night.

3. My job tends to directly affect my health.

4. If I had a different job, my health would probably improve.

5. I often "take my job home with me" in the sense that I think about it when doing other things.

6. I feel nervous before attending meetings in the organization.

7. I sometimes feel weak all over.

NOTE: These items reflect wording used in marketing applications of the scale.

Performance Measures

ORGANIZATIONAL CITIZENSHIP BEHAVIORS: OCBs
(MacKenzie, Podsakoff, and Fetter 1993)

Construct: Organizational citizenship behaviors (OCBs) are discretionary behaviors on the part of a salesperson that directly promote the effective functioning of an organization, without necessarily influencing a salesperson's objective sales productivity (MacKenzie, Podsakoff, and Fetter 1993, p. 71). According to Organ (1988), OCBs include altruism, sportsmanship, civic virtue, and conscientiousness. Briefly, altruism is discretionary behavior that has the effect of helping a specific other person with an organizationally relevant task. Sportsmanship is the willingness on the part of a salesperson to tolerate less than ideal circumstances without complaining. Civic virtue is behavior indicating that the salesperson responsibly participates in and is concerned about the life of the company. Conscientiousness is behavior that goes well beyond the minimum role requirements of the organization (MacKenzie et al., 1993, p. 71).

Description: OCBs have been studied in multiple contexts. Interested users of these measures are encouraged to conduct a more complete review than is provided here (cf. MacKenzie, Podsakoff, and Fetter 1991; MacKenzie et al., 1993; Podsakoff and MacKenzie 1994). Sample items are shown in Table 1 (MacKenzie et al. 1993, p. 74). Items are operationalized using 7-point Likert-type scales ranging from *strongly disagree* to *strongly agree*. The number and apparent content of items varies across the context involved in each study. The items have been summed and averaged to reflect the different behaviors and have been used in causal models as separate indicators of one of the OCB domains (e.g., sportsmanship, civic virtue).

Development: Standard scale development procedures were used in scale construction. This process is summarized by Podsakoff and MacKenzie (1994, p. 351) and MacKenzie et al. (1991). Briefly, items were developed to reflect the various OCB constructs. Items were then judged by knowledgeable colleagues and company representatives. The remaining items were subsequently subjected to measurement evaluation based largely on the results of extensive confirmatory factor analyses.

Samples: The samples used in Studies 1, 2, and 3 of MacKenzie et al. (1993) were as follows. Study 1 was based on the complete ratings of 261 multiline insurance agents provided by their managers; 82% were male, and their average age was 38 years. Study 2 involved the ratings of 204 chemical product salespersons. Their average job tenure was 5.6 years, and 93% were male. The data for Study 3 consisted of the evaluations of 108 district sales managers provided by 32 national sales managers working for an international pharmaceutical company.

Validity: Overall, there is substantial support offered for the measures in the three articles cited below. Based on Study 2 in MacKenzie et al. (1993), which included the four sets of OCBs for which example items are provided, the following evidence of measurement validity was described. (Similar support can be gleaned from the results of Study 1 and Study 3 as well as the related research reported elsewhere.) First, the internal consistency reliability for the four constructs ranged from .78 to .88. The construct reliability estimates ranged from .79 to .85. Evidence of discriminant validity was provided from tests of the intercorrelations among the OCB constructs and comparisons of these correlations with shared variance estimates. Overall measurement fit statistics for a six-factor correlated model incorporating sales productivity and overall performance included the following: CFI = .93, TLI = .91, GFI = .89, and chi-square = 230.3 (105 df). Subsequent results across the multiple studies revealed that OCBs have an important impact on managers' evaluations and that OCBs have significant effects beyond direct measures of employee performance (MacKenzie et al. 1993, p. 77).

Scores: Means and standard deviations are not reported by MacKenzie et al. (1993).

Source: MacKenzie, Scott B., Philip M. Podsakoff, and Richard Fetter. (1993). "The Impact of Organizational Citizenship Behavior on Evaluations of Salesperson Performance." *Journal of Marketing*, *57*, 70-80.

© 1993 by the American Marketing Association. Scale items taken from Table 1 (p. 74). Reprinted with permission.

Other evidence: Podsakoff and MacKenzie (1994) describe follow-up research using another mix of OCB items. Again, the scale development procedures are extensive, and substantial evidence of measurement validity is offered from confirmatory factor analysis results. Evidence of predictive validity is provided by the ability of three sets of OCBs to predict overall performance evaluations, as well as unit performance, for samples of insurance agents.

Other sources: N/A

References: MacKenzie, Scott B., Philip M. Podsakoff, and Richard Fetter. (1991). "Organizational Citizenship Behavior and Objective Productivity as Determinants of Managerial Evaluations of Salespersons' Performance." *Organizational Behavior and Human Decision Processes*, *50*(1), 1-28.

Organ, Dennis W. (1988). *Organization Citizenship Behavior: The Good Soldier Syndrome.* Lexington, MA: Lexington Books.

Podsakoff, Philip M., and Scott B. MacKenzie. (1994). "Organizational Citizenship Behaviors and Sales Unit Effectiveness." *Journal of Marketing Research*, *31*, 351-363.

ORGANIZATIONAL CITIZENSHIP BEHAVIORS: OCBS
(MacKenzie, Podsakoff, and Fetter 1993)

Civic Virtue

1. "Keeps up" with developments in the company.

2. Attends functions that are not required but that help the company image.

3. Is willing to risk disapproval in order to express his/her beliefs about what's best for the company.

Sportsmanship

1. Consumes a lot of time complaining about trivial matters.

2. Tends to make "mountains out of molehills" (makes problems bigger that they are).

3. Always focuses on what's wrong with his/her situation, rather than the positive side of it.

Altruism

1. Helps orient new agents even though it is not required.

2. Is always ready to help or to lend a helping hand to those around him/her.

3. Willingly gives of his/her time to help others.

Conscientiousness

1. Conscientiously follows company regulations and procedures.

2. Turns in budgets, sales projections, expense reports, etc. earlier than is required.

3. Returns phone calls and responds to other messages and requests for information promptly.

NOTES: Items in the Sportsmanship scale are all reverse coded. Sample items are shown in MacKenzie et al. (1993, p. 74, Table 1).

RETAIL SALESPERSON PERFORMANCE
(Bush, Bush, Ortinau, and Hair 1990)

Construct: Job performance of retail salespersons was evaluated by operationally defining the various behavioral dimensions of relevant selling activities. This approach differed from the traditional approach of evaluating outcomes to measure sales performance. The behavioral approach focused on what salespersons actually do on the job and how these activities relate to job performance. The construct's domain was defined as consisting of five behavior-based factors: (a) knowledge of merchandise procedures, (b) customer service ability, (c) sales ability, (c) product-merchandise knowledge, and (e) knowledge of store policy.

Description: The finalized version of the instrument, designed for self-administration, consisted of 22 items that represent the five dimensions stated above. All items are scored on a 5-point, Likert-type format where 5 = *very good*, 4 = *good*, 3 = *average*, 2 = *poor*, and 1 = *very poor*. Item scores can be summed within each dimension to form dimension scores or overall to form an overall performance score. Because the scale was based on management's evaluation of individual salesperson performance, each manager was instructed to appraise the salespeople directly under his/her control.

Development: Through an extensive literature review and 80 hours of focus group interviews with store managers, department sales managers, and industrial retail salespersons, Bush, Bush, Ortinau, and Hair (1990) identified work-related activities of retail salespersons that influence job performance. Items were then generated, screened, categorized, or deleted by the principal investigators and a panel of retailing experts. Forty-one scale items were included in the initial retail performance measure. Based on data from 144 salespersons, factor and item analyses were performed on the 41 items to determine a set of underlying dimensions that make up the multidimensional construct of retail sales performance. Six factors of retail job satisfaction were identified, and 32 items of the job performance scale were retained. The scale was subjected to confirmatory factor analysis (via LISREL) for data provided by 321 salespeople. After this procedure, 22 items representing five factors remained. Several reliability and validity checks followed.

Samples: A total sample of 144 salesperson evaluations was obtained from 43 department sales managers. These salespersons were employed in soft goods departments such as fashion apparel, accessories, and fragrances. The data were analyzed with respect to item purification in the pretesting phase of the study. In a further scale refinement effort, 48 additional retail sales department managers with instructions to evaluate employees yielded a sample of 321 salespeople. The final version of the 22-item job performance scale was sent to 57 retail sales department managers. A total of 285 retail salespeople were appraised.

Validity: For the sample of 285, alpha coefficients ranged from .84 to .88 across dimensions and was .86. for the total 22-item scale. Test-retest reliability was assessed based on a systematic sampling of 98 salesperson from the original sample. Test-retest correlations ranged from .61 to .70 across dimensions and was .67 for the total scale. Predictive validity was assessed by correlating contribution to gross margins of 192 salespersons with each of the five scale dimensions (all significant at $p < .05$ with a range from .24 to .36) and a correlation of .39 ($p < .05$) with the total scale of job performance. Concurrent validity was assessed by correlating the need for achievement of 285 salespeople with the five scale dimensions of retail sales performance. These correlations ranged from .19 to .39 across the five dimensions, and the correlation was .38 for the total scale, suggesting concurrent validity.

Scores: Mean scores and standard deviations were not reported in the Bush et al. (1990) article.

Source: Bush, Robert P., Alan J. Bush, David J. Ortinau, and Joseph F. Hair. (1990). "Developing a Behavior-Based Scale to Assess Retail Salesperson Performance." *Journal of Retailing*, *66*, 119-129.

       © 1990 by *Journal of Retailing*. Scale items taken from Table 2 (p. 129-130). Reprinted with permission.

Other evidence: N/A

Other sources: N/A

References: N/A

RETAIL SALESPERSON PERFORMANCE
(Bush, Bush, Ortinau, and Hair 1990)

Merchandise Procedure Ability
1. Employee accuracy in counting and inventorying merchandise.
2. Prevents merchandise shrinkage due to mishandling of merchandise.
3. Keeps merchandise in a neat and orderly manner on sales floor.
4. Gets merchandise on sales floor (shelves, racks, displays) quickly after merchandise arrival.
5. Knows the design and specifications of warranties and guarantees of the merchandise groups.

Customer Service Ability
1. Provides courteous service to customers.
2. Handles customers' complaints and/or service problems as indicated by store procedure.
3. Follows proper procedures concerning merchandise returns and lay-aways when conducted through credit transactions.
4. Suggests add-on or complimentary merchandise to customers.

Sales Ability
1. Has strong ability to close the sale.
2. Promotes sales of merchandise items having profit margins.
3. Acts as a resource to other departments or other salespeople needing assistance.
4. Works well with fellow workers in primary merchandise department.

Product-Merchandise Knowledge
1. Knowledge of design, style, and construction of merchandise group.
2. Knowledge of special promotions and/or advertised sale items.
3. Knowledge of material (fabric), color coordination, and complimentary accessories related to merchandise group.
4. Provides accurate and complete paperwork related to work schedules.

Knowledge of Store Policy
1. Provides accurate and complete paperwork related to work schedules.
2. Provides accurate and complete paperwork for cash and credit transactions.
3. Shows up on time for work, sales meetings, and training sessions.
4. Accurately follows day-to-day instructions of immediate supervisor.
5. Employee's overall job-related attitude.

NOTE: Item 4 of the "product-merchandise knowledge" factor is also part of the "knowledge of store policy" factor (item 1).

SALES PERFORMANCE SCALE
(Behrman and Perreault 1982)

Construct: This scale was designed to measure the job performance construct as it relates to the industrial salesperson. Differences in such variables as sales territories, product lines, customer accounts, and length of selling cycles can make generalizations about performance quite tenuous. Because quantitative sales data may be deceptive as performance indicators due to factors beyond the control of the individual, a performance evaluation based on self-report was constructed as one possible measurement of performance. The construct's domain was defined as consisting of the following five categories: (a) sales presentation, (b) providing information, (c) technical knowledge, (d) sales objective, and (e) controlling expenses.

Description: The finalized version of the instrument consisted of 31 items that represent the five components listed above. A 7-cue rating scale format was used, with possible responses ranging from *outstanding* to *needs improvement*. Item scores are summed within factors to form factor indices, or they can be summed over all items to form an overall performance measure.

Development: A review of the literature and an analysis of the job of industrial salespersons served as stimuli in developing the initial set of statements, resulting in seven categories of items. A panel of judges reviewed the statements, and 65 items remained for the seven performance areas. Data were collected from the salespersons and their sales managers using self-administered questionnaires. The purification study, which used item and factor analysis, reduced the set of items to 31 that represented five aspects of industrial sales performance. Reliability and validity estimates followed.

Samples: Five noncompeting industrial companies were selected to participate in the study. Across these five firms, 219 salespersons and 43 managers were invited to participate. Of these subjects, 200 (91%) salespersons and 42 (98%) managers returned completed questionnaires.

Validity: Alpha coefficients ranged from .81 to .90 across the facets and was .93 for the overall scale. Test-retest estimates across the facets ranged from .54 to .77, and the estimate was .70 for the overall scale. The scale was significantly correlated with manager's evaluation (.26 for the total sample), profitability data (.21), and a need for achievement measure (.25). Individually, these relationships were not strong, but in combination they suggest that the self-report captured some common variance with other surrogate indicators of sales performance. The 31 items were also factor analyzed with a holdout sample, and the five extracted factors were consistent with the expected structure.

Scores: The means (std. dev.) for the subcomponents were as follows: sales presentation 33.46 (4.69), providing information 26.52 (4.48), technical knowledge 32.41 (5.52), sales objectives 38.15 (5.82), and controlling expenses 39.96 (5.05). The overall scale mean and standard deviation were 170.51 and 19.46, respectively.

Source: Behrman, Douglas, and William D. Perreault, Jr. (1982). "Measuring the Performance of Industrial Salespersons." *Journal of Business Research, 10,* 355-370.
  © 1982 by Elsevier Science. Scale items taken from Table 3 (pp. 366-367). Reprinted with permission of Elsevier Science.

Other evidence: N/A

Other sources: N/A

References: N/A

SALES PERFORMANCE SCALE
(Behrman and Perreault 1982)

1. Producing a high market share for your company in your territory

2. Making sales of those products with the highest profit margins

3. Generating a high level of dollar sales

4. Quickly generating sales of new company products

5. Identifying and selling major accounts in your territory

6. Producing sales or blanket contracts with long-term profitability

7. Exceeding all sales targets and objectives for your territory during the year

8. Knowing the design and specifications of company products

9. Knowing the applications and functions of company products

10. Being able to detect causes of operating failure of company products

11. Acting as a special resource to other departments that need your assistance

12. Keeping abreast of your company's production and technological developments

13. When possible, troubleshooting system problems and conducting minor field service to correct product misapplications and/or product failures

14. Carrying our company policies, procedures, and programs for providing information

15. Providing accurate and complete paperwork related to order, expenses, and other routine reports

16. Recommending on your own initiative how company operations and procedures can be improved

17. Submitting required reports on time

18. Maintaining company specified records that are accurate, complete, and up to date

19. Operating within the budgets set by the company

20. Using expense accounts with integrity

21. Using business gift and promotional allowances responsibly

22. Spending travel and lodging money carefully

23. Arranging sales call patterns and frequency to cover your territory economically

24. Entertaining only when it is clearly in the best interest of the company to do so

25. Controlling costs in other areas of the company (order processing and preparation, delivery, etc.) when taking sales orders

26. Listening attentively to identify and understand the real concerns of your customer

27. Convincing customers that you understand their unique problems and concerns

28. Using established contacts to develop new customers

29. Communicating your sales presentation clearly and concisely

30. Making effective use of audiovisual aids (charts, tables, and the like) to improve your sales presentation

31. Working out solutions to a customer's questions or objections

NOTE: The factors and item numbers are as follows: (a) sales objectives 1-7, (b) technical knowledge 8-13, (c) providing information 14-18, (d) controlling expenses 19-25, and (e) sales presentations 26-31.

SALESPERSON PERFORMANCE
(Sujan, Weitz, and Kumar 1994)

Construct: This measure is used to assess salesperson self-evaluations of their own performance relative to other salespersons working for their company (Sujan, Weitz, and Kumar 1994, p. 42).

Description: The measure consists of seven items, each operationalized using a scale ranging from *Much Worse* (–5) to *Average* (0) to *Much Better* (+5). Item scores are apparently summed (cf. Table A1, Sujan et al. 1994, p. 47).

Development: Five of the seven items were taken from Behrman and Perreault (1982). The items for identifying attractive prospects and assisting the sales supervisor to meet his or her goals were added.

Samples: Participants in the research were 190 salespersons from eight different firms in diverse industries (Sujan et al. 1994, p. 41). The respondents were predominantly male (78%). On average, they were 35 years of age and had 9 years of sales experience.

Validity: All measures, including performance, demonstrated acceptable levels of unidimensionality, reliability, and convergent and discriminant validity (Sujan et al. 1994, p. 42). Based on a series of confirmatory factor analysis models, the following results were reported regarding the performance measure. The reliability for the seven-item scale was .91 (all t values > 6.50). The phi loadings between performance and working hard, positive feedback, and negative feedback were 0.50, 0.29, and 0.15, respectively. Evidence for discriminant validity was provided because each of these phi values plus or minus twice their standard error did not include 1. Additional evidence of validity is offered from the results that supported hypotheses in which theoretical antecedents (e.g., working smart and working hard) were predictive of performance, as expected.

Scores: The mean and standard deviation for the scale were 7.93 and 1.36, respectively.

Source: Sujan, Harish, Barton A. Weitz, and Nirmalya Kumar. (1994). "Learning Orientation, Working Smart, and Effective Selling." *Journal of Marketing*, *58*, 39-52.
 © 1994 by the American Marketing Association. Scale items taken from Appendix A (p. 47). Reprinted with permission.

Other evidence: The seven-item scale was also used by Challagalla and Shervani (1996) in their study of supervisory control. Tests of measurement validation were said to support the validity of all measures, including the performance scale. A number of antecedents of performance were correlated as predicted. Example correlations with performance included the following: supervisor role ambiguity (–.32), customer role ambiguity (–.34), and satisfaction with supervisor (.17).

Other source: Challagalla, Goutam N., and Tasadduq A. Shervani. (1996). "Dimensions and Types of Supervisory Control: Effects on Salesperson Performance and Satisfaction." *Journal of Marketing*, *60*, 89-105.

Reference: Behrman, Douglas N., and William D. Perreault, Jr. (1982). "Measuring the Performance of Industrial Salespersons." *Journal of Business Research*, *10*, 355-370.

SALESPERSON PERFORMANCE
(Sujan, Weitz, and Kumar 1994)

1. Contributing to your company's acquiring a good market share

2. Selling high profit-margin products

3. Generating a high level of dollar sales

4. Quickly generating sales of new company products

5. Identifying major accounts in your territory and selling to them

6. Exceeding sales targets

7. Assisting your sales supervisor meet his or her goals

NOTE: The scale for Performance went from *Much Worse* (–5) to *Average* (0) to *Much Better* (+5).

Control and Leadership

CONTROL: SUPERVISORY CONTROL
(Challagalla and Shervani 1996)

Construct: The model that guided the scale development efforts of Challagalla and Shervani (1996) consisted of nine facets, with three types of control (i.e., output, activity, and capability control) and three facets for each type of control (i.e., information, rewards, and punishments). Two of the control types reflect behavior control—activity control and capability control. Activity control refers to the specification of the activities a person is expected to perform on a regular basis, the monitoring of actual behavior, and the administration of rewards and punishments on the basis of specified activities. Capability control involves setting goals for the level of skills and abilities people must possess, monitoring their skills and abilities, providing guidance for improvement if needed, and rewarding and punishing persons on the basis of their skills and abilities (Challagalla and Shervani 1996, p. 90). Information control involves goal setting, monitoring, and feedback.

Description: A total of 34 items are used as indicators of the nine output, activity, and capability control variables. All items are operationalized using 5-point Likert-type scales anchored by *strongly disagree* and *strongly agree*. Items for the different facets are summed to represent independent variable predictors.

Development: As indicated in Appendix A, the output information items, the activity information items, and the capability information items were based on Jaworski and MacInnis (1989). The remaining facets were based on Podsakoff, Tudor, Grover, and Huber (1984). Pretesting was done in four stages. These efforts included protocol interviews with salespersons and academic experts, as well as reactions to firm managers from the participating firms. These responses resulted in the addition and deletion of several items. Lastly, survey responses from 32 industrial salespersons were used to make several final scale refinements. Initial exploratory factor analyses reduced the final set of items to 34 (Challagalla and Shervani 1996, p. 101).

Sample: Usable responses were obtained from 270 salespersons employed in one of five industrial product divisions of two *Fortune* 500 companies. In all five divisions, the salespersons acted independently (Challagalla and Shervani 1996, p. 95).

Validity: The measures for the nine facets of control were evaluated using confirmatory factor analysis. The measures were said to demonstrate adequate levels of unidimensionality, reliability, and convergent and discriminant validity (Challagalla and Shervani 1996, pp. 95, 103). The coefficient alpha reliabilities for the nine facets ranged from .72 to .90. A nine-factor correlated model provided the best fit to the data. The following fit statistics were offered: chi-square = 995 (491 df), GFI = .80, RNI = .88, TLI = .87, and CFI = .88. The composite reliabilities all exceeded .70; the variance extracted estimates were above .50 with only two exceptions. For each pair of constructs, the average variance extracted exceeded the squared structural link between each pair, and all indicator t values were greater than 2.0. Lastly, the nomological validity of the measures is supported by the ability of the measures to predict outcomes as hypothesized.

Scores: Item and scale means and standard deviations are not reported. Factor intercorrelations are shown in Table B1 (Challagalla and Shervani 1996, p. 103).

Source: Challagalla, Goutam N., and Tasadduq A. Shervani. (1996). "Dimensions and Types of Supervisory Control: Effects on Salesperson Performance and Satisfaction." *Journal of Marketing*, *60*, 89-105.

   © 1996 by the American Marketing Association. Scale items taken from Appendix A (pp. 100-101). Reprinted with permission.

Other evidence: N/A

Other sources: N/A

References: Jaworski, Bernard J., and Deborah J. MacInnis. (1989). "Marketing Jobs and Management Controls: Toward a Framework." *Journal of Marketing*, *26*, 406-419.

Podsakoff, Philip M., William D. Tudor, Richard A. Grover, and Vandra L. Huber. (1984). "Situational Moderators of Leader Reward and Punishment Behaviors: Fact or Fiction?" *Organizational Behavior and Human Performance*, *34*, 21-63.

CONTROL: SUPERVISORY CONTROL
(Challagalla and Shervani 1996)

Output Control

Output Information

1. My manager tells me about the level of achievement expected on sales volume or market share targets.

2. I receive feedback on whether I am meeting expectations on sales volume or market share targets.

3. My manager monitors my progress on achieving sales volume or market share goals.

4. My manager ensures I am aware of the extent to which I attain sales volume or market share goals.

Output Rewards

1. I would get bonuses if I exceed my sales volume or market share targets.

2. Promotion opportunities depend on how well I perform on sales volume or market share targets.

3. I would be recognized by my company if I perform well on sales volume or market share targets.

4. There are pay increases if I do well on sales volume or market share targets.

Output Punishments

1. I would receive an informal warning if sales volume or market share targets were not achieved.

2. I would receive a formal warning if sales volume or market share targets were not achieved.

3. I would be put on probation if sales volume or market share targets are not achieved with some consistency.

4. My pay increases would suffer if sales volume or market share targets are not met.

Activity Control

Activity Information

1. My manager informs me about the sales activities I am expected to perform.

2. My manager monitors my sales activities.

3. My manager informs me on whether I meet his/her expectations on sales activities.

4. If my manager feels I need to adjust my sales activities, he/she tells me about it.

5. My manager evaluates my sales activities.

Activity Rewards

1. How well I perform specified sales activities would be considered when awarding bonuses/financial rewards.

2. If I perform sales activities well my supervisor would commend me.

3. I would be recognized by my supervisor if s/he were pleased with how well I perform sales activities.

Activity Punishments

1. I would receive an informal warning if my manager is not pleased with how I perform sales activities.

2. I would receive a formal reprimand if my supervisor were unhappy with how I perform sales activities.

3. I would be put on probation if my manager is unhappy with how I perform specified sales activities.

Capability Control

Capability Information

1. My manager has standards by which my selling skills are evaluated.

2. My supervisor periodically evaluates the selling skills I use to accomplish a task (e.g., how I negotiate).

3. My manager provides guidance on ways to improve selling skills and abilities.

4. My supervisor evaluates how I make sales presentations and communicate with customers.

5. My manager assists by suggesting why using a particular sales approach may be useful.

Capability Rewards

1. Assignment to better territories or accounts depends on how good my selling skills are.

2. I would be commended if I improved my selling skills.

3. Promotion opportunities depend on how good my selling skills and abilities are.

Capability Punishments

1. I would receive an informal warning if my manager is not pleased with my selling abilities.

2. I would receive a formal reprimand if my supervisor is not pleased with my selling skills and abilities.

3. I would be put on probation if my manager is not happy with my selling abilities.

LEADERSHIP ROLE CLARITY AND LEADERSHIP CONSIDERATION
(Schriesheim 1978)

Construct: Similar to House and Dessler's (1974) path-goal theory leadership concepts, Schriesheim (1978) offers leadership role clarity and leadership consideration constructs. Leadership role clarity refers to the extent to which a supervisor is perceived by subordinates as clearly establishing the tasks and performance level required of a job. Leadership consideration refers to the extent to which a supervisor is perceived by subordinates as providing coaching, guidance, support, and rewards necessary for high job satisfaction and performance.

Description: Leadership role clarity and consideration are measured using 5- and 11-item scales, respectively. The items can be scored on 5-point scales ranging from *very true* (5) to *very false* (1). Item scores are summed within each scale to form indices of leadership role clarity and consideration. Thus, they are considered separate dimensions of perceived leadership.

Development: Because the leadership role clarity and leadership scales were developed as part of the author's doctoral thesis, extensive information on the development of the scales was not available. However, other sources suggest that stringent psychometric procedures were used in scale development and numerous estimates of validity exist (e.g., Fry, Futrell, Parasuraman, and Chmielewski 1986).

Samples: N/A

Scores: N/A

Source: Schriesheim, Chester A. (1978). *Development, Validation, and Application of New Leadership Behavior and Expectancy Research Instruments.* Doctoral dissertation, College of Administrative Science, Ohio State University.

Other evidence: Two applications in marketing will be discussed as other evidence. Fry et al. (1986) reported coefficient alpha internal consistency estimates of .93 and .84 for the role clarity and consideration leadership scales, respectively. Standardized path coefficients showed that for the prediction of role conflict, role ambiguity, job stress, and job and supervisor satisfaction, the two leadership scales exhibited predictive validity. For example, coefficients of −.36, −.57, .11, .32, and .41 were found for the prediction of role conflict, role ambiguity, job stress, job satisfaction, and satisfaction with supervisor, respectively, with leadership role clarity as the predictor. Corresponding coefficients with leadership consideration as the predictor were −.21, −.11, −.10, .22, and .55. Fry et al.'s sample was composed of 216 salespeople.

   In another study, Johnston, Parasuraman, Futrell, and Black (1990), with a longitudinal sample of 102 salespeople, reported composite reliabilities of .81 and .90 for leadership consideration, and .92 and .85 for leadership role clarity. Correlations of leadership consideration with role conflict, role ambiguity, job satisfaction, and organizational commitment were −.50, −.28, .43, and .43, respectively. Correlations of role clarity leadership with role conflict, role ambiguity, job satisfaction, and organizational commitment were −.27, −.30, .39, and .36. These results offer evidence for the nomological validity of the leadership scales.

Other source: Johnston, Mark W., A. Parasuraman, Charles M. Futrell, and William C. Black. (1990). "A Longitudinal Assessment of the Impact of Selected Organizational Influences on Salespeople's Organizational Commitment During Early Employment." *Journal of Marketing Research, 27,* 333-344.

References: Fry, Louis W., Charles M. Futrell, A. Parasuraman, and Margaret A. Chmielewski. (1986). "An Analysis of Alternative Causal Models of Salesperson Role Perceptions and Work-Related Attitudes." *Journal of Marketing Research*, 23, 153-163.

House, Robert J., and Gary Dessler. (1974). "The Path-Goal Theory of Leadership: Some Post Hoc and A Priori Tests." In James G. Hunt and Lars L. Larson (Eds.), *Contingency Approaches to Leadership*. Carbondale: Southern Illinois University Press.

LEADERSHIP ROLE CLARITY AND CONSIDERATION
(Schriesheim 1978)

Role Clarity

My supervisor . . .

1. Gives me vague explanations of what is expected of me on my job.*

2. Gives me unclear goals to reach on my job.*

3. Explains the level of performance that is expected of me.

4. Explains the quality of work that is expected of me.

5. Explains what is expected of me on my job.

Leadership Consideration

My supervisor . . .

1. Helps make working on my job more pleasant.

2. Says things to hurt my personal feelings.*

3. Considers my personal feelings before acting.

4. Maintains a friendly working relationship with me.

5. Behaves in a manner which is thoughtful of my personal needs.

6. Looks out for my personal welfare.

7. Acts rudely toward me.*

8. Does things to make my job less pleasant.*

9. Treats me without considering my feelings.*

10. Shows respect for my personal feelings.

11. Acts without considering my feelings.*

NOTES: *Denotes items requiring reverse scoring. These items reflect the wording used in the marketing applications of the measures.

LEADERSHIP: TRANSACTIONAL AND TRANSFORMATIONAL LEADERSHIP
(Bycio, Hackett, and Allen 1995)

Construct: Bass (1985) originally applied the concepts of transactional and transformational leadership to business. In an extension, Bycio, Hackett, and Allen (1995) report the results of a confirmatory factor analysis of the Bass (1985) conceptualization. Transactional leaders are described as those leaders who identify the needs of their followers and exchange rewards for appropriate levels of effort and performance. Transformational leaders try to increase the level of followers' awareness for valued outcomes by expanding and elevating their needs and encouraging them to transcend their self-interests (Bycio et al. 1995, p. 468). Three factors are seen as being transformational: charismatic leadership, individualized consideration, and intellectual stimulation. Two factors are seen as being transactional: contingent reward and management-by-exception.

Description: Bycio et al. (1995) used the subset of items that defined the factors in the original Bass (1985) exploratory analysis. The five factors and the number of items per factor that were studied by Bycio et al. (1995) are as follows: charismatic leadership, 17; individualized consideration, 7; intellectual stimulation, 3; contingent reward, 7; and management-by- exception, 6. Each item is rated on the following 5-point scale: 0 (not at all), 1 (once in a while), 2 (sometimes), 3 (fairly often), and 4 (frequently). The items composing this scale are shown in Table 2 of Bycio et al. (1995). Because the measures are copyrighted, they are not reproduced here.

Development: Coefficient alpha estimates of reliability ranged from .71 to .97 across the five factors. Confirmatory factor analysis was used to test a series of factor models. Although the five-factor correlated model provided the best fit to the data, a two-factor Active-Passive model also provided a reasonable representation of the data. In this model, examination of relative model fit and correlations among the five factors revealed that, except for the management-by-exceptions factor, the remaining factors were highly correlated. For the two-factor model, the following fit statistics were reported: chi-square = 4,683 (730 *df*), NNFI = .89, CFI = .90, GFI = .82, and RSMR = .10. Item loadings and error variances for the five-factor model and two-factor Active-Passive model are shown in Table 2 (Bycio et al. 1995, p. 473).

Sample: The analyses are based on the complete responses of 1,376 registered nurses to a mail questionnaire. Responses showed that 97% of the respondents were female, with a mean age of 37 years and mean length of organizational tenure of 9 years (Bycio et al. 1995, p. 470).

Validity: A series of hierarchical regressions was run to test if the transformational scales added to the prediction of the outcome variables. The transformational scales had strong positive relationships with extra effort, satisfaction with leader, and subordinate-rated leader effectiveness (Bycio et al. 1995, p. 472). The contingent rewards factor was somewhat less correlated. Overall, charismatic leadership was found to be the dominant predictor. A number of other correlational tests provided supportive evidence of the scales' validity. However, concerns were raised about the high item error variances and the discriminant validity of the transformational factors, given the large phi coefficients. In addition, an expected strong relationship between contingent reward and continuance commitment did not materialize. These and a large number of other correlational tests are described in detail by Bycio et al. (1995).

Scores: Item means and standard deviations are presented in Table 2 (Bycio et al. 1995, p. 473). The five factor means (std. dev.) were as follows: charismatic leadership, 1.62 (1.06); individualized consideration, 2.08 (0.93); intellectual stimulation, 1.32 (1.06); contingent reward, 1.05 (0.78); and management-by-exception, 1.87 (0.80).

Source: Bycio, Peter, Rick D. Hackett, and Joyce S. Allen. (1995). "Further Assessments of Bass's (1985) Conceptualization of Transactional and Transformational Leadership." *Journal of Applied Psychology*, *80*(4), 468-478.

Other evidence: N/A

Other sources: N/A

Reference: Bass, B. M. (1985). *Leadership and Performance Beyond Expectations.* New York: Free Press.

PERCEIVED LEADER BEHAVIOR SCALES
(House and Dessler 1974)

Construct: The perceived leadership construct has its conceptual base in the path-goal theory of leadership (House 1971; House and Dessler 1974). Leader behavior is conceived as an explanatory variable that directly affects the psychological states and performance of subordinates. Furthermore, this leadership focuses on subordinates' *perceptions* of their leader with respect to the following three aspects of leadership (House and Dessler 1974, pp. 40-43).

Instrumental leadership: leader behavior directed at clarifying expectations, assigning specific tasks, and specifying procedures to be followed. (Also referred to as initiating structure.)

Supportive leadership: the degree to which leader behavior can be characterized as friendly and approachable, and considerate of the needs of subordinates. (Also referred to as leadership consideration.)

Participative leadership: a nondirective form of role clarifying behavior analogous to the more directive instrumental leadership. It considers the degree to which leaders allow subordinates to influence decisions by asking subordinates for input and suggestions. (Also referred to as leadership participation.)

Description: The perceived leadership behavior scale is a three-factor scale comprising the three aspects of perceived leadership described above. Across factors, items have been scored on a 5-point format of *always* = 5, *often* = 4, *occasionally* = 3, *seldom* = 2, and *never* = 1. Item scores can be summed within each factor to form indices for each of the three aspects of leadership. Thus, the scale is considered multidimensional.

Development: Based on path-goal theory and an extensive literature review, a pool of 35 items was generated to reflect the aspects of perceived leadership. Several of these items were taken from earlier research on leadership theory (Fleishman 1957; Stogdill 1963). Via factor and reliability analyses over two samples, the number of items was trimmed and the final scales were derived. Numerous tests of validity were also assessed.

Samples: Two samples of 206 and 96 were used in scale development and validation. These samples were employees from two electronics firms and consisted of managers, professionals, foremen, blue-collar workers, technicians, and others.

Validity: Principal components factor analysis revealed three factors corresponding to the three aspects of perceived leadership. Estimates of internal consistency reliability for subsets of the two samples were reported to be .72 and .76 for instrumental leadership (also referred to as initiating structure), .81 and .79 for supportive leadership (also referred to as leader consideration), and .67 and .68 for participative leadership (also referred to as leadership participation). These three factors were significantly intercorrelated (the actual correlations were not specified). Thus, partial correlations were used to examine the nomological validity of the leadership factors. To examine validity, the two samples were split into high, medium, and low task structure groups. Then, partial correlations of the three factors with a number of dependent variables were reported that offered evidence for the validity of the perceived leadership scales. For example, correlations of instrumental leadership with a measure of intrinsic job satisfaction for the low task structure group were .26 and .40 for the two samples. Correlations of supportive leadership with intrinsic job satisfaction for the high task structure group were .52 and .36 for the two samples. Numerous other estimates of validity were offered.

Scores: Neither mean nor percentage scores were reported by House and Dessler (1974).

Source: House, Robert J., and Gary Dessler. (1974). "The Path-Goal Theory of Leadership: Some Post Hoc and A Priori Tests." In James G. Hunt and Lars L. Larson (Eds.), *Contingency Approaches to Leadership*. Carbondale: Southern Illinois University Press.

© 1974 by Southern Illinois University Press. Scale items taken from Tables 8 and 9 (pp. 46-48). Reprinted with permission.

Other evidence: Although the scales have been used on many occasions in the organizational behavior literature, our discussion of other evidence will be restricted to marketing applications of the perceived leadership behavior scales. Teas (1981), with a sample of 171 industrial salespeople, examined the relationship of the leadership behavior scales (modified versions) with various job-related attitudes and outcomes. He reported coefficient alpha estimates of .84, .51, and .82 for supportive leadership (i.e., leadership consideration), instrumental leadership (i.e., initiation of structure), and participative leadership (i.e., participation), respectively. For these three scales as dependent variables, R^2 estimates ranged from .24 to .44 with predictor variables that included job self-esteem, experience, and company feedback, among others. Thus, some evidence for the nomological validity of the perceived leadership measures was found.

In another marketing application of 114 salespeople, Kohli (1989) used the modified initiation structure and leadership consideration measures of Teas (1981). Reliability estimates were reported to between .64 and .84 (across all measures in the study). The initiation of structure and leadership consideration scales were used as independent variables across high and low group splits of several moderator variables. With job satisfaction and role clarity as dependent variables, regression coefficients ranged from .51 to 1.08 for initiation of structure and .30 to .79 for leadership consideration, offering evidence of predictive validity.

Other sources: Teas, R. Kenneth. (1981). "An Empirical Test of Models of Salespersons' Job Expectancy and Instrumentality Perceptions." *Journal of Marketing Research*, *18*, 209-226.

Kohli, Ajay. (1989). "Effects of Supervisory Behavior: The Role of Individual Differences Among Salespeople." *Journal of Marketing*, *53*, 40-50.

References: Fleishman, E. A. (1957). "A Leader Behavior Description for Industry." In R. M. Stogdill and A. E. Coons (Eds.), *Leader Behavior: Its Description and Measurement* (pp. 103-119). Columbus: Ohio State University Bureau of Business Research.

House, Robert J. (1971). "A Path-Goal Theory of Leader Effectiveness." *Administrative Science Quarterly*, *16*, 321-338.

Stogdill, R. M. (1963). *Manual for Leadership Behavior Description Questionnaire Form XII*. Columbus: Ohio State University Bureau of Business Research.

PERCEIVED LEADER BEHAVIOR SCALES
(House and Dessler 1974)

Instrumental Leadership (Initiating Structure)

1. He lets group members know what is expected of them.

2. He decides what shall be done and how it shall be done.

3. He makes sure that his part in the group is understood.

4. He schedules the work to be done.

5. He maintains definite standards of performance.

6. He asks that the group members follow standard rules and regulations.

7. He explains the way any task should be carried out.

Supportive Leadership (Leadership Consideration)

1. He is friendly and polite.

2. He does little things to make it pleasant to be a member of the group.

3. He puts suggestions made by the group into operation.

4. He treats all group members as his equals.

5. He gives advance notice of changes.

6. He keeps to himself.

7. He looks out for the personal welfare of group members.

8. He is willing to make changes.

9. He helps me overcome problems which stop me from carrying out my task.

10. He helps me make working on my tasks more pleasant.

Participative Leadership (Leadership Participation)

1. When faced with a problem, he consults with his subordinates.

2. Before making decisions, he gives serious consideration to what his subordinates have to say.

3. He asks subordinates for their suggestions concerning how to carry out assignments.

4. Before taking action he consults with his subordinates.

5. He asks subordinates for suggestions on what assignments should be made.

NOTES: Although not specified by the authors, it seems that item 6 of the supportive leadership factor requires reverse scoring. Items 2, 4, 5, 6, and 7 compose Teas's (1981) version of instrumental leadership. Items 1, 2, 4, 5, 7, and 10 compose Teas's supportive leadership items. Teas used the entire leadership participation scale. Also, the Teas items used a slightly modified wording format to better fit the industrial salespeople sample, and they used a *very true* (5) to *very false* (1) scoring format.

Organizational Commitment

OCCUPATIONAL AND ORGANIZATIONAL COMMITMENT
(Meyer, Allen, and Smith 1993)

Construct: Organizational commitment refers to employees' commitment to their employers. Occupational commitment refers to commitment to a particular line of work (Meyer, Allen, and Smith 1993, pp. 538-540). Both types are assumed to consist of three dimensions. This conceptualization is based on the three themes identified by Meyer and Allen (1991): affective commitment, continuance commitment, and normative commitment. Briefly, employees with a strong affective commitment remain with the organization because they want to, those with a strong continuance commitment remain because they need to, and those with a strong normative commitment remain because they feel they ought to do so (Meyer et al. 1993, p. 539).

Description: The measures consist of six factors and a total of 36 items evenly distributed across the six factors (i.e., six items per factor). Responses are operationalized using 7-point scales ranging from *strongly disagree* to *strongly agree*. The items are averaged to yield composite commitment scores for both occupational and organizational commitment (Meyer et al. 1993, pp. 541-542).

Development: Thirty items designed to assess commitment to nursing were administered to student nurses. These data were used to select the best six items for each occupational commitment dimension. Examination of item loadings from principal components analysis was used to select the 18 occupational commitment items. Confirmatory factor analyses involving different factor structures for all three samples were used to support the three-factor correlated structure for the occupational commitment scales. The corresponding organizational commitment items administered to the registered nurse sample were taken from earlier research and modified to reflect the three-dimension model of organizational commitment. Additional confirmatory factor analyses revealed that a six-factor correlated model provided the best fit for the registered nurse sample data (Meyer et al. 1993, pp. 542-543). Overall fit statistics for the six-factor model were as follows: chi-square = 1,588 (579 *df*), RNI = .97, and PNFI = .89.

Samples: Two student nurse samples (*n* = 312 and *n* = 275) and a sample of 530 registered nurses were used in scale development and validation (see Table 1, p. 543). The latter sample was randomly chosen from the membership of the College of Nurses of Ontario. For the registered nurses, the average tenure in the nursing profession was 15 years. Of the respondents, 98% were female and 56% worked full-time. Most were staff nurses in general hospitals (Meyer et al. 1993, p. 541).

Validity: A substantial amount of supportive evidence is described by Meyer et al. (1993). For the registered nurse sample, some of that evidence included the following. First, the reliabilities for the six factors ranged from .74 to .83. For both organizational and occupational commitment, the affective and normative dimensions were positively correlated with job satisfaction and a measure of loyalty. The two measures of continuance commitment were negatively correlated with satisfaction and loyalty. Supportive correlations with neglect and exit were reported as well (Meyer et al. 1993, p. 548). Propensity to leave the organization and the occupation were negatively correlated as well. Evidence of discriminant validity was offered by the modest factor correlations across all measures and samples.

Scores: Mean scores and standard deviations for the six facets are presented in Table 7 (Meyer et al. 1993, p. 547) for the registered nurses. Mean scores ranged from 5.38 for affective occupational commitment to 3.04 for both organizational and occupational normative scales.

Source: Meyer, John P., Natalie J. Allen, and Catherine A. Smith. (1993). "Commitment to Organizations and Occupations: Extension and Test of a Three-Component Conceptualization." *Journal of Applied Psychology*, *78*(4), 538-551.

   © 1993 by the American Psychological Association. Scale items taken from Table 3 (p. 544). Reprinted with permission.

Other evidence: The validity of the three-component model of occupational commitment was further investigated in detail by Irving, Coleman, and Cooper (1997). Their research revealed evidence of discriminant validity for the three components, adequate measures of overall model fit, and significant correlations with related constructs as predicted. For example, the three-factor correlated model fit statistics included the following: RNI = .96, NFI = .93, and CFI = .95. The correlation of the affective component with job satisfaction was stronger than the correlation between the normative occupational component and satisfaction, as predicted. Occupational differences were also reported, along with a number of other correlations with the three occupational commitment dimensions.

Other source: Irving, P. Gregory, Daniel F. Coleman, and Christine L. Cooper. (1997). "Further Assessments of a Three-Component Model of Organizational Commitment: Generalizability and Differences Across Occupations." *Journal of Applied Psychology*, *82*(3), 444-452.

Reference: Meyer, John P., and Natalie J. Allen. (1991). "A Three-Component Conceptualization of Organizational Commitment." *Human Resource Management*, *1*, 61-98.

OCCUPATIONAL AND ORGANIZATIONAL COMMITMENT
(Meyer, Allen, and Smith 1993)

Factor 1: Affective Occupational

   1. Nursing is important to my self-image.

   2. I regret having entered the nursing profession. (R)

   3. I am proud to be in the nursing profession.

   4. I dislike being a nurse. (R)

   5. I do not identify with the nursing profession. (R)

   6. I am enthusiastic about nursing.

Factor 2: Continuance Occupational

   1. I have put too much into the nursing profession to consider changing now.

   2. Changing professions now would be difficult for me to do.

   3. Too much of my life would be disrupted if I were to change my profession.

   4. It would be costly for me to change my profession now.

   5. There are no pressures to keep me from changing professions. (R)

   6. Changing professions now would require considerable personal sacrifice.

Factor 3: Normative Occupational

1. I believe people who have been trained in a profession have a responsibility to stay in that profession for a reasonable amount of time.

2. I do not feel any obligation to remain in the nursing profession.

3. I feel a responsibility to the nursing profession to continue in it.

4. Even if it were to my advantage, I do not feel that it would be right to leave nursing now.

5. I would be guilty if I left nursing.

6. I am in nursing because of a sense of loyalty to it.

Factor 4: Affective Organizational

1. I would be very happy to spend the rest of my career with this organization.

2. I really feel as if this organization's problems are my own.

3. I do not feel a strong sense of "belonging" to my organization. (R)

4. I do not feel "emotionally attached" to this organization

5. I do not feel like "part of the family" at my organization.

6. This organization has a great deal of personal meaning for me.

Factor 5: Continuance Organizational

1. Right now, staying with my organization is a matter of necessity as much as desire.

2. It would be very hard for me to leave my organization right now, even if I wanted to.

3. Too much of my life would be disrupted if I decided I wanted to leave my organization.

4. I feel that I have too few options to consider leaving this organization.

5. If I had not already put so much of myself into this organization, I might consider working elsewhere.

6. One of the few negative consequences of leaving this organization would be the scarcity of available alternatives.

Factor 6: Normative Organizational

1. I do not feel any obligation to remain with my current employer.

2. Even if it were to my advantage, I do not feel it would be right to leave my organization now.

3. I would feel guilty if I left my organization now.

4. This organization deserves my loyalty.

5. I would not leave my organization right now because I have a sense of obligation to the people in it.

6. I owe a great deal to my organization.

NOTE: (R) denotes items requiring reverse scoring to reflect higher levels of commitment.

ORGANIZATIONAL COMMITMENT: OCQ
(Mowday, Steers, and Porter 1979)

Construct: Organizational commitment (OC) is defined as the relative strength of an individual's identification with and involvement in a particular organization. OC can be characterized by three related factors: (a) a strong belief in and acceptance of the organization's goals and values, (b) a willingness to exert considerable effort on behalf of the organization, and (c) a strong desire to maintain membership in the organization (Mowday, Steers, and Porter 1979, p. 226). For an expanded discussion of OC, see Mowday, Porter, and Steers (1982).

Description: The OCQ is composed of 15 Likert-type items scored on scales from *strongly disagree* (1) to *strongly agree* (7). Although the scale was originally designed to tap the aforementioned three factors, item scores are summed and divided by 15 to form an overall OC index. A reduced, nine-item version of the scale is also tenable in which item scores are summed and divided by nine to form an index.

Development: The approach to developing the scale was to identify 15 items that tapped the three factors of commitment. Thus, 15 items were generated by the authors and then checked for factor structure, reliability, and validity over numerous samples.

Samples: Nine samples totaling 2,563 subjects were used to examine the reliability and validity of the OCQ. These samples were 569 public employees, 243 university employees, 382 hospital employees, 411 bank employees, 119 scientists and engineers, 115 auto company managers, 60 psychiatric technicians, 59 retail management trainees, and 605 telephone company employees.

Validity: Coefficient alpha across the samples ranged from .88 to .90 for the 15-item version and .82 to .93 for the 9-item version. Item-to-total correlations ranged from .36 to .72 across samples. Factor analyses generally supported a single dimension, as the general factor (first factor) explained from 83.2% to 92.6% of the variance in the data. Test-retest reliabilities for the psychiatric technician sample were .53, .63, and .75 over periods of 2, 3, and 4 months, respectively. Test-retest reliabilities for the retail management employees were .72 and .62 over 2- and 3-month periods.

Convergent validity with a measure of organizational attachment ranged from .63 to .74 (for six of the samples). OCQ also had a correlation of .60 with an independent commitment rating measure for the retail trainees sample. Evidence of discriminant validity was found by correlations ranging from .30 to .56 (for four of the samples) between OCQ and job involvement, and correlations ranging from .01 to .68 (over five of the samples) between OCQ and the JDI. OCQ was also correlated with a measure of career satisfaction for two of the samples. These correlations of .39 and .40 also offered evidence of discriminant validity.

Predictive validity of the OCQ was also supported. Across nine data points, OCQ was significantly correlated with turnover eight times. The significant correlations ranged from –.17 to –.43. Similar correlations were found between OCQ and measures of tenure (.23 and .26), absenteeism (.08 to –.28), and performance (.05 to .36).

Scores: Mean scores and (std. dev.) were reported for each sample. The mean scores ranged from 4.2 (.90) to 5.3 (1.05) for eight of the samples. For the psychiatric technician sample, mean scores were reported for "stayers" and "leavers" across four time periods. For "stayers," the mean score across the four time periods ranged from 4.0 (3.0) to 4.3 (3.5). For "leavers," corresponding scores ranged from 3.0 (.98) to 3.5 (1.00).

Source: Mowday, Richard T., Richard M. Steers, and Lyman W. Porter. (1979). "The Measurement of Organizational Commitment." *Journal of Vocational Behavior, 14*, 224-247.

© 1979 by Academic Press. Scale items taken from Table 1 (p. 228). Reprinted with permission.

Other evidence: In the organizational behavior literature, the OCQ has been used and examined numerous times. For an excellent review, see Mathieu and Zajac (1990). Although OCQ has been used several times in the marketing literature, our discussion here will be limited to just three marketing applications of the OCQ.

Michaels, Cron, Dubinsky, and Joachimsthaler (1988) reported an alpha of .90 for the 15-item OCQ. They also reported correlations of .32, −.47, −.48, and −.53 between OCQ and measures of organizational formalization, role ambiguity, role conflict, and work alienation (retail sales setting where $n = 330$).

Good, Sisler, and Gentry (1988), using a sample of 595 department store employees, reported an alpha of .91 for the 15-item OCQ. Correlations of −.59, −.60, −.41, −.77, and −.81 were reported between OCQ and measures of role ambiguity, role conflict, work-family conflict, job satisfaction, and intention to leave, respectively.

Johnston, Parasuraman, Futrell, and Black (1990), using a sample of 102 retail salespeople, reported composite reliability estimates (via LISREL) of .88 and .93 for the 15-item OCQ over two time periods. OCQ correlations with role conflict, role ambiguity, job satisfaction, propensity to leave, and turnover were −.49, −.45, .58, −.73, and −.33, respectively. In sum, these three marketing studies provided evidence for the reliability and nomological validity of the OCQ.

A six-item version of the Mowday, Steers, and Porter (1979) organizational commitment (OC) scale was used by Singh, Goolsby, and Rhoads (1994) in their research on the consequences of boundary personnel burnout. A scale reliability of .79 was reported. The mean and standard deviation scores were 3.12 and 0.76, respectively. Correlations with other constructs also supported the validity of the measure. For example, negative correlations with the three burnout dimensions averaged .43. In addition, the OC scale was positively correlated with job satisfaction ($r = .55$).

Other sources: Good, Linda K., Grovalynn F. Sisler, and James W. Gentry. (1988). "Antecedents of Turnover Intentions Among Retail Management Personnel." *Journal of Retailing, 64*, 295-314.

Johnston, Mark W., A. Parasuraman, Charles M. Futrell, and William C. Black. (1990). "A Longitudinal Assessment of the Impact of Selected Organizational Influences on Salespeople's Organizational Commitment During Early Employment." *Journal of Marketing Research, 27*, 333-344.

Michaels, Ronald E., William L. Cron, Alan J. Dubinsky, and Erich A. Joachimsthaler. (1988). "The Influence of Formalization on the Organizational Commitment and Work Alienation of Salespeople and Industrial Buyers." *Journal of Marketing Research, 25*, 376-383.

Singh, Jagdip, Jerry R. Goolsby, and Gary K. Rhoads. (1994). "Behavioral and Psychological Consequences of Boundary Spanning Burnout for Customer Service Representatives." *Journal of Marketing Research, 31*, 558-569.

References: Mathieu, John E., and Dennis M. Zajac. (1990). "A Review and Meta-Analysis of the Antecedents, Correlates, and Consequences of Organizational Commitment." *Psychological Bulletin, 108*, 171-194.

Mowday, Richard T., Lyman W. Porter, and Richard M. Steers. (1982). *Employee-Organizational Linkages: The Psychology of Commitment, Absenteeism, and Turnover.* New York: Academic Press.

ORGANIZATIONAL COMMITMENT: OCQ
(Mowday, Steers, and Porter 1979)

1. I am willing to put in a great deal of effort beyond that normally expected in order to help this organization be successful.

2. I talk up this organization to my friends as a great organization to work for.

3. I feel very little loyalty to this organization.*

4. I would accept almost any type of job assignment in order to keep working for this organization.

5. I find that my values and the organization's values are very similar.

6. I am proud to tell others that I am part of this organization.

7. I could just as well be working for a different organization as long as the type of work was similar.*

8. This organization really inspires the very best in me in the way of job performance.

9. It would take very little change in my present circumstances to cause me to leave this organization.*

10. I am extremely glad that I chose this organization to work for over others I was considering at the time I joined.

11. There's not too much to be gained by sticking with this organization indefinitely.*

12. Often, I find it difficult to agree with this organization's policies on important matters relating to its employees.*

13. I really care about the fate of this organization.

14. For me, this is the best of all possible organizations for which to work.

15. Deciding to work for this organization was a definite mistake on my part.*

NOTES: *Denotes items that are reverse scored. The nine-item version of the OCQ is composed of those items that *are not* reverse scored.

ORGANIZATIONAL COMMITMENT
(Hunt, Chonko, and Wood 1985)

Construct: Organizational commitment was defined as a strong desire to remain a member of a particular organization, given opportunities to change jobs (Hunt, Chonko, and Wood 1985). The actual scale was developed to measure the degree of loyalty marketers would have to an organization, given attractive incentives to change companies. These incentives to change include higher pay, more creative freedom, more job status, and a friendlier environment.

Description: A four-item scale was designed to measure the degree of loyalty marketers would have to an organization, given attractive incentives to change companies. These incentive included higher pay, more freedom, more job status, and friendlier work environment. All items are rated using seven Likert-type response categories ranging from 1 = *strongly agree* to 7 = *strongly disagree*, and item scores are summed to form an overall score.

Development: Little detail as to scale development procedures was provided by Hunt et al. (1985), as the purpose of the study was to develop a model of the relationships among organizational commitment and various other job characteristics. Factor analysis was used to assess the scale's dimensionality, and alpha was used to assess its reliability. Checks for validity were performed by positing that commitment in marketing is a positive function of the personal attributes of income and age and a negative function of education; commitment is a positive function of the job characteristics of variety, autonomy, identity, and feedback; and satisfaction is a positive function of commitment.

Sample: A self-administered questionnaire was mailed to 4,282 marketing professionals who were members of the American Marketing Association. A total of 1,706 usable questionnaires were received.

Validity: Results of a factor analysis indicated a unidimensional factor structure accounting for 69% of the variance and having a high degree of internal consistency. The reported coefficient alpha was .85. An overall finding of this study was that while relationships among personal characteristics, job characteristics, and satisfaction exist, commitment is also a consistent predictor of satisfaction. Marketers who reported a high level of commitment tended to be more satisfied with their pay, job security, jobs in general, and choice of careers in marketing. This provided evidence for the validity of the scales. Furthermore, with commitment as the dependent variable and a number of demographic (i.e., age, education, income) and work-related variables (i.e., variety, autonomy, feedback) as predictors, R^2 estimates ranged from .02 to .17 over various splits of the $n = 1,706$ sample.

Scores: Table 4 (Hunt et al., p. 118) presents an ANOVA analysis of the Commitment and Job Characteristic Inventory. Means and standard deviations were reported for the total sample and for the classification of job types. The total sample mean and standard deviation for the commitment scale were 4.17 and 1.44, respectively.

Source: Hunt, Shelby D., Lawrence B. Chonko, and Van R. Wood. (1985). "Organizational Commitment and Marketing." *Journal of Marketing*, *49*, 112-126.

© 1985 by the American Marketing Association. Scale items taken from Table 3 (p. 117). Reprinted with permission.

Other evidence: N/A

Other sources: N/A

References: N/A

ORGANIZATIONAL COMMITMENT
(Hunt, Chonko, and Wood 1985)

1. I would be willing to change companies if the new job offered a 25% pay increase.

2. I would be willing to change companies if the new job offered more creative freedom.

3. I would be willing to change companies if the new job offered more status.

4. I would be willing to change companies if the new job was with people who were more friendly.

Sales/Selling Approaches

ADAPTIVE SELLING: ADAPTS
(Spiro and Weitz 1990)

Construct: Adaptive selling is defined as the "degree to which salespeople alter sales behaviors during a customer interaction or across customer interactions based on perceived information about the nature of the selling situation" (Spiro and Weitz 1990, p. 62). Five facets of adaptive selling were retained: (a) recognition that different sales approaches are needed for different customers, (b) confidence in ability to use a variety of approaches, (c) confidence in ability to alter approach during an interaction, (d) collection of information to facilitate adaptation, and (e) actual use of different approaches.

Description: The final version of the instrument consisted of 16 items that represent the five facets of adaptive selling listed above. Presumably, the items are scored on 7-point disagree-agree scales. Although five facets are specified, item scores are averaged over the 16 items for an overall ADAPTS score.

Development: Initially, the construct's domain was defined as consisting of six facets to assess adaptive selling. Items were generated for each facet, and the initial instrument consisted of 42 scale items. During the purification study, these 42 items were subjected to a principal component analysis and factor analysis. The pattern of loadings did not correspond to the conceptualized facets of adaptive selling discussed before; however, items representing five of the six facets did load highly on the first component. Therefore, one scale incorporating all the facets, rather than separate scales for each facet, was developed. The final 16-item scale contained at least two items from five of the six facets described before. The original fourth facet, knowledge structure, was not represented in the final scale because the items assessing categorization of sales situations were unrelated to the 16 items forming the final scale. Additionally, Spiro and Weitz (1990) discussed antecedents and consequences of the adaptive selling construct. The nomological validity of these measures was assessed by examining relationships of the adaptive selling measure to antecedents, consequences, and general personality measures of interpersonal flexibility.

Sample: A sample of 500 salespeople in 10 divisions of a major national manufacturer of diagnostic equipment was contacted. Pretest interviews confirmed that these salespeople continually encountered a wide variety of selling situations in which the practice of adaptive selling should be beneficial. Of the 500 questionnaires distributed, 268 were returned in a usable form for a 54% response rate.

Validity: After the purification study, item-to-total correlations ranged from .33 to .61. The reliability of the 16-item scale, calculated by using Cronbach's alpha, was .85. However, because this scale is not unidimensional on the basis of confirmatory factor analysis, caution is warranted when using Cronbach's alpha as a reliability measure. When the 16 items were subjected to a principal component analysis, the eigenvalues of the first two components were 4.59 and 1.12. Support for the nomological validity of the scale was found by correlating it with a number of constructs. Correlations of ADAPTS with measures of performance, self-monitoring, sensitivity to others, androgyny, social self-confidence, and interpersonal control were .26, .46, .41, .45, .36, and .42, respectively.

Scores: The mean response for the total scale (sum divided by number of items) was 5.51. The standard deviation was .66. Individual item score are offered in Table 1 (p. 66).

Source: Spiro, Rosanne L., and Barton A. Weitz. (1990). "Adaptive Selling: Conceptualization, Measurement, and Nomological Validity." *Journal of Marketing Research*, 27, 61-69.

© 1990 by the American Marketing Association. Scale items taken from Table 1 (p. 66). Reprinted with permission.

Other evidence: N/A

Other sources: N/A

References: N/A

ADAPTIVE SELLING: ADAPTS
(Spiro and Weitz 1990)

1. Each customer requires a unique approach. 1

2. When I feel that my sales approach is not working, I can easily change to another approach. 3

3. I like to experiment with different sales approaches. 6

4. I am very flexible in the selling approach I use. 6

5. I feel that most buyers can be dealt with in pretty much the same manner.* 1

6. I don't change my approach from one customer to another.* 6

7. I can easily use a wide variety of selling approaches. 2

8. I use a set sales approach.* 6

9. It is easy for me to modify my sales presentation if the situation calls for it. 3

10. Basically I use the same approach with most customers.* 6

11. I am very sensitive to the needs of my customers. 5

12. I find it difficult to adapt my presentation style to certain buyers.* 2

13. I vary my sales style from situation to situation. 6

14. I try to understand how one customer differs from another. 5

15. I feel confident that I can effectively change my planned presentation when necessary. 3

16. I treat all of my buyers pretty much the same.* 6

NOTES: *Denotes reverse-scored items. The original six facets' numbers are at the end of each item and correspond to the facets listed below. As previously stated, only five facets were retained (1-3 and 5-6 below).

1. A recognition that different selling approaches are needed in different sales situations.
2. Confidence in the ability to use a variety of different sales approaches.
3. Confidence in the ability to alter the sales approach during a customer interaction.
4. A knowledge structure that facilitates the recognition of different sales situations and access to sales strategies appropriate for each situation.
5. The collection of information about the sales situation to facilitate adaptation.
6. The actual use of different approaches in different situations.

CUSTOMER ORIENTATION OF SALESPEOPLE: SOCO
(Saxe and Weitz 1982)

Construct: The SOCO scale (Sales Orientation-Customer Orientation) was designed to measure the degree to which a salesperson engages in customer-oriented selling (i.e., the degree to which salespeople practice the marketing concept by trying to help their customers make purchase decisions that will satisfy customer needs). Highly customer-oriented salespeople avoid actions that might result in customer dissatisfaction. Specifically, the SOCO scale measures six components: (a) a desire to help customers make good purchase decisions, (b) helping customers assess their needs, (c) offering products that will satisfy those needs, (d) describing products accurately, (e) avoiding deceptive or manipulative influence tactics, and (f) avoiding the use of high pressure.

Description: The SOCO scale consists of 24 items related to specific actions a salesperson might take when interacting with buyers. The items are scored on 9-point scales ranging from *true for none of my customers-NEVER* to *true for all my customers-ALWAYS*. Negatively stated items were reverse scored, and a total score can be derived by summing the item scores.

Development: Initially, the construct's domain was characterized as consisting of seven components that described attitudes and behaviors that distinguish high and low customer-oriented salespeople. Items were generated for each component, and the initial pool contained 104 scale items. Then, an assessment of the content validity of these items was made by surveying expert judges. After this assessment, 70 items were retained and distributed to salespersons. Based on an analysis of corrected item-to-total correlations, the 12 positively stated and 12 negatively stated items with the highest corrected item-to-total correlations were chosen for the second instrument. The 24-item scale was then distributed to the second sample, and the original conception of the components underlying customer orientation was largely supported by the data with only one exception (i.e., matching sales presentation to customer interests was not revealed as a distinct component). A second group of salespeople was used to assess scale properties and hypotheses related to validity.

Samples: Following a survey of the literature, the concept of customer orientation was investigated and scale items were generated by interviewing 25 salespeople and sales managers. Then, 11 sales managers and 13 faculty were used as expert judges to assess content validity of these items. Salespersons from 48 firms returned a total of 119 usable responses. The scale was revised for a second study and was distributed to four uniquely different sales forces, resulting in 95 usable responses. After 6 weeks, 46 salespeople in the second sample were retested to assess test-retest reliability.

Validity: The administration of the 24-item SOCO scale to the second sample resulted in a coefficient alpha estimate of .83. The scale was readministered to part of the second sample to assess test-retest reliability. A correlation of .67 ($p < .01$, one-tailed) indicated a reasonable degree of stability. A series of tests of nomological validity indicated that the SOCO scale was related to the ability of salespeople to help their customers and the quality of customer-salesperson satisfaction. For example, the correlation of SOCO with a measure of long- versus short-term orientation was .56, and correlations of the SOCO scale with Machiavellianism and social desirability were −.47 and .00. (Correlations of SOCO with 18 other variables are in Table 3, p. 349.) Known group validity was examined by comparing SOCO mean score across seven different sales positions. The pattern of means ranged from 159 to 187, providing evidence of known group validity.

Scores: For the 9-point items used in the final instrument, the mean score and standard deviation for the first sample were 183 and 24, respectively. The mean score for the second sample was 186, and the standard deviation was 18. (Table 2, p. 347 presents means across seven sales positions.)

Source: Saxe, Robert, and Barton A. Weitz. (1982). "The SOCO Scale: A Measure of the Customer Orientation of Salespeople." *Journal of Marketing Research*, *19*, 343-351.

© 1982 by the American Marketing Association. Scale items taken from Table 1 (pp. 345-346). Reprinted with permission.

Other evidence: Michaels and Day (1985) used a national sample of purchasing professionals to replicate the SOCO scale with buyers assessing the customer orientation of salespeople who made calls on them. A total of 1,005 responses were usable. The factor structure and reliability results were almost identical to those obtained when salespeople assessed their own degree of customer orientation. The internal consistency reliability for the scale was .91, and a unidimensional factor structure was found. The mean score and standard deviation for the salespeople were 138 and 22.

A refined version, named COVS (for customer orientation of vendor salesperson), was tested on 345 purchasing managers by Tadepalli (1995). The adapted scale consists of 21 items with a Likert-type agreement response format (Tadepalli 1995, p. 181). Reliability for the unidimensional scale was .94. Item-to-total and inter-item correlations are reported. A correlation of .31 was reported between the revised scale and a measure of similarity between the buyer and the seller.

Williams and Attaway (1996) used an 18-item version of the SOCO scale in their research involving customer orientation as a mediator of organizational culture's effects on buyer-seller relationships. Based on the responses of 153 buyers, a coefficient alpha estimate of .97 was reported. Although their findings were generally mixed in support of their proposed model, supportive evidence was provided for the use of customer orientation as a mediator of firm culture on relationship development.

Other sources: Michaels, Ronald E., and Ralph L. Day. (1985). "Measuring Customer Orientation of Salespeople: A Replication With Industrial Buyers." *Journal of Marketing Research*, *22*, 443-446.

Tadepalli, Raghu. (1995). "Measuring Customer Orientation of the Salesperson." *Psychology and Marketing*, *12*, 177-187.

Williams, Michael R., and Jill S. Attaway. (1996). "Exploring Salespersons' Customer Orientation as a Mediator of Organizational Culture's Influence on Buyer-Seller Relationships." *Journal of Personal Selling and Sales Management*, *16*, 33-52.

References: N/A

CUSTOMER ORIENTATION OF SALESPEOPLE: SOCO
(Saxe and Weitz 1982)

INSTRUCTIONS:

The statements below describe various ways a salesperson might act with a customer or prospect (for convenience, the word "customer" is used to refer to both customers and prospects). For each statement please indicate the proportion of your customers with whom you act as described in the statement. Do this by circling one of the numbers from 1 to 9. The meaning of the numbers are:

    1 - True for NONE of your customers-NEVER
    2 - True for ALMOST NONE
    3 - True for A FEW
    4 - True for SOMEWHAT LESS THAN HALF
    5 - True for ABOUT HALF
    6 - True for SOMEWHAT MORE THAN HALF
    7 - True for a LARGE MAJORITY
    8 - True for ALMOST ALL
    9 - True for ALL of your customers-ALWAYS

For example, if you circled 6 below, you would indicate that you ask **somewhat more than half** of your customers a lot of questions.

	NEVER							ALWAYS	
I ask customers a lot of questions.	**1**	**2**	**3**	**4**	**5**	**6**	**7**	**8**	**9**

Stem-Positively Stated Items

8. I try to help customers achieve their goals.

21. I try to achieve my goals by satisfying customers.

13. A good salesperson has to have the customer's best interest in mind.

2. I try to get customers to discuss their needs with me.

5. I try to influence a customer by information rather than by pressure.

16. I offer the product of mine that is best suited to the customer's problem.

23. I try to find out what kind of product would be most helpful to a customer.

9. I answer a customer's questions about products as correctly as I can.

14. I try to bring a customer with a problem together with a product that helps him solve that problem.

15. I am willing to disagree with a customer in order to help him make a better decision.

1. I try to give customers an accurate expectation of what the product will do for them.

12. I try to figure out what a customer's needs are.

Stem-Negatively Stated Items

19. I try to sell a customer all I can convince him to buy, even if I think it is more than a wise customer would buy.

6. I try to sell as much as I can rather than to satisfy a customer.

24. I keep alert for weaknesses in a customer's personality so I can use them to put pressure on him to buy.

3. If I am not sure a product is right for a customer, I will still apply pressure to get him to buy.

22. I decide what products to offer on the basis of what I can convince customers to buy, not on the basis of what will satisfy them in the long run.

20. I paint too rosy a picture of my products, to make them sound as good as possible.

7. I spend more time trying to persuade a customer to buy than I do trying to discover his needs.

17. It is necessary to stretch the truth in describing a product to a customer.

10. I pretend to agree with customers to please them.

4. I imply to a customer that something is beyond my control when it is not.

18. I begin the sales talk for a product before exploring a customer's needs with him.

11. I treat a customer as a rival.

NOTE: Item numbers are as they originally appeared in the Saxe and Weitz (1982) article.

INSTRUMENTAL AND EXPRESSIVE PERSONALITY TRAITS OF SALESPERSONS
(Jolson and Comer 1997)

Construct: Based on the original conceptualization of Bem (1974), instrumentality is defined as a masculine orientation characterized as providing for the economic and security needs of the family. Associated traits include assertiveness, independence, and dominance. The corresponding more feminine traits associated with expressiveness include compassion, warmth, sympathy, and sensitivity to the needs of others (Jolson and Comer 1997, p. 30). Both sets of traits are argued to have relevance to personal selling.

Description: The instrumentality and expressiveness subscales each comprise 10 items operationalized using a 7-place response format labeled *never or almost never true* to *always or almost always true*. Overall scores are based on averages across the 10 items (Jolson and Comer 1997, p. 33). A person is said to be of either orientation depending on which score is higher. If both scores are high and not significantly different, the individual is classified as androgynous (Jolson and Comer 1997, p. 30). Using the same response format, a series of selling behaviors characteristic of the different traits were also evaluated by the sales managers. These items are shown in Appendixes A and B (Jolson and Comer 1997, pp. 42-43).

Development: The 20 items were selected from the original Bem Sex Role Inventory. Several wording changes were made to enhance applicability to the sales force context.

Sample: The responses to 98 dyads comprising sales managers and salespersons were used to evaluate the measures. The median ages for the sales managers and salespersons were 44 and 38 years, respectively. The corresponding percentages of males within each sample were 65 and 55. For the managers, the median length of time supervising the target salesperson was 2 years.

Validity: Coefficient alpha estimates of internal consistency reliability for the salespersons ratings were .86 and .86 for instrumentality and expressiveness, respectively. No differences in median scores between males and females were found. The same estimates for the sales managers' ratings were .92 and .91. Jolson and Comer (1997) summarize estimates of reliability from previous research as well. Supportive evidence for the personality trait measures was also provided by significant positive correlations between the salespersons' self-ratings and the managers' ratings, plus the managers' sales behavior ratings.

Scores: Self-ratings and manager ratings for both sets of 10 items are presented in Table 1 (Jolson and Comer 1997, p. 35). Manager median scores were 5.25 and 5.14 for the instrumentality and expressiveness factors. In general, salesperson self-ratings were higher than the corresponding manager ratings.

Source: Jolson, Marvin A., and Lucette B. Comer. (1997). "The Use of Instrumental and Expressive Personality Traits as Indicators of a Salesperson's Behavior." *Journal of Personal Selling and Sales Management*, *17*, 29-43.

    © 1997 by the *Journal of Personal Selling and Sales Management*. Scale items taken from Appendixes A and B (pp. 42-43). Reprinted with permission.

Other evidence: N/A

Other sources: N/A

Reference: Bem, Sandra L. (1974). "The Measurement of Psychological Androgyny." *Journal of Consulting and Clinical Psychology*, *42*, 155-162.

INSTRUMENTAL AND EXPRESSIVE PERSONALITY TRAITS OF SALESPERSONS
(Jolson and Comer 1997)

Instrumental Items

Defends own beliefs

Is independent

Is assertive

Has strong personality

Is forceful

Has leadership ability

Is willing to take risk

Is dominant

Is willing to take a stand on issues

Is aggressive

Expressive Items

Is affectionate

Is sympathetic

Is sensitive to the needs of others

Is understanding

Is compassionate

Is eager to soothe hurt feelings

Is warm

Loves people

Is gentle

SELF-EFFICACY FOR NEGOTIATION
(Chowdhury 1993)

Construct: Self-efficacy is an individual difference that refers to a person's perception of her or his own level of mastery within a limited task domain. Self-efficacy is conceptualized as a global and enduring variable whose values remain relatively unaltered over a range of quota levels for a given task (Chowdhury 1993, pp. 31-32). The concept then reflects the individual's overall impression of his or her capabilities in the performance domain of negotiation. For a given level of quota, individuals high in self-efficacy will have a higher level of expectancy of task success than those low in self-efficacy and will exhibit greater increases in effort.

Description: The self-efficacy for negotiation scale consists of 20 items, operationalized with a 7-place response format bounded by *strongly disagree* (1) and *strongly agree* (7) (cf. Sujan, Weitz, and Kumar 1994, p. 47).

Development: Domain specific measures were developed for the selling negotiation experiment (cf. Bandura 1984). Item generation and scale refinement procedures were not reported.

Samples: Undergraduate business students ($n = 113$) participated in the experimental study. A second student "holdout" sample ($n = 136$) was used in measurement validation.

Validity: Coefficient alpha estimates of reliability for the holdout ($n = 136$) and experimental ($n = 113$) samples were both .92. The construct validity of the scale was said to be supported by positive correlations with measures of self-esteem ($r = .41$ and .27) and sphere of control ($r = .59$ and .42). Further evidence of validity was provided by tests of stability between the before and after conditions in the experiment (Chowdhury 1993, p. 33). In addition, subjects high in self-efficacy reported significantly higher expectancy of task success, more confidence in their probability estimates, more time negotiating, more rounds of negotiations, and higher selling prices at the conclusion of their negotiations (Chowdhury 1993, p. 35). Overall, the results demonstrate the ability of the self-efficacy measure to successfully moderate, as predicted, the relationship between assigned quotas and the level of expended effort.

Scores: Estimates of central tendency and variance were not provided.

Source: Chowdhury, Jhinuk. (1993). "The Motivational Impact of Sales Quotas on Effort." *Journal of Marketing Research*, *30*, 28-41.
     © 1993 by the American Marketing Association. Scale items taken from Appendix B (p. 39). Reprinted with permission.

Other evidence: Sujan et al. (1994) used a modified seven-item version of the scale to represent self-efficacy as a salesperson. The seven-item scale had a reliability of .77 and was significantly correlated with related constructs, as expected. The mean score (std. dev.) for the modified scale was 5.45 (0.70). The scale was positively correlated with performance ($r = .30$), working smart ($r = .51$), and working hard ($r = .49$).

Other sources: N/A

References: Bandura, Albert. (1984). "Recycling Misconceptions of Perceived Self-Efficacy." *Cognitive Theory and Research*, *8*(3), 231-255.

     Sujan, Harish, Barton A. Weitz, and Nirmalya Kumar. (1994). "Learning Orientation, Working Smart, and Effective Selling." *Journal of Marketing*, *58*, 39-52.

SELF-EFFICACY FOR NEGOTIATION
(Chowdhury 1993)

1. I am good at negotiating tasks.

2. It is easy for me to get others to agree to my terms or see my point of view.

3. I find it difficult to convince someone else, when that person's point of view conflicts with mine. (R)

4. In any negotiation situation, I find it relatively easy to refuse an offer I do not like.

5. I find it very difficult to refuse an offer if the person I am negotiating with is very persistent. (R)

6. It is easy for someone else to take advantage of me when he (or she) is bargaining with me. (R)

7. In most bargaining situations I am likely to come out as the "winner" when the deal is concluded.

8. I can put pressure on someone I am bargaining with to get him or her closer to my terms.

9. I do not possess the skills that are required to be a good negotiator. (R)

10. A person has to be a really good negotiator to persuade me to accept his or her terms (or point of view) that I started out disagreeing with.

11. My friends consider me to be a good negotiator.

12. I cannot bring myself to apply pressure on another person in order to get a better deal for myself in a bargaining situation. (R)

13. Because I am not a good bargainer, I am likely to do poorly in situations involving bargaining. (R)

14. If a situation calls for negotiating, my friends would consider me to be the right person to deal with it.

15. I usually come out better off in situations in which I have the opportunity to negotiate terms.

16. My closest friends do not consider me to be a good negotiator. (R)

17. I find it difficult to continue bargaining for long over any issue. (R)

18. I do not give up easily in the course of negotiation until the conditions and terms that I am looking for have been met.

19. In the course of a negotiation, I am good at "reading" an opponent with regard to what terms he or she is actually interested in.

20. I can easily conceal my own minimum acceptable terms and make offers and bids that will give me a substantially greater advantage.

NOTE: (R) denotes items requiring reverse scoring.

Inter- Intrafirm Issues of Influence and Power

INFLUENCE STRATEGIES IN MARKETING CHANNELS
(Boyle, Dwyer, Robicheaux, and Simpson 1992)

Construct: The following definitions are based on the taxonomy of Frazier and his colleagues (e.g., Frazier and Rody 1991). Boyle, Dwyer, Robicheaux, and Simpson (1992, p. 463) summarize these definitions as follows:

Promise: source certifies to extend specified rewards contingent on the target's compliance.

Threat: source informs the target that failure to comply will result in negative sanctions.

Legalistic plea: source contends that target compliance is required by formal agreement.

Request: source asks target to act with no mention of subsequent sanctions.

Information exchanges: source supplies information with no specific action requested or otherwise indicated.

Recommendation: source stresses that specific target action is needed for the latter to achieve desired outcomes.

Description: Twenty-nine items are used to operationalize the six influence strategies: recommendations (4 items), information exchange (4 items), promises (6 items), requests (4 items), legalistic pleas (5 items), and threats (6 items). Influence is assessed as the average of the item responses used to represent each influence type. Responses are assessed using the following 5-place response format: *always*, *usually*, *sometimes*, *rarely*, and *never*. To ensure a common referent, responses referred to the dealership's top volume manufacturer (Boyle et al. 1992, p. 465).

Development: Thirty-five items were originally developed to represent the six strategies. Pretest analyses using 92 MBA students were conducted to assess dimensionality and reliability, as well as comparative responsiveness to experimental treatments. These efforts resulted in the final set of 29 items. Subsequent analyses based on the main study data resulted in only 25 items actually being used to operationalize the influence strategies.

Samples: Study 1 was based on the responses of 198 automobile dealer representatives from 15 metropolitan areas. The dealerships averaged 67 employees, $32 million in sales, and 18 years in business (Boyle et al. 1992, p. 465). The second study was based on the responses of 686 automobile replacement tire dealers. The dealers were grouped according to the mode of channel governance: corporate systems, 172; franchise systems, 84; aligned systems, 206; and market systems, 224. Of the respondents in Study 2, 57% were owner/president and 38% were tire dealer managers.

Validity: LISREL analysis of the Study 1 data revealed that the indicators were reliable measures of their respective constructs. The pattern of mean scores (i.e., rank order and differences between strategy types) was offered as evidence of discriminant validity. Composite reliabilities ranged from .75 to .93. Significant negative correlations for four of the influence strategies with a measure of relationalism were reported. For the 25 items eventually used in the second study, composite reliabilities ranged from .85 to .91. All factor loadings were significant, and tests of factor correlations revealed support for discriminant validity. Overall fit statistics for a model including relationalism as a factor included the following: GFI = .91, AGFI = .89, and CFI = .95. Lastly, hypothesis tests revealed that related constructs were correlated as predicted with the six measures of influence.

Scores: Means scores for Study 1 were as follows: recommendations (3.37), information exchange (2.97), promises (2.58), requests (2.35), legalistic pleas (1.75), and threats (1.37). See also Tables 1 and 3 (Boyle et al. 1992, pp. 466, 468).

Source: Boyle, Brett, F. Robert Dwyer, Robert A. Robicheaux, and James T. Simpson. (1992). "Influence Strategies in Marketing Channels: Measures and Use in Different Relationship Structures." *Journal of Marketing Research, 29*, 462-473.

    © 1992 by the American Marketing Association. Scale items taken from Appendix (pp. 470-471). Reprinted with permission.

Other evidence: N/A

Other sources: N/A

Reference: Frazier, Gary L., and Raymond C. Rody. (1991). "The Use of Influence Strategies in Relationships in Industrial Product Channels." *Journal of Marketing, 55*, 52-69.

INFLUENCE STRATEGIES IN MARKETING CHANNELS
(Boyle, Dwyer, Robicheaux, and Simpson 1992)

Recommendation Items

My primary supplier . . .

RC1   makes it clear that by following their recommendations, our business would benefit.

RC2   makes it explicit, when making a suggestion, that it is intended for the good of our operation.

RC3   provides a clear picture of the anticipated positive impact on our business a recommended course of action will have.

RC4   outlines the logic and/or evidence for expecting success from the specific programs and actions suggested.

Information Exchange Items

IX1   focuses on *general* strategies (as opposed to specific tactics) as to how to make our business more profitable.

IX2   concentrates more on strategic, long-term issues, rather than specific courses of action our business should take.

IX3   discusses the orientation our management personnel should take with regard to long-term planning, rather than daily activities.

IX4   attempts to change our perspective by looking at how our business decisions affect the "big picture."

Promise Items

P1   makes promises to give something back in return for specific actions of our dealership.

P2   provides price breaks or other incentives for our participation in manufacturer promos, showroom design, and other programs.

P3   emphasizes what they will offer in return for our cooperation or participation when presenting a . . .

P4   offers specific incentives for us to make changes in marketing and/or operating procedures.

P5   uses bonuses for meeting sales or profit quotas.

P6   offers incentives to us when we initially had been reluctant to cooperate with a new program or policy.

Request Items

R1   asks for our compliance to their requests, *not* indicating any positive or negative outcome for our business contingent upon our compliance.

R2   asks us to accept new ideas without an explanation of what effect it will have on our business.

R3   asks our cooperation in implementing new programs *without* mentioning rewards for complying, *or* punishments for refusing.

R4   expects that their requests do not require an incentive for us to comply.

Legalistic Plea Items

LP1   refers to portions of our franchise agreement which favor their position to gain our compliance on a particular demand.

LP2   makes a point to refer to any legal agreements we have when attempting to influence our actions.

LP3   "reminds us" of any of our obligations stipulated in our sales agreement.

LP4   uses sections of our sales agreements as a "tool" to get us to agree to their demands.

LP5   makes biased interpretations of our selling agreement in order to gain our cooperation in following a request.

Threat Items

T1   makes it clear that failing to comply with their requests will result in penalties against our business.

T2   threatens poorer service to our business should we fail to agree to their requests.

T3   uses threats of disturbing our business, such as higher prices for supplies, slow delivery times, and lower fill rates.

T4   communicates their ability to "make things difficult" for our business if specific demands are not met.

T5   states that specific services will be discontinued for not complying to requests.

T6   threatens to reduce the amount of business they will do with our firm, should their demands not be met.

MULTIPLE INFLUENCES IN BUYING CENTERS
(Kohli and Zaltman 1988)

Construct: Influence of an individual in a buying center was defined as the changes in purchase decision–related opinions and behaviors of buying center members as a consequence of the individual's participation in the decision making. This definition tapped the notion of how different buying center members' opinions and behaviors would have been if the individual had not been involved in the decision making. The definition provided for intentional as well as unintentional change resulting from the individual's participation (Kohli and Zaltman 1988, p. 198). Furthermore, the measure was designed to assess the influences exerted by an individual in a specific purchase decision rather than in purchase decisions in general.

Description: The buying influence scale consists of nine items scored on 5-point scales ranging from *very small* to *very large*. It is important to recognize that the measure was primarily designed to assess influence in the final evaluation and selection phase of decision making. Item scores are summed to form an overall total score.

Development: After an extensive review of the literature, scale development proceeded by selecting the specific stage of the decision-making process for which the measure would be designed. The final evaluation and selection phase of the decision process was selected because it was felt that this phase was the richest with respect to group dynamics. A panel of judges was asked to critique the structure and content of the initial set of items designed to measure influence. The revised set of items went through several phases of pretesting. The final set of items contained nine items. Via factor, item, and reliability analyses, the final scale was derived and evaluated.

Samples: Five hundred randomly selected members of the National Association of Purchasing Management were surveyed. A total of 251 usable responses were obtained for an effective response rate of approximately 55%.

Validity: Alpha for the nine-item scale was .93. The dimensionality of the measure was assessed by performing a factor analysis. The general factor had an eigenvalue of 5.48 and accounted for more than 60% of the variance, suggesting a unidimensional structure. Face validity, content validity, and aspects of construct validity (including convergent, discriminant, and nomological validity) were also assessed. The results suggested support for convergent and discriminant validity. Also, findings were consistent with prior expectations on theoretical grounds and provided strong support for nomological validity of the influence scale. For example, the correlation between the scale and a single-item measure of influence was .66, indicating convergent validity. Lower correlations were found with size, risk, and time pressure measures, indicating discriminant validity. Lastly, nomological validity was provided by correlations of the scale with expertise (.45), reward power (.34), and coercive power (.25).

Scores: Means scores and standard deviations were not cited in the Kohli and Zaltman (1988) article.

Source: Kohli, Ajay K., and Gerald Zaltman. (1988). "Measuring Multiple Buying Influences." *Industrial Marketing Management 17*, 197-204.
    © 1988 by American Marketing Association. Scale items taken from Appendix (p. 203). Reprinted with permission.

Other evidence: N/A

Other sources: N/A

References: N/A

MULTIPLE INFLUENCES IN BUYING CENTERS
(Kohli and Zaltman 1988)

1. How much weight did the committee members give to his opinions?

2. How much impact did he have on the thinking of the other members?

3. To what extent did he influence the criteria used for making the final decision?

4. How much effect did his involvement in the purchase committee have on how the various options were rated?

5. To what extent did he influence others into adopting certain positions about the various options?

6. How much change did he induce in the preferences of other members?

7. To what extent did others go along with his suggestions?

8. To what extent did his participation influence the decision eventually reached?

9. To what extent did the final decision reflect his views?

NOTE: Items were scored on a 5-point scale ranging from *very small* to *very large*.

POWER: SOCIAL POWER SCALES
(Swasy 1979)

Construct: An instrument to measure perceived interpersonal social power was developed based on the French and Raven (1959) conceptualization of six interpersonal power types. These included reward, coercive, referent, legitimate, expert, and informational (Swasy 1979). It is important to note that the power one individual (person A) holds over another (person B) is *perceived* and not necessarily absolute. Brief definitions of each power type follow.

Reward power of person A over person B is based on the ability to mediate positive outcomes and to remove or decrease negative outcomes received by B.

Coercive power rests on B's belief that A will punish him for not complying.

Referent power results largely from a person B's feelings of identification with person A and the desire to maintain similarity with person A.

Legitimate power stems from internalized values of person B which dictate that person A has the right of influence and that person B is obligated to obey.

Expert power stems from person B's attribution of superior skills or knowledge to person A.

Informational power stems from the "logic," "reasoning," or importance of the communication provided by the influencing agent (person A) and independent of the communicator.

Description: The final version of the instrument consisted of 31 items in a Likert-type disagree-agree format. Items are summed within factors to form total scores for each factor. Each item was scored 1 to 5, with higher numbers reflecting higher power. The author also suggested that using only the three highest loading items for each of the six power bases resulted in a scale of more reasonable total length and acceptable levels of internal consistency.

Development: After a review of the literature, 150 items which reflected different characteristics of a social power situation were generated. Six judges rated these items, resulting in 85 items having reasonably high interjudge consistency. Items were designated by the author as acceptable indicators if the following criteria were met: (a) A minimum of five of the six judges classified each item as an indicator for the same power type and (b) each item also was not classified as an indicator in the other categories a total of three or more times (either within another category or over several categories). Two scenarios per power type were developed and subsequently rated by judges. The final situations were selected on the basis of being a clear representation of one social power type. Two scenarios depicting each power type were developed so that the scales would have some degree of generalizability. The final questionnaires were then completed by 321 students. Items reflecting each power basis were factor and item analyzed to determine the most reliable statements for the final scales. Reliability and predictive validity estimates were reported.

Samples: Six judges who were familiar with the French and Raven typology participated in the first phase of the study. Subjects were undergraduate accounting majors at UCLA. A total of 321 students were used in the final analysis of the scales.

Validity: Cronbach's coefficient alpha for each power component, as well as three-item versions of each component, were reported. The three-item legitimate power scale had an alpha level of .59. (This low estimate was attributed to the rather unique nature of a scenario used for legitimate power.) The other alpha levels for the power types are as follows: coercive—.84 for the overall scale and .81 for a three-item version; expertise—.86 overall and .74 for a three-item version; referent—.83 overall and .79 for a three-item version; and reward—.82 and .74 for a three-item version. The three-item information dimension had an alpha of .74. In addition, significant

F ratios based on mean scores for the three-item versions of the scale across situations suggested that the scales were valid operationalizations of the power constructs.

Scores: Table 3 on page 345 of the Swasy (1979) article presents the results of a one-way ANOVA and Newman-Keuls test of differences in social power scores across situations. These mean scores are based on the three-item versions of the scales and range from 5.03 to 12.17 across the six power dimensions.

Source: Swasy, John L. (1979). "Measuring the Bases of Social Power." In William L. Wilkie (Ed.), *Advances in Consumer Research* (Vol. 6, pp. 340-346). Ann Arbor, MI: Association for Consumer Research.

    © 1979 by the Association for Consumer Research. Scale items taken from Table 2 (p. 344-345). Reprinted with permission.

Other evidence: N/A

Other sources: N/A

Reference: French, John R., and Bertram Raven. (1959). "The Basis of Social Power." In D. Cartwright (Ed.), *Studies in Social Power* (pp. 150-167). Ann Arbor, MI: Institute for Social Research.

POWER: SOCIAL POWER SCALES
(Swasy 1979)

Reward

1. If I do not comply with A, I will not be rewarded.

2. The only reason for doing as A suggests is to obtain good things in return.

3. I want to do as A suggests only because of the good things A will give me for complying.

4. A has the ability to reward me (in some manner) if I do as A suggests.

5. If I do not do as A suggests I will not receive good things from A.

6. In this situation I am dependent on A's willingness to grant me good things.

Referent

7. In general, A's opinions and values are similar to mine.

8. Being similar to A is good.

9. I want to be similar to A.

10. In this situation my attitudes are similar to A's.

11. I would like to act very similar to the way A would act in this situation.

12. In this situation my behavior is similar to A's.

Information

13. The information provided by A about this situation makes sense.

14. The information A provided is logical.

15. I will seriously consider A's request because it is based on good reasoning.

Coercion

16. A can harm me in some manner if I do not do as A suggests.

17. If I do not do as A suggests, A will punish me.

18. Something bad will happen to me if I don't do as A requests and A finds out.

19. I had better do as A suggests in order to prevent something bad from happening to me.

20. A might do something which is unpleasant to those who do not do as A suggests.

Expertise

21. I trust A's judgment.

22. A's expertise makes him/her more likely to be right.

23. A has a lot of experience and usually knows best.

24. A knows best in this situation.

25. A's knowledge usually makes him/her right.

26. I trust A's judgment in this situation.

27. In this situation I don't know as much about what should be done as A does.

28. A is intelligent.

Legitimate

29. It is my duty to comply with A.

30. Because of A's position he has the right to influence my behavior.

31. I am obligated to do as A suggests.

NOTES: Items 1 through 3 represent the three-item version of reward; items 7, 8, and 10 represent the three-item version of referent; items 16 through 18 represent the three-item version of coercion; and items 21 through 23 represent the three-item version of expertise.

POWER: DEPENDENCE-BASED MEASURE
OF INTERFIRM POWER IN CHANNELS
(Frazier 1983)

Construct: The role performance of a firm in its primary channel responsibilities is assumed to drive the level of the other firm's dependence in a dyad. This dependence, in turn, determines the former firm's level of power over the latter firm (Frazier 1983, p. 158). Power has been defined in the channels literature as the ability of one channel member to influence decision variables of another channel member, and a potential for influence on another firm's beliefs and behaviors. However, the manner in which power has been operationalized has varied considerably in field studies. The measures proposed here assess auto dealer perceptions of manufacturer (or their boundary personnel) performance relative to industry average performance as reflecting levels of dealers' dependence on their manufacturer. The assumption is made that role performance appears to be critical in explaining the level of another firm's dependence and goal attainment.

Description: Two versions of the scale are tenable. In one version, dealers indicate how well their manufacturer or boundary personnel perform in comparison with industry average performance on each of six elements (e.g., manufacturer generated demand for the make). Two elements (items) are designed to reflect corporate center performance, and four reflect boundary personnel performance. Eleven-point scales ranging from −5 = *very poor* through 0 = *average performance* to +5 = *very good* were used to evaluate performance. Although not specified, it looks as though scores on this version are derived by summing and averaging over the items. The second version of the scale is an importance weighted measure of the first version. The importance of the six elements (i.e., the importance scores used in computing the weighted performance ratings) are operationalized using 11-point scales ranging from 0 = *not important at all* to 10 = *extremely important*. Each element is weighted (i.e., multiplied) by its importance score for the second version of the scale (importance scores are not normalized prior to weighting).

Development: Development of the six items was based largely on prior research involving channel power issues and a series of "prestudy" interviews. These interviews revealed two aspects of the manufacturer's organization where role performance is critical: the corporate strategic center and boundary personnel tactical center (Frazier 1983, p. 161). Items 1 and 4 (i.e., generation of consumer demand and high-quality assistance) were felt critical for the performance of the manufacturer's corporate center. The remaining items were found to be critical to the role of the boundary personnel of the manufacturer. Tests of reliability and validity were performed.

Sample: Data were collected from 423 automobile dealer "principals" from an original sample of 944 dealers. Follow-up mailings and comparison data revealed that the sample was generally representative. Responses were obtained for the dealership's primary make of vehicle (Frazier 1983, p. 161).

Validity: Coefficient alpha was reported to be .81 for the weighted measure of role performance at the boundary personnel center and .83 for the unweighted measure (Frazier 1983, p. 162). The weighted and unweighted split-half reliability estimates for the two-item measures of performance at the corporate level were .66 and .70, respectively.

Discriminant validity was assessed by estimating a confirmatory factor model of the role performance elements, role performance at the corporate strategy level, and role performance at the boundary spanner level. The fit of this model and the variance explained (67% for the weighted version and 71% for the unweighted version) supported the discriminant validity of the power measure. The correlations between a measure of "chances of switching" suppliers and the unweighted and weighted dimensions of role performance and boundary personnel ranged from −.39 to −.55, offering evidence of convergent validity. Finally, correlations of the total weighted and unweighted versions of the scale with measures of dealer satisfaction ranged from .27 to .57, and for measures of manufacturer interests, corresponding correlations ranged from .32 to .50. These results offer evidence of nomological validity.

Scores: Overall means across the performance ratings for the six items were as follows: generated demand, 1.5; assistance, 2.1; car allocation and delivery, –.3; warranty claims, –.4; advice, –.2; and cooperation, 1.3. For the same pattern of the six items, the mean overall performance ratings were 8.4, 6.9, 8.9, 8.5, 6.8, and 8.0 (Frazier 1983, p. 163).

Source: Frazier, Gary L. (1983). "On the Measurement of Interfirm Power in Channels of Distribution." *Journal of Marketing Research, 20,* 158-166.
    © 1983 by the American Marketing Association. Scale items taken from Table 2 (p. 163). Reprinted with permission.

Other evidence: N/A

Other sources: N/A

References: N/A

POWER: DEPENDENCE-BASED MEASURE OF INTERFIRM POWER IN CHANNELS
(Frazier 1983)

1. Manufacturer-generated demand for the make.

2. Cooperativeness of the manufacturer reps on interfirm issues.

3. Car allocation and delivery.

4. Interfirm assistance.

5. Quality of advice from the manufacturer reps.

6. Reimbursement for warranty claims and vehicle preparation.

NOTE: These are the six elements on which dealers rate their manufacturers.

POWER: DISTRIBUTOR, MANUFACTURER, AND CUSTOMER MARKET POWER
(Butaney and Wortzel 1988)

Construct: Within the channels of distribution literature, power and power types have been defined in various ways. Butaney and Wortzel (1988, pp. 54-55) define and measure three types of power operative in channels of distribution.

Distributor power (DP) is the extent of the distributor's freedom in making marketing decisions about the manufacturer's product. Distributor power is considered a form of "exercised" power as it represents an outcome, the power successfully achieved by a channel member to alter the behavior of another channel member.

Customer market power (CMP) is defined as those characteristics having the potential to affect the customer's power in the marketplace.

Manufacturer market power (MMP) is defined as those industry characteristics or conditions having the potential to affect the manufacturer's power in the marketplace.

Description: The DP is composed of 17 items scored on 5-point scales (see the scale items). Item scores are summed to form an overall index of DP. CMP is a three-dimensional scale. The dimensions are knowledgeable customers (CMS), large customers (CL), and customer switching costs (NCDS). There are 2, 3, and 4 items for the dimensions. CMS, CL, and NCDS items are scored on 5-point scales and summed within dimensions to form CMS and CL indices. MMP is composed of two dimensions labeled manufacturer low concern for competition (NMI) and concentrated industry structure (MI). NMI and MI are composed of 4 and 2 items, respectively, scored on 5-point scales. Item scores are summed within dimensions to form indices for the dimensions.

Development: For the DP, an original pool of 27 items was generated. Using a panel of expert judges, this pool was trimmed to 22 items. The 22 items were then subjected to factor analysis, and items with loadings greater than .40 on the first factor were retained, resulting in the final 17-item DP. For CMP and MMP measures, a pool of 40 items was generated and then trimmed to 21 after expert panel judging. These items were factor analyzed and reduced to the final CMP and MMP dimensions of 2 items for CMS, 3 items for CL, 4 items for NCDS, 4 items for NMI, and 2 items for MI. For all scales, reliability and nomological validity were assessed.

Samples: The panel of experts used to trim the initial item pools was composed of members of an industrial electronic distributors association and two professors familiar with the channels literature. The main sample, with which the factor, reliability, and validity analyses were performed, was composed of 83 managers from the electronics components industry.

Validity: Coefficient alpha for the 17-item DP scale was .76. (Alpha based on a weighted DP scale, in which each item is also evaluated on an 11-point scale as to its importance, was .85.) Alphas for the CMS, CL, and NCDS dimensions of customer market power were .74, .55, and .57, respectively. Alphas for the NMI and MI dimensions of manufacturer market power were .58 and .56, respectively.

Using DP as the dependent variable and CMS, CL, and NCDS as independent variables in a regression equation, only NCDS had a significant beta coefficient (−.28). With NMI and MI as predictors of DP, both variables had significant beta coefficients (−.34 and −.22, respectively). Thus, some evidence of nomological validity among the variables was provided.

Scores: Neither mean nor percentage scores were reported.

Source: Butaney, Gul, and Lawrence H. Wortzel. (1988). "Distributor Power Versus Manufacturer Power: The Customer Role." *Journal of Marketing*, 52, 52-63.

© 1988 by the American Marketing Association. Scale items taken from Table 2 (p. 56) and Table 3 (p. 57). Reprinted with permission.

Other evidence: N/A

Other sources: N/A

References: N/A

POWER: DISTRIBUTOR, MANUFACTURER, AND CUSTOMER MARKET POWER
(Butaney and Wortzel 1988)

Instructions and DP items: To market and distribute a product, several marketing decisions have to be made. In making these decisions, a distributor may have almost complete responsibility, or freedom to make a decision may be shared with the manufacturer, or the manufacturer may have almost complete responsibility. For each of the marketing decisions and activities listed below, please indicate the level of freedom or responsibility you have as compared to the selected manufacturer (in marketing the manufacturer's brand). Please check the appropriate response category where . . .

> 1 = manufacturer has almost complete responsibility
> 2 = manufacturer has more responsibility than myself
> 3 = manufacturer and I share equal responsibility
> 4 = I have more responsibility than the manufacturer
> 5 = I have almost complete responsibility

Distributor Power (DP)

1. Choosing geographic territories to sell in.

2. Setting sales targets or goals.

3. Setting selling prices to customers.

4. Determining distribution policies to customers.

5. Determining the training program for your salesforce to sell the product.

6. Keeping the manufacturer from selling direct in your territory.

7. Product return-related issues.

8. Choosing customers to sell to.

9. Determining pricing policies (e.g., quantity discounts to customers).

10. Deciding to join in cooperative advertising with the manufacturer.

11. Keeping the manufacturer's other distributors from selling in your territory.

12. Accommodating customer's request for product modification.

13. Margins allowed by the manufacturer.

14. Providing presale customer services (e.g., product information).

15. Attending sales meetings organized by the manufacturer.

16. Resolving customers' product-related technical problems.

17. Determining sales strategies/policies (e.g., frequency of sales calls to customers).

Customer Market Power Items (CMP)

CMS Dimension

1. The customers possess a great deal of market information.

2. The customers possess a good idea about the costs of the product to the distributor.

CL Dimension

3. Customers are able to bargain the terms of the sale.

4. 20% of my customers account for 80% of my total product sales.

5. Most of my customers can buy the product directly from manufacturers.

NCDS Dimension

6. Supplier's name and brand are not very important purchasing criteria for customers.

7. Customers' cost of finding and qualifying other suppliers is low.

8. Customers' importance for the product quality in their purchasing criteria is low.

9. The customers in the industry do not insist on buying a specific manufacturer brand.

Manufacturer Market Power Items (MMP)

NMI Dimension

1. When one manufacturer reduces the product price, the other manufacturers do not reduce their prices.

2. When the manufacturer increases price, the customers do not switch brands.

3. Competition among manufacturers in the industry is not strong.

4. The manufacturer possesses a great deal of industry information (e.g., trends, problems, competitive brands).

MI Dimension

5. Only a few manufacturers produce a large volume of the product in the industry.

6. Industry sales are not equally distributed among the manufacturers.

NOTES: All CMP and MMP items are scored on 5-point scales from *strongly disagree* (1) to *strongly agree* (5). Item 4 of the NMI dimension had a negative loading on its factor.

POWER: HOLZBACH'S ATTRIBUTED POWER INDEX: API
(Comer 1984)

Construct: The primary purpose of Comer's research was to examine the properties of Holzbach's (1974) multi-item API in a sales manager-sales representative setting. (The original source of the scale is Holzbach [1974]; however, because Holzbach's work is an unpublished dissertation, the API examined here is from Comer [1984].) Holzbach (1974) constructed a multi-item attributed power scale (API) as a measure of interpersonal power relations in an organizational environment. Specifically, the API measures the power of the sales manager. It is also important to note that the items reflect not only the sources of power but also the exercise of that power. This scale was predicated on the French and Raven (1959) power bases model.

Description: Using Busch's (1980) single-item power scales as a point of reference, Comer (1984) examined the quality of Holzbach's multi-item API. The Holzbach scale, designed for self-administration, consists of 25 individual statements measuring aspects of the power bases of French and Raven. Items are scored on 7-point scales ranging from *extremely inaccurate* to *extremely accurate*. Respondents are asked to circle an item on a mnemonic scale consisting of EI (extremely inaccurate), VI (very inaccurate), I, ?, A, VA, and EA (extremely accurate). Item scores can be summed within power dimensions to form indices of each dimension.

Development: A questionnaire was constructed for the purpose of evaluating the dimensions of sales representatives' jobs and their relationships with their managers, as well as surveying key demographic data. The survey included both the Holzbach scale and the five Busch power statements. Via factor, item, multitrait-multimethod, and reliability analyses, the API's appropriateness to a sales setting was examined.

Samples: Mail questionnaires were sent to sales representatives employed by three companies. Two companies were engaged in the sale of industrial products; the other sold consumer goods. Of 333 questionnaires sent, 207 were usable.

Validity: Cronbach's alpha was used to measure the internal consistency of the Holzbach scale in each company. The alpha values were extremely consistent across power bases and companies. The alpha value ranges were as follows: expert .89-.90, reward .88-.90, coercive .69-.75, referent .75-.90, and legitimate .64-.76. Both convergent and discriminant validity for the Holzbach scales were assessed by examining the API with Busch's measures via the multitrait-multimethod matrix method. Although the results failed to establish discriminant validity (i.e., some of the API power bases were too highly correlated to infer discriminant validity), four of the five convergent validity estimates (i.e., correlations of the API measures with Busch's measures) were significant, ranging from .29 to .71.

Factor analysis was used to explore the API structure. The factor loadings indicated that the reward, coercive, expert, and referent power results were similar to those found by Holzbach (1974). That is, the items loaded as hypothesized on their respective factors. However, the legitimate power factor did not reproduce cleanly.

Nomological validity was assessed by correlating the API dimensions with the INDSALES satisfaction measure (Churchill, Ford, and Walker 1974). The correlations between INDSALES and expert, referent, and coercive power across the three subsample groups ranged from .69 to .72, .72 to .80, and −.18 to −.57, respectively. In summary, the API represents an improvement in the measurement of power-base utilization in sales manager-sales representative relationships.

Scores: Means (std. dev.) were reported by Comer for each power dimension and were 26.09 (4.80), 25.05 (3.91), 21.80 (5.16), 25.54 (5.26), and 24.36 (5.25) for expert, legitimate, coercive, referent, and reward power, respectively.

Source: Comer, James M. (1984). "A Psychometric Assessment of a Measure of Sales Representatives' Power Perceptions." *Journal of Marketing Research*, 21, 221-225.

© 1984 by the American Marketing Association. Scale items taken from Table 2 (p. 224). Reprinted with permission.

Other evidence: N/A

Other sources: N/A

References: Busch, Paul. (1980). "The Sales Manager's Bases of Social Power and Influence Upon the Sales Force." *Journal of Marketing*, 44, 91-101.

Churchill, Gilbert A., Jr., Neil M. Ford, and Orville C. Walker. (1974). "Measuring the Job Satisfaction of Industrial Salesmen." *Journal of Marketing Research*, 11, 254-260.

French, John R., and Bertram Raven. (1959). "The Basis of Social Power." In D. Cartwright (Ed.), *Studies in Social Power* (pp. 150-167). Ann Arbor, MI: Institute for Social Research.

Holzbach, Robert L. (1974). *An Investigation of a Model for Managerial Effectiveness: The Effects of Leadership Style and Leader Attributed Social Power on Subordinate Job Performance*. Doctoral dissertation, Carnegie-Mellon University.

POWER: HOLZBACH'S ATTRIBUTED POWER INDEX: API
(Comer 1984)

Reward

2. Gives credit where credit is due

12. Recognizes achievement

13. Willing to promote others

16. Rewards good work

23. Offers inducement

Coercive

3. Rules by might

11. Retaliative

17. Overly critical

21. Disciplinarian

24. Strict

Legitimate

7. Have obligation to accept his/her orders

14. Duty bound to obey him/her

15. Has authority

19. Entitled to direct my actions on the job

20. Authorized to command

Expert

4. Skilled

5. Knowledgeable

8. Experienced

10. Proficient

22. Qualified

Referent

1. Admire him/her

6. Identify with him/her

9. Respect him/her as a person

25. Likable

18. Friendly

NOTE: Item numbers are as they appeared in the Comer (1984) article.

POWER AND INFLUENCE IN GROUP SETTINGS
(Kohli 1989)

Construct: A number of power and influence types operate in organizational buying, and purchase decisions in organizational buying are often greatly affected by these different types of influence and power. Consistent with existing literatures (e.g., French and Raven 1959; Gaski 1984; Kohli and Zaltman 1988), Kohli (1989, pp. 51-53) defines several sources of individual power and influence operating in organizational buying, as follow.

Manifest influence refers to changes in purchase decision-related opinions and behavior of buying center members that result from the individual's participation in a buying center.

Influence attempts refers to the amount of effort exerted by an individual to influence a purchase decision.

Self-perceived influence is the influence an informant believes he or she exerted on a decision.

Reinforcement power refers to the ability to mediate positive and negative reinforcements. In essence, reward and coercive power are components of reinforcement power, where *reward power* refers to an individual's ability to provide material and nonmaterial rewards to other individuals (generally in compliance to his/her requests), and *coercive power* refers to an individual's ability to mete out material and nonmaterial punishments to others.

Referent power is the extent to which others like and identify themselves with a person and have regard for his/her personal qualities.

Legitimate power refers to the extent to which others feel that they ought to comply with the wishes of an individual and derives from both formal and informal social norms.

Expert power refers to the extent to which an individual is perceived by others as being knowledgeable about other issues.

Information power refers to an individual's access to and control over relevant information.

Departmental power is the relative importance of a department in general to an organization.

The above definitions and their corresponding measures represent an extension of the Kohli and Zaltman (1988) manifest influence measures.

Description: For each of the above definitions, multi-item scales were developed. Across scales, all items were scored on 5-point formats (see scale items). Item scores are summed within each scale to form an index for each power or influence type.

Development: Through an extensive literature search and existing measures, a pool of items was generated to reflect each type of power and influence. An expert panel of academicians was used to revise the items. The items were further refined via a three-wave pretest of personal interviews with managers involved in joint purchase decisions. Then, in a large study, the items were tested for factor structure, reliability, and validity. This resulted in the elimination of several items to form the final versions of the scales.

Samples: Fourteen managers participated in the personal interviews to refine the items. A sample of 251 from the National Association of Purchasing Management was used in the study examining the scales' factor structure, reliability, and validity.

Validity: Factor analysis revealed a six-factor structure for the power measures reflecting the six power components defined above. Coefficient alpha estimates were .95, .86, .80, .85, .90, and .88 for reinforcement power, referent power, legitimate power, expert power, information power, and departmental power, respectively. Alpha estimates for manifest influence, influence attempts, and self-perceived influence were .93, .90, and .86, respectively.

Using manifest influence as the dependent variable, with the six influence types and self-perceived influence as independent variables, the relationships among power and influence were examined. For the overall sample (214 of 251), 38% of the variance in manifest influence was explained by the predictor variables, with reinforcement power (beta = .33) and expert power (beta = .49) as the major contributors. The sample was also split into high and low groups across several contingency variables. R^2 estimates across the groups ranged from .26 to .56. Furthermore, the correlations among the independent variables ranged from .03 to .48, suggesting low multicollinearity. These results show predictive validity for the measures.

Scores: Various mean scores were offered. A split of the large sample based on influence versions of the questionnaire as high or low (see Table 4, p. 58) offered mean scores as shown in Table 7.1.

TABLE 7.1

Scale	Low Influence		High Influence	
	Mean	SD	*Mean*	SD
Manifest influence	24.0	7.2	34.6	4.7
Self-perceived influence	19.0	3.7	18.5	3.7
Influence attempts	10.7	3.9	12.8	4.0
Reinforcement power	19.4	8.8	26.6	12.5
Referent power	16.2	4.1	16.4	4.7
Legitimate power	4.0	1.9	5.4	2.4
Expert power	13.8	3.6	16.6	3.5
Information power	9.8	5.2	9.8	5.1
Departmental power	12.1	4.1	13.0	4.3

Source: Kohli, Ajay. (1989). "Determinants of Influence in Organizational Buying: A Contingency Approach." *Journal of Marketing, 53*, 50-65.
© 1989 by the American Marketing Association. Scale items taken from Appendix (pp. 62-63). Reprinted with permission.

Other evidence: N/A

Other sources: N/A

References: French, John R., and Bertram H. Raven. (1959). "The Bases of Social Power." In D. Cartwright (Ed.), *Studies in Social Power.* Ann Arbor, MI: Institute for Social Research.

Gaski, John F. (1984). "The Theory of Power and Conflict in Channels of Distribution." *Journal of Marketing, 48*, 9-29.

Kohli, Ajay, and Gerald Zaltman. (1988). "Measuring Multiple Buying Influences." *Industrial Marketing Management, 17*, 197-204.

POWER AND INFLUENCE IN GROUP SETTINGS
(Kohli 1989)

Manifest Influence

1. How much weight did the committee members give to his opinions?

2. How much impact did he have on the thinking of the other members?

3. To what extent did he influence the criteria used for making the final decision?

4. How much effort did his involvement in the purchase committee have on how the various options were rated?

5. To what extent did he influence others into adopting certain positions about the various options?

6. How much change did he induce in the preferences of other members?

7. To what extent did others go along with his suggestions?

8. To what extent did his participation influence the decision eventually reached?

9. To what extent did the final decision reflect his views?

Influence Attempts

Relative to others . . .

1. he spent more time to impress his views on the committee members.

2. he tried harder to shape the thinking of others.

3. he spent more energy to make sure his opinions were taken into account.

4. he exerted more effort to make sure the final decision reflected his views.

Self-Perceived Influence

1. How much weight did the committee members give to your opinions?

2. To what extent did you influence the criteria used for making the final decision?

3. How much effort did your involvement in the purchase committee have on how the various options were rated?

4. To what extent did your participation influence the decision eventually reached?

5. To what extent did the final decision reflect your views?

Reinforcement Power

1. They believed he was capable of getting them pay raises.

2. They felt he could improve their standing in the organization.

3. They felt it was desirable to be approved by him.

4. They valued receiving recognition from him.

5. They felt that he could arrange desirable assignments for them.

6. They believed he was capable of getting them promoted.

7. They believed he was capable of interfering with their promotions.

8. They felt he could take them to task.

9. They felt he could make life difficult for them.

10. They thought he could block their salary increases.

11. They believed he could arrange for them to be assigned to unpleasant tasks.

Legitimate Power

1. They felt that the purchase decision should reflect his preferences because he had more at stake than others.

2. They felt they ought to comply with him because the purchase decision would affect him more than others.

Referent Power

1. They disliked him as a person.*

2. They thought highly of his personality.

3. They shared his personal values.

4. They identified with him as a person.

5. They had a high regard for his personal qualities.

Expert Power

1. They felt he was knowledgeable about the organization's needs with respect to the product.

2. They thought he was competent to make an assessment of the various options.

3. They felt he knew exactly how the product would be used.

4. They felt he had the expertise to make the best decision.

Departmental Power

1. The functions performed by this department are generally considered to be more critical than others.

2. Top management considers this department to be more important than others.

3. This department tends to dominate others in the affairs of the organization.

4. This department is generally regarded as being more influential than others.

Information Power

1. He served as a communication link between the suppliers and the committee members.

2. He was in direct contact with the suppliers.

3. He was responsible for obtaining information about suppliers for the committee members.

4. He held independent discussions with the various suppliers on behalf of the purchase committee.

NOTES: The items in Manifest Influence are scored from *very small* (1) to *very large* (5). Items in Influence Attempts are scored from *strongly disagree* (1) to *strongly agree* (5). Items in Self-Perceived Influence are scored from *very small* (1) to *very large* (5). Items in Reinforcement Power are scored from *none* (1) to *all* (5); items 1 through 6 reflect the reward power component, and items 7 through 11 reflect the coercive power component. Items in Legitimate Power are scored from *none* (1) to *all* (5). Items in Referent Power are scored from *none* (1) to *all* (5), and item 1 requires reverse scoring. Items in Expert Power are scored from *none* (1) to *all* (5). Items in Departmental Power are scored from *strongly disagree* (1) to *strongly agree* (5). Items in Information Power are scored from *strongly disagree* (1) to *strongly agree* (5).

POWER SOURCES IN A MARKETING CHANNEL
(Gaski and Nevin 1985)

Construct: Gaski and Nevin (1985) examined the concepts of perceived and exercised reward/coercive power in a dealer-supplier relationship (i.e., a channels framework). Specifically, perceived reward/coercive power is viewed as the dealer's perception of the ability of the supplier to mediate rewards and punishments (i.e., considered as "sources" of power). Exercised reward/coercive power is viewed as the actual granting of rewards and imposition of punishment by the supplier (cf. Hunt and Nevin 1974). Another power measure, based on the dealer's perception of the potential influence that a supplier has over the dealer's business, was also conceptualized. This power measure assesses the supplier's ability to get the dealer to do what he would not have done otherwise.

Description: In essence, Gaski and Nevin's power measure is composed of five separate indices: perceived reward power (a source), perceived coercive power (a source), exercised reward power, exercised coercive power, and a supplier's ability to potentially affect the dealer's business. The perceived reward power index is composed of 15 items scored from *no capability* to reward (0) to *very much capability* to reward (4). The perceived coercive power index is composed of 6 items also scored on the aforementioned 0 to 4 format. The exercised reward power index is composed of 15 items scored from *never* exercises the power (0) to *often* exercises the power (3). The exercised coercive power index is composed of 6 items also scored on the 0 to 3 format. The supplier's ability to affect the dealer's business is measured with 10 items scored from *not at all* (0) to *as much as they wanted* (3). Item scores within each index are summed to form an overall score for each power index.

Development: The initial pool of items for the indices was drawn from extant channels literature (e.g., Hunt and Nevin 1974; Lusch 1976). The items were screened, modified to fit the research setting, and checked for face validity. Then, with a large sample, the measures were assessed for reliability and validity.

Sample: The large sample consisted of 238 dealers of heavy industrial machinery (i.e., dealers who handled the Melroe products of the Clark Equipment Company, the supplier).

Validity: Coefficient alpha estimates for the perceived reward power, perceived coercive power, exercised reward power, and exercised coercive power indices were .87, .69, .83, and .62, respectively. The alpha for the supplier's ability to affect the dealer's business index was .86. Discriminant validity was said to be evidenced by the fact that the correlations among indices were not as high as the lowest coefficient alpha of the indices. These correlations ranged from −.16 to .56. The power indices were used as independent variables to predict dealer satisfaction with the supplier, conflict with the supplier, and dealer performance. For dealer satisfaction, significant regression coefficients were −.12, −.30, .31, and .35 for perceived coercive power, exercised coercive power, perceived reward power, and exercised reward power, respectively. For conflict, significant regression coefficients were .19, .43, −.30, and −.37 for perceived coercive power, exercised coercive power, perceived reward power, and exercised reward power, respectively. For performance, only exercised reward power showed a significant regression coefficient (−.11). These results show support for the predictive validity of the power indices.

Scores: Neither mean nor percentage scores were reported.

Source: Gaski, John F., and John Nevin. (1985). "The Differential Effects of Exercised and Unexercised Power Sources in a Marketing Channel." *Journal of Marketing Research*, 22, 130-142.
    © 1985 by the American Marketing Association. Scale items taken from Figure 4 (p. 135). Reprinted with permission.

Other evidence: N/A

Other sources: N/A

References: Hunt, Shelby, and John R. Nevin. (1974). "Power in a Channel of Distribution: Sources and Consequences." *Journal of Marketing Research*, *11*, 186-193.

Lusch, Robert F. (1976). "Sources of Power: Their Impact on Intra-channel Conflict." *Journal of Marketing Research*, *13*, 382-390.

POWER SOURCES IN A MARKETING CHANNEL
(Gaski and Nevin 1985)

Perceived Coercive Power (Source)

Please check (✓) the appropriate space to indicate **how much capability** Clark Equipment has to take each of the following kinds of action in their dealings with your organization.

	no *capability*			*very much* *capability*
	____	____	____	____	____

Delay delivery
Delay warranty claims
Take legal action against you
Refuse to sell
Charge high prices
Deliver unwanted products

Perceived Reward Power (Source)

Please check (✓) the appropriate space to indicate **how much capability** Clark Equipment has to take each of the following kinds of action in their dealings with your organization.

	no *capability*			*very much* *capability*
	____	____	____	____	____

Provide advertising support
Give trade allowances/incentives
Train personnel
Provide sales promotion materials
Grant favors (golf, lunches, etc.)
Give inventory rebates
Provide financing/credit
Furnish supplies
Give business advice
Provide service
Give pricing assistance
Give free samples
Provide ordering assistance
Provide inventory management assistance
Demonstrate products

Exercised Coercive Power

Please indicate (✓) **how often** Clark Equipment takes each of the following kinds of action in their dealings with your organization.

	never			*often*
	⎯⎯	⎯⎯	⎯⎯	⎯⎯

Delay delivery
Delay warranty claims
Take legal action against you
Refuse to sell
Charge high prices
Deliver unwanted products

Exercised Reward Power

Please indicate (✓) **how often** Clark Equipment takes each of the following kinds of action in their dealings with your organization.

	never			*often*
	⎯⎯	⎯⎯	⎯⎯	⎯⎯

Provide advertising support
Give trade allowances/incentives
Train personnel
Provide sales promotion materials
Grant favors (golf, lunches, etc.)
Give inventory rebates
Provide financing/credit
Furnish supplies
Give business advice
Provide service
Give pricing assistance
Give free samples
Provide ordering assistance
Provide inventory management assistance
Demonstrate products

Supplier's Ability to Influence the Dealer's Business

Please indicate (✓) your response to each of the following.

	not at all	*slightly*	*moderately*	*as much as they wanted*
	____	____	____	____

If Clark Equipment wanted you to raise the prices you charge for their products, what is the maximum amount you would raise prices?

If Clark Equipment wanted you to lower the prices you charge for their products, what is the maximum amount you would lower prices?

If Clark Equipment wanted you to increase the quantity of their products you order, what is the maximum amount you would increase order quantity?

If Clark Equipment wanted you to decrease the quantity of their products you order, what is the maximum amount you would decrease order quantity?

If Clark Equipment wanted you to change the composition of your product line, what is the maximum amount you would change your product line?

If Clark Equipment wanted you to change the type of advertising and sales promotion you do for their products, what is the maximum amount you would change your advertising and sales promotion?

If Clark Equipment wanted you to change your customer service policy, what is the maximum amount you would change your customer service?

If Clark Equipment wanted you to change your inventory procedures, what is the maximum amount you would change your inventory procedures?

If Clark Equipment wanted you to change your customer credit policy, what is the maximum amount you would change your customer credit?

If Clark Equipment wanted you to change the way you display their products, what is the maximum amount you would change your display of their products?

Other Measures Related To Interfirm Issues

BUYCLASS FRAMEWORK SCALES
(Anderson, Chu, and Weitz 1987)

Construct: The "buyclass framework" (Robinson, Faris, and Wind 1967) posits that different organizational buying approaches are required for different purchase situations. The different purchase situations can range from a "straight rebuy" to a "modified rebuy" to a "new task" purchase. These three buyclass decisions are defined and determined along three dimensions: (a) how much information the prospective buyer needs to make a good decision, (b) the seriousness with which the prospective buyer considers all alternatives, and (c) how familiar the purchase situation is to the prospective buyer. The "straight rebuy" is low on all three dimensions, the "modified rebuy" is in the midrange of all three dimensions, and the "new task" is high on all three dimensions (Anderson, Chu, and Weitz 1987, p. 72). Anderson et al. (1987) construct measures that reflect the three dimensions.

Description: The buyclass scales are actually two sets (i.e., versions) of the same scale. Both versions are represented by two, rather than the original three, dimensions specified. One dimension is titled "NEWNESS + INFO" and reflects the original dimensions 3 and 1 above. The other dimension, "ALT," reflects dimension 2 listed above. All items are scored on 7-point scales ranging from *0%* to *100%* of the time (see instructions). Item scores can be summed within dimensions to form indices of each dimension.

Development: The academic and trade literatures were used to generate a large pool of items. Then, a sample of 12 sales managers, using a sequential editing process over several months, was used to refine and trim the items. A large sample of sales managers from a number of different electronic component firms responded to the items. Via factor analysis, reliability, and validity checks, Version 1 of the scales was derived. In a replication study, the procedures for scale development and validation were repeated with a variety of manufacturing firms, and Version 2 of the scale was derived.

Samples: For deriving Version 1 of the scale, a sample of 169 sales managers from 16 electronic component firms were used in the main study. For Version 2, a sample of 158 sales managers from a variety of manufacturing firms were used in the main study.

Validity: For the Version 1 sample ($n = 169$), factor analysis revealed a two-factor structure (i.e., "NEWNESS + INFO" and "ALT"). The NEWNESS + INFO factor had a coefficient alpha of .73, and the ALT factor had an alpha of .57. The correlation between these two factors was .14. Nomological validity was assessed by correlating the two factors with several buyer behavior statements. These correlations ranged from −.17 to .49 (in the predicted direction) for the buyer behavior statements and the NEWNESS + INFO factor, and from −.05 to .18 for the buyer behavior statements and the ALT factor. These results offer evidence for the nomological validity of the NEWNESS + INFO factor.

For Version 2, factor analysis again revealed the two-factor NEWNESS + INFO and ALT structure. Coefficient alpha was .71 and .53 for these two factors, respectively. Nomological validity was again assessed by correlating the two factors with several buyer behavior statements. These correlations ranged from −.63 to .61 (in the predicted direction) for the buyer behavior statements and the NEWNESS + INFO factor, and from −.18 to .18 for the buyer behavior statements and the ALT factor. These results are supportive of the nomological validity of the NEWNESS + INFO factor.

Scores: Neither mean nor percentage scores were reported.

Source: Anderson, Erin, Wujin Chu, and Barton Weitz. (1987). "Industrial Purchasing: An Empirical Exploration of the Buyclass Framework." *Journal of Marketing*, *51*, 71-86.
© 1987 by the American Marketing Association. Scale items taken from Appendices A-E (p. 84-85). Reprinted with permission.

Other evidence: N/A

Other sources: N/A

Reference: Robinson, Patrick, J., Charles W. Faris, and Yoram Wind. (1967). *Industrial Buying and Creative Marketing.* Boston: Allyn and Bacon.

BUYCLASS FRAMEWORK SCALES
(Anderson, Chu, and Weitz 1987)

Instructions: The following statements describe circumstances which might exist when one of your salespeople is trying to make a sale. Please indicate **how frequently** the salesperson would face the situation described in the statement. This can be indicated by circling the number that most accurately indicates the percentage of sales situations that fit the statement. Each question is independent: Your answers do not need to add to 100% or any other number.

EXAMPLE: It is hard to get an appointment to see the account.

Percentage of Situations

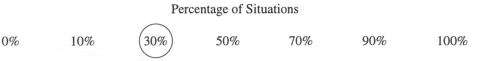

This manager indicates that in 30% of the selling situations, the salesperson has difficulty getting an appointment. Notice that "account" means customer or prospect. Those 30% of selling situations that are difficult could be cold calls, follow-ups with a regular customer, or some combination of prospects and customers.

Version 1

NEWNESS + INFO Items

1. The account seldom purchases this type of product.

2. The product is the first purchase of its kind for the account.

3. The account has not dealt with this product class or requirement before.

4. This is still a rather new purchase for the account.

5. The account's requirements have changed since the product was purchased last.

6. The account has complete knowledge about what product characteristics are needed to solve the problem.*

7. The account knows exactly what is needed.*

8. The purchase decision demands a lot of information.

9. The account is willing to gather and consider a lot of information before deciding.

10. The account is willing to consider new information in making a decision.

ALT Items

1. The account is seriously interested in alternatives to the present supplier.

2. The account wants to consider all the alternatives carefully.

3. The account is interested in salespeople calling to propose changing suppliers.

4. The account is open to suggestions for change in the current purchase pattern.

5. The account has considerable experience with the product class but is considering new options, new suppliers, or new products.

NOTES: Items 1 through 5 of NEWNESS + INFO reflect the newness of the buying situation. Although five newness items are listed in the Appendix (see Anderson et al. 1987, p. 84), the text states that four items reflect newness. Items 6 through 10 reflect the information items of the NEWNESS + INFO factor. All items are scaled such that higher values represent greater frequency of encountering new tasks and lower values reflect more routine purchases. Thus, items with a "*" require reverse scoring.

Version 2

NEWNESS + INFO Items

1. The customer seldom purchases this type of product.

2. The customer considers the purchase decision to be routine.*

3. The customer has not dealt with this product class or requirement before.

4. The customer has routinized the purchase decision so that it no longer requires a lot of attention.*

5. The customer's requirements have changed since the product was purchased last.

6. The customer has complete knowledge about what product characteristics are needed to solve the problem.*

7. The customer needs a lot of information before making a purchase decision.

ALT Items

1. The customer is seriously interested in alternatives to the present supplier.

2. The customer has considerable experience with the product class but is considering new options, new suppliers, or new products.

NOTES: Items 1 through 5 of NEWNESS + INFO reflect the newness of the buying situation. Items 6 and 7 reflect the information items of the NEWNESS + INFO factor. All items are scaled such that higher values represent greater frequency of encountering new tasks and lower values reflect more routine purchases. Thus, items with a "*" require reverse scoring.

BUYING: ORGANIZATIONAL BUYING SCALES
(Bunn 1994)

Construct: Bunn (1994) defines and then develops measures for four distinct constructs that underlie many of the activities involved with organizational buying: procedural control, proactive focusing, use of analysis techniques, and search for information. Procedural control captures the extent to which buyers rely on policies, procedures, or informal "rules of thumb" when approaching a specific purchase decision. Proactive focusing includes those activities involved with establishing objectives, planning for contingencies, and maintaining good supplier relationships. Use of analysis techniques is the extent to which quantitative and structured tools/techniques for analyzing a purchase are used. Finally, search for information reflects extent of usage for a series of sources of information including personal, impersonal, commercial, and noncommercial sources (Bunn 1994, pp. 161-162).

Description: Procedural control is operationalized as the average of 10 items using a 7-point scale anchored by 1 (*strongly disagree*) and 7 (*strongly agree*). Proactive focusing is measured using the average of 9 items and the same response format. Use of analysis techniques and search for information were assessed as the average of 10 and 9 items, respectively. Items for these latter two constructs employed scales anchored by 1 (*not at all*) and 7 (*very much*).

Development: An initial pool of 45 items was developed from an intensive literature review and the responses from 11 field interviews. The final set of 38 items (i.e., 10, 9, 10, and 9 across the four factors) was based on a series of purification analyses. Briefly, 7 items with low factor item-to-total correlations and items with low or cross loadings in subsequent factor analyses were deleted.

Samples: A series of personal interviews with 11 purchasing executives was conducted as part of the item generation process. Purification and validation of the four measurement scales were based upon 636 complete responses from a random sample chosen from the roster of the National Association of Purchasing Management. The majority of respondents had more than 5 years of purchasing experience and represented companies with between 200 and 5,000 employees. More than half the firms were from manufacturing industries (Bunn 1994, p. 163).

Validity: The four construct internal consistency estimates ranged from .75 for search for information to .87 for procedural control. In follow-up factor analysis, most items loaded as predicted. In tests of discriminant validity using LISREL, some evidence was provided from model comparisons in which correlations between factors were set to 1. However, only analyses involving procedural control satisfied the comparisons recommended by Fornell and Larcker (1981) involving average variance extracted and correlations between factors. Lastly, significant correlations with length of decision process, dollar amount of purchase, annual purchasing responsibility, and multiple influence were offered as evidence of nomological validity (Bunn 1994, p. 166).

Scores: Means (std. dev.) for the four constructs were reported in Table 1 as follows: procedural control, 5.1 (1.3); proactive forecasting, 4.6 (1.3); use of analysis techniques, 3.3 (1.2); and search for information, 3.4 (1.2) (Bunn 1994, p. 163).

Source: Bunn, Michele D. (1994). "Key Aspects of Organizational Buying: Conceptualization and Measurement." *Journal of the Academy of Marketing Science, 22*(2), 160-169.

© 1994 by Sage Publications. Scale items taken from Table 2 (p. 165). Reprinted with permission.

Other evidence: N/A

Other sources: N/A

Reference: Fornell, Claes, and David F. Larcker. (1981). "Evaluating Structural Equation Models With Unobservable Variables and Measurement Error." *Journal of Marketing Research, 18*, 39-50.

BUYING: ORGANIZATIONAL BUYING SCALES
(Bunn 1994)

Procedural Control

1. The procedure for buying this product was straightforward.

2. The terms and conditions for this purchase order were standard.

3. The standard operating procedures did not tell us what to do for this purchase. (R)

4. Each step in the purchase process required new decisions. (R)

5. We didn't have clear-cut rules about how to make this purchase. (R)

6. When the need arose, there were no existing guidelines about how to fill it. (R)

7. This purchase is made the same way each time.

8. The organization didn't have an established way of doing things for this purchase situation. (R)

9. Responsibility was not clearly defined for the accomplishment of each step of the purchase procedure in this situation. (R)

10. All the conditions that arose in this purchase situation were covered by an established procedure.

Proactive Focusing

1. It was not necessary to consider long-range purchasing objectives when making this purchase. (R)

2. Contingency plans were considered for problems that might be related to this purchase.

3. We had to make certain that this purchase fit with our forecasts.

4. We didn't give any thought to our long-range supply of this product. (R)

5. Consideration was given to the long-range supply of this product.

6. Future plans were not an important issue in purchasing this product. (R)

7. We considered how this purchase would impact the organization's long-range profitability.

8. Input from the corporate planning process was an essential prerequisite for this purchase.

9. We didn't need to develop plans for possible supply disruptions. (R)

Use of Analysis Techniques

1. Price analysis.

2. Cost analysis.

3. Extrapolation of historic trends.

4. Comparison of alternative methods of contract pricing.

5. Make or buy analysis.

6. Spreadsheet analysis.

7. Value analysis.

8. Economic analysis.

9. Computer modeling or simulation.

10. Other mathematical analysis.

Search for Information

1. Sales representatives of selected vendor.

2. Sales representative of other vendor.

3. Outside business associate.

4. Your top management.

5. Users of the product.

6. Others inside our organization.

7. Trade publications.

8. Sales literature.

9. Other commercial source.

NOTE: (R) denotes items requiring reverse scoring.

LEADERSHIP: CHANNEL LEADERSHIP BEHAVIOR
(Schul, Pride, and Little 1983)

Construct: Channel leadership behavior is defined as activities carried out by a channel member to influence the marketing policies and strategies of other channel members for the purpose of controlling various aspects of channel operations (Schul, Pride, and Little 1983, p. 22). The focus taken here is on the leadership behavior of the franchiser (not franchisee).

Description: The channel leadership scale is composed of nine items, each scored on a 5-point basis where franchisees rate their franchisers from *completely agree* to *completely disagree* with the item. Furthermore, the scale has three dimensions (i.e., participative leadership, supportive leadership, and directive leadership) with three items reflecting each dimension. Item scores can be summed within each dimension to form indices for each dimension.

Development: After a review of the organizational behavior literature and interviews with franchisees, 19 items were generated to reflect the construct. These items were administered to a sample of franchisees and trimmed to the final nine-item measure via factor analysis and coefficient alpha. Face validity of the items was also checked using 50 unstructured interviews. Lastly, the scale was administered to another sample and correlated with conflict measures and checked for validity.

Samples: For item generation, the sample size of the franchisees was not specified. A sample of 85 franchisees was used in trimming the scale to nine items, and a sample of 50 was used to check face validity. Lastly, a sample of 349 franchisees responded to the main study where the scale was correlated with conflict measures.

Validity: Factor analyses supported a three-dimensional measure that represented the three dimensions of channel leadership. The three factors accounted for 82.53% of the variance in the scale items. Correlations among the three factors ranged from .35 to .52. Coefficient alpha for the three dimensions ranged from .80 for the directive leadership dimension to .92 for the supportive leadership dimension ($n = 85$). Face validity was also confirmed with the sample of 50. Canonical correlation of the three participative leadership items with a measure of administrative and product-service conflict within a channel was .49. The canonical correlation between the supportive leadership items and the conflict measures was .57, and the canonical correlation between the directive leadership items and the conflict measure was .45, providing evidence of nomological validity.

Scores: Neither mean nor percentage scores were reported.

Source: Schul, Patrick L., William H. Pride, and Taylor L. Little. (1983). "The Impact of Channel Leadership Behavior on Intrachannel Conflict." *Journal of Marketing, 47*, 21-34.
© 1983 by the American Marketing Association. Scale items taken from Table 2 (p. 26). Reprinted with permission.

Other evidence: N/A

Other sources: N/A

References: N/A

CHANNEL LEADERSHIP BEHAVIOR
(Schul, Pride, and Little 1983)

In my franchise arrangement . . .

Participative Leadership

1. Franchisees have major influence in the determination of policies and standards for this franchise organization.

2. Good ideas from franchisees often do not get passed along to franchise management.*

3. Franchisees are not allowed to provide input into the determination of standards and promotional allowances.*

Supportive Leadership

4. There is a definite lack of coaching, support, and feedback.*

5. Once they've sold you the franchise, they forget all about you except when your fees are due.*

6. This franchise organization is highly interested in the welfare of its franchisees.

Directive Leadership

7. I am provided sufficient guidelines and careful instructions on how to manage my franchise operations.

8. The rights and obligations of all parties concerned are **clearly** spelled out in the franchise contract.

9. I am encouraged to use uniform procedures.

NOTES: *Denotes items requiring reverse scoring. Items 1 through 3 compose the participative leadership dimension, items 4 through 6 the supportive dimension, and items 7 through 9 the directive dimension. All supportive leadership items loaded negatively on the supportive factor, and item 7 loaded negatively on the directive leadership dimension.

NORMS: RELATIONAL NORMS
(Heide and John 1992)

Construct: Relational norms are defined as a higher order construct consisting of the dimensions flexibility, information exchange, and solidarity (Heide and John 1992, p. 37). Norms are defined generally as expectations shared by a group of decision makers. Specifically, flexibility defines a bilateral expectation of willingness to make adaptations as circumstances change. Information exchange defines the expectation that parties will provide information useful to the partner. Solidarity reflects a high value being placed on the relationship (Heide and John 1992, pp. 35-36).

Description: A total of 10 items are used to assess the three relational norm factors: flexibility, 3 items; information exchange, 4 items; and solidarity, 3 items. Each statement is operationalized using a 7-point scale anchored by *completely inaccurate description* and *completely accurate description*. The three norm types were subsequently combined into an equally weighted composite score for hypothesis tests (Heide and John 1992, p. 39).

Development: The specific items used are based on the items developed earlier by Kaufmann and Stern (1988) and Noordewier, John, and Nevin (1990). (See Heide and John [1992, p. 38].)

Samples: Participants in the research were 155 representatives of buying firms. The initial sampling frame was a national list of purchasing agents and directors of manufacturing in the two-digit SIC major groups 35, 36, and 37. Sixty-one key informants from supplier firms were also surveyed. The initial buying firm respondents identified this latter group representing the supplier firms.

Validity: Unreported item-to-total correlations were used initially to evaluate the items. Test of a 10-item, three-factor higher order model (Heide and John 1992, p. 39) resulted in the following fit statistics: chi-square = 40.40 (32 *df*, $p = .15$), GFI = .95, and RMSR = .04. All item and second-order factor loadings were significant (*t* values > 4.6). The correlation between the composite relational norm measures across the buyer-seller dyads was .50. Additional evidence of measurement validity is provided by the tests of hypotheses in which relational norms moderate the effects of buyer specific assets.

Scores: Means and standard deviations were not provided.

Source: Heide, Jan B., and George John. (1992). "Do Norms Matter in Marketing Relationships?" *Journal of Marketing*, *56*, 32-44.
    © 1992 by the American Marketing Association. Scale items taken from Table 1 (p. 37). Reprinted with permission.

Other evidence: N/A

Other sources: N/A

References: Kaufmann, Patrick J., and Louis W. Stern. (1988). "Relational Exchange Norms, Perceptions of Unfairness, and Retained Hostility in Commercial Litigation." *Journal of Conflict Resolution*, *32*, 534-552.

Noordewier, Thomas G., George, John, and John R. Nevin. (1990). "Performance Outcomes of Purchasing Arrangements in Industrial Buy-Vendor Relationships." *Journal of Marketing*, *54*, 80-93.

NORMS: RELATIONAL NORMS
(Heide and John 1992)

Norm of Flexibility

1. Flexibility in response to requests for changes is a characteristic of this relationship.

2. The parties expect to be able to make adjustments in the ongoing relationship to cope with changing circumstances.

3. When some unexpected situation arises, the parties would rather work out a new deal than hold each other to the original terms.

Norm of Information Exchange

1. In this relationship, it is expected that any information that might help the other party will be provided to them.

2. Exchange of information in this relationship takes place frequently and informally, and not only according to a prespecified agreement.

3. It is expected that the parties will provide proprietary information if it can help the other party.

4. It is expected that we keep each other informed about events or changes that may affect the other party.

Norm of Solidarity

1. Problems that arise in the course of this relationship are treated by the parties as joint rather than individual responsibilities.

2. The parties are committed to improvements that may benefit the relationship as a whole, and not only the individual parties.

3. The parties in this relationship do not mind owing each other favors.

PERFORMANCE: SUPPLIER PERCEPTIONS OF RESELLER PERFORMANCE
(Kumar, Stern, and Achrol 1992)

Construct: Kumar, Stern, and Achrol (1992, p. 241) postulate that an effective reseller from the supplier's perspective plays an instrumental role in helping the supplier meet the four functional imperatives of goal attainment, integration, adaptation, and pattern maintenance. Based on a summary of four effectiveness models, reseller performance is defined by Kumar et al. (1992) as consisting of eight facets: contribution to profits, contribution to sales, reseller competence, reseller loyalty, reseller compliance, contribution to growth, reseller adaptability, and customer satisfaction.

Description: The final measures consist of a five-item global performance scale and seven three-item facet scales. All items are assessed using 7-point Likert-type scales.

Development: An initial set of 100 items was developed from a review of the extant literature. Executives from Firms 1 and 2 judged the content validity of the items, and 62 items remained. Twenty-one graduate students reduced the pool further to 34 items via an item sort pretest. These 34 items were used In the subsequent field study (Kumar et al. 1992, p. 242). Confirmatory factor analyses and item-to-total correlations then were used to reduce the reseller performance measures to 21 items distributed evenly across seven facets. (The reseller loyalty facet was dropped entirely due to correlations of items with other facets.) The reliabilities for the remaining individual facets ranged from .68 to .82 for Firm 1. The reliabilities ranged from .68 to .96 for Firm 2.

Samples: Data analysis was conducted on 98 resellers for Firm 1 and 63 resellers for Firm 2. Firm 1 was a major vehicle leasing company with more than 5,000 independent business dealers. Firm 2 was a division of a multinational firm that manufacturers and distributes a portable telecommunications product through approximately 1,000 dealers. The input for the data analysis consisted of organizational level responses averaged over key informants within each reseller. The data for Firm 2 were used to assess the generalizability of the measures of reseller performance that had acceptable levels of validity in Sample 1 (cf. Kumar et al. 1992, pp. 241-244).

Validity: Evidence of convergent validity is offered by the correlation of a unit performance measure with the global performance measure (.78). Additional supportive evidence is provided by predictive and nomological validity tests involving correlations with other measures (i.e., consideration of dropping reseller, influence over the supplier, supplier satisfaction, and conflict). These results are summarized in Table 4 (Kumar et al. 1992, p. 246). Evidence of discriminant validity was provided by tests of models in which pairs of facets were alternatively allowed to be correlated or the phi between each facet in the pair constrained to unity. Other evidence of discriminant validity is cited in the discussion of Table 5. These results involve the pattern of correlations between the facet performance measure, the global performance measure, and the other constructs. Support for criterion-related and nomological validity is offered from the significant and expected gamma path coefficients from each facet, the unit measure, and the global measure to the three constructs—reseller influence over supplier, supplier satisfaction, and conflict (Kumar et al. 1992, pp. 247-248).

Scores: Overall measure means and standard deviations were not provided. However, the responses from 21 executives reflecting perceptions of the relative importance of the different facets are described in Table 2 (Kumar et al. 1992, p. 244).

Source: Kumar, Nirmalya, Louis W. Stern, and Ravi S. Achrol. (1992). "Assessing Reseller Performance From the Perspective of the Supplier." *Journal of Marketing Research*, 29, 238-253.
     © 1992 by the American Marketing Association. Scale items taken from Appendix (pp. 251-252). Reprinted with permission.

Other evidence: N/A

Other sources: N/A

References: N/A

PERFORMANCE: SUPPLIER PERCEPTIONS OF RESELLER PERFORMANCE
(Kumar, Stern, and Achrol 1992)

1. Contribution to Sales: Sales

    1. Over the past year, the dealer has been successful in generating high [rental revenues/sales volume] for *the supplier*, given the level of competition and economic growth in his market area.

    2. Compared to competing dealers in the [district/territory], this dealer has achieved a high level of market penetration for *the supplier*.

    3. Last year, the revenue that this dealer generated from *the supplier* was higher than what other competing dealers within the same [neighborhood/territory] generated.

    4. Relative to his size, his available resources, and the competition he faces, the dealer could have generated greater [sales volume/revenues] for *the supplier* last year.*

    5. Last year, the dealer did not meet the sales target that *the supplier* had set for it.*

2. Contributions to Profits: Profits

    1. *The supplier's* cost of servicing the dealer is reasonable, given the amount of business which the dealer generates for *the supplier.*

    2. The dealer's demands for support [some examples] have resulted in inadequate profits for *the supplier*.

    3. *The supplier* made inadequate profits from this dealer over the past year because of the amount of time, effort, and energy which *the supplier* had to devote to assisting him.

    4. Last year, the revenues generated by this dealer were not commensurate with *the supplier's* effort to stimulate that revenue.*

3. Reseller Competence: Competence

    1. The dealer has the required business skills necessary to run a successful [kind of business the supplier is in] business.

    2. The dealer [has amassed/demonstrates] a great deal of knowledge about the features and attributes of *the supplier's* products and services.

    3. The dealer and his personnel have poor knowledge of competitors' products and services.

    4. The dealer has not invested enough time or money in educating or training himself or his employees to be more competent in selling *the supplier's* products and services.*

4. Reseller Compliance: Compliance

    1. In the past, *the supplier* has often had trouble getting the dealer to participate in its [some program important to the supplier] program.

    2. The dealer almost always conforms to *the supplier's* accepted procedures.

    3. The dealer has frequently violated [stipulations/terms and conditions] contained in his [contract/agreement] with *the supplier*.

    4. The dealer accurately [files some reports required by the supplier] and gets them in on time.*

5. Reseller Loyalty: Loyalty

    1. The dealer clearly wants to [rent/sell] *the supplier's* products and shows his desire to do so in a number of positive ways.*

    2. It takes an inordinate amount of time, effort, and energy to get the dealer's attention on *the supplier*.*

3. The dealer shows greater motivation to [sell competing brands or] engage in other business rather than in furthering *the supplier's* business.*

4. The dealer places a disproportionately higher amount of time and effort behind *the supplier* relative to other businesses that he engages in.*

6. Reseller Adaptation: Adapt

1. The dealer senses long-term trends in his market area and frequently adjusts his selling practices.

2. The dealer is very innovative in his marketing of *the supplier's* products and services in his [neighborhood/territory].

3. The dealer makes an effort to meet competitive changes in his [neighborhood/territory].

4. The dealer could be more responsive (by changing hours of operations, staff, and local advertising) to seasonal sales fluctuations.*

7. Contribution to Growth: Growth

1. The dealer will either continue to be or will soon become a major source of revenue for *the supplier*.

2. Over the next year, *the supplier* expects its revenue generated from this dealer to grow faster than that from other competing [of the supplier] dealers within the same [district/territory].

3. In the past *the supplier's* [business with the dealer/market share through the dealer] has grown steadily.

4. Over the years, the dealer has been successful in his efforts to expand *the supplier's* business.*

5. Through its association with this dealer, *the supplier* has generated [large/significant monthly] increases in revenues.*

Customer Satisfaction: CusSat

1. *The supplier* has [frequently] received complaints from customers regarding this dealer.

2. The dealer goes out of his way to make his customers happy.

3. The dealer provides [customers/end users] with good assistance in the solution of any problems involving *the supplier's* products and services.

4. The dealer helps his customers reduce their concerns about [buying or renting the supplier's products] by providing useful information.*

Global Performance: GlobPerf

1. *The supplier's* association with this dealer has been a highly successful one.

2. If I had to give the dealer a performance appraisal for the past year, it would be (where 1 was poor and 5 was outstanding).

3. The dealer leaves a lot to be desired from an overall performance standpoint.

4. Taking all the different factors into account the dealer's performance has been (where 1 was excellent—couldn't be better and 7 was bad—couldn't be worse).

5. Overall, how would you characterize the results of *the supplier's* relationship with the dealer (where 1 was it has fallen short of expectations and 5 was it has greatly exceeded our expectations).

NOTE: *Items not included in final scale.

SATISFACTION-CHANNEL SATISFACTION: SATIND AND SATDIR
(Ruekert and Churchill 1984)

Construct: Channel member satisfaction is defined as the domain of all characteristics of the relationship between a channel member (the focal organization) and another institution in the channel (the target organization) which the focal organization finds rewarding, profitable, instrumental, and satisfying or frustrating, problematic, inhibiting, or unsatisfying (Ruekert and Churchill 1984, p. 227). Two operationalizations of the construct were presented. One is an indirect evaluation of the focal organization's beliefs. This scale is labeled SATIND. The other operationalization reflects a more direct approach to obtain the focal organization's evaluation of the target organization (i.e., satisfaction is asked for directly), and the scale is therefore labeled SATDIR. The dimensionality of each of the measures includes the following five components:

Social interaction: how satisfactorily interactions between focal organization and manufacturer are handled, primarily through the sales representative servicing the account.

Product: the demand for, awareness of, and quality of the manufacturer's products.

Financial: the attractiveness of the arrangement with respect to such matters as the focal organization's margins and ROI.

Cooperative advertising: how well the manufacturer supports the focal organization with co-op ad programs.

Other assistance: satisfaction with other promotional materials such as consumer promotions and point-of-purchase displays.

Description: Both the finalized versions of the SATIND, containing 21 items, and the SATDIR, containing 16 items, were designed for self-administration. A 5-point Likert-type scale format was used for items in both scales, with possible responses ranging from *strongly agree* to *strongly disagree* for SATIND items and from *very dissatisfied* to *very satisfied* for SATDIR. Item scores can be summed within the five SATDIR and SATIND components to form dimension indices, or overall to form overall SATDIR and SATIND scores.

Development: Based on expert interviews and an extensive literature review, the construct's domain was originally defined as consisting of four components. Thirty-six items for SATIND and 16 for SATDIR served as the initial pool of items. The dimensionality of the SATIND measures was assessed via the following steps: (a) Item-to-total correlations were examined, and any item that did not have a statistically higher correlation with the dimension to which it was hypothesized to belong was eliminated from the analysis; and (b) the internal homogeneity of items belonging to each dimension was then examined via coefficient alpha, plots of the item-to-total correlations, and principal factor analysis with oblique rotation. After these procedures were performed, 21 of the original 36 items remained for the SATIND scale. A final assessment of dimensionality (via LISREL) was conducted. The results of the confirmatory factor analysis showed that the items loaded as hypothesized on the five SATIND dimensions.

A set of similar procedures was applied to the 16 items making up the SATDIR scale. The subsequent factor analysis indicated that the SATDIR items reflect five dimensions of satisfaction. The five factors together account for slightly more than 67% of the total variation in the items. In summary, the evidence indicated that the SATDIR measure has five dimensions, and the labels are similar to the labels one would attach to those of the SATIND measure. In the confirmatory factor analysis though, one item from the SATDIR product dimension was switched to the other assistance dimension. Additionally, the convergent, discriminant, and nomological validity of SATDIR and SATIND were assessed.

Samples: The research setting for testing the conceptualization was a field study of the perceptions of retailers and wholesalers toward the manufacturer of consumer batteries and ancillary products. After measures were developed, a total of 173 diverse organizations, representing 32% of the sample organizations, provided usable questionnaires. These organizations included both retailers and wholesalers. Also, four distinct lines of trade were represented, including food, drugs, hardware, and mass markets.

Validity: The reliability of the 21-item linear combination for SATDIR was .89. Individual dimension alphas were .87, .76, .67, .56, and .73 for social interaction, product, financial, cooperative advertising, and other assistance, respectively. The reliability for a 15-item (though 16 items are specified) linear combination of SATDIR was .90, and dimension reliabilities were .70, .68, .79, and .75 for social interaction, financial, cooperative advertising, and other assistance. (Only one item was retained for the SATDIR product dimension.) The correlation between the overall SATIND and SATDIR measures was .63, and the correlations between the overall SATIND and SATDIR measures and a single-item global satisfaction measure were .68 and .58, respectively, offering evidence of convergent validity. Nomological validity was assessed by correlating SATIND and SATDIR with various constructs. For example, the overall SATIND had correlations of −.52 and −.55 with measures of role ambiguity, and −.43 and −.46 with domain descensus measures. SATDIR correlations with these constructs were −.58 and −.57, and −.39 and −.48, respectively.

Scores: Means scores and standard deviations were not reported in the Ruekert and Churchill (1984) article.

Source: Ruekert, Robert W., and Gilbert A. Churchill, Jr. (1984). "Reliability and Validity of Alternative Measures of Channel Member Satisfaction." *Journal of Marketing Research*, *21*, 226-233.

    © 1984 by the American Marketing Association. Scale items taken from Table 1 (p. 229) and Table 2 (p. 230). Reprinted with permission.

Other evidence: N/A

Other sources: N/A

References: N/A

SATISFACTION-CHANNEL SATISFACTION: SATIND AND SATDIR
(Ruekert and Churchill 1984)

SATIND Scale Items

Social Interaction

1. My manufacturer's sales representative isn't well organized.

2. My manufacturer's sales representative doesn't know his products very well.

3. Manufacturer's salespeople are helpful.

4. Manufacturer's sales representatives have my best interests in mind when they make a suggestion.

5. My manufacturer's sales representative is always willing to help me if I get into a tight spot.

Product

6. Manufacturer's products are asked for by our customers.

7. Manufacturer's products are a good growth opportunity for my firm.

8. Manufacturer's products are not well known by my customers.

9. My customers are willing to pay more for manufacturer's products.

10. I would have a difficult time replacing manufacturer's products with similar products.

11. Manufacturer's products perform much better than their competition.

Financial

12. Manufacturer's everyday margins are lower than industry margins.

13. Manufacturer provides very competitive margins on their products.

14. There is poor return for the amount of space I devote to manufacturer's products.

15. Some of the manufacturer's products aren't worth carrying because their margins are too small.

16. I am very happy with the margins I receive on manufacturer's products.

Cooperative Advertising Support

17. Manufacturer should have better cooperative advertising program.

18. Manufacturer should provide better cooperative advertising allowances.

Other Assistance

19. Manufacturer conducts excellent consumer promotions.

20. Manufacturer provides adequate promotional support for their products.

21. Manufacturer provides excellent point-of-purchase displays.

SATDIR Scales Items

Social Interaction

1. Personal dealings with manufacturer's sales representatives.

2. Assistance in managing your inventory of manufacturer's products.

3. Order handing by manufacturer.

4. Manufacturer's handling of damaged merchandise.

Product

5. The quality of manufacturer's products.

Financial

6. Income received from the sale of manufacturer's products.

7. Everyday margins on manufacturer's products.

8. Manufacturer credit policies.

Promotional Support

9. Manufacturer's national advertising support.

10. Manufacturer's cooperative advertising support.

11. Consumer promotion support by manufacturer (coupons, rebates, displays).

12. Off-invoice promotional allowances.

13. How promotional payments are made.

Other Assistance

14. Order handling by manufacturer.

15. Level of backorders of manufacturer's products.

16. Speed of delivery of manufacturer's products.

NOTE: Although not specified by the authors, items 1, 2, 8, 12, 14, 15, 17, and 18 of SATIND seem to require reverse scoring.

APPENDIX TO INTER-/INTRAFIRM ISSUES (ARTICLES CONTAINING INTER-/INTRAFIRM RELATED MEASURES)

Numerous articles use multi-item measures to assess aspects of power, conflict, and influence strategies in the channels literature. Most of these measures, though, were derived for the specific research setting or product being studied. Application of these measures to other products and settings could be problematic, and, thus, we have chosen not to summarize these types of measures here. However, the interested reader is referred to the following articles as a partial guide to some of these study/product specific channel measures.

Anderson, James C., and James A. Narus. (1984). "A Model of the Distributor's Perspective of Distributor-Manufacturer Working Relationships." *Journal of Marketing*, *48*, 62-74.

Anderson, James C., and James A. Narus. (1990). "A Model of Distributor Firm and Manufacturer Firm Working Partnerships." *Journal of Marketing*, *54*, 42-58.

Frazier, Gary, and John O. Summers. (1984). "Interfirm Influence Strategies and Their Application Within Distribution Channels." *Journal of Marketing*, *48*, 43-55.

Frazier, Gary, and John O. Summers. (1986). "Interfirm Power and Its Use Within a Franchise Channel of Distribution." *Journal of Marketing Research*, *23*, 169-176.

Gaski, John. (1984). "The Theory of Power and Conflict in Channels of Distribution." *Journal of Marketing*, *48*, 9-29.

Gaski, John. (1986). "Interrelations Among a Channel Entity's Power Sources: Impact of the Exercise of Reward and Coercion on Expert, Referent, and Legitimate Power Sources." *Journal of Marketing Research*, *23*, 62-77.

Hunt, Shelby, and John R. Nevin. (1974). "Power in a Channel of Distribution: Sources and Consequences." *Journal of Marketing Research*, *11*, 186-193.

Kale, Sudhir. (1986). "Dealer Perceptions of Manufacturer Power and Influence Strategies in a Developing Country." *Journal of Marketing Research*, *23*, 387-393.

Lusch, Robert F. (1976). "Sources of Power: Their Impact on Intrachannel Conflict." *Journal of Marketing Research*, *13*, 382-390.

INDEX OF SCALES

INDEX OF SCALE AUTHORS

ABOUT THE AUTHORS

William O. Bearden (Ph.D., University of South Carolina, 1975) is a Distinguished Faculty Fellow and holder of the NationsBank Chair in Marketing. He served on the faculties of Western Kentucky University and the University of Alabama from 1976 to 1978. He has been on the faculty of the University of South Carolina since his return in 1978. He is on the editorial review boards of *Journal of Marketing Research, Journal of Marketing, Journal of Consumer Research, Journal of Retailing, Journal of the Academy of Marketing Science,* and *Marketing Education Review*. He has served on the board of directors for the American Marketing Association and as president of the Academic Division of the American Marketing Association. He has received the University of South Carolina Amoco Teaching Award, presented annually to one faculty member, as well as the Outstanding MBA Teacher Award and the Alfred G. Smith College of Business Administration Teacher of the Year Award. His teaching and research interests include consumer behavior, marketing research, and the evaluation of marketing promotions. He was faculty codirector for the University of South Carolina Lilly Teaching Fellows from 1982 to 1995. He has published numerous articles in *Journal of Marketing Research* and *Journal of Consumer Research*, as well as a number of publications in other marketing and consumer research journals. He recently coauthored the second edition of *Marketing Principles and Perspectives* (1998).

Richard G. Netemeyer (Ph.D., University of South Carolina, 1986) is Professor in the Department of Marketing, E. J. Ourso College of Business at Louisiana State University (LSU). His research interests include measurement and scaling, public policy, maladaptive behaviors, and consumer behavior in general. His research has been published in *Journal of Consumer Research, Journal of Marketing Research, Journal of Marketing, Journal of Applied Psychology,* and *Journal of Public Policy and Marketing*. He is a member of the editorial review boards of *Journal of Consumer Research* and *Journal of Public Policy Marketing*.

ASSOCIATION FOR CONSUMER RESEARCH

The Association for Consumer Research (ACR) is a society of individuals who have a professional interest in consumer research. The objectives of this association are

1. To provide a forum for exchange of ideas among academics and policy officials in business as well as government who are interested in consumer research.

2. To stimulate research focusing on a better understanding of consumer behavior from a variety of perspectives; for example, marketing, psychology, sociology, anthropology, consumer sciences, economics, etc.

3. To disseminate these research findings through publications and conferences.

For more information, please contact

H. Keith Hunt, Executive Secretary

Association for Consumer Research

Graduate School of Management, 632 TNRB

Brigham Young University

Provo, UT 84602

Website: http://acr.webpage.com

MKT 319
REF COPY
Handbook of Marketing Scales